ESSAYS IN HONOR OF
EDWIN MANSFIELD

ESSAYS IN HONOR OF EDWIN MANSFIELD:
The Economics of R&D, Innovation, and Technological Change

Edited by
ALBERT N. LINK
University of North Carolina at Greensboro, Bryan School of Business and Economics, USA

F. M. SCHERER
Harvard University, Kennedy School of Government, Emeritus, USA

Library of Congress Cataloging-in-Publication Data

A C.I.P. Catalogue record for this book is available
from the Library of Congress.

ISBN-10: 0-387-25010-7   e-ISBN-10: 0-387-25022-0   Printed on acid-free paper.
ISBN-13: 978-0387-25010-6   e-ISBN-13: 978-0387-25022-9
© 2005 Springer Science+Business Media, Inc.
All rights reserved. This work may not be translated or copied in whole or in part without the written permission of the publisher (Springer Science+Business Media, Inc., 233 Spring Street, New York, NY 10013, USA), except for brief excerpts in connection with reviews or scholarly analysis. Use in connection with any form of information storage and retrieval, electronic adaptation, computer software, or by similar or dissimilar methodology now know or hereafter developed is forbidden.
The use in this publication of trade names, trademarks, service marks and similar terms, even if the are not identified as such, is not to be taken as an expression of opinion as to whether or not they are subject to proprietary rights.

9 8 7 6 5 4 3 2 1   SPIN 11372202

springeronline.com

ESSAYS IN HONOR OF EDWIN MANSFIELD:
The Economics of R & D, Innovation, and Technical change

Edited by Albert N. Link and F.M. Scherer

Preface	vii
Introduction	
F.M. SCHERER / Edwin Mansfield: An Appreciation	1–7
Innovation, Technology, and Economic Growth	
ROBERT M. SOLOW / Flexibility and Endogenous Innovation	9–13
F.M. SCHERER / Schumpeter and the Micro-foundations of Endogeous Growth	15–26
DAVID J. TEECE / Technology and Technology Transfer: Mansfieldian Inspirations and Subsequent Developments	27–43
JOACHIM HENKEL AND ERIC VON HIPPEL / Welfare Implications of User Innovation	45–59
GREGORY TASSEY / Underinvestment in Public Good Technologies	61–85
ALBERT N. LINK AND JOHN T. SCOTT / Evaluating Public Sector R&D Programs: The Advanced Technology Program's Investment in Wavelength References for Optical Fiber Communications	87–97
Research and Development and Innovation	
JAMES D. ADAMS / Industrial R&D Laboratories: Windows on Black Boxes?	99–107
JOHN T. SCOTT / Public Policy and Environmental Research and Development	109–127
JACQUES MAIRESSE AND PIERRE MOHNEN / The Importance of R&D for Innovation: A Reassessment Using French Survey Data	129–143
GIUSEPPE MEDDA, CLAUDIO PIGA AND DONALD S. SIEGEL / University R&D and Firm Productivity: Evidence from Italy	145–151
PHILIP E. AUERSWALD AND LEWIS M. BRANSCOMB / Reflections on Mansfield, Technological Complexity, and the "Golden Age" of U.S. Corporate R&D	153–171
KATHRYN L. COMBS / The Welfare Effects of Research and Production Joint Ventures	173–185
ALBERT N. LINK / Research Joint Ventures in the United States: A Descriptive Analysis	187–195
Patenting and the Diffusion of Knowledge	
BRONWYN H. HALL / Exploring the Patent Explosion	195–208
JOSH LERNER / The University and the Start-Up: Lessons from the Past Two Decades	209–216
WESLEY M. COHEN / Patents and Appropriation: Concerns and Evidence	217–231
DAVID C. MOWERY AND BHAVEN N. SAMPAT / The Bayh-Dole Act of 1980 and University–Industry Technology Transfer: A Model for Other OECD Governments?	233–245
ALESSANDRA CANEPA AND PAUL STONEMAN / Financing Constraints in the Inter Firm Diffusion of New Process Technologies	247–257
J.S. METCALFE / Ed Mansfield and the Diffusion of Innovation: An Evolutionary Connection	259–269

DAVID B. AUDRETSCH AND ERIK E. LEHMANN / Mansfield's Missing Link: The Impact of Knowledge Spillovers on Firm Growth … 271–274

KENNETH L. SIMONS / Predictable Cross-Industry Heterogeneity in Industry Dynamics … 275–279

DAVID B. AUDRETSCH AND ERIK E. LEHMANN / Mansfield's Innovation in the Theory of Innovation … 281–290

MICHAEL GALLAHER AND K. CASEY DELHOTAL / Modeling the Impact of Technical Change on Emissions Abatement Investments in Developing Countries … 291–305

Index of Names … 307

Preface

Edwin Mansfield was a pioneer in researching the economics of R & D, innovation and technological change. His findings and his methodologies have influenced countless scholars in both economics as well as in management, public administration, public policy, and other social sciences. The essays in this volume were written by appreciative friends and former students (although in a broader sense, all of us have been students of Mansfield at one point or another in our careers). The collection is intended as a tribute to Mansfield's many contributions. We hope it will also provide a roadmap for future generations of scholars to topics in need of further investigation and appropriate methodologies.

A number of the papers in this volume were previously published, in January 2005, in a special issue of the *Journal of Technology Transfer*. The collection here also contains several additional papers, some prepared for the *Journal of Technology Transfer* special issue.

The collection is divided into four major parts. It begins with F.M. Scherer's overview of Mansfield's many contributions. Each subsequent paper reflects in some way at least one of the Mansfield insights that Scherer chronicles. The second part is broadly related to topics in Innovation, Technology, and Economic Growth. Part three addresses Research and Development and Innovation, the roots of economic growth as Mansfield reminded us many times. And part four focuses on Patenting and the Diffusion of Knowledge.

The editors are grateful for the moral support of Lucile Mansfield, Ed's wife, throughout this project.

Edwin Mansfield: An Appreciation

F. M. Scherer

In January of 1985, I received from the committee in Sweden an invitation to nominate candidates for the Nobel Prize in Economic Science. The instructions made it clear that my nominations were to be strictly confidential. But nothing should be kept secret for more than two decades, so now I tell my tale. I nominated two persons, listed in alphabetical order: Edwin Mansfield and Robert Solow. As a preface to my exposition of reasons why those two should receive the Nobel Prize, I observed that "It is now generally accepted that in advanced economies, the growth of material well-being has depended critically upon technological change." Solow's 1957 article, I have observed frequently, was a shot heard 'round the world, elevating the study of technological change to a status far above what it had been — a neglected sideshow attraction in economics. My rationale for Mansfield was as follows:

> "Professor Mansfield has painstakingly collected and analyzed within-the-firm microdata to illuminate the nature of industrial research and development, revealed in numerous scholars' studies to be a key, if not the most important, institution through which technological change is effected. His work on uncertainty, decision-making criteria, market structure, the speed of diffusion, R&D — productivity links, and much else is collected in 1968, 1971, 1977, and 1982 books."

In 1987, Bob Solow received the Nobel Prize, which pleased me greatly. But in its infinite wisdom the committee chose not to have Ed Mansfield share the prize. Perhaps the fault was mine for saying that Mansfield's work was summarized in books, ignoring the scores of articles on which those books were based. The committee may have been showing its change of heart toward blockbuster books and its increasing emphasis on articles with an important but sharply focused contribution to knowledge. Whatever the reason, I continue to believe that the committee made a mistake in not honoring Ed Mansfield and his research.

1. Beginnings

It remains somewhat of a mystery, at least to me and many who were close to him, how Mansfield was inspired to begin his research on the economics of technological change. In tributes to Eugen von Boehm-Bawerk and later to Carl Menger, Joseph A. Schumpeter characterized the third decade of a scholar's life as "that period of sacred fertility which, in the case of every thinker, creates what is subsequently worked out." Mansfield (1961) was in substantative respects a disciple of Schumpeter, but he did not conform to the master's biographical paradigm. His first publication on the economics of technological change appeared in Econometrica in 1961, when he had passed through his third decade to the age of 31.

Mansfield's first publications, extending his Duke University dissertation on city size and per capita income, were in urban and labor economics. When he arrived at Carnegie-Mellon University (called at the time the Carnegie Institute of Technology) in 1955, he joined senior colleague Harold H. Wein in a study of decision-making in railroad switching yards. Wein's specialty was public utility economics, which may explain the railroad focus and the supporting grant from a Pittsburgh railroad equipment supplier. The

601 Rockbourne Mills Court
Wallingford, PA 19086
E-mail: fmscherer@comcast.net

research, however, exhibited classic Carnegie-Mellon methodology of the time, emphasizing in an operations research framework managerial risk aversion and adaptive expectations.

The first visible indication that Mansfield had shifted his focus to technological innovation was his participation as a discussant at the famous spring 1960 National Bureau of Economic Research conference at the University of Minnesota, leading to the classic 1962 compendium (edited by Richard R. Nelson), *The Rate and Direction of Inventive Activity*. That conference marked a beginning point for scholarly interaction among economists on technological change. In what would prove to be a Mansfield hallmark, he devoted only the first four paragraphs of his commentary to the William Fellner paper he was assigned to discuss and then turned to his own work modelling company research and development expenditure patterns, "only the first parts [of which] have been completed." The research was conducted under a grant from the National Science Foundation Office of Special Studies, which was responsible for the first systematic surveys of research and development expenditures in American industry. Much of Mansfield's later work was supported under grants from the successors to that organization as well as the Economics branch of the NSF Social Sciences division.

From the timing of that presentation and the assertion that it was in its early stages, one infers that Mansfield turned to technological innovation and imitation questions in 1958 or at the latest in early 1959. At the time Carnegie-Mellon had no tradition of work on technological change. One might guess that he was introduced to the field's research agenda by Richard Nelson, a pioneering contributor, but Nelson said in an interview that Mansfield was already well underway on his new research by the time Nelson first visited Carnegie-Mellon in 1959, joining the faculty formally in 1960. In the prefaces to his first two books on innovation, Mansfield thanks George Leland Bach for encouraging him to work in the area. At the time Bach, a monetary economist with no professional publications in the field of technical change, was dean at Carnegie-Mellon. It is possible that he participated in a Ford Foundation committee concerned with technological change during the 1950s. We remain in doubt as to how much of Mansfield's agenda was self-initiated and how much came from Bach's suggestions. Mansfield's wife Lucile reported that a relevant element in Ed's change of field was his desire to be his own master and not to play a supporting role under another scholar's grant. The grant supporting Mansfield's work with Wein had run out, so the availability of research funds from the National Science Foundation may have influenced his choice. I know from later conversations that he maintained close relationships with several National Science Foundation grant officers. But it is impossible in hindsight to disentangle demand-pull influences from the science-push that came inter alia from Leland Bach and Mansfield's reading of the nascent literature. What is clear is that he thereupon persisted in pursuing his technology agenda for nearly four decades.

2. Methodologically pioneering

Mansfield's typical research methodology differed by several robust standard deviations from what has been conventional in economics, and especially for fellows of the Econometric Society, which he was. His initial work was conventional enough. For the preliminary work he presented at the 1960 *Rate and Direction* conference, Mansfield drew data on company R&D expenditures from an M.I.T. dissertation by Charles Langenhagen, applying to them an adaptive expectations analytic framework. Langenhagen obtained his data in part from published corporate reports, but in those pre-1975 days before the Financial Accounting Standards Board required companies to disclose "material" R&D expenditures in their annual reports, he filled in data gaps by asking companies for the needed figures. It is not unreasonable to infer that Mansfield recognized he could do the same thing, and so for the extension of that research published as Mansfield (1964), he asked companies for supplemental data. These included R&D data and also, from face-to-face interviews with a subset of companies, estimates of the frequency distribution of expected profit returns from R&D, how difficult it was to expand research efforts, and how actual R&D

expenditures varied in two years from originally planned outlays. Thus emerged the epitome of Mansfield's methodology: if you want to know something, ask the people who know.

It is a methodology used far too infrequently by economists. Indeed, it warrants a digression. In 1963, a group of economists including Mansfield, Alf Conrad, Zvi Griliches, Jesse Markham, Richard Nelson, M.J. Peck, Jacob Schmookler, and myself obtained what was at the time a generous grant from the Ford Foundation to pursue and encourage economic research on technological change. We met regularly and called ourselves the Inter-University Committee on the Micro-Economics of Technological Change and Economic Growth. The capstone of our effort was a conference, held in May 1966 at the University of Pennsylvania and hosted by Mansfield, bringing together some 40 economists to present and discuss relevant work. I recall that in a planning meeting, one member of our committee, probably Mansfield, suggested that we invite some company R&D vice presidents. Another member replied, "But who would talk to them?" None were invited. Only in the late 1990s did the National Bureau of Economic Research group on productivity growth begin a program of arranging visits by NBER affiliated economists to technologically interesting companies.

From his initial research on company R&D expenditures, Mansfield branched off in several directions. The first fairly comprehensive view of which I know was provided by a paper Ed presented at Ohio State University in October 1962. Published in Tybout (1964), it outlined six ongoing research strands: the R&D expenditure project already described, how the number of significant innovations related to company R&D expenditures in three industries, the relationship between innovative leadership and firm size in four industries, how innovation affected firm growth rates, the relationships between innovation and company investment, and the speed at which twelve important innovations diffused through relevant industries. Many of the data were obtained from a wide diversity of published sources, some seldom used for economic research. But in addition, information was obtained through company interviews on the dates at which innovations were introduced by particular firms, the production volume needed to warrant adopting an innovation, the size of investment required to adopt an innovation, the durability of older equipment, and the anticipated payoff period for a new investment, among others. Using these variables quantified through interviews, Mansfield was able to make econometric estimates quite unlike anything conventional in the economic literature.

This approach was not uncontroversial. In his comment on the October 1962 paper (Tybout, 1964, p. 148), Zvi Griliches observed:

"Mansfield ... should be congratulated for working, almost alone, in this very important area and for producing so many interesting and significant results. All I can do in this context is to reiterate Mansfield's caveat that some of his conclusions rest on quite shaky data ... To illustrate ... the important variables in his [R&D] model ... were derived from answers to a questionnaire or interview. They are not "data" in the usual sense.... [What firms say] does not prove that profitability affects investment, it tells only that when asked to explain why they invest in research, these firms can provide a sensible answer."

I heard similar criticisms at many other fora in which Mansfield's results were presented. To deal with them Ed developed a standard defense mechanism, appending toward the end of each study a caveat of the general tenor (I quote from Mansfield, 1968, p. 207):

"The mathematical models that are used are often very simple, in part because of necessity, in part because of choice. Although these models seem to be useful approximations, their roughness should be noted. Also, the data that could be obtained are sometimes limited in both quantity and quality. In some studies, we were forced to use rather small samples, because no published data were available and it was necessary to collect the data ourselves – a very time-consuming and expensive process... The studies contained here are tentative in a great many respects... No pretense is made that they are close to the last word on the subject. Hopefully, however, they represent some of the most advanced work that has yet been attempted."

All I can add is that he was right, in every respect.

As his research progressed over the years, Mansfield built a rich network of industrial R&D managers who trusted him, believed that he was doing important work, and were willing to reciprocate by taking time to answer the increasingly intricate questions he posed. In other words, the work reinforced itself. The network's hubs originated in Pittsburgh and Philadelphia, where Ed had teaching appointments, but branched out from there to encompass wider geographic space. One observes too that many of the industries on which his research focused most intensely had major companies located in or around those two cities.

The network effect created by Mansfield had at least two further noteworthy ramifications. As it became clear that his methodology could illuminate questions on which economists knew little or nothing, others emulated it and added significantly to the stock of knowledge. Second, Ed helped make that happen. Of special significance is what occurred at a conference on the economics of pharmaceutical innovation in 1969 (Cooper, 1970). As discussant, Ed presented some results from his own recent research, estimating the R&D costs, development times, and success rates for a sample of new therapeutic molecules developed by a single drug company. The conference was probably the first one in which economists met with pharmaceutical executives and individuals responsible for public policy toward that intensely controversial industry. Debate over claims and counter-claims was intense but in the end satisfied no one. As the conference end drew near, Ed and I met privately with Harold Clymer, author of the paper Ed discussed and research vice president at Smith Kline & French Laboratories (located in Philadelphia). My supposition, without definitive support, is that SKF was also the source of Mansfield's data. Ed's formal comment included an observation (Cooper 1970, p. 150) that:

> "[I]t should be noted that this seems to be the first study of its kind. Or at least I haven't heard of any other investigators who have managed to get inside one of the major ethical drug firms. Putting it differently, they haven't arranged to get out alive with their data and analyze it, so far as I know."

In our private conversation with Clymer, Ed reiterated this point and insisted that if the pharmaceutical industry wanted to bridge the wide gap between its assertions and public perceptions, it had to let economists and other scholars inside its walls and give them access to data with which a balanced picture of the drug R&D process could be obtained. Clymer was well-positioned in the industry and its trade association. Whether it was through his intervention or for some independent cause, I do not know. What I know is that shortly thereafter industry members did begin letting economists such as Henry Grabowski, John Vernon, Joseph di Masi, Rebecca Henderson, and Iain Cockburn in to use their data subject to reasonable confidentiality restraints. The result has been an enormous increase in our understanding of the industry's economics. I hasten to add, as nearly every Mansfield article concluded, that much remains to be learned.

As Mansfield's network of industry insiders evolved, it became possible for him to contact industry sources by telephone, obtain new qualitative insights on the phenomena he was beginning to investigate, and secure their cooperation in completing written questionnaires providing among other things the desired quantitative estimates. This method enhanced research efficiency and reduced onerous travel, but it had its dangers. The most important adverse case known to me occurred in connection with Mansfield (1988), in which he compared the characteristics of R&D in Japanese firms with those of their American counterparts. Deeply impressed by it, I observed and made the basis of a further analysis (Scherer, 1992):

> "Ferguson's thesis is consistent with Edwin Mansfield's remarkable finding ... from a survey of 100 matched Japanese and American corporations, that on average Japanese firms devoted 64 percent of their R&D budgets to internal process development and improvement, while their U.S. counterparts spent only 32 percent."

In a footnote, Mansfield cautioned (1988, note 26) that it was difficult to design a survey instrument to be administered in two different languages and that "there is no way to eliminate completely the possibility of errors of interpretation by respondents." Later, I learned from an expert on the Japanese economy that the words used to designate product innovations had a very different interpretation in Japanese, and that differences in the fraction of R&D resources devoted to internal process work between the two nations were actually insignificant.

3. Selected contributions

The analyses completed by Edwin Mansfield, in many cases with the assistance of nearly a dozen of his graduate students, cover most of the important themes in the microeconomics of technological innovation. They have been summarized admirably, and the considerable extent to which they have been cited in the scholarly literature is shown, in a review by Arthur Diamond (2003). Given this, it would be redundant for me to attempt a comprehensive review here. Instead, I focus more subjectively on three that I have found most useful in my own research and teaching.

One of the most paradigm-altering in my view was an ambitious analysis, jointly with Richard Brandenburg, of R&D project outcomes in the Pittsburgh central research laboratory of Westinghouse Electric Co. See Mansfield and Brandenburg (1966). Up to the time of that study, the literature on industrial research and development was replete with wild but unsupported statements about the costs and risks of industrial R&D. Not atypical of the muddle was the statement of a company research manager that between one and 80 percent of research projects were technically successful, depending upon how the words "success" and "project" are defined. Conference on Industrial Research (1951, p. 190). Mansfield and Brandenburg offered four particularly noteworthy new insights: (1) In roughly three fourths of the 70 projects surveyed, the ex ante probability of technical success was predicted to be 0.80 or higher; (2) after-the-fact, 44% of the projects undertaken yielded technical success in the sense of meeting their initial objectives; (3) unforeseen technical difficulties were responsible for less than half of the failures to meet technical goals; in many other cases, there were strategic reasons for diversions from the technical initial plan; and (4) annual spending on the projects surveyed averaged about $70,000. The implication was that the risks, technical and financial, of typical projects in the laboratory studied were well within the risk-taking capabilities of both large and small corporations. Later extensions of the research to a sample of 16 companies revealed that post-technical contingencies (e.g., in the marketing stage) reduced over-all economic success ratios from an average of 57% considering technical goals alone to 27% of all projects initiated. Recognition of the appreciable slippage from technical to economic success was an impetus to my work with Dietmar Harhoff on the distribution of profit returns from innovation projects and the stochastic processes generating that distribution. See e.g. Scherer et al. (2000).

Economists had long recognized that there was likely to be a divergence between the private returns from an innovation project, i.e., the profits realized by the innovator, and the society-wide benefits. Mansfield and associates were the first to undertake a systematic quantification. In Mansfield et al. (1977, Chapter 8), novel methodologies were formulated to discover for a sample of 17 innovations that the median private return (before taxes) was 25%, whereas the median social return (including of course private returns) was 56%. This finding, replicated successfully in two other studies financed by the National Science Foundation, supported a widely-accepted policy view that private incentives may be too weak to support the socially optimal amount of R&D investment. A caveat is frequently ignored. In four of the cases analyzed by Mansfield and associates, the private rate of return exceeded the social rate of return, apparently because innovators cannibalized substantial private rents from products already on the market before the innovation in question, and such cannibalization cannot be reckoned as a social gain.

The third contribution I would emphasize is Mansfield's study of how academic research provided foundations for innovations made by commercial firms. See e.g. Mansfield (1995). From 76 companies he elicited estimates of the fraction of their new products and processes introduced between 1975 and 1985 that could not have been developed without substantial delay in the absence of academic research conducted during the preceding 15 years. The mean for all product innovations was 11% in pharmaceuticals it was 27%. For industrial processes, the average science-dependence figure was 8%. A later survey covering 1986–94 innovations (Mansfield, 1998) found generally increasing links to the academic science base, e.g., for pharmaceuticals, 31 percent, reflecting the increasing orientation over time of pharmaceutical firms toward "rational drug design" rooted in basic science. The analysis in Mansfield (1995) revealed that universities made greater contributions to industrial innovation, the higher they were rated in faculty quality surveys, the more they spent on research, and when they were geographically proximate to the innovating companies.

There are, of course, many more topics in the field of technological change on which Mansfield and his associates contributed important insights. In addition, he wrote textbooks on the principles of microeconomics and macroeconomics, intermediate microeconomics, managerial economics, statistics for business and economics, and related topics. Many of these were carried into iterated editions.

One of the things I have found striking about Mansfield's publication history is the unusual concentration of books with a single publisher, W.W. Norton & Co. A search of Harvard University's computerized catalogue revealed 51 listings (many of them duplicates or revised editions), of which 46 bore the Norton imprint. From conversations I know that Ed had an unusually close working relationship with Norton's chairman, Donald Lamm. For Ed, turning to Norton as publisher was virtually a reflex action. I confess envy, having lurched from one unsatisfactory experience with U.S. textbook publishers to another. (I expressly exclude from this negative record a U.K. house, Edward Elgar, along with my numerous highly competent academic publishers.) My two most negative experiences were the result of sell-offs, in one of them replacing a competent and enthusiastic editor with one who lacked either of those virtues.

4. Idiosyncracies

Although he did more than any other economist to illuminate the nuts and bolts of technological change, Ed himself was not what the innovation literature would call an early adopter. He didn't drive a car, but lived conveniently near a commuter rail line that transported him swiftly to the University of Pennsylvania. He greatly preferred railroad transportation – a 19th century technology – over flying. He didn't use credit cards; and he didn't type. Once I was riding with him in a hotel elevator. He looked peaked. I asked, "Ed, is there something wrong?" "I never did like elevators," he replied. When the personal computer age dawned, he had a computer on his desk. But he seldom if ever used it and among other things chose not to join the e-mail craze.

On e-mail, I suspect, he would eventually have hurdled the digital divide, had he not died in 1997. When he was diagnosed with a dangerous late-stage cancer, he shunned the use of chemotherapy, whose expected outcome was a few months of additional life at a high quality-of-life cost. His death deprived the world of an economist who generated superlative spillover benefits. He is sorely missed.

References

Conference on Industrial Research, 1951, 'Project Selection and Review,' *Costs, Budgeting, and Economics of Industrial Research*, New York: King's Crown Press.

Cooper, J. (ed.), 1970, *The Economics of Drug Innovation*, Washington: American University.

Diamond, A.M., Jr. 2003, 'Edwin Mansfield's Contributions to the Economics of Technology,' *Research Policy* **32**, 1607–1617.

Mansfield, E. 1961, 'Technical Change and the Rate of Imitation,' *Econometrica* **29** (October), 741–766.

Mansfield, E., and Brandenburg, R. 1966, 'The Allocation, Characteristics, and Success of the Firm's R and D Portfolio: A Case Study,' *Journal of Business* **39** (October), 447–464.

Mansfield, E., 1968, *Industrial Research and Technological Innovation: An Econometric Analysis*, New York: W.W. Norton.

Mansfield, E., J. Rapoport, J. Schnee, S. Wagner, and M. Hamburger, 1971, *Research and Innovation in the Modern Corporation*, New York: Norton.

Mansfield, E., J. Rapoport, A. Romeo, E. Villani, S. Wagner, and F. Husic, 1977, *The Production and Application of New Industrial Technology*, New York: Norton.

Mansfield, E., A. Romeo, M. Schwartz, D. Teece, S. Wagner, and P. Brach, 1982, *Technology Transfer, Productivity, and Economic Policy*, New York: Norton.

Mansfield, E., 1988, 'Industrial R&D In Japan and the United States: A Comparative Study,' *American Economic Review* **78** (May), 223–228.

Mansfield, E., 1995, 'Academic Research Underlying Industrial Innovations: Sources, Characteristics, and Financing,' *Review of Economics and Statistics* **77** (February), 55–65.

Mansfield, E., 1998, 'Academic Research and Industrial Innovation: An Update of Empirical Findings,' *Research Policy* **26** (April), 773–776.

Nelson Richard R. (ed.), 1962, *The Rate and Direction of Inventive Activity* Princeton: Princeton University Press.

Scherer, F.M., 1992, 'Schumpeter and Plausible Capitalism,' *Journal of Economic Literature*, **30** (September), 1416–1433.

Scherer, F.M., 2002, Dietmar Harhoff, and Joerg Kukies, 2000 'Uncertainty and the Size Distribution of Rewards from Technological Innovation,' *Journal of Evolutionary Economics*, **10**, 175–200.

Tybout, R.A., (ed.), 1965, *Economics of Research and Development*, Columbus: Ohio State University Press.

Flexibility and Endogenous Innovation

Robert M. Solow

ABSTRACT. The trail I want to follow leads from Stigler to Mansfield with few, if any, intermediate stops. That should sound like a pretty good genealogy.

I

Long ago (1939 to be exact) George Stigler published an important article called "Production and Distribution in the Short Run" (*Journal of Political Economy*, XLVII (1939), 305–27). I want to extract just one simple but fruitful point from many. Imagine a firm that is about to choose among several available technologies, build the suitable plant, or otherwise fix its method of production for some appreciable time to come. Focus on two alternatives. One of them yields an average cost curve that has a very low unit cost at its minimum point, but rises sharply at smaller or greater outputs. The other can not achieve such a low unit cost anywhere. Its minimum average cost, which we can take for simplicity (and to avoid irrelevant questions about scale) to occur at the same output as the first, is noticeably higher; but the average cost curve is much flatter, so that it achieves a lower unit cost than the first technology for outputs that are some distance from the least-cost level.

It makes sense to say that the second technology is more flexible than the first. A firm choosing between them would take the first technology if it were pretty sure that it would be producing an amount close to the least-cost output most of the time. A firm with greater uncertainty about its output pattern over time would be more likely to prefer the second, more flexible, technology. Of course the firm *chooses* its output each period, so that it is not really satisfactory to make the distinction in those terms. What one really has in mind is that the flexible technology is better for a firm facing highly variable demand conditions; the sharply targeted technology is more suitable for a firm that expects to face a stable demand.

That is simple and straightforward, and does not need even an example to clinch the point. But I want to provide an example anyway, precisely because it is elementary-textbook stuff, and can serve as an analogy when we come to a more complicated setting. I do not even have to make the contrast between the two cost curves very pronounced, though of course it could be. So, suppose the targeted technology has a total cost curve $t(x) = a + bx^2$, where x is output. Thus the average and marginal cost curves are $a(x) = a/x + bx$ and $m(x) = 2bx$. The least-cost output is $x = (a/b)^{1/2}$, and at that output unit cost is $2(ab)^{1/2}$. Figure 1 gives the familiar picture: $a(x)$ goes to infinity as x vanishes, and is asymptotic to the ray bx as x gets large.

For the flexible technology, I might as well go whole hog and make average and marginal cost constant at c. So $t(x) = cx$. It is only necessary that $c > 2(ab)^{1/2}$, or else the flexible technology dominates its rival. For an elementary reason that will be obvious in a moment, I suppose that the flexible technology has an inviolable capacity limit at $x = M$. So average cost is horizontal for $x < M$ and turns vertical at $x = M$.

Now suppose the firm is a price-taker. If it adopts the targeted technology, it will not produce unless p exceeds $2(ab)^{1/2}$, but at higher prices it will produce $x = p/2b$ and earn positive profits of $p^2/4b - a$. If it uses the flexible technology, it will not produce at all unless p exceeds c, but at higher prices it will produce at capacity and earn profits $(p-c)M$. (Of course this is why we need a finite capacity. If the flexible

Massachusetts Institute of Technology,
Department of Economics
50 Memorial Drive
Cambridge, MA 02142
U.S.A.

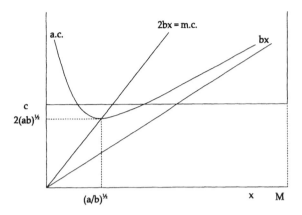

Figure 1. Targeted and flexible static average and marginal costs curves.

technology came with a flattish saucer-shaped average-cost curve instead of a horizontal line, there would be more arithmetic to do but the broad picture would be similar. It is not worth the trouble.)

The firm's decision problem turns on its *ex ante* probability distribution of the market price. (Under imperfect competition, the firm would have to have an *ex ante* joint distribution over at least two parameters of its demand curve, one for level and one for slope or elasticity.) Under risk neutrality, it will choose the technology giving the higher expected profit. This cannot depend solely on the variability of price, because any location parameter of the price distribution will also be relevant. (For example, if the largest possible price exceeds $2(a/b)^{1/2}$ but falls short of c, the flexible technology loses regardless of variability.) The point of the exercise, however, is not any such simple theorem, but rather a feeling for the way the story goes.

There is no need actually to carry out the expected-profit calculations. The situation can be easily read from Figure 2. We already know the *profit function* of each of the eligible technologies. For the targeted technology it is $\pi(p) = p^2/4b - a$ if $p > 2(ab)^{1/2}$, and zero otherwise. It is plotted in Figure 2. For the flexible technology, $\pi(p) = (p-c)M$ if $p > c$ and zero otherwise, and it is plotted in the same diagram. The advantage of one choice over the other is easily read off for each possible price. Any notion of likely price behavior over time can be translated into a choice of one technology over the other.

There is one qualification, however. From the diagram, it looks as if the profit function for the targeted technology will eventually overtake the other, so it will be preferred for all very high prices as well as for low prices. But this apparent paradox is an artifact of the arbitrary capacity limit M imposed on the flexible technology. From general duality theory, or direct calculation, we know that $\pi'(p) = x$; the slope of the profit function at any price is the profit-maximizing output at that price. Consider the point in the diagram where the targeted profit function is momentarily parallel to the flexible one. That is to say, its slope is M (and increasing). At that price, a firm operating the targeted technology would already be producing and selling M units of output. So the targeted technology's profit function only begins to catch up with its rival at the rival technology's capacity output. If the makeshift flexible technology, with a flat average cost and an absolute capacity limit, were replaced with the shallow saucer-shaped average cost curve it is intended to suggest, the capacity limit could be dispensed with. The apparent anomaly would disappear and the Stigler calculation would be routine.

II

Examples like the one just examined can be generated from a standard two-factor production function with one factor fixed and the other variable. The details may not always be so convenient, but the qualitative properties can be preserved. In fact, the quadratic-total-cost case

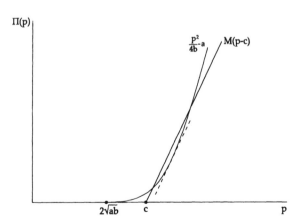

Figure 2. Profit functions associated with targeted and flexible cost curves.

just analyzed emerges directly from a constant-returns-to-scale Cobb-Douglas production function in (fixed) capital and (variable) labor, with elasticities 1/2 and 1/2 But I will want to make use, in a different context, of the broader class of production functions with constant elasticity of substitution between capital and labor, and always with constant returns to scale, though that restriction could profitably be lifted. In that context, the elasticity of substitution can serve as an indicator of technological "flexibility."

So start with the CES production function

$$x = \gamma[\delta K^p + (1-\delta)L^p]^{1/p}; \qquad (1)$$

here γ is a Hicks-neutral efficiency parameter, and $p = (\sigma-1)/\sigma$ where σ is the elasticity of substitution. If we think of capital as being temporarily fixed at K_0 and incurring a regular fixed cost F, we can solve for

$$L = \{[(x/\gamma)^p - \delta K^p]/(1-\delta)\}^{1/p}. \qquad (2)$$

Then, in a self-defining notation, we can write

$$t(x) = F + w(Ax^p - B)^{1/p}. \qquad (3)$$

From this point, it would clearly be possible to rework Stigler's calculation within this broader class of cost functions. But that is not the direction that leads toward Mansfield's terrain.

III

There is a fair amount of literature on the endogenously created *bias* of technological change. It concerned itself first with the proper definition of "labor-saving" and "capital-saving" innovations, and then with the forces that might lead profit-seeking firms to chase one kind of innovation rather than the other. The problem has more recently been cast in terms of the choice between "labor-augmenting" and "capital-augmenting" innovations (expressible as combined changes in the parameters γ and δ of the CES function, for instance). The culmination of that literature, so far, is a series of papers by Daron Acemoglu: "Labor- and Capital-Augmenting Technical Change," *Journal of the European Economic Association*, 1 (2003) 1–37; "Factor Prices and Technical Change," in *Knowledge, Information and Expectations in Modern Macroeconomics: In Honor of Edmund Phelps*, ed. Philippe Aghion et al. "Directed Technical Change," *Review of Economic Studies* 69 (2002) 781–810.

All such innovations are meant to represent gains in productive efficiency. They move the unit isoquant *inward* in the capital-labor plane; the bias has to do with whether the inward shift is greater in one direction or another. It is here that I want to suggest a Stigler twist. Is there a sense in which, given a choice, a profit-seeking firm might be pleased to discover a new technology that sacrifices some productive efficiency in exchange for greater flexibility?

The first step is to be more explicit about the meaning of "flexibility" in this context. This is not as obvious as one might at first think. I shall take it that a flexible technology is one that can easily accommodate fairly large changes in the capital-labor ratio. More formally, one might say that a flexible technology requires a relatively small change in the wage-rental ratio to induce a substantial change in the cost-minimizing capital-labor ratio. And this is precisely the definition of a production function with a large elasticity of substitution. In still other words, the marginal rate of substitution increases slowly with factor-intensity.

What is slightly counterintuitive about this definition is that the "necessity" to make large changes in factor intensity in response to small changes in factor prices sounds somehow problematic. I think the correct intuition here has to allow for the fact that, in the static production-function model, changing factor intensity is a frictionless, costless process. Indeed, the whole point about a flexible technology is that it squeezes the largest possible cost reduction (or gets away with the smallest possible cost increase) out of any change in relative factor prices.

The geometry of a changing elasticity of substitution has been closely explored by Olivier de La Grandville: "In Quest of the Slutzky Diamond," *American Economic Review*, 79 (1989) pp. 476–81. A sketchier version as shown in Figure 3 starts with a unit isoquant exhibiting fixed proportions ($\sigma_0 = 0$, $p = -\infty$). It then shows two more unit isoquants going through the initial vertex and having the same slope at that point ($\sigma_1 < \sigma_2$), and then the other limiting case of a linear isoquant at the same point with the same slope ($\sigma_3 = \infty$, $p = 1$).

As de La Grandville pointed out clearly, for these comparisons the shift to a higher elasticity of substitution is a gain in efficiency as well as a gain in flexibility, and therefore an unambiguous improvement for the firm. That is because the unfolding unit isoquants all have one input configuration in common, along with the marginal rate of substitution at that common point. At every other point, a higher elasticity of substitution moves the unit isoquant closer to the origin.

Now suppose that the choice of a technology is more complicated: one of them has a higher σ and a lower γ than the other, so that the efficiency gain shown in Figure 3 is partially offset. Both have the same value of δ, so there is no factor-saving bias in the comparison. Then Figure 4 is the picture that corresponds, in a way, to Figure 1. The targeted technology is more efficient for an interval of capital-labor ratios, but less efficient outside that interval. Which unit isoquant should a profit-seeking firm prefer? (Constant returns to scale determines the rest.)

The answer clearly depends on the firm's expectations about future factor intensities. But

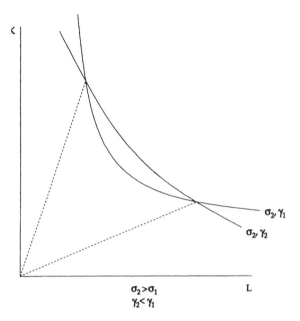

Figure 4. Isoquants for a flexible and targeted technology.

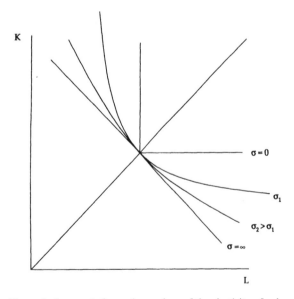

Figure 3. Isoquants for various values of the elasticity of substitution, restricted to pass through a common point with common slope.

the firm chooses its factor intensity whichever technology it operates, although the factor intensity it chooses will obviously depend on the technology it has previously chosen. From the point of view of a firm, it makes more sense to think in terms of expectations about the range of future factor prices. (For macroeconomic issues and more technical detail, see de La Grandville and Solow "Capital-Labor Substitution and Economic Growth," forthcoming.)

This problem is best discussed in terms of the dual cost function corresponding to the CES production function; it gives the smallest unit cost achievable when the price of capital services is q and the wage is w:

$$a(q, w) = \gamma^{-1}[\delta q^{1-\sigma} + (1-\delta)w^{1-\sigma}]^{1/(1-\sigma)}. \quad (4)$$

A level curve of this function shows the combinations of q and w that permit a unit cost of k, say, but nothing lower. Combinations to the SW of the level curve allow a unit cost less than k. Thus it is an unambiguous improvement when a level curve shifts *away from* the origin. Figure 5 shows a pair of such level curves for the same value of k. In this picture, the flatter curve corresponds to a *lower* value of σ. The more angular curve has

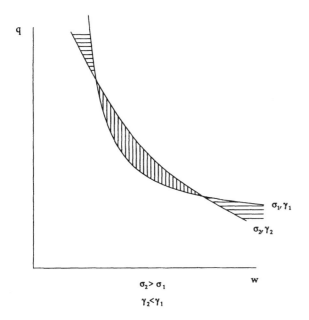

Figure 5. Unit cost functions (as a function of factor prices) for the same technologies.

higher σ, but lower γ, than the flatter one. The lower elasticity of substitution allows a lower unit cost when q/w happens to be between slopes of the two dotted rays shown in the diagram. (The values of q and w in the central vertically-striped sliver between the two curves lead to average cost less than k with the low-σ, high-γ technology, but not with the high-σ, low-γ technology. But the roles are reversed with more extreme values of q/w in either direction. Factor prices in the two horizontally-striped wedge-shaped regions between the curves lie below the angular curve and above the flatter curve. That is, they yield unit cost less than k for the high-σ case, but not for the low-σ.

If factor prices are expected to stay mostly in the narrow central range shown in the diagram, a firm would prefer the targeted low-σ technology if it had the choice. If there is much more uncertainty, if the firm expects wide swings in the factor-price ratio, it would be more likely to prefer the flexible technology. An interesting question for Mansfield's successors in the study of induced technological change is whether the incentive to look for new, flexible technologies is comparable in force to an incentive to seek a particular bias in new technologies.

Perhaps it is far-fetched, but I wonder if the conjunction of the ubiquitousness of information technology and the increased weight of the service sector in modern economies might not add to the importance of flexibility as a desirable characteristic of production processes. The classical mass-production combination of high capital-intensity and long production runs seems, on the surface at least, to be the natural habitat of the targeted technology. Even that is not a sure thing. Targeted technologies are always vulnerable to big changes in factor prices. It is possible that service industries are more exposed to changes in consumer tastes and the accompanying volatility of prices. We are certainly told nowadays that nimbleness and adaptability are keys to business success, presumably more so than in earlier times. What is not obvious is how to capture these notions in the vocabulary of the theory of production, and whether these same notions, once they are made more precise, are likely to have an influence on the direction of technological change and the course of technology-transfer.

Schumpeter and the Micro-foundations of Endogenous Growth*

F.M. Scherer

ABSTRACT. This chapter traces the idea that technological change is endogenous to microeconomic roots considerably earlier than those emphasized in the "new" macroeconomic theories of economic growth. Building upon contributions by Richard Nelson, Jacob Schmookler, F.M. Scherer, and Yoram Barzel, it presents a lean model of how incentives for technological innovation arise endogenously from the interplay of changes in knowledge and demand. Paradoxes attributable to monopoly, parallel but independent technical initiatives, uncertainty, and the divergence between social and private benefits are resolved. A simulation analysis explores the implications of skew stochastic payoff distributions for the optimal number of R&D approaches.

Key words: Endogenous technical change, innovation, Schumpeterian system, technology-push, demand-pull

JEL Classification: L10, O31

Beginning in the late 1980s, a "new" essentially macroeconomic theory of economic growth began to materialize. As characterized in a memoir by one of its founders (Romer, 1994), the new theory distinguished itself from neoclassical theories "by emphasizing that economic growth is an endogenous outcome of the economic system," and not simply the result of superior technology descending like manna from heaven, to be exploited at will by one and all.

One premise of the new endogenous growth theory is that newly discovered knowledge spills over to facilitate technological innovations by the profit-seeking firms that invest in them and which, by securing patent protection on details of the innovations even if not on the facilitating

Aetna Professor Emeritus John F. Kennedy School of Government Harvard University
E-mail: fmscherer@comcast.net
* This article was written for, and is reprinted with permission from, Horst Hanusch and Andreas Pykas, eds., *The Elgar Companion on Neo-Schumpeterian Economics* (Cheltenham: Edward Elgar, 2005).

knowledge, earn what are hoped to be supra-normal profits from them. A curiosity of the new theory is that, despite placing so much emphasis on the facilitating role of knowledge as a basis for subsequent innovations, it largely ignores the vast stock of knowledge contributed over previous decades on technological innovation and its essentially endogenous character. It in effect purports to reinvent the endogenous innovation wheel. This, as an old curmudgeon who participated in laying the earlier theoretical foundations, I recognize, may come from ignorance of previous scholars' contributions. But it ought to be taken into account by historians of thought attempting to survey the advance of economic theory during the 20th century. In this paper, I attempt at least in a limited way to set matters straight and to identify some of the persisting puzzles.

1. Schumpeter's pioneering role

Proponents of "new" endogenous economic growth theories do acknowledge, typically in a cursory way, one predecessor: Schumpeter (1912).[1] From the time of his *Habilitationsschrift* (1912), Schumpeter argued correctly that innovation, and in particular technological innovation, is one of the main driving forces underlying economic growth. In the English translation of his classic Schumpeter (1934, p. 60), acknowledges his intellectual debt to Karl Marx and criticizes John Stuart Mill's view that technological improvement "is something which just happens and the effects of which we have to investigate, while we have nothing say about its occurrence *per se*". Thus, technological change does not occur exogenously, or as one of the "given" conditions in an economy. Rather, innovation is a profit-seeking activity carried out by business firms, and in particular, entrepreneurial business firms. In modern language, it is endogenous. In his later popularization Schumpeter (1942, p. 110) makes the point even more bluntly:

> Was not the observed [economic growth] performance due to that stream of inventions that revolutionized the technique of production rather than to the businessman's hunt for profits? The answer is in the negative. The carrying into effect of these technological novelties was of the essence of that hunt. And even the inventing itself ... was a function of the capitalist process which is responsible for the mental habits that will produce invention. It is therefore quite wrong – and also quite un-Marxian – to say, as so many economists do, that capitalist enterprise was one, and technological progress a second, factor in the observed development of output; they were essentially one and the same thing or, as we may also put it, the former was the propelling force of the latter.

In other chapters of his 1942 book, Schumpeter advanced an additional set of hypotheses sharply at odds with the position he took in 1912. The 1912 book argued that innovations arose most frequently through new firms entering from outside the main stream of economic activity. However, he asserted in 1942 that the most likely innovators in a world of complex and costly modern technology were well-established firms, and indeed, those that not only anticipated obtaining new monopoly power as a result of patents or other elements of "monopolistic strategy" (p. 102) following their innovations, but those that enjoyed some degree of monopoly power before, and as a basis for, making investments in innovation. This claim spawned a vast literature on which I shall be able here to draw only a few limited insights.

Schumpeter provides in his various books little of what today would pass for a rigorously specified economic theory. A small part of that gap will be addressed here. More importantly, his theoretical "vision" does not make clear how, in their profit-seeking innovative efforts, entrepreneurs choose which potential avenues of technological change they will pursue and which they will ignore. In other words, his theory lacks a clear statement of how the "invisible hand" guides innovation efforts. One might analogize firms' innovative efforts to the search for still-undiscovered oil deposits. The opportunities are put there by nature; firms merely need to find them and perfect the means of exploiting them. But such a model would sooner or later run into diminishing marginal returns, which are clearly inconsistent with the Schumpeterian vision. Thus, it remained for later scholars to elaborate the entrepreneurial search mechanism and explain why technological change might be self-regenerating.

2. Early builders on the Schumpeterian vision

One theoretical track initiated by Hicks (1932) asked how changes in wages induce technological changes in the factor bias of production functions. Most of the substantial literature on this point excepting perhaps Fellner (1961) emerged after the contributions that will be reviewed here, so it will be given short shrift.[2]

The first known contribution that provided a fully articulated view of how market forces influence innovative efforts was a 1959 article by Nelson (1959). Two major themes are stated in the first two paragraphs and elaborated both conceptually, with careful recognition of precursor authors, and extensive case study evidence, in the remainder of the article. To paraphrase the first two paragraphs:

> [I]nvention is strongly motivated by perceived profit opportunities. Demand and cost factors play major roles with the state of scientific knowledge significantly affecting the cost and hence the profitability of invention... [S]econd, ... invention ... is an activity often carried on under conditions of great uncertainty.

George Stigler once said that "It's all in Adam Smith". Smith in fact had important things to say about the precursors of modern industrial research and development laboratories. However, for the roots of endogenous innovation theory, one can justifiably say that "it's all in Nelson".

The "demand factors" examined in Nelson's contribution went beyond prior authors' vague notions of "need" as inducements to technological innovation. The role of demand was suggested in tentative form by Schmookler (1954) and then elaborated by Schmookler (1966) into a conceptualization supported by an ambitious analysis of patent data.[3] Among other things, in his 1966 book Schmookler showed how supply- and demand-side influences interacted to induce technological changes and how the uneven distribution of technological knowledge and capabilities affected the industrial loci from which entrepreneurs responded to demand-side stimuli.

Neither Nelson nor Schmookler formulated an explicit economic model of how demand and supply influenced, separately or together, the allocation of resources to technological innovation. It is here that I creep into the picture. As an extension of my work modelling the allocation of resources to the development of new weapons systems, I began systematic research in 1963 on how market structure affected the pace of innovation – a classic Schumpeterian theme. My work was supported by a grant from the Inter-University Committee on the Economics of Technological Change, funded in turn by the Ford Foundation, and was enriched by discussions in 1964 and 1965 between Schmookler and myself in the off-hours at committee meetings, usually held in Cambridge or Princeton.[4] Schmookler stressed the importance of demand and I the role of supply-side (knowledge side) advances. It was Schmookler who provided the synthesizing metaphor, one adopted previously in a different context by Alfred Marshall: just as it took two blades of a scissors to cut paper, so both supply (knowledge base) and demand changes affected the profitability of technological innovations and hence the pace at which they were undertaken.

Following similar concepts applied to weapons R&D, my main theoretical model viewed business firms' investment in research and development as a capital investment problem. Under it, firms attempted in any given project to maximize the discounted surplus of quasi-rents $v(t)$ less R&D costs $C(t)$, with the key novelty being the assumption that the quasi-rents depended in fairly intricate ways on the timing of rivals' competing innovations. Footnote 11 to the resulting article (Scherer, 1967) stated that:

> Continuous exogenous technological progress can be represented by an additional term – λt in the exponent of [the market value term]. Developments made worthwhile mainly because of a shift in the time–cost tradeoff [$C(t)$] function can be called

"technology-push" innovations. Those made worthwhile because firms find themselves entering a period of especially high $v(t)$ values can be called "demand-pull" innovations. On these two notions a more general theory of technological innovation can be built, although the task lies beyond the scope of the present paper.

After completing that paper, I turned to other lines of research and did not return to the problem as posed above until several years later.[5] A year after my 1967 paper was published, the *Review of Economics and Statistics* included an article by Yoram Barzel building upon my "more general theory" suggestion, but with no citation to my prior work. Since Barzel attended the May 1966 conference (hosted at the University of Pennsylvania by Edwin Mansfield) at which I presented oral and written versions of the 1967 paper, he could scarcely have been unaware of my formulation. However, his model utilized a competitive equilibrium assumption I did not and would not have conceived. Those two contributions provide the foundation upon which I shall elaborate here.

3. The basic dynamic model

The basic dynamic model is illustrated in Figure 1. On the supply side, suppose that carrying out in the current time period ($T = 0$) the research and development (RD) required successfully to commercialize a new product or production process is RD_0, or, with the numerical assumptions of Figure 1, 2500. To keep matters simple, we assume with some violence to realism that the R&D project, once undertaken, is carried out instantaneously. As time goes on, exogenous advances in the knowledge base reduce the cost of performing the required R&D. These advances may come from the progress of relevant scientific and technological knowledge and/or through clues spilling over costlessly from successful solution of the technical problems confronting prior product or process development generations. The advances are assumed (somewhat implausibly) in Figure 1 to occur continuously and smoothly at the rate of (100 a) percent per year, or, as Figure 1 is drawn, at 3% annually. Thus, from year zero's vantage point, the cost of performing the requisite R&D in year T is $RD_0 \, e^{-0.03T}$. But from that vantage point, a

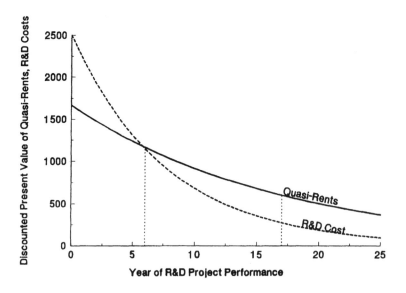

Figure 1. How changes in demand and technology induce innovation. Demand grows at 4%; R&D cost declines at 3%; Discount Rate = 10%.

dollar spent in year T must be discounted to present value at the interest rate r, assumed in the Figure 1 illustration to be 10% per year. Thus, at year zero, the equation for the R&D cost curve shown by the dashed line in Figure 1 is $RD_0\, e^{-(a+r)T} = 2500\, e^{-0.13T}$.

On the demand side, suppose the quasi-rents realized from having a successful new product or process amount to $v_0 = 100$ per year in year zero and grow (e.g., because of general demand expansion) at a rate of $100\,g = 4\%$ per year thereafter.[6] Assuming for algebraic simplicity an infinite time horizon, the discounted present value of benefits expected from an R&D project completed in year T amount to:

$$V(T) = \int_T^\infty v_0\, e^{(g-r)t}\, dt = 100\, \frac{e^{(g-r)T}}{(r-g)} \quad (1)$$

The graph of this discounted quasi-rent function, again viewed from the perspective of time zero, is shown by the solid line in Figure 1.

At time zero, discounted R&D costs exceed the discounted present value of anticipated quasi-rents, and so the project is not profitable to a would-be innovator. As the years advance, however, discounted quasi-rents fall less rapidly than discounted R&D costs. In year 6, or more precisely, at $T = 5.8$, discounted costs and quasi-rents are equal, and so the project becomes economically feasible.[7] The combination of technology-push (falling R&D costs) and demand-pull (rising quasi-rents) provides the required economic stimulus to innovation. If conduct of the R&D project can be delayed beyond year 6, there is an increasing surplus of discounted anticipated quasi-rents over R&D costs, so the project yields profits that, at least for some time, are rising. On this, more later.

With the assumptions of Figure 1, there is no unicausal inducement mechanism. Figures 2 and 3 alter the picture. Figure 2 superimposes upon the numerical assumptions of Figure 1 a sudden knowledge breakthrough during year 3 that sharply reduces R&D costs. Once the implications of the breakthrough are recognized, a project that was previously considered unprofitable becomes profitable. This illustrates the pure technology-push case. In Figure 3, discounted quasi-rents jump upward because e.g. of a sudden change in current and expected energy costs, rendering an energy-saving innovation profitable that previously failed the profitability test.[8] This is the pure demand-pull inducement scenario.

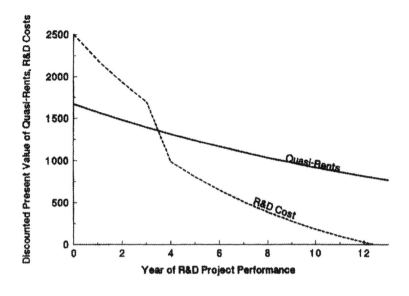

Figure 2. Technology-push innovation inducement.

4. Market dynamics and market structure

We return now to Figure 1. As we saw, discounted quasi-rents first exceed discounted R&D costs after year 6. But at that early date, there is room in the market for only one firm carrying out the R&D project. If more firms conducted independent R&D projects, their combined discounted R&D costs would exceed discounted quasi-rents and the project would be unprofitable in the aggregate at, say, year 7. For reasons other than those advanced by Schumpeter, monopoly appears necessary to achieve the earliest possible technological progress. But if the firm conducting R&D were a monopolist unconcerned by threats of losing its would-be monopoly position to faster-acting rivals, the monopolist would not choose to innovate when the project first crosses the profitability threshold at year 6. Rather, seeing discounted R&D costs falling more

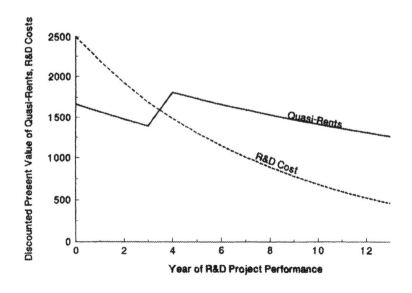

Figure 3. Demand-pull technology inducement.

rapidly than discounted quasi-rents, the monopolist would wait until it could achieve the maximum possible discounted difference between the two – given the numerical assumptions underlying Figure 1, at year 17, eleven years later than the time when the innovation first becomes profitable.[9]

Barzel's escape from this paradox is to assume that only one firm conducts the required R&D, after which it secures patent protection permitting it to monopolize the newly developed product or process market. But it can only attain this favored position by preempting all would-be rivals with an early R&D date – indeed, if pre-innovation competition exhausts all supra-normal profits, with the earliest possible (six-year) innovation timetable. Ex ante competition to achieve a monopoly position forces the pace of innovation toward completion in year six, at which time either of two things must happen to validate the model's assumptions: rival firms whose presence forces the pace withdraw before significant R&D costs have been sunk, or they are forced to withdraw, e.g., because the government grants an exclusive franchise to carry out the necessary R&D to the firm offering the earliest innovation date in some kind of competitive bidding context.[10]

Needless to say, satisfaction of these conditions is problematic. The feasibility of awarding an exclusive R&D franchise to the firm offering the fastest innovation pace is especially doubtful, since entrants into a government choice process are likely to propose R&D schedules more ambitious than those they actually intend to pursue, or they may deliver results qualitatively inferior to (and less costly than) those they promise. Such optimistic bidding biases are a chronic feature of competitions organized by the U.S. Department of Defense in choosing contractors for individual weapons R&D programs. See Peck and Scherer (1962, pp. 411–420). Thus, in a world of steady but slow change in technological possibilities and demand stimuli, it may be difficult to achieve conditions conducive to the earliest profitable exploitation of new technological possibilities. At best, a considerable degree of indeterminacy in the inducement mechanism must be acknowledged.

The dilemma fades when demand or supply conditions change abruptly with scientific breakthroughs or demand-side shocks, as illustrated in Figures 2 and 3. Then for a project that was unprofitable at one moment in time, a gap between quasi-rent and R&D cost functions suddenly opens up, perhaps to a magnitude allowing several firms to complete fast-paced competing R&D projects without exhausting the over-all profit potential, or at least, to permit several independent strands of low-cost preliminary research, after which most abandon the field for the more costly final development phases to the firms that have achieved the best early results.[11] This view is consistent with statistical evidence indicating systematically more intense R&D efforts in concentrated industries when advances in underlying scientific knowledge come gradually, but with a deterioration or even reversal of the relationship – i.e., with more intensive R&D in less tightly oligopolistic industries – when the science base is rapidly changing.[12] That a rapid pace of technological innovation can be sustained in fragmented or easily entered industries is also suggested by the predominant role of new and small firms in the U.S. information technology and biotechnology industries during the last two decades of the 20th century.

5. Uncertainty and social welfare maximization

Figures 1–3 oversimplify reality in an important way, ignoring the pervasive role of uncertainty in technological innovation. Encountering unexpected technical problems is not uncommon in R&D projects, although research by Edwin Mansfield *et al.* (1977a) suggests that a majority of projects do achieve their technical goals. Uncertainties in predicting whether a contemplated technical advance will satisfy the demands of the marketplace are without doubt much greater than uncertainties in determining whether a stated technical goal can be reached. This is shown inter alia by the experience of 110 U.S. high-technology startup companies floating common stock offerings between 1983 and 1986. Scherer *et al.* (2000). By the time an initial public offering (IPO) is launched, the typical startup company has progressed sufficiently far in its R&D efforts to have surmounted most of the purely technical hurdles. But after public stock offerings were launched, 35 of the 110 companies

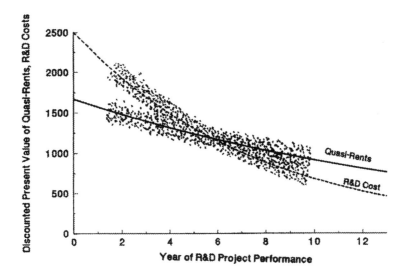

Figure 4. The impact of uncertainty.

failed altogether – usually because their products failed to gain substantial consumer acceptance. If initial $1000 investments had been made in the 52 1983–1986 IPO companies whose securities continued to be traded to the end of 1995, the most successful five companies accounted for 70% of the total December 1995 value of the 52 companies' stock market value. Analysis of month-by-month changes in individual companies' stock prices revealed a noisy random walk as the passage of time resolved market uncertainties.

Figure 4 adds the fog of uncertainty to the R&D cost and market payoff trajectories illustrated originally in Figure 1. The range of outcomes that might plausibly be foreseen ex ante is shown by clusters of points scattered about the expected cost and quasi-rent functions. With the addition of uncertainty, we see that benefits might be seen to exceed costs as early as year three, but the anticipated breakeven date might also come as late as year 10. If competition to be the first with the relevant new product or process is strong and a winner's curse prevails, the R&D project might be undertaken well in advance of the true breakeven point at year 5.8.

This outcome might at first glance seem undesirable, since projects are undertaken whose costs exceed their benefits. But here a distinction must be made between private and social benefits. The anticipated payoffs that induce commercial innovation are those that the entity making an investment in R&D can expect to appropriate to its own benefit. These are called "private" benefits. It is well-accepted that the benefits realized by all participants in the economy (including the innovator) from successful new products exceed, often by substantial ratios, the benefits appropriated by the innovator. If the new product is priced monopolistically, consumers realize a consumers' surplus from it (measured in the standard diagram by a triangular area) in addition to the profit or producer's surplus retained by the innovator. The more competition there is in pricing the new product, the larger will be the magnitude of the consumers' surplus relative to the producer's surplus. Also, the solution of technical problems in development and the identification of unmet consumer needs provide knowledge spillovers of value to other market participants. Mansfield et al. (1977b) found that at the median for a sample of 17 innovations, discounted social (i.e., private plus external) benefits exceeded private benefits by a ratio of 2.25–1, with a range of from 0.73 (for an innovation that cannibalized other products' surpluses) to 11.37.

To reflect the surplus of social over private benefits, one could add to Figure 1 (or similar diagrams) an additional function lying at most or all points above the discounted quasi-rents function. The simplest case is one in which the social benefits function exceeds the private quasi-rents function by a constant fraction k, with a slope for any given year steeper than that of the quasi-rents function. From this possibility emerge two new insights. First, social benefits normally begin to exceed R&D costs at an earlier date than the one (6 years in Figure 1) at which breakeven occurs in the relationship between private quasi-rents and R&D costs. Thus, "premature" innovation because of uncertainty and the winner's curse need not be undesirable from a broader social perspective. Second, a social planner with complete information would seek not only to ensure that social benefits exceed R&D costs, but to choose an innovation date maximizing the surplus of discounted *social* (not private monopoly) benefits minus discounted private R&D costs.[13]

This welfare-maximizing innovation date will under normal circumstances occur later than the social breakeven date. Whether it occurs before or after the date at which private quasi-rents first exceed R&D costs is ambiguous. For the case in which costs are declining and discounted benefits changing smoothly over time, it depends upon the year zero variable values, the rates at which costs and benefits are changing over time, and the size of the wedge between the social and private benefit curves. If the ratio of social benefits (including the innovator's producer surplus) to private benefits is k, the value of k at which the *socially* optimal R&D date coincides with the "breakeven" year at which discounted *private* quasi-rents equal discounted R&D costs, can be expressed by the formula:

$$k^* = (r + a)/(r - g), \qquad (2)$$

where r is the relevant time discount rate (assumed to be the same for innovators and social welfare-maximizers), a as before is the rate at which R&D costs fall annually, and g is the rate at which private quasi-rents grow per year.[14] For the parameter values assumed in constructing Figure 1, $k^* = (0.10 + 0.03)/(0.10 - 0.04) = 2.167$, which is close to 2.25 the median social/private benefits ratio determined empirically by Mansfield *et al.* (1977b). Thus, for plausible parameter values, competition that leads to innovation dates sooner than those at which private breakeven occurs can at least in principle be socially optimal. For given parameter constellations, the more the actual value of k exceeds k^*, the more desirable is an innovation pace faster than the private breakeven pace. However, the more rapidly private benefits are growing and/or the more rapidly R&D costs are falling over time, the larger the wedge between private and social benefits must be to let the socially optimal innovation date precede the private breakeven date.

Recognition of uncertainty leads to the identification of two additional general cases in which competitive "duplication" of R&D projects leads to general welfare gains.

First, because R&D projects fail, especially when the correct technological path to a successful solution is difficult to identify ex ante, pursuing multiple, diverse R&D approaches in parallel is often desirable. In this instance, the quasi-rent function in Figure 1 might be reinterpreted as the expected value of the cost of the multiple R&D approaches required to achieve the desired end product. "Required" here can be a misleading term, since the number of parallel approaches pursued affects both the probability of success and the speed at which a good solution emerges – variables which themselves are susceptible to strategic choice. See Nelson (1961) and Scherer (1965). In this additional sense, both the number of projects and the timing of their outcome are endogenous variables. The lower is the ex ante probability that a single R&D approach will be successful and the deeper the stream of anticipated benefits is from a successful solution, the larger the profit-maximizing number of parallel approaches will be.

Second, the approach pursued thus far has implicitly assumed that there is only one satisfactory solution to an innovative quest. But in fact, consumers have variegated tastes (and the purchasers of innovative producer's goods have variegated needs). Some specific innovative outcomes may satisfy few consumers, others many consumers. For such cases of what has been called "horizontal product differentiation," diversity of consumer preferences combines with uncertainty as to which solutions best satisfy the wants of particular consumer clusters to make investing in R&D like throwing darts with imprecise aim at a dartboard, over which payoffs are distributed more or less randomly.

A dartboard experiment

To illustrate this second proposition, a Monte Carlo experiment was conducted. One hundred possible R&D outcomes were identified, with each of which a randomized discounted quasi-rent payoff was associated. Consistent with a considerable amount of empirical evidence, the distribution of payoffs was highly skew, following a log normal distribution of the form $10^{normal(0,1)} \times 1000$. For the payoff matrix used in all iterations of the experiment, the mean payoff was $5490, the median $1310, and the maximum payoff $91700. The top ten payoffs accounted for 63.1% of the total across all 100 payoffs. This degree of concentration in a relatively few "winners" is typical of the outcome distributions resulting from investments in individual high-technology startup companies. See Scherer *et al.* (2000, p. 177).

If innovative projects could be targeted precisely toward the most lucrative products or processes, innovators would in effect direct darts toward all prospects with expected quasi-rents exceeding R&D costs. Assuming a uniform R&D cost of $5000 per project, the payoff distribution described in the previous paragraph would present 24 attractive targets. A precise single-shot "hit" on each of these would yield summed quasi-rents of $346,070, from which R&D costs of 24 × 5000 = $120,000 must be subtracted to yield a net profit of $226,070.

If the R&D dart throwers are unable to aim with such perfect precision, but instead strew their thrusts randomly over the dart board's payoff space, a quite different outcome ensues. This process was simulated by assuming that each R&D project or dart throw landed at some random coordinate in payoff space. The distribution of possible coordinate "hits" was assumed to be uniform random with replacement. The simulation was performed across an array of eight different sample sizes (i.e., number of dart throws), and for each such sample, the procedure was replicated ten times with a fresh sample of randomly determined coordinate "hit" locations. Multiple hits on a single coordinate location were assumed to add no quasi-rent value, e.g., as if the payoffs from a double hit were shared between two firms marketing a product with identical characteristics.

With R&D costs of $5000 per dart throw and assuming 24 throws, as in the perfect-aim case

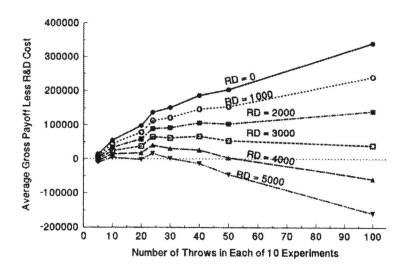

Figure 5. Net payoffs from dartboard experiment.

above, the average quasi-rent sum per iteration across ten 24-throw iterations was $137,020. Subtracting from this average payoff total R&D costs of 24 × 5000 = $120,000, the average net profit per iteration was $17,030. Thus, the innovative efforts yielded on average only slight supra-normal profits, analogous to a single-shot innovation at approximately year 7 under the conditions graphed in Figure 1. However, as one expects in sampling from highly skew potential payoff distributions, the results of the ten 24-shot iterations varied widely, with net profits after the deduction of R&D costs ranging from $146,75 down to -$73,010.

The strategy pursued by dart-throwing R&D managers depends not only upon the distribution of potential payoffs but on the cost per R&D project (dart throw), which together determine the optimal number of throws. Figure 5 illustrates the dependency of net profits (i.e., summed quasi-rents less total R&D costs) upon the average cost per R&D project. With zero cost per R&D project (the top solid line in Figure 5), one continues throwing darts beyond 100 darts per iteration in the hope of hitting previously untouched payoff coordinates.[15] However, when each dart throw entails cost, the attractiveness of large-numbers attacks eventually diminishes, the more so, the higher the cost per throw. With R&D cost of $1000 per dart throw, an extension of the experiments recorded in Figure 5 shows, it is profitable to increase the number of throws per iteration to at least 200. A similar extension reveals that with an R&D cost of $2000 per throw, the net income-maximizing number of throws is on the order of 100. With costs of $3000 per throw, the profit maximum lies in the range of 24 to 40 throws. (It is impossible to be more precise because, with such a highly skew payoff distribution, considerable variability of outcomes remains even after the experiment is iterated ten times.) With even higher R&D costs per throw, the profit maxima lie in the range of 10 to 24 throws, although again, the intrinsic variability of the results precludes greater precision. Quite generally, and completely consistent with the results of less richly specified models of optimal parallel paths strategies in research and development, the greater is the surplus of average payoffs over R&D costs for any given number of trials, the larger is the profit-maximizing number of trials.

When average payoffs are large relative to R&D costs, undertaking numerous trials (dart tosses) may be attractive not only because total payoffs rise by more than R&D costs, but also because proliferation of attacks on skew-distributed payoff targets reduces the relative variability of project outcomes. For the experiments described here, the coefficient of variation (i.e., the ratio of the standard deviation of payoffs to the average payoff) for repeated dart-tossing iterations ranged from 0.79 (for five tosses per iteration) down to 0.20 (for 100 tosses). This hedging benefit is clearly sought by the managers of high-technology venture fund portfolios in the United States. On average, the typical venture fund invests in roughly 40 individual start-up enterprises. Beyond this, the costs of overseeing and managing the diverse investment targets tend to increase disproportionately, discouraging further portfolio diversification.

Such a portfolio strategy can seldom be pursued by individual entrepreneurs who invest most or all of their personal assets and their time in innovation projects. But the innate variability of R&D project outcomes may in itself be an inducement to those entrepreneurs. I have argued previously, citing inter alia statistical evidence that horse race bettors exhibit a skewness-loving propensity along with risk (i.e., standard deviation) aversion, that the entrepreneurs who initiate high-technology ventures in the United States respond positively to the known skewness of high-technology venture payoffs (assuming as before that *average* expected rewards exceed R&D costs).[16] If there is any truth in this hypothesis, we come full circle back to the speculations of Schumpeter (1942, p. 75) six decades ago:

> Spectacular prizes much greater than would have been necessary to call forth the particular effort are thrown to a small minority of winners, thus propelling much more efficaciously than a more equal and more "just" distribution would, the activity of that large majority of businessmen who receive in return very modest compensation or nothing or less than nothing, and yet do their utmost because they have the big prizes before their eyes and overrate their chances of doing equally well.

Conclusion

This analysis of the dart-throwing metaphor leaves unanswered a question raised earlier: why large gaps between R&D payoffs and costs open up to induce the exploration of multiple R&D paths by technological entrepreneurs. Competition among entrepreneurs pursuing parallel R&D projects can accelerate the pace at which innovative opportunities are exploited, but if it proceeds too far, squeezing to nothing the expected gap between minimal R&D costs and payoffs, it undermines the very logic of its existence. The answer may lie in the existence of discontinuities, e.g., as scientific or applied research breakthroughs or abrupt changes in demand conditions create previously unavailable profit opportunities. Or it may result from uncertainty and the great difficulty of identifying the most lucrative targets for innovative investments. Until we know more about how opportunity-generating processes function, perplexities will remain in our microeconomic analyses of how innovation proceeds endogenously.

Notes

1. In four survey articles on "New Growth Theory" in the *Journal of Economic Perspectives*, Winter 1994, Paul Romer refers without a citation to his models as "neo-Schumpeterian," and one other article cites Schumpeter (1934).
2. For a thorough literature review, see Thirtle and Ruttan (1987). For a brief but remarkably perceptive early insight, see also Plant (1934).
3. For the most extensive confirming evidence, see Scherer (1982).
4. The other committee members were Alf Conrad, Zvi Griliches, Edwin Mansfield, Jesse Markham, Richard Nelson, and M.J. Peck.
5. Notes written for "job talks" I gave in Berkeley and Ann Arbor during January 1996 reveal that I presented a geometric version of the model. My first published extension was in Scherer (1970, pp. 426–432).
6. It is assumed throughout that monetary values are measured in units of constant purchasing power; i.e., compensating for whatever general inflation may be occurring.
7. As usual, the discount rate r implies that the firm making an investment is realizing a normal risk-adjusted rate of return.
8. See Popp (2002).
9. For an algebraic proof, see Scherer and Ross (1990, pp. 639–641). The delay with secure monopoly might be less if monopolists had lower R&D costs, e.g. because of scale economies or the ability to attract superior talent, or because of lower interest rates, than firms in more fragmented markets. These advantages were suggested in Schumpeter (1942, p. 101), but countervailing arguments can also be advanced.
10. This "exclusive prospect" scenario was proposed as a practical policy model by Kitch (1977). It is also implicit in the theory of optimal patent life articulated by Nordhaus (1969).
11. On the characteristic low-early expenditure, high final expenditure spending pattern in R&D projects, see Peck and Scherer (1962, p. 313).
12. See Scherer and Ross (1990, pp. 648–649).
13. For the relevant calculus in the zero quasi-rent growth case, see Scherer and Ross (1990, p. 641, note 71).
14. The proof is obtained by a simple extension of the methods used in Scherer and Ross (1990, p. 641, note 72), recognizing that the breakeven equation is equation (2) in note 68.
15. There can be numerous multiple hits (ex post, duplicative R&D projects). With 100 trials or darts, the number of "missed" payoff cells ranged from 35 to 40, implying at least that number of multiple hits.

For the experiments with smaller samples, there was substantial outcome variability among the experiments. The initial result with samples of 20 was particularly low, kinking the lines in Figure 5 downward. Three additional runs of 10 experiments each were conducted for the $n = 20$ case, with the average result substituted in the version of Figure 5 presented here.
16. See Scherer (2001), citing Golec and Tamarkin (1998).

REFERENCES

Barzel, Y., 1968, 'Optimal Timing of Innovations,' *Review of Economics and Statistics*. **50**, 348–355.

Fellner, W.J., 1961, 'Two Propositions in the Theory of Induced Innovations,' *Economic Journal*, **71**, 305–308.

Golec, J. and M., Tamarkin, 1998, 'Bettors Live Skewness, Not Risk, at the Horse Track,' *Journal of Political Economy*, **106**, 205–225.

Hicks, J.R., 1932, *The Theory of Wages*. London: Macmillan.

Kitch, E.W., 1977, 'The Nature and Function of the Patent System,' *Journal of Law & Economics*, **20**, 265–290.

Mansfield E. *et al.*, 1977a, *Research and Innovation in the Modern Corporation*. New York: Norton.

Mansfield E. *et al.*, 1977b, 'Social and Private Rates of Return from Industrial Innovations,' *Quarterly Journal of Economics*, **91**, 221–240.

Nelson, R.R., 1959, 'The Economics of Invention: A Survey of the Literature,' *Journal of Business*, **32**, 101–127.

Nelson, R.R., 1961, 'Uncertainty, Learning, and the Economics of Parallel Research and Development Projects,' *Review of Economics and Statistics*, **43**, 351–368.

Nordhaus, W.D., 1969, *Invention, Growth, and Welfare: A Theoretical Treatment of Technological Change*. Cambridge: MIT Press.

Peck, M.J. and Scherer, F. M. 1962, *The Weapons Acquisition Process: An Economic Analysis*. Boston: Harvard Business School Division of Research.

Plant, A., 1934, 'The Economic Theory Concerning Patents for Inventions,' *Economica*, new series, **1**, 30–51.

Popp, D., 2002, 'Induced Innovation and Energy Prices,' *American Economic Review*, **92**, 160–188.

Romer, P.M., 1994, 'The Origins of Endogenous Growth.' *Journal of Economic Perspectives*, **8**, 3–22.

Scherer, F.M., 1965, 'Time-Cost Trade-offs in Uncertain Empirical Research Projects,' *Naval Research Logistics Quarterly*, **13**, 71–82.

Scherer, F.M., 1967, 'Research and Development Resource Allocation under Rivalry,' *Quarterly Journal of Economics*, **81**, 359–394.

Scherer, F.M., 1970, *Industrial Market Structure and Economic Performance*. Chicago: Rand McNally.

Scherer, F.M., 1982, 'Demand-Pull and Technological Innovation: Schmookler Revisited,' *Journal of Industrial Economics*, **30**, 225–237.

Scherer, F.M., 2001, 'The Innovation Lottery,' in Rochelle Dreyfuss *et al.*, (eds.), *Expanding the Boundaries of Intellectual Property* (New York: Oxford University Press), 3–21.

Scherer, F.M. and Ross, D. 1990, *Industrial Market Structure and Economic Performance*. Third ed., Boston: Houghton-Mifflin.

Scherer, F.M., D. Harhoff, and J. Kukies, 2000, 'Uncertainty and the Size Distribution of Rewards from Innovation,' *Journal of Evolutionary Economics*, **10**, 175–200.

Schmookler, J., 1966, *Invention and Economic Growth*. Cambridge: Harvard University Press.

Schumpeter, J.A., 1912, *Theorie der wirtschaftlichen Entwicklung*. Leipzig: Duncker & Humblot.

Schumpeter, J.A., 1932, *The Theory of Economic Development*. Translated by Redvers Opie; Cambridge: Harvard University Press.

Schumpeter, J.A., 1942, *Capitalism, Socialism, and Democracy*. New York: Harper.

Thirtle, C. G. and Ruttan, V.W. 1987, *The Role of Demand and Supply in the Generation and Diffusion of Technical Change*. Chur: Harwood Academic Publishers.

Technology and Technology Transfer: Mansfieldian Inspirations and Subsequent Developments

David J. Teece

ABSTRACT. This paper discusses the foundational work and ideas of Edwin Mansfield to the economics of technological change and innovation, and introduces some of the recent work in the field. I argue that much of the recent work on patenting, technology strategy and the economics of knowledge has roots to the early Mansfield contributions, and that he should be recognized as a pioneer for these recent developments.

Key words: economics of innovation, knowledge, intangible assets, R&D management

JEL Classification: O32, O34, L10

1. Introduction

At least since Joseph Schumpeter, scholars have struggled to understand the nature and the dynamics of the economics of technical change. Edwin Mansfield was born into that struggle and was for many decades a true pioneer in the study of the economics of technological change. His early books including 'The Economics of Technological Change' (1968), and 'Technological Change: An Introduction to a Vital Area of Modern Economics' (1971) summarize his early insights and display his passionate desire to wake up the field of economics to a critical area of research. He undoubtedly was the leader in the study of the nature of industrial research in America, certainly during the period of his active scholarship, and arguably to this day.

Although both classical economists and 'modern' economists such as Solow, Nelson, David, Rosenberg, and Kuznets had recognized the

Director, Institute of Management
Innovation and Organization Professor
Haas School of Business
University of California
Berkeley, U.S.A.

importance of innovation and understood it's key role in economic growth and wealth creation, it was not until Mansfield that anyone had performed serious empirical studies of industrial research. Mansfield provided leading insights into issues such as the role of academic and basic research in increasing innovation and productivity, the diffusion of technological innovations, the private and social returns to innovation, and the role of patents and the patent system. With great wisdom, Mansfield chose areas of study that have emerged as being critically important to managers and policy makers.

However, Ed Mansfield showed considerable frustration with modern economics and the work of economic theorists. Indeed, by the 1970s Ed openly displayed almost a disdain for modern economic theory because of the field's infatuation with static analysis, and its abject failure to embrace the study of technology and technological change.

As one of Ed Mansfield's students, I must first acknowledge my huge dept to him personally and intellectually. As a graduate student at Penn in the early 1970s, I was fortunate to end up in his Ph.D. class on the economics of technological change. He opened my eyes to a set of issues for which I had no previous exposure. Because I had a background in international trade and finance and economic development, he encouraged me to study technology transfer. No one at that time, including Ed, knew much about the topic. We learned together, with Ed sending me into the field to collect data and absorb what I could from corporate R&D managers, from licensing executives, and from the experiences of the international departments of the Fortune 500. Some of my findings, along with my reflections on those findings, are discussed in Section 3.

Besides developing a substantive understanding of technology transfer, I learned quite a lot methodologically from Ed. He was a well-recognized statistician with a good nose for data. He was comfortable working with small samples. He let the data, not theory, lead him to answers. In fact, much of my work and methodological approaches can be seen as combining Mansfield's insights and approaches with other traditions, in particular transaction cost economics, and evolutionary and behavioral theory.

In the rest of this paper I shall describe in more detail the intellectual influence of Ed Mansfield on my work on the economics of technological change and technology transfer. I shall track some of the recent developments with respect to these early ideas and mention how recent work builds on the early Mansfield studies. In doing so I hope to demonstrate that his influence was substantial, and that his legacy in the field deserves more recognition. If Schumpeter founded the study of the economics of innovation,[1] then Mansfield was the first to give it empirical meaning at the micro level.

2. Mansfield's vision and early work

One of many lessons that I learned from Mansfield—and he in turn was undoubtedly shaped by his early years at Carnegie Mellon University (which in the late 1950s and early 1960s when Mansfield was there had scholars such as Herb Simon, Dick Cyert, Jim March, Franco Modigliani and Bill Cooper, among others)—was the importance of interdisciplinary research. As a young graduate student, I wanted to believe that the hard problems of the world were solvable. I came to realize with Ed's help that this would require a multidisciplinary approach. Mansfield always made the case for interdisciplinary research. In his later years he wrote:

> "[the economics of technological change] remains an area where there is particular need for people who are comfortable working in, and drawing on, a variety of disciplines. Very few problems of any consequence can be solved within the confines of a single discipline. It continues to require persons who have a lively interest in both basic and applied work, and who are able to use each to enrich the other. It is still an area needing people who like to work on ill-defined problems where little is known and nothing is tidy, but where the rewards for even a partial solution are very high. Those with such attributes should be encouraged to enter this field because the opportunities continue to be enormous. While a lot more is known now than 40 years ago, the truth is that economists have only scratched the surface' (Mansfield, 1995, p. xxi)."

This was the mantra Mansfield had been advancing to his students for over 20 years. It was good advice, although risky for a young economist to follow. Ed was keenly aware how little was known about innovation and industrial research. Mansfield, like March and Simon and the Carnegie School, was ahead of his time, substantively and methodologically. Half a century later David Kreps would write: 'I am increasingly convinced that economists should—and will—have to change large pieces of the paradigm that has kept us relatively monolithic for the past 50 years.- We'll increasingly look like and work with our colleagues in the other.. social sciences' (2004). Were David Kreps a Mansfield student, he would have realized this much earlier.

Thinking outside the box of conventional economics was particularly necessary when it came to issues of the economics of technical change. For one thing, neoclassical economics can not address issues of change other than comparative statics (Machlup, 1967) because even adjustments to equilibrium are outside the domain of neoclassical economics. As a result, neoclassical theory can not really deal with issues of innovation. Ed recognized this, but few others did.[2]

Mansfield's methodological response was always to start first with observation (influenced, perhaps, by the 'problem driven' research that was present at Carnegie). He encouraged me—as well as his other students and colleagues—to collect data in the field. This was extremely wise. Late in life he reflected on this method, in the introduction to the two volumes of collected papers of his:

> "In general, my approach has been to try to get a reasonably solid empirical footing before attempting to model complex phenomena about which very little is known; to keep the theoretical apparatus as simple, transparent and robust as possible;

to collect data directly from firms (and other economic units) carefully tailored to shed light on the problem at hand (rather than to try to adapt readily available general-purpose data, which often is hazardous), and to check the results as thoroughly as possible with technologists, executives, government officials and others who are close to whatever phenomenon is being studied'. (Mansfield, 1995, p. ix).''

'It was', Mansfield continued, 'a privilege and a great pleasure to have contributed to the formation and growth of this young field, which is now a major and vibrant sector of economics' (1995, p. ix). Similarly, I must say it was a privilege and a great pleasure to study under Mansfield, and help advance understanding of technological change and technology transfer. I only wish many more scholars had followed Ed's lead. The field would be further ahead had they done so.

My own work in technology transfer (and technological change in general) took Mansfield's advice to heart: it was interdisciplinary in the sense that it endeavored to reach out to other disciplines (although there was not much at the time to reach out to); and it tried to be methodologically rigorous. I will first summarize this work and then link it to recent developments in the economics and management of knowledge (including industrial knowledge). In particular, I shall focus on issues relating to the nature of knowledge and the importance of intellectual capital and intellectual property.

3. The economics of (international) technology transfer

In the early 1970s, literature on (international) technology transfer was basically non-existent. Indeed, to the extent that there was a literature, the focus was on the challenges of transferring know-how from the laboratory into practice. Indeed, there was almost no conceptual apparatus available to help one think through the issues.

The doctoral thesis I wrote under Ed Mansfield was an early effort to understand technology transfer. It truly involved writing on a clean sheet of paper. Doing research in an area where there had been almost no scholarly exploration is a daunting task, even to an established scholar, let alone a graduate student. But as Ed explained, it was sometimes a little easier to receive recognition if you were the first into a field or a new subject matter area. This has been my research strategy and my comparative advantage ever since.

My doctoral thesis, published as a book (Teece, 1976) and as journal articles (Teece, 1977a, b) was ably guided by Ed.[3] It was the first, and I believe the only study to date directed at measuring the costs associated with the (international) transfer of industrial knowledge. The topic was important because scholars at the time really had no idea as to what was the true state of affairs. Many economic theorists treated technology transfer as though it was costless—and while good intuition might suggest that the process was somewhat costly, there were no empirical studies to settle the issue. It's not like it was a hotly debated issue—the zero transfer cost assumption was made, and just not challenged. Undoubtedly, there are instances where assuming zero transfer cost is a sufficiently good approximation. For instance, once certain scientific knowledge is published, it can sometimes be absorbed at low cost by other scientists knowledgeable in the field. But there were no studies at the time with respect to the transfer and absorption costs associated with replicating industrial knowledge in different contexts.

Mansfield's instinct was that technology was expensive to transfer; and his instinct turned out to be well founded. However, what my dissertation study did unearth was that there was a learning curve with respect to technology transfer—the more experience (as measured by number of transfers) a transferor had at replicating a particular technology, the lower the cost of transfer/replication. The data showed that industrial enterprises simply got better at the transfer process the more they worked on it—so long as the technology in question did not change very much, and the environment to which it was transferred was familiar. Put differently, if companies could 'freeze' designs and transfer technology only to familiar 'places', in familiar configurations, then replication costs would decline with each instance of replication (replication is a topic returned to in Section 4 'Replicability, imitabililty, and appropriability of knowledge').

A rather counterintuitive finding of my study was that the costs of international technology transfer were sometimes (although not generally) less than the costs of domestic transfer. This result follows naturally if either (i) skills abroad are better than skills at home/or (ii) the factor (resource) cost of offshore skills are cheaper than equivalent domestic skills (these two factors mean that absorption costs could be lower abroad).

Another implicit finding of my study—which with three decades of refection I can now appreciate much better—is that learning industrial knowledge often involves expensive lessons. Industrial knowledge cannot generally be transferred just with the transfer of blueprints or even the transfer of people. It frequently involves the actual running (i.e. operating) of industrial facilities in a quasi-experimental way before yields/performance become acceptable. 'Switching on' a plant, however, can be a very expensive operation if non-marketable (i.e. substandard) products are produced during the startup period. This can lead to the waste of large amounts of resources, and cost overruns associated with the replication of manufacturing plants.

Indeed, some of the anecdotes I remember from my field research relate to the horrific expenses that Rolm and Haas experienced in starting up chemical (industrial) processes in the U.K. Differences in materials and environmental factors often led to surprising cost overruns, particularly if a technology was transferred and embedded in a plant configuration which had not already been tested and validated close to the home R&D facility. Another way to state this is that learning how to apply and reapply industrial knowledge can be costly—and in my study tens of millions of dollars of cost overruns in a technology transfer project were not uncommon, especially if a technology not properly understood was transferred prematurely. Upon reflection, this remains an important insight.

My doctoral dissertation study actually endeavored to measure various components of transfer costs. I endeavored to measure not just from the actual costs of transfer activities, but also the costs flowing from the consequences of poorly executed transfer activities. For many years I felt awkward about my results because my methodology included project startup costs as part of transfer (replication) costs. However, upon further reflection, I'm increasingly comfortable with this definition. The results simply drive home that transfer costs can be high because of the 'knock on' effects if replication/transfer is not properly accomplished. This is a lesson worth remembering. Put differently, the failure to achieve smart transfer can have very serious cost implications.

Needless to say, these insights required scores of interviews to develop. I remain forever grateful for Ed Mansfield's mandate that I do field research. I'm also grateful to scores of unnamed executives who gave of their time without recognition or reward, and to the Penfield Traveling Fellowship in International Affairs and Lettres (at the University of Pennsylvania) which provided the financing for me to travel throughout the U.S., interview executives, and collect data. The process itself was insightful and valuable.[4]

After I had completed my doctoral dissertation, an independent of my own efforts, a literature began to emerge on the nature of knowledge. For some reason, I did not know of Polyani (1966) even by the time I had finished by Ph.D My dissertation would have displayed better conceptual underpinnings had I been a bit more aware of the concept of tacit knowledge, and Polyani's teachings. It was too early to benefit from Nelson and Winter's work, but I have subsequently learned that they were incubating similar ideas.

Indeed, post-1980 there has been a flowering of work on the nature of know-how and the problems of replication. In what follows I introduce some of the learning which has emerged in the last 25 years on the nature of innovation—and knowledge replication/transfer, some of it having been leveraged off of Mansfield's early contributions.

4. Summarizing elements of received wisdom on replication and transfer

Developing an understanding of knowledge and intangible assets is critical to the formulation of technology strategy and the management of R&D. I will endeavor to summarize some of this literature below, and where appropriate make connections to some of Ed's contributions.

Understanding the nature of knowledge and other intangible assets remains perplexing.

Know-how, whether scientific or industrial, is not a physical commodity—it is arguably not a commodity at all. Accordingly, new concepts, language and terminology have had to be developed so that one can begin to understand and grasp the fundamental nature of knowledge. Key concepts that have developed over the years and accepted into the literature are outlined below.

Ed Mansfield's early efforts to come to grips with technology transfer benefited from the field research done at Penn. He was amongst the first to note:

"Economists sometimes assume that technology is like a sheaf of blueprints and that all one has to do is ship off the right set of papers. Unfortunately, it isn't that simple or costless. For one thing, the available evidence, both recent and for earlier periods, indicates that publications and reports are a much less effective way of transferring technology than the movement of people. To transfer 'know-how', much of which is not written down in any event, there is frequently no substitute for person-to-person training and assistance, some of which may have to go on for extensive periods of time' (Mansfield, 1975, p. 373)."

We can address these issues better now, leveraging off of the work of many who either walked in Ed's footsteps, or were fellow travelers. Important concepts that help in the understanding of innovation and technology transfer include the following:

Codified/tacit knowledge

Tacit knowledge is (as Mansfield hints) that knowledge which is difficult to write down in a way that is meaningful and readily understood.[5] It is often hard to explain to others things which one only knows intuitively (Polyani, 1966; Teece 1981). The fact that we know more than we can tell speaks to the tacit dimension of knowledge. Moreover, stand-alone codified knowledge—knowledge which can be written down such as blueprints, formulas, or computer code—need not convey much meaning. It's more akin to information than knowledge.

Consider how to sail a yacht. It can be readily written down and explained by simple mechanics. But if one simply provides 'the book' and puts the student into a sailing dinghy with a good breeze afoot, for sure the dinghy will soon be capsized. The transfer of codified knowledge is insufficient. Tacit knowledge built with just a few hours of real experience—how to hold the mainsheet, where to put ones weight, just how to 'point' as the wind shifts, etc.—is critical to establish even a modest level of proficiency.

It is now recognized that there is a simple but powerful relationship between the codification of knowledge and the cost of its transfer. Simply stated, the more a given item of knowledge or experience has been codified, the more economically at least that part of it can be transferred. This is a purely technical property that depends on the ready availability of channels of communication suitable for the transmission of well-codified information—for example, printing, radio, telegraph, and data networks. However, it has long been recognized that whether information so transferred will be considered meaningful by those who receive it will depend on whether they are familiar with the code selected as well as the different contexts in which it is used (Shannon and Weaver, 1949).

Tacit knowledge is especially slow and costly to transmit (Teece, 1976, 1977, 1981a). Ambiguities abound and can be overcome only when communications take place in face-to-face situations. Errors or interpretation can be corrected by a prompt use of personal feedback. Mansfield (1975) pointed to the differences between types of (technology) transfer in the context of the transfer of know-how.

Other scholars have built on the earlier Mansfield and Teece work on technology transfer, and have shown that knowledge does not necessarily flow easily, even from unit to another within the firm (Grant, 1996; Szulanski, 1996).

The transmission of codified knowledge, on the other hand, does not necessarily require face-to-face contact and can often be carried out largely by impersonal means, such as when one computer 'talks' to another, or when a technical manual is passed from one individual to another. Messages are better structured and less ambiguous if they can be transferred in codified form.

Observable(not-observable) in use

Much technology is available for public examination and reverse engineering can be enabled the moment the product which embodies it is sold into the market. This is simply an unavoidable consequence of engaging in commerce; reverse engineering and copying, with or without improvements, is the harsh reality that must often be faced. For example, a new CT scanner, laser printer, or microprocessor is available for conceptual imitation and reverse engineering once it has been released in the market. The technology behind new products is typically ascertainable and, absent patents, may well be immitable.[6] In the studies conducted by Mansfield and his colleagues (Mansfield *et al.*, 1982, Chapter 2) reverse engineering was the most frequent channel by which technology leaked out.

Process technology, however, is often different. You can not easily find out the manufacturing process by which something was made simply by inspecting the product. It is rare that the 'signature' of a process is ascertainable through reverse engineering. While clues about a manufacturing process may sometimes be gleaned by closely inspecting the product, much about process technology can be protected if the owners of process technology are diligent in protecting the trade secrets used in the factory. In short, absent patents, process technology is inherently more protectable than product technology.

Positive/negative knowledge

Technological innovation involves considerable uncertainty. Research efforts frequently go down what turns out to be a blind alley. It is well recognized that a discovery (positive knowledge) can focus research on promising areas of inquiry, thereby avoiding blind alleys. However, it is frequently forgotten that negative knowledge —knowledge of failures ('this approach does not work')—is also valuable, as it can help steer resource allocation into more promising avenues. For this reason, firms often find it desirable to keep their failures as well as their successes secret, even setting to one side issues of embarrassment.

The paradigmatic nature of technological innovation

One of the best modern contributions to understanding technological change comes from Dosi's analogy between technological evolution and Thomas Kuhn's view on scientific evolution.'In broad analogy with the Kuhnian definition of a 'paradigm', we shall define a 'technological paradigm' as 'model' and a 'pattern' of solution of selected technological problems, based on selected principles derived from the natural sciences and on selected material technologies' (Dosi, 1982, p. 152). Even more Kuhnian is the view that a technological paradigm is constituted by the existence of an 'exemplar' and a set of heuristics for elaborating the relevant paradigm. The broad characteristics of technological evolution begin with a pre-paradigmatic phase where product design and technology is flexible, then a paradigmatic phase follows with the emergence of a standard.[7]

Intangible assets, tangible assets, and intellectual property

Knowledge assets are simply one class of intangible assets; they differ from tangible assets in several important respects. These are summarized in Figure 1.

First, knowledge has aspects of what economists refer to as public goods—when consumption by one individual does not reduce the amount left for another. This is especially true for scientific knowledge. One engineer's use of Newton's laws does not subtract from the ability of others to use the same laws. However, the distinction erodes quickly as one moves towards

CHARACTERISTICS	KNOW-HOW/ IP	PHYSICAL COMMODITIES
1. Recognition of trading opportunities	Inherently difficult	Posting frequent
2. Disclosure of attributes	Relatively difficult	Relatively easy
3. Property Rights	Limited [patents, trade secrets, copyright, etc.]	Broad
4. Item of Sale	License	Measurable units
5. Variety	Heterogeneous	Homogeneous
6. Unit of consumption	Often Unclear	$, Value, weight
Inherent tradability:	**Low**	**High**

Figure 1. Inherent tradeability of different assets.

industrial knowledge and away from scientific knowledge. While multiple use need not take away from knowledge—indeed it may well be augmented—the economic value may well decline with simultaneous use by multiple entities. This is saying little more than the obvious. Imitators can dramatically lower the market value of knowledge by augmenting its supply in the market.

Competition simply drives down the price of knowledge, even though its utility has not declined. Relatedly, while knowledge does not wear out as do most physical assets (like tractors, trucks, refrigerators, and disk drives), it is frequently exposed to rapid depreciation because of the creation of new knowledge. Thus leading edge products in the computer industry are often obsolete in a matter of months, not years. In fact, the depreciation may be so radical that a technological breakthrough drops the value of current practice technology to zero, or very nearly so.

An important difference between intangible and tangible assets is the availability and enforceability of property rights. Physical assets (land, cars, yachts, etc.) are generally well protected. Ownership is relatively easy to define, and the 'boundaries' of the property can be clearly delineated. Whether theft has occurred is relatively easy to ascertain, and in many jurisdictions there is a decent chance of getting police assistance in property recovery if the asset is of significant value. Not so with intangibles.

It may be natural to think that the different forms of intellectual property (patents, trade secrets, trademarks, copyrights, etc.) as providing similar ownership rights, with readily available protection against theft and misuse; but this is not so. There can be 'holes' and 'gaps' in intellectual property coverage,[8] and ascertaining whether trespass or theft has occurred can be difficult. Moreover, patents and copyrights eventually expire and cannot be extended. This is generally not so for physical assets.

Patents, trade secrets, trademarks provide protection for different mediums in different ways. The strongest form of intellectual property is the patent. The importance of patents for innovation was recognized by Mansfield (1986): 'The patent system', he noted, 'is at the heart of our nation's policies toward technological innovation. Consequently, it is of widespread interest to managers, management scientists, and economists, among others' (1986, p. 173).

A valid patent provides rights for exclusive use by the owner, although depending on the scope of the patent it may be possible to invent around it, albeit at some cost. Trade secrets do not provide rights of exclusion over any knowledge domain, but they do protect covered secrets in perpetuity. Trade secrets can well augment the value of a patent position. Different knowledge mediums quality for different types of intellectual property protection. The degree that intellectual property keeps imitators at bay may also depend on other external factors, such as regulations, which may block or limit the scope for invent-around alternatives.[9]

Replicability, imitability, and appropriability of knowledge

The economic value of knowledge depends not just on its ultimate utility, but on the case of transfer and replicability. If it can be replicated it can be 'scaled' and applied in new contexts. Replicability is closely related to transferability. If it can be transferred, from one geography to another, or from one product market context to a different one, then technology can potentially yield more value. But the catch is that if it can be readily transferred, it is often also prone to being lost to ones competitors through easy imitation (see Section 'Imitation').[10]

Replication

The replication of know how involves transferring or redeploying competences from one economic setting to another. Since productive knowledge is typically embodied, this cannot be accomplished by simply transmitting information. Only in those instances where all relevant knowledge is fully codified and understood can replication be collapsed into a simple problem of information transfer. Too often, the contextual dependence of original performance is poorly appreciated, so unless firms have replicated their systems of productive knowledge on many prior occasions, the act of replication is likely to be difficult (Teece,

1977a, 1993). Indeed, replication and transfer are often impossible without the transfer of people, though this can be minimized if investments are made to convert tacit knowledge to codified knowledge. However, this may not be possible.

In short, knowledge assets are normally rather difficult to replicate. Even understanding the relevant routines that support a particular competence may not be transparent. Indeed, Lippman and Rumelt (1982) have argued that some sources of competitive advantage are so complex that the firm itself, let alone its competitors, does not understand them.

Imitation can also be hindered by the fact that few routines work well in all contexts. Thus, imitating a part of what a competitor does may not enhance performance at all. Understanding the overall causal structure of processes, organization and superior performance is often critical to successful imitation and replication. This observation provides the foundation for the concept of uncertain immitability (Lippman and Rumelt, 1982). Because key performance factors in an organization are not understood (externally and possibly internally as well), replicating observable attributes is not guarantee of success.

At least two types of benefits flow to the firm from expertise in replication if it can be achieved. One is simply the ability to support geographic and product line expansion ('scalability'). To the extent that the organizational capabilities in question are relevant to the customer needs elsewhere, replication can confer value. Another is that the ability to replicate indicates that the firm has the foundations in place for learning and improvement.

Secondly, understanding processes, both in production and in management, is the key to process improvement; an organization cannot improve what it does not understand. Deep process understanding is often required to accomplish codification and replication. Indeed, if knowledge is highly tacit, it indicates that the phenomenon may not be well understood, except at an experiential level. When knowledge is tacit, the rate of learning may be limited because scientific and engineering principles cannot be systematically applied. Instead, learning is confined to proceeding through trial-and-error, and the amplification to learning that might otherwise come from the application of modern science is denied.

Imitation

Imitation is simply replication performed by a competitor. If self-replication is difficult, imitation is likely to be even harder. In competitive markets, it is the ease of imitation that determines the sustainability of competitive advantage. Easy imitation leads to the rapid dissipation of supernormal profits.

Factors that make replication difficult also make imitation difficult. Thus, the more tacit the firm's productive knowledge, the harder is replication by the firm itself, or by it's competitors. When the tacit component is high, imitation may well be impossible, absent the hiring away of key individuals and the transfer of key organizational processes.

In advanced industrial countries, intellectual property rights may impede imitation of certain capabilities.[11] Nevertheless, imitation lags tend to be short (Mansfield *et al.*, 1982, Chapter 2). These rights present a formidable imitation barrier in certain particular contexts. Several other factors, in addition to the patent system, cause there to be a difference between replication costs and imitation costs. The observability of the technology or the organization is one such important factor. As mentioned earlier, while insight into product technology can be obtained thorough strategies such as reverse engineering, this is not the case for process technology, as the firm need not expose its process technology to the outside in order to benefit from it. Firms with product technology, on the other hand, confront the unfortunate circumstances that they must expose what they have got in order to complete a sale. Secrets are thus more protectable if there is no need to expose them in contexts where competitors can learn about them.

Appropriability

Appropriability is a function of both the nature of knowledge, ease of replication, and the efficiency of intellectual property rights as a barrier to imitation. Appropriability is strong when a technology is both inherently difficult to replicate and intellectual property systems provides legal barriers to imitation. As shown in Figure 2, there are different layers of 'protection' which owners of valuable intangibles might enjoy. If technology is inherently easy to replicate and the intellectual property protection is either unavailable or ineffectual, then appropriability is weak.[12]

Much confusion has been caused by ignoring the significant distinction between an innovation and the intellectual property which embodies that innovation. The latter is merely a legal right (or, more precisely, a collection of various legal rights, some procedural, and some substantive).

An inventor develops say, a new technology for cracking petroleum. The technology exists when it has been developed and tested. But it only becomes covered by intellectual property once it is legally recognized as such—in the case of patents, when a particular country's patent office recognizes the inventor's application and grants a patent. An issued patent is presumed to be valid, but its ultimate validity is never established until it is challenged, and validity subsequently upheld in a court of law.

The distinction between the innovation and legal 'intellectual property' rights is most readily seen when the property right grant expires. Beethoven's copyright in his compositions has long since expired. But Beethoven's creations live on.

An innovation may be just as valuable to society—in the sense that it represents an advance over the available alternative technologies—the day after the patent on that innovation expires as it was the day before the patent expires. But the legal rights of the innovator are radically different before and after the expiration date; after that date, the innovator has no right to exclude others from using the innovation. The private value falls, but the social value does not decline, and may in fact increase.

One other key distinction is that the innovation and the legal rights are often not coextensive. An innovator may only obtain legal rights over part of the totality of the innovation. Confusion can sometimes arise when individuals seek to assess the value of the 'technology' *per se*, rather than the value of the patent rights—namely, the right to exclude others from using the patented aspects of the technology. If the two are sold together it may not matter. When they are not, it does.

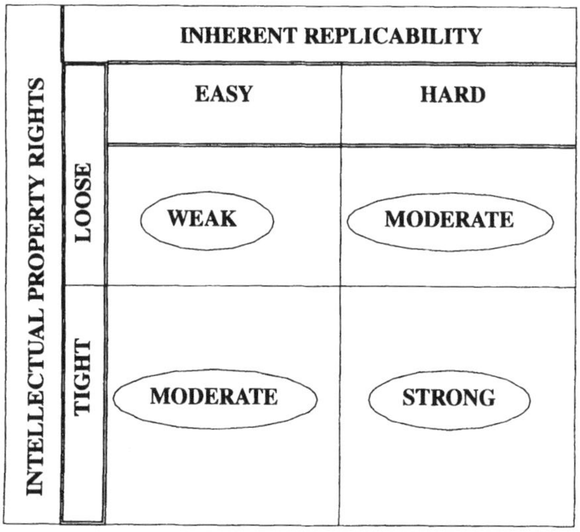

5. Capturing value from intellectual capital

As mentioned earlier, extracting value from intangible capital is a much more complicated and risky process than extracting value from tangible (physical) capital. Intellectual property, standing alone, generates little or no value to the final consumer. A patent, for instance, is merely a piece of paper that conveys the right to exclude others. The vast majority of patents are never practiced. Rather, value typically arises only after inventions are embedded in devices which are then combined with other (complementary) assets to produce a product or service which is sold in a market.

To take a simple example: merely coming up with an idea for a new semiconductor device, or even obtaining a patent or copyright on a design for a better semi-conductor device, does not generate economic value. What generates value is when some entity combines an invention or a new design with the manufacturing, marketing, after sales support and other capabilities that are necessary to actually produce and sell semiconductors. Complementary assets typically assist in

| | INHERENT REPLICABILITY ||
	EASY	HARD
INTELLECTUAL PROPERTY RIGHTS — LOOSE	WEAK	MODERATE
INTELLECTUAL PROPERTY RIGHTS — TIGHT	MODERATE	STRONG

Figure 2. Appropriability regimes for knowledge assets.

the extraction of value from intellectual property. Such assets generate a return which is analytically separate from the intellectual property itself.

In short, there are often significant hurdles that have to be cleared, and significant risks that must be undertaken, before an innovative idea can be successfully commercialized. Often, the individual(s) or firm(s) which supplies the necessary complementary assets and skills needed in order to commercialize the innovation, or which takes the necessary risks, are not the same as the inventor. When this is the case, the gains from innovation get split not only with the consumer, but also with the owners of the relevant complementary assets. Getting the commercialization strategy right is thus very important, as discussed in Teece (1986).

Appropriability regimes

One of the most fundamental reasons why innovators with good marketable ideas fail to open up markets successfully is that they are operating in an environment where appropriability is weak. This constrains their ability to capture the economic benefits arising from their ideas. As shown in Figure 2, the two most important environmental factors conditioning this are the efficacy of legal protection mechanisms and the nature of technology (including it's inherent replicability).

It is well known that patents do not generally block competitors. As Mansfield taught (1985, 1988), they can often (but not always) be worked around. Rarely, if ever, do patents confer perfect appropriability, although they do afford considerable advantage in some industries, such as with new chemical products, pharmaceuticals, and rather simple mechanical inventions (Levin *et al.*, 1987). They are especially ineffective at protecting process innovations. Often patents provide little protection because the legal and financial requirements for upholding their validity or for proving their infringement are high.

The degree of legal protection a firm enjoys is not necessarily a 'god given' attribute. The inventor's own intellectual property strategy itself enters the equation. The inventor of core technology need not only seek to patent the innovation itself, but can also seek complementary patents on new features and/or manufacturing processes, and possibly on designs.

Of course, the more fundamental the invention, the better the chances that a broad patent will be granted, and granted in multiple jurisdictions. It must be recognized that exclusionary rights are not fully secured by the mere issuance of a patent. While a patent is presumed to be valid in many jurisdictions, validity is never firmly established until a patent has been upheld in court. The strongest patents are those that are broad in scope, and have already been upheld in court.

In some industries, particularly where the innovation is embedded in processes, trade secrets are a viable alternative to patents. Trade secret protection is possible, however, only if a firm can put its product before the public and still keep the underlying technology secret. Usually only chemical formulas and industrial-commercial processes can be protected as trade secrets after they' are 'out'.

The degree to which knowledge about an innovation is tacit or easily codified also affects the ease of imitation. Tacit knowledge is, by definition, difficult to articulate and so is hard to pass on unless those who possess the know-how can demonstrate it to others. It is also hard to protect using intellectual property law. Codified knowledge is easier to transmit and receive and is more exposed to industrial espionage. On the other hand, it is often easier to protect using the instruments of intellectual property law.

As shown in Figure 2, appropriability regimes can be divided into 'weak' (innovations are difficult to protect because they can be easily codified and legal protection of intellectual property is ineffective) and 'strong' (innovations are easy to protect because knowledge about them is tacit and/or they are well protected legally). Despite recent efforts to strengthen the protection of intellectual property, strong appropriability is the exception rather than the rule. This has been so for centuries, and it will never be substantially different in democratic societies, where the migration of individuals and ideas face few governmental constraints.

Standards and timing issues

The success of the strategies, methods, and procedures by which innovators endeavor to develop new technology and capture value from it are frequently severely impacted by factors over which it may have little control. Standards and timing issues are amongst such factors.

Standard issues are particularly important when technologies must work closely together as a coupled or intertwined 'system'. Examples include telecommunications and computer equipment (interconnection is usually required) or even photocopiers—the 'aftermarket' products e.g. paper, toner must all conform to certain standards for the machine to work, or at least work well.

These factors lead to efforts by companies to promote proprietary standards (when they believe they have a good chance of success) or open standards when it's the success of a competitor's proprietary standard which is of greater concern. There are many factors which impact a firm's success, or lack thereof, in establishing standards. Achieving overall critical mass is frequently an issue, particularly when the phenomenon of two sided (or multisided) markets is at issue (Evans 2003; Rochet and Tirole, 2004). When standards are at issue, success may beget further success and dominant standards may emerge. When customers adopt a standard, they implicitly (and sometimes explicitly) abandon others. Inasmuch as innovations are often developed around existing or prospective standards, the rise and decline of certain standards is likely to have an impact on competitive outcomes, and possibly also on the value of technology.

6. Valuation issues: accounting and market metrics

It is undisputed that the creation of intangible assets and intellectual capital are sources of economic growth and productivity enhancement. It is also undisputed that private enterprise businesses in aggregate generate value from various investments, including investments aimed at creating valuable technological assets. Quite simply, firms would stop investing in R&D unless they continued to perceive that as a result they were generating an acceptable rate of return; and venture capitalists would not be able to raise money if they could not deliver the prospect of a positive return, commensurate with the risk.

Quantifying the value of intangibles and the returns they generate isn't easy.[13] However, as Mansfield recognized that it is a very important matter. One reason is that it's extremely hard to manage assets that you cannot describe or measure. Not only will one have difficulties in setting priorities, but one will also have difficulty determining success and/or failure in asset management activities. Also, if intangibles are not measured correctly, it might appear that an organization is doing poorly when it fact it is simply investing in intangibles. Accounting practices in the U.S. and elsewhere do not recognize many forms of intangibles, and this renders accounting data of limited value, and causes discrepancies to emerge between the market value and the book value of the business enterprise. Finally, to the extent that social returns exceed private, there is a case for government policies favoring innovation.

In recent decades, scholars have extended Mansfield's early work and embarked on inquiries as to the quantitative importance of intangibles, and their impact on the performance of the business enterprise. Four performance measures have received attention: (1) internal rates of return, as measured by the examination of the R&D portfolios of individual firms (2) market value, as established in (public) stock markets (3) gross margins (4) patents (5) direct measures of innovation such as innovation counts. The latter is deeply imbued with judgmental assessment and will only be dealt with in a cursory fashion.

Internal (private and social) rates of return

Ed Mansfield was the pioneer in demonstrating empirically that private rates of return from investment in R&D were in the double digits for selected industrial enterprises, but that the social rates of return were many times the private rates of return. The latter findings were the first clear measurement of spillovers associated with R&D. These results have been cited extensively in the past. They undergrid the case for government support of R&D, and for policies that favor innovation. In an important paper, Mansfield and his co-authors (1977) made perhaps the first study of the social returns from a sample of industrial innovations, using a model that measured the social benefits from innovations. Social benefits included both the profits of the innovator plus the benefits to consumers due to reduction in prices due to the innovation. The median social rate of return for the 17 innovations reported in the study was 50%; about twice the median private return.

Two follow-up studies supported by the NSF supported and even strengthened Mansfield's findings. They showed that the median social rate of return to be 70% and the median private rate of return to be 36 (Mansfield himself reflected on these findings and subsequent studies in his 1991 paper, 'Social Returns from R&D: Findings, Methods and Limitations'). Moreover, several other studies have confirmed and extended the ideas and results, including two papers in the proceedings of the AER by Scherer (1983) and Piekarz (1983). Piekarz also discusses some of the policy issues associated with Mansfield's (and other's) findings. The findings support the case that government policy should favor innovation.

Stock market valuations

If the stock market is strongly efficient, the market value of a company is at all times equal to it's fundamental value, where fundamental value is defined as the expected present discounted value of future payments to shareholders. Assuming further the absence of market power, adjustment costs, and debt and taxes, then under the efficient market thesis a company's value as determined by investors pricing decisions will equate to enterprise value—that is, the replacement cost of it's assets. Put differently, the ratio of it's market value to the replacement cost of capital—known as Tobin's Q—should equal 1.

An inference is that if the market value of the firm is greater than the replacement cost of it's tangible assets, the difference must reflect the value of intangibles. Furthermore, since accounting standards require a very conservative treatment of intangibles, corporate balance sheets of publicly traded companies are believed to in the main capture tangible assets. Because intangibles are not properly reflected on balance sheets, researchers argue that the informativeness of financial information is compromised.

Nevertheless, the difference between market value and the replacement cost of tangible assets on the balance sheet has come to be used as a proxy for the value of intangibles. However, absent specification of what these intangibles are, it is very difficult to disaggregate and assign values to particular intangibles. Moreover, the inference that the difference between a firm's market value and the replacement cost of it's physical assets represents the value of it's intangibles require the assumption of 'strong form' market efficiency (where prices reflect all information, public as well as private)—but this may be difficult to accept if investors do not have good information about the firm's intangibles.

Nevertheless, researchers have begun to explore the empirical relevance of (stock) market values. For instance, studies have established that investors regard R&D expenditures as a significant value enhancing activity, presumable because they build (intangible) technological assets (Chan *et al.*, 1992). Also, econometric studies that explore relationships between market-to-book ratios and R&D-to-sales ratios show positive and statistically significant associations (see Hirchey and Weyganat, 1985). The evidence is clear that investors view R&D as on average as being value enhancing. Moreover, the magnitude of the contribution for the investing enterprise appears considerably higher than the cost of capital.

Gross margins

Another approach utilizes accounting data, and in particular gross margins (the differences between revenues and cost of goods sold), to assess how investment in intangibles affects performance. One basic approach offered by Hand (2003) is to use econometric analysis and to regress current year dollar gross margin on current and lagged R&D, advertising, and general and administrative expenses. Hand's analysis yielded several findings (p. 304): over the period 1980–2000, the mean yearly NPV of $1.00 spent on R&D, advertising, and personnel were $0.35, $0.24, and $0.14, respectively. Scale also mattered, at least for R&D and advertising activities. Based on his findings, Hand concludes:

'Overall, my findings support the view that R&D and advertising intangibles have emerged over the past 20 years to become a critical means by which firms today create value and that one mechanism of value creation is that of increasingly profitable returns-to-scale' (Hand, p. 304).

Patent and patent citation counts

The issuance of patents, and the size of a firm's patent portfolio, is also a measure, albeit a noisy one, of innovative output. Because of the skewness in patent values—many patents are quite worthless, but a few extremely valuable—it has turned out to be necessary to impose some at least crude measure of quality in order to make sense of the data. The most common measure of quality is the number of citations to a patent included in other subsequent patent applications. A number of studies have demonstrated that quality adjusted patents capture some element of the firm's R&D asset value. For instance, Hall et al. (2000) show that citation accepted patent counts help explain Tobin's Q values.

Innovation counts

Another way to measure innovative output is directly i.e. to map significant technological innovations, and then to assign them to particular firms responsible for their creation and commercialization. While this approach is at one level superior—it actually highlights innovation rather than say R&D expenditure (expenditure measures the cost of inputs into innovative activities)—it suffers from the lack of comparability i.e. there is no easy way to compare innovations, and to quantify their significance, except possibly through panels of experts who make qualitative judgments.[14]

Organizational capital

The primary focus in this very short survey of measurement issues has been on technological assets. However, it is well recognized that organizational innovation is as significant (if not more so) than technological innovation in creating value. Cole has asserted that 'if changes in business procedures and practices were patentable, the contribution of business change to the economic growth of the nation would be as widely recognized as the influence of mechanical inventions (1968, p. 61-62).

As an example, consider Henry Ford's invention of the moving assembly line. This was unquestionably one of the greatest innovations in the automobile industry, with ramification for other industries too. However, this invention was not technological, it was organizational. The Ford Motor Company's entire system of production had to be modified to accommodate it.

Another organizational innovation was the adaptation of the M-Form structure. The transition from corporations organized in a unitary structure to corporations organized in a decentralized profit center oriented multidivisional structure had a salutary effect on business performance. In a study of the adaptation of this new structure in the petroleum industry (Armour and Teece, 1978) the innovation was shown to produce a statistically significant improvement in return on equity of approximately two percentage points during the diffusion period 1955 – 1968. A subsequent study (Teece, 1981b) of the pair wise differential performance of the two leading firms in a number of industries yielded a similar finding. This study, which used a sample of the largest firms and most important U.S. industries, that the M-form innovation displayed a statistically significant improvement in firm performance amounting to 2.37 and 1.22% for return on equity and return on assets, respectively. These results held while the innovation was being diffused. Both studies support the insights from Chandler (1968) and Williamson (1975) on the importance of organizational innovation and organizational design on economic performance.

Also, the diffusion path of the M-Form innovation was not unlike diffusion paths that Mansfield identified for technological innovations. Teece (1980) argued that such similarities between the diffusion processes affecting technological and administration/organizational innovations indicates the broader potential of insights from the economics of technological change literature. Indeed, we may see recent work examining issues regarding the relationship between organizations and performance as contributors to this stream of ideas in the Mansfield/Teece tradition.

Recently, other (indirect) measures of the impact of organizational innovation have been attempted. Brynjolfsson and Yang (1999), have showed that a $1.00 investment in computers has about a $10.00 impact on market value. This has been interpreted to reflect positive results from new business processes which the installation of enterprise software frequently requires. The author's explanation is as follows:

'Our deduction is that the main portion of computer related intangible assets comes from the new business processes, new organizational structure and new market strategies—computer use is complementary to new workplace organization—Wal-Mart's main assets are not the computer software and hardware, but the intangible business processes they have built around those computer systems (1999, p. 30).

Furthermore, recent evidence (Morck and Yeung, 2003) supports earlier work (Teece, 1982) indicating that know-how transfer inside firms (across jurisdictions and product space) is value enhancing. In this earlier study, internal technology transfer processes were seen as more efficient and effective than arms length transfers across organizational boundaries. Morck and Yeung's recent work supports this analysis by showing a positive contribution of diversification to value when it is aimed at scaling intangibles.

7. The multinational firm, internalization, and R&D activity

My work with Ed on international technology transfer also helped lay the foundations for new thinking on the distinctive role of the multinational firm. While it is true that knowledge need not move freely inside the firm, as Szulanski and others have demonstrated, it generally does move easier inside firms than between unrelated entities. This is not only because it is easier to marshal the necessary transfer of people internally, but also because of common language and control the latter softening intellectual property ('leakage') concerns. Shared values and goals inside the firm also assist technology transfer, at least when they exist.

In the 1950s and 1960s, and 1970s, Hymer (1976) and others were trumpeting that the multinational firm was an instrument for exploiting monopoly power, in part through the manner in which it exploited technology developed at home. The Mansfield–Teece–Williamson tradition, focusing on the multinational firm as a relatively efficient mechanism for transferring technology,[15] was a significant counterpoint to the Hymer argument. Not only was Hymer's argument poor competition policy analysis (competition policy experts would not automatically conclude that a firm had (antitrust) market power simply because it had valuable intangibles and intellectual property, but the proper question to ask is whether it has market power in a *relevant* (antitrust) market, not simply whether it has hard to imitate assets.

In a series of articles (Teece 1981a, b, 1985, 1986a, b) I built upon insights by two of my teachers, Ed Mansfield and Oliver Williamson, to identify particular failures in the market for know-how. I used this in turn to explain the horizontal and vertical expansion of the multinational enterprise. While it is true that others had identified internalization efficiencies as the basis of multinational enterprise and foreign direct investment (e.g. Buckley and Casson, 1976) my work explicitly focused on technology transfer issues. These issues remain compelling explanations for the international scope of the firm. Indeed, subsequent work on appropriability (Teece, 1986) provided additional generality to these explanations. When combined with Mansfield's work on spillovers and high social rates of return to innovation, this broader body of work strongly supports the thesis that the multinational firm can be an instrument of economic development, not a tool for the extraction of monopoly rents and the amplification of poverty. While Mansfield chose to stay away from some of these broader policy issues, it is rather transparent that his work is relevant to many of the great policy debates we are currently experiencing.

With respect to the focus of R&D in the multinational firm, Mansfield *et al.* (1979) were amongst the first to examine the reasons why firms 'outsourced' R&D (i.e. conducted it abroad). This work is now an important historical benchmark, as it shows that in the 1970s most foreign R&D was aimed at adapting technology to local market conditions. However, even back then some firms performed R&D abroad to access particular R&D resources not otherwise available. While this early work did not ask the theoretical/design question around what R&D should be done offshore, Mansfield's early interest in offshore R&D did stimulate me and one of my former students (Chesbrough) to design a framework to help answer those questions (Teece and Chesbrough, 1996). Indeed, much of my subsequent work has involved trying to stitch together Mansfieldian issues and ideas with those of his early contemporaries (Oliver Williamson from Penn and Nelson and Winter from Yale).[16] Indeed, I for one have taken Ed's admonition to be interdisciplinary very seriously, and have found ways to weave his ideas and findings into the broader tapestry of innovation studies. I am most grateful to have had such helpful early guidance from a great master.

8. Closing

Much progress has been done in recent years in the area of the economics of technology, but it still builds on the foundational work that Schumpeter and Mansfield and others did. Ed was undoubtedly the pioneer in the study of industrial research, and one of a few leading scholars in the economics of technological change. In 1996 Medoff reports that Mansfield received the 26th highest number of citations from 1971 to 1992 among non Nobel prize winning economists younger than 70. But in the economics of technological innovation, Grandstrand (1994) reports Mansfield was the most cited author in each of the 4 years he examined (also see Grandstrand, 2004). But this only confirms what his friends and students already knew: Ed was second to none in his field, and he chose a field of compelling significance to understanding the business enterprise, economic growth, and the future of Western Civilization.

Acknowledgment

I wish to thank Mie Augier for many helpful comments and suggestions on early drafts. Patricia Lonergan supplied helpful technical support.

Notes

1. Mansfield acknowledges Schumpeter as founding the field of the economics of technology (1995, p. ix).
2. But see for instance Nelson and Winter's (1977) early critique of neoclassical theory of innovation: 'to the extent that technical advance is important [in neoclassical theory], the set of ideas built into the formulation that individual firms are maximizing profits over a common .. choice set, and that the industry is in .. competitive equilibrium can be seen as serious structural misspecifications. It is exactly that some firms see alternatives that others do not, and that imitation is costly and takes time, that provides the incentive to try to innovate. It is a key structural characteristic ... of growth in a competitive market economy that there is a diversity of behavior (technologies used) by firms in the industry at any time. A chronic disequilibrium is what is driving the growth process. To assume .. equilibrium is to structurally misspecify the process'.
3. My doctoral work was referred to by Mansfield on several occasions; see for instance Mansfield (1975).
4. Ronald Coase admits to a similar benefit from his early field research in the U.S. in the 1930s (Coase, 1988).
5. The classical insights on the nature of tacit knowledge were provided by Hayek (1945) and Polyani (1966) and early applications to the study of technology include Mansfield (1975) and Teece (1981a).
6. Mansfield touched on some of the issues relating to imitation in an early paper 'Technical change and the Rate of Imitation' (1961).
7. Dosi's use of technological paradigms as a frame for understanding technological change can also accommodate the insights of dominating designs, technological regimes, etc. See Dosi (1982) for details.
8. In one of Ed's studies (Lee and Mansfield, 1996), it was established that the lack of intellectual property protection in certain host countries slowed technology transfer and direct foreign investment.
9. Contributions to the discussions of patent and patent protection include the early survey data from Mansfield et al., 1981, Levin et al., 1987. An extension and discussion of these studies can be found in Schankerman (1998). Moreover, Mansfield (1986) examined survey data of 100 manufacturing firms and found that—with the exceptions of the pharmaceutical and chemical industries—the firms found that most of their innovations would have been introduced even in the absence of patent protection.
10. Whether or not technology is exposed in this way is likely to depend in part on whether or not the technology enjoys intellectual property protection.
11. For Mansfield's most recent work on IP, see in particular Mansfield 1993, 1994.
12. A description of the results of an inquiry into appropriability conditions in manufacturing industries is found in Levin et al. (1987). Their data and discussion is consistent with the views discussed below.
13. As discussed below, Mansfield work on the private and social returns to innovation was pioneering (see in particular Mansfield 1977).
14. There have been very few studies of this kind. The most notable study was done by Mansfield (1968) where he

examined innovation in the petroleum industry. This study was extended and updated by Teece (1977b).

15. In Teece (1976, 1977a) I showed that internal transfer costs were generally less than the cost of transfer to unrelated entities.

16. In addition, much of Mansfield's early ideas on R&D originated while he was a consultant at the RAND Corporation—Winter and Nelson were also doing pioneering work on R&D there.

References

Armour, H. and D. Teece, 1978, 'Organizational Structure and Economic Performance: A Test of the Multidivisional Hypothesis,' *The Bell Journal of Economics* **9** (2), 106–122.

Brynjolfsson, E. and S. Yang, 1999, '*The Intangible Costs and Benefits of Computer Investments: Evidence From Financial Markets,*' Working Paper, Sloan School, Massachusetts Institute of Technology.

Buckley, P. and M. Casson, 1976, *The Future of the Multinational Enterprise,* London: MacMillan.

Coase, R.H., 1988, 'The Nature of the Firm: Origin, Meaning, Influence,' *Journal of Law, Economics, and Organization* **4** (1), 3–47.

Chan, S., J. Kesinger, and J. Martin, 1992, 'The Market Rewards Promising R&D,' *Journal of Applied Corporate Finance* **5**, 59–62.

Chandler, A., 1968, *Strategy and Structure,* Cambridge: Harvard University Press.

Cole, A.H., 1968, 'The Entrepreneur, Introductory Remarks,' *American Economic Review* **58** (2), 60–63.

Dosi, G., 1982, 'Technological Paradigms and Technological Trajectories. A Suggested Interpretation of the Determinants and Directions of technical Change,' *Research Policy* **11**, 147–162.

Evans, D., 2003, 'The Antitrust Economics of Multi Sided Platform Markets,' *Yale Journal of Regulation* (forthcoming).

Grandstrand, O., 1994, 'Economics of Technology: An Introduction and Overview,' in Idem (ed.), *Economics of Technology,* Amsterdam: North-Holland.

Grandstrand, O., 2004, *Economics, Law, and Intellectual Property,* Boson: Kluwer.

Grant, R.M., 1996, 'Prospering in Dynamically Competitive Environments: Organizational Capability as Knowledge Integration,' *Organization Science* **7** (4), 375–387.

Hall, B., A. Jaffee, and M. Trajtenberg, 2000, *Market Value and Patent Citations: A First Look,* Working Paper, National Bureau of Economic Research.

Hand, J. and B. Lev, 2003, *Intangible Asset Values, Measures, Risks,* Oxford: Oxford University Press.

Hayek, F.A., 1945, 'Economics and Knowledge,' in F.A. Hayek, (ed.), *Individualism and Economic Order,* University of Chicago Press.

Hymer, S., 1976, *International Operations of National Firms: A Study of Direct Investment,* Cambridge, MA: MIT Press.

Lee, J.Y. and E. Mansfield, 1996, 'Intellectual Property Protection and US Direct Investment,' *Review of Economics and Statistics* **78** (2), 181–186.

Kreps, D., 2004, 'Beliefs and Tastes: Confessions of an Economist,' in Augier and March (2004), *Models of a Man: Essays in Memory of Herbert Simon,* Cambridge: MIT Press.

Levin, R., C. Klevorick, R. Nelson, and S.G. Winter, 1987, 'Appropriating the Returns from Industrial Research and Development,' *Brookings Papers on Economic Activity* **3**, 783–820.

Lippman, S. and R. Rumelt, 1982, 'Uncertain Imitability: An Analysis of Interfirm Differences in Efficiency Under Competition,' *Bell Journal of Economics* **13**, 418–438.

Machlup, F., 1967, 'Theories of the Firm: Marginalist, Behavioral, Managerial,' *American Economic Review* **57**, 1–33.

Mansfield, E., 1961, 'Technical Change and the Rate of Imitation,' *Econometrica* **29** (40), 714–766.

Mansfield, E., 1968, *The Economics of Technological Change,* New York: W.W. Norton & Company Inc.

Mansfield, E., 1975, 'International Technology Transfer: Forms, Resource Requirements, and Policies,' *American Economic Review* **65** (2), 372–376.

Mansfield, E., 1986, 'Patents and Innovation: An Empirical Study,' *Management Science* **32**, 173–181.

Mansfield, E., 1991, 'Social Returns from R&D: Findings, Methods and Limitations,' *AAAS Science and Technology Policy Yearbook* **24**, 24–27.

Mansfield, E., 1993, 'Unauthorized use of Intellectual Property: Effects on Investment, Technology Transfer, and Innovation,' in M.B. Wallerstein et al. (eds.), *Global Dimensions of Intellectual Property Rights in Science and Technology,* Washington: National Academy Press.

Mansfield, E., 1994, *Intellectual Property Protection, Foreign Direct Investment, and Technology Transfer,* IFC discussion papers, No. 19, Washington, D.C.: The World Bank.

Mansfield, E., 1995, 'Introduction,' in Idem (ed.), *Innovation, Technology and the Economy: The Selected Essays of Edwin Mansfield, Vol. 1,* Brookfield: Edward Elgar.

Mansfield, E., A. Romeo, M. Schwartz, D. Teece, S. Wagner, and P. Brach, 1982, *Technology Transfer, Productivity, And Economic Policy,* New York: W.W. Norton & Company.

Mansfield E., D. Teece and A. Romeo, 1979, 'Overseas Research and Development by U.S.-Based Firms,' *Economica* **46** (May), 187–196.

Mansfield E., M. Schwartz and S. Wagner, 1981, 'Imitation Costs and Patents: An Empirical Study,' *The Economic Journal* **91**, 907–918.

Mansfield, E., R. John, R. Anthony, W. Samuel, and B. George, 1977, 'Social and Private Rates of Return from Industrial Innovations,' *Quarterly Journal of Economics* **91**, 221–240.

Medoff, M., 1996, 'A Citation-Based Analysis of Economists and Economics Programs,' *The American Economist* **40** (1), 46–49.

Morck, R. and B. Yeung, 2003, *Why Firms Diversify: Internalization v. Agency Behavior.*

Nelson, R. and S. Winter, 1977, 'In Search of a Useful Theory of Innovation,' *Research Policy* **6**, 36–76.

Piekarz, R., 1983, 'R&D and Productivity Growth: Policy Studies and Issues,' *American Economic Review* **73**, 210–214.

Polyani, M., 1966, *The Tacit Dimension,* New York: Doubleday.

Scherer, F., 1983, 'R&D and Declining Productivity Growth,' *American Economics Review* **73**, 215–218.

Schankerman, M., 1998, 'How Valuable Is Patent Protection? Estimates by Technology Field', *Rand Journal of Economics* **29** (1), 77–107.

Shannon, C. and W. Weaver, 1949, *A Mathematical Theory of Communication*, Urbana: University of Illinois Press.

Szulanski, G., 1996, 'Exploring Internal Stickiness: Impediments to the Transfer of Best Practice Within the Firm,' *Strategic Management Journal* **17**, 27–43.

Rochet, J. and J. Tirole, 2004, *Two Sided Markets: An Overview*, Mimeo, University of Toulouse.

Teece, D.J., 1976, *The Multinational Corporation and the Resource Cost of International Technology Transfer*, Cambridge, MA: Ballinger.

Teece, D.J., 1977a, 'Technology Transfer by Multinational Firms: The Resource Cost of Transferring Technological Know-how,' *The Economic Journal* **87**, 242–261.

Teece, D.J., 1977b, 'Time-Cost Tradeoffs: Elasticity Estimates and Determinants for International Technology Transfer Projects,' *Management Science* **23** (8), 830–837.

Teece, D.J., 1980, 'The Diffusion of an Administrative Innovation,' *Management Science* **26** (5) (May), 464–470.

Teece, D.J., 1981a, 'The Market for Know-how and the Efficient International Transfer of Technology,' *The Annals of the Academy of Political and Social Science* **458**, 81–196.

Teece, D.J., 1981b, The Multinational Enterprise: Market Failure and Market Power Considerations,' *Sloan Management Review* **22** (3), 3–17.

Teece, D.J., 1982, 'Towards an Economic Theory of the Multiproduct Firm,' *Journal of Economic Behavior and Organization* **3**, 39–33.

Teece, D.J., 1985, 'Multinational Enterprise, Internal Governance, and Industrial Organization,' *American Economic Review* **75** (2), 233–238.

Teece, D.J., 1986, 'Profiting from Technological Innovation,' *Research Policy* **15** (6), 285–305.

Teece, D.J. and H. Chesbrough, 1996, 'Organizing for Innovation: When is Virtual Virtuous?,' *Harvard Business Review*.

Williamson, O.E., 1975, *Markets and Hierarchies: Analysis and Antitrust Implications*, New York: The Free Press.

Welfare Implications of User Innovation

Joachim Henkel[1]
Eric von Hippel[2]

ABSTRACT. Innovation by users is now understood to be an important part of innovative activity in the economy. In this paper we explore the implications of adding innovation by users to existing models of social welfare that currently assume innovation by manufacturers only. We find this addition removes several inefficiencies, and that social welfare is likely to be increased by the presence of user innovation. Implications for policies that can impact users' freedom to innovate are discussed.

Key Words: user innovation, product diversity, social welfare, inefficiencies

JEL Classification: D62, O31

1. Introduction

Innovation by users is an important part of overall innovative activity in the economy. Users have been found to be the developers of many commercially important innovations and, in fields studied to date, from 10% to nearly 40% of users have been found to have developed or modified products for their own use (see Table I). However, this source of innovation has received little attention in economics research. Indeed, to paraphrase Solow's famous quip, user innovations appear everywhere but in the economic literature. In particular, evidence regarding the existence and importance of innovation by users has not yet been incorporated in the literature on product diversity, innovation, and social welfare. In this paper, we begin to fill this gap.

---

[1] Institute for Innovation Research, Technology Management and Entrepreneurship
University of Munich, Kaulbachstraße 45
D-80539 Munich, Germany
E-mail: henkel@bwl.uni-muenchen.de
[2] MIT Sloan School of Managent Cambridge, MA 02139, USA

The central question addressed by the literature on product diversity, innovation, and social welfare is whether, from a societal perspective, a particular market organization yields too much or too little variety or innovation. Effects that would create both over-provisioning and under-provisioning of variety, such as business stealing and the consumer surplus effect, have been identified. Adding another source of innovation—users—to the welfare analysis of new goods might exacerbate a tendency towards overprovision of new goods. Or, it might result in a crowding-out of innovation incentives for manufacturers, potentially increasing a bias towards underprovision of product diversity. In this paper we analyze the impact on social welfare associated with product developments by users. We do this by comparing user innovators to manufacturer innovators with respect to their incentives to innovate and also their innovation-related knowledge. In addition, we explore free revealing of user innovations and its implications. We present and discuss this phenomenon comprehensively via a broad qualitative analysis. Formal models of specific aspects can flow from this analysis, but are not presented here.

Our analyses show user innovation to have several positive effects on social welfare. First, we find that user innovation *complements* manufacturer innovation in two ways. Manufacturers and users tend to create *different* innovations. Manufacturers tend to develop products that many will want, and where they see a chance to capture a large share of the surplus the innovations will create. In contrast, users tend to develop innovations that only they or a few may want, and that create a high consumer surplus for themselves.

Second, the two sources of innovation complement each other with respect to *knowledge*

TABLE I
Studies of user innovation

Innovation area	No. users sampled	% Developing and building innovation for own use
Industrial products		
Printed Circuit CAD Software (a)	136 user firm attendees at PC-CAD conference	24.3
Pipe Hanger Hardware (b)	74 Pipe hanger installation firms	36
Library Information Systems (c)	102 Australian Libraries using computerized library information systems	26
Apache OS server software security features (d)	131 Apache users	19.1
Medical Surgery Equipment (e)	261 clinic surgeons	22
Consumer products		
Outdoor Consumer Products (f)	153 outdoor specialty mail order catalog recipients	9.8
"Extreme" sporting equipment (g)	197 expert users	37.8
Mountain biking equipment (h)	291 expert users	19.2

Sources of Data: (a) Urban and von Hippel (1988), (b) Herstatt and von Hippel (1992), (c) Morrison *et al.* (2000), (d) Franke and von Hippel (2003), (e) Lüthje (2003), (f) Lüthje (2004), (g) Franke and Shah (2003), and (h) Lüthje *et al.* (2002).

and *capabilities*. Users tend to develop new functionality which they require. Manufacturers can study these early user innovations to gain information about both emerging market needs and possible solutions that would be difficult to obtain otherwise. They can then advance the users' work by turning it into a robust product, producible at low cost. User innovation thus helps to reduce information asymmetries and increase efficiency of the innovation process. It can enable manufacturers to produce a higher fraction of new products that are marketplace successes.

Third, we find that the inefficiency called *"business stealing"* in the social welfare literature is absent for user innovation. This effect is known to bias the number of new goods towards excessive levels in the case of manufacturer innovation.

Fourth and finally, user innovations tend to be *freely revealed* more often than manufacturer innovations. Free revealing of innovation-related information creates positive welfare effects for users of the innovation as well as for second-generation innovators.

We conclude that an innovation system where user innovation is present is welfare superior to one where it is not. This conclusion has important policy implications. Policies related to intellectual property and innovation such as patent and copyright law as well as tax breaks and subsidies strongly influence users' and manufacturers' relative ability to innovate. There is good reason to assume that the current tendency towards stronger intellectual property protections (e.g., Gallini, 2002) has a negative impact on user innovation. In particular, policies that restrict product modification by users, or that allow manufacturers to do this, must be considered very carefully. Benkler (2002) makes a related point by showing the impact of IP policies on the innovative potential of small versus large firms.

In Section 2 we review the literature. In Section 3 we explore welfare aspects of user innovations. In Section 4 we conclude with a discussion of some implications of our findings for both innovators and policymakers.

2. Literature review

In this section we first review the literature on innovation by users (in section Innovation by users). Next, we review the literature on the tendency of users to "freely reveal" their innovations (in section Free revealing of innovation by users). Finally, we review the literature on the gains and losses in social welfare associated with the introduction of new goods to the marketplace (in section Product diversity, innovation and welfare).

Innovation by users

Innovation by end users of products and processes has been shown to be an important phenomenon within economies. Studies in a range of fields have show that many major and minor innovations are first developed and applied by firms or individuals seeking to use them rather than by firms seeking to profit from their manufacture and sale. Industrial fields in which this question has been systematically explored include oil processing (Enos, 1962), the early history of computing (Knight, 1963), machine tool innovations (Rosenberg, 1976), scientific instrument innovations and semiconductor and electronic sub-assembly processing equipment (von Hippel, 1988). In consumer products, the question has so far been explored with respect to sports equipment only (Shah, 2000). It has also been found that a considerable fraction of users—from 10% to nearly 40%—engage in developing or modifying products in fields sampled to date (Table I)[1]. Given the ratio of users to manufacturers in the economy, it is possible that *most* innovative effort and investment may well be attributable to users rather than manufacturers—largely unnoticed and untabulated in present economic data series.

The empirical studies listed in Table I, and other studies as well, consistently find that innovation is concentrated among the "lead users" in a user population. Lead users are members of a user population with two distinguishing characteristics. First, they are at the leading edge of important trends, and so are currently experiencing needs that will later be experienced by many users in that marketplace. Second, they anticipate obtaining relatively high benefits from obtaining a solution to their needs, and so may innovate (von Hippel, 1986). The effect size found in these studies tends to be very large. For example, in a study of CAD software used for printed circuit design, Urban and von Hippel (1988) found that 82% of the lead user cluster in their sample had developed their own version of or had modified the specific type of industrial product they employed, while only 1% of the non-lead users had done this.

The concentration of innovation activity among lead users within a user population can be understood from an economic perspective. Given that innovation is an economically motivated activity, users expecting relatively high economic or personal benefit from developing an innovation—one of the two characteristics of lead users—have a higher incentive to and so are more likely to innovate. Also, given that lead users experience needs in advance of the bulk of a target market, the nature, risks, and eventual size of that target market are often not clear to manufacturers. This lack of clarity can reduce manufacturers' incentives to innovate, and increase the likelihood that lead users will be the first to develop their own innovative solutions for needs that later prove to represent mainstream market demand (Franke and von Hippel, 2003).

Finally, we note that the nature of innovations developed by users and manufacturers has been found to systematically differ according to the character of "sticky" information users versus manufacturers tend to possess. Much information used by innovators has been found to be "sticky" or costly to transfer from site to site (von Hippel, 1994). Thus it is reasonable that users, generators of need-related information, will tend to be the developers of innovations having novel functionality. Such innovations tend to require access to rich need information. Similarly, it is reasonable that manufacturers will tend to be the source of innovations based heavily upon novel solution information that they generate (Riggs and von Hippel, 1994).

Free revealing of innovation by users

Empirical studies show innovating users often choose to freely reveal details of their innovations to other users and to manufacturers as well. Thus, Allen (1983) found furnace design information openly revealed by iron producers in the 19th century iron-making industry; the practice has been found among users of clinical chemistry analyzer equipment (von Hippel, 1988); Lim (2000, p. 41) reports that IBM freely revealed information on its "copper interconnect" semiconductor process and equipment innovations to equipment manufacturing firms and thereby to competing users; Morrison *et al.* (2000) found improvements to library information software freely revealed by libraries; Franke and Shah (2003) found user-developed innovations being freely revealed within communities of sports enthusiasts. Contributors to open source software projects also reveal the "source code" of the software they have developed at private expense and convey rights to use and modify that software to others without charge (e.g., Raymond, 1999).

When we say that an innovator freely reveals proprietary information, we mean that all intellectual property rights to that information are voluntarily given up by the innovator and all interested parties are given access to it—the information becomes a public good. Thus, free revealing of information by a possessor is defined as the granting of access to all interested agents without imposition of any direct payment. For example, placement of non-patented information in a publicly accessible site such as a journal or public website would be free revealing under this definition (Harhoff et al., 2003).[2]

To economists free revealing is, at first glance, surprising, because it violates a central tenant of the economic theory of innovation. In this classical view, returns to innovation can be appropriated to a larger extent the better the knowledge underlying an innovation is kept secret or protected by other means. After all, non-compensated spillovers of innovation-related information should represent a loss that innovators would seek to avoid if at all possible, even at some cost. Recent work seeks to explain free revealing on the basis of two considerations. First, if a user is to benefit from *non-free* diffusion of an innovation to the other users in a marketplace, some form of intellectual property protection followed by licensing is required. Both have been found to be costly to attempt for user innovators, with very uncertain outcomes (Harhoff et al., 2003). Second, it has been found that some forms of private rewards to innovators survive the act of free revealing— are even enhanced by it. When benefits from free revealing exceed the benefits that are *practically* obtainable from other courses of action such as licensing, then free revealing should be the preferred course of action for a profit-seeking firm.

Examples of forms of private rewards to innovators that survive are enhanced by the act of free revealing include the fact that user innovations are developed to precisely suit the private needs of the innovator—and may serve the needs of free riders less well. Also, some forms of rewards may be linked to the development process itself rather than to its result. E.g., the learning and enjoyment that programmers of open source software gain from actually writing the code cannot be shared by free riders who only adopt the completed product (Lakhani and Wolf, 2005). Open source programmers, and other innovators as well, can benefit from free revealing due to a gain in private reputation among peers (Raymond, 1999) or on the job market (Lerner and Tirole, 2002). Finally, a strong potential benefit of free revealing is that adopters of the innovation can improve it, develop it further, and reveal their improvements in turn. Such open and "collective" innovation processes are common in the case of open source software (Raymond, 1999), even when most contributors are commercial firms (Henkel, 2003). However, they have also been found in iron making and steam engines, i.e., industries that strongly differ from software (Allen, 1983; Nuvolari, 2004).

Product diversity, innovation and welfare

The issue of socially optimal product diversity has concerned economists for a long time (Chamberlin, 1950). A larger diversity is, other things being equal, assumed to be desirable. This may be so either because each consumer benefits from larger variety in his or her shopping basket, and/or because a larger selection on offer allows, on average, a better match between each user's needs and the respective consumed good. These beneficial effects of diversity are counteracted by the higher cost that a large variety presumably brings with it. Producing many goods in small quantities means scale economies are less fully exploited than when production is focused on larger outputs of fewer goods.[3] Scale economies may be caused by specificities of the production technology and/or by innovative activity required to develop new products. More recently, the conflict between diversity and returns to scale has been somewhat alleviated by the introduction of flexible manufacturing (see, e.g., Röller and Tombak, 1990; Eaton and Schmitt, 1994). However, while modern manufacturing technologies do shift the optimal degree of diversity upwards, the conflict persists.

The trade-off between diversity and returns to scale forms the basis for several modeling approaches tackling the issue of optimum product variety. Eaton and Lipsey (1989) subsume them under the headings of "address branch" and "non-address branch". Address models follow Hotelling's (1929) approach of describing goods, as well as tastes, as points on a line. Related to this is Lancaster's product characteristics approach (1975). Contributions in this branch of the literature commonly assume that each consumer buys only one good; put differently, goods are not combinable. This means that diversity in these models is valuable because it allows each consumer to, on average, better satisfy his or her taste. In contrast, papers in the non-address branch employ utility functions in which quantities of several goods enter (Spence 1976a, b; Dixit and Stiglitz, 1977). The most obvious interpretation is that of a representative consumer who values diversity in her shopping basket. Alternatively, the utility function may be the result of an aggregation of diverse consumer tastes (Sattinger, 1984; Hart, 1985; Perloff and Salop, 1985; Anderson et al., 1988).

The literature cited above explains the higher cost of larger variety by production non-convexities such as indivisibilities of fixed capital or development cost. However, the approach is static in the sense that implications of new product development for subsequent innovations are not considered. These are the subject of a broad literature on growth, innovation, and intellectual property (see, in particular, Arrow, 1962; Schmookler, 1966; Nordhaus, 1969; Romer, 1990; Grossman and Helpman, 1991; Aghion and Howitt, 1992; Oi, 1997; Bessen and Maskin 2000). While there are (few) models in this strand of the literature that assume horizontal differentiation between goods (e.g., Grossman and Helpman, 1991, p. 43), vertical differentiation seems more appropriate to the idea of technical progress. If new goods are superior to existing goods to such a degree that the latter become obsolete, then the issue is no longer product variety but rather innovation and technical progress. The principal trade-offs, however, persist (while additional ones appear), as we will discuss below.

The central question of all the research outlined above is whether, from a social welfare perspective, a particular market organization yields too much or too little variety or innovation. Researchers have identified effects that would create both over-provisioning and under-provisioning of variety, the most important of which are business stealing and the consumer surplus effect. When new goods are considered as innovations that following innovators can build upon, intertemporal spillovers and a number of further effects appear. The net result is that the answer to this question is generally unclear.

3. Welfare aspects of user and manufacturer innovation

In this section we assess the impact on social welfare resulting from adding an additional source of product innovations—innovations developed by users—to the manufacturer source of innovations that has been traditionally considered in the literature. In our analysis we will separately consider the impact of this added source of innovations upon each of the several major effects that have been discussed in the literature on product diversity, innovation, and social welfare as inducing either over-provisioning or under-provisioning of product variety or innovation. We will find that the introduction of user innovation eliminates some deleterious effects and ameliorates others.

We will begin by discussing two types of effect, consumer surplus and information asymmetries, where social welfare is affected by attributes that inherently differ between users and manufacturers. Next we will briefly review the impact of three factors with well-known impacts on social welfare: business stealing, monopoly distortions and impacts on second-generation innovators. These are relevant to our present discussion because all are affected by free revealing and, as we have argued, users are more likely to freely reveal the innovations they develop than are manufacturers.

In the analysis that follows, by "innovation" we mean information sufficient to build a novel product. We will use the term to denote both minor variations of existing products as well as radically new ones. We assume that both user and manufacturer innovators are solely motivated by their own utility gains and profits, and neither by gains or losses that their innovation might cause for others. We also abstract from uncertainty by assuming that innovators correctly anticipate the cost and outcome of their activity (or that they know the expected values and are risk-neutral).

Inefficiencies related to appropriation of innovation rents

Consumer surplus effect. Manufacturing firms generally cannot capture the entire consumer surplus created by new products they introduce to the marketplace. As a consequence, the number of products it pays them to develop is biased downwards to sub-optimal levels. In particular, manufacturers will have a bias against development of products which only allow them to capture a small share of the surplus these goods create. Under some additional assumptions (e.g., with constant elasticity of demand), these are products with relatively inelastic demand (Spence, 1976a).

User innovators make a completely different calculation with respect to the desirability of developing innovations—and this has the interesting consequence that user and manufacturer innovations will in general be of a different nature. Consider that an end-user captures none of the consumer surplus that its innovation generates for others, but does capture the full surplus that it generates for itself via in-house use. Thus, a user with a high and very inelastic in-house demand for an innovation will have an incentive to "price discriminate" against itself by investing a high proportion of its anticipated consumer surplus into the development of the innovation it requires. That is, users will tend to develop products having (so far) relatively small marketplace demand—because manufacturer products are not likely to be present there—and for which the user itself has high and inelastic demand (very precise requirements). Manufacturers, in contrast, will tend to prefer to develop products intended for relatively large markets having relatively elastic demand. The consequence is that product innovations developed by users will tend to fill small niches of high need left open by commercial sellers—the two sources of innovation are complementary to each other.

Note that the argument so far does not prove existence of innovations that are profitable for user innovators but not for manufacturer innovators. With full information and equal cost on both sides, and ignoring transaction cost, the locus of innovation should be irrelevant (we will show in section Information asymmetry-related inefficiencies, though, that these issues do make a difference). However, the argument does prove that typical user innovations are *relatively* less attractive for a manufacturer innovator than other types of innovations. Taking, in addition, information and cost aspects into account it will become clear that users, and not manufacturers, are the likely originators of the type of innovation we focus on.

Hence, the introduction of a user innovation can have an offsetting effect to the tendency of manufacturers, due to the *consumer surplus effect*, to underprovide product diversity to a marketplace. This positive welfare effect is strengthened by the fact that, as was discussed in section Innovation by users, user needs evolve over time and innovations created by "lead users" for market niches tend to become of interest to the bulk of the market later. Of course, an innovation system with *only* user innovators would just as well lead to an underprovision of variety, however, for different reasons. The point is that incentives for user and manufacturer innovators differ in such a way as to make their innovative activities complementary to each other.

Business stealing. By introducing an additional product to a market, an innovator diverts sales from substitute products already on the market to its own product, thus exerting a negative externality on incumbents. A commercial innovator, selling its product above marginal cost, benefits from this negative externality of "business stealing". Since the diverted gross profit will, at least partly, be used to pay for the development and other fixed cost of the new product, this causes a bias towards excessive product diversity and a related loss in net social welfare (Spence, 1976a).

This bias towards socially excessive diversity is absent for user innovations. Consider that a user innovator adding a new product to a marketplace may exert the same negative externality on incumbent manufacturers in a marketplace that was described above—or an even greater one if the user innovation is made available without charge. However, the lost profits of incumbent manufacturers do not benefit a user innovator (assuming potential sales to the user innovator itself are negligible). They therefore are not spent by that user on product development costs. Instead, such costs are fully covered by the benefit the user innovator derives from in-house use of the innovation: if not, the user would not find it profitable to innovate in the first place. As a result, the profit loss to incumbents due to the introduction of the user innovation does not imply a loss of social welfare, but rather a redistribution of surplus to users. This conclusion holds independent of whether the user-developed innovations are used only by the user innovator or are diffused in the marketplace.

Now consider the reverse case: a marketplace with only user-developed products present to which a manufacturer-developed product is added. Depending on the relative quality of the goods and users' tastes, the commercial product may be preferred by some or even all users. However, while there is business stealing in the sense of "units adopted", there is no business stealing in terms of margins and profits, since the user innovations are given away at marginal cost. As a result, there is no negative externality exerted by the manufacturer on the user innovators.[4] The manufacturer will only introduce the additional product if the surplus that it creates is at least as great as the cost of doing this. Hence, if the innovation is profitable, then it is also welfare enhancing. In particular, the increase in variety is not excessive.

Information asymmetry-related inefficiencies

As was laid out in Section 2, user innovators often have "sticky", need-related information that manufacturers lack. On the other hand, manufacturers typically know more about how to turn a prototype into a robust product, and how to manufacture it at low cost. Two implications of these patterns are discussed in this section. First, innovative activity by users can embody sticky user need information in a form that can be easily transferred to manufacturers, enabling manufacturers to become more successful in new product development. Second, user and manufacturer knowledge concerning innovations are to some degree complementary. This implies that users and manufacturers can benefit from each others' innovations rather than compete with each other. This in turn implies a welfare-enhancing (partial) internalization of spillovers.

Reduction of information asymmetries. It is commonplace knowledge in industry that many—perhaps most—new products developed and introduced to the marketplace by manufacturers fail commercially. Since much development investment is product-specific, this represents a huge inefficiency in the conversion of R&D investment to useful output. It is difficult to put a firm number on the proportion of R&D investment lost in this manner, because there clearly is some recycling of knowledge from failed to successful projects, some projects are deemed failures and stopped before commercial marketplace introduction, etc. However, studies of the matter clearly show the scope of the problem. Thus, Mansfield and Wagner (1975) studied the project portfolios of three industrial development labs and found an overall probability of success for new industrial products to be 27%; Elrod and Kelman (1987) find an overall probability of success of 26% for consumer products. More recent reviews by Balachandra and Friar (1997), Poolton and Barclay (1998), and Redmond (1995) confirm high failure rates in new product commercialization. Clearly, an improvement in these statistics would be socially desirable.

The primary reason for the commercial failure of manufacturer-developed products has been found to be inaccurate understanding of user needs by manufacturer-innovators. Mansfield and Wagner (1975) found that 62% of the technical projects they studied were terminated because of poor commercial prospects rather than technical problems. A major study of product pairs with very similar function—one pair member a marketplace success and one a market failure (Achiledelis *et al.*, 1971, Rothwell *et al.*, 1974) came to the same conclusion: the primary cause of commercial failure was a lack of market and need understanding, not a lack of technical understanding. As Poolton and Barclay (1998) phrase it in their review, "new products failure has been demonstrated to be highly associated with a 'we know best' attitude, especially where technical inventors fail to consult with potential users regarding new innovations."

We propose that the presence of user innovations in a marketplace will reduce this important cause of commercial failure of new products that are developed by manufacturers. Our reasoning is that users (individuals or firms) have better information about their needs than do manufacturers. After all, as was discussed in Section 2, users are the *generators* of information regarding their needs, and the quality of this information can only degrade during the process of collecting it and transmitting it to manufacturer-innovators. The degree of degradation is likely to be substantial, because much of this information has been found to be "sticky," costly to transfer from one locus to another (von Hippel, 1994; Ogawa, 1997).

How will this improvement in user need information for manufacturer product development be effected? As we saw earlier, much innovation by users is carried out by lead users. These lead users encounter needs that later are felt by many in a market—and a significant number of them innovate in order to develop a solution to their needs in advance of the availability of commercial solutions from manufacturers. Innovating users test their solutions in their own use environments, and thereby learn more about the real nature of their needs and appropriate solutions. They also often freely reveal information about their innovations. Other users then either do or do not begin to adopt that innovation and perhaps modify it in turn.

All this user activity gives manufacturers a great deal of useful information. They no longer need to understand user needs very accurately and richly in order to innovate successfully. Instead they have the easier task of replicating the functionality of user prototypes that users have demonstrated to be responsive to their needs. User innovation and adoption activity also gives manufacturers a better understanding of marketplace potential. Projections of product sales have been shown to be much more accurate when they are based on actual behavior—information regarding early adoption and actual value in use—rather than on pre-use expectations by potential buyers. Monitoring of field use of user-built prototypes and their adoption by other users gives manufacturers rich data on precisely these matters and so should improve manufacturer commercial success records. (Certainly it is difficult to imagine a scenario in which this improved information would *reduce* manufacturer success rates.) Hence, innovation-related inefficiencies due to information asymmetries will in general be reduced by user innovations.

Complementarity between user and manufacturer innovations. While users often have an advantage over manufacturers with respect to need information, they will in general lack knowledge of the most efficient technical solutions both with respect to the product itself and with respect to processes to manufacture it. The resulting potential inefficiency is resolved by manufacturers' building upon and improving the user innovation, provided user innovations are revealed to them. When user innovations are revealed, the manufacturer might either develop a complement or modify the user innovation and introduce an improved substitute to the market. Only in the latter case can there be a negative effect on the user innovator. This will be so when the negative effect from competitors' using the manufacturer-improved product—assuming that the manufacturer offers it to the entire market—outweighs the positive effect that the improved product has on the user innovator. It is hard to quantify how often one effect or the other dominates. However, one can make a relative statement: The positive effects of free revealing on the innovator will dominate for user innovations more often than for manufacturer innovations. This has to do with differing roles of second-generation innovators in the two cases, the existence of non-financial user innovators, and aspects of competition (see section Free revealing-related effect for a detailed discussion).

Hence, we argue that the user innovator often benefits from having a commercial vendor (or follow-on user innovators) modify and improve its innovation. In other words, spillovers to subsequent innovators will often actually *increase* a user's incentive to innovate, since the positive externality exerted on subsequent innovators is partly internalized. This helps explain why user innovations are often *actively* diffused by their originators (Harhoff et al., 2003). In addition, there will likely be a welfare increase resulting from a cost-reduction in this "staged" innovation process as compared to one where all steps are performed by a manufacturer innovator.

Now consider the reverse case. Suppose that a manufacturer anticipates that users might develop a substitute for *or* a complementary innovation or improvement to a commercial innovation it is considering developing—and that the user's efforts will be aided by information spillovers from manufacturer to user. If the user exploits spillover information from manufacturer innovators to develop a *substitute* product, the net effect on manufacturer incentives to innovate is likely to be negative. Further, if user innovators freely reveal their developments while competing manufacturers do not, the negative impact on the manufacturer's profits is likely to be larger than if the substitute had been introduced by a competing manufacturer.

On the other hand, if the user exploits the information contained in a manufacturer innovation to develop innovations *that improve or complement* the manufacturer-developed innovation, the effect on a manufacturer's incentive to innovate—and on social welfare—will in general be positive (assuming the improvement comes as an add-on, not as a substitute). Such improvements and complements will increase sales of the manufacturer's innovation and make it more valuable to users. Indeed, there are many examples in which manufacturers consciously employ a strategy to encourage the development of complements by users. Thus, Stata, a software vendor specializing in statistical software, has created a proprietary "platform" product to which users can add new and better statistical tests. Users encode these in a software language proprietary to Stata. This increases the value of and sales of Stata's platform product. Add-ons developed by users that are freely revealed will increase Stata profits more than will equivalent add-ons developed and sold by manufacturers. As a consequence, Stata is more likely to innovate if it anticipates the likelihood of follow-on complementary and improvement innovations by users (Jokisch, 2001). Similar strategies are pursued by manufacturers of simulator software who provide tools to their users to develop add-ons (Henkel and Thies, 2003; Jeppesen, 2002).

In sum, we see that there are both positive and negative effects from intertemporal spillovers of innovation-related information in a world containing both user and manufacturer innovators. Manufacturer incentives to innovate—and social welfare—are likely to be *increased* if manufacturers anticipate that users will develop innovations that they can learn from—and/or develop complements and improvements to innovations that manufacturers develop. In contrast, manufacturer incentives to innovate—and social welfare—are likely to be *decreased* if manufacturers anticipate that users benefit from information spillovers from a manufacturer innovation in order to develop substitutes that are possibly even freely revealed. In net across the economy, we think that the effects associated with social welfare enhancement will dominate. As was discussed earlier, users-innovators tend to be lead users. Lead users tend to develop innovations that manufacturers have not yet had the "sticky" need information to develop and/or the market size incentive to want to develop. In such cases manufacturers will tend to benefit rather than suffer from spillovers.

Free revealing-related effects

User innovations are often freely revealed, as was noted and explored in Section 2. When user *or* manufacturer-developed innovations are freely revealed, a number of positive welfare effects appear. These are relevant to our discussions here because we think that user innovators are more likely to freely reveal their innovations than manufacturer innovators. We see two reasons for this. First, as was pointed out earlier, "second-generation innovation" can be of value to both users and manufacturers. However, user innovators must reveal *more* information than manufacturers to induce such innovations and channel them in directions they will find profitable. User innovators tend to benefit from having their innovations converted from "home-made" devices into more robust commercial products. If manufacturers are to rebuild user innovations into a more robust form, their inner workings must generally be revealed in detail. In contrast, a manufacturer-innovator typically seeks to benefit from subsequent user innovations in the form of valuable "add-ons" to a platform product (Jokisch, 2001). For this purpose a user need only be provided with appropriate interface specifications: complete details of the platform's inner workings need not be revealed. Second, some user innovations but no manufacturer innovations are developed for a non-financial end use. For example, individual end users may develop novel sports equipment simply to enjoy it rather than use it as a competitive tool. When this is so, there is no competition among users that would induce them to protect rather than freely reveal their innovations.

Monopoly distortion. If user innovations are made publicly available for free (become "public" innovations), a potential user only has to bear the cost of adoption. This is statically efficient if, as we assume, the marginal cost of revealing an innovation (i.e., the respective information) is zero. As a consequence, for public user innovations there is no dead-weight loss from above-marginal-cost pricing. A second positive welfare effect of public user innovations is that they might induce sellers of competing commercial offerings to reduce their prices, thus indirectly leading to another reduction in dead-weight loss.[5] Finally, prices above marginal cost can induce excessive variety by shifting up the demand curve for substitutes, which might make the introduction of the latter profitable (Tirole, 1988). Again, this inefficiency is absent for public user innovations.

Restrictions imposed on second-generation innovators. Manufacturer innovators would usually price information sought by potential second-generation innovators above marginal cost, by either charging licensing fees and/or by keeping the innovation secret or protected by legal means. This causes a static inefficiency.[6] In contrast, a public user innovation can be freely used by agents other than the original innovator as a basis for new products and further developments, since it is neither protected by legal means nor by secrecy. Hence, the introduction of goods building upon the original innovation is simplified compared to a situation where the latter is brought forth by a manufacturer. This efficient use of the information describing public user innovations implies an increase in social welfare relative to a situation in which only manufacturer-developed innovations are present in a marketplace. Goods will be developed which otherwise would not have been, and/or the same goods will be developed while avoiding either licensing fees and transaction cost or a wasteful multiplicity of innovation expenditures.

4. Discussion

In this paper we have explored the impact of user-developed innovations on effects that tend to drive the economy to overprovide or underprovide product variety. We conclude that the addition of user innovation to models that have previously incorporated only innovations developed by manufacturers is likely to result in an increase in welfare. A central observation is that user and manufacturer innovations tend to be of a different nature, with product innovations developed by users tending to fill small niches of high need left open by commercial sellers. Furthermore, innovation-related knowledge of users and manufacturers complement each other. Hence, the introduction of a user innovation can have an offsetting effect to the tendency of manufacturers to underprovide product diversity to a marketplace. This positive welfare effect is strengthened by the fact that, due to user needs evolving over time, innovations created by "lead users" for market niches often become relevant to the bulk of the market later.

Given that user innovation is welfare enhancing, policymakers may find it useful to encourage product (and process and service) development and modification by users followed by free revealing. In this section we consider positive steps that can be taken to this end, and social policies likely to have negative impacts that should be avoided. We also note that manufacturers can enhance their benefits from user innovation by developing strategies that integrate user innovation more closely (and consciously) with their own product development efforts.

Implications for social policy

Currently, manufacturer firms are rewarded for their innovative activity by R&D subsidies and tax credits. Such measures can make economic sense if median social returns to innovation are significantly higher than median private returns, as has been found by Mansfield et al. (1977) and others. Ignoring the issue of the optimal level of this support, we want to point out the strong discrepancy that exists between the high importance of user innovations for the economy—as evidenced by the number of important commercialized innovations whose roots can be traced to user-developed prototyping and learning by doing—and the low level of public support they receive. This at least raises the question as to whether tax dollars paid to manufacturers—sometimes to subsidize development of proprietary "me too" products—might be better spent on incenting additional user innovation.[7] Bresnahan and Greenstein (1996a) make a similar point. They investigate the role of "co-invention" in users' move from mainframe to client–server architecture.[8] By co-invention they mean organizational changes and innovations developed and implemented by users that are required to take full advantage of that new invention. The authors point out the high importance that co-invention has for realizing social returns from innovation. They consider the federal government's support for creating "national information infrastructures" as insufficient or misallocated, since "[co-invention] is the bottleneck for social returns and likely the highest value locus for non-commercially motivated invention." (p. 69).

If a user innovation is kept private it can lead to even more duplicative work and less subsequent innovations than a comparable manufacturer innovation, since the latter will more likely be sold or licensed. To avoid the welfare loss this entails, public policy should think about how to strengthen users' incentives both to innovate and to freely reveal their innovations when this behavior is not already present due to insufficient reward.

Policymaking for other purposes should also be examined for any deleterious side effects on user innovation, such as are present in current technical and legal efforts to prevent users from reverse-engineering manufacturer-supplied products or modifying them. Users often modify existing products to serve as low-cost components for their own novel prototypes. Technical barriers inserted by manufacturers such as controls to prevent the refilling of manufacturer-supplied ink-jet printer cartridges with low-cost ink can also prevent other forms of user activity such as innovation by users who wish to fill them with novel materials for novel applications. Similarly, efforts to prevent copying of digital information such as the Digital Millennium Copyright Act (DMCA) can prevent users from modifying and adapting existing material to new purposes (Varian, 2002).

In a more general context, Benkler (2002) argues that institutional changes strengthening intellectual property protection tend to foster concentration and homogenization of information production. This happens to the detriment of alternative (and complementing) information production strategies. User innovations are a case in point, or even *the* case in point. Lessig (2001) and Boldrin and Levine (2002) arrive at a similarly negative valuation of overly strong IP protection.

Implications for innovators

User innovations can have both positive and negative aspects for a manufacturer that offers a commercial partial or full substitute to the user-developed product. On the positive side, there can be cost savings when a manufacturer develops a product after a user innovation has been made available. Since the later will often be freely revealed, the manufacturer can build upon information about needs and solutions developed by the innovating user. Importantly, manufacturers—that commonly devote a high share of their innovation-related efforts to products that fail commercially when introduced to the marketplace—gain "free market research" from observing user product prototyping, product use and product adoption activities.

However, we also saw that the presence of user innovations can also affect manufacturers negatively, in cases where they represent increased market competition.[9] When a user developed product and a commercial substitute exist alongside, some buyers might prefer the user development, causing a loss of market share and profit to the manufacturer. The profit maximizing price will, in general, be reduced due to competition from the user development (but could be increased in particular cases). And even if, at the profit maximizing price, no one prefers the user development, it might still be so attractive for some users that it restricts the manufacturer's pricing power. Finally, the mere threat of users developing a free substitute limits the manufacturer's pricing power, similar to the way a threat of entry works in the theory of contestable markets (Baumol *et al.*, 1982). In particular, this means that price discrimination (which is likely to be difficult anyway) becomes harder, because those users with a high willingness to pay might find innovating for themselves an attractive alternative.

The impact of a reduction in a manufacturer's pricing power might be particularly significant for manufacturers that create "platform" products linked to separately sold enhancements or complementary products. Often, a manufacturer of such a product will want to sell the platform—the razor, the ink-jet printer, or the videogame player—at a low margin or a loss, and then price the add-ons at a much higher margin. Obviously, this strategy will work less well if users can develop free add-ons for the same platform. However, the overall effect depends on details: the availability of user-developed add-ons may indirectly increase demand for commercial add-ons for which no free substitute exists, thus again benefiting the manufacturer.

If the possibility of free add-ons developed and made generally available by users makes development of a platform unprofitable for a manufacturer, social welfare can thereby be reduced. However, it is only the razor versus blade pricing scheme that may become unprofitable. If the manufacturer makes positive margins on the platform, then the availability of user-developed add-ons has an additional positive effect: it increases the value of the platform to users, and so allows manufacturers to charge higher margins on it and/or sell more units. Indeed, manufacturers can profit by taking proactive steps to make their platform more hospitable to userdeveloped add-ons ("this platform is 'open'") and thus more valuable to users. Such a strategy is systematically pursued, e.g., in the cases of Stata statistical software and consumer simulator software mentioned above.

Finally, we note that free revealing of innovations bears a potential that is often not exploited by user innovators. There obviously are cases where it makes sense for a user to keep an innovation secret. However, it is likely that user innovations are sometimes kept private not so much out of rational motives, but either because of a general, not thought-through attitude "we do not give away our intellectual property", or because the (administrative) cost of revealing are deemed higher than its perceived benefits. We propose that firms that develop user innovations should develop a conscious strategy as to what should be kept private and what should be freely revealed. For example, firms often have employee non-disclosure agreements that prevent their programmers from publicly revealing changes they have made to *any* software—yet it can be beneficial to reveal improvements employees make to open source software.

We conclude by noting again that user innovation is an important—and welfare enhancing—phenomenon in economic life. We propose that it will be valuable to study this phenomenon more deeply, and to integrate it more fully into economic theory, policy making, and innovator practices.

Acknowledgments

We thank James Bessen, Dominique Foray and Jacques Mairesse for helpful comments and suggestions. Of course, all remaining errors are ours.

Notes

1. In some studies shown in Table I, the proportion of users innovating in the general user population will be lower than that reported in the study due to intentionally introduced sample biases. For example, the study of mountain biking by Lüthje *et al.* (2002) was intentionally directed towards mountain bikers who were members of biking clubs located in a known "hot spot" for user innovation. Other studies without such biases, however, also report high proportions of users innovating. Thus a study of the *entire* population of Australian libraries found that 26% had made in-house modifications

to the computer software of the "OPAC" systems they use for record-keeping and patron information searches (Morrison et al., 2000). On the basis of present data, therefore, it seems safe to conclude that "many" users do engage in product development and modification in many fields.

2. "Free revealing" as so defined does not mean that recipients necessarily acquire and utilize the revealed information at no cost to themselves. Recipients may, for example, have to pay for a journal subscription or an Internet connection or a field trip to acquire the information being freely revealed. However, if the information possessor does not profit from any such expenditures made by information adopters, the information itself is still freely revealed, according to our definition. Conversely, note that innovators may sometimes choose to subsidize the acquisition and evaluation and use of their freely revealed information by others. For example, a firm may invest in lobbying to get others to adopt an technical standard it has developed.

3. When goods exhibit network externalities, and when product diversity implies a certain degree of incompatibility, then the benefits of product variety will also be reduced. Our analysis abstracts from this aspect. The goods we consider either do not exhibit network externalities, or we look at diversity *within* a group of compatible types of network goods.

4. There may be a negative externality when the user innovator benefits from diffusion of its innovation. However, unlike for a commercial innovator, such diffusion-related benefits will be minor for a user innovator compared to the direct benefits derived from own use. In addition, as we will discuss in section Information asymmetry-related inefficiencies, there will often be a *positive* externality exerted by a commercial second-generation innovator on the user innovator.

5. While a price reduction of competing commercial goods is plausible, it can not generally be proved. Under some circumstances, commercial sellers might react to the introduction of a substitutive user innovation by increasing their prices.

6. See Gallini and Scotchmer (2002) for an extensive discussion of the effects of different aspects of IP protection.

7. As in other cases of public subsidies there are potential downsides of government support for user innovation, as laid out by Schmidt and Schnitzer (2003) for the case of open source software. Without entering the debate on whether and to what extent government subsidies are desirable, we simply note that *given* the considerable level of government support for innovation in general, a re-allocation of some of this support to user innovators might well make sense.

8. See also Bresnahan and Greenstein (1996b), Bresnahan and Saloner (1997), and Saloner and Steinmueller (1996).

9. Saint-Paul (2003) focuses on this issue in a model of growth and innovation, finding that "philanthropical" innovation—developed and diffused for free, without any profit motive—may even reduce growth and welfare. However, his assumptions differ from ours, and they do not fit the real-world cases we are studying. First, user innovators are not philanthropists, but profit-oriented economic agents; second, their innovations and those of manufacturers tend to be of a complementary nature, as we have seen.

References

Achilladelis, B., A.B. Robertson, and P. Jervis, 1971, *Project SAPPHO: A Study of Success and Failure in Industrial Innovatio*, 2 vols, London: Centre for the Study of Industrial Innovation.

Aghion, P. and P. Howitt, 1992, 'A Model of Growth through Creative Destruction,' *Econometrica* **60**, 323–351.

Allen, R.C., 1983, 'Collective Invention,' *Journal of Economic Behavior and Organization* **4** (1), 1–24.

Anderson, S.P., A. de Palma, and J.F. Thisse, 1988, 'A Representative Consumer Theory of the Logit Model,' *International Economic Review* **29**, 461–466.

Arrow, K.J., 1962, 'Economic Welfare and the Allocation of Resources for Invention,' in: Richard Nelson (ed.), *The Rate and Direction of Inventive Activity*, Princeton, NJ: Princeton University Press.

Balachandra, R. and J.H. Friar, 1997, 'Factors for Success in R&D Projects and New Product Introduction: A Contextual Framework,' *IEEE Transactions on Engineering Management* **44** (3), 276–287.

Baumol, W., J. Panzar, and R. Willig, 1982, *Contestable Markets and the Theory of Industry Structure*, New York: Harcourt Brace Jovanovich.

Benkler, Y., 2002, 'Intellectual Property and the Organization of Information Production,' *International Review of Law and Economics* **22** (1), 81–107.

Bessen, J. and E. Maskin, 2002, 'Sequential Innovation, Patents, and Imitation,' MIT Dpt. of Economics Working Paper, revised version.

Boldrin, M. and D. Levine, 2002, 'The Case against Intellectual Property,' AEA Papers and Proceedings, May, pp. 209–212.

Bresnahan, T.F. and S. Greenstein, 1996a, 'Technical Progress and Co-invention in Computing and in the Uses of Computers,' *Brookings Papers on Economic Activity. Microeconomics*, 1996, pp. 1–77.

Bresnahan, T.F. and S. Greenstein, 1996b, 'The Competitive Crash in Large-scale Commercial Computing,' in R. Landau, T. Taylor, and G. Wright (eds.), *The Mosaic of Economic Growth*, Stanford: Stanford University Press, pp. 357–397.

Bresnahan, T.F. and G. Saloner, 1997, 'Large firms' demand for computer products and services: competing market models, inertia, and enabling strategic change,' in D.B. Yoffie (ed.), *Competing in the age of digital convergence*, Cambridge, MA: Harvard Business School Press.

Chamberlin, E.H., 1950, 'Product Heterogeneity and Public Policy,' *American Economic Review* **40** (2), 85–92, Papers and Proceedings.

Dixit, A.K. and J.E. Stiglitz, 1977, 'Monopolistic Competition and Optimum Product Diversity,' *American Economic Review* **67** (3), 297–308.

Eaton, B.C. and R.G. Lipsey, 1989, 'Product Differentiation,' in R. Schmalensee and R.D. Willig (eds.), *Handbook of Industrial Organization*, Vol. 1, Elsevier Science Publishers, pp. 723–768 (Chapter 12).

Eaton, B.C. and N. Schmitt, 1994, 'Flexible Manufacturing and Market Structure,' *American Economic Review* **84** (4), 875–888.

Elrod, T. and A.P. Kelman, 1987, 'Reliability of New Product Evaluation as of 1968 and 1981,' Working Paper, Owen Graduate School of Management, Vanderbilt University.

Enos, J.L., 1962, *Petroleum Progress and Profits: A History of Process Innovation*. Cambridge, MA: MIT Press.

Franke, N. and S. Shah, 2003, 'How Communities Support Innovative Activities: An Exploration of Assistance and Sharing Among End-Users,' *Research Policy* **32** (1), 157–178.

Franke, N. and E. von Hippel, 2003, 'Satisfying Heterogeneous User Needs via Innovation Toolkits: The Case of Apache Security Software,' *Research Policy* **32** (7), 1199–1215.

Gallini, N.T., 2002, 'The Economics of Patents: Lessons from Recent U.S. Patent Reform,' *Journal of Economic Perspectives* **16** (2), 131–154.

Gallini, N.T. and S. Scotchmer, 2002, 'Intellectual Property: When is it the best incentive system?,' in A. Jaffe, J. Lerner, and S. Stern (eds.), *Innovation Policy and the Economy*, Vol. 2, Cambridge, MA: MIT Press.

Grossman, G. and E. Helpman, 1991, *Innovation and Growth in the Global Economy*, Cambridge, MA: MIT Press.

Harhoff, D., J. Henkel, and E. von Hippel, 2003, 'Profiting from Voluntary Information Spillovers: How Users Benefit by Freely Revealing their Innovations,' *Research Policy* **32** (10), 1753–1769.

Hart, O.D., 1985, 'Monopolistic Competition in the Spirit of Chamberlin: Special Results,' *Economic Journal* **95**, 889–908.

Henkel, J., 2003, 'Embedded Linux – Informal Collaborative Software Development by Commercial Firms,'in *Proceedings of the 12th International Conference on Management of Technology (IAMOT2003)*, Nancy, France, May 2003.

Henkel, J. and S. Thies, 2003, 'Customization and Innovation – User Innovation Toolkits for Simulator Software,'in *Proceedings of the 2003 Congress on Mass Customization and Personalization (MCPC 2003)*, Munich, Germany, October 2003.

Herstatt, C. and E. von Hippel, 1992, 'From Experience: Developing New Product Concepts Via the Lead User Method: A Case Study in a "Low Tech" Field,' *Journal of Product Innovation Management* **9**, 213–221.

Hotelling, H., 1929, 'Stability in Competition,' *Economic Journal* **39**, 41–57.

Jeppesen, L.B., 2002, 'The Implications of "User Toolkits" for Innovation,' *Copenhagen Business School*. www.cbs.dk/departments/ivs/wp/wp02-09.pdf.

Jokisch, M., 2001, *Open Source Software-Entwicklung – Eine Analyse des Geschäftsmodells der STATA Corp*. Unpublished Master thesis, University of Munich.

Knight, K.E., 1963, *A Study of Technological Innovation: The Evolution of Digital Computers*. Unpublished Ph.D. dissertation, Pittsburgh, PA: Carnegie Institute of Technology.

Lakhani, K.R. and B. Wolf, 2005, 'Why Hackers Do What They Do: Understanding Motivation and Effort in Free/Open Source Software Projects,' in J. Feller, B. Fitzgerald, S. Hissam, and K.R. Lakhani (eds.), *Perspectives on Free and Open Source Software*, Cambridge, MA: MIT Press.

Lancaster, K., 1975, 'Socially Optimal Product Differentiation,' *American Economic Review* **65** (4), 567–585.

Lerner, J. and J. Tirole, 2002, 'Some Simple Economics of Open Source,' *Journal of Industrial Economics* **50** (2), 197–234.

Lessig, L., 2001, *The Future of Ideas: The Fate of the Commons in a Connected World*, New York: Random House.

Lim, K., 2000, 'The Many Faces of Absorbtive Capacity: Spillovers of Copper Interconnect Technology for Semiconductor Chips,' MIT Sloan School of Management Working Paper # 4110.

Lüthje, C., 2003, 'Customers as Co-Inventors: An Empirical Analysis of the Antecedents of Customer-Driven Innovations in the Field of Medical Equipment,' in *Proceedings from the 32th EMAC Conference* 2003, Glasgow.

Lüthje, C., 2004, 'Characteristics of Innovating Users in a Consumer Goods Field: An Empirical Study of Sport-Related Product Consumers', *Technovation*, forthcoming.

Lüthje, C., C. Herstatt, and E. von Hippel, 2002, 'Patterns in the Development of Minor Innovations by Users: Bricolage in Mountain Biking,' MIT Sloan School Working Paper #4377-02.

Mansfield, E., J. Rapoport, A. Romeo, E. Villani, S. Wagner, and F. Husic, 1977, *The Production and Application of New Industrial Technology*, New York: Norton.

Mansfield, E. and S. Wagner, 1975, 'Organizational and Strategic Factors Associated With Probabilities of Success in Industrial R&D,' *Journal of Business* **48**, 179–198.

Morrison, P., J. Roberts, and E. von Hippel, 2000, 'Determinants of User Innovation and Innovation Sharing in a Local Market,' *Management Science* **46**, 1513–1527.

Nordhaus, W.D., 1969, *Invention, Growth, and Welfare: A Theoretical Treatment of Technological Change*, Cambridge, MA: MIT Press.

Nuvolari, A., 2004, 'Collective Invention During the British Industrial Revolution: The Case of the Cornish Pumping Engine,' *Cambridge Journal of Economics* **28** (3), 347–363.

Ogawa, S., 1997, 'Does Sticky Information Affect the Locus of Innovation? Evidence from the Japanese Convenience-store Industry,' *Research Policy* **26**, 777–790.

Oi, W.Y., 1997, 'The Welfare Implications of Invention,' in Timothy F. Bresnahan (ed.), *The Economics of New Goods*, Chicago, IL: University of Chicago Press, pp. 109–141.

Perloff, J.M. and S.C. Salop, 1985, 'Equilibrium with Product Differentiation,' *Review of Economic Studies* **52**, 107–120.

Poolton, J. and I. Barclay, 1998, 'New Product Development From Past Research to Future Applications,' *Industrial Marketing Management* **27**, 197–212.

Raymond, E.S., 1999, *The Cathedral & the Bazaar: Musings on Linux and Open Source by an Accidental Revolutionary*, Cambridge, MA: O'Reilly.

Redmond, W.H., 1995, 'An Ecological Perspective on New Product Failure: The Effects of Competitive Overcrowding,' *Journal of Product Innovation Management* **12**, 200–213.

Riggs, W. and E. von Hippel, 1994, 'Incentives to Innovate and the Sources of Innovation: The Case of Scientific Instruments,' *Research Policy* **23** (4), 459–469.

Röller, L.-H. and M.H. Tombak, 1990, 'Strategic Choice of Flexible Manufacturing Technology and Welfare Implications,' *Journal of Industrial Economics* **35**, 417–431.

Romer, P.M., 1990, 'Endogenous Technological Change,' *Journal of Political Economy* **98**, 71–102.

Rosenberg, N., 1976, *Perspectives on Technology*, Cambridge, MA: Cambridge University Press.

Rothwell, R., C. Freeman, A. Horsley, V.T.P. Jervis, A.B. Roberts, and J. Townsend, 1974, 'SAPPHO Updated – Project SAPPHO Phase II,' *Research Policy* **3**, 258–91.

Saint-Paul, G., 2003, 'Growth Effects of Non-proprietary Innovation,' *Journal of the European Economic Association* **1** (2–3), 429–439.

Saloner, G. and W.E. Steinmueller, 1996, 'Demand for Computer Products and Services in Large European Organizations,' Research paper 1370, Stanford Graduate School of Business.

Sattinger, M., 1984, 'Value of an Additional Firm in Monopolistic Competition,' *Review of Economic Studies* **51**, 321–332.

Schmidt, K.M. and M. Schnitzer, 2003, 'Public Subsidies for Open Source? Some Economic Policy Issues of the Software Market,' *Harvard Journal of Law and Technology* **16** (2), 473–505.

Schmookler, J., 1966, *Invention and Economic Growth*, Cambridge, MA: Harvard University Press.

Shah, S., 2000, 'Sources and Patterns of Innovation in a Consumer Products Field: Innovations in Sporting Equipment,' MIT Sloan School of Management Working paper # 4105 (March).

Spence, M., 1976a, 'Product Differentiation and Welfare,' *American Economic Review* **66** (2), 407–414, Papers and Proceedings.

Spence, M., 1976b, 'Product Selection, Fixed Costs, and Monopolistic Competition,' *Review of Economic Studies* **43** (2), 217–235.

Tirole, J., 1988, *Theory of Industrial Organization*, Cambridge, MA: MIT Press.

Urban, G.L. and E. von Hippel, 1988, 'Lead User Analyses for the Development of New Industrial Products,' *Management Science* **34**, 569–582.

Varian, H.R., 2002, 'New Chips Can Keep a Tight Rein on Consumers,' *New York Times,* July **4**, 2002.

von Hippel, E., 1986, 'Lead Users: A Source of Novel Product Concepts,' *Management Science* **32** (7), 791–805.

von Hippel, E., 1988, *The Sources of Innovation*, New York: Oxford University Press.

von Hippel, E., 1994, 'Sticky Information and the Locus of Problem Solving: Implications for Innovation,' *Management Science* **40** (4), 429–439.

Underinvestment in Public Good Technologies

Gregory Tassey

ABSTRACT. Although underinvestment phenomena are the rationale for government subsidization of research and development (R&D), the concept is poorly defined and its impact is seldom quantified. Conceptually, underinvestment in industrial R&D can take the form of either a wrong amount or a suboptimal composition of R&D investment. In both cases, R&D policy has not adequately modeled the relevant economic phenomena and thus is unable to characterize, explain, and measure the underinvestment. Four factors can cause systematic underinvestment in R&D-intensive industries: complexity, timing, existence of economies of scale and scope, and spillovers. The impacts of these factors vary in intensity over the typical technology life cycle, so government policy responses must be managed dynamically. In addition to understanding the causes of underinvestment in R&D, the magnitude of the deficiency relative to some "optimum" must be estimated to enable a ranking of technology areas with respect to expected net economic benefits from a government subsidy. Project selection criteria must therefore be based on quantitative and qualitative indicators that represent the nature and the magnitude of identified market failures. The major requirement for management of R&D policy therefore is a methodology that regularly assesses long-term expected benefits and risks from current and proposed R&D portfolios. To this end, a three-stage process is proposed to effectively carry out R&D policy analysis. The three stages are (1) identify and explain the causes of the underinvestment, (2) characterize and assess the investment trends and their impacts, and (3) estimate the magnitude of the underinvestment relative to a perceived optimum in terms of its cost to the economy. Only after all three stages of analysis have been completed can the underinvestment pattern be matched with the appropriate policy response.

Key words: R&D innovation, underinvestment, policy

JEL Classification: O3, O2

1. Introduction

Understanding the role of technology in economic growth requires the development and application of microeconomic theory. This is because each technology has unique characteristics, which interact iteratively over the technology's life cycle with unique industry structures and technical infrastructures. The microeconomic character of such an evolutionary model is further enhanced by the fact that the majority of technology investment decisions are made by individual companies and external financing is often supplied by individuals and small venture capital firms, with much of the financing for particular technologies limited to specific geographic regions.

Economists have explored the numerous elements of the microeconomics of technology-based growth, including the determinants of research and development (R&D) spending, project selection, the tradeoffs between R&D costs and time within a portfolio management context, the interactions of this activity with firm size and market structure, and the responses of R&D investment decisions to different financial and regulatory incentives. In addition, the results of such investments have been estimated using several analytical frameworks.

However, no one has surpassed Mansfield *et al.* (1968, 1971, 1982) in the number of these elements analyzed with respect to both investment and results, the level of disaggregation explored, and the collection and use of industry data to enlighten the proposed frameworks. Mansfield *et al.* (1977) have had a particularly pronounced effect on the analysis of the results of innovation. Their work in the late 1970s in which social and private rates of return were estimated for a range of R&D investments in manufacturing technologies followed Griliches' (1958) path breaking work in agriculture and collectively drew attention to the "gap" between social and private rates of return. This gap has spawned several decades of debate over

Stop 1060
National Institute of Standards and Technology
Gaithersburg, MD 20899
E-mail: tassey@nist.gov

government roles in supporting various amounts and types of R&D [including Mansfield et al., (1982)]. Economists [including Mansfield, (1980, 1991a, b)] subsequently disaggregated R&D into basic research and applied R&D to examine the differences in rates of return between the "pure public good" (basic science) and the target of applied R&D ("proprietary technology").

Mansfield's broad and highly microeconomic analysis has provided an analytical platform for needed progress in assessing the implications of the "gap" for public policy. This paper focuses on barriers to R&D investment that result in suboptimal distributions of R&D investments across different types of R&D and thereby reduce potential long-term economic growth. The point of departure is the proposition that the gap between the social and private rates of return to R&D investments is not automatically an indicator of underinvestment and, at least as important, it is not an indicator only of potential underinvestment in the amount of R&D. Barriers arise that affect the composition of R&D and this class of market failures can have significant long-term negative effects on economic growth. The resulting added complexity to R&D policy analysis requires a more microeconomic approach in the Mansfield tradition.

2. R&D market failure analysis

Firms conduct R&D for two reasons: (1) to develop new products, services, or processes, and (2) to maintain a capability to identify and assimilate technologies from external sources (Cohen and Levinthal, 1989). Governments of industrialized nations obviously consider these activities to be essential for economic growth because they maintain various sets of R&D support policies. Yet, the theoretical and operational frameworks for managing such policies are incomplete.

Economists have consistently estimated the rates of return from R&D to be considerably above those obtainable from other assets. However, for R&D in aggregate, significant rate of return (RoR) differentials for social (industry) versus private (innovator) R&D investments have been found.[1] Moreover, among types of R&D, basic research and long-term, high-risk technology research have yielded particularly high rates of return (Griliches, 1995). The implication of these persistent rate-of-return differentials is the existence of systemic "market failure." However, the interpretation and policy implications of these RoR differentials are poorly defined because the majority of the economics literature has misspecified the knowledge production and innovation processes, resulting in inaccurate R&D policy prescriptions for dealing with the implied underinvestment.

Assessments of private sector underinvestment have been based largely on the neoclassical concept of externalities (Pigou, 1932) and defined as differences between actual investment patterns and an optimum rate of investment. However, this concept of market failure has not been made operational in the sense that specific roles for government can be deduced (Ruffin, 1996). Coase (1960, 1992) made a huge contribution toward resolving the problem by emphasizing that overcoming the difficulties in estimating the amount and nature of underinvestment mechanisms resulting from externalities requires the definition and then the assignment of property rights and associated transaction costs. The institutional (government) role therefore becomes extremely important and also case specific. Consequently, a microeconomic analysis of each specific case is required.

For R&D, analysis of market failure mechanisms and the consequent need for government intervention require accurate models of the unique set of factors determining this category of investment. If the needed models were straightforward, government R&D strategies would be relatively simple to design and manage. However, private investment incentives respond negatively to the public good content of technology and this content is distributed among elements of the typical industrial technology in more complex ways than generally realized. In particular, most industrial technologies (or, more accurately, elements of them) have a quasi-public good character, which complicates and thus inhibits addressing property rights issues, thereby substantially raising transaction costs, as originally identified by Coase.

Moreover, other factors besides property rights are important in determining R&D

investment patterns, such as the relationship between the nature of a technology and the industry and market structures that deliver it. In addition, defining an optimum rate of investment is a particularly challenging problem for R&D policy, but this is a necessary analytical step independent of identifying the factors determining private sector investment. Assessment of the time-cost trade-off is one of the many contributions by Mansfield to understanding the technology life cycle.

In the Coase tradition, R&D policy requires a set of analytical tools that can efficiently identify and assess the characteristics of an industrial technology that affect investment patterns over time. Thus, this paper seeks to provide more structure and rigor to the analysis of underinvestment in R&D. Specifically, the framework developed emphasizes underinvestment in the major elements of the typical industrial technology and examines how investment patterns change over a technology's life cycle relative to an optimum. The focus is on underinvestment relative to the optimal *composition* of R&D, as opposed to underinvestment in the aggregate *amount* of R&D.[2]

Beginning with Arrow (1962a), economists developed explanations of underinvestment in R&D based on the indivisibility and inappropriability of information and the excessive risk involved in its creation. These factors were developed largely as if technical information were a homogeneous entity and therefore so would be the process (R&D) that produces it. Some research has identified two or more distinct elements of technical information.[3] Tassey (1997) characterizes these elements in terms of uniquely different investment incentives, responding to differing public good content. It remains to develop a framework based on the composition of R&D that identifies specific underinvestment phenomena associated with each element, thereby enabling accurate policy analysis.

That is, to identify, characterize, and understand the sources and impacts of market failures with respect to the composition of R&D investment and eventually match underinvestment phenomena with efficient policy response mechanisms, an analytical framework is needed that emphasizes analysis at the technology-element level, where the elements are distinguished by unique investment incentives and patterns. A "technology-element" framework is different from the more traditional "R&D-phase" approach used by Mansfield *et al.* (1971) and a few others, even though the proposed elements are to a degree the outputs of the conventional phases of R&D. The technology element approach is preferred because it is more closely related to corporate R&D investment decision making, a fact which facilitates investment analysis.

To provide this framework, the analysis takes a three-stage approach: (1) use of conceptual models that allow specification of the causes and effects of underinvestment by major technology element; (2) selection of indicators of suboptimal investment patterns and resultant impact trends; and (3) construction of practical quantitative approaches for defining and estimating the economic impacts of the underinvestment. Collectively, these three steps provide an empirically based "cause-and-effect analysis," which becomes the basis for ranking targets for government funding and matching underinvestment mechanisms with the appropriate policy responses. The following sections discuss these three stages that lead up to the policy response decision.

3. Underinvestment in generic technologies

For policy analysis purposes, a conceptual model must be selected that portrays the typical industrial technology in terms of its public and private good elements and thereby focuses policy analysis on the process creating systematic underinvestment. Such a model is also essential for interpreting the results of this analysis for policy makers, and ultimately helping to select the appropriate policy response.

A quasi-public good model of a technology-based industry

A static representation of a typical technology-based industry is shown in Figure 1. This conceptual approach is significantly different from the "black box" model, which has influenced R&D policy for the past 50 years.[4] The black box model regards technology as a homogenous entity and thereby prohibits consideration of the

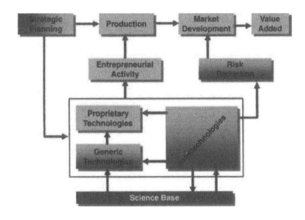

Figure 1. Economic model of a technology-based industry.

existence of distinct elements within the typical industrial technology, each of which responds to distinctly different investment incentives.

In a more realistic model, the typical industrial technology is separated into a set of private and quasi-public elements to reflect the different investment incentives and R&D management practices associated with the provision of each of these elements (Tassey, 1991, 1997). R&D policy is complicated not only by their existence, but also by the fact that these elements vary with respect to their public good content.[5] The specified elements are not arbitrary; rather, they represent distinctly different investment incentives faced by industry and therefore different underinvestment phenomena appear for each element.[6]

This last point is critical because success of a public role in supporting industrial R&D depends on demonstrating both theoretically and empirically that public R&D is a complement rather than a substitute for private R&D. However, disaggregating technology into publicly funded and privately funded components can imply a dichotomous model consisting of a pure public good and a pure private good.[7] Some of the required interaction issues (in particular, complementarity) can be assessed in such a model, but the quasi-public good nature of several common technology elements is obscured and therefore an assessment of investment incentives and subsequent underinvestment behavior is compromised.

In Figure 1, the darker shading indicates the degree of public good content for a technology element. In both the black box and technology element models, funding of basic science is a relatively straightforward policy issue because scientific knowledge is generally regarded as a strong public good. Thus, basic research is largely the responsibility of government to fund. This characterization of science simplifies policy management, with the only issues being the amount of funding and the distribution of this funding across fields of science.[8]

The first step in applying scientific knowledge (i.e., conducting *technology* research) is to prove the concept of the new technology. The end point of such an effort is frequently a laboratory prototype or some other form of "proof of concept."[9] If the resulting fundamental or "generic" technology is deemed to have sufficient potential commercial value, companies assign the substantial follow-on R&D to one of the company's line-of-business units to turn the laboratory prototype into a commercial product. Investment decisions in this phase of the R&D cycle use the more quantitative portfolio management tools of corporate finance, such as net present value and internal RoR metrics. The outcome of applied R&D is represented by the proprietary technology box in Figure 1.

The importance for industrial competitiveness of investment in generic technologies is that this first phase of technology research provides the basis for "next generation" or radically new ("disruptive") products, processes, and services.[10] Developing new technology platforms (generic technologies) and market applications derived from these platforms (proprietary technologies) are two very different investments and are managed quite differently within large R&D-based companies.

In addition, a third element is represented by the "infratechnologies" box in Figure 1. Infratechnologies are a diverse set of technical tools that are necessary to efficiently conduct all phases of R&D, to control production processes, and to execute marketplace transactions for complex technology-based goods.[11] These tools are called infratechnologies because they provide a complex but essential technical infrastructure.

Many infratechnologies are adopted as industry standards, emphasizing their public good content (Tassey, 2000). Without the availability of this technical infrastructure, especially codified as standards, transaction costs for all three major stages of economic activity—R&D, production, and marketing—would be much higher, thereby significantly slowing the evolution of technology life cycles.[12] The multiple economic roles of infratechnologies in the typical technology-based industry are indicated in Figure 1 by the several arrows pointing from the infratechnology box to the target areas of impact.

Looking at a technology-based economy more broadly, most small companies do not attempt much generic technology research, relying on assimilating the required technical knowledge from external sources. Large companies may undertake more of this type of research, but a number of factors related to its public good content result in underinvestment.[13] Thus, the proposed taxonomy is essential for R&D policy analysis because it has implications for the sources of radically new technology platforms, access to these generic technologies (property rights issues), process efficiencies and the transaction costs associated with market access.

Dynamics of R&D and underinvestment

The above conceptual model identifies the major technology elements relevant for policy analysis as a static framework. However, beginning with Mansfield *et al.* (1971), economists have shown that complex relationships exit between R&D investment over time and industry structure, risk preferences, strategic and project management capabilities, and the availability of a supporting technical infrastructure. A static framework overlooks the dynamic process by which new technology is created and utilized and thus how underinvestment can occur over the technology life cycle.

Corporate and government R&D investment decisions are made at the microeconomic level. Many attempts have been made to incorporate cause-and-effect relationships for the impact on output of an aggregate (firm- or industry-level) technology variable through the use of production functions, including the acquisition and use of a stock of knowledge. However, most of this literature assumes a continuous, steady-state stream of "opportunities" that, in turn, drive an optimal R&D intensity. The result of such a model is that the "stock of knowledge" grows steadily over time in response to a homogenous R&D process.

In fact, the dynamics of technological change are far from a continuous flow. Rather, "lumpy" advances in generic technical knowledge drive applied R&D for periods of time, after which diminishing returns set in. This requires refurbishment of the generic technology base or the optimal R&D intensity declines (Klevorick *et al.*, 1995).

Such a pattern implies a life cycle model of technological change. The richness of the underlying science base, the pattern of refurbishment of the generic technologies derived from this science base, and the efficiency of the process of creating market applications (innovations) combine to determine the optimum R&D intensity within and across life cycles.[14] Therefore, because the required analytical framework must be based on a technology life cycle concept, it requires a dynamic component.

Collectively, investments in the several phases of R&D determine the technology life cycle's trajectory and longevity and appropriate analysis can occur at several levels of aggregation.[15] The majority of research with a life-cycle dimension has characterized innovation as endogenously generated by competing firms that draw upon a knowledge base where the knowledge base is largely fixed. In such a framework, firms have limited windows of opportunity to apply this knowledge and earn a profit before new technologies mysteriously appear and a subsequent new wave of innovations takes their market shares away.

Schmookler (1966) partially solved this problem by introducing the concept of an accumulating knowledge base over time that innovators utilize to execute the process of creative destruction. Critically important is the proposition that accessing this knowledge base is affected by its public good character, which implies spillovers and increasing returns to subsequent innovators later in the life cycle (Caballero and Jaffe, 1993). However, although R&D or the resulting stock of knowledge has been incorporated into partial and general equilibrium growth models, the mechanisms by which this knowledge base evolves and is drawn upon have not been specified.[16]

Klevorick *et al.* (1995) point out that R&D investment (measured as an intensity ratio to indicate reliance on R&D as a competitive strategy) has been explained by either *search* models (technical knowledge is drawn from a fixed generic knowledge base) or *capital* models (technical knowledge is characterized as an evolving stock, augmented by flows of R&D investment). The former focuses on the efficiency of search mechanisms and the richness of the underlying generic technology base to explain R&D intensity. The latter uses production functions to first relate R&D investment to increases in the stock of applied knowledge and then indicate how this knowledge is used to produce new products/services or increase the efficiency of producing existing products/services.

Search models assume a fixed knowledge base and hence a fixed set of technological opportunities. Thus, diminishing returns are implied. The capital model also embodies diminishing returns through fixed relationships with other factors of production. These fixed relationships imply a constant set of technological opportunities, that is, a fixed generic technology base from which firms can develop market applications (innovations).

In reality, the generic technology base of an industry does not remain constant. The set of technological opportunities available to a firm or an industry changes over time. The rate of change, that is, the refurbishment of the opportunity set, determines the range of expected rates of return from investment in innovations and therefore the R&D intensity of the industry that draws upon this technology base. A central challenge for R&D investment theory is to explain the difference in incentives to invest in the opportunity set versus applications of this set (actual innovations).

Unfortunately analysis of the dynamics of investment in generic technologies (the opportunity set) has been limited. To understand potential constraints on private investment in the generic technology base requires a disaggregated technology model (Figure 1) coupled with a life-cycle framework to show how the major technology elements evolve over time and interact with each other. Investment in the major elements are affected by the functional linkages among these elements (indicated by the arrows in Figure 1), which evolve over the technology's life cycle.[17] The nature of an element or its linkages to other elements can cause underinvestment, as described in the following section.

Causes of underinvestment

Beginning with Nelson (1959) and Arrow (1962a), economists have attempted to explain the causes of underinvestment in R&D. Nelson focused on basic science and its pure public good content. Arrow identified "technical" risk and appropriability (the existence of spillovers) as major causes of underinvestment in R&D generally. The inability of investors to manage technical risk and the inability or unwillingness of property rights systems to prevent spillovers ("market" risk) can combine to create underinvestment.[18] While virtually all investments entail some degree of aggregate risk, the high levels and interactions of technical and market risk intrinsic to individual R&D investments impinge upon the ability to manage or insure against R&D risk.[19]

The sources of technical and market risk need to be specified to eventually provide quantitative cause-and-effect assessments over a technology's life cycle. These sources are more diverse than commonly believed. Specifically, R&D risk arises from

(1) *Technical Complexity:* Complexity and thus technical risk increase with the magnitude of the targeted advance and the complexity of the technology's interfaces with other technologies within a broader technology system;
(2) *Timing:* R&D investment time horizons, based on a combination of acceptable technical and market risk, are often shorter than those required to successfully develop radically new technologies;
(3) *Economies of Scale and Scope:* Some R&D is capital-intensive, which unbalances or limits diversification in R&D portfolios. This accentuates the tendency of R&D strategies to focus on achieving scale efficiencies to reduce both technical and market risk associated with specific applications, at the expense of potential economies of scope enabled by

an emerging technology; the result is to reduce incentives to invest in generic technologies with multi-market potential;

(4) *Spillovers:* Leakage or spillover of technical knowledge to companies that did not contribute to the research project creating the knowledge is typically greater the earlier in the R&D cycle an investment is undertaken, thereby increasing market risk.

Any one of these four sources of R&D risk can have serious negative impacts on the composition of private-sector R&D investment. Moreover, the severity of their impacts varies over technology life cycles and across technologies. Their impacts are particularly pronounced in the early phases of R&D aimed at next generation or radically new technologies and at supporting technology elements with a strong infrastructure character (infratechnologies). The four categories are discussed in more detail below.

Complexity. Complexity affects risk in a number of ways. The greater the targeted advance or the more multidisciplinary the R&D process, the greater the technical risk. The result can be market failure of the Arrow risk management type. Complexity is an especially vexing problem early in the technology life cycle because such research typically requires multidisciplinary research teams and unique research facilities that do not exist. Making such investments requires a positive assessment of a distant and uncertain potential market. Thus, firms react to research efficiency barriers by not undertaking more radical research projects, even though the potential RoR is high. As the technology life cycle evolves, companies often are caught between inefficient R&D processes and the intense competitive dynamics of high-tech markets, with the result that products are rushed to market with multiple performance defects.[20]

Moreover, most technologies driving advanced economies are complex systems in that a number of different technologies come together to eventually meet final demand.[21] The response has been specialization of private sector R&D on specific components of the overall system technology. Specialization creates inefficient R&D investment at the component level due to inadequate system-level performance specifications and system integration requirements. These economic impacts result from an increase in the public good content of both generic technologies and infratechnologies at the systems level.

Biotechnology is a dramatic example of the impacts of complexity leading to market failure. Using Figure 1 as a taxonomy, Table I lists multiple areas of bioscience (column 1) that have had to advance before a larger set of generic product and process technologies (columns 3 and 4) could be developed. These generic technologies have evolved over the past 25 years and slowly attracted private R&D funds, which are just now beginning to yield significant numbers of proprietary market applications (column 5).

However, lack of focus on and research tools for advancing complex generic technologies before attempting the development of specific innovations (new drugs) led to attempts to leap from advances in basic science to product development.[22] The result has been a very low success rate for biotechnology firms. In fact, 25 years after Genentech became the first public biotech company, only 12 of the 50 largest companies are profitable and the industry as a whole is still losing money.

Table I also shows the other category of industrial technology with significant public good content—infratechnologies (column 2). The demand for infratechnologies is derived from the demand for the generic technologies and its applications. However, the public good character of these technical tools results in significant underinvestment, thereby further reducing the productivity of R&D.[23]

In summary, dealing with complexity is made more difficult by the lumpy nature of technological advance (periodic quantum advances in the generic technology) and the increasing systems nature of modern technologies. These factors are pushing companies toward more focused R&D and market strategies within technology life cycles. Efficient technology systems require multiple components to be developed simultaneously and optimized so that maximum system performance is achieved.

Timing. Because technologies evolve in cyclical patterns, timing of R&D is critical. Underinvestment mechanisms can affect the rate of market

Table I
Interdependency of public–private technology assets: biotechnology

Science Base	Science Base	Generic Technologies Product	Generic Technologies Process	Commercial Products

• cellular biology
• genomics
• immunology
• microbiology/
  virology
• molecular biology
• nanoscience
• neuroscience
• pharmacology
• physiology
• proteomics
	• bioinformatics
	• biospectroscopy
	• combinatorial chemistry
	• DNA sequencing,
	  profiling
	• electrophoresis
	• fluorescence
	• gene expression
	  analysis
	• bioinformatics
	• magnetic resonance
	  spectrometry
	• mass spectrometry
	• nucleic acid diagnostics
	• protein structure
	  modeling/analysis
		• antiangiogenesis
		• antisense
		• apoptosis
		• bioelectronics
		• biomaterials
		• biosensors
		• functional genomics
		• gene delivery systems
		• gene testing
		• gene therapy
		• gene expression
		  systems
		• monoclonal antibodies
		• pharmacogenomics
		• stem-cell
		• tissue engineering
			• cell encapsulation
			• cell culture
			• DNA arrays/chips
			• fermentation
			• gene transfer
			• immunoassays
			• implantable delivery
			  systems
			• nucleic acid amplification
			• recombinant DNA
			• separation technologies
			• transgenic animals
				• coagulation inhibitors
				• DNA probes
				• drug delivery
				• inflammation
				  inhibitors
				• hormone restorations
				• mRNA inhibitors
				• nanodevices
				• neuroactive steroids
				• neuro-transmitter
				  inhibitors
				• protease inhibitors
				• vaccines

penetration *within* technology life cycles ("life cycle evolution") or the transition *between* two distinctly different technologies and their respective life cycles ("life cycle transition"). Life cycle evolution is determined both by macroeconomic factors (general capital market risk, which primarily affects the amount of R&D investment) and by the efficiency of R&D processes.

Life cycle transition is an R&D efficiency issue is affected by the public good characteristics of the generic technology and associated infratechnologies. At life cycle initiation, corporate decision making targets investments in new generic technologies in order to prove concepts before deciding to commit much larger funding to actual innovation efforts. Generic technology research not only involves greater technical risk but also requires longer R&D investment time horizons. Hence, excessive discounting for both risk and time results in underinvestment during this early phase of R&D.

More specifically, a company evaluating the risk of investing in a new technology faces a set of projected performance/cost ratios, represented by curve 2 in Figure 2. Initially the performance/price ratio for the new technology (point B) will be below the current ratio for the defender technology (point A on curve 1).[24] The consequent risk of lower technical and cost performance, possibly for some time, pushes estimates of positive rates of return into the future, which in turn lowers the estimated net present value of the R&D investment.

Moreover, the innovator's risk assessments are compounded by the fact that the defender technology seldom gives up without a fight. For example, in the face of a challenge from flat-panel displays, manufacturers of cathode-ray tubes continued to reduce costs and improve picture quality, thereby raising the hurdle for the invading technology (by continuing to move up Curve 1, even as the curve flattens). Thus, although diminishing returns for the defender technology have typically set in when the new technology appears, potential advances contrib-

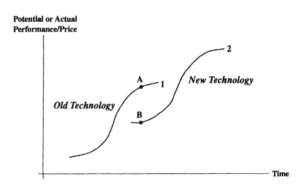

Figure 2. Translation between two technology life cycles.

ute to the risk of investing in the new technology at an early point in its life cycle.[25]

Transitioning *across* technology life cycles is a particularly difficult issue for R&D policy process to address. A number of high-tech companies manage transitions among successive *product* life cycles quite effectively. However, the transition to a radically new *technology* life cycle is seldom achieved by the majority, if any, of the firms applying the defender technology. Many of these companies lose out to small, innovative firms that are willing to take on the high risk posed by the initial performance/price gap. In cases of radically new technologies, the established companies may be replaced by new industries—either domestic or foreign.

This aspect of creative destruction occurs in part because current suppliers are focused on enhancements of the defender technology in an attempt to maximize short-term cash flows. They consequently wait too long to undertake research targeting the new technology. This pattern also occurs in part because the established industry is organized to develop and market the defender technology and does not have all of the required R&D skills and facilities needed to migrate to the new technology.[26] In summary, the *composition* of R&D investment is inadequate from a long-run (multi-cycle) perspective.[27]

Companies with long investment time horizons and high risk tolerances (and hence relatively low discount rates) might be able to make sufficient investments in the new technology (and associated R&D capabilities) before the old technology matures. This would allow innovation to take place higher on performance/price curve 2 than point B. Such a strategy seems logical because market penetration can occur more rapidly. However, with the typical R&D life cycle about 10 years (Branscomb and Auerswald, 2002; Cannon, 2002) and increasing competitive pressures raising discount rates, even large, R&D-intensive companies with substantial central research labs are decreasing investment in the longer-term research that produces most new technologies.

The problems in moving up the performance/price curve from point B are evident in the biotechnology example. The evolving structure of this industry (small firms focusing on individual drug candidates) accentuates an inefficient tendency exhibited in all high-tech industries to varying degrees toward a forced approach to product development; that is, attempting to develop proprietary products with an inadequate underlying generic technology and supporting infratechnologies. This raises product failure rates due both to inadequate proof of concept (generic technology) and to inefficient research methods that increase R&D costs leave excessive uncertainty with respect to research outcomes. These higher failure rates discourage risk capital needed for follow-on investments.

Economies of scale and scope. Arrow (1962) first identified the problem of indivisibility of technical information and its consequent effect on R&D investment. All other factors aside, the typical firm tries to fully utilize its resource base; that is, it seeks to capture the benefits from the entire scope of potential market applications that arise from a generic technology and supporting infratechnologies. Time and considerable resources are needed to acquire a unique set of technology assets, so maximum efficiency in utilizing these assets is essential. First mover and sustained leadership strategies lead firms to seek to reduce risk by concentrating on the development of a relatively limited set of technology assets and related market applications (so-called "core competence" strategies).

In contrast, portfolio theory preaches diversification into multiple product fields to diversify market risk. However, firms have found that this strategy can entail substantial technical risk due to the increased level of resources required to achieve and maintain competency in multiple technologies, each requiring somewhat different sets of research skills and facilities. Moreover, diversified portfolios also can require multiple sets of production and marketing assets. Such risk presents a disincentive to diversify horizontally or vertically. Increased global competition in technology-based markets has accentuated this risk. Thus, firms seek to reduce risk by concentrating on the development of technology assets for a limited set of market applications (so-called "core competence" strategies).

A narrower technology focus often includes downsizing central corporate research laboratories and shifting the composition of the research to more applied topics that directly support the remaining lines of business. Less generic technology research is conducted because a narrower market focus implies less opportunity for economies of scope. Many firms, especially small and medium ones, do little or no generic technology research, instead relying on external sources for new technology platforms.

In summary, such strategic shifts can be a two-edged sword. On the one hand, concentrating R&D resources on fewer technologies and their market applications can increase economies of scale. Such a strategy reduces technical risk (core competence is emphasized) and possibly market risk (due to specialization). On the other hand, market risk may actually be increased because product/service diversification has been reduced; that is, the firm's portfolio of technologies and subsequent market applications is more narrowly focused and therefore more dependent on a smaller number of markets.

Evolving industry structures offer a partial adjustment mechanism. In the last two decades, forms of collaboration for cost sharing and risk pooling have proliferated, including multi-company consortia and partnerships with universities and government. However, these complex entities have contractual, organizational, and management problems that can cause inefficiencies in the R&D undertaken and thus can lead to suboptimal results (Miotti and Sachwald, 2003).

Thus, while specialization may enhance short-term performance, it accentuates "path dependence" and thereby reduces firms' and entire industries' ability to adapt to new technology life cycles by reducing generic technology research capabilities. Such propositions are reflected in evolving "evolutionary theories" of technology-based growth (Nelson, 1995) in which acquired assets and supporting infrastructure tend to maintain technological pathways as a conscious attempt to fend off the Schumpeterian process of creative destruction. However, the life cycle nature of technological change eventually leads to the very destruction that such strategies seek to avoid. The incumbents and their defender technology inevitably lose out to the emerging technology.

Spillovers. In the economics literature, market failure in the technology-based sector of the economy is most often related to the existence of externalities called "spillovers," defined as technical knowledge and thus presumably economic benefits that are not captured by the firm creating the knowledge. That is, portions of these benefits accrue (spill over) to other firms, so that these firms "free ride" on the R&D of the innovating firm.

Unfortunately, economists have not reached a consensus on a taxonomy for characterizing and analyzing R&D spillovers. The literature identifies several types of R&D spillovers that are not necessarily distinct from one another. Most directly associated with R&D investment are "price" or "market" spillovers and "knowledge" spillovers (Griliches, 1979; Mohnen, 1996). In both cases, technical knowledge passes from the originator to other economic agents without full compensation.

Price spillovers occur when the increased value of new or improved products or services is not fully reflected in the price differential between the old and the new versions of the product or service. The portion of the benefits captured, but not paid for, by the user diminishes the reward to the supplier (innovator). In both cases, the return on investment for the innovator is reduced, which, if sufficiently pronounced, can constrain incentives for further R&D investments.

Knowledge spillovers occur when technical knowledge itself leaks or spills over from the innovator to competing firms without compensation to the innovating firm. The competing firms use the knowledge to imitate the innovation and thereby potentially reduce the innovating firm's return on investment. To the extent that the firms imitating the technical advance do not compensate the innovating firm (such as through licensing arrangements), a "reward-capture" problem can arise which inhibits private investment in R&D.[28]

Finally, this literature also identifies "production" spillovers in which knowledge diffuses into an industry in purchased capital goods embodying new technology developed in the capital goods industry. Such spillovers result from synergistic interactions within the purchasing industry (such as learning by doing) and are argued to be independent of any knowledge spillovers in the capital goods industry or price spillovers in the custody exchange due to market dynamics. Empirical studies have not shown that production spillovers present a significant disincentive or occur with any regularity.[29]

Spillovers create several problems for R&D policy analysis. On the one hand, they are viewed negatively because, when excessive, the expected RoR to the prospective innovator is lowered to the point that the contemplated investment in R&D is not undertaken. On the other hand, it is this unique characteristic of technology—the fact that it diffuses widely—that enables large and diffuse economic impacts to be realized.[30] Moreover, spillovers do not have to mean one-for-one subtraction of benefits from the innovator. For example, network externalities can result from imitation by other firms coupled with the establishment of an efficiency-enhancing infrastructure that enable increasing returns for many firms from serving a larger user population.

The form of technical knowledge influences the spillover pattern. Technical knowledge has been classified as either "embodied" or "disembodied". Production spillovers are a market transfer of embodied technology. Price spillovers usually refer to this type of technical knowledge, as well. In contrast, technical knowledge developed within or somehow acquired by an industry can be disembodied in that the knowledge is known and used independently of any physical structure. The industry's own generic product and process technologies fall into this category, as do many types of nonproprietary technology infrastructure (infratechnologies). Such disembodied knowledge tends to "leak" or spillover, causing the frequently referenced appropriability problems.

Knowledge has also been classified as tacit or codified.[31] These terms refer to the form of technical knowledge, that is, whether or not the knowledge has been formalized as a commodity in the sense defined by Arrow. Much tacit technical knowledge is embodied in human capital. Romer (1990) refers to such tacit knowledge as "rival technical knowledge" in that its use in one application (assigning human research capital to a particular R&D project) prevents its use in alternative applications. Such knowledge only diffuses slowly from one person to another usually and requires close contact between parties executing the transfer. Thus, spillovers occur slowly. Generic technology is largely of this type (Darby and Zucker, 2003).

The previously discussed concept of "technological opportunity" is a means of characterizing the potential inflows (inward spillovers) of technical knowledge. For example, Klevorick et al. (1995) used the Yale Survey of R&D managers to analyze inter-industry differences in technological opportunity. They concluded that these sources lie primarily outside the industry and that levels of opportunity result from intrinsic differences in knowledge spillovers.

Finally, adoption of the disaggregated technology model summarized in Figure 1 allows the observation that the infratechnology element is a case where spillovers are largely desirable. The strong infrastructure character of infratechnologies, frequently manifested in the form of standards, means that significant economic benefits are realized only when all participants in a market (both demand and supply sides) have access to the same infrastructure (Tassey, 2000).

For example, using the same acceptance test method to consummate a market transaction for a technologically complex product reduces transaction costs and thereby increases the rate of market penetration of the new technology. Thus, policy makers must ensure the availability of an efficient standards infrastructure to achieve utilization of these infratechnologies. However, the optimal achievement of such is not easy, as timing and content of standardization (and hence the derived demand for the underlying infratechnologies) are difficult investment objectives to define and hence to manage. "Free riding" with respect to the standard is actually encouraged to increase economic efficiency, but this objective guarantees underinvestment in the underlying infratechnology.

In summary, the evolving literature on spillovers implies a model in which technical information diffuses in specific channels and at non-negligible cost. Rate and direction depend on the degree to which the information is generic or applied and on its ultimate use (proprietary product/process development or infrastructure). The implied disaggregated model leads to a differentiated public policy perspective. That is, spillovers of generic technologies and infratechnologies are desirable because of their public good content, whereas proprietary technologies require assignment of property rights to provide incentives for market applications. This critical distinction allows a significant improvement in R&D policy over that implied by the Arrow-type conclusion in which property rights result in underutilization of this information.

Defining underinvestment for government policy development

Having identified the causes of underinvestment in R&D, a method for estimating underinvestment can now be discussed.

A major analytical challenge for R&D policy analysis is to assess the extent to which the innovator (private) rate of return (PRR) falls below the hurdle rate (HR) for corporate R&D investment. The analysis also must determine the reason for the sub-threshold PRR. A low projected PRR could simply be due to inadequate technical and/or market appeal, which means the technology has a relatively low potential social rate of return (SRR). Alternatively, intrinsic or externally imposed market failures of the type discussed above could be substantially suppressing the PRR below a relatively high SRR.

While recognizing the existence of a rate-of-return gap and noting that the magnitude of underinvestment can be related to this gap, a more accurate representation of underinvestment phenomena is possible. In Figure 3, four R&D projects are shown.[32] The vertical arrows represent the possible SRR and the horizontal arrows indicate the possible PRR. Hence, the lengths of the arrows represent the ranges of potential outcomes from a particular R&D investment. Risk is the probability of an outcome (RoR) being below the HR.[33]

These two required elements of policy analysis are incorporated in Figure 3. The first three projects (A, B, and C) have ranges of expected PRR below the corporate HR and therefore would likely not receive significant or sustained private-sector funding. Project A is an early-phase (generic) technology research project, which has significant economic potential. How-

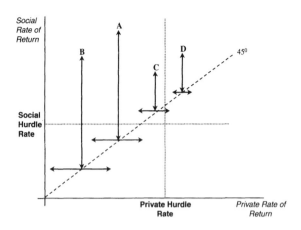

Figure 3. Government R&D project selection: rate-of-return criteria.

ever, at this point in that technology's development, the actual (or uncertainty about the actual) levels of technical and market risk are beyond the ranges acceptable to corporate R&D managers. That is, the risk-adjusted PRR estimate is lower than individual firms' HRs, and thus a corporate commitment to funding this project in response to conventional decision criteria will be limited.

Such a project is a candidate for government financial assistance, usually in the form of cost-shared funding for the conduct of generic technology research. Cost sharing reduces risk enough to stimulate initial private investment in applied R&D (in Figure 3, Project A shifts to the right toward the innovator's HR). If successful, this early-phase technology research will reduce uncertainty about the probability distribution of technical and market outcomes and shift the distribution above the innovator's HR. Conversely, this research could result in an insufficient increase in the expected PRR and might also reduce the expected SRR below its HR, causing termination of R&D in the particular technology by both industry and government.

Project B also has a very low expected PRR, while at the same time exhibiting a high SRR. A policy analyst might conclude that too large an investment of government funds would be required to reduce both uncertainty and risk and thereby raise the expected PRR above the private-sector HR. However, such projects are typical of elements of an industrial technology that have a strong infrastructure character and exhibit a high SRR. For example, the network externalities resulting from standardization greatly increase the SRR for this type of infrastructure, but simultaneously prevent ownership of the embedded intellectual property by any one firm. In such cases, the PRR may never be permanently raised above the HR. Thus, the R&D may be funded largely by government to capture the high SRR from eventual adoption by industry of the resulting infratechnology as an industry standard.

Projects C and D are quite different from either A or B. Project D is a typical R&D project found in a business unit of an R&D-intensive company. Its range of expected PRR is more than high enough to receive adequate private R&D funding. Project C is a marginal project under existing corporate R&D investment criteria; that is, its expected RoR does not quite exceed the private-sector HR, so this project is not funded.

However, projects such as C can have sufficient SRR (above the social HR) to warrant government investment incentives. In such cases, because C falls within the general category of applied R&D projects that a firm's business unit would typically consider, the R&D policy response should be directed at conventional corporate R&D investment criteria (as opposed to the distinctly different criteria used to evaluate long-term, exploratory technology research). For situations such as project C, a tax credit rather than direct funding is the correct policy response.[34]

R&D cycle analysis

The above discussion focuses on relationships between the nature of the R&D project and its risk-adjusted expected RoR at different points in the technology life cycle. Such comparative static analysis is important for identifying the factors that determine underinvestment.

In addition, the analyst must also analyze the dynamic element of underinvestment; that is, how the *pattern* of underinvestment affects the evolution of the technology. In essence, this analysis is an assessment of both technical and market risk management by industry over the technology life cycle.

As previously defined, generic technologies (proof of concept) provide the basis (technology platforms) for an array of market-specific applications (collectively, the technology trajectory). Although amounts invested in generic technologies are small relative to those for applied R&D, these investments are the first step in *technology research*. The distinction between scientific research and technology research is extremely important for market failure analysis. Scientific research seeks to advance *knowledge*. The concept of risk is relevant only in the sense that funding decisions are based on the expectation that scientific knowledge will be advanced.

In contrast, risk assessments are continually made by industry over the remainder of the technology life cycle based on estimates of the probability distributions of future market returns. These estimates drive R&D investment decisions. The nature of this risk is twofold: the probability of achieving the technical objectives perceived to be required for the target markets and the probability that when commercialization occurs, the market will be receptive.[35] As long as reward-risk ratios exceed private and social HRs, R&D funds will continue to be allocated to the technology's development. Patterns of R&D by which technology becomes progressively more applied is evident in the technology life cycles underpinning the major technology drivers of the last 60 years.[14]

However, the conventional characterization of a technology's evolution as a steady increase in its applied character masks a fundamental discontinuity in the pattern of risk reduction that strongly affects investment behavior. As discussed above, the technical complexity of the proof-of-concept objective of generic technology research, its frequent mismatches with existing corporate market strategies and internal research capabilities, and its distance in time from potential commercialization combine to cause a spike in both technical and market risk. By occurring early in the technology research cycle, this "risk spike" can block substantial private R&D investment.

Such a discontinuity in risk reduction is portrayed in Figure 4 for two hypothetical corporate R&D projects, A and B. In both cases, the assumption is that the underlying science base has been advanced over time to a point at which corporate managers can make initial assessments of the technical and market risk associated with the development of technologies derived from on this science.

Based on the body of scientific knowledge acquired through basic research, the decision making process might be said to face a purely "technical" risk, R_0, that summarizes estimates of the probability that a technology could be developed that performs some generalized function. However, the characteristic that distinguishes technology research from scientific research is the fact that the ultimate intent is commercialization. Thus, an additional amount of technical risk must be estimated and added to R_0 because the scientific principles presented now have to be proven capable of conversion into specific technological forms with specific performance attributes that meet specific market needs. Several of the factors cited in Section "Dynamics of R&D and underinvestment" can raise this technical risk. Moreover, total risk is now reassessed in view of the need to meet production cost objectives.

A "market" risk also must be estimated to allow for the significant probability that demand for the new technology will be overestimated or that market penetration will be slower than projected due to the factors cited in Section "Dynamics of R&D and underinvestment" such as improvements in the defender technology. Slower market penetration could mean that production costs will be high relative to the defender technology for a longer period of time due to failure to realize economies of scale or scope. This market risk must be added to technical risk.

In Figure 4, the risk spikes RS_A and RS_B represent the combined increase in technical and market risk for projects A and B, respectively. Such risk spikes might be thought of as the "public (or social) risk" component because they occur in the early generic technology research phase, which has the public good dimension described earlier. Project A is the more radical innovation and so it presents a greater initial risk spike, RS_A.

Without the risk spike, firms would be faced only with a reduction in the "private risk" component, RP, associated with applied R&D. Project A also requires greater risk reduction during applied R&D, RP_A.

In the absence of the risk spike, conventional R&D investment criteria would deal with RP because it falls within acceptable reward-risk ratios. Thus, if at the level of pure technical risk, R_0, conventional corporate R&D criteria result in private investment based on risk-adjusted rate-of-return estimates, the policy problem is to overcome the risk spike so that these criteria can be applied. The importance of overcoming the risk spike for the more radical technology, A, is increased by the fact that the overall risk associated with project A will actually decline to a lower level than that for Project B. This occurs because, if Project A is successful technically, the resulting set of market applications will likely have a larger collective value than B, hence increasing the probability of a RoR above the firm's HR.[36] This is depicted in Figure 1 by a greater decline in private risk for Project A, indicated by RP_A.

Current R&D policy tools do not fully recognize the large discontinuity in the risk reduction process occurring at the transition between scientific and technology research. If this risk spike did not occur, the risk curves in Figure 4 would have steadily declining slopes and would support proponents of little government R&D funding beyond basic science. However, the substantial jump in total risk caused by the potential divergence between technical and market requirements on the one hand and research capabilities, time discounting, and corporate strategy mismatches

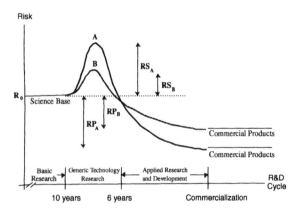

Figure 4. Risk reduction in the R&D process.

on the other can and do lead to substantial underinvestment.[37]

In summary, the advancement of basic science sufficient to allow technology development to begin does not guarantee immediate or even eventual commitment of adequate private sector funds. Reducing risk spikes through early-phase generic technology research is necessary to enable optimal private sector R&D spending. However, the fact that specific elements of an industrial technology are quasi-public goods means that their efficient development over the entire life cycle requires a mixture of public and private funding, distributed according to the magnitude and duration of various market barriers.[38]

4. Defining and measuring underinvestment

Having identified the critical quasi-public elements embedded in the typical industrial technology, the policy analyst ideally should then estimate an optimal level of investment for specific technology elements against which to assess actual investment behavior. For identified underinvestment mechanisms (the "cause"), such analysis requires the selection of impact metrics and measures that enable quantification of the economic impact (the "effect") of identified barriers. The resulting quantitative estimates are combined with qualitative analyses of the identified barriers to enable appropriate policy responses to be selected and then to allocate resources for those responses across technologies. Ranking for policy purposes will be a function of the estimated SRR and the difference between the PRR and the private HR.

However, economic research has made only partial progress in developing and applying the required analytical tools. An overall optimal R&D intensity has been correlated with assessments of technological opportunities (Klevorick et al., 1995) and estimated at the national level by Jones and Williams (1998, 2000).[39] At the microeconomic (technology) level, the opportunity set determines the distribution of possible rates of return from applied R&D (innovation investments) and thus implies an optimal R&D intensity for that technology-based industry. Based on initial rankings of technological opportunity, the policy analyst ideally would estimate SRRs and PRRs for each technology and compare them with appropriate HRs. However, arriving at an optimal R&D intensity to use as a benchmark for underinvestment analysis, estimating the appropriate investment "gap," and then explaining this gap in terms of a market failure mechanism are extremely difficult analytical and empirical steps.

Rate-of-return analysis

To some extent, the use of return-on-investment techniques (borrowed from corporate finance) has proved useful for demonstrating retrospectively the range of economic impacts from specific technology investments.[40] However, this approach is burdened with several conceptual and empirical issues, especially when applied to prospective (strategic planning) exercises.

One problem with prospective analyses for R&D policy decisions is the fact that several significant and uncertain phases of R&D must take place followed by investments in production and marketing capabilities before commercialization can occur. This problem is particularly severe for basic and early-phase (generic) technology research. In the latter case, the analysis is complicated by the fact that the additional R&D following investment in the generic technology is typically much larger, but its amount, composition, and timing are driven by the direction and timing of generic technology research.

Moreover, the time to commercialization from generic technology research is quite long. Rate-of-return analysis is sensitive to the assumed time series of R&D investment and the subsequent commercialization and market penetration patterns. Moreover, use of rate-of-return techniques or discounted cash flow/net present value measures produce a negative bias for prospective R&D investments through their treatment of risk and reward. Specifically, these techniques do not ascribe value to the intellectual capital created by the R&D cycle as it reduces technical risk (Boer, 1998, 2000). That is, at best only an incomplete market exists for technology capital.

Nevertheless, even for prospective analyses, the conventional rate-of-return method can be useful for the development and management of government R&D support roles.[41] To this end, rate-of-return analysis can be applied in two ways. One way is to compare rates of return between major categories of investment. If the SRR from a category of investment (say, R&D) is higher than that from another category, the suspicion is that some barrier is preventing efficient allocation of resources in the private sector. That is, underinvestment is occurring in the category with the higher SRR due to a suppressed PRR. Otherwise, funds would flow into the investment lowering the SRR until the marginal RoR was reduced to the opportunity cost of capital.

The relationship between the rate at which the expected PRR declines with increased R&D investment and the HR (the opportunity cost of capital for private sector investors) is shown in Figure 5. The two negatively sloped lines, P and P', are marginal efficiency of investment (MEI) curves. Firms rationally invest in the R&D projects with the highest expected PRR first and then select projects with the next highest PRRs and so on until the opportunity cost of capital (HR) is reached. The actual slope of an MEI curve can be steep or shallow depending on technological and market opportunity, efficiency of R&D, etc. The entire curve can shift up or down depending on intrinsic characteristics of the technology and its associated infrastructure. Figure 5 also shows two alternative HRs, HR and HR'.

For an MEI curve P and a hurdle rate HR, this industry will invest an amount Q in R&D. If one or more of the types of market failure discussed in Section "Causes of underinvestment" intensifies, the entire MEI curve could shift downward to P' causing a reduction in R&D investment to Q'. Similarly, if market conditions change so that either the PRR on alternative investments or general risk averseness increases, the HR could shift upward to HR' causing an equivalent reduction in R&D investment to Q'.

A second application of rate-of-return analysis is to represent the amount of underinvestment in R&D by the "gap" between the SRR and PRR for the same category of investment. The implication is that if industry can only earn the PRR, then less R&D investment will be forthcoming.

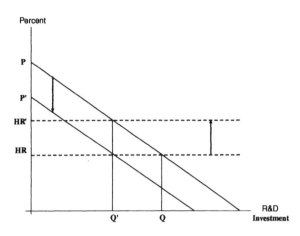

Figure 5. Marginal efficiency of R&D investment (expected private rate of return).

This conceptual approach would be represented in Figure 5 if innovating firms are assumed to capture all the returns generated by their R&D; that is, the curve P is also the SRR. If some barrier (typically assumed to be spillovers) causes a downward shift in the PRR curve to P', then a "gap" appears leading to a reduction in R&D of QQ' (for a HR).

However, this characterization of underinvestment is simplistic along several dimensions, especially with respect to the implied assumption of a fixed gap and the implications of a gap for policy:

(1) The "gap" is important only to the extent that it pushes the PRR below the HR. Obviously, the closer the PRR is to the HR, the fewer additional projects will be undertaken before the marginal PRR declines to the HR. The slope of the MEI curve is clearly important in this regard.

(2) From an economic growth perspective, "outward" spillovers can actually have a beneficial effect because they create opportunities for new firms to enter the market for the technology, which thereby expands competition and hence the range and amount of economic benefits delivered. That is, the reverse concept of "inward" spillovers to other firms in the industry needs to be taken into account. Moreover, to the extent that inward price or production spillovers are

realized from supplying industries, the innovating industry benefits in the form of higher PRR, thereby leading to more R&D in that industry.[42] The implication is that the size of the gap and hence the PRR relative to the HR will likely vary over the technology life cycle.

(3) A larger market resulting form spillovers can also allow network externalities to be realized or a general risk reduction to occur that opens that market to more risk-adverse groups of buyers. The result may be an increasing PRR for the initial innovators, as well as for imitators. Moreover, less steep MEI curves resulting from additional and larger markets derived from the generic technology lead to more applied R&D. Such effects usually are significant in the middle and later portions of the technology life cycle, where applications become "commoditized" and competition is based more on cost (personal computers are an example). Thus, the dynamics of technology-based markets can keep the PRR above the HR and maintain reasonable levels of private R&D investment for a longer period of time (extending the technology life cycle).

(4) Whereas the SRR is a single aggregate return on an industry's R&D investment, the PRR varies among firms in that industry, including the primary innovator, which makes the estimate of a PRR for the purpose of "gap analysis" difficult. In the end, what counts for policy analysis is the number of firms for which the PRR exceeds the HR at each phase in the R&D cycle.

Estimating underinvestment

Ideally, estimates of the PRR associated with each technology element would be obtained at different points in time as part of the underinvestment analysis. Such estimates would be compared with both the industry's average HR and the estimated SRR to determine if a government policy response might be warranted and, if so, over what period of time.

However, conventional applications of rate-of-return analysis, especially in the early phases of the R&D cycle, are difficult to execute. For example, because generic technology research is the first phase of technology R&D and is aimed at a next generation or an emerging technology, significant markets typically do not yet exist. Point estimates for dates in the future are highly uncertain and, if relied upon as the sole basis for initiating an R&D project, can lead to expensive long-term commitments with frequent negative outcomes.

Modified techniques are therefore required. One alternative approach involves regular assessments of progress toward technical goals and preliminary estimates of market opportunities. Repeated revisions of assessments of the extent to which technical and market risks are being reduced in effect segment the R&D funding processes with zero-based decisions occurring at each check point. Such "real options" tools can continue to be used until individual companies are able to apply conventional investment criteria to estimate PRRs.[43] As these PRRs rise above HRs, government subsidies can be phased out.

The relative funding contributions of government and industry will be determined by the subsidies required to elevate the PRR above the HR (or to reach a termination decision). Real options models exist that are highly quantitative, although application of this approach to early-phase generic technology research will likely entail some compromises. The major management requirement is periodic review of technical risk reduction and observance of industry's behavior with respect to its internal R&D strategies (evidence of reductions in both technical and market risk).

Still, the more quantitative the selected approach, the better. For infratechnologies, a quantitative approach can frequently be used. Here, markets are often established for a high-tech product or service, but inadequate technical infrastructure of some type is creating significant inefficiencies and thereby retarding market penetration.[44] Thus, direct estimates of the cost of the inadequate infrastructure are obtainable from industry surveys. Removing or at least reducing the costs constitute an economic benefit and such estimates can be related to projected research program cost estimates to calculate an expected RoR.[45]

With respect to identifying, characterizing, and estimating the magnitude of underinvestment in infratechnologies, NIST has conducted several prospective economic analyses of the adequacy of existing infratechnologies in order to provide inputs for its strategic planning function. Table II summarizes five studies of the economic costs of underinvestment in infratechnologies.[46] The choice of topics for such studies is based on a somewhat unstructured process of background analyses, consultations with industry, reviews of other studies (if they exist), and higher order policy directives.

The scope of such studies can vary significantly, making their use in ranking underinvestment phenomena difficult. For example, the first study in Table II examined the costs of inadequate standards for the exchange of electronic product design data between automobile companies and their parts and subsystems suppliers. The estimated annual cost is only for that supply chain, even though other manufacturing supply chains (such as aerospace) are known to have similar interoperability problems. In contrast, the software testing study conducted two larger case studies—one in manufacturing and the other in services—which provided a sufficiently broad base (along with some other data) to rationalize extrapolation to the national economy level. Hence, this study not only produced cost estimates for the two case studies, but also a much larger (national) estimate of the costs of underinvestment in testing infratechnologies.

Examples of government responses to the "risk spike"

Several decades of large-scale funding of molecular biology research by NIH were required before private investment kicked in and spawned a biotechnology industry. A recent analysis of U.S. patent citations in biotechnology found that more than 70% of them were to papers originating solely at public research institutions (McMillan et al., 2000). And, 20 years after the first biotechnology company went public, NIH still provides research funding to dozens of the more than 300 biotechnology companies.

The tremendous growth in health care productivity being made possible by a radically new technology also is creating a new industry with substantial economic growth potential. This phenomenon is occurring to a greater extent in the United States in large part because the U.S. Government funded both the science base and portions of the subsequent early phases of technology research (i.e., the quasi-public good element). This funding coupled with other factors such as clustering and a robust venture capital market has allowed U.S. industry and U.S. capital markets to reach positive investment decisions ahead of the rest of the world.[47]

Table II
Economic studies of costs due to inadequate infratechnology investment

Focus of study	Infrastructure studied	Industries covered	Estimated annual costs $billions
interoperability costs	product design data exchange	automotive supply chain	1.0
deregulation	metering, systems monitoring/control	electric utilities	3.1–6.5
software testing	all stages of the testing cycle	transportation equipment	1.8
		financial services	3.3
		extrapolation to U.S.	59.5
interoperability costs	business data exchange: demand, production, inventory, procurement, & distribution	automotive supply chain	5.0
		electronics supply chain	3.9
medical testing	quality of measurement assurance (calcium)	medical testing laboratories	0.06–0.199

In the past, non-market motivations (primarily national defense) allowed Federal funding of major new technologies at above-threshold levels, which subsequently drove economic growth for decades. The fields of computing and communications provide compelling examples of how government funding plays a critical role in advancing generic technologies and achieving minimum thresholds of R&D capability necessary to stimulate takeoff in private sector investment. Federal funding for electrical engineering in areas such as semiconductors and communications technologies (major components of computing technologies) has fluctuated between $800 million and $1 billion since the 1970s. Funding for computer science increased from $10 million in 1960 to approximately $1 billion in 1995. Over these time periods, such amounts have represented a major fraction of all early-phase technology research funding in information technology.[48]

The majority of this funding went to industry and university researchers. Not only did the government-sponsored research advance key areas of the underlying science and technology, but it also fostered a broad and deep R&D capability that leveraged follow-on private investment by industry. An extremely important aspect of this support is the extension of Federal funding beyond basic scientific research to generic technology and even experimental deployment. For example, before 1970, the Federal government sponsored individual researchers who developed generic network technologies, such as queuing theory, packet switching, and routing. During the 1970s, experimental networks, notably the ARPANET, were constructed. These networks were primarily research tools, not service providers. Most were federally funded because, with a few exceptions, industry had not realized the potential of the technology.[49]

During the 1980s, networks were widely deployed, initially to support scientific research. The National Science Foundation (NSF) was the major supporter of networking during this period, primarily through the NSFNET, which evolved into the Internet. At this point in networking technology's evolution, industry began to see the enormous economic potential. Companies such as IBM, Digital Equipment Corp., and Compuserve established proprietary networks. These networks were rapidly utilized worldwide for email, file transfers, and electronic funds transfers.

However, as often happens in the evolution of a major new technology, companies with a large share of the initial proprietary applications displayed little interest in the even greater potential of the generic technology. To be broadly successful and thereby have large economic impact, systems technologies such as the Internet have to be based on open architectures. This type of technical infrastructure greatly expands markets for system technologies by facilitating network externalities. Unfortunately, such a requirement presents a negative investment incentive to firms with substantial commitments to proprietary networks. Moreover, telephone telecommunications companies resisted computer networks, including the Internet, because the nature of voice communications networks is strikingly different from data networks.[50]

Similarly, IBM pioneered the concept of relational databases but did not pursue commercialization of the technology because of its potential to compete with established IBM products. NSF-sponsored research at UC-Berkeley allowed continued exploration of this concept and brought the technology to the point that it could be commercialized by several start-up companies and then by more established suppliers, including IBM. This pattern was also evident in the development of reduced instruction set computing (RISC). Though the concept was originally developed at IBM, RISC was not commercialized until DARPA funded additional research at UC-Berkeley and Stanford as part of its Very Large Scale Integrated Circuit (VSLI) Program in the late 1970s and early 1980s.[51]

Other examples of critical government funding of generic technology research include expert systems, speech recognition, and image processing. Industry began to invest in these and other areas of artificial intelligence (AI) in the 1960s but scaled back when the long time periods required for commercialization became apparent. Federal investments continued in these generic technologies for a decade or more until conventional industry R&D criteria could rationalize investments in applied R&D (i.e., projected PRRs exceeded HRs). Now, private investment is driving the commercialization of many AI technologies.

Thus, government R&D is frequently the mechanism to reduce uncertainty through support of basic research and then technical and market risk (the risk spike) in the early (generic) phases of a technology's development. However, this policy response does not guarantee commercialization in a fixed period of time, if ever. Technical and market risk may be reduced more slowly than anticipated, or market risk may actually be increased by unforeseen developments in competing technologies. In the case of gallium arsenide, the Department of Defense spent $570 million on research between 1987 and 1995, but the overall market had not reached $1 billion in annual sales by 1996.[52] Two reasons for this pattern were slower-than-anticipated progress in R&D and repeated extensions of the silicon-based semiconductor life cycle.

5. Summary

The analytical framework presented provides an approach to explaining and estimating R&D underinvestment trends in a cause-and-effect framework. Emphasis is on underinvestment in the early phases of technology R&D (generic technology research) and in technology infrastructure (infratechnologies); that is, the focus is on R&D composition distortions. The final stage of the policy process, not addressed here, is the selection, design, and implementation of policy responses—primarily the forms and management of government-funded research. The complexity of this last stage requires separate treatment. Also not analyzed are market failures associated with the aggregate amount of industrial R&D, which means primarily applied R&D. The cause-and-effect phenomena are significantly different from those associated with composition failures and therefore so are the appropriate policy responses.

Economic theory needs advancement in the area of R&D underinvestment phenomena. The underinvestment mechanisms are not well defined, with the literature focusing largely on spillovers. Even spillovers are not sufficiently treated, as several types exist and the relationships to private sector R&D investment behavior are not adequately specified. Moreover, the economic impact of spillovers has positive as well as negative dimensions. This complexity, coupled with the quasi-public good nature of technology research, has limited progress in developing models and useful tools for R&D policy analysis.

The approach taken in this paper involves three analytical steps. First, the identification and analysis of the causes of underinvestment is undertaken to enable ultimate selection of a policy response mechanism. Second, indicators of underinvestment in R&D are constructed to allow a scan of relevant private R&D investment patterns and supporting infrastructure trends and thereby identify broad investment categories for more intensive analysis. These indicators are then compared to data on economic performance in the relevant industries to prioritize and focus subsequent analysis. Third, based on these analyses, technology-specific impact metrics and measures are selected to allow quantification across technologies of the net benefits of past policy implementations and the expected net benefits from candidate policy initiatives.

If these three stages of analysis are successfully carried out, the results can significantly enhance the selection of policy response mechanisms and the levels of resources required for candidate initiatives; that is, a match can be achieved between different types and modes of underinvestment and the most efficient policy responses.

Acknowledgement

The author is indebted to David Leech and Andrew Wang for comments on previous drafts.

Notes

1. Early studies at the microeconomic level (individual innovations) are Griliches (1958) and Mansfield et al. (1977). This literature has been reviewed by Griliches (1995) and Hall (1996).
2. Because of this dichotomy in underinvestment phenomena, government policies fall into two major categories—tax incentives and direct funding. Aggregate underinvestment in R&D is usually the result of broad capital market failure characterized by excessive aversion to risk and/or the lack of appropriate institutional mechanisms for funding high-risk investments (Hall and van Reenen, 2000; Hall, 2002). The appropriate policy response is a tax incentive and is distinctly different from the direct funding response that addresses

underinvestment phenomena in the form of suboptimal composition of R&D. However, tax incentives and direct funding mechanisms often are incorrectly considered interchangeable (Tassey, 1997).
3. Link and Tassey, (1987), Tassey, (1982, 1991, 1997), Nelson, (1992, 1993), Nadiri, (1993), Teubal et al. (1996).
4. The "black box" model has been discarded when a social objective (national defense, energy independence, health care) is the ultimate objective. However, when economic growth is the target, its philosophical hold has been much stronger.
5. Public good content gives an element an infrastructure character. As with any type of infrastructure, technological infrastructure can be defined in terms of institutional capabilities rather than the type of technical knowledge. The former approach has been taken by Justman and Teubal (1995). Here, the emphasis is on the characteristics of the specific infrastructure element, which, in turn, implies a set of optimal institutional capabilities.
6. An alternative four-phase R&D cycle has been proposed by Branscomb and Auerswald (2002). Their model (pp. 30–34) uses different labels for the four phases because their focus is on small R&D firms and the supply of venture capital. However, the end points of the four phases in their model are similar, so their framework is functionally identical to the one used here for corporate R&D generally.
7. See David et al. (2000) for a comprehensive review of this funding-based approach.
8. However, the distribution of government funds across areas of science can be a hotly debated issue, as has been the case with the skewed distribution of U.S. Government funding toward life sciences. For example, in fiscal year 2001, Federal funding for life sciences was about $13 billion greater than funding for all other areas of science combined.
9. Generic technology research is typically done in central corporate laboratories using techniques based on real options models to manage the research portfolio. Data on corporate investment in generic technologies is poor. What data are available indicate that companies conducting such research allocate anywhere from 1 to 12% of total R&D spending for this phase of R&D.
10. Kim and Morbougne (1997) provide evidence of the economic importance of investment in such technologies. R&D-intensive companies in the United States and Europe were surveyed to obtain sales and profits data on investments in incremental improvements in the current generation of technology (product line extensions) and in radically new products based on next generation (i.e., new generic) technologies. For the average firm in the survey, product line extensions dominate both in terms of number and sales. This result is hardly surprising, as companies focus most of their resources on extracting value from their current technology portfolios. However, a majority of profits were found to be attributable to the relatively few "discontinuous" (new generic technology-based) innovations.
11. Examples are measurement and test methods, process and quality control techniques, evaluated scientific and engineering data, and the technical basis for product interfaces (Tassey, 1997). As quasi-public technology goods, they are co-supplied by industry and government. In the United States, the major government source is the National Institute of Standards and Technology (NIST).
12. The typical high-tech industry depends on a large number of infratechnologies whose collective economic impact is substantial. For example, a NIST study (Finan, 1998) estimated that the U.S. semiconductor industry would spend $5.5 billion in 2001 on measurement (an important type of infratechnology, much of which ends up as industry standards).
13. In other words, firms are largely "takers" with respect to the longer-term and higher-impact "natural trajectories" (Nelson and Winter, 1977) that sustain high R&D intensities and these trajectories usually derive to a significant extent from external sources (Klevorick et al., 1995). This literature implies the model proposed here. Once a technology life cycle is initiated (i.e., proof of concept is established), subsequent applied R&D investments are driven by the generic technology. Even though the generic technology can itself evolve to a degree over successive sub-cycles, it provides the platform that determines the trajectory of applications.
14. Case studies of the major technologies driving modern economies show this pattern quite clearly; for example, digital computers (Flamm, 1988), network communications (National Research Council, 1999), and biotechnology (Henderson, et al., 1999).
15. At one extreme, Mansfield et al. (1971), Abernathy and Utterback (1978) and Utterback (1979) provide a detailed framework and analysis of the impact of the evolution of individual technologies on specific product life cycles. At the other, proponents of broad-based "long waves", such as Mensch (1979) and Graham and Senge [1980], have documented the bunching of related technologies that appear after a period of advances in the underlying science and when existing capital stocks (and their associated technologies) have significantly depreciated.
16. As pointed out earlier, the conventional approach to microeconomic analysis of analyzing R&D investment by phase (basic, applied, development) is inadequate because it ignores the output of each phase and the implications for investment in subsequent or complementary phases.
17. For simplicity, Figure 1 omits feedback loops, which are critical sources of information relevant for investment decision making over a technology's life cycle.
18. Mansfield et al. (1971) made a major contribution to the understanding of R&D investment patterns by disaggregating risk into three types: technical, commercialization (innovation), and market. The conceptual framework developed in this paper considers commercialization and market risk to be the same.
19. A distinction should be made between "uncertainty" and "risk." The two terms are frequently used interchangeably, but they have distinctly different meaning. Risk is the probability of not achieving a technical or market goal; it implies a known probability distribution (for each objective). Uncertainty refers to the lack of knowledge of the probability distribution. In the R&D cycle, technical uncertainty is progressively reduced as knowledge is gained about the probability distribution associated with the technical objectives being pursued. Continued progress in defining this probability distribution and a similar distribution for market success will eventually permit the conventional decision tools of corporate

finance to be applied and a risk-adjusted expected rate of return estimated (based on the product of technical and market risk estimates).

20. Software is a prime example. A NIST study by RTI International (2002) estimated that limited and ineffective testing of software during the R&D stage costs the U.S. economy at least $60 billion per year, with the users of software absorbing over 60% of these costs. This estimate is for direct costs only (the costs of detecting and fixing errors) and does not include estimates of the ultimate losses in revenues and value added.

21. Kash and Rycroft (1998) define complexity as the degree to which one individual cannot have a total grasp of all elements of a technology. The implications are that communications (including risk assessments) among specialists is important and research coordination is hard to achieve. Locating and accessing technical infrastructures also becomes more difficult.

22. For example, a company may develop a drug candidate that is effective in terms of the intended impact, say, blocking a specific RNA pathway that influences unwanted protein production by a tumor, only to discover after multiple phases of expensive clinical trials that the specific pathway (one of many within the tumor cell) is not solely or even particularly instrumental in the growth of the tumor. The market failure results from the fact that the generic technology research on the relationships between different pathways and tumor growth ("antisense" technology) is too broad and complex for individual companies to undertake and involves significant spillovers. Moreover, the associated infratechnologies are frequently not adequate, reducing the efficiency (increasing the time and expense) of conducting this research. Companies, therefore, often guess at the underlying generic technology (the overall pathway structure and the interacting roles of all proteins), as well as the infratechnologies for mapping these relationships. The result that the efficiency of R&D at the industry level is reduced. The lack of an explicit disaggregated R&D model such as the one presented here appears to have led to underinvestment in generic technologies and subsequent wasted efforts by biotechnology firms in applications (drug) development.

23. Using biotechnology as an example is particularly revealing because it is heavily supported by government funding, but the complexity of the technology still appears to result in mismatches in the rates of progress among the three major technology elements identified in Figure 1.

24. This phenomenon can result from several factors: (1) technical problems that typically are present in newly commercialized technologies; (2) higher cost due to a manufacturing process that has not been optimized for the new technology (small initial markets do not provide sufficient incentive or cash flow to invest in the necessary process R&D); and (3) interfaces between the new technology and other components in the broader technology system are typically not defined (i.e., as standards) early enough in the technology's life cycle, thereby raising system integration (and, in effect, product) costs.

25. For example, reaching the physical limits of silicon-based semiconductor technology has been predicted for some time, but advances in the underlying generic technology keep pushing that occurrence farther into the future (new sub-cycles keep appearing), thereby raising the risk of investing in radically new semiconductor technologies such as gallium arsenide.

26. From an economic growth policy perspective, one set of firms replacing another is not a negative result under "creative destruction" models of technology-based competition. However, if the new set of firms resides in another economy, a loss of domestic value added occurs in the first economy and it experiences a reduction in its growth rate.

27. Of course, having the generic technology in place does not guarantee market success for the innovating firm or even the entire domestic industry. The video cassette recorder (VCR) is one of the best known examples, but there are many others. A major type of semiconductor manufacturing equipment called a stepper was invented in the United States, but market share is now almost totally Japanese. Oxide ceramics, which every commercial wireless communication system incorporates, was discovered in the United States but Japanese industry today dominates commercial markets. See Tassey (1999, pp. 29–31) for additional examples.

28. One distinction between these two types is that price spillovers occur through the market mechanism, while knowledge spillovers do not (Jaffe, 1996).

29. For example, Jorgenson and Stiroh (2000) and Stiroh (2001) find little evidence of production spillovers from purchases of IT capital goods.

30. In particular, some price spillovers are desirable if users are to benefit substantially from innovations. Thus, market dynamics are relied upon to effect some reasonable distribution of benefits.

31. See Dasgupta and David (1994).

32. Adapted from Tassey (1997). The figure assumes that the minimum expected SRR for an R&D project is at least equal to the PRR (the SRR is above the 45° line). This assumption follows Jaffe (1996, 1998), who used a similar diagram to analyze the relationships between spillovers and rates of return on government funding decisions. See also Link and Scott (2001, pp. 776–777). This assumption holds over the technology life cycle, even though new technologies often impart negative externalities to the technologies they are replacing during the transition period (see Figure 2 and associated discussion). Note that the range of expected SRR (vertical arrows) straddles the social HR. This simply reflects the fact that government R&D investment entails risk, just as private investment does.

33. Conventional underinvestment analysis simply makes a judgement that the PRR has been suppressed relative to the SRR. This is an inaccurate approach for two reasons. First, the role of the private HR is not accounted for and, second, the dynamics of the technology life cycle is ignored, one aspect of which is that the PRR changes over this cycle. See the previous discussion on timing (pp. 96–97) and the next section.

34. Unlike direct funding of R&D, a tax credit is not applied to particular projects such as C, but rather provides an incentive for all such projects by nudging their expected RoR above the corporate HR. A tax incentive therefore has the advantage of being technology neutral. However, this

mechanism has the disadvantage of significant leakage (excess tax expenditures) because all projects (not only like C but also like D) can potentially benefit from the tax incentive—whether or not these projects require the incentive. The conditions under which each of these two policy mechanisms (direct funding and tax incentives) should be used are discussed in more detail in Tassey (1997).

35. The relationship between technical and market risk was defined and examined empirically by Mansfield et al. (1971, pp. 50–54). The probability of commercialization of an R&D investment is determined by the product of the probability of technical completion and the probability of commercialization (given technical completion).

36. For example, Mansfield et al. (1971, p. 53) found that the probability of commercialization was higher for "large or medium" technical advances than for "small" ones.

37. The position and slope of the risk reduction curve vary depending on a number of R&D efficiency factors, in particular, the availability of a range of infratechnologies.

38. This phenomenon is recognized to varying degrees by virtually every industrialized nation, as evidenced by the existence of technology research support programs. Examples are the Framework Program in Europe and NIST's Advanced Technology Program in the United States.

39. Such estimates are averages across all technologies and are useful as general targets. However, a macroeconomic target does not take into account varying levels of technological opportunity among individual technologies.

40. Griliches (1988, 1995), Mansfield (1991b), Nadiri (1993), Hall (1996), and Cameron (1998) have assessed the literature on the rates of return from R&D investment and find both the private rate of return (PRR) and social rate of return (SRR) to be high relative to other types of investment.

41. For further discussion of these tools and applications to analyses of specific government R&D programs, see Tassey (2003).

42. The SRR for the generic technology is also likely to be higher when the contributions of supplying industries are taken into account. See Schankerman (1981), Hall and Mairesse (1995), and Jones and Williams (1998). This relationship increases the importance of the supply chain (as opposed to a single industry) as the unit of analysis for R&D policy.

43. See Angelis (2000) and Boer (2000).

44. Biotechnology is a prominent example of such a situation, as inefficiencies in technical infrastructure supporting both R&D and manufacturing abound and collectively are significantly restraining the evolution of this industry. See Lagace (2003).

45. Once a research program has been completed, retrospective impact assessments use just this approach. See Tassey (2003) for detailed descriptions of impact assessment methodologies and examples of both retrospective and prospective impact studies of NIST research programs.

46. These studies can be accessed at http://www.nist.gov/public_affairs/budget.htm.

47. Approximately $1 billion of NIH research funding goes directly to industry each year.

48. National Research Council (1999, p. 2).

49. National Research Council (1999, p. 169).

50. For example, voice traffic is handled by a continuous connection (a circuit) for the duration of the transmission, while computers communicate in bursts. Unless a number of these bursts or "calls" can be combined on a single transmission path (seldom the case in complex, high-capacity transmission systems), line and switching capacity is wasted. Telecommunications engineers were primarily interested in improving the voice network and were skeptical of alternative technologies. Thus, although telephone companies provided point-to-point communications in the ARPANET, the industry switching technology was not used. National Research Council (1999, p. 172).

51. National Research Council (1999, p. 9).

52. Elias and Hinzmann (1996, pp. 2, 5).

References

Abernathy, W. and J. Utterback, 1978, 'Patterns of Industrial Innovation,' *Technology Review* **80** (June-July), 40–47.

Angelis, D., 2000, 'Capturing the Options Value of R&D,' *Research Technology Management* **43** (July–August), 31–34.

Arrow, K., 1962, 'Economic Welfare and the Allocation of Resources for Invention,' in *The Rate and Direction of Inventive Activity: Economic and Social Factors*, Princeton: Princeton University Press, pp. 609–625.

Boer, F.P., 1998, 'Traps, Pitfalls and Snares in the Valuation of Technology', *Research Technology Management* **41** (September–October), 45–54.

Boer, F.P., 2000, 'Valuation of Technology Using 'Real Options,'' *Research Technology Management* **43** (July–August), 26–30.

Branscomb, L. and P. Auerswald, 2002, *Between Invention and Innovation: An Analysis of Funding for Early-Stage Technology Development*, National Institute of Standards and Technology, Advanced Technology Program (November).

Caballero, R. and A. Jaffe, 1993, 'How High Are the Giants Shoulders: An Empirical Assessment of Knowledge Spillovers and Creative Destruction in a Model of Economic Growth' in O.J. Blanchard and S. Fischer (eds.), *NBER Macroeconomics Annual 1993*, Cambridge, MA: The MIT Press.

Cameron, G., 1998, 'Innovation and Growth: A Survey of the Empirical Evidence' Neufield College, United Kingdom (July).

Cannon, P., 2002, 'Tell Your Legislator the Truth about R&D,' *Research Technology Management* **45** (November–December), 9–11.

Coase, R., 1960, 'The Problem of Social Cost,' *Journal of Law and Economics* **3**, 1–44.

Coase, R., 1992, 'The Institutional Structure of Production,' *American Economic Review* **82**, 713–719.

Cohen, W. and D. Levinthal, 1989, 'Innovation and Learning: The Two Faces of R&D,' *The Economic Journal* **99** (September), 569–596.

Darby, M. and L. Zucker, 2003, 'Grilichesian Breakthroughs: Inventions of Methods of Inventing and Firm Entry in

Nanotechnology', NBER Working Paper 9825 (July). Cambridge, MA: National Bureau of Economic Research.

Dasgupta, P. and P. David, 1994, 'Towards a New Economics of Science,' *Research Policy* **23**, 477–521.

David, P., B. Hall, and A. Toole, 2000, 'Is Public R&D a Complement or Substitute for Private R&D? A Review of the Econometric Evidence,' *Research Policy* **29** (April), 497–529.

Dosi, G., 1988, 'Source, Procedures, and Microeconomic Effects of Innovation,' *Journal of Economic Literature* **26** (September), 1120–1171.

Elias, E. and B. Hinzmann, 1996, *The Hype Curve: New Technology as the Modern-Day Gold Rush*. Menlo Park, CA: SRI International.

Finan, W., 1998, *Metrology-Related Cost in the U.S. Semiconductor Industry, 1990, 1996, and 2001* (NIST Planning Report 98-4). Gaithersburg, MD: National Institute of Standards and Technology.

Flamm, K., 1988, *Creating the Computer: Government, Industry, and High Technology*. Washington, DC: The Brookings Institution.

Graham, A. and P. Senge, 1980, 'A long-Wave Hypothesis of Innovation,' *Technological Forecasting and Social Change* **17** (August), 283–311.

Griliches, Z., 1958, 'Research Costs and Social Returns: Hybrid Corn and Related Innovations,' *Journal of Political Economy* **46** (October), 419–431.

Griliches, Z., 1979, 'Issues in Assessing the Contribution of Research and Development to Productivity Growth,' *Bell Journal of Economics* **10**, 92–116.

Griliches, Z., 1988, 'Productivity Puzzles and R&D: Another Non-explanation,' *Journal of Economic Perspectives* **2**, 9–21.

Griliches, Z., 1992, 'The Search for R&D Spillovers,' *Scandinavian Journal of Economics* **94** (1992, Supplement), 29–47.

Griliches, Z., 1995, 'R&D and Productivity: Econometric Results and Measurement Issues,' in P. Stoneman, (ed.), *Handbook of the Economics of Innovation and Technological Change*, Malden, MA: Blackwell Publishers, Ltd. pp. 52–89.

Hall, B., 1996, 'The Private and Social Returns to Research and Development,' in B. Smith and C. Barfield, (eds.), *Technology, R&D, and the Economy*. Washington, DC: Brookings Institution and the American Enterprise Institute, pp. 140–183.

Hall, B., 2002, 'The Financing of Research and Development,' NBER Working Paper No. 8773 (February). Cambridge, MA: National Bureau of Economic Research.

Hall, B., and J. Mairesse, 1995, 'Exploring the Relationship between R&D and Productivity in French Manufacturing Firms,' *Journal of Econometrics* **65**, 263–293.

Hall, B. and J. van Reenen 2000, 'How Effective are Fiscal Incentives for R&D? A New Review of the Evidence,' *Research Policy* **29** (April), 449–469.

Henderson, R., L. Orsenigo, and G. Psiano, 1999, 'The Pharmaceutical Industry and the Revolution in Molecular Biology: Interactions among Scientific, Institutional, and Organizational Change,' in D. Mowery and R. Nelson, (eds.), *Sources of Industrial Leadership*, Cambridge, MA: Cambridge University Press.

Jaffe, A., 1996, *Economic Analysis of Research Spillovers: Implications for the Advanced Technology Program* (report prepared for NIST's Advanced Technology Program). Gaithersburg, MD: National Institute of Standards and Technology.

Jaffe, A., 1998, 'The Importance of 'Spillovers' in the Policy Mission of the Advanced Technology Program,' *Journal of Technology Transfer* **23**, (Summer), 11–19.

Jones, C. and J. Williams, 1998, 'Measuring the Social Returns to R&D,' *Quarterly Journal of Economics* **113** (November), 1119–1135.

Jones, C. and J. Williams, 2000, 'Too Much of a Good Thing?: The Economics of Investment in R&D,' *Journal of Economic Growth* **5** (March), 65–85.

Jorgenson, D. and K. Stiroh, 1999, 'Raising the Speed Limit: U.S. Economic Growth in the Information Age', *Brookings Papers on Economic Activity* **31**, 125–211.

Justman, M. and M. Teubal, 1995, 'Technological Infrastructure Policy (TIP): Creating Capabilities and Building Markets,' *Research Policy* **24** (March), 259–281.

Kash, D. and R. Rycroft, 1998, 'Technology Policy in the 21st Century: How Will We Adapt to Complexity?' *Science and Public Policy* **25** (April).

Kim, W. Chan and R. Mauborgne, 1997, 'Value Innovation: The Strategic Logic of High Growth', *Harvard Business Review* **75** (1) (January–February), 102–112.

Klevorick, A., R. Nelson, and S. Winter, 1995, 'On the Sources and Significance of Inter-Industry Differences in Technological Opportunities,' *Research Policy* **24** (March), 185–205.

Lagace, 2003, 'Innovation and Change: Making Biotech Work as a Business,' *HBS Working Knowledge* (http://hbswk.hbs.edu/item.jhtml?id = 3247&t = innovation).

Link, A., and G. Tassey, 1987, *Strategies for Technology-based Competition*, Lexington, MA: D.C. Heath.

Link, A., and J. Scott, 2001, 'Public/Private Partnerships: Stimulating Competition in a Dynamic Market,' *International Journal of Industrial Organization* **19**, 763–794.

Mansfield, E., 1968, *Industrial Research and Technological Innovation*. New York, NY: W. W. Norton.

Mansfield, E., 1980, 'Basic Research and Productivity Increase in Manufacturing,' *American Economic Review* **70** (December), 863–873.

Mansfield, E., 1991a, 'Academic Research and Industrial Innovation,' *Research Policy* **20**, 1–12.

Mansfield, E., 1991b, 'Social Returns from R&D: Findings, Methods, and Limitations,' *Research Technology Management* **34** (November–December), 24–27.

Mansfield, E., J. Rapoport, J. Schnee, S. Wagner, and M. Hamburger, 1971, *Research and Innovation in the Modern Corporation*, New York: W. W. Norton.

Mansfield, E., J. Rapoport, A. Romero, S. Wagner, and G. Beardsley, 1977, 'Social and Private Rates of Return from Industrial Innovations,' *Quarterly Journal of Economics* **91**, 221–240.

Mansfield, E., A. Romeo, M. Schwartz, D. Teece, S. Wagner, and P. Brach, 1982, *Technology Transfer, Productivity, and Economic Policy*, New York: W. W. Norton.

McMillan, S., F. Narin, and D. Deeds, 2000, 'An Analysis of the Critical Role of Public Science in Innovation: The

Case of Biotechnology,' *Research Policy* **29** (January), 1–8.

Mensch, G. 1979, *Stalemate in Technology*, Cambridge, MA: Ballinger.

Miotti, L. and F. Sachwald, 2003, 'Co-operative R&D: Why and with Whom? An integrated Framework of Analysis,' *Research Policy* **32** (September), 1481–1489.

Mohnen, P., 1996, 'R&D Externalities and Productivity Growth,' *STI Review* **19**, 39–66.

Nadiri, I., 1993, 'Innovations and Technological Spillovers,' (NBER Working paper No. 4423), New York: National Bureau of Economic Research (August).

National Research Council, 1999, *Funding a Revolution: Government Support for Computing Research*, Washington, DC: National Academy Press.

Nelson, R., 1959, 'The Simple Economics of Basic Scientific Research,' *Journal of Political Economy* **67**, 297–306.

Nelson, R., 1992, 'What Is 'Commercial' And What Is 'Public' About Technology, And What Should It Be?,' in N. Rosenberg, R. Landau, and D. Mowery (eds.), *Technology and the Wealth of Nations*, Stanford, CA: Stanford University Press.

Nelson, R., (ed.), 1993, *National Systems of Innovation*, New York: Oxford University Press.

Nelson, R., 1995, 'Recent Economic Theorizing about Economic Change,' *Journal of Economic Literature* **30** (4), 48–90.

Nelson, R. and S. Winter, 1977, 'In Search of a Useful Theory of Innovation,' *Research Policy* **6**, 36–76.

Pigou, A.C., 1932, *The Economics of Welfare*, 4th ed. London: Macmillan.

RTI International, 2002, *The Economic Impacts of Inadequate Infrastructure for Software Testing* (NIST Planning Report 02-3). Gaithersburg, MD: National Institute of Standards and Technology. (http://www.nist.gov/director/prog-ofc/report02-3.pdf)

Romer, P., 1990, 'Endogenous Models of Technological Change,' *Journal of Political Economy* **98**, S71–S102.

Rosenberg, N., 1982, *Inside the Black Box: Technology and Economics*, Cambridge, UK: Cambridge University Press.

Ruffin, R., 1996, 'Externalities, Markets, and Government Policy,' *Federal Reserve Bank of Dallas Economic Review* (Third Quarter), 24–29.

Schankerman, M., 1981, 'The Effect of Double Counting and Expensing on the Measured Returns to R&D,' *Review of Economics and Statistics* **63**, 454–458.

Schmookler, J., 1966, *Invention and Economic Growth*, Cambridge, MA: Harvard University Press.

Stiroh, K., 2001, 'What Drives Productivity Growth,' *Federal Reserve Bank of New York Economic Policy Review* **7** (March).

Tassey, G., 1982, 'Infratechnologies and the Role of Government,' *Technological Forecasting and Social Change* **21**, 163–180.

Tassey, G., 1991, 'The Functions of Technology Infrastructure in a Competitive Economy,' *Research Policy* **20**, 345–361.

Tassey, G., 1997, *The Economics of R&D Policy*, Westport, CT: Greenwood Publishing Group (Quorum Books).

Tassey, G., 1999, *R&D Trends in the U.S. Economy: Strategies and Policy Implications* (NIST Planning Report 99-2), Gaithersburg, MD: National Institute of Standards and Technology. (http://www.nist.gov/director/prog-ofc/report99-2.pdf)

Tassey, G., 2000, 'Standardization in Technology-Based Markets,' *Research Policy* **29**, 587–602.

Tassey, G., 2003, *Assessing the Impacts of Government Research: Methods, Results, and Interpretations*. (NIST Planning Report 03-1), Gaithersburg, MD: National Institute of Standards and Technology (June).

Tassey, G., 2004, 'Policy Issues for R&D Investment in a Knowledge-Based Economy,' *Journal of Technology Transfer* **29**, 153–185.

Teubal, M., D. Foray, M. Justman, and E. Zuscovitch, (eds.), 1996, *Technological Infrastructure Policy: An International Perspective*, Boston: Kluwer.

Utterback, J., 1979, *The Dynamics of Product and Process Innovation in Industry*, Cambridge, MA: The MIT Center for Policy Alternatives (February).

Evaluating Public Sector R&D Programs: The Advanced Technology Program's Investment in Wavelength References for Optical Fiber Communications

Albert N. Link[1]
John T. Scott[2]

ABSTRACT. Griliches (1958) [*Journal of Political Economy*, 66: 419–431] and Mansfield *et al.* (1977) [*Quarterly Journal of Economics*, 91: 221–240] pioneered the application of fundamental economic insight to the development of measurements of private and social rates of return to innovative investments. This paper illustrates field-based methods for measuring the social rates of return to innovative investments by the public sector. The case study described herein relates to the development of an improved standard reference material for the measurement of the wavelength of light in an optical fiber network.

Key words: social rate of return, benefit-cost analysis, internal rate of return, net present value, program evaluation, innovation

JEL Classification: O33, H54

1. Introduction

Fundamental to an evaluation of any federal program, research program or otherwise, is that the program is accountable to the public. For research programs, such accountability refers to being able to document and evaluate research performance using metrics that are meaningful to the institutions' stakeholders—the public, including the taxpayers.[1] Metrics developed for assessing returns to private investment have been adapted to public investments using case-study techniques that emphasize analysis of public benefits to research users and taxpayers.

With any performance evaluation, it is generally assumed that the government has an economically justifiable role in supporting innovation because of market failures stemming from, among other things, the private sector's inability to appropriate returns to investments, the public-good nature of the research focus, or the riskiness of those investments.[2] Ignoring such an assumption may imply that any evaluation of a public research program is wanting in the sense that the program should initially be scrutinized on first principles as to why it is even undertaking research.

Griliches (1958) and Mansfield *et al.* (1977) pioneered the application of fundamental economic insight to the development of measurements of private and social rates of return to innovative investments. Streams of investment costs generate streams of economic benefits over time. Once identified and measured, these streams of costs and benefits are used to calculate such performance metrics as social rates of return and benefit-to-cost ratios.

For example, for a process innovation adopted in a competitive market, using the traditional framework, the publicly-funded innovation being

---

[1] Department of Economics
University of North Carolina at Greensboro
Greensboro, NC 27412
and Max Planck Institute, Jena, Germany
E-mail: al_link@uncg.edu
[2] Department of Economics
Dartmouth College
Hanover, NH 03755
E-mail: john.t.scott@dartmouth.edu

evaluated is thought to lower the cost of producing a product to be sold in a competitive market. As the innovation lowers the unit cost of production, consumers will actually pay less for the product than they paid before the innovation and less than they would have been willing to pay—a gain in consumer surplus. The social benefits from the innovation include the total savings that all consumers and producers receive as a result of producers adopting the cost-reducing innovation. Depending on the extent to which reduced costs are reflected in the price charged to consumers, social benefits are shared by producers who adopt the innovation and consumers of their products. Thus, the evaluation question that can be answered from this traditional approach is: Given the investment costs and the social benefits, what is the social rate of return to the innovation?

This paper, written in honor of Ed Mansfield, illustrates—in the context of a public sector investment—the Griliches/Mansfield pioneering field-based methods for measuring the social rates of return to innovative investments. The case study described herein relates to the development of an improved standard reference material (SRM) for the measurement of the wavelength of light in an optical fiber network. That research, which was conducted at the National Institute of Standards and Technology (NIST), was funded by an intramural grant through NIST's Advanced Technology Program (ATP).

The following Section 2 briefly describes ATP's intramural research program. Section 3 overviews the case study, and relevant social rate of return metrics are presented in Section 4. Section 5 concludes the paper with general observations about the evaluation of public sector R&D.

2. ATP's intramural research program

Since its inception in 1990, ATP has stimulated economic growth through the development of innovative technologies that are high in technical risk and enabling in the sense of having the potential to provide significant, broad-based economic benefits.[3] Industry proposes research projects to ATP in competitions in which proposed projects are selected for funding based upon both their technical and economic or business merits.

The ATP intramural research program provides funding to NIST laboratories to conduct research to advance the U.S. technology infrastructure in order to assist industry in continually improving products and services. Under the statute governing ATP, up to 10% of ATP's budget could be allocated for this research. Since 1997, ATP required that these intramural projects:

- emphasize generic basic research,
- relate to groups of ATP extramural projects, and
- focus on measurement and standards that would facilitate the deployment and diffusion of technologies developed in ATP extramurally-funded projects.

3. Case study of wavelength references for optical fiber communications

The goal of this research project was to develop an improved SRM for the measurement of the wavelength of light in an optical fiber network.

The Optoelectronics Division of the Electronics and Electrical Engineering Laboratory began research on optical communications in the mid-1970s and expanded its research program substantially in the late 1980s. The Optical Fiber and Components Group of the Division began research on SRMs in 1991. The Group's first SRM became available in 1993; with SRM 2520, an optical fiber diameter standard. Since then the Group has produced a number of optoelectronic standards. SRM 2517 was issued in 1997; it was intended for use in calibrating the wavelength scale of wavelength measuring equipment in the spectral region from 1510 to 1540 nm.

In 1998, Dr. Sarah Gilbert in the Optical Fiber and Components Group began a two-year ATP intramural project to develop a more accurate version of SRM 2517. Dr. Gilbert received $145,000 over two years—$70,000 in fiscal year 1998 and $75,000 in fiscal year 1999. The project produced the new SRM for calibration of wavelengths in the spectral region from 1510 to 1540 nm. The references in the 1500 nm region are important to support wavelength division multiplexed (WDM) optical fiber communications systems. In a WDM system, many channels, each associated with a different wavelength, of communication information are sent down the same fiber. Thus, WDM in effect increases the bandwidth of the communications system, because any given spectral region will support more channels through which communications information can be sent. A WDM system requires stable wavelengths throughout the components of the system, and equipment must be calibrated to measure those wavelengths. The wavelength references provided by NIST are needed to calibrate the instruments—such as optical spectrum analyzers, tunable lasers, and wavelength meters—that are used to characterize the components of WDM optical fiber communications systems. The wavelength references are also used to monitor the wavelengths of the channels while the system is in use, because if one channel's wavelength were to shift, crosstalk could occur between it and a neighboring channel, thus disrupting the accurate flow of communications information through the channels of the system.

The output of Dr. Gilbert's ATP-funded NIST research with William Swann was Standard Reference Material 2517a, High Resolution Wavelength Calibration Reference for 1510—1540 nm Acetylene ($^{12}C_2H_2$). Quoting NIST's description of the new SRM provides an exact description of the artifact—an "absorption cell" filled with acetylene gas that produces characteristic "absorption lines" in the readouts resulting when lasers project light of various wavelengths through the gas-filled cell. The absorption lines observed can then be used to identify the wavelengths for the laser emitting device being calibrated.[4] NIST's description of the artifact is as follows.[5]

"Standard Reference Material 2517a is intended for wavelength calibration in the spectral region from 1510 nm to 1540 nm. It is a single-mode optical-fiber-coupled absorption cell containing acetylene ($^{12}C_2H_2$) gas at a pressure of 6.7 kPa (50 Torr). The absorption path length is 5 cm and the absorption lines are about 7 pm wide. The cell is packaged in a small instrument box (approximately 24 cm long × 12.5 cm wide × 9 cm high) with two FC/PC fiber connectors for the input and output of a user-supplied light source. Acetylene has more than 50 accurately measured absorption lines in the 1500 nm wavelength region. This SRM can be used for high resolution applications, such as calibrating a narrow-band tunable laser, or lower resolution applications, such as calibrating an optical spectrum analyzer."

The primary difference between the new wavelength calibration standard, SRM 2517a, and its predecessor, SRM 2517, is the use of lower pressure in the acetylene cell to produce narrower lines. Because of that difference, SRM 2517a can be used in higher resolution and higher accuracy applications.

This ATP intramural project complemented the SRM-related research of the Optical Fiber and Components Group and was a natural extension of previous research related to SRM 2517. While research on SRM 2517a would have occurred in the absence of ATP's support, it would not have progressed as rapidly. According to Dr. Gilbert: "The ATP funding accelerated this project and enabled us to complete the development of a new wavelength calibration SRM about 1 year faster that we would have without this funding."

Thus, if ATP had not funded the project, in the course of its ongoing operations, the NIST laboratory would have invested a similar amount, but the streams of costs and benefits would have begun roughly a year later. In this paper, we evaluate the social rate of return from the investment in the project. We do not try to identify the incremental gain from having the project funded by ATP rather than the NIST laboratory that performed the research. NIST has been selling SRM 2517a at a rate of two to three per month since it was introduced in late 2000.[6]

4. Estimating the social rate of return

The traditional evaluation method pioneered by Griliches and Mansfield is used in this case study to estimate the social rate of return to ATP's (i.e. the public sector's) investments in SRM 2517a.[7] To implement that method, two general data series are needed. One data series is related to investment costs, and in the case of this study the relevant investment costs are those associated with the ATP intramural project.[8] The other data series is related to the benefits realized by society, net of society's costs to use the innovation (i.e. pull costs). Society includes both private sector companies and consumers. ATP's investment costs are known.

Benefit data have to be collected, and these data can be of two types. Benefit data can be retrospective in nature, meaning that the company or consumer who has benefited from the ATP project has already realized benefits; or benefit data can be prospective in nature, meaning that the company or consumer who will benefit in the future from the ATP project can estimate when and to what degree benefits will be realized.[9] Both types of benefit data were collected in this study.

Benefit and cost information[10]

Detailed descriptions of the uses of SRM 2517a are provided below, but in overview NIST's experience suggests that most of the test equipment manufacturers in industry use the SRM units to conduct periodic calibration checks on their equipment. The calibration checks with the SRM are not typically in the production line where various intermediate standards are used for routine calibration checks. Rather, the SRM is used to check those intermediate standards. Some of these test equipment manufacturers make absorption cells—commercial versions of the SRM 2517a artifact described above—to incorporate into their products. In those situations where the absorption cells are purchased, discussions with industry experts reveal that SRM 2517a is used both to check the commercial versions of the absorption cells and for study as a manufacturing guide in the production of the commercial high-volume versions of the cell. Discussions with industry show that the component manufacturers often integrate the SRM 2517a into their production lines to continuously calibrate their equipment. Network systems providers use the SRMs to calibrate their test equipment.

The industry costs and benefits for SRM 2517a are based on estimates—obtained through detailed telephone interviews—from industry respondents that collectively have purchased about 30% of the SRM 2517a cells.[11]

Discussions with industry identified several types of benefits and costs associated with SRM 2517a. Benefits fall within five general categories: production related engineering experimentation cost savings, calibration cost savings, yield, negotiation, and marketing. Costs are the ATP development costs plus the pull costs associated with using the SRM purchased from NIST.

Separating the benefits from SRM 2517a from the benefits from other SRMs in the 25xx family was often difficult for industry respondents.[12] Some use the entire set of SRM 25xx artifacts; those respondents sometimes think of the set of artifacts as an integrated whole, covering different parts of the spectrum of wavelengths to which equipment must be calibrated. Thus, to some extent the benefit estimates below reflect a joint benefit from the set of NIST SRM 25xx artifacts. However, there are also major sources of unmeasured industrial benefits from SRM 2517a. As a result, the benefit estimates used are, on balance, conservative for at least three reasons. First, the estimates are truncated after 10 future years, even though some respondents believed that the commercial usefulness of SRM 2517a would extend well beyond that period. Second, and more importantly, many respondents could not quantify the loss in sales, and therefore profits, that would occur without traceability to NIST of their wavelength calibrations. And third, the benefit estimates reflect only the benefits to the purchasers of the NIST SRM 2517a artifacts; they do not capture the additional benefits to users further down the supply chain.[13] Given these sources of downward bias, we believe that, on balance, the benefit estimates used to compute the evaluation metrics to characterize the outcomes of SRM 2517a are conservative.

Use of SRM 2517a results in:

- *Production related engineering and experimentation cost savings:* Users of SRM 2517a regularly conduct what we call production related engineering experimentation.[14] These activities are an important aspect of production. The new more accurate measurement technology associated with SRM 2517a lowered the cost of these activities and hence represents a cost-savings benefit. Also experimentation costs for industry have been lowered because of industry's interaction with the NIST scientists that developed the artifact.[15]

- *Calibration cost savings:* SRM 2517a reduces the costs of calibrating production equipment and products. It is not uncommon to recalibrate production devices for an optical fiber network on a daily basis, or even more frequently. SRM 2517a reduces the cost of each calibration; it permits equipment to be calibrated on the production floor. The alternative would be to purchase tunable lasers, which not only are more costly but also must be set for one frequency at a time, whereas the SRMs provide a fingerprint covering a whole range of the spectrum of wavelengths. In addition, tunable lasers entail additional operating time using well-trained technicians involved in production.[16]
- *Increased production yields:* Production yields have increased because SRM 2517a improved process control and thereby reduced the costs of product failure. Manufacturers of optical fiber network components manufacture to the customer's specifications and needs. SRM 2517a, as well as other SRMs in the 25xx series, provide useful reference points across a stable wavelength range for the tuning of the components for optical communications systems. As a costly and less accurate alternative, the points of reference could be simulated with expensive cascades of optical filters strung together.[17]
- *Negotiations cost savings:* Negotiation with customers over disputes about the performance attributes of products are reduced because of SRM 2517a and the traceability to the NIST standard that it provides. In the absence of wavelength stability, manufacturers and customers would both have grounds to disagree about performance characteristics. Without SRM 2517a and the traceability that it provides, costly negotiations and testing would occur.[18]
- *Reduced marketing costs:* Marketing costs are reduced because of the traceability of an important new standard to NIST that SRM 2517a allows, and sales are greater than for SRM 2517 because of the confidence inspired by the new standard traceable to NIST.[19]

Quantitative estimates of each of the above categories of benefits were obtained from the five manufacturers with whom we spoke. According to Dr. Gilbert, these five companies collectively have purchased about 30% of the SRM 2517a cells sold to date. The benefit data in Table I captures industry-wide benefits. Each datum in Table I is the product of the sum of the dollar values for each respondent multiplied by 3.33 (3.33 = 1/0.30), and all dollar values are converted to year 2000 dollars.

To be conservative, the estimated benefits from SRM 2517a are truncated after ten years.Respondents indicated that the SRM 2517a provided knowledge that would be commercially useful for the foreseeable future. Some respondents emphasized that, as a standard, the knowledge embodied in SRM 2517a would last and be useful virtually forever. However, industry may require even more development of the standards for measuring the wavelength of light as time passes, and the respondents as a group believed that a commercial lifetime of ten years would be a conservative estimate for the period of industrial use of SRM 2517a.

The observed variance through time in the benefits (in year 2000 dollars) reflects three key things. First, there are different periods of primary incidence for the various cost savings. For example, production-related engineering cost savings occur primarily in the early years of the time series and in some cases even before the introduction of SRM 2517a.[20] In contrast, the costs of reduced yields (benefit of increased yields) are avoided throughout the time series after SRM 2517a was introduced and the technology transferred to industry. Second, the introduction of SRM 2517a occurred in late 2000 and partial-year benefits are reported; benefits increase in subsequent years since the SRM is used throughout each year. Third, the variance over time reflects the collapse of optical fiber communications industry sales from record highs in 2000–2001 to low levels in 2002. Projections by industry then reflect an expected recovery of industry sales to the levels experienced in 1999—levels that in 1999 were between one-third and one-half of their subsequent peaks in 2000–2001 before the bubble burst—by 2004–2005. Thereafter, the projections reflect

TABLE I
Industry benefits truncated at 10 years (year 2000 dollars)

Year	Production cost savings ($1000s)	Calibration cost savings ($1000s)	Increased production yield ($1000s)	Decreased negotiation costs ($1000s)	Decreased marketing costs ($1000s)
1999	$3,193.9				
2000	$3,266.5	$401.0	$2,613.3	$245.0	$473.7
2001	$1,388.3	$1,832.6	$10,531.7	$1,094.3	$1,894.7
2002	$1,682.3	$353.5	$2,106.3	$218.9	$383.0
2003	$1,388.3	$441.8	$2,632.9	$273.6	$478.8
2004	$1,388.3	$589.7	$3,514.2	$365.2	$639.0
2005	$1,388.3	$735.8	$4,384.6	$455.6	$797.3
2006		$846.8	$5,046.5	$524.4	$917.7
2007		$973.8	$5,803.2	$603.0	$1,055.2
2008		$1,119.9	$6,673.7	$693.4	$1,213.5
2009		$1,287.8	$7,674.7	$797.5	$1,395.6

Note: Production related engineering and experimentation cost savings decrease in 2001 because, although some experimental production uses of the measurement technology were reported after the introduction of the SRM, the most intense realization of such experimental benefits came from the application of the new measurement technology—gained in industry's interaction with NIST through publications, presentations, and ongoing interaction with the researchers—to production problems encountered by industry as it coped with the need for the actual improved SRM and substituted experimentation for it. Publications about the SRM 2517a technology started appearing in 1999. The other categories of industry benefits increase after the introduction of the SRM 2517a because those benefits reflect the actual use of the SRMs once they were available for use.

TABLE II
Estimated costs associated with SRM 2517a (year 2000 dollars)

Year	ATP Funds ($1000s)	Industry pull cost ($1000s)
1998	$72.6	
1999	$76.7	
2000		$16.3
2001		$73.5

TABLE III
Estimated total costs and estimated total industry benefits associated with SRM 2517a (year 2000 dollars)

Year	Total costs ($1000s)	Total industry benefits ($1000s)
1998	$72.6	
1999	$76.7	$3,193.9
2000	$16.3	$6,999.5
2001	$73.5	$16,741.6
2002		$4,744.0
2003		$5,215.4
2004		$6,496.4
2005		$7,761.6
2006		$7,335.4
2007		$8,435.2
2008		$9,700.5
2009		$11,155.6

what knowledgeable industry observers expect to be a 15% rate of growth.

The costs associated with the SRM 2517a project are in Table II. The actual costs of the ATP intramural project are shown along with estimates of the pull costs for industry. Respondents were asked to estimate any initial costs, over and above any fees paid to NIST for SRM 2517a to be able to use (i.e., pull in) the artifact in production. These pull costs are one-time costs.

Table III aggregates the cost and benefit estimates from Tables I and II.

Results of the economic analysis

Table IV summarizes the four evaluation metrics calculated for this case study.[21] Clearly, based on one or all of the metrics in Table IV, the ATP intramural funded SRM 2517a project was successful from society's economic perspective. The internal rate of return is 4,400%, the benefit-to-cost ratio is 267 to 1, and the net present value in 2002 in year 2000 dollars is 76 million.

The metrics in Table IV reflect the social return on investments, and these are the returns

TABLE IV
Evaluation metrics for the SRM 2517a case study

Metric	Estimate
Real internal rate of return	4,400%
Benefit-to-Cost ratio	267 to 1
Net present value using 1998 as base year in year 2000 dollars	$58.1 million
Net present value using 2002 as base year in year 2000 dollars	$76.2 million

TABLE V
Revised evaluation metrics for the SRM 2517a case study using total benefits (net gains in the total of producer surplus and consumer surplus) (year 2000 dollars)

Metric	Estimate
Real internal rate of return	5,500%
Benefit-to-Cost ratio	331 to 1
Net present value using 1998 as the base year in year 2000 dollars	$72.0 million
Net present value using 2002 as the base year in year 2000 dollars	$94.4 million

that economists call producer surplus. Producer surplus is the profit resulting because of the use of the infratechnology embodied in SRM 2517a. Although the estimate will be a rough one, we are also able to provide a first-order approximation of the consumer surplus gains as well. Figure 1 represents the situation for the typical company selling a differentiated product that uses SRM 2517a in the production process.[22] The availability of the new standard reference material lowers the unit costs as shown in the figure from "unit cost 2517" to "unit cost 2517a." Consequently, the company chooses a lower price and sells more of its product or service.[23] The company's profit maximizing price falls from P_1 to P_2, and the optimal output increases from Q_1 to Q_2. The new surplus—resulting because of the new lower unit costs of production enabled by SRM 2517a—is the sum of the areas A, B, C, and D. Area A represents the new producer surplus on sales of the original amount of output. Area B plus area C represents the new producer surplus from the sale of additional output. Finally, area D represents the net gain in consumer surplus (new consumer surplus that does not simply offset a loss in previously existing producer surplus).

Details about price, output and unit cost are considered highly confidential and the industry respondents were typically unwilling to provide such information. However, one of the respondents was willing to provide detailed information, for its own production, about P1, P2, Q1, Q2, and unit cost both before SRM 2517a was introduced and then after it replaced SRM 2517. For that company, the ratio of net new consumer surplus to new producer surplus, $D/(A + B + C)$, equals 0.238. That company conjectures that its experience with the cost lowering effect of replacing SRM 2517 with SRM 2517a would be similar to the experiences of others in the industry. Therefore, as a first-order approximation of consumer surplus gains because of the process innovations from applying SRM 2517a, we multiply the new producer profits—the industry benefits column of Table III—by 0.238. Table V recalculates the metrics for the SRM 2517a project by using the total of the net gains in producer and consumer surplus (the industrial benefits from Table III multiplied by 1.238) as the social return on the investment.

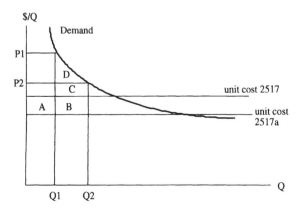

Figure 1. Demand, unit cost and net gain in producer and consumer surplus from the use of SRM 2517a.

5. Concluding observations

Public agencies have taken their own idiosyncratic approaches to respond to the Government Performance and Results Act of 1993 (GPRA), and researchers have offered a variety of evaluation methods in the pages of this journal and others. Whatever the merits of the numerous alternatives to the approach based on the Griliches/Mansfield estimation of the social rate of return for the public investments, the Griliches/Mansfield method is the preeminent way to evaluate public investments' social value from an economic perspective.[24] The Griliches/Mansfield methodology is so important that it could usefully have a category of its own among the subset of categories in the *Journal of Economic Literature* category for technological change (O300—Technological Change; Research and Development: General). We hope that our case study has illustrated the usefulness of their methodology for evaluating public investments.

Appendix: Quantifying Social Rate of Return Metrics

Using the time series for costs and benefits, measured in constant dollars, the internal rate of return, the benefit-to-cost ratio, and the net present value for the project were calculated in this case study using the year when each project began as the base year. In addition to those three customary metrics, net present value referenced to year 2002 was also computed since it is the year in which the calculations were originally performed.

The metrics are calculated from the time series of costs and benefits in year 2000 dollars. Costs and benefits were converted to constant dollars to allow all dollar figures to be directly comparable. All dollar figures have been converted to year 2000 dollars using the chain-type price index for gross domestic product provided in the *Economic Report of the President*.[25] Year 2000 was chosen because, at the time that the case study was conducted, that was the most recent year for which complete annual data were available.

Internal rate of return[26]

The internal rate of return (IRR) is the value of the discount rate, i, that equates the net present value (NPV) of the stream of net benefits associated with a research project to zero.[27] The time series runs from the beginning of the research project, $t = 0$, to a terminal point, $t = n$.

Mathematically,

$$\mathrm{NPV} = [(B_0 - C_0)/(1+i)^0] + \cdots + [(B_n - C_n)/(1+i)^n] = 0 \quad (1)$$

where $(B_t - C_t)$ represents the net benefits associated with the project in year t, and n represents the number of time periods—years in the case study evaluated in this paper—being considered in the evaluation.

For unique solutions for i, from equation (1), the IRR can be compared to a value, r, that represents the opportunity cost of funds invested by the technology-based public institution. Thus, if the opportunity cost of funds is less than the internal rate of return, the project was worthwhile from an *ex post* social perspective.

Benefit-to-cost ratio

The ratio of benefits-to-costs (B/C) is the ratio of the present value of all measured benefits to the present value of all measured costs. Both benefits and costs are referenced to the initial time period, $t = 0$, when the project began as:

$$B/C = \left[\sum_{t=0}^{t=n} B_t/(1+r)^t\right] \Big/ \left[\sum_{t=0}^{t=n} C_t/(1+r)^t\right] \quad (2)$$

A benefit-to-cost ratio of 1 is said to indicate a project that breaks-even. Any project with $B/C > 1$ is a relatively successful project as defined in terms of benefits exceeding costs.

Fundamental to implementing the ratio of benefits-to-costs is a value for the discount rate, r. While the discount rate representing the opportunity cost for public funds could differ across a portfolio of public investments, the calculated metrics in this paper follow the guidelines set forth by the Office of Management and Budget (1992), which states that: "Constant-dollar benefit-cost analyses of proposed investments and regulations should report net present value and other outcomes determined using a real discount rate of 7%."

Net present value

The information developed to determine the benefit-to-cost ratio can be used to determine net present value (NPV) as:

$$\text{NPV}_{\text{initial year}} = B - C \tag{3}$$

where, as in the calculation of B/C, B refers to the present value of all measured benefits and C refers to the present value of all measured costs and where present value refers to the initial year or time period in which the project began, $t=0$ in terms of the B/C formula in equation (2). Note that NPV allows, in principle, one means of ranking several projects *ex post*, providing investment sizes are similar.

To compare the net present values across different case studies with different starting dates, the net present value for each can be brought forward to the same year—here year 2002. The $\text{NPV}_{\text{initial year}}$ is brought forward under the assumption that the NPV for the project was invested at the 7% real rate of return that is recommended by the Office of Management and Budget as the opportunity cost of government funds. NPV_{2002} is then a project's NPV multiplied by 1.07 raised to the power of 2002 minus the year that the project was initiated as:

$$\text{NPV}_{2002} = \text{NPV}\,(1.07)^{2002-\text{initial year}} \tag{4}$$

Acknowledgment

This paper is based on research conducted under the sponsorship of the National Institute of Standards and Technology's Advanced Technology Program. We are grateful for comments and suggestions from Stephanie Shipp and Jeanne Powell on earlier versions.

Notes

1. The Government Performance and Results Act of 1993 (GPRA) required that public institutions' research programs identify outputs and quantify the economic benefits of the outcomes associated with such outputs. Some public agencies have skirted the issue by arguing that the research they do or that they fund is peer reviewed, and thus it is sound; and if the research is sound, it must be socially valuable. Many embrace the importance of having research peer reviewed both at the pre-funding stage as well as upon completion. However, the peer review process certainly does not address in any precise or reliable way whether or not the research is socially valuable from an economic standpoint. It is not so much that a formal analysis of social economic rates of return is officially out of bounds for the peer review process; rather, such an analysis is simply not a part of the peer review process as it currently exists. Other public agencies are attempting to be more exact in their approach to meeting the GPRA requirement to quantify outcomes' benefits. However, the hurdle that is difficult to clear for most public agencies is how to quantify benefits in a methodologically sound and defensible way.

2. The origin of this assumption can be traced at least to Bush (1945), although Link and Scott (1998, 2001) have placed this assumption in a specific policy context.

3. For background information about ATP see, for example, Link and Scott (1998, 2001).

4. Because of fundamental molecular absorptions when light is projected through the absorption cell filled with acetylene gas, the power transmitted through the cell is distinct at specified wavelengths, allowing accurate references to those wavelengths. Those references can then be used to calibrate instruments for industry.

5. Gilbert, Sarah L., and Swann, William C., Acetylene $^{12}C_2H_2$ Absorption Reference for 1510 nm to 1540 nm Wavelength Calibration—SRM 2517a, NIST Special Publication 260–133, 2001 Edition, Standard Reference Materials, Issued February 2001 (Washington, D.C., U.S. Government Printing Office, 2001), p. 2.

6. The rough breakdown of all of the SRM 2517a sales by industry category is 45% to manufacturers of test equipment, 30% to manufacturers of components, 10% to companies providing network systems, and 15% to other users—mostly research laboratories—of the SRM. According to Dr. Gilbert, a company will typically purchase one SRM 2517a.

7. Link and Scott have developed, through ongoing evaluations of federal research programs, an alternative approach to the *economic* evaluation of publicly-funded research. This approach differs from traditional evaluation methods that have been used in addition to peer review. The alternative approach is needed to provide additional insights because the traditional evaluation methods are limited in an evaluation world that is performance accountable. The genesis of this approach is in Link (1996a), and recent applications are in Link (1996b) and Link and Scott (1998, 2001). Link and Scott, and others, have used this approach in a number of the evaluation studies sponsored by the Program Office at NIST, as well as in several ATP-sponsored projects. More specifically, and in general terms, Link and Scott argue that asking what is the social rate of return to an innovation and asking how that compares to the innovator's private rate of return may not always be the most appropriate question to ask. The fact that the social rate of return is greater than the private rate of return does indeed provide evidence that there are benefits spilling over to society. However, the fact that the social rate of return is greater than the private rate of return ignores consideration of the cost effectiveness of the public sector undertaking the research as opposed to the private sec-

tor. In other words, the Griliches/Mansfield traditional evaluation method does not address the efficiency with which social benefits are being achieved. Two alternative evaluation methods could be more appropriate for publicly-funded research. When publicly-funded publicly-performed investments are being evaluated we argue that our Counterfactual Evaluation Method could be appropriate. Holding constant the economic benefits that the Griliches/Mansfield model measures, and making no attempt to measure that stream, the counterfactual evaluation question is: What would the private sector have had to invest to achieve those same benefits in the absence of the public sector's investments? See as an example of the Counterfactual Evaluation Method Link and Scott (1998). Alternatively, when publicly-funded privately-performed investments are being evaluated, we argue that our Spillover Evaluation Method could be appropriate. The question asked is one that facilitates an economic understanding of whether the public sector should be underwriting a portion of private-sector firms' research, namely: What proportion of the total profit stream generated by the private firm's R&D and innovation does the private firm expect to capture; and hence, what proportion is not appropriated but is instead captured by other firms that imitate the innovation or use knowledge generated by the R&D to produce competing products for the social good? The part of the stream of expected profits captured by the innovator is its private return, while the entire stream is the lower bound on the social rate of return. The extent of the spillover of such knowledge with public good characteristics could determine whether or not the public sector should have funded the research. See as an illustration of the Spillover Evaluation Method, Link and Scott (2001).

8. As relevant, other investment costs will be discussed below. Such investment costs are costs that the private sector will incur to utilize the ATP project's output. These are, stated differently, the costs incurred by the private sector to pull in ATP's output and utilize it efficiently. Hence, these costs are referred to as pull costs.

9. Of course, it is assumed that the benefit information provided by interviewed individuals is accurate and reproducible should subsequent interviews by others take place.

10. The data developed for discussion of the outcomes in this case study are based on discussions with Dr. Gilbert and several industry experts from Wavelength References, Burleigh Instruments, Corning, Agilent, and Chorum Technologies.

11. The information about the industry-wide coverage of our sample of respondents in industry was provided by NIST.

12. For a discussion of other optoelectronics SRMs, see:http://patapsco.nist.gov/srmcatalog/tables/view_table.cfm?table=207-4.htm.

13. As one respondent whose company manufactures commercial gas cells (based on SRM 2517a) for use in instruments stated: "If there were no SRM 2517a, all along the way through the supply chain the additional calibration expenses (suites of equipment and extra labor costs) would be incurred. Roughly half of the optical spectrum analyzers sold to industry incorporate the SRM 2517a technology to calibrate better. There would be extra expense and time at each research site."

14. Our understanding is that these activities fall under the rubric of research and development (R&D), but absent information about how companies classify these activities we refrain from using the policy-sensitive term "R&D."

15. To paraphrase one industry expert: SRM 2517a reduced our investigation costs; we would have invested additional engineering person-years with equipment to maintain production. See also the note to Table I.

16. One respondent, whose company manufactures locked lasers and gas cells, observed that the alternative to SRM 2517a for calibration is to invest in a suite of equipment and then take the extra time to get the calibration results. A telecommunications company responded that prior to SRM 2517a it relied on its own internal standards based on one frequency and then extrapolated to other frequencies. The company's expert stated that the SRM 2517a standard, with multiple indicators of various frequencies, is a critically important advance for telecommunications.

17. A manufacturer of narrow band optical filters told us: SRM 2517a provides narrow line widths for reference to absolute vacuum wavelengths and this is critical to meeting the performance specification needs of our customers. This artifact gives us an unquestionable reference to absolute wavelengths so that secondary standards can be recalibrated as they drift. Our alternative, over say 30 nm of wavelength range for a particular product, maybe 10 optical filters would be strung together. While the cost of this alternative is not that great, performance tolerances and wavelength stability would be lost. Using the alternative would have resulted in a yield loss of about 30%.

18. One respondent noted that without NIST traceability through SRM 2517a, interactions with the customers over performance characteristics would be like dealing with "a wound that would not heal."

19. Paraphrasing a component manufacturer: There are two parts to the sales/marketing impact of SRM 2517a for our company. First, there is a savings in personnel costs because there is less effort needed to convince customers about the quality and reliability of our products. More importantly, there is a positive effect on our reputation and the customers' confidence in our product line because of having NIST standards integrated in the production process. That positive effect translates into extra sales and extra profits. Paraphrasing a manufacturer of wavelength meters: We use SRM 2517a as we manufacture wavelength meters. SRM 2517a is used to check periodically the calibration of test lasers and equipment used for the qualification of our wavemeters. We can claim traceability to NIST. There are cost savings to us in the sales/marketing category.

20. Industry interacts with NIST and stays abreast of the latest developments through direct communication with NIST scientists, and through scientists' presentations and publications. In this case, some respondents reported that they began benefiting from the new knowledge—gained from interaction with NIST researchers—about wavelength calibration even before SRMs were sold, as industry coped with the need for the actual SRMs but substituted experimental work in their absence.

21. Regarding evaluation metrics, see the appendix to this paper.
22. As is seen in Figure 1, in addition to gaining new profits that we have identified as industrial benefits, industry loses some of its previous profits on the previous amount sold before unit costs fell because the use of SRM 2517a lowers costs and consequently price falls. However, those lost profits (lost producer surplus) are completely offset by a gain of exactly that amount in consumer surplus, leaving just the new profits measured in Table III and represented by A + B + C in Figure 1 as the increase in total surplus because of increased producer surplus. The net gain in consumer surplus (represented by D in Figure 1) is then added to get the change in total economic surplus that is the social return to the use of SRM 2517a—consumers gain more than D, but that additional gain is exactly offset by an equal amount of lost previously existing surplus for producers, leaving D as the net gain in consumer surplus.
23. Note that Figure 1 depicts optimal output in the long run when all costs are variable.
24. As we have noted above, for GPRA purposes, it will sometimes be appropriate to use the development of the Griliches/Mansfield methodology that we have incorporated in our Counterfactual Evaluation Method and our Spillover Evaluation Method.
25. See CEA (2002), Table B-7, "Chain-type price indexes for gross domestic product, 1959–2001." The index number for 2001 was estimated as the average of the three quarterly observations available.
26. The characterization of the three metrics follows Link and Scott (1998).
27. Using the constant dollar figures for costs and benefits, the internal rate of return is a "real" rate of return. In contrast, some economic impact assessments (including many conducted for NIST's Program Office) have presented "nominal" rates of return that were based on time series of current dollars (the dollars of the year in which the benefits were realized or the costs were incurred).

References

Bush, V., 1945, *Science—the Endless Frontier*, Washington, DC: U.S. Government Printing Office.

Council of Economic Advisers (CEA), February 2002, *Economic Report of the President*, Washington, D.C.: United States Government Printing Office.

Griliches, Z., 1958, 'Research Costs and Social Returns: Hybrid Corn and Related Innovations,' *Journal of Political Economy* **66**, 419–431.

Link, A.N., 1996a, 'Economic Impact Assessments: Guidelines for Conducting and Interpreting Assessment Studies,' NIST Planning Report 96-1.

Link, A.N., 1996b, *Evaluating Public Sector Research and Development*, New York: Praeger Publishers.

Link, A.N. and J.T. Scott, 1998, *Public Accountability: Evaluating Technology-Based Institutions*, Norwell, MA: Kluwer Academic Publishers.

Link, A.N. and J.T. Scott. 2001, 'Public/Private Partnerships: Stimulating Competition in a Dynamic Economy,' *International Journal of Industrial Organization* **19**, 763–794.

Mansfield, E., J. Rapoport, A. Romero, S. Wagner, and G. Beardsley, 1977. 'Social and Private Rates of Return from Industrial Innovations,' *Quarterly Journal of Economics* **91**, 221–240.

Office of Management and Budget (OMB), 1992, 'Guidelines and Discount Rates for Benefit-Cost Analysis of Federal Programs,' Circular No. A-94, October 29.

Industrial R&D Laboratories: Windows on Black Boxes?

James D. Adams

ABSTRACT. This paper provides an overview of the survey-based literature on industrial Research and Development (R&D) laboratories, beginning with the work of Edwin Mansfield. Topics covered include R&D projects, new products, and new processes; the appropriability of intellectual property; the limits of the firm in R&D; and spillovers of knowledge from other firms and universities into the laboratories. I discuss the value of collecting information from industrial R&D managers, who participate in a wide range of R&D decisions and are the natural best source of information on these decisions. I also emphasize gaps in our knowledge concerning R&D from past studies, such as the private and social returns to R&D, the nature of firms' R&D portfolios, and other topics. The paper closes with a discussion of the benefits from building a national database on R&D laboratories that could be shared among researchers and that could take this area of research to a new and higher level of achievement.

Key words: industrial research and development, management of R&D, spillovers, technology transfer, survey data

JEL Classification: L2, L3, O3

1. Introduction

The opportunity to learn firsthand how firms invent and innovate is one that should not be missed. It is surely a unique window on the black box of the firm, one that can be looked through from any angle to study interactions between the firm's innovative establishments, other divisions of the firm, and the rest of the economy. We owe this opportunity to Edwin Mansfield and his students. It is their field work that brought the study of R&D laboratories into economics, opened up research opportunities for the investigators that followed them, and created an economic literature on the subject. In this paper, mindful of this huge contribution, I survey some of the economic research that has illuminated the black box of industrial R&D. Along the way I shall comment on questions raised by this research that in my opinion remain unanswered.

The topic is important for several reasons, all of them based on the inability to substitute other information for data from R&D laboratories. This special attribute of the data rests on the extraordinary skills of their source, the laboratory managers of R&D.[1] An argument can be made that the data are irreplaceable because R&D managers are Renaissance individuals who engage in project selection, negotiate with operating divisions of the company, and work co-operatively with universities, federal laboratories, and other firms (Adams, 2002; Adams 2005, forthcoming; Adams et al. 2003; Cohen et al. 2002; Mansfield and Brandenburg, 1966). Questions such as the efficient management of industrial R&D, the returns to R&D projects, the nature of co-operative research, and the role of universities, government, and other firms in invention and commercialization are best answered by asking those who know about them. And R&D managers specialize in functions of the kind just described.

Field research in this area has uncovered critical findings on industrial R&D that could not have been obtained using received data.[2] In practice this approach has relied on data collection by many different researchers and this has its advantages as well as disadvantages. The data are heterogeneous and as a result are exceptionally rich. Also, the data are designed from the start to address the relationships of interest rather than designed for an unrelated purpose. The questions posed are limited only

---

Department of Economics,
Rensselaer Polytechnic Institute,
3504 Russell Sage Laboratory,
Troy, NY 12180-3590
E-mail: adamsj@rpi.edu

by the ingenuity of investigators and the patience of respondents. But these same qualities make it hard to compare results, and confidentiality places strong restrictions on data access. However, given sufficient community, field work can have recombinant properties. Learning by one researcher passes to the next, lending a cumulative increasing returns to scale property to the investigations as a whole.

The rest of the paper consists of five sections. The next four sections form the heart of this paper. Each explores a specific topic related to R&D laboratories. I chose these topics because they have attracted attention and I am familiar with them. Section 2 samples the literature of R&D projects, products, and processes. Section 3 reports some of what we have learned about the appropriability of intellectual property from R&D laboratory studies. Section 4 explores what studies of laboratory R&D have taught us about the limits of the firm in R&D. Evidence for spillovers of outside knowledge into the laboratory is examined in Section 5. Section 6 is a summary, discussion, and conclusion.

2. R&D projects, products and processes

R&D projects

During the 1960s and 1970s Edwin Mansfield and his co-workers undertook a series of studies of R&D projects. I begin with Mansfield and Brandenburg (1966). Its subject is the decision-making process that governs projects in the R&D laboratory of a large manufacturer. Its findings are that forecasted profits are a key driver of project expenditures, along with the scientific appeal of projects to researchers and the practical needs of manufacturing divisions. Other findings are that laboratory managers are risk-averse and take on projects that are short-term (less than five years from development) and low on technical risk. As a result, projects are completed rapidly and rarely fail for technical reasons, though the risk of commercial failure remains. The paper raises questions having to do with the portfolio aspects of R&D projects. What is the correlation matrix of returns on the projects? What is the overall level of risk of the portfolio compared with individual projects? Questions like this are of interest to the Real Options approach to investment (Dixit and Pindyck, 1994) given that R&D projects are a collection of real assets subject to uncertainty.

The uncertainty of R&D projects is further highlighted by Mansfield and Beardsley's (1978) study of industrial forecasts of their returns in a large company. One finding is that forecasted profits on new products are poorly explained by actual profits. While this explanatory power of actual for forecasted profits is higher in process-oriented R&D, in both cases forecasted profits are under-predicted. Thus considerable uncertainty and discounting apply to the projects. To my knowledge little if any work has since been done that covers the portfolio of a firm's R&D. Only in this way can the entire landscape of its research can be understood.

A recent study of project-level R&D, though not of the portfolio of a single firm, is by Bizan (2003). He explores the determinants of technical and commercial success of Israeli–American research alliances. He finds that projects are more likely to be a success when one partner is a subsidiary of the other, when the two firms have complementary capabilities, and when project size and duration increase.

New products and processes

Mansfield et al. (1977) estimate the private and social returns to industrial innovation. The work is based on a sample of 17 innovations in several industries that consist of new products and processes. The remarkable finding is that the median (pre-tax) *private* rate of return on the projects is 25%. The median *social* return is 56%. The figures seem to justify public subsidies for industrial R&D, and yet the high private rate of return calls for an explanation. Is it the risk characteristics of R&D projects and their hurdle rates that bring about a return of this size? The question harks back to whether the firm's R&D portfolio diversifies risk away, or not. Otherwise, are the private returns upward biased, perhaps because a new product replaces an older one in the same firm? How do these rates of return compare with returns on other industrial investments? Another issue concerns whether the social rate of return includes the creative destruction of profit streams on earlier products and processes by other firms. Our ability to resolve these issues seems limited at present.

Recent papers based on extensive field research explore the determinants of new drug discovery. Cockburn and Henderson (1994) find the empirical relevance of R&D racing in pharmaceuticals to be limited, suggesting instead that firms specialize according to comparative advantage. Henderson and Cockburn (1996) suggest that economies of scale, scope, and industry spillovers operate within and across drug programs in the companies.

3. Appropriability of industrial R&D

Methods of intellectual property protection

Research on industrial R&D laboratories has shed light on the means of protection of firms' intellectual assets. The Yale Survey on Industrial R&D seems to have been the first to do so. Levin et al. (1987) find that patents are neither the only nor the most important means of intellectual property protection. Instead, being first to market and ranking highest in sales and service play a more important role in this regard. The finding is significant because it shows that the role of patents can be overstated by failure to consider less visible means of securing appropriability of R&D.

Cohen et al. (2000) revisit this subject using the Carnegie–Mellon Survey on Industrial R&D. In their findings, patents continue to be less emphasized by the majority of industries than advantages of lead time and secrecy. In large companies, though, patents seem to be a more important source of protection than in the Yale Survey, mainly for purposes of patent blocking and in negotiations that lead to cross-licensing. In addition, secrecy appears to have grown more important over time.

One question raised by both studies is the comparative effectiveness of the different methods of protecting intellectual property for the propensity to invent and the value of inventions. I am not aware of any studies that have probed this question on a large scale.

Evidence on the security of intellectual property

Research on R&D laboratories has contributed to what we know about security of intellectual property. At issue is the length of time over which firms' innovations are secure and the degree of that security. Mansfield et al. (1981) examine the relationship between imitation costs and patents. Their main finding is that imitation costs are large, about two-thirds of original innovation costs. Another result is that imitation costs increase if inventions are patented. This suggests a different mechanism by which patents protect intellectual property. The mechanism is even more important in view of Mansfield (1985), which finds that knowledge of a firm's development efforts are in the hands of competitors within 18 months. The evolution of imitation costs seems an interesting topic to explore further. This is especially true given the arrival of the Internet, which may have lowered imitation costs.

Teece (1977) and Arora (1996) expand the study of appropriability to international technology transfer. Under consideration is the North–South question of whether returns to innovation can be protected when innovative firms build manufacturing plants in developing countries. Teece (1977) shows that despite (or because of) the help of the innovator, costs of technology transfer are one-fifth of total project costs. Thus fixed costs of technology transfer are large. Arora (1996) seconds this point and offers an interpretation. His view is that innovators can and do design projects to overcome problems of appropriating the returns to innovation. They do so by deliberately packaging technology with training, quality control, and plant set-up services. This might explain why costs of technology transfer are high in Teece (1977): the costs reflect a deliberate strategy of bundling service with knowledge transfer. The same point can be made more generally and it is not limited to technology transfer between developed and developing countries.

4. The limits of the firm in R&D

In this section I discuss findings from R&D laboratory studies on research alliances and joint ventures, R&D sourcing, and public–private partnerships. Two general references on this subject are by Mowery (1992, 1995). Mowery (1992) discusses the rapid growth of international collaborative research ventures. He finds that international ventures are increasing because capabilities of overseas partners are increasing, because of a rise in non-tariff barriers that foreign partners can help overcome, because of increasing complexity of technologies, and because of rising costs of commercializing new products. The increasing complexity of technologies and the value of complementary capabilities are common motives for both domestic and foreign collaborative research. Mowery (1995) discusses the R&D limits of U.S. firms in history. For most of the 20th century antitrust policy discouraged horizontal mergers, encouraged product diversification, and encouraged R&D as a means of entry into new lines of business. Court decisions showed leniency towards patent licenses and encouraged firms to accumulate patent portfolios. Only since 1980 has increasing leniency of antitrust reversed conglomeration and reduced the demand for central R&D laboratories. In this way antitrust and patent policies have shaped the limits of the firm in R&D over the very long term.

Research alliances and joint ventures

Using case studies Von Hippel (1988) has documented the sources of innovation outside the firm, in the R&D of suppliers and customers and has uncovered general information sharing among suppliers, manufacturers, and customers, including competitors. The point is that R&D used in the firm commonly originates outside the firm. Findings of Cohen et al. (2002) confirm this view, again using the Carnegie–Mellon Survey on Industrial R&D. Their results are that customers suggest new R&D projects more often than the firm's manufacturing operations, and that suppliers and competitors also suggest new projects, even if less often than customers and the firm's operating divisions.

Using a sample of firms Link (1988) finds that merger and acquisition are ranked as more important in R&D-intensive industries. Indirectly this finding suggests that research alliances and joint ventures are at least in part motivated by the option to purchase. Link and Bauer (1989) suggest as well that co-operative R&D is defensively motivated by foreign competition.

Adams and Marcu (2004) study the relationship between objective indicators of R&D outsourcing and a subjective indicator of the importance of research joint ventures, which is found to be a key driver of outsourcing. This and other papers raise the question, so far unanswered, of the sequence of events involved in the different arrangements. Does the chain of arrangements run from informal sourcing to joint research, to the possibility of acquisition? The dynamics of the different arrangements are imperfectly understood, in part because current surveys are cross-sections rather than panels of the same R&D laboratories followed over time.

R&D sourcing

A number of papers have examined R&D sourcing, as opposed to joint research. Pisano (1990) explains the motivations for R&D sourcing using a sample of biotechnology projects. In addition he identifies the source of complementary capabilities in the industry: at this time pharmaceutical firms lack knowledge of the key process technology, biotechnology, while new biotechnology firms lack marketing and distribution divisions. Consistent with this, sourcing decreases when in-house biotechnology expertise and biotechnology focus increase. The paper offers a clue as to why sourcing might precede joint research and acquisition in rapidly changing industries: old-line firms purchase expertise and learning opportunities from newcomers, deciding only later whether to expand the research or bring the partner permanently within the firm. Another finding is that greater competition among R&D suppliers increases sourcing.

Azoulay (2003) examines R&D outsourcing of drug clinical trials. He emphasizes the buffering motive for outsourcing, in which contract research absorbs demand shocks rather than core R&D. Consistent with this motive he finds that outsourcing increases with the volatility of firm sales. However, larger firms respond less to demand shocks because they can buffer research groups through reassignment. These findings bring to mind the R&D portfolio analysis of Mansfield and Brandenburg (1966).

Adams and Marcu (2004) explore multiple indicators of R&D sourcing using a sample of 200 R&D laboratories in several industries. Their data include the percent of R&D budget insourced and outsourced and the percent of engineering hours on new products contributed by customers and suppliers. They find that percents of budget outsourced are small and respond to indicators of diversity of local suppliers and customers. This form of outsourcing appears transitory and occasional. In vivid contrast the engineering contributions of customers and suppliers are much larger, are not localized, and appear to be relatively permanent. Sourcing in its several forms is directly associated with the importance of research joint ventures and merger and acquisition, suggesting that sourcing could be a prelude to more formal R&D arrangements. However, more work is needed to verify this claim. Another finding is that sourcing has no bearing on new products by the laboratories, whereas joint ventures do. This implies that sourcing and joint ventures have differing functions, with joint ventures specialized in commercialization and sourcing specialized in cost-saving.

Public–private partnerships

Public–private partnerships are another boundary of the firm's R&D. An element of strategy enters into both sides of the partnership. To see this consider industry–university co-operative research centers as in Adams *et al.* (2001). Faculty members are interested in the centers because they provide opportunities to consult, engage in joint research, and place Ph.D. students. Firms are interested in gaining preferential access to students and university research.

Siegel *et al.* (2003) consider university science parks, another kind of highly focused public–private initiative. Their interest lies in the impact of the parks on research productivity of firms, holding constant firms' R&D expenditures. Their results (using British data) are as follows. Using new product counts and patents as measures of innovation they find that location in a science park increases research output and technical efficiency in producing this output. Siegel (2003) surveys the literature of public–private partnerships. He is specifically concerned with data collection by government agencies. The paper points out that the private and social returns to public–private relationships are largely unknown. It goes on to offer suggestions for the collection of data on output and performance including qualitative data of the type favored by respondents.

Adams *et al.* (2003) study the influence of federal laboratory R&D on industrial research. They find that Co-operative Research and Development Agreements, or CRADAs, are the primary channel by which federal laboratories increase patents and company-financed R&D. This result is consistent with the view that arrangements requiring mutual effort by firms and federal laboratories are the most likely to increase the R&D efforts of both parties. As before little is known about the private and social rates of return from CRADAs.

5. Spillovers of outside R&D

In this section I discuss some of what has been learned about spillovers of outside R&D based on field studies of R&D laboratories. By spillovers I mean the acquisition of useful information at a cost that is substantially less than the original cost of discovery. The topic has many dimensions, in terms of lag structure, the identity of the sending sector (industry, university, government; domestic or foreign), and the specific sciences or technologies that spill over to R&D laboratories. A sample of background papers are these: Adams (1990) uncovers long lags in the peak effect of spillovers to industry from academic research while Jaffe (1989) finds a localized effect of university research spending on industrial research spending. Griliches (1992) surveys the difficulties that are involved in measuring knowledge spillovers and provides back-of-the-envelope estimates of their contribution to growth in per capita income.

Mansfield (1991) considers the effect of recent academic research, from the past 15 years, on new products and processes introduced by industry. His sample consists of U.S. firms in several industries. His findings are that 11% of new products, and 9% of new processes, could not have been developed without substantial delay in the absence of recent academic research. Another 8% of new products and six of new processes are would have been considerably more expensive in the absence of recent scientific research. These percentages are highest in drugs, followed by instruments, metals, and information processing. Other findings are that roughly 5% of the value of new products, and another 2–3% of the value of new processes, could not have been developed at all, or else with very substantial increases in cost, without the assistance provided by recent academic research. One issue, though, is whether old or new scientific research plays the larger role in industry.

Mansfield (1995a) details the characteristics of universities and academic researchers that contribute to industrial innovation in a sample of firms. Findings are that location of researchers within the same state as the R&D laboratory significantly increases firm "citations" in several industries. Also important are research spending by a university. The effect of locality is greater for applied than for basic academic research.

Klevorick et al. (1995) use the Yale Survey on Industrial Research and Development to explore sources of interindustry differences in technological opportunities. The three sources are: advances in scientific understanding and technique, technological advances in other firms and other industries, and feedbacks from earlier research within the same industry. Beginning with science, as in other studies, only a few fields—chemistry, computer science, materials science, and metallurgy—are viewed as highly relevant in most industries. A few industries rate more selected fields of science highly. For example, drugs and medical products rank biology and medicine highly, but few other industries do. Thus, relatively few sectors show close proximity to basic science and the majority of influence appears to be filtered through engineering disciplines and computer science. Nearly all industries view other firms in the same industry as important sources of technological advance. Firm also rely on other industries, especially materials and equipment suppliers, for technological knowledge. There is also the suggestion that certain technological activities are repetitious ('natural trajectories')

within the industry and thus not subject to diminishing returns. In an indirect sense feedbacks could be implicated in the trajectories. The comparative importance of science, between firm, between industry, and within firm sources of technological opportunity remains an open question, though interindustry effects appear to be important.

Cohen et al. (2002) examine the influence of public research on industrial R&D. One finding is that public research findings are three to four times more likely to be used in industrial R&D projects than publicly derived prototypes. Instruments and techniques derived from the public sector are two to three times more likely to be used than prototypes. Results on scientific fields used in industry are similar to those of Klevorick et al. (1995). The majority of industries rely on fields such as materials science, computer science, chemistry, electrical engineering, and mechanical engineering. Only a few rely on basic disciplines such as biology, physics, and mathematics and statistics. Pharmaceuticals, which have been intensively studied by economists, are in this respect an outlier and are not at all representative.

Another finding is that the most common channels of influence from public research are papers and reports, meetings, informal interactions, and consulting. Licenses and formal co-operative research are in this respect strictly secondary. It is informal and unregulated interactions that are the chief avenues of knowledge spillovers. This to an extent argues that the strategic public–private interactions of recent years—industry–university co-operative research centers, patents and licenses, and science parks—are overrated as spillover sources. Another observation is that larger firms, aside from university-based startups in drugs and biotechnology, are the firms that are most likely to utilize scientific research. This finding is contrary to opinions on the absorptive advantages of small firms, but appears well-grounded.

In a pair of papers I have carried out geographic and institutional comparisons of the sources of knowledge spillovers to R&D laboratories. In Adams (2002) I find evidence that spillovers from universities are more localized than spillovers from the rest of industry. This is true in the sense that R&D laboratories target learning efforts on universities to a greater extent within 200 miles than their learning efforts about firms. It is true also in the sense that closely affiliated universities are closer than the average university to the laboratories. And finally it is true in the sense that closely affiliated universities are closer to the laboratories than are closely affiliated firms.[3] The results are consistent with the free flow of information under Open Science, and with the Land Grant movement, which favors local consulting and joint research by universities. Other findings are that localization of learning effort by laboratories is driven by local pools of R&D, outsourcing, consulting, and university Ph.D. placements.

In Adams (2003, forthcoming) I find that academic spillovers appear to selectively drive learning about universities, while industrial spillovers appear to selectively drive learning about industry. If these findings hold up under additional tests, then they suggest, plausibly enough, that the direction as well as rate of industrial research is driven by those sectors whose research is increasing the most. Put differently, if the above results are true, then overall research responds by more than the sum of its parts to research opportunities, since individual parts of the research respond to the rest of research.

6. Summary, discussion, and conclusion

In this paper I have discussed the literature of technical change by R&D laboratories. The subject touches on industrial R&D that lies deep within the firm. For this reason it must be approached through field work and survey research. Much of the analysis is inspired by Edwin Mansfield, who believed that survey research was essential to progress in understanding the sources of technological change. Starting from Mansfield's premise that R&D managers possess a store of knowledge that economists cannot replace, I hope to have demonstrated the value and relevance of this approach as well as the element of sheer surprise that the research delivers at its best.

A few examples may suffice to illustrate value, relevance, and surprise. Industrial R&D projects are neither risky, nor long-term, nor are they dogged by technical failure (Mansfield and Brandenburg, 1966). The ability of firms to predict the returns from product R&D is very limited, and the returns are underestimated or discounted (Mansfield and Beardsley, 1978). Knowledge of industrial R&D leaks out to competitors within 18 months or so (Mansfield, 1985), but a countervailing force is the high cost of imitation: two-thirds of original imitation cost (Mansfield et al. 1981). Industrial R&D projects in pharmaceuticals seem to have little to do with R&D races (Cockburn and Henderson, 1994), and projects in this industry benefit from economies of scale and scope and spillovers (Henderson and Cockburn, 1996). The main pay-off to industrial R&D from federal laboratories seems to derive from co-operative agreements, or CRADAs (Adams et al., 2003), an arrangement that has sometimes been derided as ineffective. The primary benefits to firms from university research do not come from patents or formal patent licensing. Instead they derive informally from academic publications and research instruments (Cohen et al., 2002).

Despite this seeming value-added, several difficulties have stood in the way of acceptance of field research on industrial R&D. First, the research is costly and the data sets small. The data are cross-sections that cannot be analyzed using the more powerful methods of panel data econometrics, which control for unobserved individual effects and are better able to address problems of endogeneity. Confidentiality restrictions entailed in the data collection limit access by other researchers, and expose the research to the charge of non-reproducibility. Because of the individual design of the surveys issues of comparability hinder attempts to generalize across studies.

Besides all the above—and for good reasons—research on R&D laboratories has typically not conformed to the standard paradigm of empirical work in economics. In that ideal short chains of reasoning are tested in tightly specified environments in which a few variables fit the data well and satisfy the predictions of the model in repeated applications (Sutton, 2000).[4] These conditions are almost met in "quasi-natural" experiments with convincingly exogenous variables. A good example is the dominance of Microsoft in PC operating systems and the subsequent expansion of its R&D laboratory, which proves in the singular that appropriability increases R&D (Stix, 2004). But R&D data in the plural that satisfy quasi-natural experiments are rare. One exception is a recent study of the effect of market size on the invention of new drugs, specified in terms of exogenous age-related demographics, that seems to meet these requirements (Acemoglu and Linn, 2004).

One solution to some of the difficulties listed in this conclusion is to initiate large-scale panel data collection of U.S. industrial R&D laboratories that can be linked to data on parent firms. Government has a comparative advantage in this activity for several reasons. Government is more capable of enforcing confidentiality of the data, and its horizon and resources exceed those of individual researchers. Furthermore, using as a model the Center for Economic Studies of the U.S. Census Bureau of years past, anyone swearing to observe confidentiality under penalty of law can in principle test empirical results by going to the sponsoring agency and working with the data. The situation in principle gets better if academics work jointly with statistical agencies on an ongoing basis to improve the data. This setting conduces to large cross-sections that form panels over time. Moreover, the data are more comparable and more representative than individually collected data, and conclusions drawn from them can be cross-checked. But the catch is the sustained commitment of time, imagination, and money by both universities and government that such data would require to be useful.

Acknowledgement

I am indebted to the National Science Foundation for support, under NSF Grant SBR-9502968, of my research on industrial R&D laboratories. Eleanora Voelkel, Meg Fernando, and Richard Anderson administered the *Survey of Industrial Laboratory Technologies 1996* that yielded the data. I am solely responsible for any opinions expressed in this paper.

Notes

1. By industrial R&D laboratory I mean any research group within the firm, and not necessarily a formal, separately dedicated research establishment. Thus the data are not restricted to central research laboratories.
2. The idea that field research is necessary for the study of industrial R&D is a major point of Mansfield's introduction to his collected works. See Mansfield (1995b), volume I. Also see Scherer (2005) in this issue for a discussion of the controversies that followed Mansfield's adoption of this approach.
3. The exceptions to this rule are top universities. Their influence, as one might expect, is not localized, because firms go further to work with researchers at the top of their professions.
4. Sutton (2000) discusses the option pricing and auction models as case studies that fit these requirements.

References

Acemoglu, D. and J. Linn, 2004, 'Market Size in Innovation: Theory and Evidence from the Pharmaceutical Industry,' *Quarterly Journal of Economics* **119** (August), 1049–1090.

Adams, J.D., 1990, 'Fundamental Stocks of Knowledge and Productivity Growth,' *Journal of Political Economy* **98**, (August), 673–702.

Adams, J.D., 2002, 'Comparative Localization of Academic and Industrial Spillovers,' *Journal of Economic Geography* **2** (July), 253–278.

Adams, J.D., 2005, 'Learning, Internal Research, and Spillovers: Evidence from a Sample of R&D Laboratories,' Working Paper, Rensselaer Polytechnic Institute, October Forthcoming in *Economics of Innovation and New Technology*.

Adams, J.D., E.P. Chiang, and J.L. Jensen, 2003, 'The Influence of Federal Laboratory R&D on Industrial Research,' *Review of Economics and Statistics* **85** (November), 1003–1020.

Adams, J.D., E.P. Chiang, and K. Starkey, 2001, 'Industry-University Co-operative Research Centers,' *Journal of Technology Transfer* **26**, (January) 73–86.

Adams, J.D. and M. Marcu, 2004, 'R&D Sourcing, Joint Ventures, and Innovation: A Multiple Indicators Approach,' Cambridge, Massachusetts, NBER Working Paper W10474, May 2004.

Arora, A., 1996, 'Contracting for Tacit Knowledge: the Provision of Technical Services in Technology Licensing Contracts,' *Journal of Development Economics* **50**, 233–256.

Azoulay, P., 2003, 'Acquiring Knowledge Within and Across Firm Boundaries: Evidence from Clinical Development,' Cambridge, Massachusetts, NBER Working Paper 10083, November 2003.

Bizan, O., 2003, 'The Determinants of Success of R&D Projects: Evidence from American-Israeli Research Alliances,' *Research Policy* **32**, 1619–1640.

Cockburn, I.M. and R.M. Henderson, 1994, 'Racing to Invest? The Dynamics of Competition in the Ethical Drugs Industry,' *Journal of Economics and Management Strategy* **3**, 481–519.

Cohen, W.M., R.R. Nelson, and J.P. Walsh, 2000, 'Protecting their Intellectual Assets: Appropriability Conditions and Why U.S. Manufacturing Firms Patent (Or Not),' National Bureau Of Economic Research. Cambridge, Massachusetts, Working Paper No. 7552.

Cohen, W.M., R.R. Nelson, and J.P. Walsh, 2002, 'Links and Impacts: The Influence of Public Research on Industrial R&D,' *Management Science* **48**, 1–23.

Dixit, A.K. and R.S. Pindyck, 1994, *Investment under Uncertainty*, Princeton, New Jersey: Princeton University Press.

Griliches, Z., 1992, 'The Search for R&D Spillovers,' *Scandinavian Journal of Economics* **94**, 29–47.

Henderson, R.M. and I.M. Cockburn, 1996, 'Scale, Scope, and Spillovers: The Determinants of Research Productivity in Drug Discovery,' *RAND Journal of Economics* **27**, (Spring) 32–59.

Jaffe, A.B., 1989, 'Real Effects of Academic Research,' *American Economic Review* **79**, (December) 957–970.

Klevorick, A.K., R.C. Levin, R.R. Nelson, and S.G. Winter, 1995, 'On the Sources and Significance of Inter-industry Differences in Technological Opportunities,' *Research Policy* **24**, 185–205.

Levin, R.C., A.K. Klevorick, R.R. Nelson, and S.G. Winter, 1987, 'Appropriating the Returns from Industrial Research and Development,' *Brookings Papers on Economic Activity* **1987** (3), 783–820.

Link, A.N., 1988, 'Mergers and Acquisitions as a Source of Innovation,' *Mergers & Acquisitions* **23**, (November–December) 36–39.

Link, A.N. and L. Bauer, 1989, *Co-operative Research in U.S. Manufacturing*, Lexington, Massachusetts: Lexington Books.

Mansfield, E., 1985, 'How Rapidly Does New Industrial Technology Leak Out?' *Journal of Industrial Economics* **34**, (December) 217–223.

Mansfield, E., 1991, 'Academic Research and Industrial Innovation,' *Research Policy* **20**, 1–12.

Mansfield, E., 1995a, 'Academic Research Underlying Industrial Innovations: Sources, Characteristics, and Financing,' *Review of Economics and Statistics* **77**, (February) 55–65.

Mansfield, E., 1995b, *Innovation, Technology, and the Economy, Volumes I and II: The Selected Essays Of Edwin Mansfield*, Aldershot, UK: Edward Elgar.

Mansfield, E. and G. Beardsley, 1978, 'A Note on the Accuracy of Industrial Forecasts of the Profitability of New Products and Processes,' *Journal of Business* **51**, 127–135.

Mansfield, E. and R. Brandenburg, 1966, 'The Allocation, Characteristics, and Outcome of the Firm's Research and Development Portfolio: A Case Study,' *Journal of Business* **39**, 447–464

Mansfield, E., J. Rapoport, A. Romeo, S. Wagner, and G. Beardsley, 1977, 'Social and Private Rates of Return from Industrial Innovations,' *Quarterly Journal of Economics* **91**, (May) 221–240.

Mansfield, E., M. Schwartz, and S. Wagner, 1981, 'Imitation Costs and Patents: An Empirical Study,' *Economic Journal* **91**, 907–918.

Mowery, D.C., 1992, 'International Collaborative Ventures and the Commercialization of New Technologies,' in *Technology and the Wealth of Nations*, N. Rosenberg, R. Landau, and D. Mowery, (eds.), Stanford, California: Stanford University Press.

Mowery, D.C., 1995, 'The Boundaries of the U.S. Firm in R&D,' in *Coordination and Information: Historical Perspectives on the Organization of Enterprise*, N. Lamoreaux and D. Raff, (eds.), Chicago: University of Chicago Press for NBER.

Pisano, G.P., 1990, 'The R&D Boundaries of the Firm: An Empirical Analysis,' *Administrative Science Quarterly* **35**, (March) 153–176.

Scherer, F.M., 2005, 'Edwin Mansfield: An Appreciation,' *Journal of Technology Transfer*, **30** (1–2), 3–9.

Siegel, D.S., 2003, 'Data Requirements for Assessing the Private and Social Returns to Strategic Research Partnerships: Analysis and Recommendations,' *Technology Analysis and Strategic Management* **15**, 207–225.

Siegel, D.S., P. Westhead, and M. Wright, 2003, 'Assessing the Impact of University Science Parks on Research Productivity: Exploratory Firm-Level Evidence from the United Kingdom,' *International Journal of Industrial Organization* **21**, 1357–1369.

Stix, G., 2004, 'A Confederacy of Smarts,' *Scientific American* **290**, (June) 40–45.

Sutton, J., *Marshall's Tendencies: What Can Economists Know?* Leuven, Belgium: Leuven University Press; and Cambridge, Massachusetts, USA: MIT Press.

Teece, D.J., 1977, 'Technology Transfer by Multi-National Firms: The Resource Cost of Transferring Technological Know-How,' *Economic Journal* **87**, (June) 242–261.

Von Hippel, E., 1988, *Sources of Innovation*, New York: Oxford University Press.

Public Policy and Environmental Research and Development

John T. Scott

ABSTRACT. The paper evaluates several potential public policies to increase research and development (R&D) investments with the goal of introducing innovations to reduce harmful industrial emissions. The policies—new pre-innovation taxes, more stringent emissions regulations, promotion of cooperative R&D, promotion of outside financing from other companies and from the public, diplomacy to encourage emissions regulations that are more uniformly stringent worldwide, promoting dynamic competition with appropriate antitrust policy, and promoting the dissemination of fundamental knowledge about emissions and of licensable emissions-reducing technology—are evaluated by using primary data from US industry to estimate a model of the environmental R&D investments of industry.

Key words: environmental research and development (R&D), emissions reduction, environmental regulation

JEL Classification: Q550, Q580, O300, O380, L100

1. Introduction

The purpose of this paper is to develop and discuss the policy implications of a decade-long project documenting the environmental research and development (R&D) investments by U.S. manufacturing industry. The details about that project are reported in Scott (2003); this paper uses the data described there with new specifications to provide evidence focused on the possibilities for public policy to reduce hazardous emissions by promoting environmental R&D.[1] The evidence motivates discussion of several potential public policies to increase environmental R&D, which is defined broadly to include any R&D investments with the goal of introducing innovations to reduce emissions. The policies discussed are (1) new pre-innovation taxes, (2) more stringent emissions regulations, (3) promotion of cooperative R&D, (4) promotion of outside financing from other companies and from the public, (5) diplomacy to encourage emissions regulations that are more uniformly stringent worldwide, (6) promoting dynamic competition with appropriate antitrust policy, and (7) promoting the dissemination of fundamental knowledge about emissions and of licensable emissions-reducing technology. As the paper will explain, the first of these policies—the legislation of pre-innovation taxes—is quite controversial, indeed in the present environment it is an impractical policy. Nonetheless, discussing the idea of pre-innovation taxes serves to point up the limits of policy. The other policies are far less controversial; hence they are far more practical in the cases where evidence suggests the policies would be useful.

Developing public policies to stimulate environmental R&D is important. A priori, environmental R&D should, over time, reduce hazardous industrial emissions. The hypothesis that environmental R&D will reduce industrial emissions is supported by available data. For the 15 broad Standard Industrial Classification (SIC) manufacturing industries for which data are available, the simple regression of *RDCTN8899*—the percentage reduction in emissions from 1988 to 1999—as a function of *ENVRD/SALES*—an estimate of the ratio of environmental R&D to sales during the 1990s for the companies in the industry—has been estimated in alternative ways in Scott (2003, forthcoming).[2] The estimated effect of environmental R&D intensity on the percentage reduction in emissions is fairly substantial.[3] The elasticity for the effect (the percentage change in *RDCTN8899* per unit percentage change in *ENVRD/SALES*) at the sample means is 0.41.[4]

Section 2 discusses the theory behind the model of environmental R&D. The model is then esti-

---

Department of Economics
Dartmouth College
Hanover, NH 03755
USA
E-mail: john.t.scott@dartmouth.edu

mated in Section 3. The various public policies to stimulate environmental R&D are discussed in Section 4, and then the estimates from Section 3 are used to illustrate the potential effects of the policies.

2. Theoretical rationale for the estimable model

Investment in risky environmental R&D results in innovations—new processes or products with better environmental performance as indexed by the random variable x.[5] The probability distribution for the measure of environmental performance x is given by the probability density $f(x; \alpha)$, where greater values of the distribution's parameter α shift the probability distribution rightward over higher levels of environmental performance. The gamma distribution has the desired properties, and it is used for the probability density $f(x; \alpha)$.[6]

The parameter α is determined by the amount of environmental R&D investment R and an additional set of explanatory variables $\mathbf{X}$. Thus, $\alpha = \alpha(\mathbf{X}, R)$. Greater R&D investment, R, is associated with a greater α. Hence, if a company increases its environmental R&D, its distribution over environmental performance outcomes is shifted rightward over higher values of the index of environmental performance x. A measure of the environmental problems created by the company's operations would be among the distribution-shifting variables in the vector $\mathbf{X}$. Greater environmental problems would shift the distribution over environmental performance leftward over lower values of the performance index. One measure of those environmental problems is NTAPC, the number of toxic air pollutants associated with the company's operations. The more chemical emissions associated with its operations, the poorer the outcome regarding its environmental performance, other things being the same. For our estimable model using the gamma distribution, α is approximated by

$$\alpha = \alpha(\mathbf{X}, R) = A X_1^{\beta_1} X_2^{\beta_2} \cdots X_n^{\beta_n} e^{\varphi_1 D_1} \cdots e^{\varphi_w D_w} R^{\beta_R} \quad (1)$$

with the terms $X_i^{\beta_i}$ for the n positive and continuous variables, and with $e^{\varphi_i D_i}$ for each term where the explanatory variable is a qualitative (0–1 dummy) variable or where theory implies that a continuous variable should be entered in such an exponential form.

A company's market value is assumed to increase at a decreasing rate with the environmental performance x of the company's innovations. The company's market value is given by $V(x; \gamma)$, where V given x increases with the parameter γ. The value of environmental performance is modeled as

$$V(x) = \gamma - \gamma e^{-x/\theta}, \quad (2)$$

where θ is a scaling parameter.

The value parameter γ is a function of a set of explanatory variables $\mathbf{Z}$. Thus, $\gamma = \gamma(\mathbf{Z})$.

$$\gamma = \gamma(\mathbf{Z}) = a Z_1^{b_1} Z_2^{b_2} \cdots Z_m^{b_m} e^{\theta_1 S_1} \cdots e^{\theta_v S_v} \quad (3)$$

with the term $Z_i^{b_i}$ for each positive and continuous explanatory variable and with a term $e^{\theta_i S_i}$ if the explanatory variable is a qualitative (0–1 dummy) variable or, again, if theory dictates that exponential expression for a continuous variable. The value-shifting variables in the vector $\mathbf{Z}$ include, for example, the company's sales, SALES. We expect that larger firms will gain more value from an innovation.[7]

The expected value of investment in environmental R&D is

$$E = \int V(x; \gamma) f(x; \alpha) \, dx. \quad (4)$$

The company chooses its investment R to maximize the expected net value of the investment, $E - R$. Thus, the company invests until the marginal expected benefit of the last dollar invested is a dollar (that is, the company invests R such that $\partial E/\partial R = 1$). That condition for maximizing the expected net value of investment implies

$$R = g(X, Z). \quad (5)$$

With the function f being the probability density for the gamma distribution, and the function for V specified in equation (2), solving the model for a company's optimal investment in environmental R&D—that is, solving for equation (5)—in terms of the natural logarithms of the variables, we have the value of ln(R) as a function of the explanatory variables:

$$\ln R = \delta + \sum_{i=1}^{n} \omega_i \ln X_i + \sum_{i=1}^{w} \kappa_i D_i + \sum_{i=1}^{m} \tau_i \ln Z_i + \sum_{i=1}^{v} \eta_i S_i \quad (6)$$

where δ is the parameter for the intercept, ω_i is the coefficient on the natural logarithm of the ith continuous explanatory variable in the vector of probability-shifting variables **X**, and where τ_i is the coefficient on the natural logarithm of the ith continuous explanatory variable in the vector of value-shifting variables **Z**, and where κ_i and η_i denote the coefficients for the qualitative explanatory variables (or continuous variables entered in the exponential form as used for the dummy variables) for the **X** and **Z** vectors respectively.[8] The effects of the explanatory variables are shown (Scott, 2003, pp. 57–66) to be as follows.

The effect on R&D investment of increasing a value-shifting variable in **Z** (that determines γ) will be positive if increasing the variable increases value, and the effect will be negative if value falls as the variable increases. For example, we expect that firms with larger sales will derive greater benefits from an innovation, so we expect investment in R&D will increase with sales.

The effect on R&D investment of increasing a probability-shifting variable in **X** (that determines α) will be positive if increasing the variable lowers α; the effect will be negative if a greater value for the variable increases α, shifting the probability distribution rightward over better environmental performance. For example, we expect that a larger emissions problem as indicated by *NTAPC* will make the R&D research problem more challenging and result in a lower value for α, other things being the same. A lower value for α will increase the marginal benefit of doing more R&D to shift the probability distribution rightward over better environmental performance outcomes. Hence, a probability-shifting variable X_i that has a negative effect on α will have a positive effect on the investment in R&D. Analogously, a variable that has a positive effect on α will have a negative effect on R (and its logarithm) A variable can be in both **X** and **Z**, with its overall effect on R&D investment depending on the relative importance of its probability-shifting and its value-shifting roles.[9]

If the value-shifting and probability-shifting variables are sufficiently important, then the firm will do environmental R&D. In terms of an econometric model, then, the Tobit model introduced in the next section is appropriate—with the Tobit model, if the Tobit index is large enough, then we will observe positive environmental R&D investment. We turn now in Section 3 to the discussion and specification of the Tobit model.

3. The Tobit model of product R&D with selection into the sample

The Tobit models for environmental R&D are estimated using survey data. Two surveys of industry—one in 1993 and the other in 2001—were used.[10] The 1993 survey was sent to the *Business Week* R&D Scoreboard companies in the U.S. at that time, and the response provided the estimates of 1992 environmental R&D that are used in this paper. The 2001 follow-up survey was sent to a representative group of the respondents to the first survey, and the response suggested that relative to the total of R&D performed by industry, environmental R&D investments had not changed much on average across the respondents. For the 1993 survey, companies that were subsidiaries of others in the R&D Scoreboard were dropped from the sample, as were those for which a satisfactory list of four-digit Standard Industrial Classification (SIC) industries could not be developed. Of the original *Business Week* sample of 891 companies, 846 companies were surveyed in 1993 about their industrial R&D response to toxic air emissions and, to an extent, to environmental problems more generally. Of those 846 companies, 722 had a manufacturing industry as the primary four-digit SIC industry. Of the 150 responding firms, 132 firms had manufacturing lines of business. Of those 132 firms, 126 had a manufacturing industry for the primary four-digit SIC industry; six firms had significant manufacturing operations but had a nonmanufacturing industry as the primary four-digit industry.

The sample for this paper consists of the 722 manufacturing firms (that is, firms having primary four-digit SIC industry in manufacturing) among the 846 firms surveyed, plus another six nonmanufacturing firms (that is, firms having primary four-digit SIC industry in nonmanufacturing) with significant manufacturing operations.[11] From the sample of 728 firms, there is a responding sample of 132 firms—126 of the manufacturing firms and the six nonmanufacturing respondents with significant manufacturing operations. For purposes of defining their manufacturing operations for this paper, each of the six nonmanufacturing firms is assigned to the manufacturing industry where its primary manufacturing activity occurs.

Of the 132 responding firms, 71 reported environmental R&D with the goal of reducing toxic air emissions. All but three of the 71 had R&D focused on chemicals targeted by Title III of the Clean Air Act Amendments of 1990 as chemicals of concern for which new regulations should be developed.[12] The remaining 61 companies reported that they did not do any air-emissions related R&D. The data used in this paper come from the survey information along with information from the *Business Week* R&D Scoreboard, the U.S. Environmental Protection Agency, the U.S. Census, and several other sources of information about industrial companies and their industries.[13]

Scott (2003) provides simple two-step estimators of the Tobit models for environmental R&D with control for selection into the sample. Models for background research about emissions, about process R&D, and about product R&D are presented. The essential results using the simple two-step estimators remain when the models are reestimated using full information maximum likelihood (FIML) estimators that jointly estimate the parameters of the probit model of selection into the sample of respondents and the parameters of the Tobit models of R&D, including the correlation of the errors in the models.[14]

The estimated models in the present paper differ from those in the foregoing work in two ways. First, the earlier work presents the simple two-step estimations and compares them with analogous FIML estimations, while only FIML estimations are presented here. Second, the functional forms used in this paper are simpler than those in the earlier work. The earlier work uses quadratic terms to explore nonlinearities in the relations between the explanatory variables and the investments in environmental R&D. For some variables and for some types of R&D, the approach reveals nonlinearities that are present for both the two-step estimator and the FIML estimator. However, for the product R&D that is used in this paper to develop and discuss possibilities for public policy, those quadratic nonlinearities revealed are with one exception downturns in positive relations, and the downturns are associated with values of the explanatory variables that are extreme values—very much greater than the sample means. In this paper, a simpler functional form is used to capture the relationships between the explanatory variables and product R&D at settings for the explanatory variables that are not extreme values.

For the simpler functional form here, the essential results are the same—indeed, they are the same in the ranges of the variables that do not include extreme values. They have the benefit of providing a test of the robustness of the earlier findings using the more complicated functional forms. Checking that robustness is even more important because of the complexity of the two-step models and because of the difficulties obtaining convergence for estimations of complicated FIML models. On the one hand the FIML models are the most conservative way to look at the data. Yet on the other hand they are very difficult to estimate because achieving convergence for the jointly estimated parameters of the probit model, the Tobit model of R&D, and the correlation of the models' errors requires simplicity in the models estimated.[15] A simple functional form that allows for essential nonlinearities in the relations is a specification using natural logarithms—except for the one explanatory variable where the variable's effect is U-shaped (a negative sign for the coefficient on the variable, but a positive sign for the coefficient on its square) and except for qualitative (dummy, or zero-one) variables. Using such a specification with the Tobit model requires some care in stating the details of the estimable model; thus, those details are stated here now.

An appropriate procedure for analyzing the determinants of the presence of company R&D aimed at Title III chemicals is Tobit analysis (Greene, 2003a, pp. 764–766; Maddala, 1983, Chapter 6). The Tobit model makes the following assumptions for the jth observation—here the observations are companies. The model assumes that for the dependent variable y_j and the fixed $1 \times k$ vector x_j of explanatory variables, and an index function $y_j^* = x_j\beta + \varepsilon_j$, then $y_j = y^*$ if y^* exceeds 0, while $y_j = 0$ if $y_j^* \leq 0$. β is a $k \times 1$ vector of unknown parameters, while ε_j are independently and normally distributed errors with expected value of zero and homoskedastic variance σ^2.

For the present problem, y_j is either zero or, when positive, it is the observation of $\ln(PRD3RDT)$ the natural logarithm of Title III product R&D for the jth of the 132 responding companies with manufacturing operations. Thus, the index y_j* ranges from $-\infty$ to $+\infty$. If the index exceeds zero, then the jth company has positive Title III product R&D, and $y_j* = y_j = \ln(PRD3RDT)$. To accommodate this model, note that the R&D expenditure has been scaled in thousands, rather than for example millions, so that all nonzero R&D values are greater than one—that is, $PRD3RDT > 1$. Thus, all values of PRD3RDT can be captured by $y_j* > 0$ with $y_j = y_j* = \ln(PRD3RDT_j)$ in those cases where there is positive Title III product R&D. We have therefore a model of the natural logarithm of Title III product R&D when the measure of that R&D always either exceeds 1.0 or is instead equal to zero; and hence, the natural logarithm for the positive amounts of R&D (with the measure of R&D always exceeding 1.0) varies continuously in the open interval $(0, \infty)$. Thus, *PRD3RDT* is measured in thousands of 1992 dollars and is zero for 95 of the 132 observations. For the remaining 37 observations for which *PRD3RDT* exceeds zero, the mean is $12,395 thousands and the range is from $4 thousands to $367,500 thousands. The Tobit model estimates β and σ^2 using the 132 observations on *PRD3RDT* (95 at zero and 37 at positive values for $\ln(PRD3RDT)$ as shown in Table I) and the explanatory variables.

Dividing each term of the model through by σ to give normalized coefficients, one can compute the standard normal index value for an observation, and the value of the cumulative normal distribution for that index value corresponds to the probability of observing Title III process R&D for the company. The non-normalized Tobit coefficients themselves are predicting the value of *PRD3RDT* (that prediction for the observed *PRD3RDT* is zero when the regression model yields a non-positive value for the dependent variable and is $\ln(PRD3RDT)$ otherwise).

Using the Tobit model, we can combine the information about the coefficients and about the probability of doing Title III R&D and estimate the expected value of *PRD3RDT* given any specified values for the explanatory variables x_j. Following the derivation in Maddala (1983, pp. 158–159), with ϕ_j denoting the density function of the standard normal distribution evaluated at $z_j = x_j\beta/\sigma$, and Φ_j denoting the cumulative distribution function also evaluated at $z_j = x_j\beta/\sigma$, we have for the expected value of $\ln(PRD3RDT)$ given that R&D is done:

$$E(\ln(PRD3RDT_j)|y_j* > 0) = x_j\beta + E(\varepsilon_j|\varepsilon_j > -x_j\beta)$$
$$= x_j\beta + \sigma(\phi_j/\Phi_j)$$
(7)

TABLE I
Descriptive Statistics for *PRD3RDT*, Title III Product R&D in Thousands of 1992 Dollars[a]

Variable	Mean	Standard deviation	Minimum	Maximum	Number of observations
PRD3RDT	12,395.29	60,312.76	4.00	367,500.00	37
ln PRD3RDT	6.1473	2.4838	1.3863	12.8145	37

Note: [a]Note that the distribution of *PRD3RDT* is quite skewed. The average of the natural logarithms corresponds to a much smaller amount of Title III product R&D than the average value for *PRD3RDT*. The logarithms for the minimum and maximum values of course do correspond to the minimum and maximum values for *PRD3RDT*. There are 95 of the 132 responding companies that report they do not do Title III product R&D; the mean for *PRD3RDT* in the 132 observation sample is 3,474.44.

Stated differently, it is, for a given set of explanatory variables, the expected value of the index function y^* given that y^* is greater than zero. Or, equivalently, it is, for those values of the explanatory variables, the expected value of y given that y^* exceeds zero. Thus, it is the mean of the positive ys. The expected amount of Title III product R&D for a company randomly drawn from the population—and therefore that may or may not do R&D—is zero with probability $1 - \Phi_i$. There is probability Φ_i of a positive value for $PRD3RDT$; hence; with that probability the company does Title III product R&D, and the natural logarithm for that R&D has an expected value equal to $x_j\beta + \sigma(\phi_j/\Phi_j)$. Then our estimate of the expected amount of Title III product R&D for a company drawn from the population is

$$E(PRD3RDT_j) = (1 - \Phi_j)0 \\ + (\Phi_j)\exp(x_j\beta + \sigma(\phi_j/\Phi_j)), \quad (8)$$

where $\exp(p)$ denotes the base to the natural logarithms e raised to the power p.

Given that the 132 companies used in the Tobit models are selected from the original sample of 728 companies with manufacturing operations that were surveyed, we estimate the Tobit models with control for selection into the sample. To get estimates of the parameters of the Tobit model, I shall use Greene's full information maximum likelihood (FIML) estimator for the Tobit model with sample selection (Greene, 2002a, pp. E21-68–E21-74; Greene, 2003b). As Greene (2002a, pp. E21-68) explains, with the maximum likelihood estimator jointly estimating the probit model and the Tobit model (unlike the procedure used for Heckman's two-step estimators), the variable to correct for selection—the hazard rate—is not added to the model. Rather, the maximum likelihood estimator jointly estimates the parameters of the coefficients for the explanatory variables in the Tobit model, the coefficients for the explanatory variables in the probit model of response, the standard deviation ($SIGMA$) of the error in the Tobit model, and the correlation (RHO) between the standard normal error in the probit model and the normal error in the Tobit model.

For the probit model of response, DR is a dummy variable that equals one if the company responded to the survey, and it equals zero otherwise. Table II provides descriptive statistics for the explanatory variables used in the probit model of response and in the Tobit model of Title III product R&D, $PRD3RDT$. Full details about the variables, their sources, and their construction are available in Scott (2003). Here is a brief overview of the variables' definitions.

The probit model uses a measure of a company's environmental problems—measured by $NTAP$—in its primary four-digit manufacturing industry and a measure of medical concerns—measured by $MED2PR$—with those problems. $NTAP$ is the number of Title III toxic air pollutants associated with a four-digit SIC manufacturing industry. $MED2$ is a measure of the number of medical journal articles studying a chemical.[16] $MED2PR$ is the average of $MED2$ for all of the Title III chemicals associated with a company's primary four-digit industry.

The Tobit model uses the following variables.

$NTAPC$ measures the extent of a company's Title III emissions problems. It is the average value of $NTAP$, the number of Title III toxic air pollutants associated with a manufacturing industry, across the four-digit manufacturing SIC industries in which the company operates.

$SALES$ is the measure of a company's size in 1992. For each company, $SALES$ is measured as sales in millions of dollars, for the company's most recent fiscal year as of May 18, 1993.

$IMPSC$ measures average import competition faced by the company in its industries. The measure of import competition is $IMPS$, the ratio of imports to shipments for each four-digit manufacturing industry. Then, for each company $IMPSC$ is the average value of $IMPS$ across the four-digit manufacturing industries in which a company operates.

$PRODOTHER$ is a dummy variable that takes the value one if a company's product R&D to reduce emissions received additional financing from other companies or from the government; otherwise, it equals zero.

$COOP$ is a dummy variable that takes the value one if the company reported that it had at least some Title III environmental R&D that was performed in a cooperative venture with other firms.

TABLE II
Explanatory Variables for the Probit Model of Response and the Tobit Model of Title III Product R&D[a]

Variable	Mean	Standard deviation	Number of observations
Probit model			
NTAP	33.95	27.91	728
MED2PR	174.0	51.08	728
Tobit model			
ln(NTAPC)	3.229	0.6596	132
NTAPC	30.80	19.47	132
ln(SALES)	6.375	1.611	132
SALES	2721.09	7721.90	132
ln(IMPSC)	−1.913	0.9178	132
IMPSC	0.2268	0.2963	132
PRODOTHER	0.02273	0.1496	132
COOP	0.09848	0.2991	132
CR4C	36.05	11.27	132
DBACKROUND	0.3182	0.4675	132
DPROCESS	0.4394	0.4982	132
Tobit model's noncensored observations (PRD3RDT > 0)			
ln(NTAPC)	3.492	0.6673	37
NTAPC	39.92	23.90	37
ln(SALES)	7.190	1.803	37
SALES	6096.21	12971.89	37
ln(IMPSC)	−2.207	0.6899	37
IMPSC	0.1342	0.08355	37
PRODOTHER	0.08108	0.2767	37
COOP	0.2703	0.4502	37
CR4C	33.52	10.69	37
DBACKROUND	0.5946	0.4977	37
DPROCESS	0.7568	0.4350	37

[a] Note that the average of the natural logarithms for a variable does not correspond to the average value for the variable.

CRC4C measures average seller concentration for a company's industries. The concentration ratio of the value of industry shipments is *CR4*, the four-firm seller concentration ratio as a percentage for each four-digit manufacturing SIC industry. Then, for each company *CR4C* is the average value of *CR4* across the four-digit manufacturing industries in which a company operates.

DBACKGROUND is a dummy variable that equals one if a respondent reported background research on emissions; otherwise it equals zero.

DPROCESS is a dummy variable that equals one if a respondent reported process R&D to reduce emissions; otherwise it equals zero.

The industry dummy variables are for the two-digit manufacturing Standard Industrial Classification (SIC) industries. For the purpose of defining these two-digit industry dummy variables, each company is assigned to the two-digit industry in which its primary four-digit manufacturing industry is located. Thus, for example, the dummy variable *D38* takes the value of one for those observations of companies where the company has its primary four-digit manufacturing industry in two-digit SIC industry 38; otherwise it takes the value of zero. There are twenty of these industry dummy variables, and they are each defined in Table III and in the footnote to that table.

Table III shows four specifications for the jointly estimated probit model for response and Tobit model for environmental R&D. With the small sample size and also given the exploratory nature of the models (although the theory identifies the signs for the probability-shifting **X** variables and the value-shifting **Z** variables, it does not conclusively determine the variables), multiple specifications are provided. Specification (2) is a very parsimonious specification in terms of the explanatory variables, but it includes the dummy variables for broad industry effects.[17] However, for the FIML joint estimation of the response and Tobit models, none of the industry dummies in the Tobit model are significant in the presence of the other variables in the model. The qualitative results for the explanatory variables remain when the industry effects are dropped in specification (1). Specification (3) provides a more inclusive specification, adding seller concentration and its square and adding the dummy variables to indicate whether or not the company does the other types of Title III R&D. The nonlinearity in the effect on environmental R&D of the seller concentration variable is U-shaped, with the partial derivative of seller concentration being negative over the initial range of concentration and then becoming positive as seller concentration increases. To capture that nonlinear effect, seller concentration and its square are entered in the specification.[18] Finally, specification (4) adds the industry effects to the inclusive specification for the explanatory variables. Again, the industry effects are not significant, and the model has grown so large that while qualitative relations for the explanatory variables remain, the effects of the individual explanatory variables are more difficult to identify given the joint FIML estimation of the models for response and for R&D.

The probit model shows that apart from industry effects, the probability of response falls as a company's environmental problems—measured by *NTAP*—in its primary four-digit manufacturing industry increase and as medical concerns—measured by *MED2PR*—with those problems increase.

TABLE III
Full Information Maximum Likelihood Estimation of the Tobit Model with Selection for *PRD3RDT*[a]

	Coefficient (standard error)[c]			
Variable	(1)	(2)	(3)	(4)
Estimates for the selection (probit) equation for DR				
Constant	0.0935 (0.375)	0.109 (0.381)	0.0161 (0.371)	0.119 (0.387)
NTAP	−0.00538 (0.00249)****	−0.00506 (0.00258)****	−0.00546 (0.00243)****	−0.00482 (0.00259)***
MED2PR	−0.00201 (0.00114)***	−0.00216 (0.00116)***	−0.00178 (0.00112)**	−0.00221 (0.00117)***
D22 Textiles	−0.683 (0.550)	−0.641 (0.738)	−0.604 (0.534)	−0.643 (0.740)
D24 Lumber	0.532 (0.684)	0.532 (0.699)	0.637 (0.677)	0.526 (0.740)
D25 Furniture	0.0211 (0.591)	0.0537 (0.591)	0.0989 (0.577)	0.0494 (0.600)
D26 Paper	−0.259 (0.367)	−0.289 (0.389)	−0.217 (0.365)	−0.294 (0.398)
D28 Chemicals	−0.252 (0.328)	−0.268 (0.347)	−0.183 (0.325)	−0.285 (0.356)
D29 Petroleum	0.275 (0.496)	0.321 (0.505)	0.256 (0.499)	0.311 (0.510)
D30 Rubber & Plastics	−0.629 (0.352)***	−0.621 (0.364)***	−0.542 (0.351)**	−0.637 (0.374)***
D33 Primary Metals	0.222 (0.409)	0.234 (0.421)	0.253 (0.409)	0.228 (0.428)
D34 Fabricated Metals	−0.260 (0.315)	−0.250 (0.328)	−0.228 (0.316)	−0.256 (0.341)
D35 Industrial Machinery	−0.817 (0.273)*****	−0.801 (0.279)*****	−0.782 (0.273)*****	−0.807 (0.284)*****
D36 Electronics	−0.536 (0.280)***	−0.563 (0.289)****	−0.501 (0.279)***	−0.571 (0.295)****
D37 Transportation	−0.416 (0.311)*	−0.426 (0.326)*	−0.363 (0.311)	−0.435 (0.332)*
D38 Instruments	−0.539 (0.287)***	−0.510 (0.296)***	−0.510 (0.287)***	−0.517 (0.304)***
D39 Misc. Manufacturing	−0.674 (0.383)***	−0.684 (0.392)***	−0.615 (0.379)**	−0.697 (0.397)***
Estimates for the Tobit model for ln(PRD3RDT) corrected for selection				
Constant	−30.5 (13.2)****	−28.4 (15.4)***	−22.8 (12.8)***	−20.5 (14.4)*
ln(NTAPC)	2.34 (1.36)***	2.61 (2.05)*	1.80 (1.18)**	2.34 (1.91)[d]
ln(SALES)	1.47 (0.554)*****	1.52 (0.685)****	1.67 (0.646)*****	1.72 (0.793)****
ln(IMPSC)	−2.49 (1.31)***	−2.13 (1.53)*	−3.04 (1.29)****	−2.82 (1.62)***
PRODOTHER	10.0 (12.0)	10.3 (5.62)***	9.83 (6.10)**	9.19 (6.30)**
COOP	6.08 (3.17)***	5.89 (3.68)**	3.03 (2.71)[d]	2.88 (3.07)
CR4C	−	−	−0.533 (0.346)**	−0.537 (0.416)*
CR4C²	−	−	0.00506 (0.00430)[d]	0.00536 (0.00517)[d]
DBACKGROUND	−	−	2.85 (1.96)**	2.84 (2.54)[d]
DPROCESS	−	−	2.88 (1.86)**	2.95 (2.09)*

TABLE III
Continued

Variable	Coefficient (standard error)[c]			
	(1)	(2)	(3)	(4)
Industry Effects	No	Yes[b]	No	Yes[b]
SIGMA	6.47 (2.27)*****	5.81 (2.00)*****	6.45 (2.57)*****	5.30 (1.44)*****
RHO	0.478 (0.573)	0.207 (0.990)	0.627 (0.502)[d]	0.0650 (1.09)
Log likelihood	−481.45	−478.79	−473.61	−471.53
Number of observations	712	712	712	712

[a]The dependent variable for the Tobit model is ln(PRD3RDT) for the 37 nonzero observations of Title III R&D and is zero for the remaining 95 observations of companies responding to the survey. DR is a dummy variable that equals one if the firm was one of the 132 firms of the 728 that responded by answering the survey questionnaire. The model is for the 728 companies with significant manufacturing operations—722 companies with primary four-digit industry in manufacturing and an additional six with significant manufacturing operations but with primary four-digit industry in nonmanufacturing. Each of the six companies with primary four-digit industry in nonmanufacturing was classified to the broad manufacturing industry of its primary manufacturing activity. D20 is for the food industry, and those observations are in the intercept of the probit model. D21 for tobacco predicts failure perfectly, and the three observations where the sampled company had SIC 21 as its primary industry are therefore not used. The appropriate coefficient for the dummy would be negative infinity as far as the data reveal, and the probability of response from a company with its primary industry being tobacco is zero. Also predicting failure perfectly are D23 for apparel (one observation not used), D27 for printing (three observations not used), D31 for leather (two observations not used), and D32 for Stone, Clay and Glass (seven observations not used). Thus, there are 712 observations used in the probit model for selection rather than 728. The estimation of the Tobit model with sample selection uses Greene's full information maximum likelihood (FIML) estimator (Greene, 2002a, pp. E21-68—E21-74; Greene, 2003b). The maximum likelihood estimator jointly estimates the parameters of the coefficients for the explanatory variables in the Tobit model, the coefficients for the explanatory variables in the probit model of response, the standard deviation (SIGMA) of the error in the Tobit model, and the correlation (RHO) between the standard normal error in the probit model and the normal error in the Tobit model.
[b]None of the industry effects are significant in the Tobit model when estimated jointly with the probit response model.
[c]Significance levels for two-tailed tests: * $p \leq 0.20$; ** $p \leq 0.15$; *** $p \leq 0.10$; **** $p \leq 0.05$; ***** $p \leq 0.01$.
[d]This note is to indicate the p value for the ratio of the coefficient to the standard error for estimated parameters (other than the coefficients for the industry dummy variables) where the ratio is greater than one yet not great enough for a two-tailed p value ≤ 0.20. For the coefficient of $CR4C^2$ in specification (3), the p value is 0.240. For COOP in specification (3), the p value is 0.263. For RHO in specification (3), the p value is 0.212. For specification (4), we have ln(NTAPC), $p = 0.220$; $CR4C^2$, $p = 0.300$; DBACKGROUND, $p = 0.264$.

The Tobit model estimated here focuses on the parsimonious logarithmic specification to focus on the key variables that may inform public policy and to ensure convergence of the FIML estimator of the probit and Tobit models together. Some of the more complicated models that are estimated in Scott (2003) with the simpler two-step estimator of the Tobit model with selection do not converge when estimated with the FIML estimator. The more complicated models allow description of more complicated nonlinearities in the models; here, using the simpler logarithmic specification, the results for the logarithmic variables should be interpreted as holding within a standard deviation or so of the sample means for the logarithmic variables. For example, the Tobit model here should be interpreted as showing that except for extremely large values of NTAPC, Title III R&D is expected to increase as a company's pollution problems increase. Fitting a more elaborate functional form shows, however, that over very high levels of the numbers of pollutants associated with a firm's operations, the amount of R&D may begin to decrease somewhat as the pollutants increase.[19] In any case, the estimates for the simple logarithmic specification here show that environmental product R&D to address Title III pollutants increases with their importance in a company's operations. That effect for NTAPC is consistent with both R&D value-increasing effects when pollution problems are more severe and with probability distribution-shifting effects because with a bigger pollution problem to be solved, the R&D problem is more difficult.

Larger companies do more Title III product R&D. The result is consistent with greater sales having the R&D value-increasing effect described earlier. The environmental product R&D increases with company size.

The Tobit model for *PRD3RDT* shows a negative effect for import competition—measured by IMPSC—on Title III process R&D. Large U.S. corporations may be expressing their discomfort with such import competition when they voice concerns—in the context of environmental regulation—about the competitive pressures from imports. Such pressures are especially worrisome to the companies when U.S. regulations are expected to require emissions standards that the foreign competitors do not anticipate facing. The model shows that greater import competition is associated with less emissions-reducing R&D investment, *ceteris paribus*. To the extent that it is unprofitable to compete with the foreign firms and invest in R&D for improved environmental performance, the results lend support to industry's position. Jaffe *et al.* (1995) conclude that the competitiveness of firms does not appear to have suffered greatly because of environmental regulation. The result here suggests that there may well be a cost associated with maintaining that competitiveness. Namely, it appears that firms facing import competition have cut their environmental R&D.

Although the fact is clear, the reason for the reduction in environmental R&D in the face of import competition is not certain, but the model offers some potential reasons. In the context of the theoretical model, import competition would lower the value of good R&D performance because in the presence of import competition expenditures for emissions-reducing product innovations might not be recouped with sufficiently high post-innovation prices in international markets where emissions performance is not valued uniformly across nations. Further, environmental R&D is not mandated by law; it is forward-looking, with product improvements in the future and uncertain. In the present and near-term, companies doing environmental R&D would have to set product prices that meet the prices of foreign competitors who may not incur such R&D expenditures. Greater import competition reduces the pre-innovation margins of domestic firms, leaving fewer internally generated funds for the R&D investments with uncertain payouts.

The positive coefficients for *PRODOTHER* and *COOP* support the hypotheses that funding from others and cooperative activity with others make more valuable the company's own investments in product R&D to improve the emissions performance of products. Also supported are the hypotheses that the outside funding and the cooperative R&D are used with more challenging product R&D investments.

Similarly, the positive coefficients for *DBACKGROUND* and for *DPROCESS* support the hypotheses that investment in background research to understand the emissions themselves and in process R&D make more valuable the applied R&D to improve the emissions performance of a company's products. Further, again following the interpretation of the other qualitative variables' effects, there is support for the hypotheses that the understandings developed with the background research and the process R&D are used with more challenging product R&D.

Title III product R&D is least at intermediate levels of seller concentration.[20] As discussed throughout Scott (2003), the higher levels of concentration are expected to correspond to greater amounts of Schumpeterian competition while the lower levels correspond to the conventional notion of competition.[21] Therefore, the dynamic competition that spurs more R&D does not always originate in solely the "Schumpeterian" market structures. Possibly regulators impose tougher expectations for performance in markets with greater R&D competition, making the R&D problem more difficult and making more investment in R&D useful and profitable. Alternatively, and having the same effect of increasing the marginal benefit of R&D, firms facing greater dynamic competition may choose to invest more in R&D to be prepared for the future competitive threats from their rivals. It is also possible that intermediate levels of seller concentration correspond to markets where the value of R&D is less because of vigorous oligopolistic rivalry—in particular, rivalry using nonprice competition with advertising and marketing efforts more generally—in the post-innovation markets that erodes profits of innovations.[22]

4. Simulation of the effects of the policies

The evidence supports the expectation that the several public policies listed in Section 1 could be used to stimulate investments in environmental R&D. This section discusses each policy in turn and illustrates the potential effects of the policies with predictions from the model estimated in Section 3. From (8), our estimate of the expected amount of Title III product R&D for a company—say the j*th*—drawn from the population is

$$E(PRD3RDT_j) = (\Phi_j)\exp(x_j\beta + \sigma(\phi_j/\Phi_j)), \quad (9)$$

where exp(*p*) denotes the base to the natural logarithms *e* raised to the power *p*. To illustrate the policies' potential effects, the expectation stated in equation (9) will be used with the parameters estimated in the inclusive specification (4) from Table III along with appropriate settings of the explanatory variables. Specification (4) is the most conservative one to use—because all effects are controlled—and in any case the coefficients for the variables of interest are about the same as for the other specifications except that the coefficient for COOP is decidedly smaller, again making the use of specification (4) a conservative choice when reporting and assessing the predicted impacts. Although none of the industry effects are significant in the Tobit model (as contrasted with the probit model for selection), their presence does eliminate the correlation of the errors of the probit and Tobit models.

By using equation (9) for the predictions to follow, the estimate of the expected product R&D is not conditioned on the presence of the R&D. That is, the company may or may not invest in environmental R&D; the probability that a company will invest in environmental product R&D is considered. Nonetheless, we shall consider, as the base-line case for comparisons, a company with characteristics implying a relatively high probability that the R&D will be observed. We do that because the purpose of estimating the effects of different policies is to show their effects on those companies where environmental R&D is likely to be present. Thus, for the base-line case, we consider a hypothetical company that would be typical of those in the sample of the 37 responding companies that reported Title III product R&D.

The predictions in the tables to follow will consider how changes in the variables affect the predicted Title III product R&D for a firm with the average value (in the sample of the 37 responding firms that have Title III product R&D) for the natural logarithms for those continuous variables that are measured in logarithms in the model. Thus, we consider a large firm with a substantial amount of Title III emissions that faces some import competition. The company's markets will have the average amount of seller concentration for the 37 companies' markets. The dummy variables—for the presence of environmental background and process R&D, outside funding, and cooperative projects for environmental product R&D—will be set at their average for the 37 firm sample. Thus, used in the predictions are the mean values for the 37 company sample; those values are all given in Table II. The company will be in the broad two-digit manufacturing industry for chemicals, an industry left in the intercept term of the Tobit model.

Now, the foregoing hypothetical firm would be expected to have a substantial amount of Title III product R&D, but by no means would it have a large amount. Large amounts of R&D are expected when multiples of the variables are set so that each variable's setting is one implying more R&D. Thus, not only would the hypothetical company have outside financing for its environmental product R&D, it would have cooperative activity and process R&D and background research and a large number of Title III emissions, and so forth. So, although substantial, the Title III product R&D investment expected for the hypothetical company examined in the simulations is not large. It is the sort of company that public policy would target as a likely source of additional socially valuable R&D. The hypothetical company is "typical" among those having such R&D, and then the simulations examine the impacts of changing each explanatory variable while holding constant the other explanatory variables.

Table IV illustrates the effects of the explanatory variables on the predicted amount of environmental product R&D for the hypothetical company. For Table IV's experiment, while holding constant all the other explanatory variables,

TABLE IV
Predicted R&D as a Percentage of the Amount for a Hypothetical Company[a]

Variable	Low	High
ln(NTAPC)	46	227
ln(SALES)	22	541
ln(IMPSC)	280	38
CR4C	639[b]	616[b]
PRODOTHER	69	22,126[c]
COOP	68	305
DBACKGROUND & DPROCESS	15	268

[a]The hypothetical company is described in the text. Briefly, it is a company with characteristics like a typical company that has Title III product R&D. In particular, it is one characterized by the means—in the sample of 37 companies with Title III product R&D—for the explanatory variables in their modeled metrics. Thus, from Table 2, ln(NTAPC) = 3.492, ln(SALES) = 7.190, ln(IMPSC) = −2.207, CR4C = 33.52, PRODOTHER = 0.08108, COOP = 0.2703, DBACKGROUND = 0.5946, DPROCESS = 0.7568. For the continuous logarithmic variables, high and low are set as plus and minus a standard deviation for the explanatory variables measured in logarithms. For example, high SALES uses ln(SALES) = 7.190 + 1.803, and low SALES uses ln(SALES) = 7.190—1.803. The dichotomous variables are set = 1 for high and = 0 for low. CR4C is set at 20 for low and at 80 for high; it is a variable where the nonlinearity occurs over a wide range for the explanatory variable, but our functional form has let us fit the model over the extreme values and so looking at them is sensible in the case of CR4C.
[b]Because the relation between Title III product R&D and CR4C is U-shaped, predicted R&D for both low and high seller concentration is a bit more than six times as large as for the hypothetical company.
[c]The coefficient for PRODOTHER is large and the average for the variable is small because very few firms have outside finance for their environmental product R&D. The result is a large effect for changing PRODOTHER to high; the predicted Title III product R&D is 221.26 times as great as for the hypothetical company.

each variable is alternately set to be "low" or "high".[23] The resulting environmental product R&D as a percentage of the amount the hypothetical company would do demonstrates the effect of each variable. For example, a company with operations that produce a high number of pollutants in its typical industry is expected to perform 2.27 times as much R&D or 227 percent of what the hypothetical company does. With a low level of pollutants for its typical industry, the expected R&D falls to 46% of the amount done by the hypothetical company. Holding constant the number of pollutants for its typical industry, a company with high total sales is expected to do 5.41 times, or 541%, as much R&D as the hypothetical company, while a company with low sales does 22% as much.

Table V provides an alternative way to consider the effect of the variables on expected environmental R&D; it calculates the elasticity of R&D with respect to each variable as explained in detail in the table's footnotes. Turning now to the discussion of the potential effectiveness of various public policies, each explanatory variable is linked to a public policy and then the elasticity calculations are used as a way to discuss the possible effectiveness of the public policies.

Pre-innovation taxes

The most controversial of the public policies that we shall discuss is a policy of pre-innovation taxes. Arguably, environmental R&D would be increased by the implementation of a pre-innovation tax that must be paid by companies operating in specified industries until the attainment of an innovation with specified emissions-reducing attributes.[24] The theoretical discussion above implies that such a tax could increase environmental R&D as long as the tax is not so severe that there is no profit left in operating. The pre-innovation tax would be paid until a firm developed or acquired innovations that achieved desired environmental performance.[25] Thus, the "pre-innovation tax" is like a fine for poor environmental performance, just as one could think of a classic "effluent tax" as a fine for poor environmental performance. The pre-innovation tax, like an effluent tax, is ideally designed to correct firm behavior, bringing it closer to the behavior

TABLE V
The Potential Effectiveness of Public Policies

Continuous Policies (Associated Variable)	Elasticity of R&D with Respect to the Policy[a]
Pre-innovation Taxes (*SALES*)	0.974
Emissions Regulation (*NTAPC*)	1.14
Import Competition (*IMPSC*)	1.27[b]
Antitrust: Conventional (*CR4C*)	not effective

Dichotomous Policies (Associated Qualitative Variable)	Percentage Change in R&D Induced by the Policy[c]
Outside Financing (*PRODOTHER*)	199
Knowledge Dissemination (*DBACKGROUND* & *DPROCESS*)	179
Antitrust: Cooperative R&D (*COOP*)	127

[a]The elasticity here is an arc elasticity. It is the percentage change (on average over the range of the change) in predicted R&D, when an explanatory variable—the variable used to simulate the policy's effect—is changed from its low to its high setting in the experiment of Table IV, divided by the percentage change (on average over the range of the change) in the variable. For example, using the experiment of Table IV to simulate the effect of more stringent emissions regulation, ln(*NTAPC*) is increased from 3.492 − 0.6673 to 3.492 + 0.6673. That translates to a change in *NTAPC* from exp(2.8247) to exp(4.1593), or from 16.86 to 64.03. Thus, over the average value for *NTAPC* in the range of the change, the percentage change is ((64.03 − 16.86)/((16.86 + 64.03)/2)) × 100 = 117%. The percentage change in the predicted R&D induced by the change in *NTAPC* is 133%. The predicted percentage change in R&D per unit percentage change in the variable *NTAPC* is then 133/117 = 1.14, the elasticity of predicted R&D with respect the number of regulated emissions. With R_{high} and R_{low} denoting the predicted Title III R&D, and with T_{high} and T_{low} denoting the high and low values for the explanatory variable, the elasticity shown in the table here is $(R_{high} - R_{low})/(T_{high} - T_{low}) \times (T_{high} + T_{low})/(R_{high} + R_{low})$. When the continuous variable enters the model without being changed to its natural logarithm, as is the case with CR4C, the mean and the standard deviation for the variable (rather than the mean and the standard deviation for its natural logarithm) directly provide the high and low values for the variable.
[b]The elasticity of predicted R&D with respect to import competition is −1.27. However, we assume that sensible policy to level the playing field would undo the negative effect of import competition. Thus the measure of the responsiveness of R&D to the policy is positive.
[c]For each dichotomous variable, the experiment in Table IV changes the variable from 0 to 1 to predict the effects of its "low" and "high" values. The qualitative variable is "turned on" to effect its "high" setting. That is the natural experiment for the qualitative variables; a company either has cooperative R&D or not, and so forth. For the qualitative variables, the percentage change in R&D for the arc elasticity concept is again $(R_{high} - R_{low})/((R_{high} + R_{low})/2) \times 100$. That is the effect, as a percentage change, of turning on the qualitative variable. Since as far as we have defined them, the dichotomous policies are either used or not—the qualitative variable is either turned on or not—the policies have not been measured in various amounts and dividing by $(1 - 0)/((1 + 0)/2) \times 100$ to show the percentage change in R&D per unit percentage change in policy—that is, to get $(R_{high} - R_{low})/(T_{high} - T_{low}) \times (T_{high} + T_{low})/(R_{high} + R_{low}) = (R_{high} - R_{low})/(R_{high} + R_{low})$—is not sensible. Of course, if we had continuous variables corresponding to the extent of support for outside financing, the extent of the promotion of knowledge dissemination, and the extent to which cooperative activity was promoted, then the elasticity measures could be computed for the policies. Stated differently, the policies are dichotomous here simply because of the way we have estimated their effects; our information relates to whether the policies are used or not, rather than relating to the extent of their use.

that would be in the social interest. The classic effluent tax is designed to reduce emissions; the pre-innovation tax is designed to do that by encouraging innovation to avoid the creation of emissions in the first place. Scott (1995) shows that in theory a pre-innovation tax could be designed to stimulate the optimal amount of environmental R&D investment. However, in practice, such a tax would simply bring the amount of investment closer to the socially optimal amount. The effect of the policy can be explained with the model of the environmental R&D decision.[26]

Following our discussion above, the effect on R&D investment of a value-shifting variable Z_i has the sign for the derivative for the model's R&D value parameter γ with respect to the variable. The periodic pre-innovation tax is one of these value-shifting Z_i variables. The derivative of R&D value with respect to the tax is positive, because tax must be paid until the mandated innovation occurs. The tax therefore increases the value of doing R&D. R&D increases the probability of an innovation with adequate environmental performance; hence, it increases the probability of avoiding the tax—realizing the value of not having to pay it. The larger the pre-innovation tax, the greater the value of doing R&D.

Of course, there are many potential practical problems with a periodic pre-innovation tax. Those problems have been discussed in detail in Scott (1993, pp. 209–213), and they include the credibility of the policy, and issues about entry into the industries being regulated and about the informational requirements needed to fine-tune the policy. The discussion of the practical problems will not be rehashed here. Instead, I shall make two observations that point up why the policy might be feasible—the need for the policy may be great enough to support the institutional changes required for its success.

First, the earlier discussion concluded that the practical problems could be overcome, if government had a clear mandate to help steer industry toward a socially desirable R&D conclusion. The previous discussion observed (Scott, 1993, p. 212):

> The pre-innovation periodic tax might be especially appropriate for ensuring optimal investment in technologies designed to solve environmental problems ... Implementation of the pre-innovation periodic tax would be a logical step to ensure timely research, and in addition to inducing efficient R&D investment, the periodic tax could be seen as "just" in the sense that it is paid as long as the environmental problem persists.

Second, overcoming the practical problems would perhaps require changes in institutions—in particular both business and public policy institutions—that are unlikely unless the mandate for change were strong. In the context of the prominent corporate scandals featuring misbehavior by executives, Baldwin (2003, p. 849) observes that simply formulating an appropriate public policy toward industry is not sufficient to meet our collective responsibility to ensure socially responsible behavior by industry.

> Rather, reform will also require making changes in economic institutions, as was done in the early 1930s to deal with the impact of the "modern corporation" on the boom and collapse of financial markets in particular, and the economy in general, through the disclosure requirements of the Securities Act of 1933 and the reforms and regulations imposed on financial markets a year later by the Securities Exchange Act of 1934.

The theory plus the evidence in Table III that is consistent with the theoretical expectations about the incentives to do environmental R&D implies that a pre-innovation periodic tax policy "would work"—i.e., in both theory and practice it makes good sense—but it is undoubtedly impractical in the sense that it would require a dramatic change in institutions. Broadly, the law effecting such a tax would state: "If you want to produce in this industry, then you must pay this tax until innovation occurs." The U.S. government is currently unlikely to legislate sweeping reforms needed for such a tax now, given the current institutions and the need for great change in them that the reforms would require. As dramatic evidence about toxic chemicals in our environment is gathered by biomonitoring, perhaps sweeping reforms will be more likely.[27]

To consider the possible effectiveness of a pre-innovation tax as a stimulus for environmental R&D, consider the elasticity of R&D with respect to the sales of a firm. As seen in Table V, that elasticity is almost 1.0. Expected R&D increases essentially proportionately with the sales of the firm. The effect estimated shows the relation between a firm's present sales and its environmental product R&D. The estimated relation gives some insight into the unobserved relation between a pre-innovation tax and environmental product R&D. A greater pre-innovation tax affects the value of innovation because it in effect increases post-innovation revenues from sales for the company because the tax is no longer paid after the innovation occurs. There will be the revenues from sales of the product and the additional revenues accompanying the post-innovation sales because the tax is no longer being paid. Clearly the mechanics of the effects for greater sales and greater pre-innovation taxes are different. On the one hand, pre-innovation sales increase by a dollar; on the other, post-innovation taxes are down by a dollar increasing post-innovation revenues and hence post-innovation profits by a dollar, other things being the same. In what way would the effect of *SALES* on R&D mimic the effect of a pre-innovation tax on R&D—a variable that varies directly with the expectation of post-innovation profits for the firm? Ideally, we want a variable that measures expected periodic profits, since that is what is affected by the pre-innovation periodic tax vis-à-vis the value of the innovation. Well, firms with larger *SALES* have a larger post-innovation profit as a result of the innovation—including the effect of distribution and marketing enabling a rapid penetration of the market, and including larger volume on which to earn a profit. Thus, the effect of *SALES* is in part an expected profit effect, and it is then a sensible effect to use as a way to suggest the possible impact of a pre-innovation tax. With the essentially unitary elasticity—a large effect—for the associated variable, it appears the pre-innovation tax policy could be effective.

Stringent emissions regulations

The theory above also implies that increasing the stringency of emissions regulations would increase environmental R&D, as long as the policy of tougher environmental standards—the emissions regulations—were not so severe that operating leaves no profit. We can explain the effect with our model of the R&D decision, and then the evidence in support of the effect is the positive sign on *NTAPC* in the empirical test of the theory.[28]

Following the discussion earlier, in the model, the **X** variables determine α; as α increases there is a favorable shift in the probability distribution over the performance—as judged relative to the regulated environmental standards—for the innovative technology produced by a company's environmental R&D investments. As α increases, the distribution shifts to the right, centering over higher performance for the innovative technology. If a variable makes α smaller as the variable is increased, then increasing the variable will cause a company to do more environmental R&D. The company, other things being the same, will find it profitable to do more R&D to make the distribution for the performance of its innovation more favorable. The stringency of the standard for acceptable environmental performance is just such a variable. The more stringent the standard as measured by an index variable X_i, then the smaller alpha is, other things being the same.[29] The probability distribution over environmental performance x is shifted leftward; R&D then has a larger marginal benefit. Industry is given a tougher environmental problem to solve, and R&D will be greater.

Increasing the stringency of environmental regulations is analogous to increasing the number of a company's emissions that are considered to be pollutants. Therefore, the estimated positive effect of *NTAPC* on a company's environmental R&D investment suggests that more stringent regulations of emissions would increase the environmental R&D investment of industry. Table V shows the elasticity of environmental R&D to *NTAPC* is not only positive, but it is substantial, estimated to be 1.14, a bit greater than unitary elasticity.

Cooperative R&D

Policies to increase the amount of cooperative R&D could increase environmental R&D. Theoretically, we expect that cooperative R&D will increase the value of a company's individual R&D program and its R&D investments; further, cooperative R&D may enable more challenging R&D projects. The evidence for the benefits of cooperative R&D is the positive sign on the variable *COOP* in the estimates of Table III. Table V shows that the effect of cooperative R&D in the estimated model is substantial; cooperative R&D is associated with a 127% increase in a company's environmental product R&D.

Outside financing

Environmental R&D could be increased by policies to promote the availability and use of outside financing from other companies and from the public. Outside financing can enable more valuable company R&D investments; the evidence supporting the use of outside financing is the positive sign on *PRODOTHER*. Table V shows that the presence of outside financing is associated with an almost 200% increase in a company's environmental product R&D investment.

Import competition

Diplomacy to encourage emissions regulations that are more uniformly stringent worldwide could increase environmental R&D. The evidence supporting that inference is the negative sign on *IMPSC* in the estimates of Table III. The elasticity of environmental R&D with respect to import competition is negative and greater than 1.0 in absolute value. In our model, the substantial negative elasticity reflects less stringent environmental expectations in the home countries of the importers. A policy that leveled the playing field with regard to expectations about emissions performance should have the effect of increasing the environmental R&D of U.S. companies. Reversing the current effect of the divergent expectations, the policy should have a substantial effect too, as indicated by the elasticity of 1.27 reported in Table V.

Antitrust policy

Promoting dynamic competition with appropriate antitrust policy could increase environmental R&D. However, the estimates in Table III showing a U-shaped relation between seller concentration and environmental R&D imply that the use of conventional antitrust policy to promote environmental R&D is not practical. Breaking up companies to lower seller concentration in the name of better environmental R&D is simply not acceptable given the uncertainties about whether the correlation found in the sample would imply greater R&D for newly deconcentrated industries and given the possibility that efficiency consequences of the existing concentration would be lost. On the other hand, promoting extreme seller concentration in the name of Schumpeterian competition will not work either, since for many reasons—economic and social and political—the antitrust laws do not actively promote extreme concentration of resources in industry. It is simply not reasonable to expect that conventional antitrust policy toward mergers or dominant firms could be used to promote either or both of the structural environments associated with greater amounts of environmental R&D in our model.

It would not be a practical policy to promote seller concentration—several standard deviations above the mean to get the dynamic Schumpeterian competition in environmental R&D—because of other likely effects of seller concentration and simply because antitrust policy would not tolerate such concentration of sellers. Although antitrust policy traditionally works to keep seller concentration as low as practical given economies of scale or simply the historical pattern for multiplant development in an industry, typically the resulting levels of seller concentration are in the middle range where environmental R&D is expected to be least. So, as a practical matter, if limited to the traditional antitrust actions to address anticompetitive mergers or anticompetitive behavior by conspiring firms or by dominant firms, the use of antitrust policy to promote environmental R&D does not appear to be an option. However, the National Cooperative Research Act of 1984 and its sequel, the National Cooperative Research and Production Act of 1993, aimed to promote socially valuable R&D by relaxing the antitrust constraints against cooperative research joint ventures among companies. Evidence suggests that in the context of the Clean Air Act Amendments of 1990, the new antitrust policy embodied in these laws did stimulate cooperative environmental R&D projects in industry.[30] Thus, our finding, discussed above, that the presence of cooperative environmental R&D is associated with more R&D investment suggests that the relatively new antitrust policy of promoting cooperative R&D ventures in industry would be an effective policy for stimulating environmental R&D.

Knowledge dissemination

Promoting the dissemination of fundamental knowledge about emissions and licensable emissions-reducing technology could increase environmental R&D. Regarding proprietary technologies, the public policies would encourage the dissemination—"diffusion initiated or encouraged by the innovator, to distinguish it from imitation" (Baldwin and Scott, 1987, p. 114)—of the knowledge. Following Hirshleifer (1971), "dissemination" is distinguished from "imitation" which denotes (Baldwin and Scott, 1987, p. 114) "diffusion by actors other than the innovator, and without its permission or approval." Public policy would promote the dissemination of emissions technologies, with appropriate compensation to innovators. In our theoretical model, the dissemination of the knowledge about emissions-reducing technologies will increase environmental R&D if it increases the value of the R&D or makes possible more challenging R&D projects. The evidence supporting a policy of encouraging knowledge dissemination is found in the positive signs on *DBACKGROUND* and *DPROCESS* in the estimations of Table III. In the context of our theoretical model, companies that have the benefit of the knowledge from background research on emissions and from environmental process R&D are companies that find R&D more valuable and find more challenging projects doable. Consequently, those companies do more environmental product R&D. Disseminating information about the background research and the process R&D could have a similarly positive effect on the R&D of other companies. The effect could be substantial. As seen in Table V, the availability of the background and process information is associated with a 179% increase in environmental product R&D.

In all, we are left with policy options of more stringent regulations, diplomacy to make emissions regulation more uniformly stringent worldwide, and facilitation of outside finance and cooperative R&D and knowledge dissemination. Preinnovation periodic taxes would work in theory and perhaps even in practice if the law could be enacted, but given the current institutional framework, the legislature would not pass such a law.

Acknowledgment

I thank William L. Baldwin and Albert N. Link for their many helpful comments on the earlier versions of this paper.

Notes

1. Scott (2003) provides the survey instrument and a description of the population of companies surveyed and of the companies that responded.
2. Scott (2003, forthcoming) provides the alternative regressions and a detailed explanation of the estimation of the environmental R&D intensities for SIC two-digit manufacturing industries. The emissions reduction data by industry are from the U.S. Environmental Protection Agency (EPA) for the core set of chemicals traced since 1988 (see Scott, 2003, chapter 1 and chapter 8, for details).
3. As reported in Scott (2003, p. 116), *RDCTN8899* = 27.09 + 3372.6 *ENVRD/SALES* with $R^2 = 0.192$ (adjusted $R^2 = 0.130$) and with the F statistic for the equation as a whole = 3.09 with 1 and 13 degrees of freedom (the probability of a greater F given the null hypothesis is 0.102). The p-values for two-tailed tests are 0.085 for the intercept and 0.102 for the coefficient for environmental intensity. Using an alternative estimation technique to check for robustness of the results (Scott, forthcoming) reports similar estimates.
4. The effect should be viewed within the range of the observations of *ENVRD/SALES*. The sample average of *ENVRD/SALES* for the 15 two-digit SIC manufacturing industries is 0.005625 with standard deviation 0.0052609 and with range from the minimum of 0.000967 to the maximum of 0.0215. For the 15 broad industries, the sample average of *RDCTN8899* is 46.06 with standard deviation of 40.47 and a range from a negative percentage reduction (an actual increase in emissions) of −62.0 to a positive percentage reduction of 89.70. The elasticity is then: $(\partial RDCTN8899/\partial(ENVRD/SALES)) \times (0.005625/46.60) = (3372.6) \times (0.0001221) = 0.41$.
5. Some investments that might be considered environmental R&D might encompass routine engineering to improve the emissions performance for a company. Such investments might entail little or no risk, yet the improvements resulting could be considered innovations, albeit perhaps relatively minor ones. The focus of the theory and evidence in this paper is risky environmental R&D.
6. Another appropriate property of the gamma distribution is that when a company has a more challenging R&D project with the higher prospects for environmental performance (a higher alpha project), it accepts greater risk (the probability distribution has greater variance around the higher mean). Details are given in Scott (2003, pp. 59–61).
7. For development of the theory, see Kohn and Scott (1982). For review of the empirical literature, see Baldiwin and Scott (1987).
8. The explicit derivation of equation (6), including the relation of the intercept and the logarithmic derivatives to the underlying parameters of the functions for f and for V, is given in Scott (2003, pp. 60–65).
9. In Scott (2003, pp. 57–66) there is a formal development of the effects that have been described here in brief, overview form. In sum, the first and second-order conditions for the maximum, and the underlying assumptions about the variables effects on alpha and gamma, all play a role in establishing the signs.
10. The surveys, including the complete survey instruments themselves and complete description of the samples and the respondents, are described in Scott (2003). The present paper provides just a brief overview of the samples.
11. The 846 firms, including nonmanufacturing firms, were surveyed because originally I considered the hypothesis that nonmanufacturing as well as manufacturing firms would be significant sources of environmental R&D. As it turns out, purely nonmanufacturing firms did not typically report environmental R&D.
12. Scott (2003) describes Title III of the Clean Air Act Amendments and provides a complete list of the Title III chemicals and a description of their incidence in industry and in the operations of the sampled and the responding firms.
13. Scott (2003) provides complete description and documentation of these sources.
14. The FIML estimations and comparisons with the results for the simple two-step estimations in Scott (2003) are provided in Scott (forthcoming) for the process R&D; the analo-

gous comparisons for the product R&D and the background research are available on request.

15. For discussion of the need for simplicity to achieve convergence of the models, see Greene (2002b, p. R9-15).

16. See Scott (2003, chapter 2) for details; the numbers of articles were for the five year period ending at the time of the 1993 survey to which the 132 firms responded. As described there, the "2" in the variable name MED2 serves to identify the particular form of the variable.

17. The effects used are exactly as in the specification used for the two-step estimation of the Tobit model of Title III product R&D with selection in Scott (2003, Table 6.5, p. 88). Included in the specification are *D20*, *D22*, *D25*, *D26*, *D30*, *D34*, *D35*, *D36*, *D37*, *D38*, with the effects—indistinguishable from each other—for the remaining primary manufacturing industries represented in the sample in the intercept.

18. Scott (2003, p. 88) provides an alternative specification, using each of the continuous variables with its square (as done here for seller concentration where the U-shape for the relation required it) in place of the natural logarithms for those variables. That alternative specification is estimated in the context of a simpler two-step estimation of the Tobit model with selection, and the results using FIML with that alternative specification are described in Scott (forthcoming) for the process R&D and are available on request for the product R&D and background research. As explained earlier, here the more parsimonious specifications are used to simplify and check the robustness of the results in the context of the difficulty of obtaining convergence when the model of selection and the model for R&D are estimated jointly with the FIML estimator with a large number of explanatory variables. To capture the effect of seller concentration, we need to use both concentration and its square. For *NTAPC*, *SALES*, and *IMPSC*, the simpler logarithmic form captures the relationships well in the ranges of the variables we consider.

19. Scott (2003, chapter 6).

20. Some readers may believe that the result here contradicts evidence of an inverted-U relation between seller concentration and R&D intensity, but that is not really the case. First, we are examining here a very special type of R&D, and the evidence about an inverted-U is for aggregations of a company's many types of R&D. But, second, and more important, there is no evidence of an inverted-U once sufficient controls for factors other than seller concentration are introduced (Scott, 1993, chapters 7 and 10). The effects for concentration in this paper for the particular type of R&D studied occur in the presence of a large number of controls, including industry effects.

21. Schumpeterian competition refers to the dynamic rivalry—to introduce new processes and products—among large firms that dominate their markets. Baldwin and Scott (1987) provide a review of the literature about Schumpeterian competition.

22. For discussion of the inverted-U in advertising as a function of seller concentration, *ceteris paribus*, and references to the literature, see Martin (2002, pp. 174–175). Thus, an anticipated inverted-U in the relation from seller concentration to nonprice competition could explain the U-relationship seen here for R&D and seller concentration.

23. The footnote to Table IV explains the exact settings corresponding to the "low" or "high" values of the explanatory variables.

24. Note that the pre-innovation periodic tax is distinct from the conventional effluent tax. A company could clean up the emissions by capturing and storing potential effluent. It would not be released, so no effluent is released into the environment. Or a company could avoid an effluent tax by cleaning up more generally with the same result of no toxic emissions. Yet, in those circumstances there is no innovation to avoid creating any toxic byproduct in need of containment. The company, then, would still pay the pre-innovation periodic tax.

25. The periodic pre-innovation tax is developed in the context of a general R&D model in Scott (1995). In this paper, we explain the tax in the context of the model of the environmental R&D decision. Scott (1995) also discusses and compares typical public policy toward R&D, including the more conventional taxation policy of tax credits for R&D investments.

26. A more detailed explanation is provided in Scott (2003, chapter 8).

27. A dramatic example is the finding of high levels of toxic chemicals in human breast milk that evidently come in part from the flame retardants that are found in carpeting, draperies, and clothing such as sleepwear for babies. For discussion of that example in the general context of the concerns raised by the findings of biomonitoring, see Roan (2003).

28. A more detailed explanation is provided in Scott (2003, chapter 8).

29. Suppose for example that for an initial level of emissions regulation and given other factors such as the amount of R&D investment, a company expects a distribution over environmental performance implying the expectation of achieving 75% of the desired environmental goal. With more stringent emissions regulations and their concomitant greater requirements for satisfactory performance, the same amount of R&D effort might leave the company expecting to achieve just 50% of the desired environmental goal.

30. See Scott (2003, chapter 7) for the evidence.

References

Baldwin, W.L., 2003, 'The Corporation and Society: An Evolutionary/Institutional Approach,' *Vermont Law Review* **27**, 843–849.

Baldwin, W.L., and J.T. Scott, 1987, *Market Structure and Technological Change*, in the series *Fundamentals of Pure and Applied Economics*, Vol. 17, New York: Harwood Academic Publishers.

Greene, W.H., 2002a, *LIMDEP Version 8.0: Econometric Modeling Guide*, Vol. 2 Plainview, NY, USA: Econometric Software.

Greene, W.H., 2002b, *LIMDEP Version 8.0: Reference Guide*, Plainview, NY, USA: Econometric Software.

Greene, W.H., 2003a, *Econometric Analysis*, Fifth Edition, Upper Saddle River, New Jersey, USA: Prentice Hall.

Greene, W.H., 2003b, *NLOGIT 3.0* (with LIMDEP Version 8.0), Version 3.0.6 May 20, 2003, Plainview, NY, USA: Econometric Software.

Hirshleifer, J., 1971, 'The Private and Social Value of Information and the Reward for Innovative Activity,' *American Economic Review* **61**, 561–574.

Jaffe, A.B., S.R. Peterson, P.R. Portney and R.N., Stavins, 1995, 'Environmental Regulation and the Competitiveness of U.S. Manufacturing: What Does the Evidence Tell Us?', *Journal of Economic Literature* **33**(1), 132–163.

Kohn, M. and J.T. Scott, 1982, 'Scale Economies in Research and Development: the Schumpeterian Hypothesis,' *The Journal of Industrial Economics*, **30** (3), 239–249.

Maddala, G.S., 1983, *Limited-Dependent and Qualitative Variables in Econometrics*, Cambridge, England; New York, USA: Cambridge University Press.

Martin, S., 2002, *Advanced Industrial Economics*, 2nd Edition, Oxford, UK; Malden, MA., USA: Blackwell Publishers.

Roan, S., 2003, 'Testing People for Pollutants: Project Studies Breast Milk to Discern Possible Link between Pollution, Disease,' *Los Angeles Times* as reprinted in *Valley News*, October 31, p. C1.

Scott, J.T., 1993, *Purposive Diversification and Economic Performance*, Cambridge, England; New York, USA: Cambridge University Press.

Scott, J.T., 1995, 'The Damoclean Tax and Innovation,' *Journal of Evolutionary Economics*, **5**(1), 71–89.

Scott, J.T., 2003, *Environmental Research and Development: US Industrial Research, the Clean Air Act and Environmental Damage*, Cheltenham, UK; Northampton, MA, USA: Edward Elgar Publishing.

Scott, J.T., "Corporate Social Responsibility and Environmental Research and Development," *Structural Change and Economic Dynamics*, forthcoming.

The Importance of R&D for Innovation: A Reassessment Using French Survey Data

Jacques Mairesse[1]
Pierre Mohnen[2]

ABSTRACT. This paper compares the contribution of R&D to innovation in terms of the various innovation output measures provided by the third Community Innovation Survey (CIS 3) for French manufacturing firms and in terms of accounting for interindustry innovation differences.

Key words: R&D, innovation, patents

JEL Classification: C35, L60, O31, O33

1. Introduction

In this paper we want to pay tribute to Ed Mansfield for his pioneering research on the economics of technological change. We reassess the importance that R&D plays in the innovation process using the latest French data from CIS 3, the third Community Innovation Survey. We have a chosen a topic that would have been dear to Ed Mansfield since innovation, and in particular R&D, were at the center of his research for the greatest part of his career. He was also, as Mike Scherer mentions in his introductory paper to this issue, one of the first user (and producer) of survey data on R&D and innovation. Nowadays these survey data are collected in a systematic way for large samples in many countries.

Traditionally, the importance of R&D is evaluated by relating R&D and production (or cost, or profit) data, estimating the output elas-

[1] CREST-INSEE, 18, boulevard Gabriel Péri
92245 Malakoff Cedex, France
E-mail: mairesse@ensae.fr
and NBER
[2] MERIT, Maastricht University, PO Box 616, 6200 MD Maastricht, Netherlands
and CIRANO

ticity or rate of return of R&D from an extended Cobb-Douglas production (or cost, or profit) function, where a stock of R&D knowledge enters as a separate input. Ed Mansfield himself contributed to this literature (Mansfield, 1964, 1965, 1980). Another way of evaluating R&D is by estimating the value attached to R&D investment by capital markets (see the original paper by Griliches, 1981 and recent work by Hall and Oriani, 2004). Instead of being related to measures of economic performance, R&D can also be related to innovation indicators through some kind of knowledge production function. The returns to R&D have been usually estimated in this line of work in terms of patent counts or innovation counts (see for instance the debate between Jaffe, 1989, and Acs et al., 1992).

This last approach is the one we follow here. Instead of using count data, we use the five dichotomous indicators of innovation and patents, and the three shares in total sales of innovative and patent protected sales, which are provided by the third Community Innovation Survey. We can thus make the distinction between indicators related to product and process innovations, and among the former between indicators for products new to the firm only (but already known in the market) and products new to the market (new can also mean substantial modifications of existing products). And we can confront these indicators with indicators on patent applications during a given time period and on patent holdings, in a way reflecting the distinction between flows and stocks of patents.

Prior to the late eighties, innovation surveys were conducted in isolated ways. Mansfield, as already indicated, based much of his work on company survey data (e.g. Mansfield *et al.*, 1977). SPRU set up a database of innovations back in the mid 1970s, which was explored among others by Pavitt, 1984. In the early 1990s these surveys became institutionalized, in least in Europe, with the advent of the Community Innovation Surveys (CIS), which followed the guidelines of the Oslo Manual (OECD, 1992 and 1996). Up to now, there exist three official waves of CIS (CIS 1 for 1990–1992, CIS 2 for 1994–1996 and CIS 3 for 1998–2000). A few countries, notably France, Germany and the Netherlands, had actually an innovation survey prior to CIS 1. The fourth round of innovation survey is presently underway. The present study is based on the data of CIS3 for French manufacturing.

We assess the impact of R&D on innovation separately for high-tech and low-tech industries and in two ways. We first estimate the marginal effects of R&D on the various innovation output indicators, controlling for other co-determinant factors, and correcting for both the selectivity and endogeneity of R&D itself (Section 5). We then ask how much of the inter-industry difference in innovation performance can be imputed to R&D and to the other factors explicitly taken into account in the analysis and how much remains to be explained or could be attributed to innovativeness (Section 6). Before that, we give necessary explanations on our data and our model, and provide a short preliminary descriptive analysis.

2. Data

Our sample consists of French manufacturing enterprises that responded to the CIS 3 survey, covering the years 1998–2000, and that have also been surveyed by the EAE survey ("Enquête Annuelle d'Entreprise" or Annual Survey of Enterprises) in these three years.[1]

The CIS 3 survey, like the previous ones, is structured in such a way that specific filter questions lead to the selection of firms which are innovators as opposed to non-innovators. Only the former have to answer the full questionnaire. Firms are first asked whether they have introduced in 1998–2000 a new product or a new process, or whether they have had any ongoing or abandoned activities to do so during this period. If they answer positively to one of these questions (about 60% in our sample), they are asked additional information about their innovation outcomes, their R&D expenditures in 2000, and other characteristics. If they answer no to all the filter questions (about 40%), they are considered as non-innovators so to say, having to report chiefly on their size, group affiliation and industry of main activity.[2]

We are thus left with little information about the non innovating firms, and a severe selectivity problem. In particular we have the information on the R&D expenditures of the innovating firms for the year 2000, in case they have engaged in R&D, but not for the non innovating firms. We have thus been lead to consider that all R&D performers were innovators, and conversely that all non-innovators were non-R&D performers. By merging the French annual R&D survey for 2000 with CIS 3, we have been able to check that it was not far from being the case: only 2% of the R&D firms in the annual survey declare they were non-innovators in CIS 3, while about 60% of innovating firms in CIS 3 declare that they were R&D performers (on a continuous basis). Actually, in CIS 3 the innovating firms reporting R&D expenditures in 2000 are also asked whether they engaged in R&D continuously over the period 1998–2000 or only occasionally. While about 60% of them answered that they did R&D continuously and 25% occasionally, we preferred to restrict our attention here to the continuous R&D performers for two reasons. Ideally we would have like to have some measure of R&D stock. Since this is not possible without knowing past R&D expenditures for at least several years, we thought that the 2000 R&D flow number would be a much better proxy for the R&D stock in the case of the continuous R&D performers only. The second reason has to do with the timing problem. Being an innovator in CIS 3 refers to the period 1998–2000 whereas R&D expenditures are known for the year 2000 only. By focusing on continuous R&D performers we avoid attributing innovation in 1998–2000 to firms that had no R&D activity prior to the year 2000. To simplify, from now on R&D will refer to continuous R&D.

Overall, CIS 3 provides five indicators of innovation stricto sensu. The first three are dichotomous (or propensity) indicators, respectively for process innovations, product innovations new to the firm (but not necessarily to the market), and product innovations new to the market. New products refer to the three year period 1998–2000. Products new to the firm are defined as substantially improved or entirely new. Products new to the market refer to a first appearance on the market and therefore to more fundamental innovations than products new to the firm but which can already exist on the market. The other two are quantitative (or intensity) indicators measuring for product innovators (of both types) the importance of their flow of innovations, in terms of the share of their total sales in 2000 accounted by the new products.

One problem that is often raised regarding these survey innovation indicators is their subjectivity. The definition of what is and what is not an innovation remains in the end up to the appreciation of the respondent. Therefore it is interesting to compare these indicators with the more objective indicators concerning patents. At least for patents an outside patent examiner decides on the suitability of granting a patent to an invention. CIS 3 asks three indicators on patents. Two are dichotomous on whether the firm has applied or not for at least a patent in the period 1998–2000, and whether or not the firm holds at least one patent in the year 2000. The third measures the importance of the stocks of patents again in terms of the share of sales in the firm total sales in 2000, which are protected by patents. It is thus analogous to the two product innovation intensity indicators, but corresponds to a stock measure rather than a flow measure.

3. Model

Innovation survey data are qualitative and some of them are censored. These features call for a proper econometric modeling using latent variables.

Our model consists of two groups of equations. First, firms decide on whether they perform R&D and, if so, by how much. Then, depending on the extent of their R&D and other factors, they achieve a certain innovation output.

R&D is thus modeled as a generalized tobit:

(1) $\quad s_R^* = x_R^1 b_R^1 + u_R^1$ and $i_R^* = x_R^2 b_R^2 + u_R^2$

with $s_R = 1$ and $i_R^* = i_R$ if $s_R^* > 0$,

and $s_R = 0$ otherwise

where s_R is the observed dichotomous indicator for R&D doing and non R&D doing firms and i_R is the observed intensity of R&D (measured in log of R&D per employee) for R&D doing firms, s_R^* and i_R^* are the corresponding latent variables, x_R^i ($i = 1, 2$) are the explanatory variables in both equations and b_R^i the respective coefficients, and u_R^1 and u_R^2 follow a bivariate normal distribution with correlation coefficient ρ_R and standard errors 1 (for reasons of identification) and σ_R^2 respectively.

For each measure of innovation we have an innovation equation that depends on R&D. In the case of process innovation and patent application, the dependent variable is dichotomous. In that case we specify a probit model. For instance for process innovation,

(2) $\quad s_{PC}^* = b_R i_R^* + x_{PC} b_{PC} + u_{PC}$

with $s_{PC} = 1$ if $s_{PC}^* > 0$, and $s_{PC} = 0$ otherwise where s_{PC} is the observed dichotomous variable doing a process innovation or not, s_{PC}^* is the corresponding latent variable, i_R^* is the latent R&D intensity variable (as predicted by the equations (1) for all firms, that is for $s_R = 1$ and $s_R = 0$) and b_R is the corresponding coefficient of interest, x_{PC} are the other explanatory variables and b_{PC} their respective coefficients, and u_{PC} is a random variable with a standard normal distribution. A similar model holds for patent applications.[3]

If the innovation variable is filtered, as for the two types of product innovative sales and for patent-protected sales, the appropriate model is, as for R&D, a generalized tobit model, with a selection equation and an intensity equation, where the error terms of both equations are correlated and the explanatory variables are not necessarily the same. The intensity of innovation is measured respectively by the share of sales accounted for by new or substantially improved products subject to having introduced such a product on the market in the last 3 years; the share of sales accounted for by products new to the market, subject to having introduced such a product on the market in the last 3 years; and the share in sales of product protected by patents, subject to having had at least one valid patent in the last 3 years.

We explicitly treat R&D as endogenous and account for the selection of R&D performing firms. By doing this, we wish to achieve two things. On the one hand, determinants of innovation, like size, are decomposed into their direct effect on innovation and their indirect effect operating through R&D. On the other hand, common causal factors of R&D and innovation that are not included in our model either because of our lack of knowledge or a lack of appropriate data, do not bias our R&D coefficient estimates (to the extent that the explanatory variables in the R&D equations (1) are indeed exogenous).

In all equations we control for size, belonging to a French group, belonging to a foreign group, foreign exposure, and industry characteristics summarized by industry dummies. *Size* is measured by the number of employees (in logs). *Foreign groups* are distinguished from *French groups* by the location of their head office. A dummy indicates whether the *international market* is the main market. We have 10 *industry dummies* corresponding to one or more NACE (rev 1) 2-digit industries. Firms are assigned to these industries on the basis of their main activity.[4]

In the R&D selection equation we also control for demand pull, cost push, market share and diversification.[5] The French CIS 3 questionnaire contains two questions regarding the importance of *demand pull* and *cost push* as reasons for innovating. These variables can take values of 0 to 3. We have decided to isolate strong cost push and demand pull perceptions by creating dummies that take the value one when cost push (resp. demand pull) take value 3. The *market share* is constructed as the market share each firm has in each of the 227 industry segments in the NAP ("Nomenclature des Activités et Produits") 600 industrial classification, where each share is weighted by the relative importance of each market in the firm total sales. The *diversification* index is constructed as the inverse of the Herfindahl concentration index of firm sales in the different markets. The Herfindahl index takes a maximum value of 1 if sales are concentrated in one market and a minimum value of $1/n$, where n is the number of markets in which the firm is active, if sales are equally divided between all markets. The diversification index can thus be interpreted as the equivalent number of markets in which the firm would equally share its total sales. Both market share and diversification are introduced in logs. Those are basically the variables that we have for all firms (innovating or not) and that can to a large extent be considered as exogenous.

We have more explanatory variables available to explain the intensity of R&D, because R&D performers are by construction innovators. Thus we also include as explanatory variables in the R&D intensity equation whether R&D was done in *cooperation*, whether the firm was a beneficiary of *government support for innovation*, and whether it benefited from four sources of *information for innovation* (that can be considered as proxies of knowledge spillovers): the enterprise or the group, basic research institutions (universities and government labs), suppliers, and clients.

In order to better identify and estimate the R&D coefficients in the innovation equations, we chose to impose as many exclusion restrictions as we thought reasonable. In the innovation equations, we only include, besides R&D, our general control variables for industry, size, domestic and foreign groups, and foreign exposure. We thus consider that all other variables included in the R&D equations affect our innovation output indicators only indirectly through R&D.[6]

We estimate the model by asymptotic least squares (ALS), also known as minimum distance estimator (Gouriéroux et al., 1985). The idea is in a first step to estimate consistently the parameters of the reduced form, and then in a second step to estimate the parameters of the structural form by minimizing the distances between the estimated reduced form coefficients and their predictions from the structural form coefficients, weighted by the inverse of the variance–covariance matrix of the estimated reduced form coefficients. The relations between the reduced form and structural form coefficients are in our case simply obtained by substituting the expression of the latent variable for R&D intensity in equations (1) into the equations (2) for the propensity and intensity of our innovation output indicators. Since there is no feedback in our model from innovation output to R&D (the modeling of such a feedback would require sufficiently long panel data to model dynamic effects), the R&D equations are estimated consistently by a generalized tobit. The second step of the minimum distance estimator hence only concerns the coefficients of the innovation equation.[7]

4. Descriptive analysis

To have a first idea of the differences between the various measures of innovation, the characteristics of innovative and R&D firms and the interrelations between R&D and innovation, it is useful to look at some descriptive statistics. Table I presents the sample averages of the main dependent and explanatory variables on the total sample of 2253 firms, the sub-sample of 1399 innovative firms (firms that declare to have either introduced a new product or a new process or that were at some point during the 1998–2000 period trying to do so), and the sub-sample of 855 R&D performers. It is striking to notice that all variables (except of course the percentage of firms in low-tech sectors) have higher averages as we move from all firms to innovative firms and to R&D performers. A larger proportion of innovative firms (however they are measured) is thus found among R&D performers than among other firms. In addition, among the product innovators and the patent holders, the share of total sales accounted for by new products or covered by patents is higher for R&D performers than for non R&D performers. The share of total

Table I
Summary statistics: France, CIS 3, 1998–2000, manufacturing samples of all firms (TOTAL), innovative firms (INNO) and continuously R&D performing firms (R&D)

Variable	TOTAL Sample	INNO Sub-sample	R&D Sub-sample
Number of firms	2253	1399	855
% firms performing R&D continuously	37.9	61.1	100.0
R&D over sales (in%)	n.r.	n.r.	3.9
Log (R&D/Emp) (in 10^3 euros per person)	n.r.	n.r.	1.0
% firms innovating with products new to the firm* (A)	50.1	80.7	89.8
% firms innovating with products new to the market* (B)	28.3	45.5	58.0
% firms with process innovation	34.7	55.8	57.5
% firms with at least one patent applied for in 1998–2000	32.4	48.2	63.5
% firms with at least one valid patent at the end of 2000* (C)	34.6	49.6	64.7
Share of new to the firm innovative sales for firms of type (A)	n.r.	12.9	14.5
Share of new to the market innovative sales for firms of type (B)	n.r.	5.9	7.7
Share of total sales covered by patents for firms of type (C)	9.7	13.1	16.7
Number of employees: Mean/Median	410/133	541/207	727/340
% of firms in high-tech industries	39.9	48.4	57.7
% of firms in low-tech industries	60.1	51.6	42.3
% of firms for which the most significant market is international	41.8	53.0	64.1
% of firms belonging to a French group	46.7	48.4	51.2
% of firms belonging to a foreign group	27.1	33.8	36.3
% of firms with strong demand pull	37.0	59.6	67.6
% of firms with strong cost push	12.8	20.7	24.3
Diversification index	1.17	1.19	1.24
Average market share (in%)	2.6	3.4	4.3
% of firms with government support for innovation	n.r.	32.4	37.0
% of firms collaborating in innovation	n.r.	45.5	56.4
% of firms with significant source of information for innovation from:			
Within the firm or group	n.r.	74.1	84.1
Basic research institutions	n.r.	50.3	62.5
Suppliers	n.r.	47.9	49.7
Clients	n.r.	71.8	79.8

n.r.: not available or non relevant. * Indicator corrected to 0 if corresponding share = 0. All means are unweighted.

sales covered by patents is also higher for innovators than for non innovators. Moreover, R&D performers are larger, more diversified, more internationally oriented, and so on than non R&D performers.

The eight innovation indicators that we consider behave differently. There are more product innovators of all sorts (i.e. true innovators and imitators combined) than process innovators: 80.7% of all innovating firms are new to the firm products innovators whereas only 55.8% of them are process innovators. Among the R&D performers, the relative proportion of product innovators is even slightly higher. True innovators, i.e. those that introduce products new to the market, are less frequent of course (the average drops from 80.7 to 45.5%), but their relative number increases if we move to R&D performers. These simple descriptive statistics suggest that R&D is more geared towards product innovations than process innovations, and is positively correlated to the introduction of products new to the market. The proportion of firms with new patent applications is similar to the proportion of firms with valid patents, which seems to indicate that over a three year period there is persistence in patenting. What is also very interesting to notice is that the proportion of firms with new to the market product innovations is almost as high as the proportion of firms with patents. This does not imply of course that all new products are patented. Still, 72% of the firms that introduced new to the market products also applied for a patent (figure not shown in Table I).

5. Comparison of the marginal impact of R&D on various innovation measures

In this section we present the results of our econometric analysis in terms of the marginal effects of R&D intensity on the various innovation indicators. Based on previous experience (Mairesse and Mohnen, 2001) and on the large difference in the proportions of R&D performers in high-tech and low-tech sectors (see Table I), we have performed a separate analysis for the two corresponding clusters or sub-samples of firms, that is for the 899 firms in the electrical products, chemicals, machinery and vehicles industries, and for the 1354 firms in the textiles, wood, plastics, non-metallic mineral products, basic metals and not elsewhere classified industries.[8]

As appendix Table I shows, the marginal effects of the explanatory variables in the R&D equations are quite different. The propensity to engage in continuous R&D increases significantly with size, foreign exposure, demand pull and cost push, more so in high-tech than in low-tech sectors. In the high-tech sectors it also increases with diversification and in the low-tech sectors with market share. The difference between high-tech and low-tech industries is even more visible if we look at the determinants of R&D intensity. In the high-tech sectors, size, demand pull, market share and cooperation play no significant role. By contrast, in low-tech industries a 100% increase in size decreases R&D intensity by 31.2%, and demand pull, market share or cooperation are significantly positive and of a similar order of magnitude. R&D intensity is also affected by different information channels in the two sub-samples: information from basic research institutions increases R&D intensity by 29 percentage points in high-tech sectors, information from clients increases R&D intensity by 25.5 percentage points in low-tech sectors. All other information sources are not significant. The fact that the demand pull, cost push, diversification and market share effects, which are excluded from the innovation equations, are in most cases significant indicates that these variables should be good instruments to identify the R&D parameter in the innovation equation.

Table II compares the marginal effects of changes in R&D/employee and the number of employees on the different measures of innovation output. Size, if significant, has a small impact on the probability to innovate. In high-tech sectors, a one percent increase in size increases by 4.5 percentage points the probability of introducing a new process, by 6.6 percentage points the propensity to apply for a patent and by 4.8 percentage points the propensity to hold a valid patent; it has only a minor non-significant effect on new product introductions. In low-tech sectors, it increases the probability to be a product or a process innovator by 3–4 percentage points and patent applications (resp. patent hold-

Table II
Average marginal effects of R&D intensity and size, by innovation indicator, in high-tech and low-tech industries

Innovation variables	Products new to the firm		Products new to the market		Process innovation	Patent applications	Patent holdings	
In %	Yes/no	Share in sales	yes/no	Share in sales	yes/no	yes/no	yes/no	Share in sales
High-tech industries								
R&D intensity	26.5 (2.0)	3.7 (1.4)	21.6 (2.2)	7.6 (1.2)	19.5 (2.5)	19.9 (2.3)	20.4 (2.1)	13.0 (2.9)
Size	0.5 (0.8)	−0.3 (0.5)	0.7 (0.8)	0.1 (0.4)	4.5 (1.0)	6.6 (1.0)	4.8 (0.8)	4.9 (1.1)
Number of firms	899	593	899	372	899	899	899	411
Low-tech industries								
R&D intensity	27.7 (1.5)	7.9 (1.3)	45.5 (3.3)	2.2 (0.9)	34.3 (2.3)	28.5 (2.7)	39.8 (3.0)	18.5 (2.1)
Size	3.1 (0.7)	0.1 (0.5)	3.8 (1.5)	0.1 (0.3)	3.5 (1.2)	9.4 (1.4)	7.2 (1.5)	1.4 (0.9)
Number of firms	1354	536	1354	265	1354	1354	1354	283

All regressions include binary indicators for industry effects (4 in high-tech industries, 6 in low-tech industries), for the affiliation to a domestic or a foreign group, and for the importance of international market. R&D intensity is measured by R&D expenditures per employee (in logs), and size by the number of employees (in logs). All marginal effects are in percentage points: for example a 10% increase in R&D intensity has an average marginal effect of 2.6% on the propensity to innovate in new to the firm-products and of 0.4% on the corresponding intensity to innovate. Standard errors are in parentheses.

ings) by 9.4 (resp. 7.2) percentage points. Size has, in general, no significant impact on the share of innovative sales.

The effect of R&D intensity on innovation is stronger than size and more pronounced in the high-tech sectors. In high-tech sectors a one percent increase in R&D/employee increases the probability to innovate by around 20 percentage points for the five dichotomous indicators, somewhat more for new to firm product innovation. Conditional on being innovative, a one percent increase in R&D intensity increases the share in sales of products new to the firm by 3.7 percentage points, the share in sales of products new to the market by about twice as much, and the share of patented products by 13 percentage points. The effect of an increase in R&D intensity is even more pronounced in the low-tech sectors. A one percent increase in R&D/employee increases the propensity to innovate in new to the firm products by about the same amount as in the high-tech sectors but it increases the propensity to introduce a product new to the market, a new process, as well as the probability to hold a patent by twice the amount in the high-tech sectors. In the low-tech sectors R&D increases the share in total sales of new to the firm products more than the share in sales of new to the market products (7.9 versus 2.2 percentage points), and it increases even more than in high-tech sectors the share of patented products (18.5 compared to 13 percentage points).

6. Inter-industry comparisons of innovativeness

In this section we compare innovation across industries, within the high-tech and low-tech sectors, by decomposing it into the contribution from R&D, size together with other explanatory factors (being part of a domestic or foreign group and foreign exposure), and "innovativeness". The framework of this decomposition is laid out in Mairesse and Mohnen (2002). The idea is borrowed from growth accounting. Just as differences in output between two periods (years, decades) or between two spatial units (firms, industries, countries) can be ascribed to differences in the inputs and to a residual that has been named total or multi-factor productivity (TFP or MFP), or simply productivity, likewise, differences in innovation output (in terms of new products, processes or patents) between two periods or spatial units can be ascribed to differences in the factors of innovation (notably R&D) and to a residual that we call "innovativeness", or the unexplained ability to turn innovation inputs into innovation outputs.

Within the high-tech or low-tech cluster separately, we compare the inter-industry innovative performance along three measures (new to the firm product innovations, new to the market product innovations and patents) and two criteria (the probability to innovate and the intensity of innovation). As a general notation, let us write the innovation function as

$$y = f(R, Z) \tag{3}$$

where y can thus be measured in three ways and f can represent two types of functions (the propensity and the intensity of innovation). R represents R&D intensity and Z the other determinants that have been introduced as explanatory variables. Suppose we have two industries. Let y^A, y^B, and y^C represent the expected shares of innovative sales at respectively the mean values of the explanatory variables for industry A, industry B and the average industry within a cluster. By a linear approximation of each industry's average expected share of innovative sales around the cluster average we have

$$\begin{aligned}y^A &= y^C + f_R^C(R^A - R^C) \\ &\quad + f_Z^C(Z^A - Z^C) + e^A\end{aligned} \tag{4}$$

$$y^B = y^C + f_R^C(R^B - R^C) + f_Z^C(Z^B - Z^C) + e^B$$

where f_x^E represents the gradient of $f(.)$ with respect to x ($x = R, Z$) evaluated at the cluster average values for x, and x^C ($x = R, Z$) represents the cluster average of variable x.[9] The first term of the approximation is the cluster average, the second term is the R&D effect, the third term is the effect of variable Z, and the last term, which includes the industry effect and the first-order approximation error, captures innovativeness.[10] Notice that $e^E = (e^A + e^B)/2 = 0$.

The results of the innovation accounting are presented numerically in appendix Tables II (for the high-tech cluster) and III (for the low-tech cluster) and graphically in Figures 1–4. Appendix Tables II and III are organized as follows. In the first column we have the cluster average of an innovation measure, in column 2 the difference between an industry innovation and the cluster average attributable to size (group and foreign exposure) (the third term of equation (4)), in column 3 the difference attributable to R&D (the second term of equation (4)), in column 4 the sum of columns 2 and 3 (i.e. the explained difference in innovation between a given industry and the cluster average), in column 5 the expected innovation intensity (i.e. the cluster average of column 1 plus the explained effect of column 4), and in column 6 the difference between the industry innovation average of column 7 and the expected innovation intensity of column 5 (in other words, the difference in measured innovation that we cannot at this stage attribute to anything else but innovativeness). Since the comparison is always with respect to the cluster average, the average differences which are reported in the last row add up to zero and the average expected industry measure of innovation is by construction equal to the observed cluster average.

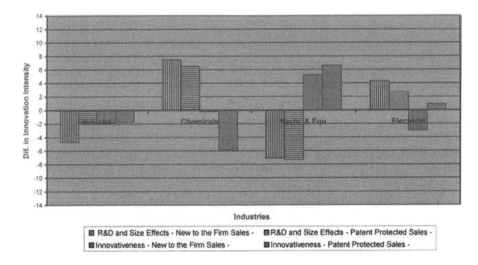

Figure 1. High-tech sectors—Innovation Propensity in terms of new to the firm innovative sales and of patent protected Sales.

The Importance of R&D for Innovation

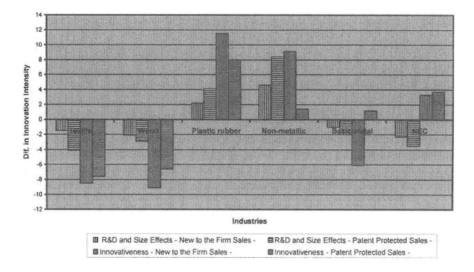

Figure 2. Low-tech sectors—Innovation propensity in terms of new to the firm innovative sales and of patent protected sales.

In Figures 1–4 we concentrate on new to the firm product innovations and patent holdings, the most subjective and the most objective of the three measures for which we have intensity of innovation measures.[11] In Figures 1–4, size and R&D are regrouped. We want to contrast the explained and unexplained portions of the interindustry innovation differences along the two innovation measures.

As the appendix Tables II and III show, R&D explains most of the inter-industry difference in the probability to innovate in the high-tech cluster. For instance, if we take the two industries with the largest and the smallest proportion of new to the firm product innovation, chemicals and vehicles, 11.9 out of a total of 13.9 percentage points difference is attributable to the R&D effect. R&D plays a less dominant role in the explanation of the intensity of innovation and in the low-tech sectors, but it still outweighs the contribution of the other explanatory variables. It is also worth noticing that enterprises are more likely to innovate than to patent, but the share in total sales due to new products is lower than the share in total sales protected by patents. For instance, in the high-tech cluster 65.6% of enterprises innovate in products

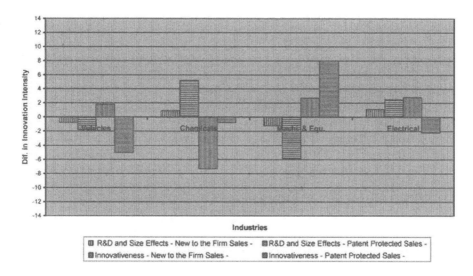

Figure 3. High-tech sectors—Innovation intensity in terms of new to the firm innovative sales and of patent protected sales.

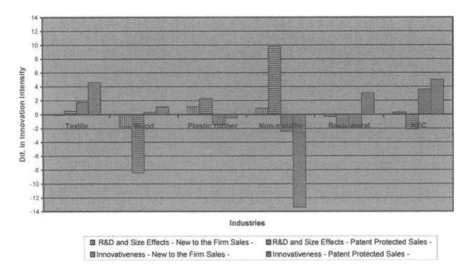

Figure 4. Low-tech sectors—Innovation intensity in terms of new to the firm innovative sales and of patent protected sales.

new to the firm but only 45.2% of them hold patents. However, whereas only 16.5% of total sales represent new products, 28.6% of total sales are patent-protected. The same pattern holds for the low-tech cluster.

Given that these magnitudes differ between indicators, it is not appropriate to compare the size of the individual contributions between the product and the patent decompositions in Figures 1–4. However, it is interesting to compare the directions of the explained and unexplained contributions and their relative magnitude for each innovation measure. With one exception (the not elsewhere classified industries in the low-tech cluster) the explained portions of the inter-industry differences in product innovation and patenting go in the same direction. With a few exceptions, the same can be said for innovativeness. If an industry is more innovative than the cluster average in terms of introducing new products, it is also more innovative in terms of patenting. The objective and subjective measures of innovation do not contradict each other. Apart from the propensity to innovate in high-tech sectors, in most other cases innovativeness is higher than the explained part of innovation. What is even more astonishing in that in some cases the unexplained part of innovation gets even larger after accounting for R&D. For instance in appendix Table III, we observe that enterprises in machinery have a higher share of new (to the firm or to the market) innovative sales than chemical firms and yet they do less R&D. The greatest part of the innovation remains to be explained. This conclusion is not very surprising, given the limited number of explanatory variables that we could introduce in this study.

7. Conclusion

We have systematically confronted all the indicators of innovation output that are provided by the French CIS 3: the five dichotomous innovation indicators for the incidence of process innovation, product innovations new to the firm, product innovations new to the market, patent applications and patent holdings and the three censored continuous indicators measuring the shares in total sales of sales accounted for by products new to the firm or new to the market, and that of patent-protected sales.

R&D is positively correlated with all measures of innovation output, and, all other things equal, more correlated than size to innovation. Innovation is generally more sensitive to R&D in the low-tech sectors than in the high-tech sectors.

The innovation indicators may differ in terms of their meaning and objective quality. The notion of product or process innovation defined in the innovation surveys is often criticized for being rather subjective, up to the respondent's appreciation, as opposed for example to a patent that has been granted by a patent officer. We nonetheless find that both measures tell a consistent story when it comes to comparing the innovation performance across industries and attribute them to explanatory factors (like size and R&D) and the unexplained innovativeness. We thus tend to downplay the skepticism on the value and meaning of subjective survey data (as expressed for example in the quote by Zvi Griliches cited by Mike Scherer in his introductory paper to this issue), and to support the faith that Ed Mansfield showed in much of his work by relying on survey data and in Scherer's acute wording by "asking the people who know".

Appendix Table I
Marginal effects of the determinants in the (generalized tobit) R&D equations—correcting for the selection of continuous R&D performing firms

Dependent variable	High-tech industries Doing continuous R&D[1]	High-tech industries Log of R&D / employee[1]	Low-tech industries Doing continuous R&D[1]	Low-tech industries Log of R&D/ employee[1]
Log of number of employees	6.8 (1.6)	0.7 (6.1)	4.3 (1.3)	−31.2 (10.8)
National group	4.5 (3.8)	−10.4 (18.4)	2.7 (2.5)	9.4 (20.6)
Foreign group	−0.6 (4.2)	−14.6 (20.1)	−1.7 (3.1)	15.7 (24.7)
International market	14.1 (2.8)	37.8 (12.5)	8.0 (2.0)	34.5 (13.4)
Demand pull	28.7 (2.7)	12.6 (12.9)	25.6 (2.0)	35.7 (16.6)
Cost push	23.1 (4.2)	60.9 (12.2)	16.7 (3.2)	43.4 (18.3)
Diversification	11.4 (5.5)	−16.0 (17.1)	6.0 (4.0)	7.1 (22.9)
Market share	0.9 (1.2)	7.6 (5.6)	4.0 (1.0)	29.6 (8.5)
Cooperation	−	14.7 (11.8)	−	33.2 (12.8)
Government support for innov.	−	8.3 (13.6)	−	−2.0 (12.8)
Information from within enter/group	−	17.5 (19.8)	−	18.1 (15.7)
Information from basic research inst.	−	29.0 (12.9)	−	11.1 (14.2)
Information from suppliers	−	−15.4 (10.8)	−	0.2 (12.3)
Information from clients	−	22.2 (18.5)	−	25.5 (12.5)
SE of regression	1	1.44 (0.13)	1	1.26 (0.08)
ρ		0.09*		0.55 (0.10)
Number of firms	899	494	1354	361

Note: All regressions include industry indicators. Standard errors are in parentheses. *imposed, [1]all marginal effects are given in %

Appendix Table II
Accounting for inter-industry differences of innovation propensity and intensity in high-tech industries

Industry	Average innovation	Size-related effects	R&D effects	Total Effects	Expected innovation	Innova-tiveness	Observed innovation
Innovation propensity (in %) in terms of new to the firm innovative sales							
Vehicles	65.6	−0.1	−4.7	−4.7	60.9	−1.9	59.0
Chemicals	65.6	0.3	7.2	7.5	73.1	−0.2	72.9
Machinery	65.6	0.1	−7.2	−7.1	58.5	5.2	63.7
Electrical	65.6	−0.3	4.6	4.3	69.9	−3.0	66.9
Average industry	65.6	0.0	0.0	0.0	65.6	0.0	65.6
Innovation intensity (in %) in terms of new to the firm innovative sales							
Vehicles	16.5	−0.2	−0.7	−0.8	15.7	1.8	17.5
Chemicals	16.5	0.1	0.8	0.9	17.4	−7.3	10.1
Machinery	16.5	0.0	−1.2	−1.2	15.3	2.7	18.0

Appendix Table II (Continued)

Industry	Average innovation	Size-related effects	R&D effects	Total Effects	Expected innovation	Innovativeness	Observed innovation
Electrical	16.5	0.1	1.1	1.1	17.7	2.8	20.5
Average industry	16.5	0.0	0.0	0.0	16.5	0.0	16.5
Innovation propensity (in %) in terms of new to the market innovative sales							
Vehicles	40.7	0.2	−3.8	−3.6	37.1	−2.6	34.5
Chemicals	40.7	0.2	5.9	6.1	46.8	−3.1	43.8
Machinery	40.7	−0.2	−5.9	−6.1	34.6	6.3	40.9
Electrical	40.7	−0.2	3.8	3.5	44.2	−0.7	43.6
Average industry	40.7	0.0	0.0	0.0	40.7	0.0	40.7
Innovation intensity (in %) in terms of new to the market innovative sales							
Vehicles	14.5	0.1	−0.8	−0.8	13.8	2.9	16.7
Chemicals	14.5	0.0	1.1	1.1	15.6	−7.2	8.5
Machinery	14.5	0.0	−2.5	−2.6	12.0	4.4	16.4
Electrical	14.5	−0.1	2.3	2.2	16.8	−0.2	16.6
Average industry	14.5	0.0	0.0	0.0	14.5	0.0	14.5
Innovation propensity (in %) in terms of patent protected sales							
Vehicles	45.2	1.8	−3.6	−1.8	43.4	−1.7	41.7
Chemicals	45.2	0.9	5.6	6.5	51.7	−5.9	45.8
Machinery	45.2	−1.8	−5.6	−7.3	37.9	6.6	44.5
Electrical	45.2	−0.9	3.5	2.7	47.9	0.9	48.8
Average industry	45.2	0.0	0.0	0.0	45.2	0.0	45.2
Innovation intensity (in %) in terms of patent protected sales							
Vehicles	28.6	1.7	−3.4	−1.8	26.8	−5.0	21.8
Chemicals	28.6	1.2	4.0	5.2	33.7	−0.8	33.0
Machinery	28.6	−1.7	−4.2	−5.9	22.7	8.0	30.6
Electrical	28.6	−1.1	3.6	2.5	31.1	−2.2	28.9
Average industry	28.6	0.0	0.0	0.0	28.6	0.0	28.6

Note: Small discrepancies are due to rounding errors

Appendix Table III
Accounting for inter-industry differences of innovation propensity and intensity in low-tech industries

Industry	Average innovation	Size-related effects	R&D effects	Total Effects	Expected innovation	Innovativeness	Observed innovation
Innovation propensity (in %) in terms of new to the firm innovative sales							
Textile	42.6	0.0	−1.4	−1.5	41.1	−8.5	32.6
Wood	42.6	1.0	−3.1	−2.1	40.4	−9.1	31.3
Plastic	42.6	−1.0	3.2	2.2	44.7	11.5	56.2
Non-metal	42.6	0.2	4.5	4.6	47.2	9.1	56.3
Basic metal	42.6	0.1	−1.0	−1.0	41.6	−6.1	35.5
Nec	42.6	−0.1	−2.1	−2.3	40.3	3.3	43.5
Average industry	42.6	0.0	0.0	0.0	42.6	0.0	42.6
Innovation intensity (in %) in terms of new to the firm innovative sales							
Textile	13.1	0.2	−0.3	−0.1	13.0	1.8	14.7
Wood	13.1	0.0	−1.8	−1.8	11.3	0.3	11.6
Plastic	13.1	−0.2	1.3	1.1	14.2	−1.4	12.8
Non-metal	13.1	−0.3	1.2	0.9	14.0	−2.5	11.5
Basic metal	13.1	0.0	−0.4	−0.3	12.7	−1.8	10.9

Appendix Table III (Continued)

Industry	Average innovation	Size-related effects	R&D effects	Total Effects	Expected innovation	Innovativeness	Observed innovation
Nec	13.1	0.2	0.1	0.3	13.4	3.6	17.0
Average industry	13.1	0.0	0.0	0.0	13.1	0.0	13.1
Innovation propensity (in %) in terms of new to the market innovative sales							
Textile	20.4	0.2	−2.3	−2.1	18.3	−3.0	15.3
Wood	20.4	1.2	−5.1	−3.9	16.5	−3.9	12.6
Plastic	20.4	−1.4	5.3	3.8	24.3	4.1	28.4
Non-metal	20.4	−0.1	7.4	7.3	27.7	1.7	29.5
Basic metal	20.4	0.1	−1.7	−1.6	18.9	1.8	20.6
Nec	20.4	0.0	−3.5	−3.6	16.9	−0.7	16.1
Average industry	20.4	0.0	0.0	0.0	20.4	0.0	20.4
Innovation intensity (in %) in terms of new to the market innovative sales							
Textile	10.8	−0.1	0.1	0.1	10.6	4.6	15.5
Wood	10.8	0.0	−1.2	−1.2	9.6	−2.1	7.5
Plastic	10.8	0.0	0.5	0.5	11.3	−1.0	10.3
Non-metal	10.8	0.1	0.6	0.7	11.5	−2.7	8.8
Basic metal	10.8	0.0	−0.1	−0.1	10.8	−1.6	9.2
Nec	10.8	0.0	0.1	0.1	10.9	2.8	13.7
Average industry	10.8	0.0	0.0	0.0	10.8	0.0	10.8
Innovation propensity (in %) in terms of patent protected sales							
Textile	22.4	−2.1	−2.0	−4.1	18.3	−7.6	10.7
Wood	22.4	1.6	−4.5	−2.9	19.5	−6.6	12.9
Plastic	22.4	−0.5	4.6	4.1	26.5	8.0	34.5
Non-metal	22.4	1.9	6.5	8.4	30.8	1.4	32.1
Basic metal	22.4	−0.5	−1.5	−2.0	20.4	1.2	21.6
Nec	22.4	−0.4	−3.1	−3.5	18.9	3.7	22.6
Average industry	22.4	0.0	0.0	0.0	22.4	0.0	22.4
Innovation intensity (in %) in terms of patent protected sales							
Textile	19.3	−1.0	1.6	0.5	19.8	4.6	24.5
Wood	19.3	0.4	−9.1	−8.4	10.7	1.1	11.8
Plastic	19.3	0.2	2.0	2.3	21.6	−0.5	21.1
Non-metal	19.3	0.7	9.1	9.8	29.1	−13.4	15.8
Basic metal	19.3	0.1	−1.9	−1.8	17.5	3.1	20.6
Nec	19.3	−0.4	−1.7	−2.1	17.2	5.0	22.2
Average industry	19.3	0.0	0.0	0.0	19.3	0.0	19.3

Note: Small discrepancies are due to rounding errors.

Acknowledgments

We are grateful to SESSI for having access to the CIS 3 and EAE data for French manufacturing under strict confidentiality requirements, and help in constructing the final working sample. We are particularly indebted to Elizabeth Kremp for her expertise and collaboration. This study builds directly on Mairesse-Mohnen (2001, 2002) and is part of an ongoing research on R&D, Innovation and Productivity. It has benefited from support by the EU Commission as part of the project on "Innovation and Employment in European Firms" (IEEF).

Notes

1. The CIS3 survey is a mandatory survey which has been conducted in 2001 (and available in its final form for research purpose in 2003). We restrict ourselves to manufacturing industries, excluding food industries, which have been surveyed by SESSI ("Service des Études et Statistiques Industrielles"). The food industries and service industries have been surveyed by other agencies than SESSI (namely the statistical offices of the Ministry of Agriculture and the Ministry of Education and

Research, and by INSEE). The SESSI survey concerns some 5500 manufacturing firms with 20 employees or more, which have been chosen randomly, using the business register based on legal units and according to the following stratified sampling design: all firms over 500 employees, 1/2 for firms from 100 to 499 employees, 1/4 for firms from 50 to 99 employees, and 1/8 for firms from 20 to 49 employees. The rate of response was 86%, corresponding to an overall coverage of 89% of the total turnover for the manufacturing sector in 2000. We have restricted our sample to the firms which have also answered the EAE surveys in 1998, 1999 and 2000, and have also eliminated a number of firms for which important variables or ratios had missing values or extreme outlier values, for example firms with an R&D to sales ratio above 50%.

2. Note that the non-innovating firms have to report also on the last group of questions of the survey, concerning patents and other protection methods. As should be expected, only very few (less than 20 in our sample) declare that they have applied for a patent in 1998–2000, and a small minority (about 80) that they hold at least one patent in 2000. We have chosen to ignore this information for these few firms, since we could not treat them in our model as the innovating firms for which we have much more information.

3. In implementing the estimation, we make a logit transformation on the share of innovative sales, so that the dependent variable would vary from minus infinity to plus infinity, i.e. over the same domain as the normally distributed random error term. To avoid infinite values, the sales shares corresponding to the various innovation indicators are truncated from below at 0.01 and from above at 0.99.

4. The ten industries we control for are non-metallic minerals (NACE 14 and NACE 26), textiles (NACE 17-NACE 19), wood (NACE 20-NACE 22), chemicals (NACE 23 and NACE 24), plastics (NACE 25), basic metals (NACE 27 and NACE 28), machinery (NACE 29), electrical products (NACE 30-NACE 33), vehicles (NACE 34 and NACE 35), and industries not elsewhere classified (NACE 36).

5. These variables are defined and included in the R&D equations (1) as in Crépon-Duguet-Mairesse, 1998.

6. Crépon-Duguet-Mairesse, 1998, have also excluded the market share and diversification variables but included the demand pull and cost push variables.

7. For R&D in the high-tech sectors, the likelihood function of the generalized tobit has a local maximum for a positive value of the correlation coefficient between the error terms of the two parts of the tobit model and a global maximum for a negative value, but the two maxima are not far apart. In that case, we have preferred to impose a priori the positive correlation coefficient in our estimation procedure, on the presumption that left out determinants affect the probability to do R&D and its intensity in the same direction. We have the same problem in the case of the generalized tobit reduced form equations for the new to the market product innovation indicators in the low-tech sectors. In the case of generalized tobit reduced form equations for the patent holdings indicators in both the high- and low-tech sectors, we also encounter a somewhat similar problem with a correlation coefficient equal to one at the maximum maximorum of the likelihood function. In all these cases the next maximum corresponded to a very close value of the likelihood function and to a positive correlation coefficient, and we just chose to impose that correlation coefficient in estimation.

8. The marginal effects for the two sub-samples are simply obtained as the sub-samples averages of the marginal effects computed for each firm. The marginal effects on the five indicators of innovation propensity are themselves equal for a given firm to the corresponding estimated coefficient multiplied by the predicted probability to innovate for this firm. Similarly, the marginal effects on the three indicators of innovation intensity are equal for a given firm to the corresponding estimated coefficient multiplied by $\exp(z)/(1+\exp(z))^2$, where z is the predicted logit transformation of innovation intensity for the firm (see Wooldridge, 2003).

9. We give each industry equal weight.

10. If the $f()$ function was linear, there would be no approximation error.

11. The numerical appendix tables also present the decomposition for new to the market product innovations, which is closer to the decomposition for new to the firm products than for patents.

References

Acs, Z., D. Audretsch, and M. Feldman, 1992, 'Real Effects of Academic Research: Comment,' *American Economic Review* **82** (1), 363–367.

Crépon, B., E. Duguet, and J. Mairesse, 1998, 'Research and Development, Innovation and Productivity: An Econometric Analysis at the Firm Level,' *Economics of Innovation and New Technology* **7**(2), 115–158.

Gouriéroux, C., A. Monfort, and A. Trognon, 1985, 'Moindres carrés asymptotiques,' *Annales de l'INSEE* **58**, 91–122.

Griliches, Z., 1965, 'Comment on Mansfield,' in R. Tybout (ed.), *Economics of Research and Development*, Columbus: Ohio State University Press, 148–150.

Griliches, Z., 1981, 'Market Value, R&D and Patents,' *Economics Letters* **7**, 183–187.

Hall, B. and R. Oriani, 2004, 'Does the Market Value R&D Investment by European Firms? Evidence from a Panel of Manufacturing Firms in France, Germany, and Italy,' NBER working paper 10408.

Jaffe, A., 1989, 'Real Effects of Academic Research,' *American Economic Review* **79** (5), 957–970.

Mairesse, J. and P. Mohnen, 2001, 'To be or not to be Innovative: An Exercice in Measurement,' *STI Review. Special Issue on New Science and Technology Indicators*, OECD **27**, 103–129.

Mairesse, J. and P. Mohnen, 2002, 'Accounting for Innovation and Measuring Innovativeness: An Illustrative Framework and an Application,' *American Economic Review, Papers and Proceedings* **92** (2), 226–230.

Mansfield, E., 1965a, 'Rates of return from industrial research and development,' *American Economic Review* **55**, 310–322.

Mansfield, E., 1965b, 'The Process of Technical Changes,' in R. Tybout (ed.), *Economics of Research and Development*, Columbus: Ohio State University Press, 136–147.

Mansfield, E., 1980, 'Basic Research and Productivity Increase in Manufacturing,' *American Economic Review* **70**, 863–873.

Mansfield, E., J. Rapoport, A. Romeo, S. Wagner, and G. Beardsley, 1977, 'Social and Private Rates of Return from Industrial Innovations,' *Quarterly Journal of Economics* **77**, 221–240.

Organization for Economic Co-operation and Development (1992, 1996), *Oslo Manual*, Paris, 1st, 2nd edition.

Pavitt, K., 1984, 'Sectoral Patterns of Technical Change: Towards a Taxonomy and a Theory,' *Research Policy* **13**, 343–373.

Wooldridge, J., 2003, *Econometric Analysis of Cross Section and Panel Data*, Cambridge: MIT Press.

University R&D and Firm Productivity: Evidence from Italy

Giuseppe Medda[1]
Claudio Piga[2]
Donald S. Siegel[3]

ABSTRACT. Ed Mansfield wrote several papers on the private returns to basic research (e.g. Mansfield, 1980) and the influence of academic research on industrial innovation (e.g. Mansfield, 1991). We extend this line of research by assessing the impact of university research on total factor productivity growth of Italian manufacturing firms. The econometric analysis is based on reduced-form estimation of the R&D capital stock model, including controls for two potential sources of sample selection bias, as proposed by Crepon *et al.* (1998) and Piga and Vivarelli (2004). Our results suggest that while there are positive returns to collaborative research with other firms, collaborative research with universities does not appear to directly stimulate productivity. We interpret this result as consistent with recent evidence (e.g. Hall *et al.*, 2001, 2003) suggesting that firms engage in collaborative research with universities when appropriability conditions are weak.

Key words: university R&D, total factor productivity, sample selection bias

JEL Classification: C21, C80, D24, O30

[1] University of Cagliari
Viale Fra' Ignazio
Cagliari, 09100
Italy
E-mail: gmedda@yahoo.it
[2] Nottingham University Business School
Wollaton Road
Nottingham NG8 1BB
United Kingdom
E-mail: Claudio.Piga@Nottingham.ac.uk
[3] Department of Economics
Rensselaer Polytechnic Institute 3502 Russell Sage
110 8th Street
Troy, NY 12180-3590
United States
E-mail: sieged@rpi.edu

1. Introduction

Ed Mansfield is probably best known for his seminal project-level research on the microeconomics of technological advance and the computation of social returns to innovation (Mansfield, 1968; Mansfield *et al.*, 1977). Professor Mansfield also wrote several papers on the private or firm-level returns to basic research (e.g. Mansfield, 1980) and also one of the first comprehensive studies of the influence of academic research on industrial innovation (Mansfield, 1991).

In this paper, we attempt to extend this line of research, by assessing the private returns to collaborative R&D with universities. Such evidence may shed light on an unexplored dimension of university technology transfer: the impact of joint research projects with universities on a firm's growth in total factor productivity (henceforth, TFP). TFP is generally regarded to be the best metric of economic efficiency.

Our empirical analysis is based on comprehensive, longitudinal surveys of Italian manufacturing firms. These files contain detailed data on output, factor inputs, and R&D investment, which we use to estimate a reduced-form version of the R&D capital stock model. The econometric analysis includes controls for two types of sample selection bias, as proposed by Crepon *et al.* (1998) and Piga and Vivarelli (2004), a variant of which was applied to an earlier version of these data in a previous paper (Medda *et al.*, 2004).

2. Econometric model

Our econometric model is a reduced-form version of the R&D capital stock model (Griliches,

1979), which asserts that there is a stock of technical capital (in addition to physical capital) in a firm's production function. If we assume disembodied, Hicks-neutral, technological progress, constant returns to scale with respect to the conventional inputs (capital, labor and materials), perfectly competitive factors markets, and we compute logarithms and differentiate the production function with respect to time, we have the following equation:

$$\text{TFPG} = \alpha + \beta_1 X_1 + u \quad (1)$$

where TFPG = growth in total factor productivity (TFP); X_1 = rate of R&D investment, typically computed as the ratio of R&D to output u = a classical disturbance term; α = the rate of disembodied external technical change.

In this type of model, TFP is computed as a Solow residual. Empirical estimates of β_1 from equation (1) have been interpreted as an estimate of the marginal private rate of return to investment in R&D. Scherer (1982) noted that if the stock of R&D capital depreciates, estimates of β_1 are downwardly biased. Schankerman (1981) discusses the impact of "double-counting" in the calculation of the private returns to R&D, since R&D expenditures are often already included in measures of capital, materials, and labor (the conventional arguments of a production function). Thus, it is common in this literature to refer to β_1 as an "excess" rate of return (in excess of normal remuneration to conventional factors of production).

As noted in Link and Siegel (2003), most researchers report estimates of β_1 that are positive and statistically significant, implying that there are positive returns to R&D. There have also been numerous studies that provide evidence on *differential* returns to R&D by type (i.e. product versus process), character of use (i.e. basic research, applied research, and development), or source of funding (i.e. privately-financed R&D versus publicly-funded R&D). For instance, Mansfield (1980), Link (1981), and Griliches (1986) find that there is a productivity premium associated with basic research. Lichtenberg and Siegel (1991) report that while company-funded R&D has a positive impact of productivity, publicly-funded R&D does not.

Another important distinction in innovative activity at the firm level is between internal and external R&D. External research projects are conducted with other firms, universities, or non-profit research organizations. Such activities might enable firms to enhance their "absorptive capacity" (Cohen and Levinthal, 1989) or result in other types of beneficial research spillovers (Kamien and Zang, 2000). Hall *et al.* (2001) found that firms typically collaborate with universities when they engage in long-term, basic research projects.

We would like to estimate equation (1), using total R&D intensity, or the ratio of R&D expenditure to sales as our proxy for the rate of investment in R&D investment. More importantly, we wish to disaggregate this intensity measure into internal and external R&D intensities, in order to assess their differential returns. Further disaggregation of external R&D is made possible by the availability of data on the research relationships companies have with research centers, universities and other firms.

It is important to note that there are two potential sources of sample selection bias associated with estimation of equation (1). The first potential source of bias relates to the fact that many firms do not conduct formal R&D activities, in the sense that they report zero expenditure on R&D. Second, as noted by Piga and Vivarelli (2004), the decision to undertake external research may be related to the antecedent decision to engage in some form of R&D. Our point is that firms reporting that they have conducted external research (as some do in our survey) are not randomly selected, but rather, constitute a sub-sample of those reporting involvement in R&D.

To mitigate these problems, we propose to estimate a two-stage, treatment effects model (Barnow *et al.*, 1981). In the first stage, we estimate a bivariate probit sample selection model, in which we jointly assess the determinants of reporting positive R&D expenditure and, conditional on non-zero R&D, the determinants of external R&D activity. Formally:

$$\begin{aligned} \text{DREEXT}_i = \beta_1 x_{i1} + \epsilon_{i1}, \quad y_{i1} = 1 \\ \text{if R\&DEXT}_i > 0, \ 0 \text{ otherwise} \end{aligned} \quad (2)$$

$$DRE_i = \beta_2 x_{i2} + \epsilon_{i2} y_{i2} = 1$$
if $R\&D_i > 0$, 0 otherwise

$$(\epsilon_1, \epsilon_2) \sim BVN(0, 0, 1, 1, \rho)$$

$(DREEXT_i, x_{i1})$ is observed
only when $DRE_i = 1$

where i is a firm subscript, DRE is a dummy variable = 1 if the firm reports positive R&D expenditure (and thus, has a positive R&D intensity—$R\&D_i > 0$); 0 otherwise, DREEXT is a dummy variable = 1 if the firm reports positive external R&D; 0 otherwise, (x_1, x_2) are vectors of variables that influence the decision to engage in R&D and external R&D activity, and (ϵ_1, ϵ_2) are classical disturbance terms, which are assumed to be jointly and normally distributed with correlation ρ. A more technical analysis of this model is presented in Greene (2003, pp. 710–712). The two Inverse Mill's Ratios (IMRs) calculated in the first stage are then inserted into equation (1), allowing us to discriminate between the impact of internal and external R&D expenditures on TFP (which is our ultimate objective) from those effects that (x_1, x_2) have on the decisions to engage in such research activity.

3. Data and empirical results

Our primary dataset is a 1998 survey conducted by Mediocredito Centrale (www.mcc.it), an Italian investment bank. The *Mediocredito Centrale* survey consists of balance sheet data, data on conventional inputs, R&D, and output, and several qualitative items relating to the firm's competitive environment and industry characteristics. These data are described in greater detail in Medda *et al.* (2004). All firms with more than 500 employees were sampled, with probability-based sampling (on the basis of firm size) for all other companies. Although the balance sheet and productivity data are available for as many as 9 years (1989–1997), we have data on R&D expenditure (and various types of R&D) for only 3 years (1995–1997).

Following Los and Verspagen (2000), we employ a gross output specification of the production function to compute TFP (rather than a value-added specification), with capital, labor, and materials (including energy) as the three factor inputs. Capital growth was calculated as the growth rate of tangible assets net of depreciation. Data on energy and materials costs were used to compute growth rates of these inputs. Labor input growth was calculated as the growth in the number of non-R&D employees, weighted by the number of part-time workers, to avoid the double counting problem cited earlier.

If we assume perfectly competitive markets for factor inputs, then the output elasticities of each of the factor inputs are equal to their respective cost shares. To compute shares for each firm over the sample period, the ratios of labor cost and materials and energy costs to total cost were calculated for the initial and final years. For the statistical analysis, we used the average values of these variables. Following Lichtenberg and Siegel (1991), the cost share of capital was calculated as a residual. All variables were deflated using an industry-specific price deflator. These deflators were also disaggregated by location to take account of regional differences in input prices in the North-West, North-East, Center, and South of Italy.

Variable definitions are provided in Table I. After eliminating outliers and firms with missing data, our final sample consists of 2222 firms. Descriptive statistics are presented in Table II. Only 687 out of 2222 firms (approximately 31%) reported positive R&D expenditure. These 687 firms had an average R&D intensity of 1.51%. The table reveals that the southern region of Italy is lagging behind other regions, in terms of various indicators of research activity. Not surprisingly, we find that large firms have a greater propensity to establish formal research projects. Recall that we can also disaggregate external R&D expenditure into three categories: expenditure on research with universities, other research centers, and other companies. First, note that a greater R&D intensity seems to characterize firms involved in both internal and external activities, suggesting a complementarity between the two. Second, the firms indicating a research collaboration with universities exhibit a greater R&D intensity.

TABLE I
Variables names and description

TFPG	Average annual growth in TFP
R&D	Ratio of R&D expenditure to Sales
DRE	Dummy = 1 if R&D > 0
R&DINT	Ratio of Internal R&D Expenditure to Sales
R&DEXT	Ratio of External R&D Expenditure to Sales
DREEXT	Dummy = 1 if R&DEXT > 0
R&DEXTRC	Ratio of External R&D Expenditure With Research Centers to Sales
R&DEXTOF	Ratio of External R&D Expenditure With Other Firms to Sales
R&DEXTUN	Ratio of External R&D Expenditure With Universities to Sales
RESERVE	Ratio of Accumulated Retained Earnings over Total Assets
HEADGR	Dummy = 1 if a firm is a Holding Company or Controls other firms within a group organization
LNEMP	Size measured as the natural log of number of employees
INTASS	Ratio of 1994 Intangible Assets over Total Assets
DINF	Dummy = 1 if firm invested in 1995–1997 to improve its Information Technology (IT) equipment.
OUTSOURCP	% of input purchases made within outsourcing agreements.
COMPABR	Index of extent of competition from foreign firms measured as the square root of the sum of the three dummy variables specifying whether the main competitors are localized, respectively, in the European Union, in other industrialized countries and in developing countries.
MAIN3CL	% of total sales to the three main clients (1992; 1995)
PRODDIVE	Index of Product diversification $= 1/(\Sigma s_i^2)$, s_i = Shares of sales from product group i (1995)
HUMDEG	Percentage of employees with degree or post-graduate qualifications (1992; 1995)
EXPFATT	Percentage of export sales over Total Sales (1992; 1995)
NWEST	Dummy = 1 if firm located in the North-west of Italy
NEAST	Dummy = 1 if firm located in the North-east of Italy
CENTRE	Dummy = 1 if firm located in the Center of Italy
SOUTH	Dummy = 1 if firm located in the South of Italy
EMPL_	Three Dummy variables for size classes ($\mathbf{1}: 11 \leq x \leq 50; \mathbf{2}: 51 \leq x \leq 250$; $\mathbf{3}: 251 \leq x$)

Table III presents estimates of Bivariate Probit Sample Selection model outlined in equation (2). In general, these coefficients have the expected signs. For example, we find that there is a positive association between export intensity and the probability of engaging in R&D. We also find that large, multi-product firms, and those that have a greater proportion of intangible assets and employees with a degree, are more likely to report positive R&D expenditure. With respect to the determinants of external relationships, it appears that exporting firms, small firms, and those companies acquiring a large proportion of their inputs via outsourcing agreements, are more likely to establish such alliances.

Table IV contains parameter estimates of the TFP treatment effects model. Not surprisingly, we find that there is a positive association between R&D and productivity growth. Our estimate of a 39.0% "return" to R&D is a bit higher than those reported in previous studies. In the second column of Table 4, we find that both internal and external R&D activities stimulate higher productivity growth. Note, however, that external R&D appears to generate a higher return than internal research, and this difference is statistically significant. The third column of Table IV indicates that engaging in external research projects with research centers and especially, other firms, significantly enhances productivity, while collaboration with universities does not. Finally, it is important to note the significance of the IMR term in the DRE equation, relating to the decision to engage in R&D. This demonstrates the need to correct for sample selection biases in estimation of the returns to R&D, thus, lending credence to our methodological approach.

5. Conclusions and suggestions for additional research

In this short paper, we have estimated a reduced-form version of the R&D capital stock model, with controls for two potential sources of sample selection bias. Our analysis is an extension of Mansfield's research of the private returns to R&D and is based on a comprehensive firm-level dataset from Italy containing information on various types of external research.

TABLE II
Industry, size, and regional distribution of firms and mean values of growth in total factor productivity growth (TFPG), Sales per worker (DLABP), and R&D Intensity

	N	TFPG Mean	DLABP Mean	N Firms with positive R&D	% Firms with positive R&D	% R&D exp./Sales
TOTAL	2222	−0.0095	−0.0330	687	30.92	1.51
Food, tobacco	239	−0.0072	−0.0581	49	20.50	0.66
Textiles, apparel	315	−0.0189	−0.0641	98	31.11	1.18
Shoes, leather	82	0.0032	0.0146	23	28.05	0.86
Wood and wood products	62	−0.0150	−0.0212	12	19.35	0.63
Paper, printing	144	−0.0038	−0.0376	18	12.50	0.72
Petroleum, coal	10	0.0434	0.0125	2	20.00	0.26
Chemicals	111	0.0106	0.0377	41	36.94	2.38
Rubber, plastics	145	−0.0168	−0.0616	36	24.83	1.21
Stone, clay, glass	143	−0.0220	−0.0509	34	23.78	1.00
Metals and Metallic products	277	−0.0002	0.0166	53	19.13	1.35
Industrial machinery	368	−0.0136	−0.0420	178	48.37	1.87
Electric and electronic equipment, instruments	139	−0.0107	−0.0347	71	51.08	2.17
Transportation	85	−0.0041	0.0141	39	45.88	1.98
Misc.: furniture, jewelry, musical instruments, toys	102	−0.0144	−0.0726	33	32.35	1.14
North-west	912	−0.0075	−0.0205	325	35.64	1.42
North-east	641	−0.0122	−0.0451	209	32.61	1.78
Centre	356	−0.0135	−0.0348	99	27.81	1.50
South	313	−0.0055	−0.0427	54	17.25	1.03
$11 \leq$ empl ≤ 50	1120	−0.0103	−0.0459	200	17.86	1.59
$50 <$ empl. ≤ 250	813	−0.0083	−0.0220	303	37.27	1.45
Empl. > 250	289	−0.0099	−0.0141	184	63.67	1.52
R&D $= 0$	1535	−0.0094	−0.0363	–	–	–
R&D > 0	687	−0.0099	−0.0257	687	30.92	1.51
Internal R&D $= 0$	1574	−0.0091	−0.0349	–	–	–
Internal R&D > 0	648	−0.0107	−0.0285	–	–	1.52
External R&D $= 0$	1899	−0.0102	−0.0364	–	–	–
External R&D > 0	323	−0.0054	−0.0132	–	–	1.81
Int.&Ext. R&D $= 0$	1938	−0.0100	−0.0353	–	–	–
Int.&Ext. R&D > 0	284	−0.0066	−0.0178	–	–	1.89
R&D with universities $= 0$	2139	−0.0097	−0.0336	–	–	–
R&D with universities > 0	83	−0.0044	−0.0179	–	–	2.38
R&D with research centre $= 0$	2084	−0.0100	−0.0342	–	–	–
R&D with research centre > 0	138	−0.0024	−0.0154	–	–	1.69
R&D with other firms $= 0$	2013	−0.0098	−0.0346	–	–	–
R&D with other firms > 0	209	−0.0071	−0.0180	–	–	1.82

We find that external R&D generates significantly higher returns than internal R&D. However, these positive returns appear to be driven primarily by external research projects with other companies and research centers. On the other hand, investment in external collaborative research with universities does not appear to generate a direct positive return to the firm.

Our evidence is consistent with Hall et al. (2003), who reported that firms are likely to collaborate with universities on basic research projects and when it is difficult for them to

TABLE III
Estimates of the determinants of R&D and external R&D aativity, based on bivariate probit sample selection model

	Coeff.	z-stat.	Sig.
External RD equation (DREEXT)			
CONST.	0.749	3.025	***
RESERVE	−1.002	−2.609	***
HEADGR	0.212	1.706	*
EMPL_1	0.428	2.593	***
EMPL_2	0.054	0.408	
INTASS	2.245	1.764	*
OUTSOURCP	0.344	2.702	***
EXPFATT	−0.471	−2.696	***
HUMDEG	0.588	0.916	
RD equation (DRE)			
CONST.	−2.809	−14.890	***
HEADGR	0.148	1.557	
LNDIP	0.300	9.149	***
HUMDEG	1.755	4.049	***
EXPFATT	0.418	3.654	***
DINF	0.511	6.486	***
PRODDIVE	11.058	2.054	**
COMPABR	0.193	3.404	***
OUTSOURCP	−0.278	−3.255	***
MAIN3CL	−0.291	−2.215	**
RHO			
(equations' disturbances' correlation)	−0.566	−3.590	***
N	2222		
Log likelihood function	−1557.432		
Wald St. (ind.; regr. DREEXT)†	20.83		**
Wald St. (ind.; regr. DRE)†	60.39		***

***, **, * Significant at the 1, 5 and 10% level respectively. Includes 13 industrial dummy variables. Variable definitions are presented in Table I. †Joint significance of industry dummies in the two equations.

TABLE IV
Regressions of TFP growth in 1995–1997 on R&D intensity dependent variable: average annual TFP growth (TFPG)
Two Stage least squares regression using bivariate selection model

	Coeff.	t-ratio	Sig	Coeff.	t-ratio	Sig	Coeff.	t-ratio	Sig.
CONST.	−0.004	−1.142		−0.002	−0.344		−0.002	−0.328	
R&D	0.39	4.885	***						
R&DINT				0.302	3.231	***	0.308	3.212	***
R&DEXT				0.632	3.031	***			
R&DEXTRC							0.542	1.875	*
R&DEXTOF							0.870	2.695	***
R&DEXTUN							−0.066	−0.059	
NWEST	−0.002	−0.533		−0.002	−0.673		−0.002	−0.708	
NEAST	−0.006	−1.769	*	−0.006	−1.815	*	−0.007	−1.853	*
CENTRE	−0.008	−2.141	**	−0.009	−2.271	**	−0.009	−2.291	**
Inverse mills ratio									
(DREEXT eq.)				0.003	1.417		0.003	1.403	
Inverse mills ration									
(DRE eq.)	−0.005	2.929	***	−0.006	−2.688	***	−0.006	−2.711	***
N	2222			2222			2222		
Adj.R^2	0.038			0.039			0.039		
F test	5.94			5.510		***	5.060		***

TABLE IV (Continued)

	Coeff.	t-ratio	Sig	Coeff.	t-ratio	Sig	Coeff.	t-ratio	Sig
Wald St. (ind)[†]	75.8		***	76.504		***	77.119		***
Wald St. (reg)[†]	7.61		*	7.792		**	7.893		**
Reset test	1.01			1.70			1.896		

***, **, * Significant at the 1, 5, and 10% level respectively. Includes 13 industrial dummy variables. Variable definitions are presented in Table I.

[†] Joint significance of industry and regional dummies.

appropriate benefits from joint research. However, if these R&D efforts significantly enhance a firm's absorptive capacity, the knowledge generated from interacting with universities may ultimately lead to higher productivity growth. If such an effect holds, it is likely to take a long time for such activities to result in a performance improvement, since basic research has a long time frame. Thus, in future work, it might be useful to extend the time frame of our analysis of productivity growth when assessing the returns to collaborative research with universities.

References

Barnow, B.S., G.G. Cain, and A.S. Goldberger, 1981, 'Issues in the analysis of selection bias' in E. Stromsdorfer and G. Farkas, (eds.), *Evaluation Studies Review*, San Francisco, Ann.5, Sage, 43–59.

Cohen, W.M., and D.A. Levinthal, 1989, 'Innovation and Learning: The Two Faces of R&D,' *The Economic Journal* **99** (3), 569–596.

Crepon, B., E. Duguet, and J. Mairesse, 1998, 'Research, Innovation and Productivity: An Econometric Analysis at the Firm Level,' *Economics of Innovation and New Technology* **7** (2), 115–158.

Greene, W.H., 2003, *Econometric Analysis*, 5th edition. Upper Saddle River, NJ: Prentice Hall.

Griliches, Z., 1979, 'Issues in Assessing the Contribution of R&D to Productivity Growth,' *Bell Journal of Economics* **10**, 92–116.

Griliches, Z., 1986, 'Productivity, R&D and Basic Research at the Firm Level in the 1970's,' *American Economic Review* **76** (1), 141–154.

Hall, B.H., A.N. Link, and J.T. Scott, 2001, 'Barriers Inhibiting Industry from Partnering with Universities: Evidence from the Advanced Technology Program,' *Journal of Technology Transfer* **26**, 87–98.

Hall, B.H., A.N. Link, and J.T. Scott, 2003, 'Universities as Research Partners,' *Review of Economics and Statistics* **85** (2), 485–491.

Kamien, M., and I. Zang, 2000, 'Meet me Halfway: Research Joint Ventures and Absorptive Capacity,' *International Journal of Industrial Organization* **18** (7), 995–1012.

Lichtenberg, F., and D. Siegel, 1991, 'The Impact of R&D Investment on Productivity – New Evidence Using R&D – LRD Data,' *Economic Inquiry* **29** (2), 203–228.

Link, A.N., 1981, 'Basic Research and Productivity Increase in Manufacturing: Additional Evidence,' *American Economic Review* **71** (5) 1111–1112.

Link, A., and D.S. Siegel, 2003, *Technological Change and Economic Performance*, London and New York, NY: Routledge.

Los, B., and B. Verspagen, 2000, 'R&D Spillovers and Productivity: Evidence from U.S. Manufacturing Microdata,' *Empirical Economics* **25**, 127–148.

Mansfield, E., 1968, *Industrial Research and Technological Change*, New York: W.W. Norton.

Mansfield, E., 1980 'Basic Research and Productivity Increase in Manufacturing,' *American Economic Review* **70**, 863–873.

Mansfield, E., 1991, 'Academic Research and Industrial Innovation,' *Research Policy* **20** (1), 1–12.

Mansfield, E., J. Rapoport, A. Romeo, S. Wagner, and G. Beardsley, 1977, 'Social and Private Rates of Return from Industrial Innovations,' *Quarterly Journal of Economics* **91**, 221–240.

Medda, G., C.A. Piga, and D.S. Siegel, 2004, 'Assessing the Returns to Collaborative Research: Firm-Level Evidence from Italy,' Rensselaer Department of Economics Working Paper #0416, June 2004.

Piga, C.A. and M. Vivarelli (2004). 'Internal and External R&D: A Sample Selection Approach,' *Oxford Bulletin of Economics and Statistics* **66** (4), 457–482.

Schankerman, M., 1981, 'The Effects of Double-Counting and Expensing on the Measured Returns to R&D,' *Review of Economics and Statistics* **63**, 454–458.

Scherer, F.M., 1982, 'Inter-industry Technology Flows and Productivity Growth,' *Review of Economics and Statistics*, **6**, 627–634.

Reflections on Mansfield, Technological Complexity, and the "Golden Age" of U.S. Corporate R&D

Philip E. Auerswald[1]
Lewis M. Branscomb[2]

ABSTRACT. We focus on two themes, among those in Mansfield's work, particularly relevant to understanding the role of large corporations in the U.S. innovation system: (1) the development of science-based inventions into market-ready innovations, and (2) the imitation by one firm of another's technology. Both of these phenomena, we propose, depend critically on the extent of technological and organizational complexity characteristic of current products and potential innovations. Reporting on recent survey research of our own, we argue that the origins and potentially the future of U.S. leadership in technology-based economic growth lie in the complementarity of large corporations and entrepreneurial startups, each exploring and exploiting the market potential of different types of science-based innovations.

Key words: complexity, corporate research and development (R&D), imitation, invention, innovation, military, technology

JEL Classification: L22, L23, O31, O32

> The management of technology entails a great deal more than the establishment of an R&D laboratory that produces a lot of good technical output. A central problem facing a firm that attempts to be innovative is to effect the proper coupling between R&D, on the one hand, and marketing and production on the other. Many R&D projects are designed without sufficient understanding of market and production and realities. Many marketing and production people are unnecessarily impervious to the good ideas produced by R&D people and people in other parts of the of the firm, there being considerable evidence that person-to-person contacts are the most effective way of transferring ideas and technology.
> —Mansfield (1993, p. xix)

[1] *School of Public Policy, George Mason University
4400 University Drive, Fairfax, Virginia 22030-4444
U.S.A.
E-mail: auerswald@gmu.edu*
[2] *Kennedy School of Government, Harvard University
79 J.F. Kennedy Street, Cambridge, MA 02138, U.S.A.
E-mail: lewis_branscomb@harvard.edu*

1. Introduction

In papers and books spanning decades, Edwin Mansfield meticulously explored the nature of the innovation process. Notably for the purposes of this paper, Mansfield's work focused on corporate research and development (R&D) in the U.S. during an era of previously unmatched U.S. scientific, technological, and economic dominance. A contribution to a volume published in Mansfield's honor is thus a natural place to raise the question: Has the golden age of science-based innovation in large corporations drawn to a close? Our paper seeks to address both policy and theoretical dimensions of this question, informed by recent research on investments in early stage technology development (ESTD) in large corporations—the "coupling between R&D, on the one hand, and marketing and production on the other" described by Mansfield in the above quote.[3]

On the policy side, we begin with the view—seemingly uncontroversial, but actually quite debatable—that to understand the future role of U.S. corporations in the innovation system, we have to understand its past. Since World War II, industry in the United States has (notably, during the Cold War) vied, successfully in the main, with other nations for leadership in technological capabilities. Once other nations recovered from World War II, particularly in the 1980s, U.S. firms in some industries failed to capture the returns from products they originally prototype as rapidly as foreign competition. Yet during what we are referring to as the "golden age" of U.S. corporate R&D from 1950 to 1980, the leadership of the U.S. in both science and commercial inventiveness was nearly absolute.

Of the themes in Mansfield's work, we focus on two that are, in our view, fundamental to understanding the role of large corporations in the U.S. innovation system past and future: (1) the development of science-based inventions into market-ready innovations by large firms (Mansfield, 1969, 1981, 1993, 1995), and (2) the imitation by one firm of another's technology (Mansfield 1961, 1963; Mansfield et al 1981).[4] Both, we will argue, depend critically on the extent of technological and organizational complexity of both current products and potential innovations. Referring to Mansfield's findings, we will suggest that the origins and potentially the future of U.S. leadership in technology-based economic growth lie in a unique complementarity between large corporations and entrepreneurial start-ups, each exploring and exploiting the market potential of different types of science-based innovations.

In Section 2, we describe the ascendancy of U.S. corporate research and development operations, which we argue was driven to a substantially extent by the disruptive impacts of World War II and subsequent military dominance of support for U.S. research and development (R&D). In Section 3, we discuss technology-based innovation in large corporations in the 1960s and 1970s, viewed via the early works of Mansfield and his contemporaries—notably, other contributors to the 1962 volume on *The Rate and Direction of Inventive Activity: Economic and Social Factors*, edited by Richard Nelson. In Section 4 we turn to current trends. We propose a conceptual model of the process of technology-based innovation in corporations, then report the findings from recent survey research based upon that conceptual model. In Section 5, we summarize the implications of the paper for the future role of large corporations in the U.S. innovation system.

2. World War II and the ascendancy of large, research intensive, U.S. firms

Rosenberg and Birdzell (1985) document the advent, at the end of the 19th century, of the corporate research laboratory. The dramatic trend toward the consolidation of American business in the first quarter of the 20th century had a direct impact upon the organization of industrial innovation. As early as 1928, Joseph Schumpeter observed that in the new era of oligopolistic markets dominated by large trusts, "innovation is ... not any more embodied *typically* in new firms, but goes on, within the big units now existing, largely independently of individual persons .... Progress becomes 'automatised', increasingly impersonal and decreasingly a matter of leadership and individual initiative" (Schumpeter, 1928, pp. 384–385).[5] To Schumpeter, the routinization of innovation was a global phenomenon with profound implications. It meant the end of entrepreneurship, and thus the *de facto* end of capitalism: "Capitalism, whilst economically stable, and even gaining in stability, creates, by rationalizing the human mind, a mentality and a style of life incompatible with its own fundamental conditions, motives and social institutions, and will be changed, although not by economic necessity and probably even at some sacrifice of economic welfare, into an order of things which it will be mere a matter of taste and terminology to call Socialism or not".

The evolutionary economic and social trajectory that Schumpeter in 1928 sought to anticipate—already volatile in the aftermath of the "Great War"—was violently disrupted by the World War II. In 1913, prior to World War I, dynamic centers of production capable of developing new products competitive in world markets existed in many countries (notably Czechoslovakia, France, Germany, Italy, Japan, the U.K., and the U.S.). The U.S. accounted for only 17% of world GDP while Western Europe, Russia, Japan, and China together accounted for 74%. World War II devastated U.S. competitors for science and technological leadership at the same time that it drove a surge in U.S. productive capabilities. By 1950, five years after the end of World War II, the U.S. was thoroughly dominant in commercial innovation. More broadly, the U.S. now accounted for 27% of world GDP while Western Europe, Russia, Japan, and China together accounted for only 50%—a degree of economic concentration exceeded in the past 500 years only in the case of China during the early 19th century.[6] The return home of 12 million veterans not only fueled an immediate demand-driven postwar boom but also created within the labor pool a deep reservoir of management and entrepreneurial talent—men experienced at a young age in assessing risk, making decisions under pressure, and mobilizing large teams. The GI bill was an additional stimulus, permitting many of those returning veterans to seek advanced degrees in science and engineering. The large scale immigration to the U.S. (during and after World War II) of scientists, engineers, executives, and entrepreneurs further deepened the talent pool.

Victory in World War II left the U.S. in the position of being the world's default economic power;[7] Federal government policies-alternately enlightened and paranoid-and aggressive corporate strategy combined to convert a potentially transient position of strength into a sustained period of U.S. economic dominance built upon leadership in science-based innovation. Investments in basic science infrastructure famously advocated by Vannevar Bush (among others) provided resources required to capitalize on the nation's wartime windfall of scientific and technological talent, rapidly building leading U.S. research institutions. Managers at many (though certainly not all) major U.S. corporations implemented farsighted strategies. At roughly the same time that Mao Zedong was pursuing an ultimately short-lived policy of "letting a hundred flowers bloom" in China, in the U.S. the flowering of greatest long-term significance was that of corporate research laboratories. At Bell Telephone Laboratories, DuPont, General Electric (GE), RCA Laboratories,[8] the IBM T.J. Watson Research Center, the Xerox Palo Alto Research Center (PARC), and elsewhere, management focused on attracting the most able researchers, then providing them with a great deal of latitude. These laboratories' scientific achievements, recognized by several Nobel prizes, brought great prestige to their parent companies.

Underlying every aspect of this developing U.S. scientific and technological leadership was military spending. By the 1960s, U.S. military funded R&D comprised more than 30% of all of the R&D conducted, not only in the United States, but in the world.[9] The military was dominant in funding research in universities, supporting more than 50% of university basic research (as compared with roughly 30% in 1998). The military was dominant in funding research and development in corporations, supporting more roughly a quarter of industry applied research (as compared with less than 6% in 1998). The military also was dominant in seeding both Silicon Valley and Boston's Route 128 research corridors. Furthermore, in high technology markets such as aircraft, integrated circuits, and computers, the government acted as a monopsonistic buyer. This substantially reduced the barriers to market entry by customer's potential reluctance to accept new and unfamiliar products and technologies (Branscomb and Auerswald 2001)."

Eisenhower's famed "cross of iron" address delivered in 1953[11] highlighted the social sacrifices inherent in sustained high levels of overall military spending. Yet the intensity of military spending on R&D contributed significantly to developing the capabilities of U.S. corporations to engage in what Kash (1989) terms complex, "synthetic" innovations—innovations whose production requires a significant quantity and diversity of knowledge, information, skills, and materials.

The economy that developed in the U.S. during the 1950s and 1960s—highly centralized in large corporations and dependent to a significant extent upon military-supported R&D—thus was arguably the fulfillment of the prediction of Schumpeter (1928). Certainly, where industrial innovation in the 19th and early 20th centuries was identified with the work of individuals—Samuel Morse, Eli Whitney, and Thomas Edison—by the 1960s and 1970s it was identified almost entirely with corporate entities. The observations of Jewes et al. (1959) are startlingly reminiscent of core Schumpeterian themes:

> In the twentieth century ... the individual inventor is becoming rare; men with the power of originating are largely absorbed into research institutions of one kind or another, where they must have expensive equipment for their work. Useful invention is to an ever-increasing degree issuing from the research laboratories of large firms, which alone can afford to operate on an appropriate scale ... Invention has become more automatic, less the result of intuition or genius and more a matter of deliberate design.
>
> (Rhodes, 1999, p. 212)

The research activity of corporations during this extraordinary era in U.S. history was Edwin Mansfield's first, and most often revisited, domain of study within the field of technological innovation.

3. Mansfield and the "golden age" of U.S. corporate R&D

The tremendously influential work of Solow (1956, 1957) spurred interest in technological change and growth theory among a remarkable generation of economists—among them Mansfield, Kenneth Arrow, Zvi Griliches, Richard Nelson, Merton Peck, Edmund Phelps, and Karl Shell—whose command over economic theory and empirics was exceed only by their drive to understand economic phenomena as they are in the world, not as we would have them be for the sake of technical convenience. Those who today seek better understanding of the economics of technological change can only be awed the output of that generation over the period of nearly a half century, beginning dramatically in the late 1950s and early 1960s with Solow (1956, 1957), Griliches (1957), Nelson (1959, 1961), Mansfield (1961, 1962, 1963, 1965), Arrow (1962a, b).[12]

This outpouring of research on technological innovation did not, of course, occur in a vacuum. The second of Solow's seminal pair of papers on technological change and economic growth was published the same year, 1957, that the USSR launched Sputnik. Over the coming three years, Federal R&D spending in the United States tripled. Meeting the Soviet scientific and technological challenge became a paramount national priority. The origins of Mansfield's study of technological innovation were thus at least contemporaneous with, if not possibly influenced by, of concern about the ability of the U.S. to maintain leadership in science and technology, and a renewed determination to do so.

Creating new combinations: system development within large corporations

The contribution by Scherer in this volume points to Mansfield's participation in the NBER research conference held at the University of Minnesota in Spring 1960 as the first evidence of his interest in technological innovation. That conference resulted in the famed 1962 volume on *The Rate and Direction of Inventive Activity: Economic and Social Factors,* edited by Richard Nelson.[13]

To revisit that volume today is striking. Many of the current focal points of research of research on innovation are all but absent from *The Rate and Direction of Inventive Activity*; other areas that are today largely ignored were then intensively studied. Of the many case studies in the volume, none primarily concern inventive activity originating from research in universities; none discuss entrepreneurship and the role of small firms; none discuss venture capital (then, admittedly, in its infancy); none discuss differences among regions in propensity to innovate (though, interestingly, Mansfield for one began his academic career with publications concerning variations in city income levels). Instead, the case studies in the 1962 volume *all* concern invention and innovation as carried out in large corporations funded either by commercial capital or by the Department of Defense. Marshak's paper examines the development by Bell Labs of a microware relay system for the transmission of telephone conversations. Nelson looks at the development of the transistor, also at Bell Labs, concluding with the question "[t]o what extent is an invention like the transistor dependent upon a sponsoring organization like the Bell Telephone Laboratories? How did the size of the Laboratories and the size of corporations owning the Laboratories affect the project? ... My feeling is that devices such as the transistor, based on fundamental new scientific knowledge, can come from small laboratories or from universities, but that a large industrial laboratory like Bell does have a comparative advantage in this business" (Nelson, 1962, p. 579). Admittedly, issues of data availability and editorial discretion no doubt played a role in the authors' selection of topics. Yet, as collected, the case studies in *The Rate and Direction of Inventive Activity* paint a coherent and consistent picture of invention and innovation in the U.S. in the later 1950s: overwhelmingly the domain of either large corporations or the military engaged in complex, large scale, system development projects.

Mansfield's brief contribution to the volume is notable in that it is one of the few papers that succeeds in establishing a bridge between the multiple case studies of invention and innovation on one side, and theoretical and quantitative papers on the other. The theoretical and quantitative papers are a diverse collection. Some of the papers—notably Arrow (1962a)—have had an enduring influence on the literature, and continue to frame discussions regarding inventive activity. Others develop themes that are only now again being taken up in the literature. The first contributed paper in the volume is by Simon Kuznets. It is titled "[i]nventive Activity: Problems of Definition and Measurement". Echoing Shumpeter (1912) and anticipating Weitzman (1998),[14] Kuznets begins by proposing a definition of invention as "a new combination of available knowledge concerning properties of the material universe". The organizational analysis by Cherington et al. (1962, p. 395) puts some applied structure on this definition, proposing that in practice the term "R&D" encompasses "a continuous spectrum of activities" that can for the purposes of exposition be expressed as discrete "steps", not necessarily sequential and interacting in various ways:

Step I. The formation of empirical verification of theories about parameters of the physical world.
Step II. The creation and testing of radically new physical components, devices, and techniques.
Step III. The identification, modification, and combination of existing components and devices to provide a distinctly new application practical in terms of performance, reliability, and cost.
Step IV. Relatively minor modification of existing components, devices, and systems to to improve performance, increase reliability, reduce cost, and simplify application.[15]

Marshak (1962, p. 509) then puts these distinctions in the context of the data, noting that "[o]f the $3.7 billion spent by private industry on research and development in 1953, about 4% ... went to basic research. A breakdown of the remainder by categories related to 'appliedness' does not yet exist. It is safe to say, however, that a large proportion went to the development of what have come to be called systems". Marshak emphasizes that the distinction between a basic research project and system project is as much one of scale as it one of the magnitude of intrinsic uncertainty, noting that where "in a basic research project, a commitment might be an order for a dozen Bunsen burners, in a system project it is likely to be the task assignment of a large team of engineers, and sometimes it is heavy investment in production facilities". It suffices, he continues, "to think of a system as a complex aggregation of components, based on established principles". By this definition, "[a]n aircraft is a system, and so are a color television set, a telephone exchange, and a synthetic fiber plant".

Technological and organizational complexity

These early discussions of technological complexity as related to system development anticipate two linked themes the find expression in Mansfield's work: industries and firms are differentiated by their underlying technological and organizational characteristics; ease of imitation is an important one of those characteristics. While in later work Mansfield became well known for measuring the extent of social returns to R&D via numerous mechanisms collectively termed "spillovers," his legacy rests equally in demonstrating the costliness of either imitating existing processes and products or of converting basic science knowledge into new production methods or new products ready for markets. Mansfield's (1961, 1963) first publications that related to technological changes were about imitation by one firm of the production methods of another. This work advanced the studies by Griliches (1957) on technological adoption.[16] Where Griliches had used published data to study the adoption of essentially modular agricultural technologies, Mansfield (1961) used questionnaires and interviews to study the adoption of new production techniques by large firms in four industries. Mansfield (1963) advanced this line of work, finding that a firm's inclination to adopt a particular innovation depended on the innovation itself: "[t]he results show quite clearly the dangers involved in the common assumption that certain firms are repeatedly the leaders, or followers, in introducing new techniques. It would be very misleading to take few innovations and assume that the firms that are quick to use them are generally leaders in this sense. Judging by our findings, there is a very good chance that these firms will be relatively slow to introduce the next innovation that comes along".

Interestingly given these findings, Mansfield (1965) seeks to estimate the marginal rate of return from R&D expenditures using two models: the first constructed from the assumption that "all technical change is organizational" and the second assuming capital-embodied technical change. Considering Mansfield's earlier work with Harold Wein on managerial decision-making in railroad yards (Mansfield and Wein, 1958), it is fair to infer that this modeling decision does not simply reflect a desire for symmetry. The insight is far from trivial. Combined with the findings from Mansfield (1963), this observation can be interpreted (with some license) as suggesting that *the disruptive impacts of technical change are experienced at least as much within the innovating firm as by the firm's competitors*. One can further hypothesize that *the larger scale of the "system" being developed by a firm and the greater its complexity, the more substantial the potentially disruptive the impact within the innovating firm of a new, substantially different proposed system*.

Technological and organizational complexity can be interpreted in a number of ways. Most simply, it may be measured in terms of the number of parts in a technological artifact (Kash and Rycroft, 1999). Alternately, increasing technological complexity may be understood as the extent to which new market innovations require the efforts of teams incorporating multiple distinct technological fields—a phenomenon sometimes referred to as "convergence". It may also be measured as the average size and/or diversity of teams involved in the creation of new technological innovations, or from a human capital standpoint as the average investment required by an individual in order to reach the technological frontier. However complexity is measured, increased complexity will be manifest in the trend toward supply chain integration, in which functional requirements are managed both up and down the supply chain from each firm in the chain. Thus all of the parts, all the transactions, at multiple levels of the chain become visible to the firm managing the chain.

Relatively recent work by Auerswald (1999, ch. 3), Auerswald *et al.* (2000) and Rivkin (2000) has taken up some of the themes suggested in Mansfield's early work on imitation. In these papers the greater the complexity of technology, the lower the correlation between the effectiveness of the original organizational "routine" (i.e. the leader's method) and that of the same recipe altered slightly (i.e. an imperfect imitation). All three of these papers represent the complexity of a production recipe in terms of both the number of "operations" or distinct units involved in the production process, and (critically) the extent of the interdependence between those units.[17] The theoretical motivation for this approach is found in Coase (1937, p. 390), who argued that in the presence of technological interdependencies, firms will expand to realize economies of scope. When firms do expand in such a manner to internalize the externalities, they create what Auerswald *et al.* (2000) term "intra-firm externalities". Indeed, if one particular unit of a firm is not linked to any other via such intrafirm externalities, then we reasonably wonder why that unit is part of the firm to begin with (rather than, for example, acting as an outside contractor). In this sense, a transactions cost theory of the firm thus predicts that, in industries where technological interdependencies abound, managers will typically be charged with solving the sort complex coordination problems alluded to by Marshak above. The premises of a transactions cost economics naturally suggest a view of the firm as a combinatorial problem solver.[18]

This framework allows for an elaboration of the contrast between Griliches (1957) and Mansfield (1961, 1963). Prior to imitating a simple technological/organizational routine, a firm can predict its *a posteriori* performance characteristics with some reliability. Based on those estimated *a posteriori* performance characteristics, a simple technological/organizational routine is either "adopted" or not. Complex technological/organizational routines can not be "adopted" in this sense. Imitation of complex technological/organizational routines is almost always imperfect—sometimes disastrously so—because modifications in the practices of one unit within the firm will affect the effectiveness of multiple other units. Because a simple technological/organizational routine can be easily imitated, it is not likely to yield persistent "above normal" profits to an early adopter. Enduring technological leadership is based on activities that require the greatest coordination, and have the greatest inherent complexity. These activities are the most potentially disruptive to the internal operations of innovating firms, but also the most difficult to imitate when successfully implemented.[19]

The complementary roles of large and small firms

A significant branch of the literature in empirical industrial organization contemporaneous with Mansfield's period of greatest research productivity was devoted to testing the Schumpeterian hypothesis that large firms were more productive in R&D activities than small ones. Mansfield (1981) took a different approach, framing the issue as less one of relative productivity in research and innovation than it was one of different roles. He found that, "[w]hereas large firms seem to carry out a disproportionately large share of the basic research (and perhaps the long term R&D) in most industries, there is no consistent tendency for them to carry out a disproportionately large share of the relatively risky R&D or of the R&D aimed and entirely new products and processes. On the contrary, they seem to carry out a disproportionately small share of the R&D aimed at entirely new products and processes".

Indeed, despite their great success in advancing scientific and technological frontiers, the great U.S. corporate research laboratories often (one might say, systematically) failed along one critical dimension: the ability to take inventions that were unrelated to "core" lines of business—those defined, and defined by, the firm's organizational capabilities in the sense of Chandler (1992)—and translate them into viable product market innovations within the sponsoring company.[20] Ample evidence exists that large firms and military contractors were (and are) willing to invest heavily in research—even basic research—supporting core lines of business. However, as Christensen (1997) and McGroddy (2001) have described, the same firms have resisted innovations that have the potential either "cannibalize" existing lines of business and/or otherwise disrupt the organization internally. It was precisely this phenomenon that has in the past led (and continues to lead) to the creation of "skunks works" within the research apparatus of large firms; or, in the cases when the innovation is completely frustrated, of spin-off firms.

With regard to the systematic hesitancy of large corporations to pursue internally disruptive innovations, the default explanation is thus neither myopia, nor risk aversion, nor bungling. It is rather that the organizational "routines' (in the sense of Nelson and Winter, 1982) or "production recipes" (in the sense of Auerswald et al., 2000) that support "core" activities are perhaps the firms most valuable assets. Technological change is often "disruptive" of organizational routines or changing production recipes, and thus can be costly.

Beginning in 1970s, deregulation and the resumption of more "normal" patterns of international competition (such as the Asian challenge in the 1980s) contributed to the erosion of the ability of U.S. technology corporations to sustain funding of basic research not linked to core corporate activities. Trends in the valuation of publicly traded companies also had indirect but significant impacts on corporate R&D. The widely observed phenomenon of "conglomerate discount"[21] indicated a general reversal of the prior trend toward consolidation as a pathway of corporate growth. Corporate managers contended with a Wall Street climate that persistently penalized those that lacked focus on near term growth and profitability. At the same time, especially in the decade of the 1980s, increased international competition in high tech product markets put tremendous pressure on costs—contributing to agglomeration of firms within well defined lines of business (merger waves), reorganizations, outsourcing, and "downsizing".

By the end of the 1980s, most U.S. research intensive firms were seeking to link research activities more closely to existing lines of business, and to put in place new management tools to match the apparent efficiency of Asian competitors. Lester's (1998) analysis of how U.S. firms were able to restore their competitiveness in the 1990s concludes that a broad variety of management tools and practices were invoked. More mature and sophisticated forms of technical management in industry focused on core business interests. While they expected the corporate laboratory to create commercializable technologies, they began increasingly to look outside the firm for innovative components and subsystems. Some (at GE for example) implemented disciplined approaches to R&D management, tightly coupled to core business interests. Many large corporations introduced formal processes of risk management and metrics for tracking progress toward documented goals.[22] Others (IBM for example) began to see the central corporate laboratory as an instrument for informing decisions about technology choices, identifying directions for new business opportunities, and evaluating the intellectual assets of competitors and potential partners. Firms also began to outsource more of their needs for component innovation to small and medium sized enterprises, both at home and abroad, reducing the dependence on corporate laboratories for component innovations.

4. The corporate role in technology development: current trends and recent findings

Has the entrepreneur-driven economic order celebrated in Schumpeter (1912) thus returned, superceding the "managed economy" of the mid-1960s that was the focus of Mansfield's early studies? There is substantial evidence that, during, the past fifteen years developed countries have undergone what Audretsch and Thurik (2001) describe as a transition from the "managed" to an "entrepreneurial" economy. Yet recent work of ours with Nick Demos and Brian Min suggests that, while significant transformations in national and international innovation systems have taken place in recent years, the role of large corporations in those systems today is as substantial as it is nuanced.[23]

Between July 2001 and January 2002, our project team conducted detailed interviews with 39 CEOs, senior executives, technology managers, and venture capitalists to identify emerging corporate trends and strategies for managing ESTD activities. Of the 39 interviews, 31 were with technology companies from across eight different industries and eight were with venture capital firms. In total, the interviewed firms account for approximately 7% of total U.S. industrial R&D expenditures. These surveys, combined with the research reported in Branscomb and Auerswald (2002), suggests that the findings of Mansfield (1963) continue to hold: the vitality of the U.S. innovation systems is based on a complementary relationship between large corporations and entrepreneurial start-ups, each exploring and exploiting the market potential of different types of science-based innovations.

Industry support of early stage technology development

A look at the numbers helps set the context. In 2000, industry (large and small firms) reported to NSF investments in R&D totaling $180.4 billion. According to the traditional three-tiered R&D classification scheme, firms allocated $6.0 billion of their R&D investments to basic research, $36.1 billion to applied research, and $138.3.4 billion to development.[24] As discussed in detail in Branscomb and Auerswald (2002), only a small portion of these massive investments is directed at the kinds of ESTD activities that transform lab bench inventions and discoveries into new radical innovations for the marketplace.[25] This is not new. Mansfield (1969) found that even during the "golden age" of corporate R&D, corporations did not fund a significant amount of long term research: "The bulk of R&D projects are relatively safe from a technical point of view" (p. 65). He elaborated: "Only a small percentage of the money spent by these firms goes for basic research. On the average 9% ... The bulk of R&D projects are expected to be finished and have an impact on profits in less than 5 years".

Marshak (1962, p. 509, quoted above) observed that a breakdown of corporate R&D spending "by categories related to 'appliedness' does not yet exist". This statement is as true today as it was over forty years ago. While corporate R&D numbers are regularly reported to NSF and other agencies, these numbers alone tell us little about how companies support and invest in truly radical (as opposed to incremental) technological innovations. The traditional categories of "basic research", "applied research" and "development" do not correspond in any meaningful way to the nature and level of risk or value of commercial investments in new product innovation.[26] Alternate approaches are required therefore, to track the levels of corporate funding and support for activities aimed at bringing disruptive innovations to market.

Corporate venturing activity has been examined in detail (most notably by Gompers, 2002). However this body of work only quantifies corporate investment in innovation activity external to the corporation. It does not attempt to distinguish investments in ESTD from other R&D funded by corporate seed venture capital. A vast literature exists on corporate resource allocation methodologies focusing on internal project investment and portfolio management (including such techniques as real options valuation), however it is difficult to apply these methodologies when assessing allocation of resources towards highly speculative ESTD activity which by its definition cannot be valued quantitatively. Others, such as Lazonick and O'Sullivan (1998), recognize the limitations of these approaches to the innovation process and prescribe alternative frameworks for corporate governance. However they do not attempt to quantify the allocation of corporate resources to this type of activity.

Analytic framework

ESTD is a subset of corporate innovation activity. Innovations are created from inventions or other ideas whose novelty may trace to new science, to new engineering concepts, or even to new and different business models.

In the spirit of the organizational analysis by Cherington *et al.* (1962, p. 395) cited above, Figure 1 illustrates the paths through which these new commercial ideas may flow. There are three kinds of technical innovations that may arise within established firms.

A. These innovations address a market within the core business of the firm and, despite their technical novelty, are sufficiently compatible with existing business models and technical capabilities that they are highly likely to be supported by an existing business unit.
B. The intended market for type B innovations is sufficiently alien to the company's existing business models and technical capabilities that, if developed at all the invention will be spun off outside the firm.
C. Innovations that address a market within the core business of the firm, but face serious obstacles from incompatibilities or displacement of current products, may, in rare cases, be pursued in a "skunk works" or some other form of protected environment.

Type A innovations take place within the normal functioning of businesses. We do not conceive of ESTD as applying to this situation.

Type B innovations may be "excubated"[27] through partnerships outside the firm, but they are rare, as McGroddy (2001) argues. Here the ESTD characteristics are closest to the circumstances surrounding new firm creations based on the ideas of technical entrepreneurs.

An example of a Type C innovation is the IBM PC, which as a computer product certainly lay within the strategic interests of the

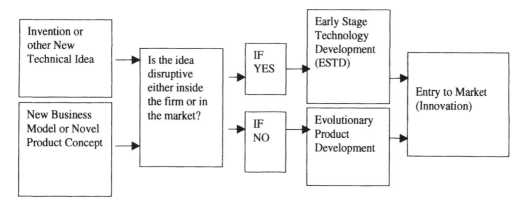

Figure 1. Paths from a creative commercial idea to an innovation.

IBM company but had to be developed in a specially formed organization free of the normal business practices of IBM.

Our definition of ESTD and the data reflecting it in Auerswald *et al.* (forthcoming) apply to Types B and C innovations but not to Type A. By ESTD we mean the technical and business activities that transform a commercially promising "invention" into a business plan that can attract enough investment to enter a market successfully, and through that investment become a successful innovation.

We define ESTD in the corporate context to refer to early development of fundamentally new products or processes that lie outside of, or might be in conflict with, the firm's current technology strategy, or that deploy current technology outside of the firms current core businesses. ESTD must address functional specifications, product manufacturability and costs, and the initial market for entry of an innovation must have at least one of the following characteristics:

- Its technical novelty promises the possibility of exclusive advantages but poses a significant risk that technical obstacles cannot be overcome.
- The intended innovation either addresses a market that lies outside the core business interests of the firm, or challenges the current business model, the current technical base, competes with current products.

Thus the concept we advance for ESTD applies to new business activities that have the characteristic either of destabilizing markets if the innovation hopes to create a market not already in existence, or of destabilizing customer behavior—posing serious barriers to acceptance—or of destabilizing the internal operations of the firm. This last obstacle might reflect a novel and unfamiliar business model,[28] a technical incompatibility,[29] or a significant impact on the sale of current mainstream products.[30]

Findings

In planning our interviews, we sought to target a qualitatively diverse sample of firms along dimensions of industry, firm size, and lifecycle stage. In the end, we relied heavily on established relationships and contacts between members of the research team and industry leaders to select our interviewees. The small number of firms in our study sample allowed us to conduct in-depth interviews with each of our respondents but does place serious limitations on our ability to assess the accuracy of our extrapolations to industry sectors as a whole.

Table I compares the R&D expenditures and sales of interviewed firms aggregated by industry, with industry totals. These data indicate that the firms interviewed are more R&D intensive than the average firm in every industry analyzed. Furthermore, for all industries with the exception computer software, the interviewed firm with the highest level of R&D intensity was also that with the greatest share of ESTD activity. To the extent that a firm's overall R&D intensity affects the *share* of R&D dedicated to ESTD activities, this difference may imply that our results *overstate* the share of corporate resources dedicated to ESTD activities

In our interviews, we made an important distinction between incremental improvements in a firm's core products and processes and disruptive innovations as defined earlier. As we define ESTD, only early stage research that is disruptive because its market lies outside that of the firm's core products or core business model, or because the introduction of the new product disrupts the firms current technology or impacts current products qualifies. This distinction is subtle, however, and in many cases, deciding what technologies and products lie within a firm's core business and what lies outside is a subjective judgment. To facilitate this discussion during interviews we often used a framework represented in Figure 2. Early development within the context of familiar technologies and familiar markets was not considered to be ESTD. Early development work oriented to new products using familiar technologies but focused on new value propositions, using new technologies deployed against a familiar value propositions, or new technologies focused on new value propositions was all considered ESTD. When using this framework most of the interviewees recognized that most of their ESTD activity was in fact focused in the upper left or

TABLE I
R&D expenditures and sales: Companies and industry totals in 2000 (dollar in millions)

Industry	R&D expenditures Surveyed companies	R&D expenditures All industry	Surveyed / All industry (%)	Sales Surveyed companies	Sales All industry	Surveyed / All industry (%)	R&D / Sales Surveyed companies (%)	R&D / Sales All industry (%)
Surveyed industries								
Electronics	1 039	30,408	3.4	7655	387,956	2.0	13.6	7.8
Biopharmaceutical	509	17,722	2.9	1096	160,252	0.7	46.4	11.1
Automotive	6 800	20,389	33.4	170,064	612,644	27.8	4.0	3.3
Telecommunications	157	13,085	1.2	514	399,607	0.1	30.5	3.3
Computer software	273	18,761	1.5	1099	104,176	1.1	24.8	18.0
Basic industries & materials	1 078	21,215	5.1	87,356	1,870,478	4.7	1.2	1.1
Machinery & electrical equipment	540	10,642	5.1	13,000	337,049	3.9	4.2	3.2
Chemicals	2 000	8 548	23.4	30,000	224,992	13.3	6.7	3.8
Subtotal	12,395	140,770	8.8	310,784	4,097,155	7.6	4.0	3.4

Source: BAH Analysis: Interviews with corporations: National Science Foundation, *Research and Development in Industry: 2000*, (Arlington VA, 2003) (NSF-03-318).

lower right hand quadrants of figure 2. These interviewees also observed that they would generally not allocate funds to activity in the upper right hand quadrant.

Moreover, the operational definition of R&D process terminology like "exploratory research" and "process development" varies widely across industries and firms. While we made efforts to ensure consistency in the way terms were defined and used in our interviews, some variation in the way our respondents categorized their research activities was to be expected. In a few exceptional situations, there were clear discrepancies in the way respondents decided what portion of their R&D investments to characterize as ESTD work. In these cases, we made slight adjustments to the categorizations to be more broadly consistent with our set of definitions.

The research suggests that of the $180 billion invested into R&D by U.S. firms in 2000, an estimated $13 billion funded the kinds of ESTD activities that are targeted at bringing radical technological innovations to the marketplace despite disruptive obstacles. This works out to about 7.3% of total corporate R&D budgets that is dedicated to ESTD activities. As noted earlier, this may be an over estimate, since the firms interviewed were somewhat more R&D intensive than the average firm in each sector, and ESTD expenditures appear to be correlated with R&D intensity. The majority of R&D spending, 86%, is for product development, and the remaining is for concept/invention. The results of our research are summarized in Table II and Figure 3.

There are significant variations in ESTD expenditures across industries and between firms within specific industries. These inter- and intra-industry variations are shaped by several forces including the increasing sophistication required to develop new technological innovations, mounting pressures on corporate R&D divisions to demonstrate financial value from R&D investments, and the importance of the lifecycle position of specific industries relative to other industries and individual companies relative to their peers.

In 2000, the two firms we interviewed in the chemicals industry invested on average 33% of their R&D dollars on ESTD activities, the highest proportion for any group of industry firms

	More disruptive	**Type B** Market is alien to company's existing business models and technical capabilities	**Type B +C** Market is outside core business and incompatible with technology
Compatibility with company's existing business models and technical capabilities	Less disruptive	**Type A** New technology easily introduced ESTD not required	**Type C** Market is in core but is incompatible with company's existing business models and technical capabilities
		Less disruptive	More disruptive
		Compatibility with core markets	

Figure 2. Four transitions to innovation; three of which require ESTD.

that we interviewed. These high ESTD expenditures were driven by a common corporate emphasis on new technology and market development and by market expectations for frequent innovation. The fact that the chemicals industry seemed to have the highest ratio of ESTD to total R&D may seem counter-intuitive, given the significant amount of bulk industrial chemicals manufactured in this industry. But it is important to observe that the R&D to sales ratio in this industry is only 3.8%. Thus the industry is not nearly as R&D-intensive as biopharmaceuticals or electronics. The R&D that they do perform is often aimed at fundamental research to spur the development of new product innovations. Firms in the chemical industry thus tend to spend a larger fraction of their modest R&D investments on early stage research than do other industries.

In sheer dollar terms, the largest ESTD spender was the electronics industry. The results from our interviews suggest that the electronics industry spent $3.5 billion, or 11% of its R&D, on ESTD activities in 2000. Among the firms we spoke with in this highly competitive industry, many insisted that while the incentives to exploit and extend existing product lines are powerful, such a short-sighted strategy could be perilous. Given the rapid pace of technological change in electronics, investments into new lines of research and the pursuit of an innovation-led growth strategy are the most viable paths to long-term survival.

On the opposite end of the spectrum, the computer software industry showed no evidence of substantive ESTD activity—a result that may be surprising to some. We found that almost all software releases, creative as they may be, are built using well-established technologies and programming languages. They are rarely based on truly novel technological innovations—indeed, most were business model or market innovations. Numerous software industry executives provided corroboration for this finding.

Overall, we found that ESTD spending is concentrated in industries based on quickly developing technologies, like electronics, specialty chemicals and materials, and biopharmaceuticals. Mature industries based on well established technologies, like the automotive and computer software industries, typically spend less on ESTD and focus more of their resources on product development.

Within individual industries, significant firm-level variations in ESTD spending also exist. A firm's relative lifecycle position, for example, is a key driver of intra-industry differences in ESTD investments. Companies in the early stages of their lifecycle are more likely to invest more heavily into ESTD in order to establish a comparative advantage than more mature companies who focus instead on protecting existing product lines through heavy spending on product and market development. As companies grow, their technology investments become increasingly targeted and they put into place disciplined processes to evaluate all research projects.

Finally—and importantly for the purposes of this paper—many respondents reported that the ability of any one company to develop all of the technological elements required to deliver signifi-

TABLE II
Estimated ESTD spending by U.S. corporations (2000)

	Average R&D spending allocation (%)				R&D Expenditures ($million)		ESTD Expenditures by industry (estimated in $million)	% Range of R&D funding for ESTD (%)
	Basic	Concept/ Invention	ESTD	Product Development	Surveyed companies	Industry		
Surveyed industries								
Electronics (8)	0	5	11	84	1 039	30,408	3 463	0–40
Chemicals (2)	3	28	33	38	2 000	8 548	2 778	25–40
Biopharmaceutical (5)	0	0	13	86	509	17,722	2 373	0–30
Basic industries & materials (3)	0	5	7	87	1 078	21,215	1 547	0–15
Telecommunications (5)	0	0	10	90	157	13,085	1 305	0–35
Machinery & electrical equipment (1)	0	0	10	90	540	10,642	1 064	10
Automotive (1)	1	3	3	93	6 800	20,389	612	3
Computer software (6)	0	0	0	100	273	18,761	71	0
Subtotal	0	4	9	86	12,395	140,770	13,213	
Non-surveyed industries								
Trade						24,929	n/a	
Services						10,545	n/a	
Aircraft, missiles, space						4 175	n/a	
Subtotal						39,649	n/a	
Total						180,419	13,213	7.3

Note: *Numbers in parentheses indicate quantity of interviews in each industry category.
Source: BA&H analysis; Interviews with corporations; National Science Foundation, *Research and Development in Industry: 2000*, (Arlington VA, 2003) (NSF-03-318). See Appendix for map of source document industry classifications to industry categories above.
Totals may not add to 100% due to rounding.

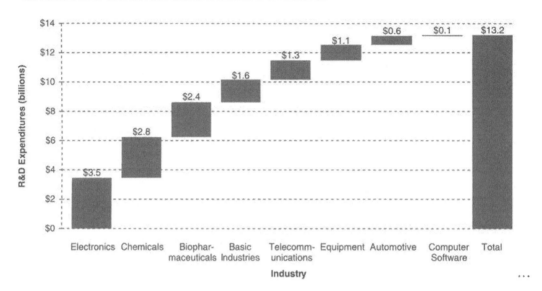
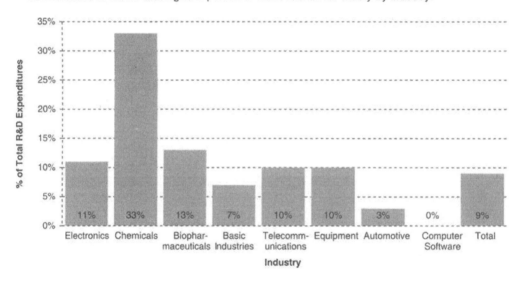

Figure 3. Estimated ESTD spending by U.S. corporations.

cant advances alone has rapidly diminished. According to a disk drive industry executive we interviewed, "[a]s technology advances, it costs more to solve successive problems. At some point, solving a new problem is beyond the capabilities of any one company". There are simply too many potential ideas and too few resources to go it alone. There was a strong sense among our interviewees that the scale of research required to create new innovations has increased as technology becomes more complex. But a firm's ability to capture the full benefits and exploit the full potential of new research has not kept pace, making ESTD investment decisions more difficult than ever before.

In Section 5, we conclude by exploring the implications of these findings for the prospects of U.S. leadership in radical innovation, focusing on the trend toward increased technological complexity.

5. Conclusion

The period from 1950 to 1980 was a legitimate "golden age" for U.S. corporate research and development. The dramatic post-war growth in the supply of scientific and technical talent available in the U.S. and the post-Sputnik surge in R&D spending were important drivers of a flowering of innovative capabilities within large firms. The growing power of the U.S. research enterprise was further enhanced by far-sighted public policies, the research intensive strategies of some leading firms, and the slow development of competition from non-U.S. firms in both domestic and overseas markets for complex, technology-intensive products.

This era of corporate-led technological dominance in the United States was paralleled by a remarkable era of breakthroughs in the study of technological change. While Edwin Mansfield earned a distinguished place among the participants to that literature by contributing in profound ways to advancing the frontier of empirical work on the economics of innovation, Mansfield differentiated himself from his peers by having retained a deep and abiding interest in the perspectives of practitioners and the actual, day to day functioning of institutions engaged in research and development.

In this paper we have discussed some conjectures regarding the impact of long term trends in technological and organizational complexity on the role of large corporations in the U.S. innovation system. Among these conjectures, one that seems to us interesting to pursue empirically is that concerning the relationship of the complexity of technology to the challenge of converting basic science breakthroughs into market-ready products. Jones (unpublished) is an important contribution in this context, documenting trends in the average age of patent recipients and the size and inter-disciplinary extent of teams named on patents.

Another relationship to explore further is that between the complexity of products and the scale and scope of the organizations that produce them. From a purely "architectural" standpoint—that is, simply in terms of the number of component parts—the complexity of the most complex products traded in the economy seems clearly to be increasing. However, that is only part of the story. The rest of the story is that subcomponents are purchased from subcontractors, who in turn purchase from their subcontractors, creating a production hierarchy (or supply chain) for a complex product that may be many layers deep. Other factors such (e.g. just-in-time delivery) may intensify the interaction between these layers. Also interesting to explore empirically is the implication that while complexity increases the potential disruption internal to a firm caused by undertaking a new innovation, it also protects successful innovators by making imitation more difficult.

A reading of Mansfield, as well as review of the contributions to the *Rate and Direction of Inventive Activity*, is a cause for some wistfulness on the part of the empirically minded with regard to the manner in which data on corporate innovation are gathered. It is still the case that we do not have any reliably gathered breakdowns of data on corporate "R&D" according to the extent of "appliednesss". Research has advanced to the point where categories such as "basic", "applied", and "development" do not begin to capture the richness of the system being studied.[31] The survey results presented in this paper are a small scale attempt at providing a more fine grained understanding of the quantitative inputs into the innovative process. However, they are clearly limited in scale and scope. The definition of ESTD needs to be more carefully elaborated, ideally into a form that is usable in large-scale surveys.

Finally there is the domain of inter-industry variation, about which we have not said a great deal. One of Mansfield's most enduring contributions was to emphasize the extent to which industries differ—an emphasis consistent with our own focus on the impact of technological and organizational complexity, and reinforced by the quantitative results derived from our interviews. Further work advancing understanding of this dimension of variation is critical to the formulation of public policy.

The findings from our recent research, reported above, do support the view that large industrial corporations continue to play an important role in converting new science into market ready innovations, especially when the innovations fit within the firm's core business strategy and can be exploited within the basic manufacturing and marketing capabilities of the firm. At the same time, large firms are hesitant now, as they were in the 1960s, to support technology development projects that have the potential to be internally disruptive, even when the product would be compatible with core business goals. Such projects are more likely to be taken up by small firms, at times in partnership with large firms.[32]

Yet today, unlike in 1960, even the largest firms can not maintain all the capabilities internally—including research capabilities—required to compete at the technological frontier. Furthermore, even the most technologically dynamic regions, such as Silicon Valley and Boston's route 128, do not contain all of the talent locally—including research talent—required to compete at all of the most interesting technological frontiers.

Appreciation for the importance of technological and organizational complexity was a common theme in early (i.e. late 1950s, and early 1960s) discussions of technological change, and was evident in Mansfield's work throughout his career. The initial survey findings we have presented in this paper and our review of Mansfield's contributions to the literature suggest to us that additional analytical attention could be paid to impact of complexity *within* innovating organizations. Combined with, and elaborating upon, the findings from Mansfield (1963), this observation can be interpreted, as we noted earlier, as suggesting that *the disruptive impacts of new technology change are experienced at least as much within the innovating firm as by the firm's competitors*. It follows that the larger scale of the "system" being developed and the greater its complexity, the more substantial the potentially disruptive the impact within the innovating firm of a new, substantially different proposed system.

The barriers to radical innovation in large firms are, therefore, by no means limited to resistance to accept new products and services, or the difficulties of absorbing new technologies and processes. Resistance to radical, science-based innovations is best characterized by the disruptive effect of their introduction, whether the resistance to innovation arises from disruption within the firm or without; or arises from radical changes in technology, markets, or in business models.

Despite the growing complexity of their businesses and the challenge that both internal and external disruptions would bring, the most competitive of the larger firms understand that they have little choice but to press on with the most promising, if difficult, innovations in order to secure competitive advantage. The results of our surveys of selected high-tech firms suggests that the more R&D intensive firms are spending over $10 billion a year on early stage technology development—funds specifically directed to projects that face barriers from internal disruption or barriers from the limited scope of the firm's established lines of business. When internal development is resisted, excubation and partnering with others may be the answer. Or internal organizational structures such as "skunk works" may be used. Finally joint ventures with firms that offer complimentary capabilities may provide a way around the internal barriers that inhibit the development of some innovations.

Government has a potential role in promoting economic growth by encouraging the development of disruptive innovations. The technical and market risks faced by smaller firms attempting radical science-based innovation have been widely discussed and are reasonably well appreciated.[34] Depending entirely on high-tech start-ups to develop disruptive innovations and introduce them to market—waiting for small technology firms to mature into, or merge with, larger firms, thereby transforming industries from the bottom up—is a strategy that is both slow and uncertain. Yet the one U.S. federal programs targeted solely at promoting high tech innovation across the economy, the Advanced Technology Program (ATP) in the Department of Commerce, has faced strong political pressure to restrict the participation of large firms. Our limited and early studies suggest that large firms increasingly also have a need for external partners to help them overcome internal, as well as external, barriers to the development of disruptive innovations.

Notes

3. See also Branscomb and Auerswald (2002) and Auerswald *et al.* (forthcoming)
4. See also Rosenberg (1970) and Teece (1977). Mansfield (1993, p. xix) summarizes the argument in Teece (1977) as follows: "[Teece] stresses that technology is by no means a set of blueprints that is usable at nominal cost to all. In his sample [of international transfers of technology], transfer costs averaged about 20% of total project costs".
5. This argument was developed more fully, and famously, in Schumpeter (1942).
6. In 1820 China dominated the world economy, accounting for an estimated 34% of world GDP (Maddison, 2001, p. 261).
7. Post Cold War reassessments of Soviet economic strength make clear that the challenge to the U.S. posed by the USSR was military and political, not economic.
8. The David Sarnoff Research Center.
9. See Alic et al. (1992, p. 6). Total U.S. R&D (government and industry) was 69% of total R&D by G7 countries in 1960; Federal R&D was 65% of total U.S R&D; military R&D was over 80% of Federal R&D. An extrapolation of recent data permits us to assume that G7 R&D was at least 90% of global in 1960.
10. See Leslie (2000).
11. Properly titled the Chance for Peace address, delivered before the American Society of Newspaper Editors, April 16,1953. See < http://www.eisenhower.utexas.edu/chance.htm >.
12. Only slightly later, Shell (1966, 1967) published the work that provided most direct antecedent to Romer's (1986, 1990) widely cited papers on endogenous growth.
13. Nelson (1999) recalls the line of work broadly represented at that conference as stemming "from the work of a group of economists working in the late 1940s and early 1950s for the National Bureau of Economic Research, using the new national product data". As notable among this group Nelson identifies Solomon Fabricant, Moses Abramovitz, and John Kendrick. Other early contributors include William Fellner, Simon Kuznets, and Schultz.
14. Schumpeter (1912, p. 14) [Oxford University Press 1961 ed.]: "Technologically as well as economically considered, production "creates" nothing in the physical sense. In both cases it can only influence or control things and processes, or 'forces' ... [T]o produce means to combine the things and forces within our reach. Every method of production signifies some definite combination".
15. That paper goes on to describe the decision-making process for weapons development as one in which "very many hands and heads participate ... with the result being a lengthy and complex decision making chain". Cherington *et al.* (1962, p. 399)
16. In a groundbreaking study of the spread of hybrid corn varieties across the agricultural regions of the U.S. from 1932 to 1956, Griliches found spatial variation in economic incentives to be a significant determinant of differences between places in the timing and pace of technological adoption.
17. The NK framework of Kauffman and Levin (1987) provides a shared inspiration for the models in these three papers.
18. Reiter and Sherman (1962) is another classic paper that anticipates current work on the firm as a solver of hard combinatorial optimization problems.
19. Auerswald (1999, ch. 3) provides a proof of this proposition.
20. Smith and Alexander (1988) offer a narrative account of failures to commercialize innovations from Xerox PARC. Chesbrough and Smith (unpublished) detail the experience of each of the 35 firms that spun out of Xerox research centers from 1978 to 1998.
21. See Berger and Ofek (1995) for empirical support.
22. Hartmann and Myers (2001).
23. Auerswald *et al.* (forthcoming).
24. National Science Foundation (2004), Tables 4-5, 4-9, 4-13, and 4-17.
25. ESTD does not correspond uniquely to any of the three categories used by the National Science Foundation (NSF) and the Organization for Economic Cooperation and Development (OECD) to categorize industrial R&D. In fact, there are no statistical collections of ESTD data in the U.S.
26. Branscomb (1998).
27. McGroddy (2001).
28. Chesborough and Rosenbloom (2001).
29. John Cocke invented the Reduced Instruction Set Computer (RISC) in IBM Research. Despite its functional advantages as a target for optimized compilers, and despite the best efforts of the company's technical executives, RISC was rejected by the product divisions because of its incompatibility with the IBM 370 architecture. The first native RISC machine was produced by Hewlett Packard, under the leadership of the former head of the IBM computer research group where RISC was developed. Later IBM did sell RISC processors and was successful using them as elements of a super computer.
30. In the 1980s, Xerox corporation suffered heavily from Asian competition at the low end of their copier product line. In the next decade Xerox introduced all digital copiers in the quest to regain lost market share.
31. Branscomb, "[f]rom Science Policy to Research Policy" in Branscomb and Keller, eds., 1998.
32. Scott Shane, in a study of inventions licensed by MIT, found that scientifically radical inventions were more successfully commercialized through new startup firms, while more evolutionary inventions were more suitable for existing firms, with their greater resources and relevant experience. See Branscomb and Auerswald (2001, p. 83).
33. Branscomb *et al.* (1999).
34. For further discussion, see e.g. Branscomb and Auerswald (2001) and Hall (2002).

References

Alic, J.A., L.M. Branscomb, H. Brooks, A.B. Carter, and G.L. Epstein, 1992, *Beyond Spinoff: Military and Commercial Technologies in a Changing World*, Boston: Harvard Business School Press.

Arrow, K.J., 1962a, 'Economic Welfare and the Allocation of Resources from Invention,' in R.R. Nelson (ed.), *The Rate and Direction of Inventive Activity: Economic and Social Factors*. Princeton, NJ: Princeton University Press.

Arrow, K.J., 1962b, 'The Economic Implications of Learning by Doing', *Review of Economic Studies* **29**, 155–73.

Audretsch, D.B., and A.R. Thurik, 2001, 'What's New About the New Economy,' Indiana University Institute for Development Strategies, Working Paper. http://www.spea.indiana.edu/ids/pdfholder/ISSN-01-1.pdf.

Auerswald, P. 1999, *Organizational Learning, Intrafirm Externalities and Industry Evolution*. University of Washington Ph.D. thesis.

Auerswald, P., S. Kauffman, J. Lobo, and K. Shell, 2000, 'The Production Recipes Approach to Modeling Technological Innovation: An Application to Learning by Doing', *Journal of Economic Dynamics and Control* **24**, 389–450.

Berger, P. and E. Ofek, 1995, 'Diversification's effect on firm value,' *Journal of Financial Economics* **37**, 39–65.

Branscomb, L.M., 1998, 'From Science Policy to Research Policy' in L.M. Branscomb, and J.H. Keller, (eds.), *Investing in Innovation: Creating a Research and Innovation Policy that Works*, Cambridge MA: MIT Press, 115–124.

Branscomb, L.M., and P.E. Auerswald, 2001, *Taking Technical Risks: How Innovators, Executives and Investors Manage High-Tech Risks*, Cambridge, MA: MIT Press.

Branscomb, L.M., and P.E. Auerswald, 2002, *Between invention and innovation: An analysis of funding for early stage technology development*. Report #NIST GCR 02–841, Advanced Technology Program, National Institute for Standards and Technology (NIST), U.S. Department of Commerce.

Branscomb, L.M., F. Kodama, and R. Florida (eds.), 1999, *Industrializing Knowledge, University-Industry Linkages in Japan and the United States* Cambridge MA: MIT Press.

Chandler, A.D. 1992. 'Organizational Capabilities and the Economic History of the Industrial Enterprise', *Journal of Economic Perspectives* **6** (3), 79–100.

Cherington, P.W., M.J. Peck, and F.M. Scherer, 1962, 'Organization and Research and Development Decision Making within a Government Department,' in R.R. Nelson (ed.), *The Rate and Direction of Inventive Activity: Economic and Social Factors*, Princeton: Princeton University Press, pp. 395–408.

Chesborough, H., and R. Rosenbloom, 2001, 'The Dual-Edged Role of the Business Model in Leveraging Corporate Technology Investment', in L.M. Branscomb and P. Auerswald (eds.), *Taking Technical Risks: How Innovators, Executives, and Investors Manage High Tech Risks*, Cambridge MA: MIT Press.

Christensen, C.M., 1997, *The Innovator's Dilemma: When New Technologies Cause Great Firms to Fail*, Boston: Harvard Business School Press.

Coase, R., 1937, 'The Nature of the Firm,' *Economica* **4**, 386–405.

Gompers, P.A., 2002, 'Corporations and the Financing of Innovation: The Corporate Venturing Experience.' Federal Reserve Bank of Atlanta, *Economic Review*, **Fourth Quarter**.

Griliches, Z., 1957, 'Hybrid corn: An exploration in the economics of technological change', *Econometrica* **25**(4), 501–22.

Hall, B.H., 2002, 'The financing of research and development,' Working Paper 8773, National Bureau of Economic Research (NBER).

Hartmann, G.C., and M.B. Myers, 'Technical Risk, Product Specifications, and Market Risk' in Branscomb, Lewis M., and Philip Auerswald, *Taking Technical Risks: How Innovators, Executives, and Investors Manage High Tech Risks* (Cambridge MA: MIT Press) 30–43.

Jewes, J., D. Sawers, and R. Stillerman, 1959, *The Sources of Invention*, New York: W.W. Norton & Company.

Kash, D.E., 1989, *Perpetual Innovation: The New World of Competition*, New York: Basic Books.

Kash, D.E., and R. Rycroft, 1999, *The Complexity Challenge: Technological Innovation for the 21st Century*, London: Printer.

Kauffman, S., and S. Levin, 1987, 'Toward a General Theory of Adaptive Walks on Rugged Landscapes,' *Journal of Theoretical Biology* **128,** 11–45.

Lazonick, W. and M. O'Sullivan, 1998, 'Corporate Governance and the Innovative Economy: Policy Implications. STEP report R-03.

Leslie, S.W., 2000. 'The Biggest 'Angel' of Them All: The Military and the Making of Silicon Valley'. in M. Kenney (ed.), *Understanding Silicon Valley: The Anatomy of an Entrepreneurial Region*, Palo Alto: Stanford University Press.

Lester, R., 1998, *The Productive Edge: How U. S. Industries Are Pointing the Way to a New Era of Economic Growth*, New York: W.W. Norton.

Maddison, A., 2001, *The World Economy: A Millennial Perspective*, Paris: Organization of Economic Cooperation and Development (OECD) Press.

Mansfield, E., 1961, 'Technical Change and the Rate of Imitation,' *Econometrica* **29**, 741–766.

Mansfield, E., 1962, 'Entry, Gibrat's Law, Innovation, and the Growth of Firms', *American Economic Review* **52** (5), 1023–1051.

Mansfield, E., 1963. 'The Speed of Response of Firms to New Techniques,' *The Quarterly Journal of Economics,* **77** (2), 290–311.

Mansfield, E., 1965, 'Rates of Return from Industrial Research and Development,' *The American Economic Review* **55** (1/2), 310–322.

Mansfield, E., 1969 'Industrial Research and Development: Characteristics, Costs, and Diffusion of Results,' *The American Economic Review* **59** (2), 65–71.

Mansfield, E. 1981, 'Composition of R&D Expenditures: Relationship to Size of Firm, Concentration, and Innovative Output,' *The Review of Economics and Statistics* **63** (4), 610–615.

Mansfield, E., 1995, 'Academic Research Underlying Industrial Innovations: Sources, Characteristics, and Financing,' *The Review of Economics and Statistics* **77** (1), 55–65.

Mansfield, E., and E. Mansfield (eds.), 1993, *The Economics of Technical Change* Aldershot: Edward Elgar.

Mansfield, E., M. Schwartz, and S. Wagner, 1981, 'Imitation Costs and Patents: An Empirical Study,' *The Economic Journal,* **91** (364), 907–918.

Mansfield, E. and H.H. Wein, 1958, 'A Study of Decision-Making Within the Firm,' *The Quarterly Journal of Economics* **72** (4), 515–536.

Marshak, T.A., 1962. 'Strategy and Organization in a System Development Project,' in R.R. Nelson (ed.), 1962, *The Rate and Direction of Inventive Activity: Economic and Social Factors*, Princeton: Princeton University Press, 509–548.

McGroddy, J., 2001, 'Raising Mice in the Elephant's Cage' in L.M. Branscomb, and P. Auerswald (eds.), *Taking Technical Risks: How Innovators, Executives, and Investors Manage High Tech Risks*, Cambridge MA: MIT Press.

National Science Foundation, *Science and Engineering Indicators 2004* (Arlington VA), NSF-04-01.

Nelson, R.R., 1959, 'The simple economics of basic scientific research,' *Journal of Political Economy* 297–306.

Nelson, R.R., 1961, 'Uncertainty, Learning, and the Economics of Parallel Research and Development Efforts,' *Review of Economics and Statistics* **XLIII**, 351–64.

Nelson, R.R. (ed.), 1962, *The Rate and Direction of Inventive Activity: Economic and Social Factors*, Princeton: Princeton University Press.

Nelson, R.R., 1999, 'Technological Advance and Economic Growth,' in National Academies of Science, *Harnessing Science and Technology for America's Economic Future: National and Regional Priorities*, Washington DC: National Academies Press.

Nelson, R.R. and S. Winter, 1982. *An Evolutionary Theory of Economic Change*, Belknap: Harvard U. Press.

Reiter, S. and G.R. Sherman, 1962, 'Allocating Indivisible Resources Affording External Economies or Diseconomies', *International Economic Review* **3** (1), 108–135.

Rhodes, R., 1999, *Visions of Technology: A Century of Vital Debate about Machines, Systems, and the Human World*, New York: Simon & Schuster.

Rivkin, J., 2000, 'Imitation of complex strategies,' *Management Science* **46**, 824–844.

Romer, P.M., 1986, 'Increasing Returns and Long-Run Growth', *Journal of Political Economy* **94** (5), 1002–1037.

Romer, P.M., 1990, 'Endogenous technological change,' *Journal of Political Economy* **98** (5), S71–S102.

Rosenberg, N., 1970, 'Economic Development and the Transfer of Technology: Some Historical Perspectives,' *Technology and Culture* **11** (4), 550–75.

Rosenberg, N. and L.E. Birdzell Jr., 1985, *How the West Grew Rich: The Economic Transformation of the Industrial World*, New York: Basic Books.

Schumpeter, J.A., 1912, *Theorie der witschaftlichen Entwicklung*, Leipzig: Duncker & Humblot. Revised English translation (1934) by Redvers Opie, *The Theory of Economic Development*.

Schumpeter, J.A., 1928, 'The Instability of Capitalism,' *The Economic Journal* **38** (51), 361–386.

Schumpeter, J.A., 1942, *Capitalism, Socialism, and Democracy*, New York: Harper and Row.

Shell, K., 1966, 'Toward a theory of inventive activity and capital accumulation,' *American Economic Review* **56** (2), 62–68.

Shell, K., 1967, 'A model of inventive activity and capital accumulation,' In K. Shell (ed.), *Essays on the Theory of Optimal Economic Growth*, Cambridge MA: MIT Press, 67–85.

Smith, D.K. and R.C. Alexander, 1988, *Fumbling the Future: How Xerox Invented Then Ignored the First Personal Computer*, New York: William Morrow & Co.

Solow, R.M., 1956, 'A Contribution to the Theory of Economic Growth,' *Quarterly Journal of Economics*, **70**, 65–94.

Solow, R.M., 1957, 'Technical Change and the Aggregate Production Function,' *Review of Economics and Statistics*, **XXXIX**, 312–20.

Teece, D.J., 1977, 'Technology Transfer by Multinational Firms: The Resource Cost of Transferring Technological Know-how,' *Economic Journal* **87**, 242–61.

Weitzman, M.L., 1998, 'Recombinant Growth', *The Quarterly Journal of Economics* **113** (2), 331–360.

The Welfare Effects of Research and Production Joint Ventures

Kathryn L. Combs

ABSTRACT. This paper develops a model to analyze behavior and welfare effects of a research and production joint venture (JV). In the model, a research dollar is more productive if spent in the joint venture because it increases the achievable probability of new product introduction. This efficiency of research and production joint ventures offsets, to some degree, the loss due to higher consumer prices. For some parameter configurations and joint venture membership rules, research and production joint ventures yield higher social welfare than research-only joint ventures (RJVs). This contrasts with some of the industrial organization literature on research collaboration and with traditional antitrust views.

Key words: R&D, research joint venture, social rate of return, welfare analysis, innovation, game theory

JEL Classification: O33

1. Introduction

Mansfield *et al.* (1977) laid out a pioneering methodology for the estimation of private and social returns from industrial innovations. The methodology identified the following factors as critical: (1) whether the innovation is a product innovation used by households, a product innovation used by firms, or a process innovation; (2) the cost and timing of unsuccessful or discontinued parallel research efforts by other firms. In his consideration of the latter factor, Mansfield acknowledges the inherent uncertainty of R&D outcomes. Yet in much recent theoretical modeling of R&D, and especially modeling of research joint ventures, this uncertainty is omitted.[1] One of the main purposes of this paper is to examine the effects of uncertainty on behavior of research and production joint ventures (JVs). Here, the uncertainty of R&D coupled with product innovation leads to welfare conclusions that contrast with some of the industrial organization literature on cooperative R&D and with traditional antitrust views. Under some circumstances, research and production joint ventures frequently outperform research-only joint ventures (RJVs) in terms of social welfare. In retrospect, Mansfield's emphasis on the details of the R&D process and its outcomes seems all the wiser.

This paper develops a model to investigate research joint venture formation when venture participants are free to cooperate in output production as well as research activity. The model is an extension of Combs (1993). In the model, endogenously formed research joint ventures and venture non-participants aim to develop and introduce new products to households. In the event that the multiple entities produce innovations (e.g. the joint venture and one or more non-participants), they compete against each other in a homogeneous product market. In other words, patent protection is ineffective.

The benefits and the opportunity costs of joining the venture are tied to the randomness of R&D outcomes. The benefits of joining are improved efficiencies of R&D stemming from a higher achievable probability of success of innovation. The cost of joining is the foregone opportunity to become a monopolist—rather than share joint venture profits—in the event that others fail to innovate. However, the opportunity cost shrinks as the joint venture grows. This occurs because a larger joint venture is more

Department of Economics
University of St. Thomas
TMH #343
1000 LaSalle Avenue
Minneapolis, MN 55403
U.S.A
E-mail: klcombs@stthomas.edu

likely to successfully develop the new product due to increased R&D efficiencies and increased spending on R&D. It should be noted that in practice, technology spillovers might also figure into the benefit of collaboration. However, this model does not consider such spillovers, so as to focus on the benefits of efficiencies related to the uncertainty of R&D.

The social benefits and costs of allowing such a joint venture to operate also stem in part from the randomness of R&D outcomes. The social benefits of the joint venture accrue from the value to the consumer of new products that are more likely to be introduced if the joint venture forms. However, the joint venture's cooperatively set output levels result in higher prices, ex post, which present a social cost.

The paper compares expected total surplus across three regimes: Regime A—cooperation in both research and production levels; Regime B—research-only cooperation with free entry to the joint venture, as examined in Combs (1993); Regime C—research-only cooperation where the joint venture is allowed to block entry, as examined in Combs (1993). Research and production ventures with entry blocking are not included in the comparison because entry blocking is not binding in equilibrium.

In Regime A, all firms join the joint venture. This formation resembles an industry-wide merger. In the grand joint venture, the industry research level is maximized due to maximum research efficiency leading to highest R&D incentives. In turn, this maximizes the probability of new product introduction. For most parameter values, expected consumer surplus is maximized. For all parameter values, both expected industry producer surplus and expected total surplus are maximized.

Comparing Regime A to the two other regimes, the results are mixed. When parameters are set to yield a low inherent probability of success, Regime A has greater expected total surplus than Regime B, because in Regime B, not many firms enter the joint venture due to low incentives, so efficiencies are not exploited. Otherwise, Regime B outperforms A, because R&D cooperation and efficiencies are maximized, and competition in the output market keeps prices low. In contrast, Regime A always outperforms C. Entry blocking will be profitable for the joint venture in Regime C, so its joint venture is small and efficiencies will be minimal, yielding a lower probability of industry innovation.

Related literature

The somewhat favorable welfare impacts of research and production cartels found here run counter to some of the cooperative R&D literature. For example, Hinloopen (2000) and Bloch (1995) find that research joint ventures always reduce welfare if collusion in the product market is allowed. But general discussions have recognized the tradeoffs between efficiencies of cooperative R&D and potential higher product prices. See, for example, Jorde and Teece (1990), Brodley (1990), Shapiro and Willig (1990), and Grossman and Shapiro (1986). Some formal models of cooperative R&D, including Ordover and Willig (1985), D'Aspremont and Jacquemin (1988), Kamien et al. (1992), Poyago-Theotoky (1997), and De Fraja and Silipo (2002) suggest that extending collaboration to the product market may improve welfare, although under restricted conditions.[2]

The model with results most similar to this paper is De Fraja and Silipo (2002), who incorporate uncertainty of R&D and product market innovation. They also incorporate technological spillovers, which are omitted in this paper. Although their model uses a different framework, they also conclude that the research and production cartel sometimes outperforms the research-only joint venture. The rationale is identical to the model here—firms spend more on R&D if they can reap more profits in the product market; this increases the probability of success in R&D which can help to benefit consumers. Poyago-Theotoky (1997) derives similar conclusions. Also using an alternative framework, she examines market outcomes for a three-firm industry that engages in cooperative research aimed at uncertain product market innovation. In her paper, if a "superproduct", developed and priced cooperatively, raises quality high enough, then welfare improves. This paper reinforces the above findings but does so with more generality in the number of potential collaborators. With n potential collaborators, richer scenarios are examined with respect to joint venture size and the influence of non-member firms.

Several other papers lend indirect support to the results here. Stennek (2003) finds that horizontal mergers may increase consumer welfare, despite reducing competition, by generating informational efficiencies. Brod and Shivakumar (1999) show that it is conceivable for a production cartel to over-invest in a competitive R&D game enough to benefit consumers. In contrast, but still showing that positive incentives can be generated through cooperation, Kaiser (2002), using a sample of German cooperating R&D partners, finds that research cooperation has a positive effect on R&D investment.[3] Also he shows that an increase in research productivity has a positive effect on research joint venture formation and expenditures. In an empirical study, Dick (1992) discovered that export volume and revenues rose when export cartels were formed. Both consumers and firms were inferred to be better off.

Unfortunately, the results of this paper muddy antitrust recommendations. In the US, for instance, significant debate was held on the form of research cooperation that the law should allow. Some proposed versions of the National Cooperative Research and Production Act of 1993—to extend the earlier National Cooperative Research Act—did not restrict the form of product market collaboration.[4] Notably, the enacted version of the 1993 legislation prohibits research and production joint ventures from setting product prices as part of their downstream collaborations. However, since tacit collusion is always a possibility as Martin (1995) shows, it is wise to consider the ramifications of product market cooperation.

The paper is laid out as follows. Section 2 defines the R&D environment. Section 3 sets up the decision problems of firms in a research and production joint venture (Regime A), finding the equilibrium size of the joint venture and firms' R&D expenditures in a very general case. Section 4 presents and analyzes computations of welfare under various sizes of the joint venture, given linear demand and constant marginal production cost. In addition, the welfare levels of the joint venture (Regime A) are compared to welfare levels of research-only joint ventures (Regimes B and C). Concluding remarks are found in Section 5.

2. The research environment for the research and production joint venture[5]

As is common in the literature on research joint ventures, the model assumes that joint venture formation, R&D investment, and market activity take place within a three-stage game. In the first stage, each of n firms individually decides whether to affiliate with a single joint venture. In the second stage, each non-cooperating firm chooses its R&D expenditure to maximize its expected net returns, and the joint venture sets its per-firm R&D expenditure allocations to maximize joint expected net returns. A firm's expected returns are explicitly affected by the cooperation and R&D expenditure decisions that firms make in the first two stages, because these decisions affect the likelihood of innovation. It is assumed that innovations are not patented; that is, multiple technologies can co-exist. Therefore, in the third stage, all successful innovators enter the new product market and compete to produce and sell the good. This would include the joint venture, which if successful, would enter the product market as a single player.

The remainder of this section of the paper specifies the research environment in stage two. R&D activity is modeled as a research draw. Each of the n firms, whether independent or a research and production joint venture member, faces the same technological opportunity set: a menu of m possible research approaches ("projects"). In particular, each firm, having a capacity constraint of one research project, draws one research project from the menu of m available projects. Whether selection of research projects is done with or without replacement depends on whether the firm is a JV member. In either case, it is common knowledge, a priori, that one of the m projects is "good" and the rest "bad", though the quality of a particular project is unknown until it is completed. A "good" project is defined as one that may yield an innovation, whereas a "bad" project never yields an innovation.

The level of research expenditures that a firm devotes to its selected research project influences the likelihood of innovation. The probability that a good project yields an innovation is $F(b) = 1-e^{-\lambda b}$, where λ is positive and b is a firm's R&D expenditure on the project. Note the presence of diminishing returns to R&D expenditure.

All told, innovation requires that the research project selected is good *and* that the expenditures on the good project are successful in bringing forth an innovation. Thus, for each non-member firm i, the probability of innovation is $P_i(b_i) = (1/m)F(b_i)$.

Firms in a joint venture have better technological opportunities than do non-cooperating firms. This is due in part to specific assumptions about the joint venture contract and R&D process. First, JV members have free use of any innovation discovered within the JV. Second, a JV with s members selects s of the m projects without replacement, allocating a unique project to each member. (For simplicity, $1 \leq s \leq n \leq m$.) In this manner, duplication of the same research project is eliminated, so that the parallel projects are conducted in a more efficient manner.[6] The probability that the joint venture selects the good project is thus s/m. Suppose further that the research expenditure per member, B, is chosen cooperatively and enforced without cost. Then, the probability that the good project yields an innovation is $F(B) = 1-e^{-\lambda B}$. Innovation for the JV requires that some firm selects the good project *and* that expenditures on that project yield an innovation. It can be shown that the probability of innovation for the JV is thus $P^{jv}(s, B) = (s/m)F(B)$. Therefore, $P^{jv} > P_i$ ceteris paribus—a research dollar has a larger impact if spent in the joint venture. Note also that the upper bound on the probability of innovation is higher for the JV (s/m) than for a non-member firm ($1/m$). The differentials in the probability of innovation generate large economies to cooperation that grow along with the size of the joint venture.

For JV members as well as non-members, the expected net benefits that are generated from R&D efforts depend on the size of the joint venture, the R&D expenditures of all firms, and the actual product market payoffs in stage three. This paper assumes that a successful JV would enter production in stage three as a single strategic player, and would divide product market returns equally among its members. The reduced-form product market payoff function for a JV member is denoted $R^I(I,K)$, where I equals one if the joint venture innovates and zero otherwise, and K is the number of innovating non-members. Using similar notation, a firm that does not cooperate has a market payoff of $R_i^O(I,K)$: the product market equilibrium assumes a symmetric product market equilibrium among non-member firms.

To state the expected net benefit function, use $\mathbf{b} = (b_1, b_2, \ldots, b_{n-s})$, and let $P(k, N, \mathbf{b})$ denote the probability that innovation occurs for k out of N firms that are not members of the JV.[7] Assuming that innovations across non-member firms are independent, and that firms who do not innovate earn zero product market profits, expected net returns for the JV member are

$$V^I(s,B,\mathbf{b}) = \left[P^{jv}(B)\sum_{k=0}^{n-s}P(k,n-s,\mathbf{b})R^I(1,k)\right] - B$$

and for a non-member firm i,

$$V_i^O(s,B,\mathbf{b}) = P_i(b_i)\left\{\sum_{k=0}^{n-s-1}P(k,n-s-1,\mathbf{b})\right.$$
$$\times \left[P^{jv}(B)R_i^O(1;k+1)\right.$$
$$\left.\left.+ (1-P^{jv}(B))R_i^O(0;k+1)\right]\right\}$$
$$- b_i$$

3. Decision problems and equilibrium for the research and production joint venture

This section defines a subgame-perfect equilibrium for the three-stage game, using the expected net return functions specified above. The equilibrium payoff functions in the final production stage are already stated in their reduced forms, $R^I(I,k)$ and $R_i^O(I,k)$. These functions are used to solve for the equilibrium expenditures in the R&D stage of the game, given the JV size. Next, the resulting values of research expenditures enter the expected net return functions, which in turn are used to solve for the equilibrium JV size. The recursive solution yields a subgame-perfect equilibrium of the three-stage game.

R&D stage

The R&D-stage decision problem of each of the non-member firms is to maximize expected net returns to R&D with respect to own R&D expenditures, given others' expenditures, the JV size, and production payoffs. That is, firm i maximizes V_i^O with respect to b_i.

The JV has a unique R&D-stage decision problem. It maximizes joint expected net returns to R&D with respect to R&D expenditure per member, taking nonmembers' expenditures and JV size as given. Given the functional form of P^{jv}, an equivalent problem is to maximize V^I with respect to B.

The solutions to the R&D decision problems lead to a Nash equilibrium in research expenditures in the research-stage subgame. The Nash equilibrium is found by solving the $n - s + 1$ equations from the first-order conditions of the R&D decision problems. $[B^*(s), \mathbf{b}^*(s)]$ denotes this equilibrium. Assuming symmetry among the non-member firms, $b_i^* = b^*$ for all i.

The size of the joint venture influences the equilibrium in research expenditures. Proposition 1 shows that an industry-wide JV induces the highest level of aggregate industry research expenditure.

Proposition 1: *Assuming an innovator's product market profits do not decrease when there are fewer competitors, total industry research expenditure is highest with an industry-wide joint venture. That is, assuming $R^I(1, k) \geq R^I(1, k-1)$ for all k between 0 and $n - s$, it follows that $nB^*(n) > sB^*(s) + (n - s)b^*(s)$, for all $s < n$.*

The proof of Proposition 1 shows that if firms were to pull out of an industry-wide JV, 1) the research expenditure of each remaining member would drop or remain the same, and 2) those that pull out would lower their research expenditures. Appendix A.1 has the full proof.

As research expenditures per firm increase with formation of an industry-wide JV, the JV also increases its probability of innovation. What is striking about the Proposition 1 result is that an industry-wide JV chooses to increase its probability of success by increasing research expenditure rather than solely relying on greater economies of scale in R&D. In fact, it is possible for the JV to increase the probability of innovation without increases in research spending. Therefore, the model generates a strong Schumpeterian effect: monopoly power in the product market elicits greater R&D spending and innovation.

Joint venture formation stage

The first-stage joint venture formation stage involves firms' unilateral decisions about whether to join the venture. When making its membership decision, a firm knows the subsequent equilibrium behavior in both research and production stages and how the behavior is affected by its membership decision. Finding the equilibrium for the membership stage thus yields a subgame-perfect equilibrium for the three-stage game.

The model seeks a "stable JV", which is a Nash equilibrium in membership decisions, along the lines of D'Aspremont *et al.* (1983). The equilibrium is found by allowing free entry and exit. Firms have no incentive to exit a JV of size s if $V^I(s, B^*(s), \mathbf{b}^*(s)) \geq V^O(s - 1, B^*(s-1), \mathbf{b}^*(s-1))$, given $n \geq s \geq 2$. In this case call the JV "internally stable". The JV is "externally stable" when no firm has an incentive to enter: $V^O(s, B^*(s), \mathbf{b}^*(s)) \geq V^I(s+1, B^*(s+1), \mathbf{b}^*(s+1))$, A JV of size $s = 1$ will be defined to be internally stable and one of size $s = n$ externally stable. A JV is "stable" if it is both internally and externally stable.[8]

Proposition 2: *For any size industry, an industry-wide JV is stable.*

The proof is in Appendix A.2. The intuition behind Proposition 2 is straightforward. Larger JVs experience a significantly greater probability of innovation, without the downside of having to compete in the product market with fellow members. A single member in an industry-wide JV weighs the tradeoffs of sharing the JV expected returns or betting on JV failure and its own success if it exits the JV. But the JV is such a research engine that a single firm would find its odds of success to be relatively small. Therefore, sharing in the JV returns outweighs going it alone.

4. Welfare analysis of the research and production joint venture and comparisons to research-only joint ventures for an example

Using an example, this section presents computations of welfare in research and production joint ventures and compares these Regime A results to Combs' (1993) results for research-only joint ventures, Regimes B and C. The example assumes linear demand for a homogeneous product, $P = a - Q$, where P is product price, Q is market output, and a is a positive constant. The average and marginal costs of production, c, are equal and constant; the fixed costs of production are assumed to be zero. For simplicity, $a - c$ is normalized to be 1.

The example for Regime A, the research and production joint venture, includes two sub-cases of product market behavior. The first case assumes that a successful JV acts as a single Cournot competitor, on equal footing with successful non-member firms.[9] The second case assumes that a successful JV acts as a Stackelberg leader in the product market, with the successful non-member firms comprising a Cournot "competitive" fringe, as formalized in Shaffer (1995). That is, the JV would be the first mover in deciding product market output. The non-member firms would then take the JV's output as given and follow by making Cournot output decisions among themselves.[10] In the Stackelberg sub-case, non-member firms engage in Cournot competition if the JV is unsuccessful.

The computations for Regime A, the research and production joint venture, are reported in Tables I–IV. The tables display equilibrium R&D expenditures for various parameter values (numbers of firms, number of JV members, probability of success parameters) for the stage-two subgame. In addition, the tables show the resulting probabilities of innovation, expected returns, and expected consumer surplus.[11] From these numerical values, the equilibrium JV size can be confirmed, and the welfare-maximizing JV size can also be determined.

The computations for Regime A illustrate three results. The first result is that expected

TABLE I
Regime A: JV. Equilibrium computations when JV is a Cournot product market competitor: $n = 3$

λ	m	s	b	B	P_i	P^{jv}	V^O	V^I	Consumer surplus	Total surplus
25	4	1	0.0144	–	0.08	–	0.0030	–	0.0279	0.0367
25	4	2	0.0140	0.0162	0.07	0.17	0.0028	0.0038	0.0297	0.0399
25	4	3	–	0.0179	–	0.27	–	0.0047	0.0338	0.0477
25	6	1	0.0014	–	0.01	–	0.0000	–	0.0021	0.0022
25	6	2	0.0014	0.0015	0.01	0.01	0.0000	0.0000	0.0022	0.0023
25	6	3	–	0.0016	–	0.01	–	0.0000	0.0025	0.0026
50	4	1	0.0192	–	0.15	–	0.0131	–	0.0559	0.0951
50	4	2	0.0188	0.0210	0.15	0.33	0.0124	0.0162	0.0583	0.1031
50	4	3	–	0.0228	–	0.51	–	0.0197	0.0637	0.1229
50	6	1	0.0129	–	0.08	0.11	0.0052	–	0.0292	0.0448
50	6	2	0.0127	0.0138	0.08	0.17	0.0051	0.0061	0.0302	0.0474
50	6	3	–	0.0147	–	0.26	–	0.0070	0.0325	0.0535
100	4	1	0.0160	–	0.20	–	0.0235	–	0.0714	0.1420
100	4	2	0.0157	0.0172	0.20	0.41	0.0225	0.0285	0.0738	0.1532
100	4	3	–	0.0183	–	0.63	–	0.0342	0.0787	0.1813
100	6	1	0.0129	–	0.12	–	0.0134	–	0.0440	0.0843
100	6	2	0.0128	0.0136	0.12	0.25	0.0131	0.0153	0.0452	0.0889
100	6	3	–	0.0143	–	0.38	–	0.0174	0.0475	0.0997
5,000	4	1	0.0011	–	0.25	–	0.0453	–	0.0880	0.2240
5,000	4	2	0.0011	0.0011	0.25	0.50	0.0439	0.0525	0.0899	0.2389
5,000	4	3	–	0.0011	–	0.75	–	0.0612	0.0934	0.2769
5,000	6	1	0.0010	–	0.17	–	0.0332	–	0.0598	0.1593
5,000	6	2	0.0010	0.0010	0.17	0.33	0.0328	0.0366	0.0606	0.1666
5,000	6	3	–	0.0011	–	0.50	–	0.0404	0.0622	0.1834

TABLE II
Regime A: JV. Equilibrium computations when JV is a Cournot product market competitor: $n = 4$

λ	m	s	b	B	P_i	P^{jv}	V^O	V^I	Consumer surplus	Total surplus
25	4	1	0.0131	–	0.07	–	0.0024	–	0.0342	0.0438
25	4	2	0.0127	0.0148	0.07	0.15	0.0023	0.0031	0.0356	0.0464
25	4	3	0.0118	0.0164	0.06	0.25	0.0019	0.0039	0.0391	0.0526
25	4	4	–	0.0179	–	0.36	–	0.0047	0.0450	0.0636
25	6	1	0.0013	–	0.01	–	0.0000	–	0.0026	0.0027
25	6	2	0.0013	0.0014	0.01	0.01	0.0000	0.0000	0.0027	0.0028
25	6	3	0.0012	0.0015	0.00	0.02	0.0000	0.0000	0.0030	0.0031
25	6	4	–	0.0016	–	0.03	–	0.0000	0.0033	0.0035
50	4	1	0.0177	–	0.15	–	0.0108	–	0.0698	0.1132
50	4	2	0.0174	0.0195	0.15	0.31	0.0103	0.0134	0.0720	0.1195
50	4	3	0.0164	0.0212	0.14	0.49	0.0091	0.0165	0.0768	0.1353
50	4	4	–	0.0228	–	0.68	–	0.0197	0.0850	0.1639
50	6	1	0.0121	–	0.08	–	0.0045	–	0.0369	0.0551
50	6	2	0.0120	0.0130	0.08	0.16	0.0044	0.0053	0.0379	0.0573
50	6	3	0.0117	0.0138	0.07	0.25	0.0042	0.0061	0.0399	0.0625
50	6	4	–	0.0147	–	0.35	–	0.0070	0.0433	0.0713
100	4	1	0.0150	–	0.19	–	0.0197	–	0.0905	0.1695
100	4	2	0.0147	0.0161	0.19	0.40	0.0189	0.0239	0.0927	0.1783
100	4	3	0.0141	0.0172	0.19	0.62	0.0170	0.0287	0.0974	0.2005
100	4	4	–	0.0183	–	0.84	–	0.0342	0.1050	0.2417
100	6	1	0.0123	–	0.12	–	0.0118	–	0.0565	0.1038
100	6	2	0.0122	0.0129	0.12	0.24	0.0116	0.0135	0.0576	0.1078
100	6	3	0.0120	0.0136	0.12	0.37	0.0111	0.0154	0.0598	0.1170
100	6	4	–	0.0143	–	0.51	–	0.0174	0.0633	0.1329
5,000	4	1	0.0011	–	0.25	–	0.0393	–	0.1135	0.2706
5,000	4	2	0.0011	0.0011	0.25	0.50	0.0381	0.0453	0.1155	0.2824
5,000	4	3	0.0010	0.0011	0.25	0.75	0.0353	0.0526	0.1193	0.3123
5,000	4	4	–	0.0011	–	1.00	–	0.0612	0.1246	0.3692
5,000	6	1	0.0010	–	0.17	–	0.0301	–	0.0781	0.1986
5,000	6	2	0.0010	0.0010	0.17	0.33	0.0298	0.0332	0.0789	0.2048
5,000	6	3	0.0010	0.0010	0.17	0.50	0.0290	0.0366	0.0806	0.2193
5,000	6	4	–	0.0011	–	0.66	–	0.0404	0.0829	0.2445

consumer surplus is highest for an industry-wide JV for many, but not all, circumstances. The outcome depends on the type of product market behavior. When the JV acts as a Cournot competitor (Tables I and II), expected consumer surplus is always highest for an industry-wide JV. This is not necessarily the case when the JV acts as a Stackelberg leader (Tables III and IV).

Table IV illustrates the first result for Regime A. For any value of λ between 25 and 100, consumer surplus increases steadily as the JV gains more members. But for a very high value of λ such as 5000, consumer surplus increases as the JV grows from one to three firms, then decreases slightly as the fourth and last firm joins. This pattern holds up for similar computations not reported here. For example, given seven firms facing ten projects, with $\lambda = 2000$, the highest consumer surplus occurs when the JV has five members.

In principle, differences in expected consumer surplus between Cournot and Stackelberg production could stem from either differences in probabilities of innovation or differences in product pricing, or both. Interestingly, in the Table IV example, product pricing differences alone are responsible for the expected consumer surplus differences. This can be seen by comparing Table II (Cournot) to Table IV (Stackelberg) for the parameter values $\lambda = 5000$, $m = 6$, and $n = 4$. The probabilities of innovation are the same,

TABLE III
Regime A: JV. Equilibrium computations when JV is a Stackelberg production leader: $n = 3$

λ	m	s	b	B	P_i	P^{jv}	V^O	V^I	Consumer surplus	Total surplus
25	4	1	0.0144	–	0.08	–	0.0029	–	0.0279	0.0367
25	4	2	0.0124	0.0165	0.07	0.17	0.0021	0.0039	0.0298	0.0398
25	4	3	–	0.0179	–	0.27	–	0.0046	0.0338	0.0477
50	4	1	0.0192	–	0.15	–	0.0131	–	0.0559	0.0951
50	4	2	0.0172	0.0213	0.14	0.33	0.0010	0.0167	0.0604	0.1038
50	4	3	–	0.0228	–	0.51	–	0.0200	0.0638	0.1229
100	4	1	0.0160	–	0.20	–	0.0235	–	0.0714	0.1420
100	4	2	0.0146	0.0173	0.19	0.41	0.0186	0.0292	0.0779	0.1549
100	4	3	–	0.0183	–	0.63	–	0.0342	0.0788	0.1813
100	6	1	0.0129	–	0.12	–	0.0134	–	0.0440	0.0843
100	6	2	0.0122	0.0137	0.12	0.25	0.0117	0.0156	0.0466	0.0894
100	6	3	–	0.0143	–	0.38	–	0.0174	0.0475	0.0997
5,000	4	1	0.0011	–	0.25	–	0.0453	–	0.0088	0.2240
5,000	4	2	0.0011	0.0011	0.25	0.50	0.0379	0.0534	0.0972	0.2419
5,000	4	3	–	0.0012	–	0.75	–	0.0612	0.0935	0.2769
5,000	6	1	0.0010	–	0.17	–	0.0332	–	0.0598	0.1593
5,000	6	2	0.0010	0.0011	0.17	0.33	0.0301	0.0370	0.0639	0.1679
5,000	6	3	–	0.0011	–	0.50	–	0.1212	0.0622	0.1834

TABLE IV
Regime A: JV. Equilibrium computations when JV is a Stackelberg production leader: $n = 4$

λ	m	s	b	B	P_i	P^{jv}	V^O	V^I	Consumer surplus	Total surplus
25	4	1	0.0132	–	0.07	–	0.0024	–	0.0342	0.0438
25	4	2	0.0114	0.0131	0.06	0.14	0.0018	0.0034	0.0358	0.0461
25	4	3	0.0093	0.0154	0.05	0.24	0.0017	0.0041	0.0390	0.0524
25	4	4	–	0.0168	–	0.34	–	0.0046	0.0450	0.0636
50	4	1	0.0177	–	0.15	–	0.0108	–	0.0698	0.1131
50	4	2	0.0158	0.0200	0.14	0.32	0.0083	0.0144	0.0754	0.1207
50	4	3	0.0135	0.0215	0.12	0.49	0.0058	0.0171	0.0790	0.1363
50	4	4	–	0.0228	–	0.68	–	0.0197	0.0850	0.1638
50	6	1	0.0121	–	0.08	–	0.0045	–	0.0369	0.0551
50	6	2	0.0113	0.0132	0.07	0.16	0.0039	0.0055	0.0387	0.0575
50	6	3	0.0105	0.0140	0.07	0.25	0.0033	0.0063	0.0405	0.0626
50	6	4	–	0.0147	–	0.35	–	0.0070	0.0433	0.0713
100	4	1	0.0150	–	0.19	–	0.0197	–	0.0905	0.1694
100	4	2	0.0136	0.0164	0.19	0.40	0.0155	0.0252	0.0997	0.1810
100	4	3	0.0121	0.0174	0.18	0.62	0.0114	0.0296	0.1026	0.2029
100	4	4	–	0.0183	–	0.84	–	0.0342	0.1050	0.2417
100	6	1	0.0123	–	0.12	–	0.0118	–	0.0565	0.1038
100	6	2	0.0116	0.0131	0.11	0.24	0.0103	0.0140	0.0602	0.1088
100	6	3	0.0110	0.0137	0.11	0.37	0.0090	0.0157	0.0618	0.1178
100	6	4	–	0.0143	–	0.51	–	0.0174	0.0633	0.1329
5,000	4	1	0.0011	–	0.25	–	0.0393	–	0.1135	0.2706
5,000	4	2	0.0010	0.0011	0.25	0.50	0.0325	0.0470	0.1285	0.2874
5,000	4	3	0.0010	0.0011	0.25	0.75	0.0263	0.0534	0.1302	0.3168
5,000	4	4	–	0.0012	–	10.00	–	0.0612	0.1246	0.3692
5,000	6	1	0.0010	–	0.17	–	0.0301	–	0.0781	0.1986
5,000	6	2	0.0010	0.0010	0.17	0.33	0.0272	0.0339	0.0849	0.2072
5,000	6	3	0.0010	0.0011	0.17	0.50	0.0249	0.0370	0.0854	0.2213
5,000	6	4	–	0.0011	–	0.66	–	0.0404	0.0829	0.2445

controlling for the JV size, regardless of the JV's product market behavior. This is not surprising, due to the high value of λ, which places the probabilities near their upper bounds for a wide range of research expenditures. That leaves pricing, in the Table IV example, as the only factor explaining the decrease in expected consumer surplus as the last firm joins the JV.

The second result for Regime A is that expected total surplus is always highest for an industry-wide JV. This is straightforward in the Cournot case, because both expected producer and consumer surplus increase as more members join the JV. In the Stackelberg case, for high λ, expected producer surplus increases but consumer surplus decreases as the last JV member joins. Numerically, the increase in producer surplus is the dominating factor. This result is robust to changes in values of demand and cost parameters, and to extreme values of the probability parameters not reported here.

The third and final result for Regime A is that an industry-wide JV is uniquely stable. Proposition 2 showed that an industry-wide JV is stable but did not examine other JV sizes for stability. The data in Table IV, with four potential entrants, illustrates the stability results. Given $\lambda = 25$, $m = 4$, and no cooperation, all earn expected net benefits of 0.0024. However, this formation is not externally stable. Two firms would choose to join with one another because each would increase its benefits to 0.0034. A third firm would also choose to join in order to increase its benefits from 0.0018 to 0.0041. Finally, the last remaining firm would choose to join because its benefits increase from 0.0017 to 0.0046. Thus, no JV structure is externally stable except the industry-wide JV, so no other size JV is stable. This result seems to be robust to changes in parameter values.

Although the welfare gains are significant when firms cooperate in research and production, could other cooperative R&D structures do better? Table V compares expected total surplus generated in equilibrium across three different regimes: Regime A—research and production cooperation (JV). Regime B—cooperation in research but not production; no venture-imposed membership restrictions ("stable RJV"), and Regime C: cooperation in research but not pro-

TABLE V
Total surplus in equilibrium for three cooperative regimes

n	m	λ	Regime A JV[a]	Regime B stable RJV[b]/ (equilibrium RJV size)	Regime C entry-blocking RJV[c]/ (equilibrium RJV size)
3	4	50	0.1229	0.0951/(1)	0.0951/(1)
		100	0.1813	0.2302/(3)	0.1764/(2)
		5000	0.2769	0.3468/(3)	0.2679/(2)
3	6	50	0.0535	0.0448/(1)	0.0448/(1)
		100	0.0997	0.0842/(1)	0.0842/(1)
		5000	0.1834	0.1593/(1)	0.1593/(1)
4	4	50	0.1638	0.1344/(2)	0.1344/(2)
		100	0.2417	0.3046/(4)	0.1984/(2)
		5000	0.3692	0.4734/(4)	0.3068/(2)
4	6	50	0.0713	0.0551/(1)	0.0551/(1)
		100	0.1329	0.1038/(1)	0.1038/(1)
		5000	0.2445	0.3137/(4)	0.1986/(2)

[a] This column shows total surplus for a stable research and production JV that acts as a single Cournot competitor. This JV is industry-wide in equilibrium; [b] This column shows total surplus for a stable, research-only RJV. Computations are from Combs (1993). Numbers in parentheses indicate the number of firms in the stable RJV; [c] This column shows total surplus for an entry-blocking, research-only RJV. The computations are from Combs (1993). Numbers in parentheses indicate the number of firms in the entry-blocking RJV.

duction; venture-imposed membership restrictions allowed ("entry-blocking RJV"). The stable RJV and entry-blocking RJV computations come from Combs (1993).

Analyzing Table 5 yields some policy recommendations that vary with the research environment, specifically with the values of the probability parameters. In environments with low research "productivity" (low λ—suggestive of basic R&D), a JV maximizes welfare. For example, for $\lambda = 50$, (say for $n = 3$ and $m = 4$), total surplus is 0.1229 for the JV but only 0.0951 for both types of RJVs. The lower total surplus for the RJVs is tied to the endogeneity of the venture's size. Product market payoffs are lower in the case of a research-only joint venture because if successful, members would compete with one another in production and have lower earnings, ex post. This reduces incentives for joining, all else constant. Thus, RJVs may not form, and the product is less likely to be introduced. Further, collaborative research efficiencies may not be realized. Together this contributes to lower total surplus in an environment of research-only joint ventures. The same type of pattern can occur if m is high enough (e.g. $n = 3$, $m = 6$). For low λ and/or high m, then, allowing JVs to cooperate in production improves welfare.

Welfare comparisons flip in the case of more productive research environments (higher λ). Depending upon whether the RJV blocks potential members from joining, the JV may under perform the RJV. For $n = 3$, $m = 4$, and $\lambda = 5000$, Table V shows that welfare is lower in the JV than in a stable RJV, but higher in the JV than in an entry-blocking RJV. For those parameter values, the entry-blocking RJV restricts membership to two of the three firms, whereas all firms join the JV and stable RJV. Industry-wide membership enhances research productivity and thereby makes product introduction more likely. Thus, in this type of environment, membership rules can influence welfare outcomes and thus are important for policy makers to take into account.

5. Conclusion

By developing a model of R&D aimed at uncertain product market innovations, this paper makes a prediction about the extent of research and production cooperation in equilibrium for a general case, and compares welfare across different cooperative regimes for an example. For the general case, the paper finds that all potential entrants to a product market will cooperate in a research and production joint venture. Computational results for an example show that research and production joint ventures can outperform research-only joint ventures in certain situations. Despite higher pricing, this can occur because the product is more likely to be offered due to significant cooperative research efficiencies in the research and production joint venture, especially when the alternative, a research-only joint venture, limits membership.

Overall, the model would not overwhelmingly support cartelization of the market. When the likelihood of innovation is relatively high, as in product development, it is difficult to judge whether allowing industry-wide research and production ventures improves welfare. It requires an analysis of what membership rules would have evolved for the alternative, research-only joint venture. In environments with lower research success probabilities, such as basic R&D, this model advises more permissive antitrust treatment of research and production joint ventures.

Therefore, in regard to policy, a case-by-case consideration of cooperative research ventures is recommended. Important considerations brought out here include endogenous joint venture formation, uncertainty of R&D results, efficiency gains from cooperation, and the gain to consumers if a new product is introduced.

However, the model is somewhat limited because of several simplifying assumptions. First, appropriability problems of R&D do not exist in the model. If they were introduced, this would provide another private benefit to firms from cooperating, and possibly give incentives for increases in research expenditures across all regimes. It is difficult to say how this would affect which regime dominates in terms of welfare.

Further limitations include the assumption that firms do not have sources of revenue from other products, that only one JV is allowed to form rather than competing JVs, and that managerial problems in overseeing an industry wide JV do not exist. Relaxing these assumptions may well cause a research and production joint venture to be smaller, and this may reduce efficiencies and welfare. Additionally, it is assumed that consumers have no alternative substitute product, so the gains to consumer surplus from a new supplier are significant. Mansfield's critique may have been that we would want to add only the net gain to consumers and the net gain to firm profits if, for example, products were displaced. Finally, Mansfield may also have wanted to know how the results differ with process innovations. The answer to that question is unfortunately beyond the scope of this paper.

Appendix

A.1. Proof of Proposition 1

First, examine industry-wide cooperation, where $s = n$. The JV's problem, maximizing the sum of V^J with respect to each member's level of research (assuming research is equal across members), is

equivalent to the problem of a single member maximizing V^I with respect to B. With industry-wide cooperation,
$V^I = (n/m)(1 - e^{-\lambda B})\pi^m/n - B$, where π^m is monopoly profit. Assuming an interior solution, the first-order condition to this problem is

$$(1/m)(\lambda e^{-\lambda B})\pi^m = 1 \tag{A.1}$$

Second, find the level of research expenditure in the JV if it has less than n firms. The first-order condition to the JV's decision problem to maximize $V^I(s,B,\mathbf{b})$, assuming an interior solution, is

$$\frac{\partial P^{jv}(s,B)}{\partial B}\left\{\sum_{k=0}^{n-s} P(k,n-s,\mathbf{b})R^I(1;k)\right\} = 1$$

or

$$(s/m)(\lambda e^{-\lambda B})\left\{\sum_{k=0}^{n-s} P(k,n-s,\mathbf{b})R^I(1;k)\right\} = 1$$

or

$$(1/m)(\lambda e^{-\lambda B})\left\{\sum_{k=0}^{n-s} P(k,n-s,\mathbf{b})sR^I(1;k)\right\} = 1 \tag{A.2}$$

Condition (A.2) is sufficient for a solution to the maximization problem because of the concavity of P^{jv}. The bracketed summation term in (A.2) is a weighted average of total earnings of the joint venture. For example, the first term of the sum, $sR^I(1,0)$, equals π^m, the total earnings of a monopoly joint venture. Under even the broadest assumptions about market behavior, subsequent joint venture earnings terms in the sum must be less than or equal to π^m, because these terms involve one or more nonmember entrants into the product market. Therefore, the entire bracketed term in (A.2) is less than or equal to π^m. A comparison of (A.1) and (A.2) shows that $B^*(s;s < n) \leq B^*(s;s = n)$. That is, the per-firm expenditure in the JV is never higher than that performed when the venture is industry-wide.

To complete the proof, examine the research level of firms outside the JV. Maximizing $V_i^o(s,B,\mathbf{b})$ with respect to b_i yields the following first-order condition for an interior solution:

$$\frac{\partial P_i(b_i)}{\partial b_i}\left\{\sum_{k=0}^{n-s-1} P(k,n-s-1,\mathbf{b})\right.$$
$$\left[P^{jv}(B)R_i^o(1;k+1)\right.$$
$$\left.\left.+(1-P^{jv}(B))R_i^o(0;k+1)\right]\right\} = 1$$

or

$$(1/m)(\lambda e^{-\lambda b_i})\left\{\sum_{k=0}^{n-s-1} P(k,n-s-1,\mathbf{b})\right.$$
$$\left[P^{jv}(B)R_i^o(1;k+1)\right.$$
$$\left.\left.+(1-P^{jv}(B))R_i^o(0;k+1)\right]\right\} = 1$$

Writing out the summation term in more detail is useful, and shows that the summation term is a weighted average of terms strictly less than π^m. That is, denoting the summation term immediately above as $\sum$, then the first order condition for an nonmember firm is

$$(1/m)(\lambda e^{-\lambda b_i})\sum = 1 \tag{A.3}$$

where

$$\sum = P(0,n-s-1,\mathbf{b})\left[\underbrace{P^{jv}\,R_i^o(1;1)}+\underbrace{(1-P^{jv})\,R_i^o(0;1)}\right]$$
$$+ P(1,n-s-1,\mathbf{b})\left[\underbrace{P^{jv}\,R_i^o(1;2)}+\underbrace{(1-P^{jv})\,R_i^o(0;2)}\right]$$
$$+$$
$$\vdots$$
$$+ P(n-s-1,n-s-1,\mathbf{b})\left[\underbrace{P^{jv}\,R_i^o(1;n-s)}+\underbrace{(1-P^{jv})\,R_i^o(0;n-s)}\right]$$

Condition (A3) is sufficient for a solution to the maximization problem because of the concavity of the exponential function. The summation term is a weighted average of the terms in square brackets. Each of these bracketed terms is strictly less than π^m, because P^{jv} is strictly less than 1, and $R_i^o(1,k)$ and $R_i^o(0,k)$ are product market profits that do not exceed π^m. Therefore, the entire summation term is strictly less than π^m.

Comparing (A.2) and (A.3), it follows that, in a symmetric $b^* = b_i$ equilibrium, $b^*(s;s < n) < B^*(s;s = n)$.

To summarize results so far, if firms leave the industry-wide JV, they reduce their research expenditures. The remaining JV members will either reduce expenditures or hold steady. Thus, aggregate research expenditures are lower when cooperation is less than industry-wide.

A.2.
Proof of Proposition 2.

Industry-wide JV

Substituting into $V^I = (1/m)(1 - e^{-\lambda B})\pi^m - B$ for π^m, from the first-order condition (A.1),

$$V^I = (1/m)(1 - e^{-\lambda B^*(n)})(m/(\lambda e^{-\lambda B^*(n)})) - B^*(n)$$

Simplifying yields

$$V^I = (1/\lambda)(e^{\lambda B^*(n)} - 1) - B^*(n) \quad (A.4)$$

Less-than-industry-wide JV

Similarly,

$$V^I = (s/m)(1-e^{-\lambda B})\left\{\sum_{k=0}^{n-s} P(k,n-s,\mathbf{b}) R^I(1;k)\right\} - B$$
$$= (s/m)(1-e^{-\lambda B^*})\left(\frac{m}{s(\lambda e^{-\lambda B^*})}\right) - B^*,$$

after substituting in from (A.2)

Simplifying yields

$$V^I = (1/\lambda)(e^{\lambda B^*(s)} - 1) - B^*(s) \quad (A.5)$$

Nonmember firm:

Following similar procedures, and substituting in from the first order condition (A.3) yields

$$V_i^o = (1/\lambda)(e^{\lambda b^*(s)} - 1) - b^*(s) \quad (A.6)$$

Note that in equilibrium, all per-firm value functions, (A.4)–(A.6), have the same functional forms. Denote the value function in these functional forms as V^*.

A couple of remaining facts need to be shown. First, simple calculus confirms that functions (A.4) and (A.5) increase in B^*, and similarly, (A.6) increases in b^*. The second fact borrows the finding from Proposition 1, that is that a JV with $s = n$ firms induces more research expenditure per member than if $s < n$. Therefore, when the "last" firm enters the now industry wide JV, it increases its research expenditures. Consequently its V^* rises, and we have the result that $V^{I*}(s = n) > V^{o*}(s = n - 1)$. Therefore, there is no incentive for a firm inside an industry wide JV to leave; the industry wide JV is stable.

Notes

1. For example, the seminal article on research joint ventures by D'Aspremont and Jacquemin (1988), and much of the literature that extends their model does not incorporate uncertainty.
2. Combs and Link (2003) summarize the literature on research partnerships in regard to several policy issues.
3. Presumably these are research-only collaborations.
4. Link and Bauer (1989) give a good description of the debate surrounding the initial National Cooperative Research Act.
5. The research environment specified here is based on Combs (1993).
6. This type of research program is not that far removed from the parallel research projects strategy in a line of literature stemming from Nelson (1961).
7. Below, the paper employs the fact that in a symmetric equilibrium in b, $P(k,N,\mathbf{b})$ follows a binomial distribution with N trials and the probability of success in each trial of P_i.
8. It is difficult to model more complicated endogenous JV formation, though significant papers in this area are Bloch (1995), Yi and Shin (2000).
9. The single-competitor nature of the JV in the product market is similar to the behavior of a product market cartel in D'Aspremont et al. (1983), or a merged firm in Salant et al. (1983).
10. Equilibrium values of output levels, etc., are identical to those in Shaffer (1995), who also uses a linear product demand and constant marginal cost.
11. Complete computational results are available from the author.

References

Bloch, F., 1995, 'Endogenous Structures of Association in Oligopolies,' *The RAND Journal of Economics* 26, 537–556.

Brod, A. and Ram Shivakumar, 1999, 'Advantageous Semi-Collusion,' *The Journal of Industrial Economics* 47, 221–230.

Brodley, J.F., 1990, 'Antitrust Law and Innovation Cooperation,' *The Journal of Economic Perspectives* 4, 97–112.

Combs, K.L., 1993, 'The Role of Information Sharing in Cooperative Research and Development,' *International Journal of Industrial Organization* 11, 535–551.

Combs, K.L. and A.N. Link, 2003, 'Innovation Policy in Search of an Economic Foundation: The Case of Research Partnerships in the United States,' *Technology Analysis and Strategic Management* **15**, 177–187.

D'Aspremont, C. and A. Jacquemin, 1988, 'Cooperative and Noncooperative R&D in Duopoly with Spillovers,' *The American Economic Review* **78**, 1133–1137.

D'Aspremont, C., A. Jacquemin, J.J. Gabszewicz, and J.A. Weymark, 1983, 'On the Stability of Collusive Price Leadership,' *Canadian Journal of Economics* **16**, 17–25.

De Fraja, G. and D.B. Silipo, 2002, 'Product Market Competition, R&D, and Welfare,' *Research in Economics* **56**, 381–397.

Dick, A., 1992, 'Are Export Cartels Efficiency-Enhancing or Monopoly-Promoting?: Evidence from the Webb-Pomerene Experience,' *Research in Law and Economics* **15**, 89–127.

Grossman, G.M. and C. Shapiro, 1986, 'Research Joint Ventures: An Antitrust Analysis,' *Journal of Law, Economics, and Organization* **2**, 315–337.

Hinloopen, J., 2000, 'Strategic R&D Co-operatives,' *Research in Economics* **54**, 153–185.

Jorde, T.M. and D.J. Teece, 1990, 'Innovation and Cooperation: Implications for Competition and Antitrust,' *The Journal of Economic Perspectives* **4**, 75–96.

Kaiser, U., 2000, 'An Empirical Test of Models Explaining Research Expenditures and Research Cooperation: Evidence for the German Service Sector,' *International Journal of Industrial Organization* **20**, 747–774.

Kamien, M.I., E. Muller, and I. Zang, 1992, 'Research Joint Ventures and R&D Cartels,' *The American Economic Review* **82**, 1293–1306.

Link, A.N. and L.L. Bauer, 1989, *Cooperative Research in US Manufacturing*, Lexington, MA: Lexington Books.

Mansfield, E., J. Rapoport, A. Romero, S. Wagner, and G. Beardsley, 1977, 'Social and Private Rates of Return from Industrial Innovations,' *The Quarterly Journal of Economics* **91**, 221–240.

Martin, S., 1995, 'R&D Joint Ventures and Tacit Product Market Collusion,' *European Journal of Political Economy* **11**, 733–741.

Nelson, R.R., 1961, 'Uncertainty, Learning, and the Economics of Parallel Research and Development Efforts,' *Review of Economics and Statistics* **43** (4), 351–364.

Ordover, J.A. and R.D. Willig, 1985, 'Antitrust for High Technology Industries: Assessing Research Joint Ventures and Mergers,' *Journal of Law and Economics* **28**, 311–333.

Poyago-Theotoky, J., 1997, 'Research Joint Ventures and Product Innovation: Some Welfare Aspects,' *Economics of Innovation and New Technology* **5**, 51–73.

Salant, S.W., S. Switzer, and R.J. Reynolds, 1983, 'Losses from Horizontal Merger: The Effects of an Exogenous Change in Industry Structure on Cournot-Nash Equilibrium,' *Quarterly Journal of Economics* **98**, 185–199.

Shaffer, S., 1995, 'Stable Cartels with a Cournot Fringe,' *Southern Economic Journal* **61**, 744–754.

Shapiro, C. and R.D. Willig, 1990, 'On the Antitrust Treatment of Production Joint Ventures,' *The Journal of Economic Perspectives* **4**, 113–130.

Stennek, J., 2003, 'Horizontal Mergers Without Synergies May Increase Consumer Welfare,' *Topics in Economic Analysis and Policy* **3**, 1074.

Yi, S.-S. and H. Shin, 2000, 'Endogenous Formation of Research Joint Ventures with Spillovers,' *International Journal of Industrial Organization* **18**, 229–256.

Research Joint Ventures in the United States: A Descriptive Analysis

Albert N. Link

ABSTRACT. This paper describes trends and characteristics of the membership of RJVs in the United States.

Key words: research joint venture, R&D

JEL Classification: 0330, 0380

1. Introduction and background public policy

The purpose of this paper is to describe the current state of descriptive information about industrial research and development (R&D) that is undertaken cooperatively in the United States through research joint ventures (RJVs).[1,2] Hopefully, researchers will respond to the paucity of empirical research, especially empirical research of a policy nature, and fill the many voids, a point emphasized by Combs and Link (2003).

The National Cooperative Research Act (NCRA) of 1984, Public Law 98-462, was legislated, as stated in the Preamble to the Act:

> to promote research and development, encourage innovation, stimulate trade, and make necessary and appropriate modifications in the operation of the antitrust laws.

While the Act sets forth these objectives, it does not place them in an historical perspective. In the early 1980s there was growing concern that the U.S. industrial sector was loosing its competitive advantage in global markets. This was explicitly noted in the Research and Development Joint Venture Act of 1983, HR 4043. In the Joint Research and Development Act of 1984, HR 5041, the supposed benefits of joint research and development were first articulated from a policy perspective:

Department of Economics
University of North Carolina at Greensboro
Greensboro, NC 27402
U.S.A
E-mail: anlink@uncg.edu

> Joint research and development, as our foreign competitors have learned, can be procompetitive. It can reduce duplication, promote the efficient use of scarce technical personnel, and help to achieve desirable economies of scale [in R&D].

After revisions, the NCRA of 1984 was passed.

The NCRA of 1984 created a registration process, later expanded by the National Cooperative Research and Production Act (NCRPA) of 1993 and recently by the Standards Development Organization Advancement Act of 2004 (SDOAA), under which RJVs can voluntarily disclose their research intentions to the U.S. Department of Justice; all disclosures are made public in the *Federal Register*.[3]

RJVs gains two significant benefits from filing with the Department of Justice, and these benefits are what could be referred to as a "safer harbor" for participants in the venture. One, if the venture is subjected to criminal or civil action, the charges would be evaluated under a rule of reason that analyzes whether the venture improves social welfare. And two, if the venture is found to fail a rule-of-reason analysis, it is subject to actual damages rather than treble damages.

There is a vast theoretical literature, recently summarized by Hagedoorn *et al*. (2000) and Combs and Link (2003), that concludes that, among other things, collaborative research increases the efficiency of the R&D conducted by the collaborating members. Link and Rees (1990) provided early empirical evidence of this proposition, but to date related empirical research has been sparse owing to the paucity of public domain data related to research collaborations.

However, there has been conspicuously absent from the policy landscape rich public domain information about cooperative research activity. The Cooperative Research (CORE) database was constructed under the sponsorship of the

National Science Foundation, and is maintained under their support by Link, for the purpose of chronicling what public information there is. Its resource base is information in the RJV filings with the Department of Justice as disclosed publicly in the *Federal Register*. The unit of observation in the CORE database is the RJV. In the following section, public domain information about disclosed RJVs is summarized.

2. An example of a research joint venture

There have been very few case studies of RJVs; this is surprising because even in the absence of rich public domain datasets on these activities, case-based information is accessible. In fact, reflecting on the Mansfield research tradition, much of his early work was case based, and from these case studies more complete datasets began to be created and analyzed systematically.

As discussed in the following section, there have been 913 RJVs filed with the Department of Justice and disclosed publicly in the *Federal Register* through 2003. One joint venture is described herein for purposes of illustration.[4]

During the late 1980s, software developers were increasingly unwilling to incur the cost of maintaining ports to the numerous and different UNIX operating systems, many of which were not identical.[5] In addition, many hardware companies were addressing specific market niches, and any given niche was generally too small to offer a critical market size to software developers to make their products successful. Thus, to maintain profitability, developers limited their software support to only a few hardware platforms.

Most of the computer industry's leading companies relied on, at that time, technology licensed from MIPS Technologies, Inc., in particular its reduced instruction-set computing (RISC) processor for use in UNIX operating systems. Since 1991, a number of the companies committed to the MIPS RISC architecture began to work together on a standardized interface to facilitate software portability in an open UNIX environment. The group's objectives were:

- to improve software availability and selection for end users
- to lower the cost of business and quicken product development for platform vendors
- to provide customers with compatible solutions, and
- to preserve customers' investments in hardware, software, and training.

Toward these objectives, a RJV was formed in 1996 and disclosed publicly in the *Federal Register* on February 20, 1996. As stated therein:

> The nature and objectives of this joint venture are developing, adopting, establishing, maintaining, publishing, promoting and endorsing UNIX SVR4 ABI [Application Binary Interface] standards (i.e., conformance specifications) for MIPS processor-based systems and to provide under appropriate transfer means (e.g., license, lease or sale), ABI specifications and other intellectual property to industry participants, including labs, universities and consultants.

The original members of the joint venture and their home country were Concurrent Computer Corporation (U.S.); Control Data Systems, Inc. (U.S.); Dansk Data Electronic A/S (Denmark); NEC Corporation (Japan); Siemens AG (Germany); Silicon Graphics, Inc. (U.S.); Sony Corporation (Japan); and Tandem Computers, Inc. (U.S.). In 1997, Concurrent Computer merged with Harris, and, due to financial difficulties, it left the joint venture. Also, in 1997, Control Data Systems dropped out of the computer business and left the venture. On March 1, 1999, the MIPS ABI Group, Inc. ceased operations because all needed standards were developed.

While operative, the MIPS ABI Group companies worked together to develop a single, binary-compatible port which was sold and supported across multiple platforms, thus making each member's own platform compatible, and thus facilitating development and support of software by key vendors.

3. General characteristics of research joint ventures

Through calendar year 2003, 913 RJVs have been registered with the Department of Justice and disclosed publicly in the *Federal Register*.[6] Figure 1 shows the number of RJVs by year since 1985.[7] Disclosures peaked around 1995 and have steadily declined.[8]

Figure 2 shows the mean number of members in an RJV, by year, and Figure 3 shows the median number. The mean size of a venture has remained relatively stable at around 14 members, with the exception of 1988, while the median size has been more variable from year to year.

As shown in Figure 4, there has been over time a mild increase in the percent of RJVs that include a U.S. federal laboratory as a member; and the same has been true, except for 1992,

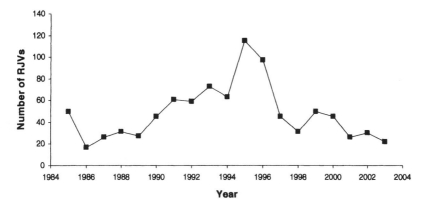

Figure 1. Number of RJV filings, by year.

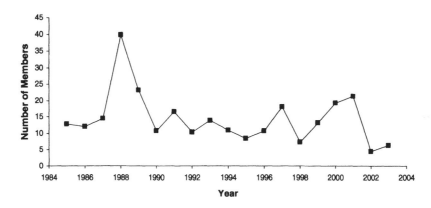

Figure 2. Mean number of members in RJVs, by year.

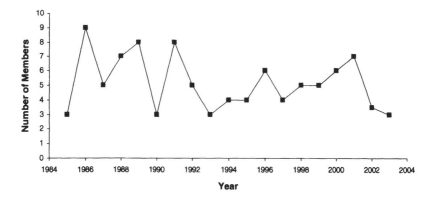

Figure 3. Median number of members in RJVs, by year.

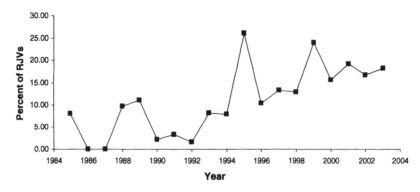

Figure 4. Percent of RJVs with U.S. Federal Laboratory as member, by year.

regarding U.S. universities (Figure 5) as research members.[9]

Foreign-owned company participation in RJVs, that is the percent of RJVs with a foreign-owned company as a member, has declined over time as shown in Figure 6.

As shown in Figure 7, the percent of RJVs with an environment focus has been declining, but the percent with a health focus, Figure 8, has been sporadic.

Finally, two outputs of RJVs can be ascertained from information in the *Federal Register*. Shown in Figure 9 is the percent of RJVs that explicitly state in their *Federal Register* disclosure an intention to patent, license, or trademark the research results. Figure 10 shows the percent of RJVs that explicitly state that protocols, standards, or infrastructure technology is an objective of the venture. No trends are evident.

4. Concluding statement

In 2000, the National Science Foundation (NSF) sponsored a workshop on strategic research partnerships in an effort to identify and discuss the innovation-related implications of collaborative research and set a direction for a more systematic collection of information–more systematic relative to studying *Federal Register* filings (Jankowski, *et al.* 2001). As a result of that workshop, NSF added a question on their 2002 survey of industrial research and development (RD-1) specifically designed to collect information on company-funded R&D done in collaboration with other research partners (e.g., for-profit companies, federal laboratories, universities and colleges, and other nonprofit organizations). These data, albeit that they will likely be reported only in aggregate form, will go a long way to supplementing what little empirical

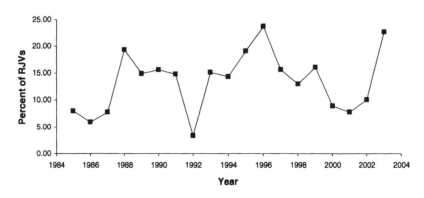

Figure 5. Percent of RJVs with U.S. University as research member, by year.

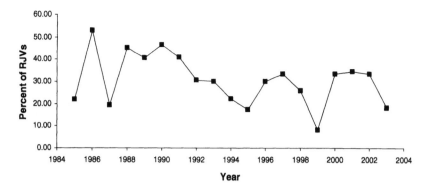

Figure 6. Percent of RJVs with Foreign-Owned Company as member, by year.

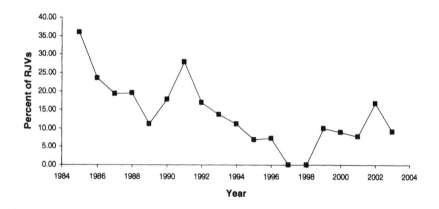

Figure 7. Percent of RJVs with Environmental Focus, by year.

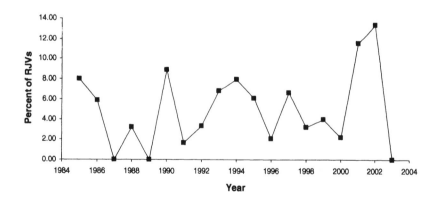

Figure 8. Percent of RJVs with Health Focus, by year.

information we have about RJV activities. There are many theoretical propositions about research collaboration that need to be tested.

Notes

1. I began to investigate RJV activity in the United States nearly two decades ago. While the National Science Founda-

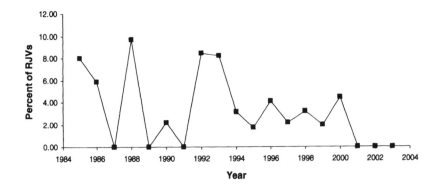

Figure 9. Percent of RJVs with Patent, License, or Trademark Output, by year.

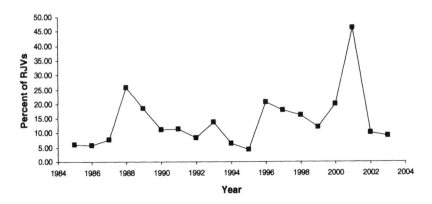

Figure 10. Percent of RJVs with Infratechnology output, by year.

tion has been extremely generous in its support of this on-going agenda, and the construction of the CORE database, were it not for Ed Mansfield's encouragement during the early 1980s to depart from the then traditional empirical studies of in-house R&D, this and related projects might never have been undertaken. For this guidance, and for his friendship, I am very appreciative.

2. Much of the material in this section draws directly from Link and Bauer (1989), Scott (1989), Link (1996), Brod and Link (2001), and especially Link and Scott (forthcoming).

3. An RJV is a collaborative research arrangement through which firms jointly acquire technical knowledge.

4. This joint venture was not randomly selected. Rather it is one of two case studies by Link and Vonortas (2000).

5. This background information came from in depth discussions with Mr. Kevin Payne of NEC Corporation and information at www.mipsabi.org (quoted from with permission of the author).

6. There has been, on average, a 2 month lag between registering the RJV with the Department of Justice and that registration being reported in the *Federal Register* (Brod and Link, 2001).

7. In Figure 1 and in subsequent figures, the data are by year of disclosure in the *Federal Register*.

8. Brod and Link (2001) show that, *ceteris paribus*, this is a countercyclical trend.

9. Link and Scott (forthcoming) showed that the probability of an RJV inviting a university to join increases with the size of the RJV, *ceteris paribus*; and Leyden and Link (1999) found the same relationship with regard to a federal laboratory being invited to join the venture, *ceteris paribus*.

References

Brod, A.C. and A.N. Link, 2001, 'Trends in Cooperative Research Activity,' in M.P. Feldman and A.N. Link (eds.), *Innovation Policy in the Knowledge-Based Economy*, Norwell, MA: Kluwer Academic Publishers.

Combs, K.L. and A.N. Link, 2003, 'Innovation Policy in Search of an Economic Foundation: The Case of Research Partnerships in the United States,' *Technology Analysis & Strategic Management*, **15**, 177–187.

Hagedoorn, J, A.N. Link, and N.S. Vonortas, 2000, 'Research Partnerships,' *Research Policy*, **29**, 567–586.

Jankowski, J., A.N. Link, and N.S. Vonortas, 2001, *Strategic Research Partnerships: Proceedings from an NSF Workshop*, NSF 01-336, Arlington, VA: National Science Foundation.

Leyden, D.P. and A.N. Link, 1999, 'Federal Laboratories as Research Partners,' *International Journal of Industrial Organization* **17**, 557–574.

Link, A.N., 1996, 'Research Joint Ventures: Patterns from *Federal Register* Filings,' *Review of Industrial Organization* **11**, 617–628.

Link, A.N. and L.L. Bauer, 1989, *Cooperative Research in U.S. Manufacturing: Assessing Policy Initiatives and Corporate Strategies*, Lexington, MA: Lexington Books.

Link, A.N. and J. Rees, 1990, 'Firm Size, University-Based Research, and the Returns to R&D,' *Small Business Economics* **2**, 25–31.

Link, A.N. and J.T. Scott, 'Universities as Partners in U.S. Research Joint Ventures,' *Research Policy*, forthcoming.

Link, A.N. and N.S. Vonortas, 2000, 'Participation of European Union Companies in U.S. Research Joint Ventures,' *IPTS Report* **43**, 1–7.

Scott, J.T., 1989, 'Historical and Economic Perspectives of the National Cooperative Research Act,' in A.N. Link and G. Tassey (eds.), *Cooperative Research and Development: The Industry-University-Government Relationship*, Norwell, MA: Kluwer Academic Publishers.

Exploring the Patent Explosion

Bronwyn H. Hall[1,2]

ABSTRACT. This paper looks more closely at the sources of patent growth in the United States since 1984. It confirms that the increase is largely due to U.S. patenters, with an earlier surge in Asia, and some increase in Europe. Growth has taken place in all technologies, but not in all industries, being concentrated in the electrical, electronics, computing, and scientific instruments industries. It then examines whether these patents are valued by the market. We know from survey evidence that patents in these industries are not usually considered important for appropriability, but are sometimes considered necessary to secure financing for entering the industry. I compare the market value of patents held by entrant firms to those held by incumbents (controlling for R&D). Using data on publicly traded firms 1980–1989, I find that in industries based on electrical and mechanical technologies the market value of entrants' patents is positive in the post-1984 period (after the patenting surge), but not before, when patents were relatively unimportant in these industries. Also, the value of patent rights in complex product industries (where each product relies on many patents held by a number of other firms) is much higher for entrants than incumbents in the post-1984 period. For discrete product industries (where each product relies on only a few patents, and where the importance of patents for appropriability has traditionally been higher), there is no difference between incumbents and entrants.

Key words: ICT, market value, entry, intellectual property

JEL Classification: O340, L100, G240

1. Introduction

A number of researchers have explored the reasons behind the recent rapid growth of patenting worldwide and especially in the United States (Hall and Ziedonis, 2001; Kim and Marschke, 2004; Kortum and Lerner, 1995, 2003). Various explanations for the phenomenon have been offered: using aggregate U.S. and international patent data, Kortum and Lerner attribute most of the growth to increases in innovation and, improvements in the management of R&D. Using data on U.S. firms during the 1983–1992 period, Kim and Marschke attribute the growth to increases in R&D in certain sectors as well as to increased patent yield in the computing, electronics, and auto sectors. Hall and Ziedonis study a single industry, semiconductors, where the patenting per R&D rate doubled over 10 years and find that the increase is associated with the assembly of large patent portfolios in order to forestall hold-up by rivals in the industry that own patents on technology that is necessary for the manufacture of semiconductor chips. Although there is no complete agreement among these authors as to the reasons for the increase, there is some consensus that the increase in patent yield is largely concentrated in computing and electronics, which suggests either that R&D has become more "fertile" in those industries or that something else having to do with patent strategy has changed.

The growth in patenting has also renewed economists' interest in evaluating the effectiveness of the patent system in promoting innovative activity among private firms. Although evidence on the effectiveness of patents for securing the returns to innovation is mixed (see the survey evidence reported by Cohen et al., 2000 and the summary of empirical work in this area in Hall, 2003a), one area where patents are widely viewed as important if not essential is for securing the financing to start a new venture (e.g., see the evidence from semiconductor firms in Hall and Ziedonis, 2001). The current paper probes the empirical validity of this assertion by examining the comparative market valuation of patents held by incumbent and entrant firms in the United States during the 1980s, a period in which the use of patents by U.S. firms increased very substantially, partly as a

---

[1] Department of Economics, 549 Evans Hall
University of California at Berkeley, Berkeley
CA 94720-3880
E-mail: bhhall@econ.berkeley.edu
[2] NBER, 30 Alta Road, Stanford, CA 94305-8715 U.S.A.

result of changes in the enforceability of patents in the courts.

As several authors have demonstrated, the creation of a centralized court of appeals specializing in patent cases in 1982, together with a few well-publicized infringement cases in the mid-1980s, have led to an increased focus on patenting by firms in industries where patents have not traditionally been important, such as computers and electronics. In the first part of the paper I show that the decomposition of the sources of patent application growth in the United States supports the interpretation that the growth has been driven by increased patenting by U.S. firms in the electric machinery, electronics, and instrument industries, broadly defined. I also show that a time series analysis of patents reveals a very significant structural break between 1983 and 1984, one that was concentrated in the electrical sector, and more particularly, that firms in that sector (broadly defined to include electric machinery, electronics, instruments, computers, and communication equipment) increased their patenting across all technologies, accounting for essentially *all* the growth in patenting by U.S. firms.

Using a large sample of publicly traded U. S. manufacturing firms, I then investigate how their patent valuations changed between the early and late 1980s, focusing on the differences between incumbent firms and new entrants to the industry. I am able to confirm that after the mid-1980s, patents held by entrants to the publicly traded sector are indeed more highly valued than those held by incumbents. An industry decomposition of this effect shows that it is concentrated in what Cohen *et al.* (2000) label complex product industries, which are industries where a single product can contain intellectual property covered by thousands of patents held by hundreds of patentholders. In such industries, patent portfolios often serve the defensive function of facilitating cross-licensing negotiations, rather than the traditional role of excluding competitors and securing the ownership of particular inventions. Although patent yield *per se* is not valued for incumbents in any of the industries, I show that in complex product industries there has been a strong positive shift in valuation for entrants as we enter the pro-patent era.

2. Changes in the U.S. patent system

A number of changes to the patent system, both legislative and via legal precedent, took place during the 1980s and more recently. These changes are summarized in Table I. A series of court decisions have expanded legitimate subject matter to include genetically modified organisms, software, and business methods.[2] Legislative changes have enhanced the ability of patentholders to enforce their patents, both via the creation of a specialized patent court, and via various procedural changes made at the same time. The Hatch–Waxman Act made patents even more important than they had been for pharmaceutical companies seeking to block generics from entering the market, by extending the lifetime of their drug patents to compensate for delays in regulatory approval.

Following these legislative changes, the demonstration effect of a series of infringement cases had a powerful effect on the thinking of some firm

TABLE I
Major changes to the U.S. patent system

Year	Event or case	Result
1980	Diamond v Chakrabarty	patentability of artificially engineered genetic organisms
1980	Bayh–Dole legislation	increase in university patenting
1981	Diamond v Diehr	patentability of software
1982	legislation	Creation of CAFC; patent validity more likely to be upheld
1984	Hatch–Waxman Act	increased importance of patents for drug firms vis a vis generic producers
1985/6	TI sues Japanese semiconductor firms	wins suits; turns to suing U.S. semiconductor firms, funding R&D from licensing royalties
1986	Kodak-Polaroid	Decision on instant camera patent; final injunction against Kodak leading to $1B judgment
1994	TRIPS agreement	harmonization drive begins
1998	State Street and ATT vs. Excel	patentability of business methods

managers. The Kodak-Polaroid case mentioned in the table ultimately cost Kodak a billion dollar judgment and shut down their instant camera business in 1986. It also demonstrated that the ability of a patentholder to obtain an injunction against the use of the supposedly infringing technology well before damages were awarded was a powerful financial weapon, and one to be avoided even at considerable cost. Fear of this strategy appears to have been a strong motivation for increased defensive patent filings, at least in the semiconductor industry (Hall and Ziedonis, 2001).

The result of all these events was a rapid increase in patent applications. In the next section of the paper I study the timing and composition of this increase in some detail.

The patent explosion

Figure 1 shows the number of applications and grants for all U.S. utility patents from 1953 to 2003. In addition it shows granted patents by application date for patents granted between January 1965 and December 2002.[3] Because of grant-application lags, the data on grants by application date are only complete through 1997. Figure 2 shows growth rates for the same data, smoothed using a moving average. Both graphs exhibit a substantial break in the mid-1980s: until then, patenting is roughly constant and after that it grows around 5% per year. Real R&D increased only about 2.4% per year during the late 1980s so that patents taken out by U.S. inventors per R&D dollar also increased.

For further investigation, I focus on the patent grants by date of application (which is relevant date for an investigation of firm behavior and abstracts from variations in the application-grant lag). The properties of the patent application series were explored in two ways: first I tested for structural breaks both in the aggregate and by region and main technology class. Then I

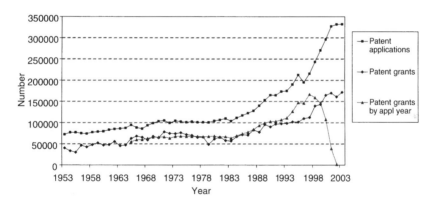

Figure 1. USPTO utiliy patents 1953–2003.

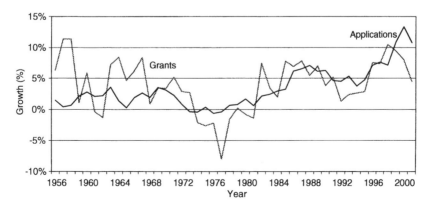

Figure 2. Growth of aggregate US patent grants and applications 1956–2001 (5-year moving average).

performed a growth accounting exercise over different 5-year subperiods to identify the sources of the growth displayed in the graphs.

Tests for structural breaks

Table II displays the results for the aggregate patent application series. Four different versions of the series were used, two in levels and two in changes, in both cases in absolute values and in logarithms. The presence of a unit root was clearly accepted for the two series in levels, so further analysis was conducted on the differenced series. The next row of the table shows the results of a simple *t*-test for a change in the mean of the differenced series between 1983 and 1984 (the choice of period was based on inspection of the graph in Figure 1). Either in levels or logs, this test rejects a constant mean resoundingly. The growth rate of patent applications jumps in 1984 from an average of 0.3% per annum to an average of 6.9% per annum. The final rows of the table give Andrews (1993) test for a structural break of unknown date. This too is highly significant, and in the case of the logged series, the break year is identified as 1984. Therefore further analysis in this section is conducted only on the first-differenced log of patent applications.

Table IIIA shows the results of tests for a structural break in patent applications by region of patent application origin, and technology class. The regional breakdown reveals unambiguous evidence of a structural break for U.S. origin patents in 1984. The remaining evidence is more ambiguous: Europe and the other developing countries have a marginally significant structural break according to the Andrews test, in 1993 and 1984 respectively. Although the other regions have no identifiable break, all but the Asian-origin patents have significantly different patenting growth rates before and after 1984. The conclusion is that the highly visible increase in growth rates in 1983/1984 is primarily due to inventors resident in the U.S.

In Tables IIB and IIIC, I show similar results for the six broad technology categories developed by Hall *et al.* (2002). The results are unambiguous: chemicals and pharmaceuticals, the industries that have traditionally identified patents as important for securing returns to innovation, exhibit little evidence of a structural break in 1984 or any other year. On the contrary, the electrical, computers and communications, mechanical and other technologies all have a significant structural break that occurs in 1984 or 1993 in the case of computers. Beginning in 1984, the growth of patent applications increased about 8–9% per annum in computing and electrical technologies, and about 6% per annum in mechanical and other technologies. The next section of the paper probes the contribution of these sectors to the aggregate growth in patenting in more detail.

TABLE II
Tests for unit roots and structural breaks in patent application series
USPTO patent applications 1967–1997 that were granted by 2002

Statistic	Patent applications	Log of patent applications	Change in patent applications	Change in logs of pat applications
Weighted symmetric unit root test	0.69	0.03	−5.08	−5.03
p-value	0.9998	0.9987	0.0002	0.0002
T-test on break between 1983 and 1984	40026 (7177)	.445 (.067)	7376 (1809)	.069 (.014)
p-value	0.0000	0.0000	0.0000	0.0000
Andrews (1993) test for unknown structural break ($T = 32$)	86.1	126.1	21.8	23.0
p-value	<.01	<.01	<.01	<.01
Break year chosen by Andrews test	1989	1988	1993	1984

TABLE III

Statistic	USA	Europe	Asia & Japan	Other Developed	Other
A. *By region*					
Total patents	1,499,517	533,614	461,575	71,688	6,445
T-test on break between 1983 and 1984	.084 (.018)	.037 (.019)	−.000 (.029)	.063 (.021)	.101 (.039)
p-value	0.000	0.068	0.990	0.006	0.016
Andrews (1993) test for structural break at unknown point ($T = 31$)	27.14	8.93	6.84	8.86	7.23
p-value	<.10	<0.5	>.10	<.0.5	>.10
Break year chosen by Andrews test	1984	1993	1972	1984	1989

Statistic	Chemical	Drugs & medicine	Computers & comm.	Electrical	Mechanical	Other
B. *By technology class*						
Total patents	542,700	219,665	325,665	470,463	604,679	568,489
T-test on break between 1983 and 1984	.045 (.023)	.035 (.040)	.090 (.023)	.075 (.014)	.059 (.013)	.058 (.011)
p-value	0.041	0.378	0.001	0.0000	0.0000	0.0000
Andrews (1993) test for structural break at unknown point ($T = 31$)	4.57	0.94	22.90	26.90	20.40	25.70
p-value	>.01	>.01	0.0000	0.0000	0.0000	0.0000
Break year chosen by Andrews test	1984	1976	1993	1984	1984	1984
C. *By technology class, US inventors only*						
Total patents	292,410	128,454	162,338	243,115	315,455	357,745
T-test on break between 1983 and 1984	.049 (.024)	.061 (.041)	.113 (.028)	.084 (.014)	.077 (.014)	0.71 (.012)
p-value	0.052	0.142	0.000	0.000	0.001	0.000
Andrews (1993) test for structural break at unknown point ($T = 31$)	5.21	2.29	32.04	37.82	29.81	33.72
p-value	>.01	>.01	<.01	<.01	<.01	<.01
Break year chosen by Andrews test	1987	1984	1987	1984	1984	1984

Accounting for patent growth

In order to carry out a simple growth accounting exercise on the patent data, I define the following:

g_t = growth of patenting from time $t - 1$ to t

g_{it} = growth of patenting in class or region i from time $t - 1$ to t

$s_{i,t-1}$ = share of patents in class or region i at time $t - 1$ (1.1)

Then the growth in patents at time t is given by

$$g_t = \sum_{i=1}^{n} s_{i,t-1} g_{it} \qquad (1.2)$$

Figures 3–5 show the results of the computations for three different decompositions of the data, by major region of patent origin, and then by broad technology class and broad industry class based on the Compustat firm sample that I use later in the paper. Both of the later breakdowns are for U.S.-origin inventors only, because of the evidence that this is the source of the patent increase and because I am unable to perform an industry class decomposition on those patents

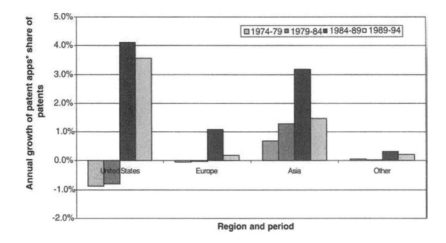

Figure 3. Accounting for U.S. patent application growth by region of inventor.

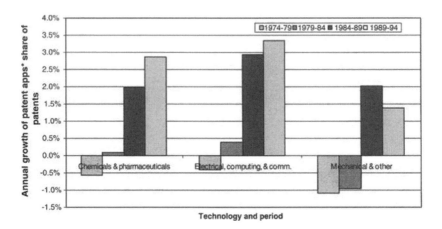

Figure 4. Accounting for U.S. inventor patent application growth by broad technology class.

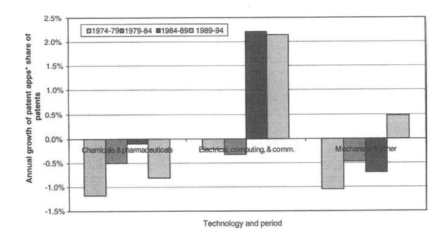

Figure 5. Accounting for U.S. inventor patent application growth compustat firms by broad industry class.

(unassigned and foreign) for which I do not have ownership information. The plots in Figures 3 to 5 show $s_{it-1}g_{it}$ for the three different decompositions.

The figures reveal the following interesting fact: although the jump in patent applications within the U.S. occurred in all technology classes, when we look by broad industry class, we find that it occurred *only* in firms that are in the electrical, computing and instruments industries. That is, the increase in chemicals, mechanical and other technologies appears to have been driven by increasing patenting activity by firms that were not traditionally in these industries. This result is consistent with the view that there has been a major strategic shift in patenting in the electrical/computing industries, but not in other industries.

One interpretation of the contrasting findings in Figures 4 and 5 is the following: the first figure suggests an increase in innovation (as measured by patents) from the 1974–1984 period to the 1984–1994 period that occurred in all technology areas. But the second says that the increase was actually concentrated in firms in one sector, which implies that these firms increased their patenting not only in their own sector but in the other technology sectors as well. This suggests that the increase is due to a strategic shift within the electrical and computing sector, rather than an increase in inventiveness across the board. Further testing of this hypothesis seems warranted, to understand what the patenting behavior of the electrical/computing firms was in the chemicals/ mechanical/ other sector before and after the shift in 1984.

What changed?

Given these findings with respect to timing of the surge, region of origin, and technology and industry origin, we can identify the following changes in the patent system as having provided an impetus for the increase in growth rate: the 1982 creation of CAFC and the litigation success of Texas Instruments against a number of firms in 1985/86 and Polaroid against Kodak in 1986. As a result of the creation of CAFC and as demonstrated by these cases, patents were now more likely to be upheld in litigation, and the consequences were likely to be more negative for alleged infringers, especially in complex product industries like electronic computing and communications.

In Ziedonis and Hall (2001) we reported the results of our interviews with patent counsel and CEOs at a number of semiconductor manufacturing firms.[4] The interviewees emphasized the important "demonstration effect" of Polaroid's successful patent infringement suit against Kodak; in 1985, the district court found Kodak liable for infringement and this decision was affirmed by the CAFC in 1986, barring Kodak from competing in the instant-film camera business. In 1989/1990 the damages portion of the case was tried, ultimately settling for almost one billion dollars.[5] The large penalties imposed in this case and the realization that U.S. courts were willing to take an aggressive stance against infringement by halting—either temporarily or permanently—production utilizing infringed technologies fueled concerns among executives in many firms, including semiconductor manufacturers, for whom it would be very costly to shut down a wafer fabricating plant for even a week.

The other widely-cited reason for intensified patenting in the industry was Texas Instruments' patent royalty strategy. During 1985–1986, Texas Instruments successfully asserted its patents in court for a range of inventions pertaining to integrated circuits (e.g., the "Kilby patent" on the basic design of the integrated circuit) and manufacturing methods (e.g., the method for encapsulating chips or transporting wafers from one manufacturing platform to another). Although the original suits were against non-U.S. (Japanese) firms, TI's successful enforcement of its patents enabled the firm to charge higher royalty rates to other firms in the industry. Indeed, our interviewees were well aware of the strategies that Texas Instruments had put in place to manage—and profit from—its patent portfolio;[6] representatives from several firms plan to adopt a similarly aggressive licensing strategy once their portfolios grow larger. Others noted that AT&T, IBM, and Motorola began asserting their patent rights more aggressively during this period in order to increase licensing revenues based on their large portfolios of semiconductor-related patents. According to several industry representatives, these large patent owners not only increased royalty rates for "rights to infringe" their patents but sought royalty-bearing licenses from smaller firms more aggressively.

As Levin *et al.* (1987) and Cohen *et al.* (2000) reported from their survey evidence, patents have not been considered the most important means for appropriating returns to R&D except in the pharmaceutical industry, although they are considered effective for over one third of innovations in several other industries: paper, chemicals, metal products and machinery, computers and electrical equipment, medical equipment, and autos. Cohen *et al.* probe this question further and find that when industries are divided into those producing discrete products and those producing complex products, important differences in the *reasons* for using patents emerge.[7] Industries with discrete products tend to patent for the traditional reasons of excluding competitors and preventing litigation, whereas those in complex product industries are significantly more likely to patent for cross-licensing and trading/negotiation purposes, as well as to prevent litigation.

Their evidence agrees with the Ziedonis and Hall finding that patents are now primarily used for defensive purposes in semiconductors, to protect against litigation and for cross licensing. But we also found that patents were considered important for securing financing for startups in this industry. The analysis in this section confirms that the overall surge in patenting is due to an increased use of patents by U.S. firms in industries similar to and including semiconductors, that is, in complex product industries. The next section explores the implications of this finding for firm valuation by the market, and attempts to shed light indirectly on the financing hypothesis.

3. The market value of patents

The findings in the previous section of the paper, together with the evidence in Hall and Ziedonis (2001) and Cohen *et al.* (2000) suggest that the value of patents to the firm may differ depending on the use to which they are put. That is, if patents are primarily valued because having a large number assists in cross-licensing negotiations and serves as insurance against threats from other patentholders, the individual patents in the portfolio may not be valued separately from the fact that they are a natural consequence of the firm's R&D. That is, once we control for the level of R&D in a market value equation, there may be no additional effect arising from patenting. In particular, firms in sectors with complex product technologies should show such an effect, because in general it is the number of patents rather than the quality of each one that is relevant for defense, at least according to the Ziedonis-Hall interviewees.

At the same time, if patents help to secure financing for entry, we expect that firms who have recently entered the publicly traded sector would have a patent portfolio that is more valuable on average than that held by other firms. That is, their R&D will have been differentially successful, compared to the incumbent firms. So the hypothesis is that patents will be related to the market value of these firms, above and beyond the value from their R&D effort. In addition, I would expect this differential to be largest in complex product industries.

In this section of the paper I test these hypotheses using a simple market to book value equation at the firm level that includes the R&D assets to tangible assets ratio, the patent stock to R&D assets ratio, a dummy for firms that do not report R&D, and year dummies to account for overall market movements. The equation is estimated for two subperiods, 1980–1984 and 1985–1989, and for incumbents entrants during the two periods separately. I then go on to estimate equations separately for firms in the three different technology classes used in the previous section (electrical, chemical, and mechanical), and for the discrete product/complex product breakdown suggested by Cohen *et al.* (2000).

Finally, I use a differences in differences approach to examine whether the differential valuation of patents for entrants and incumbents in complex product industries increased relative to that for discrete product industries between the first and the second half of the 1980s. Finding that this is so is confirmatory evidence that strategies in those industries shifted, partly as a result of changes in patent enforcement around the middle of the 1980s.

Data sample

The data sample used here is drawn from the sample described in Hall *et al.* (2002, 2005). It consists of about 1400 U.S. manufacturing firms with at least one patent and at least 5 years of data between 1980 and 1989, for a total of 9705 observations. Firms are divided into three groups: incumbents (in the sample as of 1979), entrants 1980–1984, or entrants 1985–1989. Note that being an entrant means that the number of shareholders in the firm was large enough for it to command sufficient investor interest to be followed by Standard and Poor's Compustat, which basically means that the firm is required to file 10-Ks to the Securities and Exchange Commission on a regular basis. It does not necessarily mean that the firm has just gone through an IPO, although for some of these firms that will be true. Most of them are listed on NASDAQ or the NYSE.

A table in Appendix 1 shows the industrial breakdown of these firms, and the way I classify their technologies for the tests later in this section. Not surprisingly, the industries with the highest entry rate during the period are the science-based industries in either chemical or electrical technologies: Medical Instruments, Computing Equipment, Instruments and Communication Equipment, and Pharmaceuticals. These four industries account for slightly over half of all entry during the period.

Model and estimation strategy

The model estimated is a very basic hedonic market value model, similar to that in Griliches (1981) or Hall *et al.* (2005). The market value of a firm is related to the book value of its assets via the following regression equation:

$$\log Q_{it} = \log\left(\frac{V_{it}}{A_{it}}\right)$$
$$= \delta_t + \beta_K\left(\frac{K_{it}}{A_{it}}\right) + \beta_P\left(\frac{P_{it}}{K_{it}}\right) + \varepsilon_{it} \quad (1.3)$$

where V is the market value of firm, A is the book value of tangible assets, K is the stock of R&D assets, P is the stock of patents.

The form of the specification is dictated by the fact that patents are roughly proportional to R&D for these firms, so that the separate impact of obtaining a patent successfully can be measured by including a patent productivity variable in the form of patents per R&D in the model. The stocks of both R&D and patents are constructed from the past R&D and patent applications history using a 15% depreciation rate.

The method of estimation is ordinary least squares with standard errors robust to heteroskedasticity and serial correlation reported.[8] In estimation, the slopes and the full set of time dummies δ_t are allowed to vary across the type of firm, whether incumbent or entrant, the time period (1980–1984, or 1985–1989), and the technology category (in three groups, electrical, chemical, and mechanical, or two, discrete and complex).

Comparing incumbents and entrants

A summary of the results of these estimations is shown in Table IV, which displays the patent coefficient for all firms and for the two different industry breakdowns. Several things emerge from these tables: first, during 1980–1984 period, having a higher patent productivity from R&D is not associated with an increase in market value. On the contrary, it is slightly negatively valued in electrical and chemical industries, and especially negative among entrants in the chemical sector. This latter result no doubt reflects the collapse of biotechnology valuations that occurred during this period. Except for this sector, there is no difference between incumbents and entrants in the valuation of patent per R&D yield during the first half of the 1980s.

However, during the 1985–1989 period, the patent yield of entrants in the electrical and mechanical sectors is valued at a substantial premium over incumbent firms, after controlling for their tangible and R&D assets. The difference is most stark when I distinguish between industries with discrete product technologies and those with complex product technologies. In the latter sector, having one additional patent per million dollars of R&D investment yields a market value boost of 25% for newly entered firms.

TABLE IV
Coefficient of patent stock/R&D stock

Industry	All	Electrical	Chemical	Mechanical	Discrete	Complex
			1980–1984			
Number of obs (entrants)	5037 (652)	1720 (337)	1174 (103)	2143 (212)	2622 (276)	2312 (366)
Incumbents	−.026 (.011)**	−.061 (.023)**	−.040 (.016)**	.005 (.014)	−.025 (.014)	−.027 (.023)
Entrants	−.022 (.036)	.001 (.068)	−.257 (.068)**	.021 (.040)	−.068 (.055)	.010 (.046)
Difference	.004 (.038)	.062 (.071)	−.217 (.070)**	.015 (.043)	−.043 (.057)	.037 (.052)
			1985–1989			
Number of obs (entrants)	4676 (537)	1824 (301)	1036 (85)	1821 (151)	2330 (233)	2256 (284)
Incumbents	.009 (.009)	.013 (.011)	−.072 (.043)	.039 (.025)	−.014 (.025)	.014 (.010)
Entrants	.059 (.031)	.192 (.058)**	.013 (.010)	.278 (.097)**	.023 (.015)	.272 (.062)**
Difference	.050 (.033)	.179 (.059)**	.085 (.044)	.239 (.101)**	.037 (.030)	.258 (.063)**
Difference in diffs	.046 (.050)	.117 (.092)	.302 (.083)**	.224 (.110)**	.080 (.064)	.221 (.082)**
Industries	All	Electrical; Transport eq; Computing; Inst & comm..	Chemicals; Pharma; Food; Oil; Rubber & plastics; SCG	Textiles/app; wood/furniture; paper/printing; primary & fab metals; machinery; autos	Food; textiles; wood; paper; chemicals; pharma; rubber; SCG; metals;	Machinery & eng; comp eq; elec mach; inst & comm; transport eq

**Significant at the 5% level.
Standard error estimates are robust to heteroskedasticity and first order serial correlation.

Third, there is a significant difference between the two periods. In the first, patent productivity is valued negatively or not at all by the market, whether the firm is an incumbent or an entrant. In the second period, after the changes in the patent environment have taken place, patent productivity remains negative or insignificant for the value of the incumbent firms, whereas it is now significant and positive for firms in the electrical and mechanical industries; the differences are even more striking for the discrete/complex split. The last line of Table IV shows the differences in differences estimate of the difference between incumbents and entrant firms in the two periods. The differences are most significant for the chemicals sector, where the patent valuation for entrants rose from quite negative to slightly positive, and for the complex products industry, where the patent valuation for entrants rose from zero to very positive.

Because it appears from Table IV that the discrete/complex split is more informative for patent yield valuation than the technology split, I present the complete results for this split in Table V, for the two periods and for the incumbent/entrant split in each, in order to look more carefully at the differences in results for the two sectors. The discrete product industries show the following pattern in both periods: first, firms that enter tend to have a substantial premium (about 100% above that predicted by their assets), but R&D assets are valued less for entrants than for incumbents. At the same time, not having R&D is valued very negatively. What this suggests is that entry in this sector during the period essentially requires having R&D assets, so some of the valuation is absorbed by the entry dummy. This can occur because R&D assets are an error-ridden measure of the underlying value of the firm's knowledge base. I also note that the patent yield from these assets has no impact on firm value for firms in this sector.

The results for the complex product industries are quite different: First, the results for the two periods are quite different, with both R&D and patent yield valued significantly more highly for entrants in the second period. During the first period, only entry itself receives a

TABLE V
Comparing incumbents with entrants

1980–1984

Variable	Incumbents 1979 Coeff.	S.E.	Entrants 1980–84 Coeff.	S.E.	Difference Coeff.	S.E.
Discrete Product Industries						
R&D Stock/Assets	0.882	0.119**	0.429	0.120**	−0.394	0.169**
Patent Stock/R&D Stock	−0.025	0.014	−0.068	0.055	−0.043	0.057
D(no R&D)	−0.012	0.039	−0.510	0.157**	−0.498	0.162**
Entrant dummy in first year			1.511	0.208**		
Std. error; adj. R-squared	0.609		0.264			
Firms	513		95			
Observations	2622		276			
Complex Product Industries						
R&D Stock/Assets	0.559	0.079**	0.642	0.108**	0.084	0.133
Patent Stock/R&D Stock	−0.027	0.023	0.010	0.038	0.037	0.052
D(no R&D)	−0.047	0.068	−0.269	0.188	−0.222	0.200
Entrant dummy in first year			0.469	0.201**		
Std. error; adj. R-squared	0.676		0.203			
Firms	412		126			
Observations	2312		366			

1985–1989

Variable	Incumbents 1984 Coeff.	S.E.	Entrants 1985–89 Coeff.	S.E.	Difference Coeff.	S.E.
Discrete Product Industries						
R&D Stock/Assets	0.554	0.072**	0.395	0.055**	−0.160	0.090
Patent Stock/R&D Stock	−0.014	0.025	0.023	0.015	0.037	0.030
D(no R&D)	0.016	0.045	−0.440	0.108**	−0.456	0.117**
Entrant dummy in first year			0.802	0.203**		
Std. error; adj. R-squared	0.639		0.204			
Firms	486		82			
Observations	2330		233			
Complex Product Industries						
R&D Stock/Assets	0.251	0.042**	0.513	0.076**	0.263	0.086**
Patent Stock/R&D Stock	0.014	0.010	0.272	0.062**	0.258	0.063**
D(no R&D)	−0.040	0.066	−0.002	0.158	0.038	0.170
Entrant dummy in first year			0.225	0.133		
Std. error; adj. R-squared	0.621		0.176			
Firms	456		89			
Observations	2256		284			

All equations include a full set of time dummies for each group.
Standard error estimates are robust to heteroskedasticity and first order serial correlation.

valuation premium over incumbent firms (of about 50%) and not doing R&D is somewhat negative for entrants. During the second period, the value of the incumbents' R&D has fallen, whereas that for the entrants remains about the same. And as we saw earlier, there is a substantial premium for entrants that have a higher patent yield. Hall (1993) reviews the reasons for the decline in R&D valuation during this period and shows that is was concentrated in rust belt industries (e.g., metals and automobiles) and in large scale mainframe and mini computer firms, both of which were subject to restructuring during the 1980s due to the advent of the personal computer and the rise in global competition. Many of these industries are in the complex product sector.

Thus these regressions provide some support for the hypothesis that patents may serve differing functions for incumbents and entrants in complex product industries, and that this difference may have emerged in the wake of the changes to the functioning of the U.S. patent system during the early to mid-1980s. Although the division into discrete and complex product industries is admittedly rather coarse, it seems to be revealing of a considerable difference in the role of patents.

4. Conclusions

This paper has established several facts about changes in the patenting behavior of U.S. firms during the past 20 years, some more precisely and robustly than others. First, there is clear evidence of a structural shift to a higher growth rate in overall patenting in the United States between 1983 and 1984, one that is driven for the most part by U.S. firms, but with some contribution from Asia and Europe. Second, this shift is largely accounted for by firms in the electrical and computing technology sectors, although patenting by U.S. inventors has risen in all technology classes. Although R&D has also increased in this sector, this cannot explain the size of the increase in patenting. In addition, patenting per R&D dollar has actually fallen in the chemicals sector broadly defined.

These findings are subject to a couple of competing explanations: one is that of Kortum and Lerner (1998, 2003), who argue that the management of R&D has improved during the period and who find that innovative activity has risen as much as patenting, at least in the pages of the Wall street Journal. The second is that the growth in patenting is largely driven by the needs of players in complex product industries for large patent portfolios and their consequent drive to obtain patents, even those of dubious quality, that is, even those that they have no intention of enforcing. The results thus far cannot really distinguish these two hypotheses, although we can say that if R&D management has improved, it is only in some sectors (electrical, etc.) and not in all.

The results in the second part of the paper provide some limited support for the view that patent rights themselves are not valuable assets, once we know the amount of investment that went into obtaining the innovation, but that they may be important for new entrants. That is, a possible interpretation of these results is the following: in established firms, accumulating patents for defensive reasons has little impact on market value because the past history of R&D spending is already a good indicator of the firm's technology position. In fact, an above average accumulation of patents could be slightly negative for value if it indicates the present of threatened suits for infringement.

On the other hand, for new entrants, especially in complex product industries like electronics where patents were previously unimportant, ownership of patents may have become an important signal of viability, especially because these firms have a median intangible to tangible asset ratio of above one half. That is, as the venture capitalists argue when considering funding these firms earlier in the life cycle process, patents are essential to provide a claim on the most important asset of the firm, its knowledge capital. In the market value equation, this translates into a premium for high patent productivity, especially post-1984.

Some questions remain unanswered in this paper. First and foremost, what happened during the 1990s? Did the positive premium for entry with patents continue during the rapid growth of the computing and electronics sector in the late 1990s? Has the growth in patenting continued to be due almost entirely to U.S. firms in computing and electronics?

APPENDIX 1

Sector breakdowns (number of observations 1980–1989)

	Firms	All Entrants	Obs.	By Technology Base			By Product Type	
				Electrical	Chemical	Mechanical	Discrete	Complex
Food & tobacco	58	10	420		420		420	
Textiles & apparel	67	18	455			455	455	
Lumber & wood	8	0	57			57	57	
Furniture	31	5	231			231	231	
Paper	48	6	351			351	351	
Printing	27	5	218			218	218	
Chemicals	63	10	512		512		512	
Medical instruments	85	47	516	516			516	
Pharmaceutical & soap	71	28	519		519		519	
Oil	25	3	203		203		203	
Rubber & plastics	56	13	388		388		388	
Stone, clay, and glass	24	3	163		163		163	
Primary metals	53	13	376			376	376	
Fabricated metals	85	19	543			543	543	
Machinery & engines	158	38	1,162			1,162		1,162
Computing equipment	72	39	465	465				465
Electrical machinery	90	25	642	642				642
Instruments & comm. eq.	250	104	1,716	1,716				1,716
Transportation eq.	26	2	205	205				205
Autos & auto parts	47	9	378			378		378
Misc n.e.c.	30	8	185			185		
Total	1,374	405	9,705	3,544	2,205	3,956	4,952	4,568

Notes

1. This paper was written for a special issue of the *Journal of Technology Transfer* in memory of Edwin Mansfield. The preliminary draft was presented as an invited lecture to the ZEW Workshop on Empirical Economics of Innovation and Patenting, Mannheim, Germany, March 14-15, 2003. I am very grateful to Josh Lerner and Cecil Quillen for extremely helpful comments on the first version of the paper. My first meeting with Ed Mansfield was in 1980, when he discussed the paper I presented on patenting in the computer and drug industries (which was ultimately published with data on all manufacturing industries, as Bound et al 1984, in the volume from that conference edited by Zvi Griliches). At that time, his unpublished discussion emphasized the difference between these two industries in the importance and relevance of patents as a measure of innovation. This was the first time I learned about what is now called the distinction between discrete and complex product industries. Although the use of patents in the two types of industries has certainly changed since that time, they are still quite different in their patenting behavior, as I hope this paper shows. I think Ed would have particularly liked the fact that this paper was motivated by interviews with those in the electronics industry (Hall and Ziedonis 2001; Ziedonis and Hall 2001), something he always encouraged me to undertake.

2. The "extension" of patentable subject matter to business methods is of course too late to have any effect on the data considered in this paper, but it is included for the sake of completeness, and because it is in some sense a consequence of the pro-patent shift of the 1980s and the creation of the CAFC.

3. The apparent dip and rise in applications between 1995 and 1996 is due to accelerated filing, primarily by pharmaceutical firms who wished to obtain the traditional 17 year lifetime from date of patent grant that was changed in 1996 to 20 years from date of filing. This caused a number of applications to be moved forward to the extent that was feasible. Patent applications in Hall, Jaffe, Trajtenberg technology class 31 (drugs) actually rose 45% in 1995 and fell 45% in 1996!

4. The next two paragraphs are largely drawn from Ziedonis and Hall (2001).

5. I am grateful to Cecil Quillen, who was patent counsel for Kodak during that period, for these precise recollections of the events in the case.

6. After launching its more aggressive patent licensing strategy in 1985, TI subsequently earned almost $2 billion in royalty income during 1986–1993 (Grindley and Teece, 1997).

7. The former group includes food, textiles, paper, chemicals, drugs, metals and metal products, and the latter consists of machinery, computers, electrical equipment, electronic components, instruments, and transportation equipment.

8. GMM in TSP 5.0 was used for estimation, in order to obtain the correct standard errors, but with instruments identical to the right hand side variables.

References

Barton, J.H., and S.J. Parapatt, 1998, 'Patent Litigation and Its Relationship to Industry Structure and Competition in the Photographic Film and Camera Industry,' Conference Paper, Intellectual Property and Industry Competitive Standards, Stanford University, April.

Cohen, W.M., R.R. Nelson, and J.P. Walsh, 2000, 'Protecting Their Intellectual Assets: Appropriability Conditions and Why Firms Patent or Not?,' NBER Working Paper No., 7552.

Griliches, Z., 1981, 'Market Value, R&D, and Patents,' *Economic Letters*, 7, 183–187.

Grindley, P.C., and D.J. Teece, 1997, 'Managing Intellectual Capital: Licensing and Cross-Licensing in Semiconductors and Electronics,' *California Management Review* 39 (2), 1–34.

Hall, B.H., 1993, 'Industrial Research During the 1980s: Did the Rate of Return Fall?' *Brookings Papers on Economic Activity Microeconomics* 1993 (2), 289–344.

Hall, B.H., A. Jaffe, and M. Trajtenberg, 2005, 'Market Value and Patent Citations,' *Rand Journal of Economics*, 36, (Spring).

Hall, B.H., A. Jaffe, and M. Trajtenberg, 2002, 'The NBER Patent Citations Data File: Lessons, Insights and Methodological Tools,' in *Patents, Citations and Innovations*, A. Jaffe and M. Trajtenberg (eds.), Cambridge, MA: The MIT Press.

Hall, B.H. and R.H. Ziedonis, 2001, 'The Determinants of Patenting in the U. S. Semiconductor Industry, 1980–1994,' *Rand Journal of Economics* 32, 101–128.

Kim, J., and G. Marschke, 2004, 'Accounting for the Recent Surge in U.S. Patenting: Changes in R&D expenditures, Patent Yields, and the High Tech Sector,' *Economics of Innovation and New Technology* 13 (6), 543–558.

Kortum, S., and J. Lerner, 2003, 'Unraveling the Patent Paradox,' *AEA Annual Meeting*. Washington, DC.

Kortum, S., and J. Lerner, 2000, 'Assessing the Contribution of Venture Capital to Innovation,' *Rand Journal of Economics* 31 (4), 674–692.

Kortum, S., and J. Lerner, 1998, 'Stronger Protection or Technological Revolution: What Is Behind the Recent Surge in Patenting?,' *Carnegie-Rochester Conference Series on Public Policy* 48, 247–304.

Levin, R.C., A.K. Klevorick, R.R. Nelson, and S.G, Winter, 1987, 'Appropriating the Returns from Industrial Research and Development.' *Brookings Papers on Economic Activity*, 3, 783–832.

Ziedonis, R.H., 2004, 'Don't Fence Me in: Fragmented Markets for Technology and the Patent Acquisition Strategies of Firms,' *Management Science*, 50 (6), 804–820.

Ziedonis, R.H., and B.H. Hall, 2001, 'The Effects of Strengthening Patent Rights on firms Engaged in Cumulative Innovation: Insights from the Semiconductor Industry,' in *Entrepreneurial Inputs and Outcomes: New Studies of Entrepreneurship in the United States*, Vol. 13, Advances in the Study of Entrepreneurship, Innovation, and Economic Growth, Libecap, Gary (ed.), Amsterdam: Elsevier Science.

The University and the Start-Up: Lessons from the Past Two Decades[1]

Josh Lerner

ABSTRACT. This paper explores one of Edwin Mansfield's enduring interests: the interface between academia and industry. It highlights some key lessons regarding the management of university-based spin-outs, drawing on a variety of sources. I highlight the challenges that the spin-off process poses, the impracticality of directly financing firms through internal venture funds, and the ways in which universities can add value to faculty ventures.

Key words: spin-off, venture, capitalist, entrepreneurship, venture capital

JEL Classification: O31

1. Introduction

One of Edwin Mansfield's enduring interests was the relationship between academic science and industrial development (Edwin Mansfield, 1968, 1991). In recent years, these questions have become even more urgent on many campuses: despite the recent decline in venture funding, there remains enormous interest in start-up activity on the university campuses.

University administrators see new firms as having several key benefits: they can generate considerable revenue for the institution, make the university more attractive to current and potential faculty members, and benefit the community and the nation as a whole. Faculty members often view these ventures as potential sources of both personal wealth and career fulfillment.

Meanwhile, venture capitalists have long viewed universities as a fertile source of investment ideas. The first modern venture capital firm, American Research and Development (ARD), was designed to focus on technology-based spinouts from the Massachusetts Institute of Technology. As envisioned by its founders, who included MIT President Karl Compton, Harvard Business School Professor Georges F. Doriot, and Boston-area business leaders, this novel structure would be best suited to commercialize the wealth of military technologies developed during World War II. Many of the most successful venture capital-backed firms over the decades—including Cisco Systems, Genentech, and Netscape Communications—had their origins as academic spin-outs.

Despite this interest, however, the effective management of these start-ups poses many challenges. If managed incorrectly, a start-up can cause serious disruption to the institution that spawns it. The dangers can manifest themselves in many ways:

- Boston University's venture capital subsidiary invested in a privately held biotechnology company founded in 1979 by a number of scientists affiliated with the institution. As part of its initial investment in 1987, the school bought out the stakes of a number of independent venture capital investors, who had apparently concluded after a number of financing rounds that the firm's prospects were unattractive. Between 1987 and 1992, the school, investing alongside university officials and trustees, provided at least $90 million dollars to the private firm. (By way of comparison, the school's entire endowment at the fiscal year in which it initiated this investment was $142 million.) While the company succeeded in completing an initial public offering, it encountered a series of disappointments

Harvard Business School
Arthur Rock Center for Entrepreneurship, Room 214
Boston, Massachusetts 02163
U.S.A.
E-mail: josh@hbs.edu

with its products. At the end of 1997, the University's equity stake was worth only $4 million.[2]

- The University of Illinois, having developed the Internet browser, licensed the technology to a Boston-based venture, Spyglass Technologies. When some former university employees begin a separate firm to commercialize a related technology, the University commenced litigation against them. The acrimony of the dispute may have influenced the institution's decision to reject the offer of a large block of stock in the new firm to settle the dispute—instead they demanded (and received) a relatively modest cash payment. The value of the equity in the new firm, Netscape Communications, would have exceeded the cash payment by many hundred-fold. Meanwhile, Spyglass largely abandoned its Internet browser effort and was acquired in 2000.[3]

- The University of Chicago launched the ARCH initiative in 1987 to encourage commercialization of its own technology and that of Argonne National Laboratory, a federal facility which it managed. The group was given a mandate both to license technologies to established firms and to fund start-ups. The venture fund enjoyed some modest initial successes. Shortly thereafter, however, the relationship between ARCH and the University of Chicago was restructured. The ARCH partners received permission to raise a second, more substantial, venture fund with far more generous compensation for the venture capitalists. As part of the new effort, they were allowed to invest outside the University, while retaining a formal "right of first look" at the University's technology. ARCH rapidly expanded after raising the second fund, and the share of new transactions originating from the University of Chicago and Argonne fell dramatically. Meanwhile, many at the school believed in their eagerness to become established as venture investors, the ARCH partners had neglected the more mundane—but necessary—technology licensing activities.[4]

Thus, the successful management of the relationship between universities and start-up firms is thus not a trivial or routine matter!

This article seeks to highlight some of the key lessons about the management of university-based spin-outs. It highlights a number of lessons, based on a wide variety of sources: traditional academic research, case studies on specific programs, service on advisory panels, and special projects that have sought to address the needs of particular organizations.

I highlight five lessons that emerge from these efforts:

- Starting new ventures based on university technology is hard. Despite the confidence of many academic entrepreneurs and university administrators, the process of creating a sustainable new company is a very challenging one.
- In the vast majority of cases, new firms will not generate enormous wealth for academic institutions. Much more modest returns are the norm.
- Directly financing firms through internal venture capital funds is unlikely to be a successful strategy for universities.
- Nonetheless, universities can add considerable value to young firms that faculty begin.
- Old frameworks about conflicts-of-interest must be rethought in light of the special needs of start-ups.

These issues will be explored in turn in the subsequent sections.

2. The Challenges of New Technology-Based Firms

University technology transfer offices typically focus on nascent firms in high-technology industries with tremendous promise. Unfortunately, these firms are also characterized by uncertainty and informational gaps, which make it difficult for the investors to evaluate business plans or to oversee the entrepreneurs once the investments are made. The consequences are often unfortunate. In some cases, the idea is commercialized, but the return to the academic institution is small; often these information problems discourage outside investors entirely and the discovery languishes.

To briefly review the types of conflicts that can emerge in these settings, conflicts between managers and investors can affect the willingness of both debt and equity holders to provide capital. If the firm raises equity from outside investors, the manager has an incentive to engage in wasteful expenditures from which he may benefit disproportionately—such as lavish offices. Alternatively, the entrepreneur may increase risk to undesirable levels or withhold bad news from the investors. Because providers of capital recognize these problems, outside investors demand a higher rate of return than would be the case if the funds were internally generated.

These information problems have also been shown to exist in debt markets. If banks find it difficult to discriminate among companies, raising interest rates can have perverse selection effects. In particular, the high interest rates discourage all but the highest-risk borrowers, so the quality of the loan pool declines markedly. To address this problem, banks may restrict the amount of lending to risky firms rather than increasing interest rates.

Described in this manner, these problems may appear to be abstract. But they have very real implications for university technology managers, who may find investors and corporations unwilling to invest the time and resources to examine early-stage technologies, or offering only modest payments in exchange for exclusive licenses to innovations that the technology transfer officers believe to be valuable. University-based start-ups may find it impossible to access bank loans or equity investors.

These problems in the debt and equity markets are a consequence of the information gaps between the entrepreneurs and investors. If the information gaps could be eliminated, financing constraints would disappear. Financial economists argue that specialized financial intermediaries, such as venture capital organizations, can ameliorate these problems by intensively scrutinizing firms before providing capital and then monitoring them afterwards.

To address information problems, venture capitalists employ a variety of mechanisms. First, business plans are intensively scrutinized: of those firms that submit business plans to venture capital organizations, historically only 1% have been funded. The decision to invest is frequently made conditional on the identification of a syndication partner who agrees that this is an attractive investment. Once the decision to invest is made, the venture capitalists frequently disburse funds in stages, forcing the managers of the venture-backed firms to return repeatedly to their financiers for additional capital in order to ensure that the money is not squandered on unprofitable projects. In addition, venture capitalists intensively monitor managers, demanding preferred stock with numerous restrictive covenants and representation on the board of directors. Thus, it is not surprising that the capital provided by venture capital organizations is the dominant form of equity financing for privately held technology-intensive businesses.

3. The Implications for Financial Returns

These difficulties have a stark consequence for universities. Despite the optimistic dreams of many deans, most start-ups will not generate huge returns for the academic institutions from which they spring. This harsh lesson stems from the overall returns from young firms, as well as the special circumstances of the types of firms emerging from academia.

The first reason why substantial returns are unlikely relates to the distribution of outcomes from start-up firms in general: no matter how sophisticated the investors, most start-ups yield disappointing returns. A wide variety of studies has examined the returns from investments in innovative activities, focusing on such measures such as the value of patents, the growth of young firms, and the returns to venture capitalists and to investors in stocks that have recently gone public. Despite the varying measures employed and the different industries under study, the conclusions are remarkably consistent. The returns to investment in innovative activities appear to be remarkably skewed. A small subset of projects generates the bulk of the returns.

The second reason relates to the very early stage of most academic projects. Because they are so high risk, financial investors—whether venture capitalists or individual "angels"—will demand a return commensurate with the risk. This translates to a substantial demand for equity.

Moreover, these investors are only likely to invest if the entrepreneurs are adequately rewarded. Venture capitalists typically argue that the process can only work if the key entrepreneurs in the start-up firm have a substantial equity stake. Without such holdings, these investors argue, managers are unlikely to make the huge personal and financial sacrifices necessary for the success of a new venture.

As a result, these investors are skeptical of potential investments where third parties who are not directly involved in the ongoing success of the venture have large equity stakes. Venture capitalists are likely to reject the argument that a university is entitled to a substantial equity stake in recognition of its contributions of intellectual property to the firm. Rather, they are likely to argue that the past is irrelevant—the allocation of equity should maximize the chances of the company *going forward*.

Consider the experience of a federally funded R&D facility, where an aggressive new CEO launched an initiative to grow revenues through spin-out firms. Mindful of the demands to generate substantial gains for the corporation, the business development staff sought to interest venture capitalists in transactions where the R&D organization would control much of the equity. In a typical proposed transaction, the venture capitalists would receive a 30% stake in exchange for their investment, the management team would control 10%, and the research institution would hold the remainder. Despite considerable effort for over 2 years, the organization was unable to attract any investors into their portfolio of projects.

Thus, universities should not expect rapid returns from their commercialization strategies. The equity stakes they will receive are likely to be modest, and many of the shares are likely to prove worthless. To be sure, there will be exceptions: to cite two extreme examples, the stake that MIT was granted upon the founding of Akamai Technologies was worth 6 months after its initial public offering (when it was free to sell its shares) about $60 million and Stanford's stake in Google may be worth several times this amount.[5] While the occasional successful firm is likely to yield substantial returns, the typical returns will be much more modest.

4. The Illusive Promise of University Venture Capital Funds

While the tradition of interactions between venture funds and universities has been a long one, particularly at MIT and Stanford, the relationship has undergone a fundamental change in the past decade. Universities have become increasingly interested in venture capital-backed spinouts as a mechanism to commercialize early-stage technologies and to produce the greatest returns for the institution. This trend has been manifested in numerous ways, such as increases in the staff within academic technology transfer offices devoted to working with professors to establish new firms.

The most dramatic manifestation, however, has been the proliferation of funds dedicated to investing in new firms spawned from these institutions. Increasingly, institutions are seeing internal venture funds as an avenue to generate more wealth for the university, as remarks by Greg Gardiner, at the time the director of Yale's Office of Cooperative Research, illustrates:

> It is even more instructive to look at Yale intellectual assets that could have matured into new ventures... like Human Genomic Sciences or Incyte Pharmaceuticals. Each has a market capitalization in excess of 500 million dollars. Though Yale had the ideas, technology and personnel to form such a company a year or two in advance of HGS or Incyte, it did not happen because our development strategies were limited to licensing.[6]

While this vision is a tempting one, the experience of ARCH Venture Partners alluded to in the introduction illustrates a variety of challenges faced by university-affiliated funds. With ARCH, many things went right: substantial barriers to the recruitment of personnel were overcome, regulatory barriers designed to forestall conflicts of interest and informal organizational concerns were addressed, and the investments proved to be reasonably successful. Nonetheless, the structure proved unstable.

This disappointing experience illustrates some of the challenges associated with these efforts:

- *Political interference can doom the effort*. Programs entailing the commercialization of federally funded research always risk hearing complaints from competitors. For instance, Martin Marietta, the contractor that operated Oak Ridge National Laboratory, drew fire from the U.S. General Accounting Office and Representative John Dingell of Michigan for its venture capital initiative at the laboratory. Martin Marietta had established a venture capital subsidiary, the Tennessee Innovation Center, which sought to establish new businesses around Oak Ridge. Martin Marietta had also invested in a business that later received an exclusive license to develop an Oak Ridge technology. As a result of the congressional criticism, the contractor restructured the relationship with its affiliate in a financially unattractive way. Soon after, Martin Marietta abandoned the effort.[7]

- *Regulations can severely restrict researchers' involvement with start-up firms.* In extreme cases, all formal relationships with outside start-ups are prohibited. More frequently, university or laboratory policies let publicly funded researchers serve as directors of and consultants to spin-off companies, but forbid them from holding equity in these enterprises. These same institutions often make it difficult for employees to take leaves to work with these companies. Granted, these steps may have sought to prevent abuses, but they also stifle efforts to commercialize technologies.

- *Programs may fail to recruit and retain the best talent.* This failure often stems from the limited compensation and autonomy that these programs offer investors. Forced to recruit less experienced managers, these funds suffer when the managers make unwise decisions: for instance, funding firms with limited commercial potential or exhausting the institution's resources on seed investments that they can't support with follow-on financing. In this regard, universities have run into problems similar to corporate venture programs, as corporations have frequently been reluctant to compensate their venture managers through profit-sharing ("carried interest") provisions, fearing that they might need to make huge payments if their investments were successful. Typically, successful risk-taking was inadequately rewarded and failure excessively punished. As a result, corporations were frequently unable to attract managers who combined industry experience with connections to other venture capitalists to run their venture funds; and all too many corporate venture managers adopted a conservative approach to investing.

A natural question concerns the generality of these examples. Relatively few academic-based funds have reached maturity, and data on their activities are limited to case studies of a number of programs: see Atkinson (1994). But the difficulties that the pioneering funds as faced—as well as those encountered by their closely related cousins, the corporate venture fund—lead to a dubious prognosis.

5. Better Paths to Adding Value

The skepticism expressed in the previous section about university-based venture funds does not imply that there is not an important role for university technology transfer offices in the start-up formation process. On the contrary, these offices can play an important role in alleviating the information problems discussed above. This role has two dimensions: reducing the uncertainty of academic entrepreneurs about the spin-out process and easing outside investors' and strategic partners' doubts about the new venture.

Academic entrepreneurs are frequently bright and charismatic individuals. While they have very deep knowledge of their respective fields, often their confidence outstrips their knowledge in other arenas. Examples abound of brilliant scientists who have made poor choices in managing new ventures. An academic entrepreneur, for instance, may opt for a term sheet from a little known venture capitalist who is willing to invest at a higher valuation instead of that a much more reputable group, not understanding the "stamp of approval" that the relationship with an established organization may bring. Similarly, a university spin-out may enter into a strategic alliance that entails the transfer of its key intellectual property for only a modest consideration.

Moreover, in many cases, academic entrepreneurs lack realistic expectations about their ventures. In particular, they often fail to perceive why potential investors might hesitate to provide themselves with funds. Alternatively, they may have an inflated impression of the value of their discovery.

By drawing on their experience, and placing the discovery in the context of other similar efforts, university technology transfer officers can help address these problems. This assistance is likely to have two dimensions.

The first of these relates to entrepreneurial education. A number of leading technology transfer offices have come to regard the education of academic entrepreneurs as one of their important objectives. Whether through informal counseling or structured courses, these technology offices have been able to help academic entrepreneurs come "down the learning curve" and avoid costly mistakes or misapprehensions.

The second dimension is addressing the concerns of outside investors. In many cases, venture capitalists and other financiers are inundated with proposals from young firms, many of which may have difficult-to-assess claims. As a result, they may be reluctant to fund ventures that solicit funds without a formal introduction without a trusted intermediary.

The best technology transfer offices have been able to play such an "honest broker" role. These offices have cultivated relationships with key venture capital organizations and corporations over time, building an understanding of the outlook and investment criteria of each group. When they then reach out to one of these groups with an investment opportunity in an academic spin-out, the investors are likely to consider the new venture seriously.

To play these roles effectively, however, is not easy. The effectiveness of these roles is likely to depend critically on the experience level of the technology transfer office staff. Retaining experienced staff has been difficult for many organizations. Few university technology transfer offices can offer compensation approaching the levels that corporate business development groups enjoy, much less independent venture capital firms. As a result, many offices have experienced a "revolving door" phenomenon: new staff, primarily recent Ph.D.s with little business experience, remain at the organization long enough to develop some familiarity with the licensing process, but then leave for the private sector. As a result, the institution does not glean many returns for its substantial investment in building its staff's human capital.

In many respects, this is little different from the challenges that other academic functions with private sector analogues face, such as endowment managers. The best organizations have created environments that are pleasant and rewarding workplaces, which attract and retain many talented staff members despite the disparities in financial rewards.

6. Rethinking Conflict-of-Interest Policies

The final section discusses on particular challenge that universities face in playing an active role in fomenting spin-offs: the presence of formal and informal curbs on perceived conflicts-of-interest. The rationales for such policies are easy to understand. Many academic projects are funded with public funds, which are accompanied by a variety of legal and ethical obligations. Moreover, academic institutions are themselves nonprofit entities, a special status which brings with it substantial responsibilities. Commercial activities, critics have feared, may subvert the core academic mission of the university, or at least create an unseemly appearance of impropriety.

It can be challenging, however, to reconcile the concerns about conflict-of-interest with effective fomenting of spin-outs. An example of these challenges is the Department of Energy's national laboratory system, where real and apparent conflicts have been major concerns of senior and mid-level managers for many years. In some cases, managers have insisted on a request-for-proposal process: a technology must be widely publicized and the entrepreneurial team must bid for the rights to it against established concerns. While such a process may appear on the surface "fair," the long delays associated with the process and the widespread publicity about the technology have often reduced its value considerably. Even when start-up firms have won exclusive rights to a new technology, advocates for competing firms have sometimes challenged their licenses. In extreme cases, researchers who have tried to leave the laboratory with new technologies have been unable to obtain licenses to the key technologies, despite being the only parties interested in the work. For a variety of illustration of these problems, see Adam B. Jaffe and Josh Lerner (2001).

The degree to which concerns about fomenting innovation or those about avoiding conflicts-of-interest should be paramount has been long debated. While the federal government's policies towards the commercialization of the research it funded were the subject of litigation and Congressional debate as early as the 1880s, the debate assumed much greater visibility with the onset of World War II. The dramatic expansion of federal R&D effort during the War raised questions about the disposal of the rights to these discoveries. Two reports commissioned by President Roosevelt reached dramatically different conclusions, and framed the debate that would follow in the succeeding decades.

The National Patent Planning Commission, an *ad hoc* body established shortly after the Pearl Harbor attack to examine the disposition of the patents developed during the War, opined:

> It often happens, particularly in new fields, that what is available for exploitation by everyone is undertaken by no one. There undoubtedly are Government-owned patents which should be made available to the public in commercial form, but which, because they call for a substantial capital investment, private manufacturers have been unwilling to commercialize under a nonexclusive license.[8]

A second report, completed in 1947 by the Department of Justice, took a very different tack. Rather, it argued that "innovations financed with public funds should inure to the benefit of the public, and should not become a purely private monopoly under which the public may be charged for, or even denied, the use of technology which it has financed" (U.S. Department of Justice, 1947). The report urged the adoption of a uniform policy forbidding both the granting of patent rights to contractors and exclusive licenses to federal technology in all but extraordinary circumstances. Over the ensuing 30 years, federal patent policy vacillated back and forth between these two views.

Beginning in the 1980s, policy seemed to shift decisively in favor of permitting exclusive licenses of publicly funded research to encourage commercialization. The Stevenson–Wydler Technology Innovation Act of 1980 explicitly made technology transfer a mission of all federal laboratories and created a variety of institutional structures to facilitate this mission. Among other steps, it required that all major federal laboratories establish an Office of Research and Technology Applications to undertake technology transfer activities. At about the same time, the Bayh–Dole Act allowed academic institutions and non-profit institutions to automatically retain title to patents derived from federally funded R&D. The act also explicitly authorized government-operated laboratories to grant exclusive licenses on government-owned patents. These two acts were followed by a series of initiatives over the next decade that extended and broadened their reach.

This wave of legislation did not, however, resolve the debate concerning the extent to which ownership of government-funded R&D ought to be transferred to private sector entities. Congressional and agency investigations of inappropriate behavior during the commercialization process—particularly violation of fairness-of-opportunity and conflict-of-interest regulations during the spin-out and licensing process—continued to be commonplace (Derek Bok, 2003).

It is asking too much for university technology transfer officers to resolve these debates themselves. But it is important that they realize—and communicate to administrators and faculty—the trade-offs at work. To be most effective, they must be allowed to move nimbly, serving as educators to academic entrepreneurs and information brokers to investors. Yet these types of activity are quite different from the cautious approach that substantial concerns about conflict-of-interest policies might engender. Without condoning blatant self-dealing, university administrators must nonetheless recognize that too vigorous limits on potential conflicts can have a chilling effect on entrepreneurial activity.

Notes

1. This essay is based in part on Paul Gompers and Josh Lerner, *The Money of Invention,* Boston, Harvard Business School Press, 2001, and Josh Lerner, "Venture Capital and the Commercialization of Academic Technology: Symbiosis and Paradox" in Lewis M. Branscomb, editor, *Industrializing Knowledge: University-Industry Linkages in Japan and the United States,* Cambridge: MIT Press, pp. 385–409.

2. This account is based on Seragen's filings with the U.S. Securities and Exchange Commision. In a 1992 agreement with the State of Massachusetts' Attorney General's Office, the university agreed to make no further equity investments. The school, however, made a $12 million loan guarantee in 1995 (subsequently converted into equity) and a $5 millon payment as part of an asset purchase in 1997.

3. This account is based on Goldie Blumenstyk, "Accord in the Mosaic War: U. of Illinois and Private Company Agree on Product for Navigating the Internet," *Chronicle of Higher Education*, 41 (January 6, 1995), A21–A22, "Legal Entanglements in the World Wide Web," *Investors Business Daily*, (December 28, 1995), A6, and interviews with concerned parties.

4. The ARCH Venture Partners experience is documented in Josh Lerner, "ARCH Venture Partners: November 1993," Harvard Business School Case No. 9-295-105, 1995.

5. This calculation is based on an analysis of Akamai's securities filings and daily.stanford.edu/tempo?page=content&id=14315&repository=0001_article.

6. Gregory E. Gardiner, "Strategies for Technology Development: A Presentation to the Board of the Yale Corporation" http://www.yale.edu/ocr/yalecorp.html, 1997.

7. The Martin Marietta case is discussed in U.S. General Accounting Office, *Energy Management: Problems with Martin Marietta Energy Systems' Affiliate Relationships* (GAO/RCED-87-70), Washington: U.S. General Accounting Office, 1987, and U.S. General Accounting Office, *Energy Management: DOE/Martin Marietta Earnings Limitation Agreement* (GAO/RCED-87-147), Washington: U.S. General Accounting Office, 1987.

8. U.S. House of Representatives, *The Second Report of the National Patent Planning Commision*, Document #22, 79th Congress, 1st Session, January 9, 1945.

References

1. Atkinson, S.H., 'University-affiliated Venture Capital Funds, '*Health Affairs* **13,** 159–175.
2. Bok, D., 2003, *Universities in the Marketplace: The Commercialization of Higher Education*, Princeton: Princeton University Press.
3. Mansfield, E., 1968, *The Economics of Technological Change*, New York: W.W Norton & Company Inc.
4. Mansfield, E. E., 1991, 'Academic Research and Industrial Innovation,' *Research Policy* **20,** 1–12.
5. Jaffe, A.B. and J. Lerner, 2001, 'Reinventing Public R&D: Patent Law and Technology Transfer from Federal Laboratories, *Rand Journal of Economics* **32,** 167–198.
6. U.S. Department of Justice, 1947, *Investigation of Government Patent Pratices and Policies: Report and Recommendations of the Attorney General to the President*, Washington, U.S. Government Printing Office.

Patents and Appropriation: Concerns and Evidence[1]

Wesley M. Cohen

ABSTRACT. For over the past twenty years, the United States has witnessed a pro-patent movement. In response, numerous concerns have been raised, including possible impediments to innovation in cumulative technologies, emergence of anti-commons, barriers to entry and an elevation of costs of innovation associated with defensive patenting, growth in patent litigation and poor quality patents. Although there is little systematic evidence that these concerns have materialized in any substantial way, vigilance is nonetheless warranted.

Key words: patents, R&D, innovation

JEL Classification: O34

1. Introduction

For over 20 years, the United States has witnessed a pro-patent movement, manifest in both public policy and managerial practice. In 1982, the Court of Appeals for the Federal Circuit (CAFC) was established to make patent protection more uniform, and indirectly strengthened it. Since the early 1980's, there has been an expansion of what can be patented, with the courts affirming that life forms, software and even business methods were patentable. The 1980 Bayh-Dole Amendment and related legislation has extended the eligibility of who can patent, permitting universities and other institutions receiving federal R&D support to obtain patents on the work supported by those funds. Partly stimulated by these policy changes, firms have become more aggressive in both applying for and asserting patents. Similarly, universities and other publicly supported research institutions have increased their patenting and their pursuit of licensing revenues.

This pro-patent movement has raised concerns among scholars as well as public and quasi-public agencies and authorities, including the National Research Council (2004) and the Federal Trade Commission (2003). Nelson (2004), among others, argues that now that universities and other public research institutions are patenting more aggressively, access to new scientific and technological discoveries is becoming more restricted, threatening the research enterprise itself. Heller and Eisenberg (1998) suggest that the patent landscape is becoming too fractionated in biomedicine, with too many patents associated with any one therapeutic, undermining development and commercialization of innovation. Hall and Ziedonis (2001) and Shapiro (2000) have argued that the semiconductor industry has witnessed an acceleration of patent portfolio races that stimulate both defensive patenting and the patenting of marginal innovations that may be both raising the cost of innovation and acting as a barrier to entry. Finally, Barton (2000) and others have argued that the bar for receiving a patent has fallen, potentially conferring monopoly power with little compensating innovation in exchange. Collectively, these concerns have raised the question whether, from a social welfare perspective, the pendulum has swung too far in the direction of privatization of intellectual property (IP).

In this paper, we will briefly review the broad outlines of the pro-patent movement, and the reaction against it. We will also try to assess what scholars of technological change understand empirically about these various critiques. In this context, we will review recent research that I

The Fuqua School of Business
Duke University
Box 90120
1 Towerview Drive
Durham, North Carolina 27708
E-mail: wcohen@mail.duke.edu

have conducted with colleagues on the impact of patenting and appropriability on R&D.

2. Pro-patent movement in the U.S.[2]

It is widely understood that since about 1980, likely stimulated by the competitiveness crisis of the 1980's, U.S. policy and courts have moved in a pro-patent direction. The major change in the policy environment was the 1982 creation of the CAFC, a court designed to consolidate all appeals in patent cases emerging from the Federal District Court level in the U.S. The chief purpose of the court was to make judicial decisions in patent cases more uniform, and thus diminish the incentives to "forum shop" in the U.S. In contrast to many of the Federal District Courts, the CAFC also offered the advantage of providing judges who are expert in patent law and often in the technologies that came before them. Finally, the CAFC has also been generally recognized as broadly sympathetic with the overall intent of patent law, which has not always been the case in selected courts, and certainly not the case previously in the U.S. Thus, while the major intent of the CAFC's creation was to make patent law more uniform, its creation also indirectly strengthened it.

Indeed, the creation of the CAFC is widely thought to have signaled a shift in U.S. courts' consideration of patent cases. For example, citing the work of Allison and Lemley (1998) and Koenig (1980), Jaffe (2000) notes that before 1980, "a district court finding that a patent was valid and infringed was upheld on appeal 62% of the time; between 1982 and 1990 this percentage rose to 90%. Lanjouw and Lerner (1998) note that plaintiff success rates have increased from an average of 61% in the years before the establishment of the CAFC in 1982 to 75% by 1987.

In addition to an increase in plaintiff success rates, it appears that the values of the settlements have also increased. While I have found no systematic data on trends in settlement values, it is widely acknowledged (e.g., Hall and Ziedonis (2001)) that the nearly 900 million dollar payment to Polaroid in its suit against Kodak, resolved in 1985, was a watershed event in demonstrating just how much could be won (and lost) in patent infringement cases.[3] Subsequent settlements, also in the hundreds of millions of dollars, notably in the cases brought by Texas Instruments, had a similar demonstration effect. While such settlements are unusual, it is not uncommon for substantial values to be at risk in patent suits. For example, the 1997 "Report of Economic Survey" of the American Intellectual Property Law Association reported that the "estimated average value at risk" for 42% of the patent infringement suits were in the one to ten million dollar range, 38% in the ten to 100 million dollar range, and eight percent were over 100 million dollars.

Also marking the "pro-patent" movement in the U.S. was the expansion in patentable subject matter. Patentability was extended to life forms with the landmark *Diamond v. Chakrabarty* Supreme Court case in 1980. After previously striking down patents on mathematical algorithms, the Supreme Court allowed a patent on a computer program as an adjunct to a physical process in its 1981 decision, *Diamond v. Diehr*, thus endorsing the patentability of software. The courts, however, struggled over interpretation and implementation of their decisions regarding software for many years, gradually expanding the scope of patentable subject matter. The 1998 decision in *State Street Bank and Trust v. Signature Financial Group* rejected the doctrine against patents on "methods of doing business", thus affirming the patentability of software, and dispensing with virtually all limitations on software-related subject matter.

Another of the major reforms of the pro-patent era in the U.S. was the extension of eligibility regarding who can patent. The Bayh-Dole and the Stevenson-Wydler Acts of 1980 permit universities, government research labs, and other institutions receiving federal R&D support, to obtain patent rights over the inventions developed with federal support. The impetus behind Bayh-Dole and related legislation was the assumption that there is a stock of underexploited, valuable knowledge residing in universities and other research institutions receiving federal funding, and that patents would incent the private sector to undertake the downstream R&D and related investment necessary for commercialization (Mazzoleni and Nelson, 1998). Going beyond the intent of the original legislation, by providing universities with an opportunity to realize revenues on their inventions, the Bayh-Dole Act has also created an incentive for universities to use their research to generate income.

Although universities can now realize some share of the financial fruits of their IP, they ironically find themselves liable to infringement suits due to a recent pro-patent court decision that explicitly delimits what is known as the "research exemption" from infringement liability. Until recently, university administrators and researchers alike widely believed that their uses of patented inventions in their research was shielded from infringement liability by a "research exemption". In fact, however, it was widely understood among legal professionals that such an exemption does not apply to the sorts of research, typically biomedical, that university personnel thought to be exempt. In the 2002 *Madey v. Duke* case, the CAFC unambiguously stated that no university research enjoys protection from infringement liability, notwithstanding its commercial or noncommercial character (NRC, 2004, p. 18).[4]

Other changes marking the pro-patent era are outlined in the NRC (2004, pp. 17–19) report, *A Patent System for the 21st Century*. These included, for example, the 1988 Process Patent Amendments Act that enabled U.S. process patent holders to block the import of foreign goods produced by infringing methods. The 1984 Hatch-Waxman Act extended patent terms for up to 5 years to reflect regulatory delay in approving a drug. Also, from the 1980s on, there has been a relaxation of antitrust limitations on the use of patents. The TRIPS agreement of 1994, under the GATT, also strengthened patent enforcement internationally.[5]

3. Changing practices

Coincident and subsequent to these changes in policy, the patent-related practices of management—of both firms and universities—have changed. The annual rate at which patents are issued in the U.S. has skyrocketed since 1980. Total patents issued per annum in the U.S. to both U.S. and foreign entities have increased almost 170%, jumping from 61,819 in 1980 to 166,039 in 2001 (USPTO).[6] Of that total, patents issued to U.S. inventors have increased by 135% during the same period, from 37,355 to 87,607, and patents issued in the U.S. to foreign entities have increased over 200%, from 24,464 to 78,432. This trend is much less dramatic, however, if we normalize the patent issue rate by R&D. As Jaffe (2000) notes, there is a trend increase, especially in the late 1990's, with patenting increasing at a rate exceeding the rate of increase in R&D spending. Patents per million dollars of R&D rises about 50% over the period, 1985–1998, increasing from 0.35 patents per million dollars to almost 0.50 patents per million dollars.[7]

This growth, however, has not been uniformly distributed across technology areas. Hicks et al. (2001) show that the average yearly percentage growth in the number of patents by technology area for the three areas of information technologies, health technologies, and all other areas differ considerably.[8] Of these three classes, information and health technologies account for 26% of U.S. invented USPTO patents in the period, 1980 to 1999—but 57% of the growth in patenting during the same period. Between 1980 and 1999, patenting in health and information technology grew by more than 400%, with information technology patenting growing slightly more than health technologies during the period. In sharp contrast, patenting in all other areas combined grew by 63% during the 1980–1999 period. Thus, patenting activity has progressively shifted toward health and information technologies. The rapid growth of particularly information technology related patents is also apparent in the identity of the top corporate patenters in the U.S. In 1980, of the top 10 patenting firms, only 4 were information technology firms. In 1999, of the top 10 patenting firms, all were information technology firms.[9]

As noted above, the number of patents per R&D dollar—defined by many as "patent propensity"—for U.S. corporations increased by almost 50% during the 1980—2001 period. Hicks et al. (2001) findings, though not spanning the same time period, suggest that the vast bulk of this increase in patent propensity originates from the area of information technology where patents per R&D dollar between the periods 1989–1992 (the associated patent counts are drawn from the period 1991–1994) and 1993–1996 (the associated patent counts are drawn from the period 1995–1998) increased from an average of 0.28 patents per million dollars to 0.48 patents per million dollars. In contrast, in health technologies, chemical and polymer technologies and all other technologies, the patent propensity over the same period changed, respectively, from 0.23 to 0.24, 0.38 to 0.38 (no change), and 0.37 to 0.35 (a decline).

Although patenting by U.S. universities had begun to rise even prior to the Bayh-Dole Act (see Jaffe, 2000), its growth since the mid-1980's has been enormous—though university patents still account for a very small share of U.S. patents overall. In 1985, 589 patents were issued to 111 universities. In 2002, 3109 patents were issued to 156 academic institutions, representing more than a quintupling and easily outpacing the growth in university R&D expenditures. According to the Association of University Technology Managers (AUTM) FY 2002 Licensing Survey, gross licensing income grew from almost 130 million dollars going to 97 universities in 1991 to 998 million dollars going to 156 universities in 2002.

As patenting has increased, patent litigation has also increased. The number of federal district court patent cases terminated annually grew from about 1100 in 1988 to over 2200 in the year 2000. Lanjouw and Schankerman (2003) report that, in the period 1978 to 1999, the number of patent suits filed rose almost by tenfold, with much of this increase concentrated in the 1990's. They also suggest, however, that the rise in the number of suits relative to the patenting rate has not changed much. The rate of suit filings also differs substantially across technology fields, ranging from a low of 11.8 per thousand patents in chemicals to 25–30 cases per thousand in computers, biotechnology and the non-drug health areas. Lanjouw and Schankerman (2000) also show that the increase in the aggregate number of suits has been driven partly by the shift of patenting toward technology fields with higher litigation rates. They conclude that, "...once the growth in patenting is taken into account, we find that there has been no trend increase in the filing rates in any technology field over this period." (Lanjouw and Schankerman, 2003) Although the litigation rate, expressed as a percentage of patents, may not have increased, Ziedonis (2003) shows that suits per R&D dollar, in contrast, have increased sharply in the semiconductor industry, which is one of the most patent-intensive industries in the economy. Between the periods, 1973–1985 and 1986–2000, although the number of cases per thousand patents awarded dropped 5%, the number of cases per million (real) R&D dollars increased from 7.19 to 9.26, reflecting a jump of 43%.

According to the very limited data that are available, even if the filing rate on suits per patent may not have increased, expenditures per suit may have, implying a growth in legal costs over time—an increase which is obviously all the more substantial if normalized by R&D expenditures rather than the number of patents. Out-of-pocket legal costs per patent application filed or per litigated patent case appear to be growing. For example, American Intellectual Property Law Association (2003) survey data suggest that, between 1998 and 2002, the charges associated with filing a patent application have increased in the range of 25–50%, depending on the technology. Between 1997 and 2003 the median cost for all legal charges per side in patent infringement suits with less than one million dollars at risk grew from 301 thousand dollars to 500 thousand dollars. Between 2001 and 2003, the median cost per side through the end of suit where $1 to $25 million are at risk grew 33.4% to two million dollars per side. Where there is more than $25 million at risk, the median cost per side grew from three million to almost four million dollars per side (AIPLA, 2003).

4. Concerns

The pro-patent movement has provoked criticism that some of the very legislative and court decisions that mark this movement may dampen the long run pace of innovation—contrary to the intent of the provision for IP rights in the U.S. Constitution to "advance the progress of science and the useful arts". In this section, we will briefly review some of the more prominent of these critiques.

Restricted access to upstream discoveries[10]

Due to Bayh-Dole, the coincident growth of molecular biology and related fields, and court decisions affirming the patentability of life forms, there has been a growth in the patenting of upstream scientific discoveries, particularly in the life sciences. Merges and Nelson (1990) and Scotchmer (1991), have highlighted the social welfare costs that might accrue in industries whose technologies advance cumulatively (i.e., where invention proceeds largely by building on prior invention), when a patent holder restricts access to such upstream discoveries. To illustrate, consider the case where access is restricted to either the patent holder or an exclusive licensee. From a social welfare perspective, nothing is wrong with restricted access to IP that is useful for subsequent discovery as long as the patent holder or licensee is as able as other potential downstream users to fully exploit the potential contribution of that tool or input to subsequent innovation and commercialization.[11] This, however, is unlikely for several reasons. First, firms and universities are limited in their capabilities. Second, there is often a good deal of uncertainty about how best to build on a prior discovery, and any one rights-holder will tend to be limited in its views about what that prior discovery might be best used for and how to go about exploiting it. Consequently, a restricted number of rights-holders are typically unable to exploit fully the research and commercial potential of a given upstream discovery. Thus, society is better off to the extent that such upstream discoveries are made broadly available, ceterus paribus.[12] Merges and Nelson (1990) conclude that "unless licensed easily and widely," patents—especially broad patents—on early, foundational discoveries may limit the use of these discoveries in subsequent discovery and consequently limit the pace and even direction of innovation. The notion that prior discoveries should be made broadly available rests, however, on an important assumption—that broad availability will not compromise the incentive to invest the effort required to come up with that discovery to begin with (cf. Scotchmer, 1991).

Nelson (2004) has recently extended this line of argument by observing that restricted access to upstream discoveries and research has become more commonplace as universities and their faculties, responding to the incentives put in place by Bayh-Dole, are patenting more of their findings—findings which previously would have been made freely and publicly accessible. Thus, in his view, the "scientific commons" is shrinking and that shrinkage has been abetted by university administrations that historically have served as stewards of the public domain. The consequence is that the progress of innovation that depends on that commons—and a good deal does (cf. Cohen et al., 2002)—may be impeded.

Anticommons

In response to court decisions affirming the patentability of genes and gene fragments, Heller and Eisenberg (1998) raise a different concern. They argue that biomedical innovation has become susceptible to what they call a "tragedy of the anticommons," which can emerge when there are numerous property right claims to separate elements required to pursue a line of research or develop a new product. When these property rights are held by many claimants (especially if they are from different kinds of institutions), the negotiations necessary to their combination may fail, quashing the pursuit of otherwise promising lines of research or product development. Heller and Eisenberg suggest that the essential precondition for an anticommons—the need to combine a large number of separately patentable elements—now applies to drug development due to the patenting of gene fragments or mutations (e.g., expressed sequence tags (ESTs) and single-nucleotide polymorphisms (SNPs)), and a proliferation of patents on research tools that are essential inputs into the discovery of drugs, other therapies, and diagnostic methods. Heller and Eisenberg (1998) argue that the combining of multiple rights is susceptible to a breakdown in negotiations or, to the same effect, a stacking of license fees to the point of overwhelming the value of the ultimate product.

Heller and Eisenberg (1998) argue that biomedical research and innovation may be especially susceptible to breakdowns, elevated costs and delays in negotiations over rights for three reasons. First, as noted, the existence of numerous rights holders with claims on the inputs into the discovery process or on elements of a given product increases the likelihood that the licensing and transaction costs of bundling those rights may be greater than the ultimate value of the deal. Second, when there are different kinds of institutions holding those rights, heterogeneity in goals, norms, and managerial practice and experience can increase the difficulty and cost of reaching agreement. Such heterogeneity is manifest in biomedicine given the participation of large pharmaceutical firms, small biotechnology research firms, large chemical firms that have entered the industry (e.g., DuPont and Monsanto), and universities. Third, uncertainty over the value of rights, which is acute for upstream discoveries and research tools, can spawn asymmetric valuations that contribute to bargaining breakdowns and provide opportunities for other biases in judgment. Invoking the image of the "patent thicket", Shapiro (2000) has raised similar concerns in other industries such as semiconductors when he observes that technologies that depend on the agreement of multiple parties are vulnerable to holdup by any one of them, making commercialization potentially costly and difficult.

Barrier to entry

Cohen et al. (2000) suggest that in "complex product" industries such as semiconductors, computers and communications equipment, where there are commonly hundreds of patentable elements in one product, no one firm is likely to hold all the rights necessary for a product's commercialization.[13] As argued by Cohen et al. (2000) for "complex product" industries generally, and by Hall and Ziedonis (2001) for the semiconductor industry in particular, such mutual dependence commonly spawns extensive cross-licensing. Although the kind of breakdown suggested by Heller and Eisenberg (1998) does not occur in these industries, the prospect of extensive cross-licensing, and the associated use of patents as bargaining chips may stimulate patent portfolio races among industry incumbents that can act as a barrier to entry to firms that possess relatively few patents, particularly where incumbents will only exchange "like for like" (i.e., cross-license) rather than pay licensing fees (cf. Shapiro, 2000). In this way, by impeding entry, patents may act to suppress the innovation that accompanies it. Under such circumstances, patents become one of potentially several means of protecting oligopolistic rents[14] rather than principally protecting the rents that accrue directly from the commercialization or licensing of any specific patented invention.

Portfolio races and defensive patenting imposing a tax on innovation

A related concern in complex product industries is that the way that patents are used in such industries as well as the policies that support those uses may be increasing the cost of innovation more than warranted. First, the patent portfolio races that appear to be ongoing in semiconductors and other complex product industries compel firms to patent more marginal inventions in order to increase the size of their portfolios to strengthen their bargaining positions in cross-licensing negotiations. Related, and often contributing to these portfolio races, is defensive patenting, where firms file for patents largely to prevent infringement suits and gain the freedom of design and operation that comes with the ability to countersue if sued. These costs are sometimes characterized as a "tax" on innovation that increase the costs of innovation without generating much of an offsetting benefit in the form of more innovation (cf. Hall and Ziedonis, 2001; von Hippel, 1988).

Patent quality

With the recent growth in patenting, and a perception of greater deference to the interests of patent applicants, there have been concerns that the quality of patents has declined (Barton, 2000; Kingston, 2001; Merges, 1999). Specifically, some have suggested, especially with patent application approval rates that have been estimated by some to be as high as 90% or more (Quillen and Webster, 2001), that the patent approval standards of novelty, non-obviousness and utility are not being met.

Low quality imposes social costs. First, it increases uncertainty about the ultimate validity of any given patent, which in turn can dampen investment in the development of the associated technology. It can also diminish investment in competing technologies to the degree that others believe that such investments may be at risk of a finding of infringement. That same uncertainty may also spawn litigation if would-be infringers believe that it may be worth the risk to ignore a patent given a reasonable chance of a finding of invalidity in the event of a suit.

Diminished quality may also have the effect of broadening patent scope unduly, with enduring effects for cumulative technologies. For example, to the extent that a patent need not satisfy enablement for all applications, patent scope is effectively broadened. With regard to the standard of non-obviousness, the argument is more complex. Jaffe (2000) argues that a lowering of the bar of non-obviousness means that someone else will be able to patent an invention that is technologically close—effectively limiting the scope of the patent. However, by lowering the standard of non-obviousness, the technological space a firm can claim to be within its patent will likely be larger.[15]

The recent NRC (2004) report characterizes other important welfare costs that low quality patents may impose:

> Patents on known or only trivially modified inventions would confer potential market power to restrict access and raise prices and enable the patent holder to use litigation as a competitive weapon without providing incentives for making genuine advances or disclosing such advances to the public. They offer no public benefit in exchange for the benefit given to the patentee. Granting patents for inventions that are not new, useful and non-obvious unjustly rewards the patent holder at the expense of consumer welfare. (Levin and Levin, 2003). (NRC, 2004, p. 38)

4. Evidence

All these concerns merit attention and ongoing vigilance. It is not clear, however, how important they are in fact. Indeed, one of the challenges in this area is the collection of systematic data that allow us to assess the empirical importance of these and related issues. In this section, we will briefly evaluate the strength of the empirical evidence underpinning each of these concerns.

Restrictions on upstream discoveries and anticommons[16]

The possibility that access to a patent on a key upstream technology may be blocked, impeding subsequent innovation and commercialization is not a matter of conjecture; there is historical precedent. For the Wright brothers' airplane stabilization and steering system and Edison's incandescent lamp, "broad pioneering patents were exercised in a manner that at least temporarily deterred competitors from making further improvements." (NRC, 2004, p. 20) In the view of Merges and Nelson (1990), the refusal of the Wright brothers to license their initial pioneer patent significantly retarded progress in the industry, and this hold-up was in turn compounded as improvements and complementary patents, owned by different companies, emerged. Similarly, there are instances where an anticommons impeded technological progress. Merges and Nelson (1990) and Merges (1994), for example, note the case of radio technology where the Marconi Company, De Forest and De Forest's main licensee, AT&T arrive at an impasse over rights that lasted about 10 years and was only resolved in 1919 when RCA was formed at the urging of the Navy.

These two examples show that neither restricted access nor the emergence of an anticommons need be pervasive to have an important effect on social welfare. If the technology in question is sufficiently important, only one or a few instances of either may impose considerable social cost. Yet, the alarms that have been sounded with regard to both of these issues suggest that they may be or may become widespread in their effect, impeding the broader research enterprise. Both of these concerns have attracted particular attention recently in biomedicine, especially around the impact of the patenting and licensing of "research tools," which include any tangible or informational input into the process of discovering a drug or any other medical therapy or method of diagnosing disease (cf. Heller and Eisenberg, 1998).[17]

To assess the degree to which either restrictions on access to upstream discoveries or anticommons are hampering biomedical innovation, John Walsh, Ashish Arora and I conducted and analyzed 70 interviews with scientists, executives employed by firms, intellectual property practitioners, and university and government personnel. First, we found that the preconditions for both of these concerns exist. More patents are indeed now associated with new drugs and other therapies, and there is more patenting of upstream discoveries since Bayh-Dole, especially on the part of universities. We did not find, however, that these developments are impeding the development of drugs or other therapies in a significant way, at least not yet. Also, for commercially worthwhile projects, we found no evidence of breakdowns in negotiations over rights, nor firms avoiding projects due to the prospect of an anticommons. The major reason is that firms and other institutions have developed "working solutions" that limit the effects of the IP complexities that exist. These range from the normal responses of licensing and occasional litigation to other less visible solutions.[18] The most notable of the latter is pervasive infringement of patents in the course of laboratory research at a pre-product stage. Such infringement seems to be common in both public research institutions, notably universities, and in firms. In universities, researchers would often infringe unknowingly, although, when questioned, researchers tended to rationalize their actions as causing no commercial harm, and, in any event, believed themselves to have been shielded from infringement liability by a "research exemption". Such an exemption, however, did not in fact exist according to IP experts and practitioners familiar with court decisions of the past two decades. One final reason why more serious problems have not emerged is the response by powerful private and public sector actors, including NIH and major pharmaceutical firms.[19]

There are several important qualifications to our findings. First, we did observe isolated instances of firms restricting access to potentially important upstream discoveries, which may undermine important downstream research. This may be the case, for example, with Geron's exclusive license on human embryonic stem cell technology where it had expressed the intention of working on the technology itself, at least for selected application areas. Second, a small number of patent holders, notably Myriad, did aggressively restrict the unauthorized use of IP on diagnostic tests used in clinical research, largely because such use also deprived them of the clinical market. Third, negotiations across multiple rights holders did elevate transactions costs somewhat and could quash commercially marginal projects. Fourth, our interviews were conducted prior to the CAFC's *Madey v. Duke* decision of 2002, which, as noted above, unequivocally stated that the research exemption does not shield any research conducted by universities from infringement liability. Depending on how firms, and university administrations respond, this decision could undermine the important "working solution" of informal, often unknowing, infringement on the part of academic researchers. Finally, Walsh, Arora and I consider our interview-based study to be only a pilot study. To probe the generality of our findings, a more extensive study needs to be conducted.

Our interview-based study of the impact of patenting and licensing on biomedical innovation yields, however, several broader insights. First, the fact that things may happen does not mean they will. For example, our observation of pervasive infringement as one of our "working solutions" underscores the fact that one cannot presume that policy dictates behavior. Second, to understand why policies may have certain impacts (or not) requires attention to the institutional and policy environments, and the incentives and constraints of those involved. For example, for scientists at drug firms who knew they were infringing research tool patents, we learned the risk of a lawsuit was slight since there is a 6 year statute of limitations on patent infringement cases, and typically the infringement would only be detectable when a drug was actually commercialised—commonly a decade or more after the infringement occurred. Finally, although access to IP rights on upstream discoveries can be restricted in ways that undermine innovation, and breakdowns in negotiations over rights have occurred historically in other domains, decentralized incentives can also move the parties involved toward working solutions where there is a collective surplus to be had and actors exist who are in a position to extract that surplus. Yet, one should not be sanguine that these concerns are without merit. Indeed, it was likely that some of the early expressions of concern, such as that of Heller and Eisenberg (1998), pushed powerful public institutions like the NIH to intervene to make sure that serious problems did not in fact emerge.

Entry

Do patent thickets and the extensive cross-licensing and associated accumulation of large patent portfolios among incumbents common in complex product industries create or reinforce barriers to entry, beyond the substantial barriers that are often already in place? With no systematic empirical studies on the question, it is not clear.

As noted, scholars such as Hall and Ziedonis (2001), Cohen *et al.* (2000) and Shapiro (2000) suggest that the use of patents in portfolio swapping among large incumbents, along with the convention of swapping like-for-like, may actually deter entry into the semiconductor and other complex product industries. In another study, Ziedonis (2003) reports, however, that, starting in the 1980's, there was rapid entry in the semiconductor industry by chip design firms that relied heavily on patents to protect their IP. According to Ziedonis (2003), from their first appearance in 1983, the number of semiconductor design firms grew to over 40 by 1994, which suggests that in the very industry where concerns have been raised over the effect of patent portfolio races and cross-licensing on entry, we observe entry based at least partly on the strength of patent protection.[20] Although numerous semiconductor design firms have been established since the 1980's, it was, however, only after overcoming intense resistance on the part of Intel, which sued Cyrix, one of the first such firms, for patent infringement (*Cyrix Corp. v. Intel Corp.*) (Warshofsky, 1994).

Defensive patenting and portfolio races imposing a tax on innovation

As noted above, there is some evidence suggesting that litigation costs have increased, especially per dollar of R&D spending. There is also evidence that the costs of prosecuting patents have grown rapidly, and the costs per case have grown (NRC, 2004, p. 31). Yet, it is not apparent that costs have grown due to any increase in defensive patenting or accelerated patent portfolio races.

Moreover, even if one presumes such costs have risen, this only poses a problem to the extent that benefits have not risen concomitantly, which we do not know.

Quality

Given the rapid growth in patenting, a logical question is whether the quality of patents has declined. It is not clear. Hall *et al.* (2004) provides a brief list of patents issued over the past decade that, *prima facie*, do not meet any reasonable standard for novelty. But, out of tens of thousands of patents issued per year, a culled set of relatively few patents does not make the case that overall quality is declining. Hall and Ziedonis (2001) also conjectured that much of the increase in patenting in semiconductors reflected "harvesting" behavior—that is the patenting of inventions that would have been invented in any event, and, that, as a consequence, one would have expected a decline in quality. Hall and Ziedonis (2001) did not, however, find a clear decline in quality, measured as the average number of forward citations per patent in semiconductors. Consistent with this finding, Lanjouw and Schankerman (2003) actually find a positive relationship between portfolio size and the number of forward citations per patent. In information technology more broadly, and using a normalized measure of the number of times the previous 5 years of patents are cited in the current year, Hicks *et al.* (2001) found an increase in patent quality over time.

These tests of quality that rely on forward citations, a preferred measure of patent quality, do not, however, make the case that the patents that have been issued over the recent past have not declined in terms of the standards of novelty, non-obviousness, or utility. To sum up the case, NRC (2004) states that "...the claim that quality has deteriorated in a broad and systematic way has not been empirically tested." The same report goes on to say, however, that there are reasons to suspect that "deviations from previous or at least desirable standards of utility, novelty and especially non-obviousness" may have occurred, and may be more pronounced in fast-moving technologies such as biotechnology and software (NRC, 2004, pp. 39—41). The reasons for concern include the increased workload pressures on the USPTO, and what appear to be rather high patent approval rates, according to some estimates (e.g., Quillen and Webster, 2001). Also, while many legal scholars would agree that the standards came down in the early 1990's, there have been some moves toward a restoration of standards in new technologies signaled by a strengthening of the utility standards at the USPTO for genetic patents, and a recent reform in the USPTO's examination procedure for business method patents that requires a "second look" before any patents are issued.

6. Patenting and R&D

The social costs of patents highlighted above become more troublesome to the degree that patents provide little compensating benefit in the form of a stimulus to innovation. An empirical legacy of the past forty years, reflected in the work of Scherer et al. (1959), Taylor and Silberston (1973), Mansfield (1986) and Levin et al. (1987), casts doubt on the claim that patents stimulate innovation in the preponderance of manufacturing industries. Cohen et al. (2000) more recent survey also suggests that patents are still not among the most featured mechanisms for appropriating returns to innovations. Instead, the key mechanisms in most industries are secrecy, lead time, and complementary capabilities. Patents are featured in only a small handful of industries, notably drugs and medical equipment, and play less critical roles for protecting innovation even in high tech industries such as semiconductors and communication equipment. Cohen et al. (2002) caution, however, that one cannot "...conclude from these results that patents are unimportant in stimulating innovation in most industries. The results speak only to the relative—not absolute—standing of patents." Cohen et al. (2002) go on to argue that the impact of patenting on innovation can only be assessed once one explicitly probes the relationship among patent effectiveness, patenting behavior and R&D with a model that considers the mutual causation that exists between R&D and patenting and the broad range of other factors affecting both innovation and patenting.

In Arora et al. (2004), Ashish Arora, Marco Ceccagnoli and I attempt to take one more step in using the data from the Carnegie Mellon Survey (CMS) to address the question of the effect of patenting on innovation.[21] We develop and estimate a structural model of the impact of patenting on industrial R&D in the U.S. manufacturing sector that links a firm's R&D effort with its decision to patent, recognizing that R&D and patenting affect one another and are both driven by many of the same factors. The paper first estimates "the patent premium"—defined as the proportional increment to the value of innovations realized by patenting—for the manufacturing sector as a whole, and by industry. Using our cross-sectional results, we then simulate the effect of increasing the patent premium on both R&D and patenting itself.

In our model, the patent premium represents the firm's expectations of the net payoff from applying for patent protection. That payoff is intended to reflect the returns from all the ways in which a firm may use its patents, including the protection of the commercialization of an innovation, licensing, and using the patent as a bargaining chip in cross-licensing negotiations. Our model also permits innovations to be protected by multiple patents.[22]

In our structure, a profit-maximizing firm will only patent an innovation if the premium exceeds unity. A patent premium of less than unity reflects an expected loss from patenting, perhaps due to the expected cost of applying for or defending a patent, or the cost of the information spillovers from the patent's publicaton.

We assume that each firm faces a distribution of premia across its innovations. Although we assume the premium to be normally distributed, the observed distribution of patent premia is truncated normal and positively skewed, which is consistent with prior findings of a positively skewed distribution of patent values (Schankerman and Pakes, 1986; Scherer and Harhoff, 2000). The reason for this positive skew is that the only premia that will be realized are those associated with innovations that are patented, and it is not profitable to patent all innovations.

We estimate a simultaneous system of three equations, explaining, respectively, firms' R&D decisions, their patent propensities (defined as the percentage of innovations that are patented),[23] and R&D productivity. Featured independent variables include: (1) a measure of patent effectiveness that summarizes unobserved, firm-level determinants of the patent premium in addition to firm size, technological rivalry and industry fixed effects; (2) factors affecting the gross benefits to innovation, including, for example, measures of business unit size, technological rivalry, effectiveness of rivals' patents and industry effects; and (3) factors conditioning R&D productivity, which include R&D effort itself (reflecting diminishing returns to R&D), organizational variables, as well as sources of R&D spillovers such as rival R&D and geographically proximate university R&D.

As noted, we estimate the model using data from the 1994 CMS of R&D performing units in the U.S. manufacturing sector. Our measure of patent propensity, defined here as the percentage of innovations that are patented, is vital for our empirical analysis because it permits us to analyze the patenting and R&D decisions as separate, albeit jointly determined, decisions, which, in turn, enable us to empirically distinguish the impact of the patent premium on R&D from its impact on patenting itself. Other important data elements include measures of R&D, the number of patent applications, patent effectiveness, and information flows from other firms and universities, among other variables.

The empirical analysis suggests that the unconditional expected patent premium for the sample as a whole is about 0.6. Thus, for our sample of U.S. manufacturing firms, the expected value of the typical innovation if patented (net of patenting costs) is 40% lower than without patent protection. The expected patent premium is greater than one in only one industry, medical instruments, and it is about one in biotech and drugs. An average patent premium less than unity confirms that the opportunity cost of patenting, due to the cost of information disclosure, of being "invented around" or the cost of enforcement, are substantial. This result both confirms earlier findings but also marks an advance. Earlier studies (e.g., Cohen et al., 2000; Levin et al., 1987) had found that patents are not as central to the protection of inventions as other mechanisms except in selected industries.

These estimates of the expected (unconditional) patent premium confirm that in most industries, patenting the typical innovation is indeed not profitable. However, even in these industries, some innovations are profitable to patent, thus explaining why firms may patent some innovations even while they rate patents as less effective than other appropriability mechanisms.

Although the typical innovation may not be profitable to patent, conditional on patenting an innovation, the premium from patenting is substantial. For our sample as a whole, conditional on having patented an innovation, our results suggest that firms expect on average to earn 47% more than if they had not patented those innovations. The conditional premium is highest, about 60%, in industries such as medical instruments, biotechnology, and drugs, and the lowest in food and electronic components, about 40%. As may be expected, the variation in the conditional premium across industries is much smaller than that for the unconditional premium.

We next consider the question of whether patenting stimulates R&D by using the estimates from our structural model to simulate the effect on R&D of raising the patent premium. We find increasing the expected patent premium indeed stimulates R&D for the manufacturing sector as a whole (i.e., an increase in the mean of the patent premium distribution for a typical firm in our sample of manufacturing firms significantly stimulates R&D). Increasing the patent premium by 10 basis points increases R&D spending on average by 6.6%. The expected premium also stimulates, as should be expected, patenting, which always increases more than proportionately than does R&D. Our analysis suggests that the stimulative effect of the premium on R&D is greatest in industries where patent effectiveness is reported to be high, such as drugs and medical equipment. Perhaps more importantly, we also find the premium increases R&D—though less so—even in industries such as semiconductors where the patent premium is lower and firms rely more heavily upon means other than patents to protect their inventions.

The aggregate pattern identified in Section 3 above—that R&D is rising in the 1990's, but patenting is rising more than proportionately than R&D—is consistent with what our model would suggest to be reflective of a rising patent premium. The more disaggregate patterns showing that patenting is rising much more quickly than R&D in lower patent premium industries, such as semiconductors and communications equipment, is also consistent with what our model predicts would occur when patent premia are growing economy-wide. There are, however, many other factors at work that undoubtedly affect these patterns.[24] Moreover, patent premia would not necessarily grow comparably across all industries.

We subjected the analysis in Arora *et al.* (2004) to numerous robustness checks and sensitivity analyses.[25] Nonetheless, the paper is subject to important qualifications. Most notably, the analysis does not comprehensively address the question of the effect of patenting on innovation. It ignores the impact of patents on entry and the innovation that may be associated with it. We also do not consider the role that patents may play in enhancing industry R&D efficiency by fostering the emergence of specialized technology service or research firms, as observed, for example, in biotechnology, semiconductors, scientific instruments and chemicals (cf. Arora, *et al.*, 2001). Finally, although our results appear to be robust to the use of other appropriability mechanisms at the margin, we cannot analyze the implications of the wholesale elimination of patents, which may well elicit behaviors that fall outside of our current model structure.

What does Arora *et al.* (2004) tell us about the broad range of concerns about patent policy and practice raised in the prior sections? For R&D performers at the time the CMS data were collected, it suggests that patenting tended to stimulate R&D, even in those industries such as semiconductors where the patent system and practices are argued by some to be at least somewhat dysfunctional. These results do not, however, suggest that patent policy is in any sense optimal. Thus, responding to the kinds of concerns raised in Section 4 above may well improve the performance of the patent system.

7. Conclusion

The creation of the CAFC, the policy and court decisions extending patentability to life forms and software, and the Bayh-Dole Act which permitted universities and other institutions receiving government research funds to patent their inventions all mark the pro-patent movement in the U.S. since 1980. These pro-patent shifts in policy and the courts appear to have stimulated patenting among both firms and universities.

There has been a strong reaction against this movement, highlighting possible disadvantages for the cause of technical advance. There are concerns that the growth of patenting of foundational, upstream inventions in cumulative technologies may constrain important follow-on research. The fragmentation of patent rights, especially in biomedical technologies, has raised the prospect that the costs of gathering of such rights may impede the downstream development and commercialization of drugs, other therapies and diagnostics, and undermine subsequent biomedical innovation. An apparent acceleration of patent portfolio races and the increased prominence of such portfolios in semiconductors, communications equipment and related industries raise the prospect that patents may be employed for the purpose of reinforcing barriers to entry and oligopoly rents at the possible expense of innovation. Also, the related acceleration in defensive patenting may be making innovation more costly. Finally, concerns have been expressed over a possible decline in the quality of patents issued in the U.S.

These are all very legitimate concerns. The empirical basis for these concerns is, however, far from strong. It also appears that patenting does stimulate innovation, at least among incumbent firms—even in industries such as semiconductors where the benefits of IP for innovation have been subjected to the greatest doubt. Does the absence of a strong empirical basis for these concerns warrant, however, either inaction or inattention? As noted above, in the case of restricted access to upstream discoveries for the purpose of further research, or in the case of an anticommons, it does not take a high frequency of occurrence of a problem to impose significant social costs if the problem emerges for a technology of sufficient importance. Moreover, it may take some time to collect the data required to see whether these concerns are occurring on a widespread basis—indeed, so much time that sizable social welfare costs may have already been incurred and irreversible actions taken. Thus, vigilance and prudence are indicated at this juncture. Moreover, to the extent that we observe even modest realizations of these concerns, we should not assume that what we are observing are merely infrequent and therefore insignificant occurrences because they may be harbingers of more significant problems to come. Yet, at the same time, aggressive empirical inquiry is warranted. It is too easy for academics and others to raise alarms when the bases for arguments are conjectural and understanding of the institutions and behaviors involved is so limited.

Notes

1. Originally prepared for presentation at the 10th International Joseph A. Schumpeter Society Conference, Universita Bocconi, Milan, 9-12 June 2004.
2. Much of this section is drawn from Cohen (2002).
3. Kodak also incurred the even more substantial loss of having to cease production of its instant cameras and withdraw from the business.
4. The decision went further still, arguing universities cannot enjoy such an exemption because research constitutes an integral part of the business of the university.
5. While the overall direction of change has been clearly pro-patent, one should note that the story is more complex; some policy decisions over the past two decades have departed from the overall trend. For example, the U.S. patent applications of firms that also intend to file for patent protection overseas are now automatically published after 18 months, in closer conformity with policies in Europe and Japan. Previously, such applications were only published upon the grant of the patent.
6. Patent data drawn from http://www.uspto.gov/web/offices/ac/ido/oeip/taf/us_stat.pdf.
7. The particular cause for the patent surge has not been determined. Kortum and Lerner (1999) entertained four different explanations, including "friendly courts." They end up leaning, however, toward R&D productivity (in terms of patents per dollar of R&D) growth. I would suggest that the data collected by Hicks et al. (2001) suggest a couple of reasons if we focus on the two technology areas where the preponderance of the growth occurred. First, we likely witnessed a growth in R&D productivity in the life sciences. In contrast, in the information technology industries (notably semiconductors and communications equipment), we are likely observing rapid growth due to the acceleration of patent portfolio races and defensive patenting since the mid-1980's (cf. Hall and Ziedonis, 2001).
8. Information technology includes computers, peripherals, telecommunications, semiconductors, electronics and software. Health technologies includes pharmaceuticals, biotechnology, medical electronics and medical equipment.
9. I wish to thank Diana Hicks of Georgia Tech University for having made these data available.
10. This and the next subsection draw heavily, and sometimes verbatim, from Walsh et al. (2003).
11. That patents imply some type of output restriction due to monopoly is taken as given. The question here is whether there is any social harm if the patent holder chooses to exploit the innovation himself exclusively or grant an exclusive license.
12. The premise of this argument, well recognized in the economics of innovation (e.g., Evenson and Kislev, 1973; Nelson, 1982), is that, given a technological objective (e.g., curing a disease) and uncertainty about the best way to attain it, an objective will be most effectively met to the extent that a greater number of approaches to it are pursued.
13. Cohen et al. (2000) define a complex product industry as one where there are relatively numerous patentable elements—often hundreds—in a commercializable product. For example, Hewlett Packard had over 500 patents on its original inkjet printer technology. In contrast, there are also "discrete product" industries, like drugs, where there are relatively few patentable elements in a commercializable product.
14. How big a share, however, can be affected by the size and quality of a firm's patent portfolio, which affects the terms of trade between rivals.
15. That is, with a high standard of non-obviousness, a patent holder may only be able to claim X. With a lower standard, he may be able to include $X + Y$.
16. This section draws heavily from Walsh et al. (2003), sometimes verbatim.
17. Examples of research tools include recombinant DNA (Cohen-Boyer), polymerase chain reaction (PCR), genomics databases, microarrays, assays, transgenic mice, embryonic stem cells, or knowledge of a target, that is, any cell receptor, enzyme, or other protein that is implicated in a disease and consequently represents a promising locus for drug intervention.
18. There are other examples where the preconditions for an anticommons exist, but it does not emerge. For example, in the semiconductor industry, there are numerous patents associated with a product and multiple claimants (Cohen et al., 2000; Hall and Ziedonis, 2001; Levin, 1982;), but rights over essential inputs to innovation are routinely transferred and cross-licensed.
19. Walsh et al. (2003b) state, "For example, with substantial public, private, and foundation support, public and quasi-public databases (e.g., GenBank or the SNPs Consortium) have been created, making genomic information widely available. The NIH has funded initiatives and instituted new guidelines for grantees to promote access to research tools. The NIH has also negotiated with owners of foundational technologies, such as stem cells or genetically altered mice, to ease publicly funded researchers' access to these important research tools. Scientific journals have pushed authors to deposit sequences in publicly available databases as a condition of publication." (Walsh et al., 2003b, p. 121)
20. There is also broad consensus that in the few instances where patents are especially effective, they have provided the basis for raising capital and stimulating entry, as in biotechnology (e.g., Henderson et al., 1999).

21. The description of Arora et al. (2004) that follows draws heavily from the original article, and includes numerous verbatim excerpts.
22. See Cohen et al. (2000) for a consideration of the implications of the number of patents per commercializable innovation for the uses of patents.
23. Note that this measure of patent propensity differs importantly from the conventional measure, which is the number of patents per R&D dollar.
24. Other factors would include, for example, changes in technological opportunity and aggressive government support of R&D in the health-related industries.
25. We probed assumptions of the model and checked the sensitivity of the results with regard to: 1. the interpretation of our measure of patent effectiveness; 2. the effect on the returns to patents of the use of other means of protecting innovations; 3. the potential endogeneity of patent effectiveness; 4. the assumption that the patent premium is normally distributed; and 5. the role of industry effects.

References

Allison, J.R. and M.A. Lemley, 1998, 'Empirical Evidence on the Validity of Litigated Patents,' *AIPLA Quarterly Journal* **26** (3), 185–275.

American Intellectual Property Law Association (AIPLA), 1997, 2001, 2003 'Report of the Economic Survey,' AIPLA, Washington, DC.

Arora, A., M. Ceccagnoli and W.M. Cohen, 2004, 'R&D and the Patent Premium,' Mimeo, Carnegie Mellon University.

Arora, A., A. Fosfuri and A. Gambardella, 2001, *Markets for Technology: Economics of Innovation and Corporate Strategy*, MIT Press: Cambridge.

Association of University Technology Managers (AUTM), 2002, 'The AUTM Licensing Survey, Fiscal Year 2002,' Association of University Technology Managers, Norwalk, Connecticut.

Barton, J., 2000, 'Intellectual Property Rights. Reforming the Patent System,' *Science* **287**, 1933–1934.

Cohen, W.M., 2002, 'The pro-patent movement in the United States: Indicators and Impacts,' in Institute on Intellectual Property, *Report on Patents and the Economy*, Tokyo.

Cohen, W.M. and S. Merrill, eds., 2003, *Patents in the Knowledge-Based Economy*, Washington, DC.: National Academies Press.

Cohen, W.M., R.R. Nelson and J.P. Walsh, 2000, 'Protecting their Intellectual Assets: Appropriability Conditions and why U.S. Manufacturing Firms Patent (or not),' NBER Working Paper 7522 (revised, 2004, as mimeo, Duke University).

Cohen, W.M., R.R. Nelson and J.P. Walsh, 2002, 'Links and Impacts: The Influence of Public Research on Industrial R&D,' *Management Science* **48**(1), 1–23.

Evenson, R. and Y. Kislev, 1976, 'A Stochastic Model of Applied Research,' *Journal of Political Economy* **84**, 265–281.

Federal Trade Commission, 2003, 'To Promote Innovation: The Proper Balance of Competition and Patent Law and Policy,' Washington: Federal Trade Commission, October.

Hall, B.H., S. Graham, D. Harhoff and D.C. Mowery, 2004, 'Prospects for improving U.S. Patent Quality via Postgrant Opposition,' in *Innovation Policy and the Economy*, A.B. Jaffe, J. Lerner and S. Stern (eds.), Cambridge: National Bureau of Economic Research.

Hall, B.H. and R.H. Ziedonis, 2001, 'The Patent Paradox Revisited: An Empirical Study of Patenting in the U.S. Semiconductor Industry, 1979–1995, '*R&D Journal of Economics* **32**(1), 101–128.

Heller, M.A. and R.S. Eisenberg, 1998, 'Can patents deter innovation? The Anticommons in Biomedical Research,' *Science* **280** (May 1), 698–701.

Henderson, R., L. Orsenigo and G.P. Pisano, 1999, 'The Pharmaceutical Industry and the Revolution in Molecular Biology: Interactions among Scientific, Institutional and (eds.), Organizational Change,' in D.C. Mowery and R.R. Nelson *Sources of Industrial Leadership: Studies of Seven Industries*, New York: Cambridge University Press.

Hicks, D., T. Breitzman, D. Olivastro and K. Hamilton, 2001, 'The Changing Composition of Innovative Activity in the US—A Portrait based on Patent Analysis,' *Research Policy* **30** (4), 681–704.

Jaffe, A., 2000, 'The U.S. Patent System in Transition: Policy Innovation and the Innovation process,' *Research Policy* **29**, 531–558.

Kingston, W., 2001, 'Innovation Needs Patent Reform,' *Research Policy* **30**, 403–423.

Koenig, G., 1980, *Patent Invalidity: A Statistical and Substantive Analysis*, Clark Boardman, New York.

Kortum, S. and J. Lerner, 1999, 'What is Behind the Recent Surge in Patenting?,' *Research Policy* **28**, 1–22.

Lanjouw, J.O. and J. Lerner, 1998, 'The enforcement of Intellectual Property Rights: A Survey of the Empirical Literature,' *Annales d'Economie et de Statistique* No. **49/50**, 223–246.

Lanjouw, J.O. and M. Schankerman, 2003, 'Enforcement of Patent Rights in the United States,' in W. Cohen and S. Merrill (eds.), *Patents in the Knowledge-Based Economy*, Washington, DC.: National Academies Press.

Levin, R., 1982, 'The Semiconductor Industry,' in R.R. Nelson (ed.), *Government and Technical Progress: A Cross-Industry Analysis*, New York: Pergamon Press.

Levin, R.C., A.K. Klevorick, R.R. Nelson and S.G. Winter, 1987, 'Appropriating the Returns from Industrial R&D', *Brookings Papers on Economic Activity* 783–820.

Levin, R.C. and J. Levin, 2003, 'Benefit and Costs of an Opposition Process,' in W. Cohen and S. Merrill (eds.), *Patents in the Knowledge-Based Economy*, Washington, DC.: National Academies Press.

Mansfield, E., 1986, 'Patents and Innovation: An Empirical Study,' *Management Science* **32**, 173–181.

Mazzoleni, R. and R.R. Nelson, 1998, 'Economic theories about the Benefits and Costs of Patents,' *Journal of Economic Issues* **32** (4), 1031–1052.

Merges, R., 1994, 'Intellectual Property Rights and Bargaining Breakdown: the Case of Blocking Patents,' *Tennessee Law Review* **62** (1), 74–106.

Merges, R., 1999, 'As Many as Six Impossible Patents before Breakfast: Property Rights for Business Concepts and Patent System Reform,' *Berkeley High Technology Law Journal* **14**, 577–615.

Merges, R. and R.R. Nelson, 1990, 'On the Complex Economics of Patent Scope,' *Columbia Law Review*, May.

National Research Council (NRC), 2004, *A Patent System for the 21st Century*, Washington, DC.: National Academies Press.

Nelson, R.R., 1982, 'The Role of Knowledge in R&D Efficiency,' *Quarterly Journal of Economics* **97**, 453–470.

Nelson, R.R., 2004, 'The Market Economy and the Scientific Commons,' *Research Policy* **33**(3), 455–472.

Quillen, C.D. and O.H. Webster, 2001, 'Continuing Patent Applications and Performance of the U.S. Patent Office,' *Federal Circuit Bar Journal* **11**(1), 1–21.

Schankerman, M. and A. Pakes, 1986, 'Estimates of the Value of Patent Rights in European Countries During the Post-1950 Period,' *The Economic Journal* **96**, 1052–1076.

Scherer, F.M. *et al.*, 1959, *Patents and the Corporation*, 2nd edn, Boston, privately published.

Scherer, F.M. and D. Harhoff, 2000, 'Technology Policy for a World of Skew-distributed Outcomes,' *Research Policy* **29**, 559–566.

Scotchmer, S, 1991, 'Standing on the Shoulders of Giants: Cumulative Research and the Patent Law,' *Journal of Economic Perspectives* **5**, 29–41.

Shapiro, C., 2000, 'Navigating the Patent Thicket: Cross Licenses, Patent Pools, and Standard Setting,' in *Innovation Policy and the Economy*, Vol. 1, A. Jaffe, J. Lerner and S. Stern (eds.), Cambridge, National Bureau of Economic Research and MIT Press.

Taylor, C.T. and Z.A. Silberston, 1973, *The Economic Impact of the Patent System: A Study of the British Experience*, Cambridge: Cambridge University Press.

von Hippel, E., 1988, *The Sources of Innovation*, Oxford, UK: Oxford University Press.

Walsh, J.P., A. Arora, and W.M. Cohen, 2003, 'Effects of Research Tool Patents and Licensing on Biomedical Innovation,' in W. Cohen and S. Merrill (eds.), *Patents in the Knowledge-Based Economy*, Washington, DC. National Academies Press.

Walsh, J.P., A. Arora and W.M Cohen, 2003b, 'Working through the Patent Problem,' *Science* **299** (Feb. 14), 121.

Warshofsky, F., 1994, *The Patent Wars: The Battle to Own the World's Technology*, New York: Wiley and Sons.

Ziedonis, R.H., 2003, 'Patent litigation in the U.S. semiconductor industry,' in W. Cohen and S. Merrill (eds.), *Patents in the Knowledge-Based Economy*, Washington, DC.: National Academies Press.

The Bayh-Dole Act of 1980 and University–Industry Technology Transfer: A Model for Other OECD Governments?*

David C. Mowery[1,2]
Bhaven N. Sampat[3,4]

ABSTRACT. Recent initiatives by a number of OECD governments suggest considerable interest in emulating the Bayh-Dole Act of 1980, a piece of legislation that is widely credited with stimulating significant growth in university–industry technology transfer and research collaboration in the US. We examine the effects of Bayh-Dole on university–industry collaboration and technology transfer in the US, emphasizing the lengthy history of both activities prior to 1980 and noting the extent to which these activities are rooted in the incentives created by the unusual scale and structure (by comparison with Western Europe or Japan) of the US higher education system. Efforts at "emulation" of the Bayh-Dole policy elsewhere in the OECD are likely to have modest success at best without greater attention to the underlying structural differences among the higher education systems of these nations.

Key words: Bayh-Dole, technology transfer, patents

JEL Classification: O340, O380

[1] Haas School of Business,
UC Berkeley, Berkeley, CA 94720, U.S.A.
[2] NBER. 30 Arta Road,
Stanford, CA 94305-8715, U.S.A.
E-mail: mowery@hass.berkerly.edu
[3] School of Public Policy
Georgia Institute of Technology 685 Cherry Street, NW
Atlanta, GA 30332, U.S.A.
[4] School of Public Health
Health Management and Policy
University of Michigan
109 Observatory Room M2240 Ann Arbor
MI 48109-2029, U.S.A.
*This paper draws extensively on research conducted with Professors Richard Nelson of Columbia University and Arvids Ziedonis of the University of Michigan. Much of that work appears in 'Ivory Tower' and Industrial Innovation: University–Industry Technology Transfer Before and After the Bayh-Dole Act (Stanford University Press, 2004).

1. Introduction

The relationship between academic research and industrial innovation was a central focus of Edwin Mansfield's research agenda. His papers on academic research and industrial innovation (1991, 1995) were important early contributions to the large literature on the economic benefits of US university research. Mansfield found a high social rate of return to investment in academic research performed between 1960s and 1970s, as well as important complementarities and feedbacks between the "basic" and "commercially oriented" research by academic researchers. Mansfield's findings were published near the peak of the "competitiveness debate" of the 1980s and early 1990s within the US over issues such as the alleged failure of US firms to exploit academic research more effectively for commercial advantage. These concerns contributed to the passage of the Bayh-Dole Act of 1980, which sought to facilitate patenting and licensing by US universities of inventions based on federally funded research.

The Bayh-Dole Act was followed by significant growth in patenting and licensing by US universities, and a number of assessments have argued that expansion in these activities enhanced the social returns to publicly funded research academic. Although tenuously anchored in empirical evidence, these assessments and other factors have led governments in many OECD countries to consider policy initiatives that emulate the Bayh-Dole Act. This paper examines the effects of Bayh-Dole on university–industry collaboration and technology transfer in the US. There is a long history of such collaboration and technology transfer in the US university system stretching far back into the pre-1980 period, and these activities have been rooted in the incentives created by the unusual scale and structure (by comparison with many Western European nations or Japan) of the US higher education system. Based on this analysis, we argue that efforts at "emulation" of the Bayh-Dole policy elsewhere in the OECD are likely to have modest success at best without greater attention to the underlying structural differences among the higher education systems of these nations.

The global diffusion of these policies illustrates a phenomenon that has received little attention in the literature on innovation policy—the efforts by policymakers to "borrow" policy instruments from other economies and apply these instruments in very different institutional contexts. History, path dependence, and institutional "embeddedness" all make this type of "emulation" very difficult. Nonetheless, such emulation has been especially widespread in the field of technology policy, most notably in the area of collaborative R&D policies.

Our critique of the efforts to emulate the Bayh-Dole Act relies in part on a survey of recent evidence on the characteristics of the university–industry knowledge exchange and technology transfer, discussed in Section 2. We discuss the effects of Bayh-Dole, relying on evidence from the pre- and post-1980 periods, in Section 3. Section 4 provides an overview of efforts of other OECD nations to emulate the Act, and Section 5 concludes.

2. How does academic research influence industrial innovation? A review of recent studies

A number of recent studies based on interviews and surveys of senior industrial managers in industries ranging from pharmaceuticals to electrical equipment have examined the influence of university research on industrial innovation, and thereby provide additional insight into the role of universities within the US national innovation system. All of these studies (Cohen, et al., 2002; GUIRR, 1991; Levin et al., 1987; Mansfield, 1991) emphasize the significance of interindustry differences in the relationship between university and industrial innovation. The biomedical sector, especially biotechnology and pharmaceuticals, is unusual, in that university research advances affect industrial innovation more significantly and directly in this field than is true of other sectors.

In these other technological and industrial fields, universities occasionally contributed relevant "inventions," but most commercially significant inventions came from nonacademic research. The incremental advances that were the primary focus of the R&D activities of firms in these sectors were almost exclusively the domain of industrial research, design, problem-solving, and development. University research contributed to technological advances by enhancing knowledge of the fundamental physics and chemistry underlying manufacturing processes and product innovation, an area in which training of scientists and engineers figured prominently, and experimental techniques.

The studies by Levin et al. (1987) and Cohen et al. (2002) summarize industrial R&D managers' views on the relevance to industrial innovation of various fields of university research (Table I summarizes the results discussed in Levin et al., 1987). Virtually all of the fields of university research that were rated as "important" or "very important" for their innovative activities by survey respondents in both studies were related to engineering or applied sciences. These fields of US university research frequently developed in close collaboration with industry. Interestingly, with the exception of chemistry, few basic sciences appear on the list of university research fields deemed by industry respondents to be relevant to their innovative activities.

The absence of fields such as physics and mathematics in Table I, however, should not be interpreted as indicating that academic research in these fields does not contribute to technical advance in industry. Instead, these results reflect the fact that the effects on industrial innovation of basic research findings in such areas as physics, mathematics, and the physical sciences are realized only after a considerable lag. Moreover, application of academic research results may require that these advances be incorporated into

TABLE I
The relevance of university science to industrial technology

Science	No. of industries with "relevance" scores ≥ 5	No. of industries with "relevance" scores ≥ 6	Selected industries for which the reported "relevance" of university research was large (≥ 6).
Biology	12	3	Animal feed, drugs, processed fruits/vegetables
Chemistry	19	3	Animal feed, meat products, drugs
Geology	0	0	None
Mathematics	5	1	Optical instruments
Physics	4	2	Optical instruments, electronics
Agricultural science	17	7	Pesticides, animal feed, fertilizers, food products
Applied math/operations research	16	2	Meat products, logging/sawmills
Computer science	34	10	Optical instruments, logging/sawmills, paper machinery
Materials science	29	8	Synthetic rubber, nonferrous metals
Medical science	7	3	Surgical/medical instruments, drugs, coffee
Metallurgy	21	6	Nonferrous metals, fabricated metal products
Chemical engineering	19	6	Canned foods, fertilizers, malt beverages
Electrical engineering	22	2	Semiconductors, scientific instruments
Mechanical engineering	28	9	Hand tools, specialized industrial machinery

Source: Data from the Yale Survey on appropriability and Technological Opportunity in Industry. For a description of the survey, see Levin et al. (1987).

the applied sciences, such as chemical engineering, electrical engineering and material sciences. The survey results summarized in Cohen et al. (2002) indicate that in most industries, university research results play little if any role in triggering new industrial R&D projects; instead, the stimuli originate with customers or from manufacturing operations. Pharmaceuticals is an exception, since university research results in this field often trigger industrial R&D projects.

Cohen et al. (2002) further report that the results of "public research" performed in government laboratories and universities were used more frequently by US industrial firms (on average, in 29.3% of industrial R&D projects) than prototypes emerging from these external sources of research (used in an average of 8.3% of industrial R&D projects). A similar portrait of the relative importance of different outputs of university and public-laboratory research emerges from the responses to questions about the importance to industrial R & D of various information channels (Table II). Although pharmaceuticals is unusual in its assignment of considerable importance to patents and license agreements involving universities and public laboratories, respondents from this industry still rated research publications and conferences as a more important source of information. For most industries, patents and licenses involving inventions from university or public laboratories were reported to be of little importance, compared with publications, conferences, informal interaction with university researchers, and consulting.

Data on the use by industrial R&D managers of academic research results are needed for other industrial economies. Nonetheless, the results of these US studies consistently emphasize that the

TABLE II
Importance to industrial R&D of sources of information on public R&D (including university research)

Information source	% rating it as "very important" for industrial R&D
Publications and reports	41.2%
Informal interaction	35.6
Meetings and conferences	35.1
Consulting	31.8
Contract research	20.9
Recent hires	19.6
Cooperative R&D projects	17.9
Patents	17.5
Licenses	9.5
Personnel exchange	5.8

Source: Cohen et al. (2002).

relationship between academic research and industrial innovation in the biomedical field differs from that in other knowledge-intensive sectors. In addition, these studies suggest that academic research rarely produces "prototypes" of inventions for development and commercialization by industry—instead, academic research informs the methods and disciplines employed by firms in their R&D facilities. Finally, the channels rated by industrial R&D managers as most important in this complex interaction between academic and industrial innovation rarely include patents and licenses. Perhaps the most striking aspect of these survey and interview results is the fact that they have not informed the design of recent policy initiatives to enhance the contributions of university research to industrial innovation.

3. The Bayh-Dole Act and Academic Patenting in the United States

Origins of the Bayh-Dole Act

Although some US universities were patenting patent faculty inventions as early as the 1920s, few institutions had developed formal patent policies prior to the late 1940s, and many of these policies embodied considerable ambivalence toward patenting. Public universities were more heavily represented in patenting than private universities during the 1925–1945 period, both within the top research universities and more generally. Moreover, many of the public universities active in patenting faculty inventions sought to insulate themselves from this activity by establishing affiliated but legally separate research foundations such as the Wisconsin Alumni Research Foundation to manage their patent portfolios. Other institutions relied on third-party specialists in patent management such as the Research Corporation (Mowery and Sampat, 2001a; 2001b).

The pre-1980 patenting activities of US universities built on research collaborations between university and industrial researchers that spanned many channels of technology and knowledge exchange, including publishing, training of industrial researchers, faculty consulting, and other activities. University–industry collaboration in turn was facilitated by the unusual structure of the US higher education system (especially by comparison with those of other industrial economies) during the 20th century. The US higher education system was significantly larger, included a very heterogeneous collection of institutions (religious and secular, public and private, large and small, etc.), lacked any centralized national administrative control, and encouraged considerable interinstitutional competition for students, faculty, resources, and prestige (see Geiger, 1986, 1993; Trow, 1979, 1991, among other discussions). In addition, the reliance by many public institutions of higher education on "local" (state-level) sources for political and financial support further enhanced their incentives to develop collaborative relationships with regional industrial and agricultural establishments. The structure of the US higher education system thus strengthened incentives for faculty and academic administrators to collaborate in research and other activities with industry (and to do so through channels that included much more than patenting and licensing) long before the Bayh-Dole Act's passage.

The collaboration between university and industrial researchers, combined with the focus of many US university researchers on scientific problems with important industrial, agricultural, or other public applications, meant that a number of US universities patented faculty inventions throughout the 20th century. Nevertheless, despite the adoption by a growing number of universities of formal patent policies by the 1950s, many of these policies, especially those at medical schools, prohibited patenting of inventions, and university patenting was far less widespread than was true of the post-1980 period. Moreover, many universities chose not to manage patenting and licensing themselves. The Research Corporation, founded in 1912 by Frederick Cottrell, a University of California faculty inventor who wished to use the licensing revenues from his patents to support scientific research, assumed a prominent role as a manager of university patents and licensing. Even in these early decades of patenting and licensing, however, biomedical technologies accounted for a disproportionate share of licensing revenues for the Research Corporation and other early university licensors, such as the Wisconsin Alumni Research Foundation (Mowery and Sampat, 2001b).

The decade of the 1970s, as much as or more so than the 1980s, represented a watershed in the growth of US university patenting and licensing. US universities expanded their patenting, especially in biomedical fields, and assumed a more prominent role in managing their patenting and licensing activities, supplanting the Research Corporation. Agreements between individual federal agencies and universities also contributed to the expansion of patenting during the 1970s. Private universities in particular began to expand their patenting and licensing rapidly during this decade. The number of universities establishing technology transfer offices and/or hiring technology transfer officers began to grow in the late 1960s, well before the passage of the Bayh-Dole Act. Although the Act was followed by a wave of entry by universities into management of patenting and licensing, growth in these activities was apparent by the late 1970s. Indeed, lobbying by US research universities was one of several factors behind the passage of the Bayh-Dole Act in 1980. The Act therefore is as much an effect as a cause of expanded patenting and licensing by US universities during the post-1960 period.

The Bayh-Dole Patent and Trademark Amendments Act of 1980 provided blanket permission for performers of federally funded research to file for patents on the results of such research and to grant licenses for these patents, including exclusive licenses, to other parties. The Act facilitated university patenting and licensing in at least two ways. First, it replaced a web of Institutional Patent Agreements (IPAs) that had been negotiated between individual universities and federal agencies with a uniform policy. Second, the Act's provisions expressed Congressional support for the negotiation of exclusive licenses between universities and industrial firms for the results of federally funded research.

Supporters of Bayh-Dole asserted that university contributions to innovation were limited by difficulties in patenting the outputs of federally funded research and licensing the patents exclusively to industry. This argument was particularly salient during the competitiveness crisis in the US during the 1970s, in spite of the failure of proponents of Bayh-Dole to offer much evidence in its support (see Eisenberg, 1996; Mowery et al., 2004). Moreover, the Bayh-Dole debates included no discussion of any potentially negative effects of increased patenting and licensing on the other channels through which universities contribute to innovation and economic growth.

The passage of the Bayh-Dole Act was one part of a broader shift in US policy toward stronger intellectual property rights.[1] Among the most important of these policy initiatives was the establishment of the Court of Appeals for the Federal Circuit (CAFC) in 1982. Established to serve as the court of final appeal for patent cases throughout the federal judiciary, the CAFC soon emerged as a strong champion of patentholder rights.[2] But even before the establishment of the CAFC, the 1980 US Supreme Court decision in *Diamond* versus *Chakrabarty* upheld the validity of a broad patent in the new industry of biotechnology, facilitating the patenting and licensing of inventions in this sector. The origins of Bayh-Dole thus must be viewed in the context of this larger shift in US policy toward intellectual property rights.

A number of scholars have documented the role of Bayh-Dole in the growth of patenting and licensing by universities since 1980 (Henderson et al., 1998). But Bayh-Dole is properly viewed as initiating the latest, rather than the first, phase in the history of US university patenting. And this latest phase is characterized by a higher level of direct involvement by universities in management of their patenting and licensing activities, in contrast to the reluctance of many US universities to become directly involved in patenting prior to the 1970s. Public universities were more active in patenting than private institutions during much of the pre-Bayh-Dole era, reflecting the strong incentives that they faced to reap the benefits of university research for local taxpayers and the importance of applied research at many of these institutions. By the 1970s, however, both public and private universities had become directly involved in patenting.

The effects of Bayh-Dole

How did the Bayh-Dole Act affect patenting by US universities? Since overall patenting in the US grew during this period, indicators of university patenting need to be normalized by overall trends in patenting and R&D spending. Figures 1 and 2 present two such indicators that span the period before and after the Bayh-Dole Act. Figure 1 depicts US research university patenting as a share of domestically assigned US patents during 1963–1999, in order to remove the effects of increased patenting in the US by foreign firms and inventors during the late 20th century. Universities increased their share of patenting from less than 0.3% in 1963 to nearly 4% by 1999, but the rate of growth in this share begins to accelerate before rather than after 1980. Figure 2 plots the ratio of aggregate university patenting at time t to aggregate academic R&D expenditures at time $t-1$, for application years 1963–1993.[3] The Figure reveals an increase in aggregate university "patent propensity" after 1981 (as pointed out by Henderson et al., 1998), but this is the continuation of a trend that dates at least as far back as the early 1970s; there is no evidence of a "structural break" in trends in patent propensity after Bayh-Dole.[4]

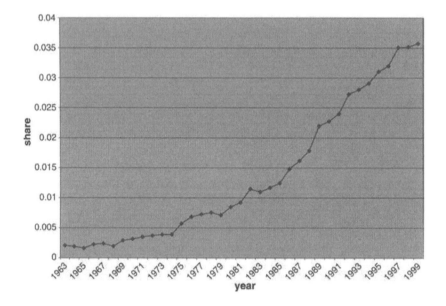

Figure 1. US research univ. patents % of all domestic-assignee US patents, 1963–1999.

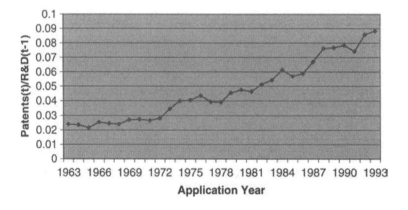

Figure 2. University patents per R&D Dollar, 1963–1993.

Another issue of interest in academic patenting is the distribution among technology fields of university patents during the pre- and post-Bayh-Dole periods. Figure 3 displays this information for US research university patents during 1960–1999, and highlights the growing importance of biomedical patents in the patenting activities of the leading US universities during the period. Non-biomedical university patents increased by 90% from the 1968–1970 period to the 1978–1980 period, but biomedical university patents increased by 295%. This rapid growth in biomedical patents also reflected growth of the IPA program of the major biomedical funding agency (HEW) during the 1970s. The increased share of biomedical disciplines within overall federal academic R&D funding, the dramatic advances in biomedical science that occurred during the 1960s and 1970s, and the strong industrial interest in the results of this biomedical research, all affected the growth of university patenting during this period.

After Bayh-Dole, universities increased their involvement in managing patenting and licensing, setting up internal technology transfer offices to manage licensure of university patents. Figure 4 shows the distribution of years of "entry" by universities into patenting and licensing, defined as the year in which the universities first devoted 0.5 FTE employees to "technology transfer activities" (AUTM, 1998). Although "entry" accelerated after Bayh-Dole, growth in this measure of university commitment to "technology transfer" predates Bayh-Dole. Longitudinal data on university licensing activities are less complete, but the available data indicate that in FY2000, US universities signed more than 4000 license agreements, representing more than a doubling since FY1991 (AUTM, 2000).

Based on these trends in university patenting and licensing, many observers have argued that Bayh-Dole was a major catalyst to university–industry technology transfer. During the late 1990s and early 21st century, many commentators and policymakers portrayed the Bayh-Dole Act as the critical catalyst to growth in US universities' innovative and economic contributions. Indeed, the OECD went so far as to argue that the Bayh-Dole Act was an important factor in the remarkable growth of incomes, employment, and productivity in the US economy of the late 1990s.[5] Implicit in many if not all of these characterizations is the argument that university patenting and licensing in particular were necessary to these asserted increases in the economic contributions of US university research.[6] Similar characterizations of the effects of the Bayh-Dole Act have been articulated by the President of the

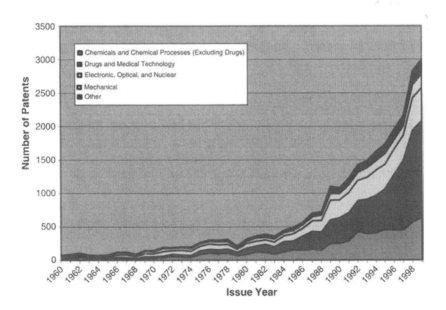

Figure 3. Technology field of carnegie university patents, 1960–1999.

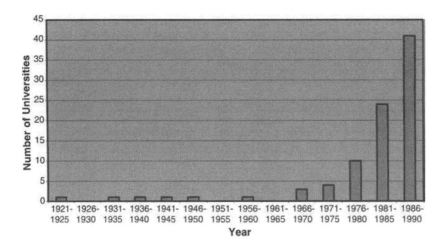

Figure 4. Year of "Entry" into technology transfer activities.

Association of American Universities,[7] the Commissioner of the US Patent and Trademark Office,[8] and the *Technology Review*, edited and published at MIT.[9]

These characterizations of the positive effects of the Bayh-Dole Act cite little evidence in support of their claims beyond simple counts of university patents and licenses. But growth in both of these activities predates Bayh-Dole and is rooted in internationally unique characteristics of the US higher education system. Nor does evidence of increased patenting and licensing by universities by itself indicate that university research discoveries are being transferred to industry more efficiently or commercialized more rapidly, as Colyvas et al. (2002) and Mowery et al. (2001) point out. Current research thus provides mixed support at best for a central assumption of the Bayh-Dole Act, i.e., the argument that patenting and licensing are necessary for the transfer and commercial development of university inventions.

In addition, of course, these "assessments" of the effects of the Bayh-Dole Act fail to consider potentially negative effects of the Act on US university research or innovation in the broader economy. Some scholars have suggested that the "commercialization motives" created by Bayh-Dole could shift the orientation of university research away from "basic" and towards "applied" research (Henderson et al., 1998), but there is little evidence of substantial shifts since Bayh-Dole in the content of academic research. Since US university patenting and licensing before and after 1980 has been concentrated in a few fields of research, notably biomedical research, a field characterized by blurry lines between "basic" and "applied" research, this finding should not come as a great surprise.

A second potentially negative effect of increased university patenting and licensing is a weakening of academic researchers' commitments to "open science," leading to publication delays, secrecy, and withholding of data and materials (Dasgupta and David, 1994; Liebeskind 2001). There are indications in this research on university patenting and licensing that the "disclosure norms" of academic research in specific fields have been affected by increased faculty patenting, but more research on this issue is needed. Moreover, the Bayh-Dole Act is not solely responsible for any such changes in disclosure norms—increased opportunities for commercial gain from basic research in such fields as academic biotechnology, as well as the overall strengthening of intellectual property rights in the US, are not themselves directly linked to Bayh-Dole. Nonetheless, given the importance assigned by industrial researchers to the "nonpatent/licensing" channels of interaction with universities in most industrial sectors, it is crucially important that these channels not be constricted or impeded by the intensive focus on patenting and licensing in many universities.

Finally, the effects of any increased assertion by institutional and individual inventors of property rights over inputs to scientific research have only begun to receive serious scholarly attention. Patenting and restrictive licensing of inputs into future research ("research tools") could hinder downstream research and product development (Heller and Eisenberg, 1998; Merges and Nelson, 1994).

Although there is little compelling evidence as yet that the Bayh-Dole Act has had negative consequences for academic research, technology transfer, and industrial innovation in the US, the data available to monitor any such effects are very limited. Moreover, such data are necessarily retrospective, and in their nature are likely to reveal significant changes in the norms and behavior of researchers or universities only after a long lag. Any negative effects of Bayh-Dole accordingly may reveal themselves only well after they first appear.

4. International "emulation" of the Bayh-Dole Act

Although the evidence on the effects of the Bayh-Dole Act suggests that its "catalytic" effects on university–industry technology transfer are limited, a number of other OECD governments are considering or have adopted policies emulating the Act's provisions.[10] In Denmark, a 1999 law gave public research organizations, including universities, the rights to all inventions funded by the Ministry for Research and Technology. Under Denmark's previous policy (established in 1957), all such rights had reverted to employees (OECD, 2003). The German Ministry for Science and Education in 2002 altered the "professor's privilege," which gave academic researchers primary responsibility for the decision to file for patent protection on inventions and granted them the rights to any resulting patents. The new policy requires that academic inventors inform their employers of potentially patentable inventions two months before papers disclosing such inventions are submitted for publication, and grants universities four months to determine whether they wish to file for patent protection.[11] In France, a 1999 law authorized the creation of technology transfer offices at universities, and in 2001 the Ministry of Research "recommended" that universities and public research organizations establish policies to assert their rights to employee inventions (OECD, 2003). The Canadian Prime Minister's "Expert Panel on the Commercialization of University Research" recommended in 1999 that universities retain ownership of inventions resulting from publicly funded research, and "be held accountable for maximizing returns to Canada," noting that "the proposed IP policy framework will inspire a transformational shift in culture within Canadian universities, as happened in the US with the passage of the Bayh-Dole Act in 1980" (Public Investments in University Research, p. 28).[12]

In varying degrees all of these initiatives cite Bayh-Dole as one justification. Nevertheless, they in fact differ significantly from the Act, which sought to transfer ownership for publicly funded inventions from government agencies to universities and other nonprofits. In contrast to Bayh-Dole, all of the policies described in the previous paragraph, along with similar new policies in other European countries (e.g., Austria, Ireland, and Spain) "have focused on changing employment laws so that university professors are no longer exempted from legislation that gives employers the IP generated by employees" (OECD, 2003, p. 11), and seek to transfer ownership from individual inventors to universities.[13] Similarly, the "Japanese Bayh-Dole Act" of 1999 shifted ownership from individual inventors to universities (http://www.nsftokyo.org/rm04-05.html). These initiatives thus ignore one of the central justifications for Bayh-Dole, i.e., that government ownership of publicly funded inventions impedes their commercialization.

In addition to changes in intellectual property policy an employment regulations, a number of related initiatives aim to stimulate the organization and activity of technology licensing offices. Thus the Swedish, German, and Japanese governments (among others) have encouraged the formation of external "technology licensing organizations," which may or may not be affiliated with a given university (see Goldfarb and Henrekson, 2003, for a comparison of Bayh-Dole and Swedish initiatives to enhance university–industry technology transfer).

As this discussion suggests, these initiatives to emulate Bayh-Dole differ from one another and from Bayh-Dole itself. The policy proposals and initiatives display the classic signs of international emulation—selective "borrowing" from another nation's policies for implementation in an institutional context that differs significantly from that of the nation being emulated. Nonetheless, these initiatives are based on the belief that university patenting was an essential vehicle for effective transfer of technology from universities to industry and that Bayh-Dole was essential to the growth of university–industry interaction in science-based industries in the US during and after the 1980s. These views appear to be based on a misreading of the limited evidence concerning the effects of Bayh-Dole, however, and on a misunderstanding of the factors that have encouraged the long-standing and relatively close relationship between US universities and industrial innovation. More importantly, like Bayh-Dole itself, these initiatives focus narrowly on the "deliverable" outputs of university research, and ignore the effects of patenting and licensing on the other, more economically important, channels through which universities contribute to innovation and economic growth.

In as much as patenting and licensing are of secondary importance in most fields, emulation of the Bayh-Dole Act is insufficient and perhaps even unnecessary to stimulate higher levels of university–industry interaction and technology transfer. Instead, reforms to enhance inter-institutional competition and autonomy within national university systems, as well as support for the external institutional contributors to new-firm formation and technology commercialization, appear to be more important.

Indeed, emulation of Bayh-Dole actually could be counterproductive in other industrial economies, precisely because of the importance of other channels for technology transfer and exploitation by industry. A narrow-minded focus on licensing as the primary or only channel for technology transfer can have a chilling effect on the operation of other important channels. There are potential risks to the university research enterprise that accompany increased involvement by university administrators and faculty in technology licensing and commercialization, and uncritical emulation of Bayh-Dole in a very different institutional context could intensify these risks.

5. Conclusion

The relationship between US university research and innovation in industry is a long and close one. Both organized industrial research and the US research university first appeared in the late 19th century and have developed a complex interactive relationship. The unusual structure of the US higher education infrastructure, which blended financial autonomy, public funding from state and local sources with federal research support, and substantial scale, provided strong incentives for university faculty and administrators to focus their efforts on research activities with local economic and social benefits. Rather than being exclusively concerned with fundamental scientific principles, much of US university research throughout the late 19th and 20th centuries focused on understanding and solving problems of agriculture, public health, and industry.

US universities have made important contributions to industrial innovation throughout the past century, not least through by combining advanced research and education. The strong links between education and research sustained a close relationship between the evolving scientific research agenda and problems of industry or agriculture, while at the same time providing a powerful and effective channel (in the form of trained students) for the transfer and application of much of this knowledge to industry and other economic sectors. In addition, many university researchers in engineering and medical schools maintained close ties with the users of their research and their graduates in industry, medical practice, and agriculture. The important role of universities in industrial innovation, particularly during the post-1945 period, also relied on institutions external to the university, including venture capitalists, equity-based financing of new firms, and high levels of labor mobility between academia and industry.

Based on these considerations, we believe that much of the growth in licensing and university-based "spinoffs" that has occurred since the passage of the Bayh-Dole Act almost certainly would have occurred in the absence of this piece of legislation. After all, US universities were active patenters and licensors for decades before 1980, and much of their patenting and licensing activity since 1980 has been highly concentrated in a few fields, at least some of which also have benefited from rapid growth in public research funding and significant advances in basic science.

The Bayh-Dole Act thus appears to have been neither necessary nor sufficient for much of the post-1980 growth in university patenting and licensing in the US. Moreover, given the very different institutional landscape in the national higher education systems of much of Western Europe and Japan, it seems likely that the "emulation" of Bayh-Dole that has been discussed or implemented in many of these economies is far from sufficient to trigger significant growth in academic patenting and licensing or university–industry technology transfer. Indeed, there is some question as to the necessity of a "patent-oriented" policy to encourage stronger research collaboration and technology transfer. And the potential risks associated with such policy changes have received too little attention.

Notes

1. According to Katz and Ordover (1990), at least 14 Congressional bills passed during the 1980s focused on strengthening domestic and international protection for intellectual property rights, and the Court of Appeals for the Federal Circuit created in 1982 has upheld patent rights in roughly 80% of the cases argued before it, a considerable increase from the pre-1982 rate of 30% for the Federal bench.
2. See Hall and Ziedonis (2001) for an analysis of the effects of the CAFC and related policy shifts on patenting in the US semiconductor industry.
3. Data on total academic R&D were obtained from National Science Board (2000), Appendix Table 4-4.
4. As we have pointed out elsewhere (Mowery et al., 2001) The Bayh-Dole Act did not dramatically affect the patenting and licensing activities of universities that had long been active in this area, such as Stanford University and the University of California. Indeed, the biomedical patents and licenses that dominated these institutions' licensing revenues during the 1980s and 1990s had begun to grow before the passage of the Bayh-Dole Act. Columbia University, an institution with little experience in patenting and licensing before 1980 (and an institution that prohibited the patenting of inventions by medical faculty until 1975), also had filed for its first "blockbuster" patent before the effective date of the Act. Nevertheless, the Act did increase patenting of faculty inventions at both Stanford and the University of California, although many of these patents covered inventions of marginal industrial value and did not yield significant licensing royalties.
5. "Regulatory reform in the US in the early 1980s, such as the Bayh-Dole Act, have [sic] significantly increased the contribution of scientific institutions to innovation. There is evidence that this is one of the factors contributing to the pick-up of US growth performance ⋯" (OECD, *A New Economy?*, 2000, p. 77).
6. "Possibly the most inspired piece of legislation to be enacted in America over the past half-century was the Bayh-Dole Act of 1980. Together with amendments in 1984 and augmentation in 1986, this unlocked all the inventions and discoveries that had been made in laboratories throughout the US with the help of taxpayers' money. More than anything, this single policy measure helped to reverse America's precipitous slide into industrial irrelevance. Before Bayh-Dole, the fruits of research supported by government agencies had gone strictly to the federal government. Nobody could exploit such research without tedious negotiations with a federal agency concerned. Worse, companies found it nigh impossible to acquire exclusive rights to a government owned patent. And without that, few firms were willing to invest millions more of their own money to turn a basic research idea into a marketable product." (Economist, 12/14/02).
7. "In 1980, the enactment of the Bayh-Dole Act (Public Law 98-620) culminated years of work to develop incentives for laboratory discoveries to make their way to the marketplace promptly, with all the attendant benefits for public welfare and economic growth that result from those innovations. Before Bayh-Dole, the federal government had accumulated 30,000 patents, of which only 5% had been licensed and even fewer had found their way into commercial products. Today under Bayh-Dole more than 200 universities are engaged in technology transfer, adding more than $21 billion each year to the economy."
8. "In the 1970s, the government discovered the inventions that resulted from public funding were not reaching the marketplace because no one would make the additional investment to turn basic research into marketable products. That finding resulted in the Bayh-Dole Act, passed in 1980. It enabled universities, small companies, and nonprofit organizations to commercialize the results of federally funded research. The results of Bayh-Dole have been significant. Before 1981, fewer than 250 patents were issued to universities each year. A decade later universities were averaging approximately 1000 patents a year."
9. "The Bayh-Dole Act turned out to be the Viagra for campus innovation. Universities that would previously have let their intellectual property lie fallow began filing for – and getting patents at unprecedented rates. Coupled with other legal economic and political developments that also spurred patenting and licensing, the results seems nothing less than a major boom to national economic growth."
10. A recent OECD report (2003) argues that these initiatives "echo the landmark Bayh-Dole Act of 1980" (11).
11. The new policy aims to ensure that "more inventions are brought to patent offices before they get published" and "is

supposed to lead to active licensing transfer from university to industry and to more companies being founded on the basis of intellectual property conceived within the university environment" (Kilger and Bartenbach, 2002).

12. Although no uniform government policy governs the treatment of university inventions in the United Kingdom, "there is now an increasing trend for Universities to claim ownership" over academic inventions (Christie et al., 2003 p. 71).

13. In contrast to these initiatives, Italy passed legislation in 2001 that shifted ownership from universities to individual researchers. According to Breschi et al. (2004), this policy change has "the declared intention of finally providing the right economic incentives for individual scientists to undertake "useful" (that is "patentable") research" (2).

References

Association of University Technology Managers (AUTM), 1998, *AUTM Licensing Survey 1998, Survey Summary.* Norwalk, CT: AUTM.

Association of University Technology Managers (AUTM), 2000, *The AUTM Licensing Survey: FY 1999*, Association of University Technology Managers.

Breschi, S., F. Lissoni, and F. Montobbio, 2004, Open Science and University Patenting: A Bibliometric Analysis of the Italian Case Mimeo.

Christie, A.F., S.D 'Aloisio, K.L. Gaita, M.J. Howlett, and E.M. Webster, 2003, 'Analysis of the Legal Framework for Patent Ownership in Publicly Funded Research Institutions,' Commonwealth of Australia, Division of Education, Science, and Training.

Cohen, W.M., R.R. Nelson, and J.P. Walsh, 2002, 'Links and Impacts: The Influence of Public Research on Industrial R&D,' *Management Science* **48**, 1–23.

Colyvas, J.M. Crow, A. Gelijns, R. Mazzoleni, R. R. Nelson, N. Rosenberg, and B.N. Sampat, 2002, 'How Do University Inventions Get into Practice?' *Management Science* **48**, 61–72.

Dasgupta, P. and P. David, 1994, 'Towards a New Economics of Science,' *Research Policy* **23** (5), 487–521.

Eisenberg, R., 1996, 'Public Research and Private Development: Patents and Technology Transfer in Government-Sponsored Research,' *Virginia Law Review* **82**, 1663–1727.

Eisenberg, R, 2001, 'Bargaining over the Transfer of Proprietary Research Tools: Is This Market Emerging or Failing?,' in D.L. Zimmerman, R.C. Dreyfuss, and H. First, (eds.), *Expanding the Bounds of Intellectual Property: Innovation Policy for the Knowledge Society*, New York: Oxford University Press.

Geiger, R. 1986, *To Advance Knowledge: The Growth of American Research Universities, 1900–1940*, New York: Oxford University Press.

Geiger, R.L., 1993, *Research And Relevant Knowledge : American Research Universities Since World War II*, New York: Oxford University Press.

Government University Industry Research Roundtable (GUIRR), 1991, *Industrial Perspectives on Innovation and Interactions with Universities*, Washington, DC: National Academy Press.

Hall, B.H. and R.H. Ziedonis, 2001, 'The Patent Paradox Revisited: An Empirical Study of Patenting in the US Semiconductor Industry, 1979–95,' *RAND Journal of Economics* **32** (1), 101–128.

Heller, M.A. and R.S. Eisenberg, 1998, 'Can Patents Deter Innovation? The Anticommons in Biomedical Research,' *Science* **280**, 298.

Henderson, R., A.B. Jaffe, and M. Trajtenberg, 1998, 'Universities as a Source of Commercial Technology: A Detailed Analysis of University Patenting, 1965–88,' *Review of Economics & Statistics* **80**, 119–127.

Henderson, R., A.B. Jaffe, and M. Trajtenberg, 1998, 'University Patenting Amid Changing Incentives for Commercialization,' in G. Barba Navaretti, P. Dasgupta, K.G. Mäler and D. Siniscalco (eds.), *Creation and Transfer of Knowledge*, New York: Springer.

Innovation's Golden Goose, 2002, *The Economist* **365**, T3.

Katz, M.L. and J.A. Ordover, 1990, 'R&D Competition and Cooperation,' *Brookings Papers on Economic Activity: Microeconomics*: 137–192.

Kilger, C. and K. Bartenbach, 2002, 'New Rules for German Professors,' *Science* **298**, 1173–1175.

Levin, R.C., A. Klevorick, R.R. Nelson and S. Winter, 1987, 'Appropriating the Returns from Industrial Research and Development,' *Brookings Papers on Economic Activity* **3**, 783–820.

Liebeskind, J., 2001, 'Risky Business: Universities and Intellectual Property,' *Academe* **87**.

Mansfield, E., 1991, 'Academic Research and Industrial Innovations,' *Research Policy* **20**, 1–12.

Merges, R. and R. Nelson, 1994, 'On Limiting or Encouraging Rivalry in Technical Progress: The Effect of Patent Scope Decisions,' *Journal of Economic Behavior and Organization* **25**, 1–24.

Mowery, D.C., R.R. Nelson, B.N. Sampat, and A.A. Ziedonis, 2001, 'The Growth of Patenting and Licensing by US Universities: An Assessment of the Effects of the Bayh-Dole Act of 1980,' *Research Policy* **30**, 99–119.

Mowery, D.C. and B.N. Sampat, 2001a, 'Patenting and Licensing University Inventions: Lessons from the History of the Research Corporation,' *Industrial and Corporate Change* **10**, 317–355.

Mowery, D. C. and B.N. Sampat, 2001b, 'University Patents, Patent Policies, and Patent Policy Debates, 1925–1980,' *Industrial and Corporate Change* **10**, 781–814.

Mowery, D.C., R.R. Nelson, B.N. Sampat, and A.A. Ziedonis, 2004, *Ivory Tower and Industrial Innovation: University Industry Technology Transfer Before and After Bayh-Dole*, Stanford University Press.

National Science Board, 2000, *Science and Engineering Indicators*, Washington, D.C.: U.S. Government Printing Office.

OECD, 2000, *A New Economy?* Paris: OECD.

OECD, 2003, *Turning Science Into Business: Patenting and Licensing at Public Research Organizations*, Paris: OECD.

Reimers, N., 1998, Stanford's Office of Technology Licensing and the Cohen/Boyer Cloning Patents, An Oral History Conducted in 1997 by Sally Smith Hughes, Ph.D., Regional Oral History Office, Berkeley, CA: The Bancroft Library, U.C. Berkeley.

Rosenberg, N, 1998, 'Technological Change in Chemicals: The Role of University–Industry Relations,' in A. Arora, R. Landau and N. Rosenberg (eds.), *Chemicals and Long-Term Economic Growth*, New York: John Wiley.

Rosenberg, N. and R.R. Nelson, 1994, 'American Universities and Technical Advance in Industry,' *Research Policy* **23**, 323–348.

Trow, M., 1979, 'Aspects of Diversity in American Higher Education,' in H. Gans (ed.), *On the Making of Americans*, Philadelphia: University of Pennsylvania Press.

Trow, M., 1991, 'American Higher Education: "Exceptional" or Just Different,' in B.E. Shafer (ed.), *Is America Different? A New Look at American Exceptionalism*, New York: Oxford University Press.

Financing Constraints in the Inter Firm Diffusion of New Process Technologies

Alessandra Canepa[1]
Paul Stoneman[2]

ABSTRACT. This paper explores why finance constraints may impact upon the inter firm diffusion of new technology, incorporates these arguments in a hazard rate formulation of a diffusion model and then estimates that model using data relating to the adoption of CNC machine tools in the UK. The results indicate that financial constraints can be a significant factor in the diffusion process.

Key words: technological diffusion, CNC, financial constraints

JEL Classification: O3

1. Introduction

Ed Mansfield stands with Zvi Griliches as a founding father of diffusion analysis in Economics. Even today, 40 years on, it is impossible to properly work in this field without referring back to Mansfield's path breaking work in the 1960s as published in Mansfield (1968). This body of work stresses that diffusion is a process driven, or at the least conditioned by, economic factors, a finding that over the years has been extended and elaborated upon but not refuted (see, for example, Hall, 2004). In one of his earliest diffusion papers, Mansfield (1963), the intra firm diffusion of new technology (in this case diesel engines) was modelled and certain firm level financial variables were included as potential determinants of the diffusion process. In particular a measure of firm liquidity (the ratio of the firm's current assets to liabilities in the 2 years prior to when it began to dieselize) was found to have a positive and significant impact upon intra firm diffusion. Although this result suggests that financial factors (defined to encompass all issues relating to the funding of those capital expenditures that are a part of the technological diffusion process) may play a role in the diffusion process, later diffusion research has not tended to pick up on Mansfield's lead, and has instead somewhat ignored this line of enquiry (Stoneman, 2001). This is despite the fact that within the literature upon investment in general (Hubbard, 1998) and even R&D (Hall, 2002) there has been a growing emphasis upon the importance of financial factors and constraints. In this paper we partially correct that omission by exploring the impact of financial constraints upon the inter (rather than intra) firm diffusion of a new process technology. We initially discuss the rationale for expecting finance constraints to have an impact and then incorporate these arguments in a reasonably standard hazard rate formulation of a diffusion model and estimate that model using data relating to the adoption of CNC machine tools in the UK.

In the following Section we discuss the nature of financial constraints and the reasons why they might exist and in Section 3 the existing empirical evidence relating to their existence and patterns. In Section 4 a diffusion model that can test for the existence of such constraints in the inter firm diffusion process is proposed and we discuss the data and estimation methods to be employed in that testing. The results are presented and discussed in Section 5 and conclusions offered in Section 6.

---

[1] University of York
Department of Economics and Department of Mathematics
Heslington, York YO10 5DD
United Kingdom
E-mail: ac48@york.ac.uk

[2] Warwick Business School, University of Warwick
Coventry CV4 7AL
United Kingdom
E-mail: paul.stoneman@warwick.ac.uk

2. What are financial constraints and why might they exist?

According to Hall (2002) a financial constraint is said to exist when, even if there are no externalities involved in the firm's investment activity, there is a wedge (perhaps even a large wedge) between the rate of return required by an entrepreneur investing his own funds and that required by external investors. Stiglitz and Weiss (1981) consider a firm to be credit rationed if it does not get as much credit as it wants although it is willing to meet the conditions set by the lender on equivalent credit contracts. In essence therefore a firm is credit or financially constrained if it cannot raise external funding at the market price or in order to raise external funding it has to pay over the market price.

There are many reasons postulated as to why such financial constraints might exist. These are reviewed in Canepa and Stoneman (2003) as well as in Hall (2002). The existence of uncertainty and thus risk is a *sine qua non* of such constraints. Beyond this, the most commonly argued reasons for such constraints are asymmetric information between borrower and lender and moral hazard resulting from the separation of ownership and control, although capital market incompleteness and inefficiency, taxes, subsidies, bankruptcy costs, and the problems of measuring risk may also have roles to play. The literature argues that the importance and relevance of such financial constraints may differ across firm sizes, industries and countries.

Smaller firms may be relatively more tightly constrained because (i) the availability of internally generated funds may be more limited for smaller firms than larger firms (ii) problems of information asymmetries for small firms may also be more severe (iii) smaller, newer firms may have no track record upon which to base a case for funding and/or there may be fewer realisable assets to use as collateral and (iv) the costs (to funding providers) of search may mean also that the supply of finance to smaller firms is more severely limited.

Differences across industries may also exist so that, for example, firms in high-tech and newer industries may face stricter constraints to raising external (and internal) funding either in terms of cost and/or availability. This is because: (i) in riskier industries it may be more difficult to raise funding from outside the firm purely because of the risk factor; (ii) in more high-tech sectors not only may risk itself be a factor but also the proportion of assets that are realisable may be lower; (iii) in high-tech industries innovation is more likely to be of a sort that has not been undertaken before elsewhere and it may be particularly difficult to observe the systematic risk of such projects (Goodacre and Tonks, 1985) and thus difficult to determine the appropriate discount rate to use in evaluating investments in the firm; and (iv) information asymmetries may also be greater in such industries.

Differences in national systems of innovation (see Nelson, 1993) across countries may lead to differing financial constraints upon firms operating in different economies (as the result, for example, of differing taxes and subsidy regimes, the completeness of markets for finance, the legal environment as regards bankruptcy, government intervention etc.). Of particular interest are differences in the financial environments in different countries (Mayer, 1990). Financial environments are both heterogeneous and changing. On the one hand, there are bank-based systems as typified by the German system and on the other, market-based systems as typified by the UK or US system. Most continental European systems are largely bank-based although there are signs of some movement in certain countries (e.g. France) from a bank-based to a market-based system. Alongside these different financial system environments there are different patterns of ownership of industry. The German system, for example, reflects greater private control, more concentrated ownership and more pyramid ownership. In the UK the pattern is for less concentrated holdings, less private control and few inter-corporate holdings. The financing of investment by firms also differs across systems. Although self-generated funds are the main finance sources for firms in all countries (except perhaps for SMEs) these are more important in the UK, for example, whereas bank finance is more important in bank-based systems.

It is argued that such differences across systems have important implications for the way firms behave. The argument is that bank-based systems with insider control are particularly favourable to longer term steady development built upon the construction of trust-based relations, firm-specific investments and gradual continual change but may generate a higher cost of capital due to bank monopoly power, informational capture (of the firm by the bank) and perhaps undue conservatism. On the other hand market-based systems with outsider control and more arms-length relationships between financiers and managers are seen as more favourable to major change and switches of strategic direction (but with no obligation for financiers to take anything other than a short-term view, encouraging liquidation of investment in the event of dissatisfaction). These arguments lead us to believe that firms will be differentially affected by financial constraints under different national financial systems.

The above discussion relates to investment in general in plant and machinery and/or R&D. However the diffusion process has a number of characteristics that might lead one to consider that financial issues will perhaps play a more important role in that process than investment in general. In particular:

- Given that diffusion is concerned with doing something new the extent of uncertainty attached to a diffusion process may be greater than that attached to replication of existing activities. For example Stoneman and Toivanen (2000) show that across countries, investment in robot technologies shows much greater volatility than investment in machine tools in general. This higher level of uncertainty may exacerbate for the diffusion of new products and processes any problems that exist in raising finance for investment. It may also cause problems in determining the appropriate cost of capital in that for new projects it may be difficult to determine the systematic risk of similar projects as there are no similar projects.
- As diffusion is concerned, by definition, with new technologies, it may well be that the suppliers and users of those technologies are much more aware of their true nature and characteristics than potential financiers. Such information asymmetries may lead to credit rationing and or difficulties for the firm in raising external finance.
- The diffusion process will generate (and require funding to acquire) a number of assets that may well be intangible, and/or firm specific (e.g. learning economies of various kinds, knowledge from search, and/or product goodwill). Such assets may not be realisable in the event of bankruptcy and/or may not be appropriately valued by the market. Once again this may make raising external finance problematic especially for firms without other assets that may act as collateral (unless, and this is possible taking a creative destruction viewpoint, successful diffusion causes losses in the value of other assets).

Taken together these factors suggest that finance constraints may play a major role in the diffusion process with firms possibly being credit rationed.[1] The importance of this role may differ across firm sizes, industries and countries.

3. Financial constraints to innovation: the evidence

There is a growing body of empirical research relating to the relationship between finance and investment in plant and machinery and or innovation (largely measured by R&D). The two main strands in the literature investigate (i) the sensitivity of the investment rate to cash flow (ii) the results of innovation questionnaire surveys.

The correlation between cash flow and investment is usually investigated by estimating a standard investment demand function (see, for example, the surveys by Hall, 2002 and Hubbard, 1998). Three main approaches can be identified:

- estimating a dynamic neoclassical accelerator model in which the profit maximizing firm equates the marginal cost of capital to the marginal product (see, for example, Carpenter and Petersen, 2002; and Fazzari et al., 1988 for the US, Devereux and Schiantarelli, 1989 for the UK).
- estimating an Euler equation derived for the profit-maximizing firm without including the shadow value of capital among the regressors (see, for example, Bond et al., 2003).
- estimating directly the investment demand function where the shadow value of capital is proxied by a VAR forecast of firm fundamentals observable to the econometrician (see, for example, Bond, et al., 1999).

These methodologies have been applied to investment data for a number of different countries. Overall the voluminous literature presents strong empirical evidence of a correlation between cash flow and investment in plant and machinery and/or R&D. For example, an early paper, Fazzari et al. (1988) found that cash flow tends to affect the investment of low-dividend firms more than that of high dividend firms leading them to conclude that finance rationing matters. An example of the later literature is Carpenter and Petersen (2002) who find that for small, quoted firms in the US, the sensitivity of growth to cash flow of firms that use external equity is lowered. Bond et al. (2003)[2] estimate accelerator, error correction model and Euler equations for different countries. Although they find that the simple accelerator equations tend to exaggerate the importance of financial variables relative to richer dynamic specifications, they also find robust results across all econometric models indicating that the sensitivity of investment to financial variables (and thus the importance of financial constraints) is both statistically and quantitatively more significant in the UK than in France, Germany or Belgium.

In contrast, Kaplan and Zingales (1997) have argued that studies such as those cited above which estimate the sensitivity of investment to cash flow are fundamentally flawed in that such sensitivities are unable to reflect financial constraints in an unbiased manner. However, the empirical evidence on the relationships between finance, investment and innovation has been further augmented and extended through the analysis of innovation survey data. Canepa and Stoneman (2003) for example explore Community Innovation Survey (CIS) questionnaire response data to investigate whether European firms consider themselves to be financially constrained in their innovative activity. They find that (i) the cost of finance or the availability of finance ranks among the more significant factors that have acted as hindrances to innovation in Europe, both in 1994–1996 and 1998–2000; (ii) the probability that a firm's innovative activity will be financially constrained is greater for small firms than for medium and larger firms, in the latter case there being only minor differences between the UK and other countries; (iii) when firms are constrained such that their innovative activity is delayed or reduced, then financial factors (the cost or availability of finance) are more likely to have a high (as opposed to medium or low) impact for small firms than for large firms. Their results also confirm that differences in financial systems also matter: the market-based economies (e.g. the UK) exhibit greater sensitivity of innovation to financial constraints than bank-based economies (e.g. Germany).

Further research also suggests that capital market imperfections affect firms more in high-tech industries than in traditional sectors.[3] For example, Westhead and Storey (1997) examine the relative importance of several potential problems faced by high-tech SMEs. Their multivariate analysis on a sample of UK firms shows that technologically sophisticated high-tech firms were significantly more likely to report the presence of a continued financial constraint than less high-tech firms. In a similar study of italian high-tech firms, Giuduci and Paleari (2000) confirm that 50% of the sample companies experienced difficulties in financing their innovative projects. The work of Canepa and Stoneman (2003) confirms these findings and extends them to the majority of European countries.

To summarise, although there is not universal agreement (see, for example, Wagenvoort, 2003), the overview of various empirical studies relating to investment in plant and machinery and R&D suggest that (Hall, 2002):

- small firms are more likely to be financially constrained in their investment activity;
- firms (especially small and start-up firms) in R&D intensive industries face a higher cost of capital;[4]
- the evidence for a financing gap for large and established firms is harder to establish; and
- the Anglo Saxon economies, with their thick and developed stock markets and relatively transparent ownership structures typically exhibit greater sensitivity of investment to cash flow than continental economies.

Despite the various studies of investment in plant and machinery and in R&D there is very little evidence directly relating to the role of financial factors in the diffusion of new technology. Differences in diffusion rates across countries are notoriously difficult to measure (Canepa and Stoneman, 2004) and to the best of our knowledge there has been no explicit testing of the impact of different financial regimes on different national diffusion experiences. The empirical work on diffusion as surveyed in Stoneman (2001) indicates that there is clear evidence that larger firms are earlier adopters and smaller firms are later adopters, which is consistent with smaller firms being finance constrained. Generally however this is attributed to scale economies rather than financial factors. Davies (1979) shows differences in the diffusion of simple and complex technologies. Stoneman and Toivanen (2000) show that uncertainty has an impact upon the diffusion process. Both observations would be consistent with financing difficulties in the face of uncertainty, however, such results are rarely considered to be the result of financial factors. One of the very few pieces of evidence available to us is that Mansfield (1968) explicitly incorporated a liquidity term (measured as the ratio of the firms current assets to liabilities) in an empirical diffusion equation explaining the intra firm spread of diesel locomotives in US railroads and found a positive and significant coefficient.

4. A model

On the basis of the arguments above the diffusion of new technology will probably not be independent of financial factors. The rest of this paper is directed towards an empirical analysis of the role of such financial factors or constraints. However the impact of such factors may differ across firms (according to, for example, size), technologies (reflecting complexity and cost), industries (reflecting technological state and/or competitiveness) countries (reflecting national systems of innovations) and time (reflecting experience and information asymmetries).

Empirical analysis of these issues is itself however constrained. Although it would have been most informative to have data across several countries such data is not generally available (see, Stoneman and Canepa, 2004). The empirical analysis below is thus restricted to one country, the UK. In addition efforts are concentrated upon one technology, Computer Numerically Controlled machine tools (CNC), this being reasonably well defined and a technology for which higher quality data is available. CNC first appeared in the early 1970s and by incorporating micro computer technology into numerically controlled machines provided the capability of automatic and flexible machining. CNC also facilitated the introduction of flexible automation systems (Cainarca et al., 1990; Mansfield, 1995). Suitable data is only available as regards inter firm rather than intra firm diffusion. The empirical analysis thus addresses the inter firm diffusion of CNC machine tools in the UK. This topic has been analysed before using the same data set but without inclusion of financial constraints (Karshenas and Stoneman, 1993, where further data details can be found).

The data that we employ was collected in three surveys undertaken by the Centre for Urban and Regional Development Studies of the University of Newcastle upon Tyne (CURDS) in 1980, 1986 and 1993 of a given sample of establishments (some stand-alone that we label firms, some part of multi establishment organisations that we label groups) in the UK engineering and metalworking industry. Although our analysis of this data may be better described as a study of inter establishment diffusion, to relate more closely to the existing literature we continue to talk throughout of inter firm diffusion, assuming[5] each establishment to be an autonomous decision making unit which we label the firm.

The surveys[6] contain information on the date at which each firm in the sample first adopted CNC. They also contain longitudinal data on establishment characteristics,[7] such as employment in 1970–1975, 1981, 1985 and 1993, year of start-up, information on R&D, whether the firm is export oriented, as well as on certain managerial and technological characteristics of the firm.

By 1993 the proportion of potential users[8] that have adopted CNC is about 80%. The revealed time profile of the whole inter firm diffusion of CNC is illustrated in Figure 1. Of the 1993 sample of 343 firms, 222 had adopted CNC at or before 1993 of whom 212 were still users in 1993 (i.e. 10 were no longer users by 1993).

The data set is quite rich and as it offers firm level data the best use of that data will be if the analysis is also undertaken at the firm level. We

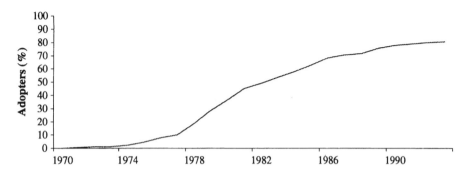

Figure 1. The Inter Firm diffusion of a new technology: CNC machine tools in the UK.

thus proceed using a hazard rate adoption model as previously employed by Hannan and Macdowell (1984) and Karshenas and Stoneman (1993). Specifically, it is assumed that the probability that a firm j will adopt a new technology at time t, conditional on not having previously adopted, is determined by a vector of covariates x_j, reflecting the costs and benefits of adoption. Defining t_j (measured from a start date $t_0 = 1981$) as the date of adoption by firm j, the estimated survival model[9] is

$$\ln(t_j) = x_j\beta_x + \ln(\tau_j), \qquad (1)$$

where τ_j is distributed as a Weibull. In order to check the parametric specification of the model the cumulative hazard function based on the non parametric Kaplan–Meier estimator was computed. The plot of the Kaplan–Meier estimates against the Cox–Snell residuals suggested that the Weibull model fitted the data better than the exponential model. Model (1) has been estimated by maximum likelihood with the likelihood function given by

$$L_j(\beta_x, \Theta) = \frac{\{\Omega(t_j|x_j\beta_x, \Theta)\}^{1-d_j}\{f(t_j|x_j\beta_x, \Theta)^{d_j}\}}{\Omega_0(t_0|x_j\beta_x, \Theta)}, \qquad (2)$$

where $f(t) = pt^{p-1}\exp(-t^p)$ is the density function of the Weibull distribution and $\Omega(t) = \exp(-t)^p$ the corresponding survivor function. The parameters β_x, and the ancillary parameters $\Theta = (\beta_0, p)$, (where β_0 is the scale parameter and p is the shape parameter) are estimated from the data. The triple (t_j, d_j, x_j) summarises the survival experience (i.e. the probability of adoption after time t) for each plant in the sample: i.e. if the plant did not adopt during the period $t_0 < t < t_j$, then at $t = t_j$ the firm either adopted ($d_j = 1$) or was censored ($d_j = 0$). If $d_j = 0$ then (2) gives the probability that the firm does not adopt from 1981 to t_j. if $d_j = 1$ then (2) is the probability of adopting at time t_j. The denominator $\Omega_0(t_0|x_j\beta_x, \Theta)$ gives the probability of not adopting up to time t_0, so when $t_0 = 1981$ then $\Omega_0(t_0|x_j\beta_x, \Theta) = 1$, for $t_0 < t < t_j$.

To apply the model requires specification of the elements of the vector x_j. The key issue addressed in this paper is the impact of financial constraints and thus although the procedure is disputed (Kaplan and Zingales, 1997) a cash flow variable is included as an element in x_j and the sensitivity of adoption times to this variable is interpreted as an indicator of the impact of financial constraints. The only variable available in the data set to reflect cash flow is the pre-tax profit, in £ 100s, declared by firms in time t, $\pi_{t,j}$.

As inter firm analysis addresses whether firms invest in CNC or not, and the size of the investment necessary to meet this requirement need not differ across different sized firms, this variable is introduced without the correction for firm size that is common in the standard investment literature. As cash flow data were not available before 1981 the sample was restricted to those firms that had not adopted CNC before 1981 yielding a usable panel of 87 establishments for 10 years of whom 25 adopt in the sample period.

The other control variables to be introduced in to the vector x_j were determined using both the literature as a guide and data availability as a constraint.[10] Many different combinations were tried and many empirical models were estimated. The results presented below relate to the most parsimonious of these models. The variables that have remained are as follows.

P_t, the quality adjusted factory gate price of CNC technology deflated by the retail price index at time t, reflecting the costs of adoption. Price data on CNC machine tools was supplied by the Office of National Statistics (ONS) but unfortunately for a number of years the data for CNC and NC (its previous non-computerised version) were not separately distinguished. The adjustment for quality has been carried out using a modified version of the hedonic price approach whereby, given that data upon CNC generations are not available, the quality change was approximated by the trend in the quality improvements of computers outsourced from Triplett (1989) and Stoneman et al. (1992). Further details can be found in Battisti (2000).

$S_{t,j}$, the size of the establishment given by the number of employees at time t sourced from the CURDS survey. This variable is usually considered as a proxy for several other factors, particularly scale and the relative risk faced by different-sized firms (see, for example, Karshenas and Stoneman, 1993). An alternative turnover measure of firm size was also tried without any significant impact on the results.

ST_j, a dummy variable taking the value one if the firm is an independent unit and zero if the establishment is part of a corporate "group", reflecting the possible impact of both internally sourced information relating to technology performance and technological competencies (and may also pick up whether there are different degrees of autonomy for firms that are independent as opposed to being part of a group) (see Astebro, 2002; Cainarca et al., 1990; and Dunne, 1994).

A dummy variable, RD_j, that takes the value unity if the number of employees engaged full time in R&D at time t is positive and zero otherwise. An alternative measure, the number of employees engaged full time in R&D at time t, was correlated with firm size. This variable reflects innovativeness (see, for example, Hall, 2004).

ED_j, the difference in years between time t and the date of start up of the establishment reflecting experience and perhaps vintage effects (see Karshenas and Stoneman, 1993).

I_j, a vector of dummies reflecting the industry within engineering and metalworking to which the establishment belonged (see Dunne, 1994).

Table I reports descriptive statistics on the explanatory variables described above.

5. Estimates

The estimating equation is given by

$$\ln(t_j) = \beta_0 + \beta_1 \pi_j + \beta_2 P_j + \beta_3 RD_j + \beta_4 ED_j + \beta_5 S_j + \beta_6 ST_j + \beta_7 I_j + \beta_7 I_j + \ln(\tau_j).$$

The model in (3) contains three dichotomous covariates (ST_j, ED_j, RD_j) plus industry dummies and three continuous variables (π_j, P_j, S_j). In order to test if the log-time ratio is linear in the covariates we used the fractional polynomial method suggested by Royston and Altman (1994).[11]

The analysis indicates that the best non-linear transformations are not significantly different from the linear model for P_t and $\pi_{t,j}$ but suggests the following specification for the variable $S_{t,j}$

$$S_{t,j,1} = (S_{t,j}/100)^{-2}, \quad S_{t,j,2} = S_{t,j,1} \times \ln(S_{t,j}/100).$$

In our unrestricted initial estimates $\pi_{t,j}$, P_t, $S_{t,j,1}$, $S_{t,j,2}$, ST_j all carried coefficients significantly different from zero.[12] However, the industry dummies were not significant and were dropped. The conventional 0.05 p-value for the covariates RD_t and ED_j suggested that these covariates did not

TABLE I
Descriptive statistics

	Mean	Std. Dev.	Min.	Max.
π_j	424.07	1022.04	−800	8000
P_j	103.32	4.240	99.88	109.45
RD_j	0.784	0.412	0	1
ED_j	31.32	156.86	1	89
S_j	117.34	0.412	1	950
ST_j	0.260	0.439	0	1
I_j	7.230769	2.99	1	13

exert a significant influence on the speed of adoption (their *p*-values being 0.057 and 0.068, respectively) although both carried positive signs. Although there is a growing literature showing (see Mickey and Greenland, 1989, for example) that strict adherence to the 0.05 *p*-value as a screening criterion for variable selection often fails to identify variables known to be important, parsimony in model specification has particular advantages in term of parameter stability. RD_t and ED_j thus were also excluded. The results of fitting the final restricted model are reported in Table I. The main difference compared to the estimates including RD_t and ED_j is that the coefficient on ST_j in the unrestricted estimates is increased by 45% and on P_t reduced by 13% (in absolute value) but the other estimated coefficients do not change significantly.

From Table II the estimated coefficient on P_t, the real quality adjusted price of CNC, is negative, with a 10-unit increase in the real price index producing a reduction in the estimated date of adoption by $0.91 = \exp[10 \times (-0.092)]$—a reduction of 9%.

The coefficient on ST_j implies that if the firm is independent rather than a member of a group the speed of adoption is reduced by about 0.5% (i.e. $0.995 = \exp[(-0.0046)]$). Both $S_{t,j,1}$ and $S_{t,j,2}$ carry positive coefficients (in line with results in the existing literature). However, given that the estimated time-ratio ($\widehat{TR}$) is modelled as a non-linear function of establishment size, $\widehat{TR}$ changes with $S_{t,j}$. The $\widehat{TR}$ resulting from five-unit increases in plant size has been calculated as follows. Let z denoted the vector of the fixed variables; then the estimated difference in the log-time function is obtained by evaluating

$$g(S_j + 5, \mathbf{z}) - g(S_j, \mathbf{z}) = a\gamma_1 + b\gamma_2,$$

where $a = ((S_{j,1} + 5) - S_{j,1})$ and $b = ((S_{j,2} + 5) - S_{j,2})$, and from Table I we have $\gamma_1 = 0.0039$ and $\gamma_2 = 0.00085$. The estimated survivor function corresponding to the accelerated failure time form of the hazard function in (2) is

$$\Omega(t, x, \boldsymbol{\beta}, p) = \exp\left\{-t^{-\beta_0/p} \exp\left[-p^{-1}(\beta_0 + (a\hat{\gamma}_1 + b\hat{\gamma}_2))\right]\right\},$$

by evaluating the survivorship function at the 50% quantile and solving for time we obtain

$$t_{50}(S_j, \boldsymbol{\beta}, p) = [-\ln(0.5)]^p e^{\beta_0 + (a\hat{\gamma}_1 + b\hat{\gamma}_2)}$$

so that the time-ratio at the median survival time is

$$TR(S_j + 5, S_j, \mathbf{z}) = \frac{[-\ln(0.5)]^p e^{\beta_0 + (\gamma_1(S_{1,j}+5) + \gamma_2(S_{2,j}+5))}}{[-\ln(0.5)]^p e^{\beta_0 + (\gamma_1 S_{1,j} + \gamma_2 S_{2,j})}} = e^{(a\hat{\gamma}_1 + b\hat{\gamma}_2)}.$$

Figure 2 shows how $\widehat{TR}$ changes as a result of a five-unit increase in establishment size keeping all the other covariates fixed. The estimated time-ratios increase quite rapidly with size up to unity at a threshold of around 60 employees, above which the marginal effect of size on the time of adoption seems to vanish. Such a non-linearity in the impact of size on the probability of adoption has not been emphasised in the literature before. The pattern suggests that the ratio of the benefits to the cost of adoption

TABLE II
Estimated coefficients for the restricted model, robust standard errors, *z*-Scores, *p*-value, 95% and confidence intervals

T	Coef.	Rob. Std. Err.	z	P > z	[Conf.	Interval]
$S_{t,1}$	0.00393	0.000021	191.16	0.0000	0.0039	0.0040
$S_{t,2}$	0.00085	0.000005	175.75	0.0000	0.0008	0.0009
P_t	−0.00916	0.000109	−83.81	0.0000	−0.0094	−0.0089
ST_t	−0.00457	0.000193	−23.66	0.0000	−0.0049	−0.0042
π_t	0.00245	0.000459	5.34	0.0000	0.0016	0.0034
Cons	5.46810	0.015116	361.75	0.0000	5.4385	5.4977
ln(p)	3.24265	0.065580	49.45	0.0000	3.1141	3.3712

Log Likelihood = −757.868, LR test: Pr ($\chi^2(5) > 12.02$) = 0.034.

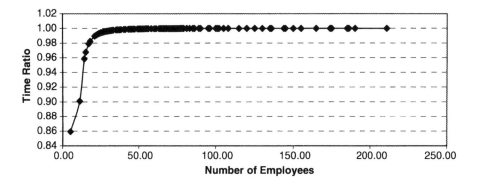

Figure 2. Estimated time ratio for five-unit increases in size as a function of firm size.

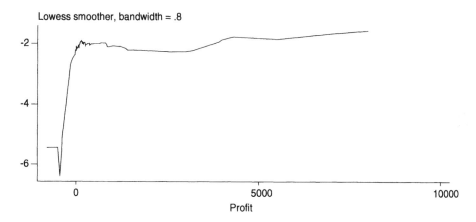

Figure 3. Univariate lowess smoothed logit scatterplot of CNC adoption versus π_j.

increases quite rapidly with size but only up to quite a low threshold.

The profit variable, our proxy for financial constraints, carries a positive and highly significant estimated coefficient, indicating that financial constraints have a significant impact upon the diffusion of new technology. The estimates indicate that a £ 100 increase in profit produces an estimated time ratio of approximately 1.00245, which is an increase in the speed of adoption of approximately 0.0025%. Testing for the interaction $\pi_{t,j} \times ST_j$ failed to give significant results, suggesting that it is establishment rather than group cash flow that matters.

To further explore the relationship between profit and CNC adoption we compute the lowess smoothed weighted average of d_j (d_j takes the value unity if the plant adopted at time t and zero otherwise) over the $\pi_{t,j}$.[13] The resulting pattern, illustrated in Figure 3, shows that the logit initially increases sharply in the profit level when profit is negative or around zero but the rate of growth of the logit is much lower when profit is positive.

This pattern suggests that in exploring the impact of financial factors upon adoption it is the difference between profit and loss that is most important. A firm that is registering negative profits is much less likely to adopt new technology than a firm making positive profits. The two obvious reasons for this are that a loss making firm: (i) will have less internal funding available for investment; and (ii) will be giving a negative signal to outside lenders and thus find it more difficult to borrow.

6. Conclusions

The literature on the diffusion of new technology has largely ignored any impact that financial factors may have upon the process whereby new technology spreads across its potential market. This is in contrast to the general literature on investment in plant and machinery and R&D where there is a growing body of evidence that financial factors do act as a constraint upon investment spending.

In this paper we have proposed a reasonably standard hazard rate formulation of an adoption model incorporating therein a cash flow covariate to reflect financial constraints and, using the example of CNC adoption in the UK metal working and engineering industry, shown empirically that such constraints have a significant impact upon the rate at which new technologies are adopted. This is confirmation in the inter firm context of a proposition first made and tested by Mansfield in the intra firm context in 1963.

Our findings suggest that the financial constraints largely impact upon firms near the break-even point and that for more profitable firms there are no such constraints. This non-linearity is also apparent in the impact of firm size upon adoption rates. The non-linearity with respect to profitability however makes policy prescriptions difficult. If there are financial constraints then government assistance to overcome such constraints appears appropriate. However, if the constraints mainly bind upon firms that are only marginally profitable, there would be considerable problems in separating out those firms that are temporarily suffering ill fortune but merit support in the adoption of new technology from those that are inefficient and for whom support is likely to be wasted.

Acknowledgment

This work has been financed under the Fifth EU Framework Programme, Contract No. HPSE-CT-1999–00039 with additional financial support provided under the project "The Euro, SMEs and Banks" by the the Department of Economics, University of Western Piedmont.

Notes

1. There is the possibility that as the diffusion process proceeds these problems will be ameliorated. For example, an increasing number of projects may help in determining systematic risk, information asymmetries may reduce and learning and intangible assets may decline in relative importance.
2. See also Bond, Harhoff, and Van Reenan (1999).
3. In reviewing the financial environment in which European SMEs operate, the European Commission (2000), using a very different methodology, argues that SMEs do face specific problems in accessing finance and early stage enterprises in particular face the most severe financial constraints.
4. Although we do not know of any particular evidence that this is true risk adjusted.
5. We do not have any data available that would generate any advantage from doing otherwise.
6. Between 1980, 1986 and 1993, the survey experienced considerable sample attrition as UK manufacturing industry declined. In a previous paper, Karshenas and Stoneman (1993) have shown that this sample attrition is independent of whether new technology was adopted and thus the attrition will not cause bias.
7. We would like to thank Guiliana Battisti who provided the actual data used.
8. The sample of potential users excludes from the full sample those firms who consider that the technology is not appropriate to their production activities (59 of the 343).
9. For an excellent reference on survival models see, for example Kalbfleisch and Prentice, 1980.
10. A number of experiments with additional independent variables were also undertaken but provide little further insight and are thus not reported here.
11. Denoting $x_{t,j}$ as the continuous covariate of interest, this method involves estimating by maximum likelihood the following set of equations

$$\ln(t_j) = \delta_0 + \sum_{i=1}^{m} G_i(x_j)\delta_i$$

where $G_1(x_{j,t}) = x_t^{n_1}$ (for $N \in \{-2, -1, -0.5, 0, 0.5, 1, 2, 3\}$). The remaining power functions are defined as $G_i(x_j) = \begin{cases} x_j^{n_i}, & n_i \neq n_{i-1} \\ G_{i-1}(x_j)\ln(x_j) & n_i = n_{i-1} \end{cases}$ for $i = 2,\ldots, m$ and $\{n\}$. The best model is chosen on the base of likelihood ratio test. The results on the LR test are available from the authors on request.
12. The LR test comparing the model to the saturated model rejects the null hypothesis that the estimated coefficients are equal to zero.
13. The lowess smoothed weighted average of d over $\pi_{t,j}$ has been calculated as follows. Let $\bar{d}_j$ the logit transformation for d_j the and assume that $d_j \leq d_{j+1}$ for $j = 1,\ldots, N-1$. For each we $d_{l,j}$ we compute a smoothed value $d_{l,j}^s$

$$\bar{d}_j^s = \frac{\sum_{j=i_l}^{i_u} w(\pi_i, \pi_j)\bar{d}_j}{\sum_{j=i_l}^{i_u} w(\pi_i, \pi_j)},$$

where $w(x_i, x_j)$ represents the weight function, i_l and i_u include the bandwidth k = 0.8 (see Cleveland (1979) for more details).

References

Astebro, T., 2002, 'Non-capital Investment Costs and the Adoption of CAD and CNC in US Metalworking Industries,' *RAND Journal of Economics* **Winter** 33 (4), 672–688.

Battisti, G., 2000, *The Intra-Firm Diffusion of New Technologies*, PhD Thesis, Warwick University.

Bond, S., J.A. Elston, J. Mairesse, and B. Mulkay, 2003, 'Financial Factors and Investment in Belgium, France, Germany and the UK: A Comparison using Company Panel Data', *Review of Economics and Statistics* **85** (1), 153–165.

Bond, S., H. Harhoff, and J. Van Reenen, 1999, 'Investment, R&D and Financial Constraints in Britain and Germany,' IFS Working Paper No. 99/5.

Cainarca, G., M.G. Colombo, and S. Mariotti, 1990, 'Firm Size and the Adoption of Flexible Automation,' *Small Business Economics* **2**, 129–140.

Canepa, A. and P. Stoneman, 2003, *Financial Constraints to Innovation in the UK and Other European Countries: Evidence from CIS2 and CIS3*, paper presented at a CIS user group conference, Modelling Innovation, DTI Conference Centre, London.

Carpenter, R.E. and B.C. Petersen, 2002, 'Is the Growth of Small Firms Constrained by Internal Finance?' *The Review of Economics and Statistics* **84** (2), 298–309.

Cleveland, W.S., 1979, 'Robust Locally Weighted Regression and Smoothing Scatterplots' *Journal of the American Statistical Association* **74**, 829–836.

Davies, S., 1979, *The Diffusion of Process Innovation*, Cambridge: Cambridge University Press.

Devereux, M. and F. Schianterelli, 1989, 'Investment, Financial Factors and Cash flow: Evidence from UK Panel Data,' NBER Working Papers No. 3116, New York: NBER.

Dunne, T., 1994, 'Plant Age and Technology Use in the U.S. Manufacturing Industries,' *RAND Journal of Economics* **Autumn**, **25** (3), 488–499.

European Commission, 2000, *The European Observatory for SMEs, Sixth Report*, Executive Summary, Enterprise Policy, Brussels.

Fazzari, S., R.G. Hubbard, and B. Petersen, 1988, 'Finance Constraints and Corporate Investment,' *Brookings Papers on Economic Activity* **1**, 141–195.

Goodacre, A. and I. Tonks, 1985. 'Finance and Technological Change,' in P. Stoneman (ed.), *Handbook of the Economics of Innovation and Technological Change*, Oxford: Blackwells, pp. 298–341.

Giudici, G. and S. Paleari, 2000, 'The Provision of Finance to Innovation: A Survey Conducted Among Italian Technology-Based Small Firms,' *Small Business Economics*, **14**, 37–53.

Hall, B., 2004, 'Innovation and Diffusion,' NBER Working Paper, No. 10212, Cambridge, MA: NBER.

Hall, B., 2002, 'The Financing of Research and Development,' *Oxford Review of Economic Policy* **18**, 35–51.

Hannan, T.H. and J.M. Mcdowell, 1984, 'The Determinants of Technology Adoption: The Case of the Banking Firm,' *RAND Journal of Economics* **15**, 328–335.

Hubbard, R.G., 1998, 'Capital Market Imperfections and Investment,' *Journal of Economic Literature* **36**, 193–225.

Kalbfleisch, J.D. and R.L. Prentice, 1980, *The Statistical Analysis of Failure Time Data*, New York: John Wiley & Sons.

Karshenas, M. and P. Stoneman, 1993, 'Rank, Stock, Order and Epidemic Effects in the Diffusion of New Process Technologies: An Empirical Model,' *RAND Journal of Economics* **24** (4), 503–528.

Kaplan, S. and L. Zingales, 1997, 'Do Investment Cash Flow Sensitivities Provide Useful Measures of Financing Constraints,' *Quarterly Journal of Economics* **112**, 169–215.

Mansfield, E., 1963 'Intrafirm Rates of Diffusion of an Innovation,' *The Review of Economics and Statistics* **XLV**, 348–359.

Mansfield, E., 1968, *Industrial Research and Technological Innovation*, New York: Norton.

Mayer, C.P., 1990 'Financial Systems, Corporate Finance and Economic Development,' in R.G. Hubbard, (ed.), *Asymmetric Information, Corporate Finance and Investment*, Chicago: NBER, and University of Chicago Press.

Mickey, J. and S. Greenland, 1989, 'A Study of the Impact of Confounder-Selection Criteria on Effect Estimation,' *American Journal of Epidemiology* **129**, 125–137.

Nelson, R., 1993, (ed.), *National Innovation Systems: A Comparative Analysis*, Oxford: Oxford University Press.

Royston, P. and D.G. Altman, 1994, 'Regression Using Fractional Polynomials of Continuous Covariates: Parsimonious Parametric Modelling,' *Applied Statistics*, **43**, 429–467.

Stiglitz, J. and A. Weiss, 1981 'Credit Rationing in Markets with Imperfect Information,' *American Economic Review* **71** (3), 393–410.

Stoneman, P., 2001, *The Economics of Technological Diffusion*, Oxford: Blackwells.

Stoneman, P. and A. Canepa, 2004, 'Comparative International Diffusion: Patterns, Determinants and Policies,' *Economics of Innovation and New Technology* **13** (3), 279–298.

Stoneman, P. and O. Toivanen, 2000, *Technological Diffusion Under Uncertainty: A Real Options Model Applied to the International Diffusion of Robot Technology*. presented at a Conference in Honour of Paul David, Turin, May 19–21, 2000.

Stoneman, P., D. Bosworth, D. Leech, and D. McCausland, 1992, 'Quality Adjusting the Producer Price Index for Computers in the UK,' *Report to the Central Statistical Office* 1–45.

Triplett, J., 1989, 'Price and Technological Change in a Capital Good. A survey on Computers,' in D. Jorgenson and R. Landau, (eds.), *Technology and Capital Formation*, Cambridge, MA: MIT Press.

Wagenvoort, R., 2003, 'SME finance in Europe, Introduction and Overview,' *EIB Papers* **8** (2), 11–20.

Westhead, P. and D.J. Storey, 1997, 'Financial Constraints on the Growth of High Technology Small Firms in the United Kingdom,' *Applied Financial Economics* **7**, 197–201.

Ed Mansfield and the Diffusion of Innovation: An Evolutionary Connection

J. S. Metcalfe

ABSTRACT. The analysis of the diffusion of innovation was a central theme in Ed Mansfield's work over many years. In this essay I summarise his analysis of logistic diffusion processes and relate his work to earlier studies of industrial retardation and subsequent work on evolutionary economic processes. A distinction has to be drawn between the logistic law and the logistic curve, the latter being only one instantiation of the more general law which is itself a signature of evolutionary selection processes within a population of rival innovations.

Key words: innovation diffusion, logistic law, evolutionary process

JEL Classification: D23, O31, O32, O33

1. Introduction

Ed Mansfield was an acknowledged pioneer in the study of technological change and its wider economic consequences. Along with Zvi Griliches, Dick Nelson and Chris Freeman he was a premier source of inspiration to the generation of scholars who began to study technical change in the 1960s. In terms of the range of his interests, the sharpness of the questions he posed and his willingness to gather the detailed micro data that is needed to make sense of technological change, he had few peers in his generation. Others have written extensively about his work (Diamond, 2003; Scherer, 2005); in this short essay I want to relate his contribution to the wider framework of evolutionary economic analysis for, unwittingly or not, it is to this field that Mansfield made a major contribution particularly though his work

ESRC Centre for Research on Innovation and Competition
School of Economic Studies
University of Manchester
U.K.
E-mail: Stan.Metcalfe@man.ac.uk

on the spread of new technology. The connection to evolutionary ideas is through Mansfield's use of the logistic curve, one of a ubiquitous family of "S" curves to which scholars have turned to summarize the evolutionary dynamics of the spread of innovations. Less well known is the fact that behind the logistic curve lies a more general logistic law describing the relative diffusion of competing innovations in a population of technologies that serve some common economic purpose. It is the logistic law that predisposes population dynamics to generate logistic curves when the diffusion data are plotted over time. The logistic has for many years been a standard tool of analysis in evolutionary ecology (Kingsland, 1985) and in evolutionary economics it is a way of capturing the dynamic response of a market system to the opportunities opened up by economic variation in the form of sequences of innovations. In this brief essay, I shall explore two particular aspects of Mansfield's work on diffusion, in relation to the further developments in diffusion theory that it stimulated, and in terms of the longer sequences of evolutionary economics that pre-date and post-date Mansfield's work. It turns out that Mansfield's work is closely connected to wider questions subsequently studied by evolutionary economists, indeed that the logistic law, the logistic process and the logistic curve are characteristic signatures of competitive selection processes in the presence of economic variation. In short, I shall argue that logistic phenomena are deeply embedded in competitive evolutionary processes but that these processes do not generate in general a logistic curve when the diffusion data is plotted over time. The logistic law and the logistic curve must be separated conceptually, and only in special cases will the later follow from the former. Indeed the logistic curve is a very special case of the more general logistic law, which is perhaps why there exists a whole family of "S" curves, Gompertz, log-logistic, log normal etc., that can provide good competing, empirical summaries of the diffusion process. The deeper content of the logistic process it turns out is that it is a natural consequence of a population approach to evolutionary dynamics.

The modern literature on innovation diffusion is immense not only in economics but in marketing management and in technological forecasting and I don't propose to review it at all.[1] However, some brief assessment of the Mansfield approach will help the subsequent discussion.

2. Mansfield on innovation diffusion

Amongst the most influential of his papers are the studies of the spread of new technology, for as he put it "Once an invention is introduced for the first time, the battle is only partly won, since it must still gain widespread acceptance and use. The rate of diffusion is of great importance. The full social benefits of an innovation will not be realised if its use spreads too slowly" (1971, p. 133). Here Mansfield identifies themes of great importance in his future work; that the economic and social payoffs from innovations depend on the diffusion of those innovations, a problem in economic dynamics, that there might be an optimal rate of diffusion which ultimately would determine the private and social returns from investments in practical knowledge and in its more abstract underpinnings in science and basic engineering.

Here I propose to focus on the 1961 paper on the diffusion of innovation since most of his subsequent ideas and studies on innovation diffusion remain framed by this seminal paper. Mansfield begins with a question "Once a new technique is introduced into an industry by a firm how quickly will others make use it?" His answer is grounded in Schumpeter's distinction between the initial innovator and the subsequent swarm of imitators who carry the innovation to its full economic significance. By taking 12 innovations in 4 industries and using data gathered from major firms he observes that the rate of adoption is generally slow with wide variations across the innovations. Clearly this is a problem in dynamic adjustment, and Mansfield's general approach to the problem is that the spread of new technology is part of a market process which sets the dynamic context in which producers and users respond to new technological opportunities. He suggests it is a process of learning, and thus of the growth of knowledge in the market context, in which producers and users improve the innovations in focus and, when they are stabilised, then shift their attention to improving the associated process technology. This is a theme that has been explored in depth in the subsequent product and technology life cycle literature (Utterback, 1994) but it is clearly contained in Mansfield's general approach, albeit in a form subdued relative to the questions to which he devoted most attention. Among these questions the three most important are "What factors explain the different rates at which innovations spread?" "What factors explain the rates at which different firms adopt innovations at different times?" and "What factors determine the speed with which a given firm substitutes new methods for old in its operations?" The answer to the first question is of course a logical extension of the second and third although the three are often treated separately. In the 1961 paper, for example, the focus is on the first question and we find that it takes 5–10 years on average before half the firms in an industry begin using an important innovation and in many cases longer, although there are wide variations around the average. On the basis of this framework one is led to a number of important distinctions. The diffusion of innovation should be distinguished from the adoption of innovation, the latter relating to the decisions by firms to incorporate an innovation in their activities, the former to the economic importance of an innovation as measured by, for example, the proportion of the output of an industry that is produced with a given innovation. Adoption obviously influences diffusion but it is the latter that embodies the economic impacts of an innovation on employment, rates of return and the competitive process. Indeed, the wider significance of these phenomena is that they provide the link between innovation and productivity growth in particular and economic growth in general. Adoption between firms is distinguished from adoption within firms since it may take many years for a firm to completely adjust its methods of production to a new innovation and, of course, the overall rate of diffusion will depend on the product of the inter-firm and intra-firm adoption rates. In a subsequent study of railroad dieselization, for example, Mansfield reports that of 30 randomly chosen railroads over 70% took more than eight years to fully adopt the innovation while 10% took more than 14 years.[2]

The characteristic feature of Mansfield's explanation of these findings is that they relate to decisions to invest by the respective firms. His innovations are typically capital goods innovations, new plant or equipment, and so the variables used to explain adoption behaviour are profitability and capital cost in some form together with a range of ancillary variables, (durability of the capital equipment is one such) that rarely find statistical significance. Thus Mansfield's principal, deterministic model twins together the theory of adoption and a theory of investment.[3] How does it work?

The explanation is built around a two stage procedure. In the first stage, he begins by defining a measure of the change in the number of adopting firms in some time interval, expressed as a proportion of the firms that had yet to adopt at the beginning of the interval. This measure of the change in "holdouts" is made to depend functionally on the proportion of firms that have adopted by the beginning of the interval (the current adoption rate), and the investment and other variables noted above. This functional dependence is approximated by a Taylor expansion in which terms of third and higher order are dropped and an initial condition is set.[4] The combination of these assumptions leads to the conclusion that the change in the number of adopting firms is defined by a logistic process with constant parameters relating to the maximum number of potential adopters of the innovation, the intrinsic rate at which adoption increases and the initial condition. The outcome is a predicted logistic curve for the diffusion process which is then fitted successfully to the data for the various innovations to obtain in particular an estimate of the intrinsic adoption rate. Having established a logistic curve as the characteristic signature of the adoption process, Mansfield moves to the second stage to explain the differences in the intrinsic rates of adoption by reference to the investment variables and finds that profitability and capital cost typically account for nine tenths of the statistical variation in the intrinsic adoption rates. In further elaborations, the durability of equipment, the rate of expansion of the adopting firm, and the phase of the business cycle are not found to provide any improvement in the statistical explanation of the cross innovation rates of adoption. This is Mansfield's general approach which he used in numerous other studies including ones where it is the diffusion rate rather than the adoption rate that is investigated.[5] In these other studies the theory of investment is embellished to consider the effects of market structure, firm and industry characteristics such as R&D expenditure, liquidity, and the dispersion of the profitability of adoption but always within the same broad framework.

The methods may look crude by today's standards but in the 1960s they were truly path breaking even acknowledging the caveats that Mansfield always applied to the quality of his data. Anyone interested in the penumbra of topics related to the spread of new technology could not but be influenced by Mansfield's work. His influence on the study of technical change was profound.[6] Almost half a century on, "What are we to make of this as a framework for explaining adoption and diffusion?" Clearly a great deal. Mansfield's insights on the link between investment and adoption have been modified by others but the broad approach remains intact. This is not to say that it cannot be improved upon as a consideration of the following issues shows.

The first general problem is that, *pace* Mansfield, there is no particular reason to expect that the parameters of the logistic process should remain constant over the adoption or diffusion process. Although the underlying process is logistic for given parameters there would be a branch of a different logistic curve for each set of those parameters and so the overall envelope of these branches need not be logistic. As Geroski (2000) points out, many empirical diffusion curves are positively skewed with an inflection point at less than half the saturation level of diffusion as, for example, with a Gompertz curve, and this degree of skewness may simply reflect the rate of time variation of the key parameters. The lesson here is simple but important; even if the underlying dynamic process is a logistic process its realization over time may not trace an exact or "naïve" logistic curve. For example, if the saturation level is growing exponentially then ultimately the intrinsic rate of diffusion rate must converge to that same exponential rate. Similarly, if the saturation level is increasing also as a logistic curve then the compound diffusion curve may appear as a logistic built on a logistic, not as a simple logistic curve.[7] Consequently, we cannot deduce the nature of the underlying dynamics simply from an observation of the shape of the diffusion curve.

This is one matter when the supposed changes in parameters are exogenous but quite another when they are varying endogenously because of the diffusion process itself. Then the ensuing diffusion envelope and the variables explaining diffusion rates are generated simultaneously by the diffusion process and again it may or may not be realized in a logistic curve even when the underlying dynamics are logistic.[8] Two broad kinds of factors may produce this result. The first recognizes that diffusion and adoption are not exclusively demand side phenomena, the capacity to supply the innovation is a coequal factor in determining the rates of adoption and diffusion. The rate of diffusion must, in general, depend on the supply capacity of the industry making the innovation and, unless this is perfectly elastic, the parameters of the diffusion process will reflect a mix of demand and supply side forces.[9] As a consequence, the economic characteristics of different innovations may be expected to vary over the diffusion process as capacity to supply is kept in balance with the growth of demand. In Mansfield's terms, both the capital cost of the innovation and the profitability of adopting the innovation will vary endogenously during the diffusion process and indeed are explained by that diffusion process in such a manner that the rates of diffusion and the values of the investment variables co-evolve. The parameters of the resulting diffusion curve have to be interpreted in terms of some amalgam of supply and demand influences, which is entirely consistent with Mansfield's general point about diffusion being embedded in market processes.[10]

The second broad set of factors that extend Mansfield's approach reflect post-innovation improvements in a technology. Any innovation is usually the prelude to a sequence of improvements, major or minor, many of which follow through learning effects by suppliers and users.[11] What is being diffused is not usually a single innovation but rather a design opportunity in which the evolution of design is not invariant to the process of diffusion but reflects diffusion induced learning. Moreover, it is misleading to focus solely on the innovation that is being diffused and thereby lose sight of any improvements that may follow from the rival technologies that it seeks to displace. The sailing ship effect has long been recognised by scholars of technical change but it should really be part of every study of innovation diffusion. Diffusion curves then reflect endogenous rates of improvement across the population of competing innovations not only improvements in the innovation that is the focus of attention. The obvious conclusion is that market and technology co-evolve and that innovation induced diffusion induces innovation.[12]

The above is only a small selection of the theoretical and empirical issues stimulated by Mansfield's pioneering work but they are sufficient to underpin the point that a logistic process and a logistic curve are quite different notions and we should be careful not to assume that one always implies the other. Moreover, what matters is the underlying dynamic process not the particular shape of the diffusion curve, and to deduce the former from the latter is not necessarily an easy task. Then we have the basis for a far richer analysis of diffusion and adoption phenomena. Rather than explore this point further in terms of work post Mansfield it will first be more instructive to go backwards in time to make the point that Mansfield's work on diffusion was part of a broader tradition in which the ubiquitous "S" curve played a central role.[13]

3. Retardation theory and the diffusion of innovation

The theme explored here is that Mansfield's diffusion work is part of a far broader tradition of work on the economic dynamics of technical change in which innovations and the response to them are emergent consequences of market processes. The link between all of these literatures is the ubiquitous "S" curve of which the logistic is one of the more easily handled examples. The origins of the logistic curve are normally associated with the biologists Pearl and Reed who were concerned to uncover laws of biological population growth at the turn of the 19th century, and whose work led to the development of a mathematical ecology in which growth curves such as the logistic played a key role. Lotka's (1924) treatise, *Elements of Physical Biology*, provided the definitive statement of this literature. It was obvious to many, including Lotka, that this analysis had strong implications for the laws of growth of an economy in which the structure is continually changing in response to innovation and the rise of new industries and firms. Numerous isolated studies of industrial growth using "S" curves followed (Prescott, 1922; Windsor, 1932; Bratt, 1936; Vianelli, 1936)[14] but it was left to the leading American interwar economists Simon Kuznets and Arthur Burns to develop a more sophisticated and general growth curve analysis applied to the output of specific industries. Kuznets and Burns each built their work around a particular property of "S" curves, including the logistic, namely the phenomena of growth rate retardation. Retardation refers to the fact that the rate of growth of the variable in question, say output, declines continually with time and with the increasing scale of output.[15] This is the phenomena that Abramovitz (1989) identified as one among eight salient empirical generalisations about the process of economic growth.

Both Burns and Kuznets were concerned with the measurement and explanation of secular or long time movements in the volume of economic activity. Both emphasised that the introduction of new activities and the disappearance of old activities are an intrinsic part of the development of capitalism. Both understood that the evidence for retardation would depend on the level of statistical definition of an industry or sector, and that the broader the aggregate the more the evidence in favour of economic evolution and their underlying causal processes will be suppressed. Accepting that the modern economic system is "characterized by ceaseless change", neither could proceed with an aggregate analysis of growth nor accept the idea of uniform progress in all branches of economic activity.

Like other empirically minded scholars, Burns gathered a great deal of evidence to establish that a central feature of modern economic development is the diversity of growth rates of output across different sub-sectors and commodities in the economy. His list of the innovations that underpin the diversity of industry growth rates has a thoroughly modern ring to it. It includes new commodities; new raw materials; changes in methods of production; new methods for the recovery of waste products; changes in forms of industrial organisation; increases in the number of uses of given materials and in the number of materials put to a given use; and, finally, the emergence of what he calls learning products and style goods. In sum, Burns claimed that "These changes have resulted in an increasing divergence of production trends for they have served to stimulate or depress but to an unequal extent, the development of various industries" (p. 63).[16]

Kuznets (1929, 1954) had independently explored the same themes and from a broadly similar perspective. He stated the problem clearly as follows:

"As we observe various industries within a given national economy, we see that the lead in development shifts from one branch to another. A rapidly developing industry does not retain its vigorous growth forever but slackens and is overtaken by others whose period of rapid development is beginning. Within one country we can observe a succession of different branches of activity in the vanguard of the country's economic development, and within each industry we can notice a conspicuous slackening in the rate of increase" (Kuznets, 1929, 1954, p. 254).

However, this recorded unevenness of growth experience is only part of the picture. For both Burns and Kuznets focused upon a consistent empirical regularity in the process of growth, namely retardation. Their explanations of retardation are remarkably similar and they include population growth (a minor element), foreign competition, inter-industry relations of competition and complementarity and, of vital importance, technical progress. Indeed, for both

Kuznets and Burns, it is retardation in the within industry rates of technical progress, which is the chief explanation of retardation in rates of output growth. Moreover, their theories of technical progress are essentially the same, namely that any industry is created by a particular broad invention, or complex of innovations that offers scope for a myriad of improvements of ever decreasing importance. Progress inevitably slackens, and unless there is some radical breakthrough in the foundations of an industry's methods it becomes increasingly difficult to extract further improvements in performance. This is a view beautifully and subsequently expressed by Hicks (1977) who wrote in terms of the "economic children" that follow the original invention. A sequence of initial inventions creates new activities and a potential design space to explore the possibilities latent in the new concepts and so provides the stimuli to maintain a trajectory of technical innovation over time within the limits resident in these new concepts. This is a theme familiar to all modern evolutionary minded scholars and students of innovation (Dosi, 1982; Georghiou et al., 1984).

Kuznets and Burns were not the only scholars to explore these themes. Fabricant (1942) too found compelling evidence for the retardation of growth in American manufacturing output and employment over the period 1899–1939, although he worked in terms of broader commodity groups rather than the individual commodities that were the focus of the Kuznet's and Burn's studies. While Fabricant does not develop the logic of the retardation thesis, being content to echo the Kuznets/Burns line on technical progress, his study is valuable for its emphasis on structural change and the shifting balance of employment within the overall growth of the economy. Subsequent studies by Hoffman (1949), Stigler (1947) and Gaston (1961) further explored the empirical basis of the retardation theme in different bodies of industrial data but without any further development of the underlying theory. Unfortunately for the study of economic change, growth theory had taken by then its macro economic turn as the consequences of the Keynesian revolution percolated through to the study of long period problems. In all its essentials, the picture of economic growth as the evolving self-transformation of an economy was lost in its entirety.[17]

What brought the logistic and retardation back into modern focus was precisely the literature on the diffusion of innovation and subsequently on industrial and technological life cycles towards which Mansfield made such an important contribution. Any analysis of the logistic curve contains within it an implicit analysis of retardation. Where Kuznets, Burns and others found this at the level of industry and sector aggregates, Mansfield discovered it at the level of individual innovations and thus brought back onto the research agenda a central characteristic of modern capitalism its capacity to self transform through innovation.

4. Logistic laws of evolution

If Mansfield continued a tradition of growth dynamics that stretched back over half a century it is also the case that his "S" curve approach is central to subsequent work carried out by evolutionary economists. In this section I develop the idea that the "logistic law" is a defining signature of an evolving population, the dynamics of which is driven by a process of competitive selection. The connection is that Mansfield's work is in the context of populations of competing innovations and measures of their changing relative importance. In many cases the populations have simple structures, firms have adopted or they have not, a fraction of industry output is produced with a certain innovation a remaining fraction is not and so on. In each case the diffusion phenomena picks up on the changing structure of the population.

The defining attribute of an important class of evolutionary models is that they deal with populations of phenomena and they provide explanations of how the structure of those populations, as measured by the relative importance of the constituent members, changes over time. Populations of innovations are the basis of all diffusion models, even if the focus is upon a single technology or innovation there are always in the background one or more other technologies that are being substituted for. Indeed a wide number of diffusion models are in fact presented as models of technological substitution (Fisher and Pry, 1971; Kwasnicki and Kwasnicki, 1996; Mahajan and Muller, 1996). It is the fact that all diffusion processes involve more than one rival technology serving the same broad function that makes a population dynamics perspective relevant, even though the levels at which the population is defined may differ widely in each case. It is the population perspective which also gives rise to the importance of the "logistic law" as a fundamental characteristic of evolving population structures.

To sharpen the argument, we now define $x_i(t)$ as the absolute scale of utilisation of a particular innovation. We also define s_i is the measure of relative importance in the market of the ith innovation ($\sum s_i = 1$), and $X(t)$ is the overall scale of output of all the innovations in the market. It follows that the diffusion path for the scale of utilisation of any one innovation is the product of changes in its relative importance in the population and changes in the overall scale of the population. The first of these is dependent on the logistic law as we now show.

A general multi-innovation diffusion process is designed to explain how the relative importance of the different innovations, s_i, is changing over time. If $g_i(t)$ is the intrinsic rate of growth in the scale $x_i(t)$ at which the ith technology is utilized, then it follows that the motion of the population structure is governed by

$$\frac{ds_i}{dt} = s_i(t)[g_i(t) - g'_s(t)] \quad (1)$$

where $g'_s(t) = g_X(t)$ is the average growth rate in the scale of utilization of all the innovations in the population such that $g'_s(t) = \sum s_i(t)g_i(t)$.

Now this relation is easily reformulated by defining $g_s(t)$ as the average growth rate in the utilization of all the innovations apart from innovation i, thus (1) can be rewritten as

$$\frac{ds_i}{dt} = s_i(t)(1 - s_i(t))[g_i(t) - g_s(t)] \quad (2)$$

where $g_s(t) = \sum_{j \neq i} s_j(t)g_j(t)$, and the term in square brackets is the intrinsic diffusion rate for the ith innovation in this population.

Relation (2) is, of course, the general logistic law that governs the evolution of the population structure for this set of innovations. The saturation level for any dominant innovation is unity but the intrinsic rate of diffusion is not a constant. Notice that (2) captures the central feature of an evolutionary dynamic in terms of the distribution of the individual growth rates around the population mean; what is called the distance from mean population dynamic. Hence, the relative importance, diffusion, of any one technology depends on how the growth rate of its utilisation compares with the population average and this measure is continually changing during the diffusion process even for a fixed set of innovations. Note also that this diffusion rate can decrease as well as increase; the diffusion of a superior innovation always has in its background the decline in the relative importance of rival, and often "hidden" innovations.

If we now define $G_{is}(t)$ as

$$G_{is}(t) = \int_o^t [g_i(t) - g_s(t)]dt$$

then, on integrating (2) and imposing the initial condition $s_i(0)$, we can write the solution as

$$s_i(t) = [1 + A \exp(-G_s(t))]^{-1} \quad (3)$$

with $A = (1 - s_i(0))/s_i(0)$.

Equation (3) summarizes the logistic law for this population, and it will be clear from relations (1) to (3) that the diffusion of a technology always follows the logistic law in terms of its relative importance in the relevant population. All

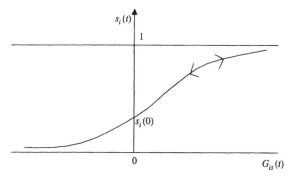

Figure 1.

the technologies in the population, therefore obey the general, reversible logistic diffusion mapping shown in Figure 1.

Provided that $g_i(t) > g_s(t)$ then $G_{is}(t)$ is increasing with time and so is $s_i(t)$. Conversely when $g_i(t) < g_s(t)$ then $G_{is}(t)$ is declining and with it $s_i(t)$. The important point to note is that the shares are not a logistic function of time, *simpliciter*, as in the usual logistic curve, but are rather a logistic function of the growth rate integrals $G_{is}(t)$. This is the logistic law which underpins all relative diffusion processes, reflecting the fact that diffusion is a problem in distance from mean population dynamics. Of course, diffusion in this relative sense is reversible, and it is typically the case that innovations once dominant in their field of application are displaced by the innovation of superior methods. This is what the logistic law allows for. This is a frequently observed phenomenon in diffusion and technology substitution analysis when say successive generations of an innovation are compared or when a sequence of rival innovations that are distributed over time is considered.[18]

Thus the logistic law captures the central principle of evolutionary analysis that populations evolve only in the presence of growth rate diversity and, ultimately, any theory of diffusion, like Mansfield's, is an explanation of that growth rate diversity. In his case the different growth rates are grounded in the relative rates of return to investment in different technologies, but many other sources of differential growth are possible depending on the innovations and the environment in which they are diffused.

Although the diffusion dynamics must follow the logistic law, as expressed in (3), it is not in general the case that the respective shares s_i trace a "naïve" logistic curve over time. The only case in which this is true is when we have just two innovations in the population and when their respective utilization growth rates are constants, for then $G_{is}(t)$ reduces to $(g_1 - g_2)t$. If $g_1 > g_2$, for example, then it is innovation one which follows the logistic curve of growth and innovation two the same logistic curve but in the direction of decline. Outside of this special case, the traditional logistic curve does not capture the evolution of any element in the population, although the underpinning logistic law always does.

Matters are even more complicated and enriched when we allow new innovations to enter the population over time for then, if the entrants have superior growth rates, those established technologies formerly ascending the curve in Figure 1 will be pushed into reverse and may even be forced out of the population.[19]

The general point is, I hope, clear; while the diffusion process is always covered by the logistic law it is only in the simplest of cases that the time dynamics generate a "naïve" logistic curve. If this is true of the population structure, it is true *a fortiori* for the levels $x_i(t)$ at which each technology is utilized. Since the respective growth rates obey the constraint

$$g_{xi}(t) = g_{si}(t) + g_x(t) \qquad (4)$$

it follows that the diffusion curve for X_i would only be a "naïve" logistic with respect to time if g_{si} follows the "naïve" logistic path and the overall scale of utilization, X, is constant.[20] An obvious counter example would be the diffusion of a particular set of technologies into a market environment that is growing at a constant rate. Then the dominant innovation would end up growing in scale in a non-logistic fashion towards an upper asymptote that is increasing at an exponential rate. To repeat, the fundamental importance of the logistic law does not imply the fundamental importance of the naïve logistic curve.

The final observation to be made is that the logistic law implies retardation in the evolution of the relative diffusion rates. When s_i is increasing it does so at a declining rate and when it is decreasing it does so at an accelerating rate. Thus, it is not surprising that Kuznets, Burns and others have found such impressive evidence in favour of the retardation hypothesis in terms of absolute scales of utilization. Whenever the overall population utilization rate $X(t)$ is changing slowly, then the logistic law does its work on the relative diffusion rates and imposes retardation on the utilization levels of the individual population components.

5. Concluding remarks

In this brief discussion of only a small part of Ed Mansfield's work we have focused on his exposition of innovation diffusion dynamics and sought to establish that it fits within a much wider tradition of evolutionary economic thought, one that stretches back to the early expositions of the logistic curve and theories of economic retardation and forward to modern evolutionary analysis. The connection should not cause the reader any surprise. Evolutionary change is change within populations and it occurs only when those populations contain economic variation within them. Deeply embedded in this dynamic of structural change is the logistic law and the related phenomena of retardation but we have seen that it is essential to distinguish between the logistic law and the naïve logistic curve. The later is a very special case and this in part explains why the logistic law may be consistent with a wide family of empirical "S" curves. By comparison, the logistic law is the signature of the evolutionary population dynamics and it follows from the nature of innovation and diffusion process in market economies. Much more important than the empirical realization is the economic explanation of the diversity in utilisation growth rates and the explanation of dynamic diversity as the fundamental evolutionary problem. Here we may find the connection between investment and diffusion that Mansfield emphasised and more generally the self transforming nature of modern capitalism in which innovation and its diffusion are of central importance. That is the value of Mansfield's legacy.

Acknowledgment

I thank Davide Consoli for excellent research assistance and Sharon Dalton for producing this draft in unusually quick time. Comments from Andrea Mina and Ronnie Ramlogan also helped, though the usual disclaimer applies.

Notes

1. See Geroski (2000) for an excellent, authoritative survey of the economics literature on diffusion and Mahajan and Peterson (1985) similarly on the marketing literature. Geroski draws attention to a wide variety of economic diffusion models, some based on processes of information spread, others based on equilibrium levels of diffusion that are disturbed by "interfering forces". *The Journal of Technological Forecasting and Social Change* is the premier source for work on diffusion interpreted in terms of technology substitution. The recent book by Geroski (2003) also provides important bridges between the more formal study of diffusion and work in strategic management. For other approaches to diffusion analysis see Antonelli et al. (1992) the survey by Lissoni and Metcalfe (1994) and Stoneman (1983, 1987). Pioneering work on the econometrics of logistic evolutionary processes may be found in Foster and Wild (1999a, b).
2. Mansfield (1971), p.178.
3. Mansfield refers to the work of Wilfred Salter (1961), who had developed a sophisticated account of the delay by firms in adopting new techniques based on Marshallian principles, but dismisses it on the grounds that it does not apply to regulated markets. Another important paper by Frankel (1955) on interrelated capital expenditures and investment in innovation was not, as far as I can ascertain, taken up by Mansfield.
4. Actually, the matter is a little more complicated, since a crucial assumption in restricting the Taylor expansion is that all terms of *second* order and higher in the current adoption rate are also dropped. Without this the adoption curve would not be a logistic. In typical, pragmatic fashion Mansfield justifies an apparently arbitrary restriction by claiming that adding a quadratic term for the adoption rate does not improve the goodness-of-fit of the investigated equations. See Mansfield 1961 reprinted in Mansfield 1968, p.139 footnote 10.
5. See the discussion in (Mansfield et al., 1977), chapters 6 and 7.
6. In my own graduate work, undertaken in 1968, on the diffusion of three innovations in the Lancashire textile industry I had four names to turn to, Everett Rogers, George Ray, Zvi Griliches and Ed. Mansfield. Each had an enormous influence but, because the later was concerned with industrial innovations and the investment processes required to adopt them, his was the dominant influence on my own thinking (Metcalfe, 1970).
7. For an example see, Meyer and Ausubel (1999).
8. Of course, the same conclusion would follow if the underlying dynamics followed a Gompertz law or any other sigmoid law for that matter.
9. See Ireland and Stoneman (1982), Metcalfe (1981) and Cameron and Metcalfe (1988) for alternative specifications of this theme.
10. Nelson (1968) explores the same theme where the inelasticity of supply of an innovation reflects factors in the labour market.
11. Classic references are Arrow (1961) and Rosenberg (1982).
12. For further discussion see Geroski (2003). Metcalfe (2003) explores endogenous, diffusion induced technological improvement in the context of a Gompertz process.
13. From henceforth I shall speak of diffusion and adoption interchangeably, the interpretation being, I hope, clear from the context.
14. Ultimately, it emerged again, in different form in the idea of an industrial, technological or product life cycle in the 1960s. See Utterback (1994) and Klepper (2002) for relevant discussion.

15. In the logistic case the growth rate declines linearly with the scale of output, in the Gompertz case it declines log linearly.
16. Glenday (1938) applied Burns' method to long production series for eight UK industries and found consistent evidence of retardation.
17. It should be noted that Samuelson (1947, pp. 291–294) devoted a section of his *Foundations* to an analysis of the mathematical properties of the logistic curve but this had little subsequent resonance on the development of economic dynamics.
18. See the examples in Kwasnicki and Kwasnicki (1996) and Mahajan and Muller (1996).
19. Equation (3) is, in fact, closely connected to the Fisher/Price theorem in evolutionary dynamics, namely that population means of some attribute evolve over time according to the magnitude of the covariance of the attribute with the growth rates across the elements in the population. This theorem and its many sequalia play an important role in many formal evolutionary models (Nelson and Winter, 1982; Andersen, 1994; Saviotti, 1996; Metcalfe, 1998; Dosi, 2000; Witt, 2002).
20. In Mansfield 1961 reprinted in Mansfield 1968, the analogue to X(t) is the number of firms in the adopting population, which he takes to be constant-the given major firms.

References

Abramovitz, M., 1989, *Thinking About Growth*, Cambridge: Cambridge University Press.

Andersen, E.S., 1994, *Evolutionary Economics: Post Schumpeterian Contributions*, London: Pinter.

Antonelli, C., P. Petit and G. Tahar, 1992, *The Economics of Industrial Modernisation*, New York: Academic Press.

Arrow, K.J., 1961, 'The Economic Implications of Learning by Doing,' *Review of Economic Studies* **29**, 155–173.

Bratt, E.C., 1936, 'Relations of Institutional Factors to Economic Equilibrium and Long-Time Trend,' *Econometrica* **4**, 161–183.

Burns, A.F., 1934, *Production Trends in the United States Since 1870*, Boston: NBER.

Cameron, H. and J.S. Metcalfe, 1988, 'On the Economics of Technological Substitution,' *Technological Forecasting and Social Change* **32**, 147–162.

Diamond, A.M. Jr., 2003, 'Edwin Mansfield's Contributions to the Economics of Technology,' *Research Policy* **32**, 1607–1617.

Dosi, G., 1982, 'Technological Paradigms and Technological Trajectories—A Suggested Interpretation of the Determinants and Directions of Technological Change,' *Research Policy* **11**, 147–162.

Dosi, G., 2000, *Innovation, Organization and Economic Dynamics*, Cheltenham: Edward Elgar.

Fabricant, S., 1942, *Employment in Manufacturing, 1899–1939*, New York: NBER.

Fisher, J. and R. Pry, 1971, 'A Simple Substitution Model of Technological Change,' *Technological Forecasting and Social Change* **3**, 75–88.

Foster, J. and P. Wild, 1999a, 'Detecting Self Organisational Change in Economic Processes Exhibiting Logistic Growth,' *Journal of Evolutionary Economics* **9**, 109–133.

Foster, J. and P. Wild, 1999b, 'Econometric Modeling in the Presence of Evolutionary Change,' *Cambridge Journal of Economics* **23**, 749–770.

Frankel, M., 1955, 'Obsolescence and Technological Change in a Maturing Economy,' *American Economic Review*, **45**, 259–268.

Gaston, J.F., 1961, *Growth Patterns in Industry: A Re-Examination*, New York: National Industrial Conference Board.

Georghiou, L., J.S. Metcalfe, J. Evans, T. Ray, and M. Gibbons, 1984, *Post-Innovation Performance*, London: Macmillan.

Geroski, P.A., 2000, 'Models of Technology Diffusion,' *Research Policy* **29**, 603–625.

Geroski, P.A., 2003, *The Evolution of New Markets*, Oxford: Oxford University Press.

Glenday, R., 1938, 'Long–Period Economic Trends,' *Journal of the Royal Statistical Society Series A.* **51**, 511–552.

Hoffman, W.G., 1949, 'The Growth of Industrial Production in Great Britain. A Quantitative Survey,' *Economic History Review* **2**, 162–180.

Hicks, J., 1977, *Economic Perspectives*, Oxford: Oxford University Press.

Ireland, N. and P. Stoneman, 1982, 'The Role of Supply Factors in the Diffusion of New Process Innovations,' *Economic Journal* **82**(conference issue), 65–77.

Kingsland, S.E., 1985, *Modelling Nature*, Chicago: Chicago University Press.

Klepper, S., 2002, 'The Capabilities of New Firms and the Evolution of the US Automobile Industry,' *Industrial and Corporate Change* **11**, 645–666.

Kuznets, S., 1929, *Secular Movements of Production and Prices*, Boston: Houghton Miflin.

Kuznets, S., 1954, *Economic Change*, London: Heinemann.

Kwasnicki, W. and H. Kwasnicki, 1996, 'Long Term Diffusion Factors of Technological Development: An Evolutionary Model and Case Study,' *Technological Forecasting and Social Change* **52**, 31–57.

Lissoni, F. and J.S. Metcalfe, 1994, 'Diffusion of Innovation, Ancient and Modern: A Review of the Main Themes,' in R. Rothwell, and M. Dodgson (eds.), *New Developments in the Economics of Innovation*, London: Francis Pinter.

Lotka, A.J., 1924, *Elements of Physical Biology*, Reprinted 1956 as *Elements of Mathematical Biology*, New York: Dover Publications.

Mahajan, V. and E. Muller, 1996, 'Timing, Diffusion, and Substitution of Successive Generations of Technological Innovations: The IBM Mainframe Case', *Technological Forecasting and Social Change,* **51**, 109-132.

Mansfield, E., 1968, *Industrial Research and Technological Innovation*, New York: W.W. Norton.

Mansfield, E., J. Rapoport, A. Romeo, E. Villani, S. Wagner, and F. Husic, 1977, *The Production and Application of New Industrial Technology*, New York: W.W. Norton.

Metcalfe, J.S., 1970, 'Diffusion of Innovation in the Lancashire Textile Industry,' *Manchester School* **38**, 145–162.

Metcalfe, J.S., 1981, 'Impulse and Diffusion in the Study of Technological Change,' *Futures* 347–359.

Metcalfe, J.S., 1998, *Evolutionary Economics and Creative Destruction*, London: Routledge.

Metcalfe, J.S., 2003, 'Industrial Growth and the Theory of Retardation: Precursors of an Adaptive Evolutionary Theory of Economic Change,' *Revue Economique* **54**, 407–431.

Meyer, P. and J.H. Ausubel, 1999, 'Carrying Capacity: A Model with Logistically Varying Limits,' *Technological Forecasting and Social Change* **61**, 209–214.

Nelson, R.R., 1968, 'A "Diffusion" Model of International Productivity Differences in Manufacturing,' *American Economic Review* **58**, 1219–1248.

Nelson, R.R. and S. Winter 1982, *An Evolutionary Theory of Economic Change*, Cambridge: Belknap Press.

Prescott, R., 1922, 'Laws of Growth in Forecasting Demand,' *Journal of the American Statistical Society* **18**, 471–479.

Rosenberg, N., 1982, *Inside the Black Box*, Cambridge: Cambridge University Press.

Salter W.E.G., 1961, *Productivity and Technical Change*, Cambridge: Cambridge University Press.

Samuelson, P.A., 1947, *Foundations of Economic Analysis*, Cambridge: Harvard University Press.

Saviotti, P.P., 1996, *Technological Evolution,Variety and the Economy*, Cheltenham: Edward Elgar.

Scherer, F.M., 2005, 'Edwin Mansfield: An Appreciation,' *Journal of Technology Transfer*, (This issue, details at proof stage).

Stigler, G.J., 1947, *Trends in Output and Employment*, New York: NBER.

Stoneman, P. 1983, *The Economic Analysis of Technological Change*, Oxford: Oxford University Press.

Stoneman, P., 1987, *The Economic Analysis of Technology Policy*, Oxford: Oxford University Press.

Utterback, J., 1994, *Mastering the Dynamics of Innovation*, Boston: Harvard Business School Press.

Vianelli, S., 1936, 'A General Dynamic Demographic Scheme and its Application to Italy and the United States,' *Econometrica* **4**, 269–283.

Windsor, C.P., 1932, 'The Gompertz Curve as a Growth Curve,' *Proceedings of the National Academy of Sciences* **18**, 1–8.

Witt, U., 2002, *The Evolving Economy*, Cheltenham: Edward Elgar.

Mansfield's Missing Link: The Impact of Knowledge Spillovers on Firm Growth

David B. Audretsch[1]
Erik E. Lehmann[2,3]

ABSTRACT. The purpose of this paper is to provide a link between two of the seminal contributions of Edwin Mansfield. The first focuses on the determinants of firm growth and the second is concerned with university-based knowledge spillovers. By linking both firm-specific characteristics as well as access to knowledge spillovers from universities, the empirical evidence found in this paper suggests that knowledge spillovers as well as firm-specific characteristics influence firm growth.

Key words: university spillovers, firm growth

JEL Classification: M13, L20, R30

1. Introduction

Among his many compelling contributions, Edwin Mansfield ranked among the pioneers in economics focusing the determinants of the evolutionary process by which firms are created and then grow through an evolutionary process. According to Mansfield (1962, p. 1023), "Because there have been so few econometric studies of the birth, growth and death of firms, we lack even crude answers to the following basic questions regarding the dynamic processes governing an industry's structure. What are the quantitative effects of various factors on the growth of firms represented by Gibrat's law of proportionate effect? What have been the effects of successful innovations on a firm's growth rate?" It required no fewer than two sweeping articles in the Journal of Economic Literature (Caves, 1998; Sutton, 1997) at the end of the last century to review the literature on empirical tests of firm growth and Gibrat's Law spawned by Mansfield's pioneering research.

Towards the end of his career, Mansfield (1995), also pioneered a very different research trajectory, which focused on external sources of R&D, and in particular universities, as inputs into firm innovation.[1] Mansfield's research was instrumental in triggering a more recent wave of studies identifying the role that knowledge spillovers play, and in particular, knowledge spillovers from universities in generating innovative activity (Audretsch and Stephan, 1996; Jaffe, 1989).

Despite the enormous literatures triggered by Mansfield's seminal contributions, these two research trajectories remain separate. As the Caves (1998) and Sutton (1997) review articles confirm, the plethora of econometric studies focusing on firm growth in general, and Gibrat's law in particular, never consider the impact of external research on the growth of firms. Instead, this entire literature consists almost exclusively of trying to link firm-specific characteristics, principally size and age, but also in some cases R&D and other types of innovative activity, to firm growth. Similarly, the literature on knowledge spillovers has concentrated mainly on performance measures such as innovation and R&D, but has yet to consider the impact on firm growth (Audretsch et al., 2005).

---

[1] Department Entrepreneurship, Growth, and Public Policy Max Planck Institute for Research into Economic Systems Jena Kahlaische Strasse 10, 07745 Jena, Germany.
Email: audretsch@mpiew-jena.mpg.de
[2] Department Entrepreneurship, Growth, and Public Policy Max dPlanck Institute for Research into Economic Systems Jena Kahlaische Strasse 10, 07745 Jena
Germany.
[3] Department of Economics
University of Konstanz
Box D-144, 78457 Konstanz
Germany.
E-mail: lehmann@mpiew-jena.mpg.de

The purpose of this paper is to provide the missing link between the literatures on firm growth and on university-based knowledge spillovers. In particular, we examine whether access to university-based knowledge spillovers has an impact on firm growth. In the second section we present the model relating not just firm characteristics, but also knowledge external to the firm, to firm growth. In the third section issues involving measurement are discussed. The results from estimating the growth rates of high-technology German firms are presented in Section 4. Finally, in the last section a summary and conclusion are provided. In particular, the results of this paper suggest that two of the seminal contributions made by Mansfield need to be linked together. Just as Mansfield discovered, not only is firm growth positively influenced by investments in knowledge, but accessing external knowledge generated by universities also contributes to firm growth.

2. Linking firm growth to university spillovers

Since the purpose of this paper is to link the two seminal contributions by Mansfield together, we introduce a model relating firm growth to characteristics specific to the enterprise as well as external knowledge from universities. The starting point is the most prevalent model for identifying the determinants of growth at the level of the firm, which has been based to test Gibrat's Law (Sutton, 1997).

Formalizing the relationship between size and growth, Gibrat's law assumes that the present size of firm i in period t may be decomposed into the product of a "proportional effect" and the initial firm size as:

$$\text{Size}_{i,t} = (1 + \varepsilon_t)\,\text{Size}_{i,t-1}, \quad (1)$$

where $(1+\varepsilon_t)$ denotes the proportional effect for firm i in period t. Here the random shock ε_t is assumed to be identically and independently distributed. Taking the natural log and assuming that for small ε, $\ln(1+\varepsilon) \approx \varepsilon_t$,

$$\ln(\text{Size}_{i,t}) = \ln(\text{Size}_{i,0}) + \sum_{k=1}^{t} \varepsilon_{ik} \quad (2)$$

It can be observed that as $t \to \infty$ a distribution emerges which is approximately log normal with properties that $\ln(\text{Size}_{i,t}) \sim N(t\mu\varepsilon, t\sigma^2_\varepsilon)$. Firm growth can then be measured as the difference between the natural log of the number of employees as:

$$\text{Growth}_{it} = \ln(S_{i,t}) - \ln(S_{i,t-1}) \quad (3)$$

where the difference in size for firm i between the current period t and the initial period $(t-1)$ equals Growth_{it}.

This equation can be empirically estimated by:

$$\text{Growth}_{i,t} = B_1 \ln(\text{Size}_{i,t-1}) + B_2 \ln(\text{Size}_{i,t-1})^2 \\ + B_3 \text{Age}_{i,t-1} + \varepsilon_i \quad (4)$$

where growth for firm i in period t is a function of initial firm size, size^2, age, and ε_i a stochastic error term.

Sutton (1997) and Caves (1998) survey and report on the large number of empirical studies estimating Equation (4). The evidence is systematic and compelling that both size and age are negatively related to firm growth.

Note that Equation (4) only considers characteristics specific to the enterprise. We extend this approach by including knowledge spillovers from universities,

$$\text{Growth}_{i,t} = B_1 \ln(\text{Size}_{i,t-1}) + B_2 \ln(\text{Size}_{i,t-1})^2 \\ + B_3 \text{Age}_{i,t-1} B_4 \text{Knowledge}_{r,t-1} \quad (5) \\ \times B_5 D_{ind} + \varepsilon_i$$

where D_{ind} is a vector of industry dummies controlling, for example, for the knowledge intensity of production in a specific sector. Knowledge$_r$, $t-1$ represents knowledge spillovers from universities.

3. Data set and descriptive statistics

To test the hypothesis that firm growth depends not only on firm size and age but also university spillovers, we use a unique dataset of 281 IPO firms in Germany. The dataset is collected combining individual data from IPO prospectuses, along with publicly available information from on-line data sources including the *Deutsche Boerse AG* (www.deutsche-boerse.com). We pooled this dataset by adding university-specific variables, which are individually collected from the 73 public universities in Germany. For each of those universities we collected the number of articles listed in the research database from the ISI (Information Sciences Institutes). Although this research database includes a small number of all the journals in one field, it ensures that it only contains the high-quality research journals. We further consider the amount of grants available to each respective university in 1997 (see Audretsch *et al.*, 2004).

We take the *log growth rates* of employees one year after the IPO as the dependent variable. The first two exogenous variables are firm age (AGE) and firm size (SIZE). Age is measured in years from foundation to IPO, and firm size by the number of employees before IPO. To capture effects from university spillovers we include the distance to the closest university as an exogenous variable. Since universities in Germany are more geographically concentrated compared to the US, we need a measure which is sensitive to small variations. The distance is measured in kilometers using the online database of the *German Automobile Club* (www.a-dac.de). All firms located within a radius of 1.5 km are classified as belonging to the distance category of 1 km.

In the first two models (models I, II), we estimate the following basic regressions to test Gibrat's Law, as proposed in the literature (see Sutton, 1997).

(I) $LnGrowth = const. + \beta_1 LnSize + \beta_2 LnSize^2 + \beta_3 LnAge + \beta_4 LnAge^2 + \varepsilon$

(II) $LnGrowth = const. + \beta_1 LnSize + \beta_2 LNAge + \varepsilon$

Then we test for the impact of university spillovers as an additional explanatory variable for firm growth (models III, IV):

(III) $LnGrowth = const. + \beta_1 LnSize + \beta_2 LNAge + (-1)\beta_3 University\ Spillovers + \varepsilon$

(IV) $LnGrowth = const. + \beta_1 LnSize + \beta_2 LnAge + (-1)\beta_3 University\ Spillovers \times (LnUniversity\ Spending; \times LnSSCI; LnSCI)$

We multiplied with (−1) to capture the effect that the closer the distance towards the next university, the higher should be the growth rate of the respective firm. Model (V), which is not explicitly shown, captures all variables.

The descriptive statistics are depicted in Table I. The closest location between firms and universities is 1 km and the maximum distance is 177 km away from the nearest university. The data also demonstrate that most of the firms are strikingly young. Half of the firms in our sample are 8 years old or less. The firms also differ extremely in their size as measured by the number of employees before IPO. The mean firm before IPO employed about 180 workers. Finally, the table shows that on average the log growth rate is about 0.475. All the variables show high differences between the minimum and maximum values.

4. Empirical evidence

Table II presents the results from the four regressions. Models (I) and (II) replicate the standard tests of Gibrat's Law as known from the literature. The negative and statistically coefficient on firm size suggests that smaller firms grow faster than do their larger counterparts. The coefficient of firm age and firm age as well as the squared term shows no statistically significant impact on firm growth.

The estimation of model (III) shows no significant impact of university spillovers as measured by the distance towards the closest university of a firm. However, if we instrument this variable model (model IV) using the spending for the

TABLE I
Descriptive statistics

Variable	Mean	SD.	Min.	Max.
Distance (km)	16.69	23.45	1	177
Firm size (#employees)	180.20	256.52	2	1,700
Firm age (years)	10.27	11.11	0.1	107
Ln growth rates	0.4969	1.6121	−4.106	7.5183

TABLE II
Regressions on firm growth

	OLS (I)	OLS (II)	OLS (III)	OLS (V)	2SLS (IV)	2SLS (V)
LnSize	−0.7895 (2.75)[b]	−0.9290 (15.33)[c]	−0.9117 (14.10)[c]	−0.8537 (1.86)[b]	−0.8554 (10.22)[c]	−1.1272 (2.31)[c]
Ln Size2	−0.0152 (0.47)			−0.0059 (0.12)		0.03133 (0.58)
LnAge	0.0859 (1.29)	0.07390 (1.40)	0.0613 (1.19)	0.0731 (0.96)	0.1688 (2.00)[b]	0.1929 (1.83)[a]
LnAge2	−0.0114 (0.41)			0.0092 (0.34)		−0.0099 (0.31)
University spillover			−0.0423 (0.92)	−0.0430 (0.92)	0.7131 (1.78)[b]	0.7263 (1.79)[b]
Const.	4.3187 (7.03)[c]	4.5762 (17.27)[c]	4.4339 (13.75)[c]	4.3289 (4.11)[c]	5.430 (8.25)[c]	6.001 (4.43)[c]
R	0.4749	0.4779	0.4856	0.4860	0.0236	0.0094

This table presents the result from OLS on firm growth. The endogenous variable is growth rates of employees one year after the IPO. University Spillover is measured in log kilometers from the next university. This variable is instrumented in the 2SLS approach by the number of research spending, the number of papers published in the natural sciences and in the social sciences. All OLS-estimations are done using the White-heteroskedasticity robust estimator. Absolute t-values in parentheses, [a, b, c] Statistically significant at the 10, 5 1% level, respective. The coefficient of university spillovers are multiplied with (−1) to capture the positive effect of a close location towards the next university.

respective university as well as the academic papers published in the natural sciences and the social sciences, we find the missing link: Spillovers matter for firm growth. The closer the distance towards the next university and the higher the amount of academic papers published, the higher the growth rates of firms. This result is also robust in model 2SLS (V), which includes all the variables.

5. Conclusion

Perhaps had Edwin Mansfield's career been extended, he would have had the opportunity to bring together two of his seminal contributions—firm growth and university research spillovers. In this paper, we have followed in the footsteps of Mansfield by linking these two seminal contributions together. Not only does firm growth depend upon characteristics specific to the firm, but also on external characteristics as well, and in particular, the spillover of knowledge from universities. We would anticipate future research to further pursue the intellectual tradition pioneered by Ed Mansfield and further examine how firm growth is shaped by other types of knowledge spillovers external to the firm.

Note

1. An earlier study focusing on knowledge spillovers is Link and Rees (1991).

References

Audretsch, D.B. and P.E. Stephan, 1996, 'Company-Scientist Locational Links: The Case of Biotechnology,' *American Economic Review* 86 (3), 641–652.

Audretsch, D.B., M. Keilbach and E.E. Lehmann, 2005, *Entrepreneurship and Economic Growth*, London: Oxford University Press (forthcoming).

Audretsch, D.B., E.E. Lehmann, and S. Warning, 2004, 'University Spillovers: Does the Kind of Knowledge Matters?,' *Industry and Innovation* (forthcoming).

Caves, R., 1998, 'Industrial Organization and New Findings on the Turnover and Mobility of Firms,' *Journal of Economic Literature* 36 (4), 1947–1982.

Hall, B.H., A.N. Link, and J.T. Scott, 2003, 'Universities as Research Partners,' *Review of Economics and Statistics* (forthcoming).

Jaffe, A.B., 1989, 'Real Effects of Academic Research,' *American Economic Review* 79, 957–970.

Link, A.N. and J. Rees, 1991, 'Firm Size, University-Based Research, and the Returns to R&D,' *Small Business Economics* 2, 24–31.

Link, A.N., and B. Bozeman, 1991, 'Innovative Behavior in Small-Sized Firms,' *Small Business Economics* 3 (3), 179–184.

Mansfield, E., 1962, 'Entry, Gibrat's Law, Innovation, and the Growth of Firms,' *American Economic Review* 52, 1023–1051.

Mansfield, E., 1995, 'Academic Research Underlying Industrial Innovations: Sources, Characteristics, and Financing,' *The Review of Economics and Statistics* 77, 55–65.

Sutton, J., 1997, 'Gibrat's Legacy,' *Journal of Economic Literature* 35, 40–59.

Predictable Cross-Industry Heterogeneity in Industry Dynamics

Kenneth L. Simons[1]

ABSTRACT. Technological change affects industry dynamics, by influencing whether an industry experiences a shakeout and attains a concentrated market structure. Decades-long competitive processes are similar for matched industries in different nations, indicating that competitive processes — not just eventual concentration levels — arise systematically from causes that might be traced. The television manufacturing industry in the United States and the United Kingdom is used to illustrate common processes at work.

Key words: industry evolution, shakeout, technological change, television receivers

JEL Classification: L10, O33, L63

Edwin Mansfield (1962) was one of the first researchers to link empirical facts on dynamics of small and large firms' entry, exit, growth, and mobility to underlying technological change. His subsequent work greatly improved understanding of decisions to conduct R&D, and of the spread of technology, among firms of differing size and nature. It is natural to return with the spirit of his methods and the wisdom of four decades' research to analyze the apparently central role of technology in the dynamics of industries.

A growing literature improves our understanding of industry competition and eventual industry outcomes by analyzing dynamic processes at work through the industry life cycle. Firm entry and exit, growth, and technological innovation are involved. One striking pattern is that, after an initial buildup, the number of firms in an industry often experiences a dramatic "shakeout" or drop-off and production ends up concentrated among few producers. Contrasting patterns also occur: some industries have little or no shakeout. Might these different outcomes be predictable?

Indeed, Joe S. Bain (1966) and Frederic L. Pryor (1972) showed evidence that industries with high or low concentration in one nation tend to have similar high or low concentration in all the industrialized nations they studied. In the words of Richard Schmalensee (1989, p. 992), this finding "suggests that similar processes operate to determine concentration levels everywhere...." Moreover, since national markets are somewhat independent, the finding suggests that concentration may be in part predictable based on traits of the technology, product, or market.

Common outcomes and predictability are important, because they underlie our ability to write down models of industries that explain structure and performance based on underlying traits. For example, Avner Shaked and John Sutton (1987) model a lower bound to industrial concentration as stemming from firms' cost of advertising and technological requirements. If we can determine realistic models of how industry outcomes stem from such underlying characteristics, we may be able to make reasonable *a priori* predictions of industry outcomes and advise accordingly on national and corporate policy.

One approach to extend this line of work is to examine the dynamic processes in industry competition. If underlying technological or other traits determine processes affecting firm entry, exit, growth, and concentration, empirical patterns should reflect this determinism in two ways. First, comparing the same industry across two or more countries, a similar competitive outcome should occur in all nations. To the extent such similarity arises, systematic causes, not differing national environments nor random successes and failures of firms, may drive industry outcomes.

---

[1] *Department of Economics*
Rensselaer Polytechnic Institute
3504 Russell Sage Laboratory
Troy, NY 12180-3590, USA.
E-mail: simonk@rpi.edu

Second, correlated patterns of entry, exit, and other outcomes might be observed, and the observer might learn something by classifying types of competition into a small number of commonly-occurring groups.

1. Multi-industry, multi-nation competitive analysis

Empirical analyses of competitive processes in industries are hindered by the lack of available competitive-level data. Data from government censuses of firms and many commercial datasets are available generally at 4-digit or more aggregated SIC levels. At these levels, most of the products made by companies are not substitutable; a customer would rarely if ever buy a hearse, bus, or military tank as a substitute for an automobile (all are in 1987 U.S. SIC 3711). Government and some commercial data sources also tend to recognize new industries only after substantial delay, making it impossible to analyze the important early years of competition.

Fortunately it has proved possible to piece together evidence that does not suffer unduly from these problems. Trade registers, industry associations, and books assembled by enthusiasts about particular products provide written records of which firms produced certain goods. The records often begin in the early years of an industry, and tend to be defined at the competitive level. For example, lists of television manufacturers analyzed later in this paper are drawn from periodic editions of *Television Factbook* in the U.S. and *Kelly's Directory of Merchants, Manufacturers, and Shippers* in the U.K.[1]

Kenneth L. Simons (unpublished manuscript) compares 18 competitive-level manufacturing industries in the U.S. and the U.K. (the two countries for which data collection was feasible) to analyze a range of industry outcomes. This is apparently the first such many-industry, multinational study of dynamics in the number of firms. It turns out that not only do industries have Bain and Pryor's common eventual concentration levels, but moreover they evolve through similar processes across both nations. Some but not all of the industries studied experienced severe shakeouts in their numbers of producers in the U.S. and the U.K. Using as a measure of severity of shakeout the percentage drop in number of firms from peak to eventual low over a common time period, a high and statistically significant correlation results in the severity of shakeouts in the U.S. and the U.K. The date of (or elapsed time until) the peak number of firms is also highly and significantly correlated. Thus, industries that ended up concentrated among a few producers in the U.S. ended up similarly concentrated in the U.K., and *vice versa*, and competitive processes played out on similar time scales in both nations.

Moreover a typology of most industries seems to be possible by classifying industries according to their degree of shakeout. Among the 18 industries, those with severe shakeouts experienced a dramatic decline in entry and an early-entry advantage manifested through low exit rates relative to later entrants. Industries with little or no shakeout, in contrast, experienced little or no drop in entry and little or no early-entry advantage. The evidence on the 18 industries therefore suggests that competitive processes generally fall along a spectrum from severe shakeout to no shakeout, and that in each case similar processes are at work regarding firm entry and exit. Furthermore, patent data that pertain to technology specific to the product area (as opposed to technology more likely to pertain to new products) show extensive patenting dominated by early entrants in industries with substantial shakeouts, consistent with technological opportunity causing the early-entry advantage.

2. Television manufacture[2]

To illustrate the findings in an industry at one extreme of the spectrum, consider the television receiver industry. Television manufacture began to take off in the 1930s in the U.K. and at the start of the 1940s in the U.S., but substantial production was delayed until after World War II. The number of television manufacturers in both countries began to rise thereafter as many firms began production. Figure 1 shows the changing number of manufacturers in the two countries. In the U.S. the number of manufacturers rose from 31 in 1947 to a peak of 92 in 1951, but then began to drop almost as rapidly. In the U.K. the number of manufacturers grew from 9 in 1947 to

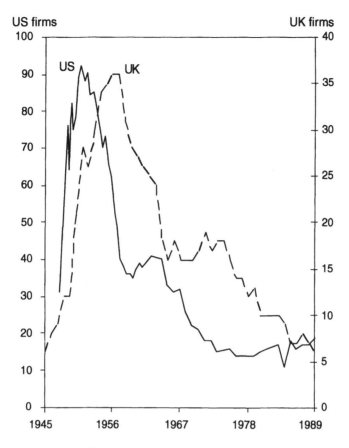

Figure 1. U.S. and U.K. Television Manufacturers, 1945–1989.

a peak of 36 in 1956 and 1957, and similarly plummeted.

The drop in the number of firms in the U.S. coincides with a leveling-off of sales, while in the U.K. sales grew rapidly through 1959, two years after the shakeout began. In both countries, the number of firms continued to fall despite later demand growth that yielded greater unit sales in the 1970s and 1980s. Market saturation presumably enhanced competition, but more than demand change caused the contraction of the number of firms.

Equivalent competitive processes

In both nations the number of firms rose and declined in an almost identical pattern, with the U.S. drop-off some 6 years ahead of the U.K. The percentage drop in number of firms was nearly identical in the two countries, 88 and 87%. An initial period of high entry preceded much-reduced entry in both countries: in 1948 through 1951 or 1957 in the U.S. or U.K. respectively entry averaged 28.3 or 4.6 firms per year, but subsequently entry fell to 5.0 or 0.4 per year in the next 5 years and 1.0 or 0.9 per year thereafter through 1989.[3] Exit rates among U.S. manufacturers averaged 11.2% per year in 1948–1950, 13.7% in 1951–1955 (the initial 5 years of the shakeout), 10.2% in 1956–1960, 10.4% in 1961–1970, and 6.5% in 1971–1988 (unweighted averages). Among U.K. manufacturers exit rates averaged 9.4% in 1947–1951, 6.6% in 1952–1956, 8.2% in 1957–1961 (the initial five years of the shakeout), 12.2% in 1962–1966, 8.2% in 1967–1976, and 14.3% in 1977–1988. These figures imply that in both countries reduced entry combined with continued exit was primarily responsible for the decline in the number of firms; variation in exit rates had relatively little impact.[4]

In both nations early entrants exited relatively infrequently. The median firm entered in 1949 in the U.S. and 1953 in the U.K. Firms entering in this year or later had an exit rate 1.67 or 1.93 times that of earlier entrants, in the U.S. or U.K. respectively, over the years 1948 through 1989. This late entry disadvantage is statistically significant at the 0.01 level (two-tailed) in exponential hazard regressions.[5]

In both nations firms made large improvements in productivity and product quality. In the U.S., labor productivity in radio and television manufacture combined grew about 5% per year from 1958 through 1980, with television prices declining similarly, and in the U.K. the real price of color televisions fell fairly steadily about 8% per year from 1968 through 1981. Televisions steadily gained reliability (in early years repairs had to be made every few months), plus product features such as improved picture tubes and sound systems, automated and improved tuning, and remote controls.

Process and product improvements were competitively important and were dominated by the leading manufacturers. For the U.S., Steven Klepper and Simons (1997) show that leading, early-entering firms dominated both product and process innovations. For the U.K., patent records show that noted early entrants dominated patenting, led by the firms Marconi E.M.I., Pye, Baird, Murphy, and Mullard. Both country's producers eventually succumbed to foreign firms, which were first to heavily use integrated circuits and remained 1–2 generations ahead in this technology, resulting in fewer set breakdowns and more efficient production.

Mode of technological competition

A U.K. committee set up in 1943 urged enactment of a 405-line screen standard, which it was hoped would establish a *de facto* worldwide standard and aid U.K. firms' exports. The U.K. enacted this standard, but other nations proceeded to adopt standards with greater resolutions. The U.K. broadcast standard remained anomalous through 1964, when some U.K. broadcasts began using the internationally common PAL 625-line color standard. Hence through 1964 and longer, many of the electronic circuits in U.K. televisions differed from those used in other nations. This helped isolate the U.K. market from import competition, which became significant in the early 1960s in the U.S. but not until 1970 in the U.K.

The establishment of a dominant product design, color broadcast standards combined with the 21-inch picture tube, has been blamed for the industry's shakeout (James Utterback and Fernando Suárez, 1993). Firms that took advantage of the standard design were deemed better able to compete. This explanation seems to be incorrect. U.S. color broadcast standards were approved by the Federal Communications Commission in 1953, just after the shakeout began, and leading firms invested in color set production, but color sales failed to materialize until the 1960s. In the U.K. color broadcasts began seven years after the shakeout started. In both nations screen sizes other than 21 inches were always common, and the 21-inch size did not remain a dominant standard.

The implementation of any one technology does not seem to have triggered the industry's shakeout. Technological analyses such as Arnold (1985) and Klepper and Simons (1997) failed to uncover an exceptional technological change at the times of the shakeouts. Moreover, if a radical technology was so important that U.S. firms had to successfully adopt it or die in the mid-1950s, surely U.K. firms would have scrambled to adopt the technology, but the U.K. shakeout did not begin until 6 years later.

Instead, technology mattered to competition in another way. Firms had to keep up with the technological frontier to remain competitive, and this required large research and engineering budgets. The literature suggests that only firms with large output chose to make such expenditures, for only they could expect to sell enough units to reap a substantial return from their investments. This seemingly propelled a rich-get-richer mechanism in which a few early entrants grew large and dominated both innovation and market share.

3. Causes of competitive dynamics

Industries with shakeouts are somewhat well understood, but why does entry decline only slightly or not at all in industries with little or no shakeout? In these industries late-entering firms do not suffer a competitive disadvantage. With little opportunity for technological improvement, or if relevant research and engineering outputs can readily be licensed and sold to other firms, there is no requirement for within-firm innovation. Persistent continued entry might then be explained, despite profit margins already driven down by entry, by sufficient market growth or by incumbent firms frequently exiting to pursue alternative market opportunities. Alternatively, a late-entrant advantage or some other process yet to be uncovered could yield continued entry.

Whatever the reasons, a spectrum or dichotomy of industry dynamics seemingly applies to most industries. This remarkable finding cannot be dismissed on the basis of minimal attention to firm size or concentration, for the limited attention is due merely to limited available data, and robust and meaningful industry processes related to size and concentration have been uncovered. Nor can industry dynamics be dismissed as a minor research topic, for static outcomes result through dynamic processes, and we must uncover how industry outcomes result. If researchers can determine with greater certainty what underlying industry traits most frequently cause different processes of industry dynamics, we might predict industry outcomes *a priori* with some accuracy, as well as design more appropriate corporate and national policy.

Notes

1. For a deeper exploration of the U.S. data see Klepper and Simons (2000).
2. For this section, data on firms, entry, and exit were compiled by the author from successive annual editions of *Television Factbook* for the U.S. and *Kelly's Directory of Merchants, Manufacturers, and Shippers* for the U.K. For the first U.S. year, 1947, a count of 31 firms was used based on the 17 January 1948 issue of *Television Digest and FM Reports* (p. 1). Major sources of other industry information include Levy (1981), Willard (1982), Arnold (1985), Wooster (1986), and Klepper and Simons (1997). The British Radio and Electronics Manufacturers Association kindly provided data on production and sales of televisions.
3. Moreover, among the few late entrants, many were overseas producers that established U.S. or U.K. production to avoid trade barriers.
4. In both countries the brief increase in number of firms during the middle of the shakeout occurred when color television sales took off.
5. Significant multiples of 1.58 and 1.71 likewise result in Cox regressions controlling for years of experience as a television manufacturer.

References

Arnold, E., 1985, *Competition and Technological Change in the Television Industry: An Empirical Evaluation of Theories of the Firm*, London: Macmillan.

Bain, J.S., 1966, *International Differences in Industrial Structure*, New Haven: Yale University Press.

Klepper, S. and Simons, K.L., 1997, 'Technological Extinctions of Industrial Firms: An Enquiry into their Nature and Causes,' *Industrial and Corporate Change*, **6**(2), 379–460

Klepper, S. and Simons, K.L., 2000, 'Dominance by Birthright: Entry of Prior Radio Producers and Competitive Ramifications in the U.S. Television Receiver Industry,' *Strategic Management Journal*, **21**(10–11), 997–1016.

Levy, J.D., 1981, *Diffusion of Technology and Patterns of International Trade: The Case of Television Receivers*, PhD Dissertation, Yale University.

Mansfield, E., 1962, 'Entry, Gibrat's Law, Innovation, and the Growth of Firms,' *American Economic Review*, **52**(5), 1023–1051.

Pryor, F.L., 1972, 'An International Comparison of Concentration Ratios,' *Review of Economics and Statistics*, **54**(2), 130–140.

Schmalensee, R., 1989, 'Inter-Industry Studies of Structure and Performance,' in R. Schmalensee and R. Willig, (eds.), *Handbook of Industrial Organization*, vol. 2. Amsterdam: Elsevier, pp. 951–1009.

Shaked, A. and Sutton, J., 1987, 'Product Differentiation and Industrial Structure,' *Journal of Industrial Economics*, **36**(2), 131–46.

Utterback, J. and Suárez F., 1993, 'Innovation, Competition, and Industry Structure,' *Research Policy*, **22**, 1–21.

Willard, G.E., 1982, *A Comparison of Survivors and Non-survivors under Conditions of Large-scale Withdrawal in the U.S. Color Television Set Industry*, PhD Dissertation, Purdue University.

Wooster, J.H., 1986, *Industrial Policy and International Competitiveness: A Case Study of U.S.-Japanese Competition in the Television Receiver Manufacturing Industry*, PhD Dissertation, University of Massachusetts.

Mansfield's Innovation in the Theory of Innovation

David B. Audretsch[1]
Erik E. Lehmann[2,3]

ABSTRACT. Edwin Mansfield combination of well-founded theoretical formulation about the process of innovation, the systematic testing of broadly accepted views in economics. His pioneering work helped to shape the theory of innovation from a primary focus on industry and firm specific characteristic as well as on the external environment, such as spillovers. The purpose of this paper is to link the seminal contributions of Mansfield. The first focuses on the determinants of firm, the second is concerned with industry context and the third is concerned with university-based knowledge spillovers. The purpose of this paper is to provide a link between these literatures spawned by Mansfield. By linking industry and firm-specific characteristics as well as access to knowledge spillovers from universities, the empirical evidence suggests that knowledge spillovers as well as firm-specific characteristics influence firm growth.

Key words: university spillover, firm growth, entrepreneurship

JEL Classification: M13, L 20, O 31

1. Introduction

Edwin Mansfield was at the cutting edge of theory and understanding concerning innovation and technological change throughout his career. He accomplished this not by taking a position and then defending it to the end, but rather by constantly scrutinizing his views by subjecting them to systematic empirical testing, allowing

---

[1]*Department Entrepreneurship, Growth, and Public Policy Max-Planck Institute for Research into Economic Systems Jena, Kahlaische Strasse 10, 07745 Jena,*
Germany
E-Mail: audretsch@mpiew-jena.mpg.de
[2]*Department Entrepreneurship, Growth, and Public Policy Max-Planck Institute for Research into Economic Systems Jena, Kahlaische Strasse 10, 07745 Jena*
Germany.
[3]*Department of Economics*
University of Konstanz
Box D-144, 78457 Konstanz,
Germany
E-mail: lehmann@mpiew-jena.mpg.de

him to either accept the prevailing thought, or else push it into a new direction.

Well into the 1970s, a conventional wisdom about the nature of technological change generally pervaded. This conventional wisdom had been shaped largely by scholars such as Alfred Chandler (1977), Joseph Schumpeter (1942) and John Kenneth Galbraith (1956) who had convinced a generation of scholars and policy makers that innovation and technological change lie in the domain of large corporations and that small business would fade away as the victim of its own inefficiencies.

At the heart of this conventional wisdom was the belief that monolithic enterprises exploiting market power were the driving engine of innovative activity. Schumpeter had declared the debate closed, with his proclamation in 1942 (p. 106) that, "What we have got to accept is that (the large-scale establishment) has come to be the most powerful engine of progress." Galbraith (1956, p. 86) echoed Schumpeter's sentiment, "There is no more pleasant fiction than that technological change is the product of the matchless ingenuity of the small man forced by competition to employ his wits to better his neighbor. Unhappily, it is a fiction."

At the same time, the conventional wisdom about small and new firms was that they were burdened with a size inherent handicap in terms of innovative activity. Because they had a deficit of resources required to generate and commercialize ideas, this conventional wisdom viewed small enterprises as being largely outside of the domain of innovative activity and technological change. F.M. Scherer (1991, p. 25) describes confronting this conventional wisdom "at a fundamentalist revival", where the Fifth Plan of the French Government had an explicit objective of promoting "the constitution, or the reinforcement where extant, of a small number of firms or groups ...".

While this conventional wisdom about the singular role played by large enterprises with market power prevailed during the first three decades subsequent to the close of the Second World War II, Edwin Mansfield, along with other leading scholars such as F.M. Scherer helped to pioneer a wave of new studies that has challenged this conventional wisdom. Most importantly, these studies identified a much wider spectrum of enterprises contributing to innovative activity, and that, in particular, small entrepreneurial firms as well as large established incumbents play an important role in the innovation and process of technological change.

Taken together, these studies comprise the foundations for understanding innovation and technological change. The purpose of this chapter is to explain how and why Ed Mansfield's work, along with that of a handful of other scholars of his generation, shaped our understanding about innovation.

2. The firm context

Mansfield's primary focus was on what influenced the innovative activity of firms. The starting point of this research was on the relationship between the most observable characteristics of a firm, principally its size, and its innovative activity. The focus on the firm as the most relevant unit of observation perhaps reflected the theoretical concern of Schumpeter's later work, which argued that "the large, monopolistic corporation provided an ideal environment for advancing technology" (Scherer, 1991, p. 24). However, testing the so-called Schumpeterian Hypothesis proved to be less than obvious. While size is not without measurement problems, measuring innovative activity is fraught with ambiguities and challenges.

The initial attempts to quantify technological change at all generally involved measuring some aspects of inputs into the innovative process (Grabowski, 1968; Mansfield, 1968; Mueller, 1967; Scherer, 1965a, b; 1967). Measures of R&D inputs—first in terms of employment and later in terms of expenditures—were only introduced on a meaningful basis enabling inter-industry and inter-firm comparisons in the late 1950s and early 1960s.

A clear limitation in using R&D activity as a proxy measure for technological change is that R&D reflects only the resources devoted to producing innovative output, but not the amount of innovative activity actually realized. As Mansfield (1981, p. 130) pointed out, these studies "focus attention solely on the total amount spent on R&D, not on its composition. This is a very important limitation. R&D includes fundamental investigations as well as superficial ones, work directed at major new products and processes, as well as projects aimed at minor modifications of existing processes and products; and long-term and risky projects as well as short-term and safe ones. It is widely recognized that attempts should be made to disaggregate R&D expenditures in studies of this type."

Kleinknecht *et al.* (1991) have systematically shown that R&D measures incorporate only efforts made to generate innovative activity that are undertaken within formal R&D budgets and within formal R&D laboratories. They find that the extent of informal R&D is considerable, particularly in smaller enterprises.[1] And, as Mansfield (1984) points out, not all efforts within a formal R&D laboratory are directed towards generating innovative output in any case. Rather, other types of output, such as imitation and technology transfer, are also common goals in R&D laboratories.

As systematic data measuring the number of inventions patented were made publicly available in the mid-1960s, many scholars interpreted this new measure not only as being superior to R&D but also as reflecting innovative output. In fact, the use of patented inventions is not a measure of innovative output, but is rather a type of intermediate output measure. A patent reflects new technical knowledge, but it does not indicate whether this knowledge has a positive economic value. Only those inventions which have been successfully introduced in the market can claim that they are innovation.

Besides the fact that many, if not most, patented inventions do not result in an innovation, a second important limitation of patent measures as an indicator of innovative activity is that they do not capture all of the innovations actually made. In fact, many inventions which result in innovations are not patented. The tendency of patented inventions to result in innovations and of innovations to be the result of inventions which were patented combine into what Scherer (1983a) has termed as the propensity to patent. It is the uncertainty about the stability of the propensity to patent across enterprises and across industries that casts doubt upon the reliability of patent measures.[2] According to Scherer (1983a, pp. 107–108), "The quantity and quality of industry patenting may depend upon chance, how readily a technology lends itself to patent protection, and business decision-makers' varying perceptions of how much advantage they will derive from patent rights. Not much of a systematic nature is known about these phenomena, which can be characterized as differences in the propensity to patent."

Mansfield (1984, p. 462) has explained why the propensity to patent may vary so much across markets: "The value and cost of individual patents vary enormously within and across industries ... Many inventions are not patented. And in some industries, like electronics, there is considerable speculation that the patent system is being bypassed to a greater extent than in the past. Some types of technologies are more likely to be patented than others." The implications are that comparisons between enterprises and across industries may be misleading.

The evidence suggested that technological change—or rather, one aspect of technological change reflected by one of the three measures discussed in the previous section, R&D—is, in fact, positively related to firm size.[3] The empirical evidence generally seems to confirm Scherer's (1982, pp. 234–235) conclusion that the results "tilt on the side of supporting the Schumpeterian Hypothesis that size is conducive to vigorous conduct of R&D".

In one of the most important studies, Scherer (1984) used the U.S. Federal Trade Commission's Line of Business Data to estimate the elasticity of R&D spending with respect to firm sales for 196 industries. He found evidence of increasing returns to scale (an elasticity exceeding unity) for about twenty percent of the industries, constant returns to scale for a little less than three-quarters of the industries, and diminishing returns (an elasticity less than unity) in less than ten percent of the industries. Mansfield (1981, 1983; Mansfield et al., 1982), showed that the relationship between firm size and R&D was considerably more nuanced. Still, the empirical evidence seems to generally support the Schumpeterian hypothesis that R&D is positively related to firm size.

The studies relating patents to firm size are even less ambiguous. Here the findings unequivocally suggest that "the evidence leans weakly against the Schumpeterian conjecture that the largest sellers are especially fecund sources of patented inventions" (Scherer, 1982, p. 235). In one of the most important studies, Scherer (1965b) used the Fortune annual survey of the 500 largest U.S. industrial corporations. He related the 1955 firm sales to the number of patents in 1959 for 448 firms. Scherer found that the number of patented inventions increases less than proportionately along with firm size. Scherer's results were later confirmed by Bound et al. (1984) in the study mentioned above. Basing their study on 2852 companies and 4553 patenting entities, they determined that the small firms (with less than $10 million in sales) accounted for 4.3 percent of the sales from the entire sample, but 5.7 percent of the patents.

Scherer (1988, pp. 4–5) has summarized the advantages small firms may have in innovative activity: "Smaller enterprises make their impressive contributions to innovation because of several advantages they possess compared to large-size corporations. One important strength is that they are less bureaucratic, without layers of "abominable no-men" who block daring ventures in a more highly structured organization. Second, and something that is often overlooked, many advances in technology accumulate upon a myriad of detailed inventions involving individual components, materials, and fabrication techniques. The sales possibilities for making such narrow, detailed advances are often too modest to interest giant corporations. An individual entrepreneur's juices will flow over a new product or process with sales prospects in the millions of dollars per year, whereas few large corporations can work up much excitement over such small fish, nor can they accommodate small ventures easily into their organizational structures. Third, it is easier to sustain a fever pitch of excitement in small organization, where the links between challenges, staff, and potential rewards are tight. "All-nighters" through which tough technical problems are solved expeditiously are common."

3. The industry context

As the evidence started to crystallize about the relationship between firm-specific characteristics, and especially size, and innovative activity, principally R&D effort and the number of patented inventions, more attention was placed on the influence of one dimension of the external environment—the industry context. In particular, the degree of competition and concentration and the impact on firm innovative performance was a central concern.

In fact, most of the focus on the innovative activity of firms remained focused on firm. In their exhaustive review of the literature, Baldwin and Scott (1987, p. 89) identify only a "miniscule" number of scholars refocused their attention to the industry context in explaining the innovative performance of firms. Once again, Mansfield was a pioneer in linking the industry context to firm innovative performance.

The most comprehensive and insightful evidence utilized the Federal Trade Commission's Line of Business Data. Using 236 manufacturing industry categories, which are defined at both the three- and four-digit SIC level, Scherer (1983a) found that 1974 company R&D expenditures divided by sales was positively related to the 1974 four-firm concentration ratio. Scherer (1983a, p. 225) concluded that, "although one cannot be certain, it appears that the advantages a high market share confers in appropriating R&D benefits provide the most likely explanation of the observed R&D-concentrator associations."

Scott (1984) also used the FTC Line of Business Survey Data and found the U-shaped relationship between market concentration and R&D. However, when he controlled for the fixed effects for two-digit SIC industries, no significant relationship could be found between concentration and R&D.

Mansfield found "little or no indication that more concentrated industries tend to provide a larger percentage of R&D expenditures to basic research and to relatively long-term, ambitious and risky projects. Instead, the results show that more concentrated industries devote a smaller, not larger, percentage of R&D expenditures to basic research. Moreover, the difference in this regard between more and less concentrated industries is statistically significant and quantitatively quite large" (Mansfield, 1981, pp. 132–133).

Overall, the research efforts of Mansfield, Scherer and others produced systematic and compelling findings, which were summarized by Scherer (1991, pp. 24–25), " The principle conclusions of this study are as follows: (1) Inventive output increases with firm sales, but generally at a less than proportional rate. (2) Differences in technological opportunity... are a major factor responsible for interindustry differences in inventive output, and (3) Inventive output does not appear to be systematically related to variations in market power, prior profitability, liquidity, or (when participation in fields with high technological opportunity is accounted for) degree of product line diversification.

These findings, among other things raise doubts whether the big, monopolistic, conglomerate corporation is as efficient an engine of technological change as disciples of Schumpeter (including myself) have supposed it to be. Perhaps a bevy of fact-mechanics can still rescue the Schumpeterian engine from disgrace, but at present the outlook seems pessimistic."

4. The university context

Mansfield was again one of the pioneers pointing out that that the industry was not the only element of the external environment affecting the innovative activity of the firm. He was one of the first to identify research laboratories of universities as providing an important source of innovation-generating knowledge that is available to private enterprises for commercial exploitation (Mansfield, 1995, 1998).

In this new dimension of his work, Mansfield (1995), pioneered a very different research trajectory, which focused on external sources of R&D, and in particular universities, as inputs into firm innovation.[4] Mansfield's research was instrumental in triggering a more recent wave of studies identifying the role that knowledge spillovers play, and in particular, knowledge spillovers from universities in generating innovative activity (Audretsch and Feldman, 1996; Audretsch and Stephan, 1996; Jaffe, 1989).

The empirical work reviewed previously supported that finding. For example, Jaffe (1989) and Acs, Audretsch, and Feldman (1992), Audretsch and Feldman (1996) found that the knowledge created in university laboratories spills over to contribute to the generation of commercial innovations by private enterprises. Even after controlling for the location of industrial R&D, knowledge created at universities results in greater innovation. The ability of research universities to create benefits for their local economies has created a new mission for research universities and a developing literature examines the mechanism and the process of technology transfer from research universities.

Mansfield's work helped to spawn a new literature has emerged suggesting that knowledge spills over from the firm or university producing it to a different firm commercializing that knowledge (Griliches, 1992). An important theoretical development is that geography may provide a relevant unit of observation within which knowledge spillovers occur. The theory of localization suggests that because geographic proximity is needed to transmit knowledge and especially tacit knowledge, knowledge spillovers tend to be localized within a geographic region. The importance of geographic proximity for knowledge spillovers has been supported in a wave of recent empirical studies by Jaffe (1989), Jaffe, Trajtenberg and Henderson (1993), Acs, Audretsch and Feldman (1992 and 1994), Audretsch and Feldman (1996), Audretsch and Stephan (1996), Hall, Link and Scott (2003) and Link (1995).

As it became apparent that the firm was not completely adequate as a unit of analysis for estimating the model of the knowledge production function, scholars began to look for externalities. In refocusing the model of the knowledge production to a spatial unit of observation, scholars confronted two challenges. The first one was theoretical. What was the theoretical basis for knowledge to spill over yet, at the same time, be spatially within some geographic unit of observation? The second challenge involved measurement. How could knowledge spillovers be measured and identified? More than a few scholars heeded Krugman's warning (1991, p. 53) that empirical measurement of knowledge spillovers would prove to be impossible because "knowledge flows are invisible, they leave no paper trail by which they may be measured and tracked."[5]

In confronting the first challenge, which involved developing a theoretical basis for geographically bounded knowledge spillovers, scholars turned to the emerging literature of the new growth theory. In explaining the increased divergence in the distribution of economic activity between countries and regions, Krugman (1991) and Romer (1986) relied on models based on increasing returns to scale in production. By increasing returns, however, Krugman and Romer did not necessarily mean at the level of observation most familiar in the industrial organization literature—the plant, or at least the firm—but rather at the level of a spatially distinguishable unit. In fact, it was assumed that the externalities across firms and even industries yield convexities in production. In particular, Krugman (1991), invoking Marshall (1920), focused on convexities arising from spillovers from (1) a pooled labor market; (2) pecuniary externalities enabling the provision of non-traded inputs to an industry in a greater variety and at lower cost; and (3) information or technological spillovers.

That knowledge spills over was barely disputed. Some 30 years earlier, Arrow (1962) identified externalities associated with knowledge due to its non-exclusive and non-rival use. However, what has been contested is the geographic range of knowledge spillovers: knowledge externalities are so important and forceful that there is no reason that knowledge should stop spilling over just because of borders, such as a city limit, state line, or national boundary. Krugman (1991), and others, did not question the existence or importance of such knowledge spillovers. In fact, they argue that such knowledge externalities are so important and forceful that there is no reason for a political boundary to limit the spatial extent of the spillover.

In applying the model of the knowledge production function to spatial units of observation, theories of why knowledge externalities are spatially bounded were needed. Thus, it took the development of localization theories explaining not only that knowledge spills over but also why those spillovers decay as they move across geographic space.

Studies identifying the extent of knowledge spillovers are based on the model of the knowledge production function applied at spatial units of observation. In what is generally to be considered to be the first important study re-focusing the knowledge production function, Jaffe (1989) modified the traditional approach to estimate a model specified for both spatial and product dimensions:

$$I_{si} = \alpha IRD^{\beta_1} * UR_{si}^{\beta_2} * (UR_{si} * GC_{si}^{\beta_3}) * \varepsilon_{si} \qquad (1)$$

where I is innovative output, IRD is private corporate expenditures on R&D, UR is the research expenditures undertaken at universities, and GC measures the geographic coincidence of university and corporate research. The unit of observation for estimation was at the spatial level, s, a state, and industry level, i. Estimation of equation (2) essentially shifted the knowledge production function from the unit of observation of a firm to that of a geographic unit. Implicitly contained within the knowledge production function model is the assumption that innovative activity should take place in those regions, s, where the direct knowledge-generating inputs are the greatest, and where knowledge spillovers are the most prevalent. Jaffe (1989) dealt with the measurement problem raised by Krugman (1991) by linking the patent activity within technologies located within states to knowledge inputs located within the same spatial jurisdiction.

Estimation of equation (1) essentially shifted the model of the knowledge production function from the unit of observation of a firm to that of a geographic unit. Jaffe (1989) found empirical evidence that $\beta_1 \geq 0, \beta_2 \geq 0, \beta_3 \geq 0$ supporting the notion knowledge spills over for third-party use from university research laboratories as well as industry R&D laboratories. Acs, Audretsch and Feldman (1992) confirmed that the knowledge production function represented by equation (2) held at a spatial unit of observation using a direct measure of innovative activity, new product introductions in the market. Feldman (1994) extended the model to consider other knowledge inputs to the commercialization of new products. The results confirmed that the knowledge production function was robust at the geographic level of analysis: the output of innovation is a function of the innovative inputs in that location.

Other studies confirmed that knowledge spillovers tend to be geographically bounded within the region where new economic knowledge was created (Autant-Bernard, 2001a, b; Black, 2003; Orlando, 2000). Scholars have continued to work in this tradition adding new measures of innovative output and refining the measures of innovative inputs and outputs. For example, Black (2003) developed a measure of innovation based on awards made in the United States Small Business Innovation Research (SBIR) Program. In estimating a knowledge production function along the lines of equation (2) for a variety of geographic units and using different measure of innovative output, the results concur that the logic of the knowledge production function is robust across geography. Autant-Bernard (2001a, b) and Orlando (2000) model the interplay between geographic and technological proximity for inter-firm spillovers. Their results suggest the importance of geographic proximity for spillovers is dependent on the propensity of similar industrial activity to agglomerate geographically.

Estimation of the knowledge production function has typically varied the spatial unit from relatively broad geographic units of observations, such as states, to much more focused geographic units of observations such as cities, counties or even zip codes. Most scholars concluded that states are probably too broad to represent an appropriate geographic unit of observation. In probing for the relevant spatial unit of observation, scholars responded by estimating the geographic extent of knowledge spillovers in miles using the concept of distance decay (Adams, 2002; Audretsch and Lehmann, 2005).

While this literature has identified the important role that knowledge spillovers play, they provide little insight into the questions of why knowledge spills over and how it spills over. What happens within the black box of the knowledge production is vague and ambiguous at best. The exact links between knowledge sources and the resulting innovative output remain invisible and unknown. None of the above studies suggesting that knowledge spillovers are geographically bounded and localized within spatial proximity to the knowledge source actually identified the actual mechanisms which actually transmit the knowledge spillover; rather, the spillovers were implicitly assumed to automatically exist, or fall like "Manna from heaven", but only within a geographically bounded spatial area.

One explanation was provided by the knowledge spillover theory of entrepreneurship, which suggests that the startup of a new firm is a response to investments in knowledge and ideas by incumbent organizations that are not fully commercialized by those organizations. Thus, those contexts that are richer in knowledge will offer more entrepreneurial opportunities and therefore should also endogenously induce more entrepreneurial activity, *ceteris paribus*. By contrast, those context that are impoverished in knowledge will offer only meager entrepreneurial opportunities generated by knowledge spillovers, and therefore would endogenously induce less entrepreneurial activity.

While this literature has identified the important role that knowledge spillovers play, they provide little insight into the questions of why knowledge spills over and how it spills over. What happens within the black box of the knowledge production is vague and ambiguous at best. The exact links between knowledge sources and the resulting innovative output remain invisible and unknown. None of the above studies suggesting that knowledge spillovers are geographically bounded and localized within spatial proximity to the knowledge source actually identified the actual mechanisms which actually transmit the knowledge spillover; rather, the spillovers were implicitly assumed to automatically exist, or fall like "Manna from heaven", but only within a geographically bounded spatial area.

What is the appropriate unit of observation to be used to frame the context and observe the entrepreneurial response to knowledge investments made by incumbent organizations? In his 1995 book, Audretsch proposed using the industry as the context in which knowledge is created, developed, organized and commercialized. The context of an industry was used to resolve the paradox concerning the high innovative output of small enterprises given their low level of knowledge inputs that seemingly contradicted the Griliches model of the firm knowledge production, "The findings in this book challenge an assumption implicit to the knowledge production function—that firms exist exogenously and then endogenously seek out and apply knowledge inputs to generate innovative output.... It is the knowledge in the possession of economic agents that is exogenous, and in an effort to appropriate the returns from that knowledge, the spillover of knowledge from its producing entity involves endogenously creating a new firm" (pp. 179–180).

What is the source of this entrepreneurial knowledge that endogenously generated the startup of new firms? The answer seemed to be through the spillover of knowledge from the source creating to commercialization via the startup of a new firm, "How are these small and frequently new firms able to generate innovative output when undertaken a generally negligible amount of investment into knowledge-generating inputs, such as R&D? One answer is apparently exploiting knowledge created by expenditures on research in universities and on R&D in large corporations" (p. 179).

The empirical evidence supporting the knowledge spillover theory of entrepreneurship was provided from analyzing variations in startup rates across different industries reflecting different underlying knowledge contexts (Audretsch, 1995). In particular, those industries with a greater investment in new knowledge also exhibited higher startup rates while those industries with less investment in new knowledge exhibited lower startup rates, which was interpreted as the mechanism by which knowledge spillovers are transmitted.

Thus, compelling evidence was provided suggesting that entrepreneurship is an endogenous response to the potential for commercializing knowledge that has not been adequately commercialized by the incumbent firms. This involved an organizational dimension involving the mechanism transmitting knowledge spillovers—the startup of new firms. In addition, Jaffe (1989), Audretsch and Feldman (1996) and Audretsch and Stephan (1996) provided evidence concerning the spatial dimension of knowledge spillovers. In particular their findings suggested that knowledge spillovers are geographically bounded and localized within spatial proximity to the knowledge source. None of these studies, however, identified the actual mechanisms which actually transmit the knowledge spillover; rather, the spillovers were implicitly assumed to automatically exist (or fall like Manna from heaven), but only within a geographically bounded spatial area. These studies do, however, suggest that the geographic space might be a relevant context for knowledge spillover entrepreneurship.

5. Conclusions

The empirical evidence provided by Mansfield and the other leaders of his generation strongly suggested that small entrepreneurial firms play a key role in generating innovations, at least in certain industries. While the conventional wisdom is derived from the Schumpeterian Hypothesis and assumption that scale economies exist in R&D effort, for which there is considerable empirical evidence, more recent evidence suggests that scale economies bestowed through the geographic proximity facilitated by spatial clusters seems to be more important than those for large enterprises in producing innovative output.

Edwin Mansfield has been a pioneer helping to shape the theory of innovation and technological change in its evolution from a primary focus on characteristics specific to the firm, such as size, to a later and broader orientation, which incorporated influences from the external environment, such as university spillovers.

Mansfield was a pioneer in economics because he tested theory with empirical data, and then subsequently let the emerging findings and results guide and revise the theoretical formulations.

Mansfield's combination of well-founded theoretical formulation about the process of innovation, combined with the development of new types of measurement and novel data bases facilitated the systematic testing of broadly accepted views in economics. Thus, Mansfield proved to be a pioneer in documenting not just how important the process of innovation and technological change is, but also the sources of innovation, as well as their impact in making markets dynamic.

Notes

1. Similar results emphasizing the importance of informal R&D have been found by Santarelli and Sterlachinni (1990).
2. For example, Shepherd (1979, p. 40) has concluded that, "Patents are a notoriously weak measure. Most of the eighty thousand patents issued each year are worthless and are never used. Still others have negative social value. They are used as "blocking" patents to stop innovation, or they simply are developed to keep competition out."
3. Fisher and Temin (1973) demonstrated that the Schumpeterian Hypothesis could not be substantiated unless it was established that the elasticity of innovative output with respect to firm size exceeds one. They pointed out that if scale economies in R&D do exist, a firm's size may grow faster than its R&D activities. Kohn and Scott (1982) later showed that if the elasticity of R&D input with respect to firm size is greater than unity, then the elasticity of R&D output with respect to firm size must also be greater than one.
4. An earlier study focusing on knowledge spillovers is Link and Rees (1990.).
5. Lucas (2001) and Lucas and Rossi-Hansberg (2002) impose a spatial structure on production externalities in order to model the spatial structure of cities. The logic is that spatial gradients capture some of the externalities associated with localized human capital accumulation.

References

Acs, Z., D. B. Audretsch, and M. Feldman, 1992, Real Effects of Academic Research: Comment, *American Economic Review*, **81**, 363–367.

Acs, Z., D. B. Audretsch, and M. Feldman, 1994, R&D Spillovers and Recipient Firm Size, *The Review of Economics and Statistics*, **76**, 336–340.

Adams, J.D., 2002, 'Comparative Localization of Academic and Industrial Spillovers,' *Journal of Economic Geography* **2**, 253–278.

Adams, J.D. and A.B. Jaffe, 2002, 'Bounding the Effects of R&D: an Investigation Using Matched Firm and Establishment Data,' *Rand Journal of Economics* **27**, 700–721.

Arrow, K., 1962, Economic Welfare and the Allocation of Resources for Invention, in R. Nelson (ed.), *The Rate and Direction of Inventive Activity*, Princeton: Princeton University Press, 609–626.

Audretsch, David B. 1995, *Innovation and Industry Evolution*, Cambridge: MIT Press.

Audretsch, D.B. and M.P. Feldman, 1996, 'R&D Spillovers and the Geography of Innovation and Production,' *American Economic Review* **86**(3), June, 630-640.

Audretsch, D.B. and P. E. Stephan, 1996, 'Company-Scientist Locational Links: The Case of Biotechnology,' *American Economic Review* **86**(3), June, 641–652.

Audretsch, D. B., and E. E. Lehmann, 2005, Do University Policies Make a Difference, *Research Policy* (forthcoming).

Autant-Bernard, C., 2001a, Science and Knowledge Flows: Evidence from the French Case, *Research Policy*, **30**, 1069–1078.

Autant-Bernard, C., 2001b, The Geography of Knowledge Spillovers and Technological Proximity, *Economic of Innovation and New Technology*, **10**, 237–254.

Baldwin, W.L. and J.T. Scott, 1987, *Market Structure and Technological Change*, London and New York: Harwood Academic Publishers.

Black G., 2003, *The Geography of Small Firm Innovation*, Dordrecht: Kluwer Academic Publishers.

Bound, J., C. Cummins, Z. Griliches, B.H. Hall, and A. Jaffe, 1984, 'Who Does R&D and Who Patents?,' in Z. Griliches (ed.), *R&D, Patents, and Productivity*, Chicago, IL: University of Chicago Press, pp. 21–54.

Chandler, A., 1977, *The Visible Hand: The Managerial Revolution in American Business*, Cambridge: Harvard University Press.

Feldman, M., 1994, *The Geography of Innovation*, Boston: Kluwer Academic Publishers.

Fisher, F.M. and P. Temin, 1973, 'Returns to Scale in Research and Development: What Does the Schumpeterian Hypothesis Imply?,' *Journal of Political Economy* **81**, 56–70.

Galbraith, J.K., 1956, *American Capitalism: The Concept of Coutervailing Power*, revised edition, Boston, MA: Houghton Mifflin.

Grabowski, H.G., 1968, 'The Determinants of Industrial Research and Development: A Study of the Chemical, Drug, and Petroleum Industries,' *Journal of Political Economy* **76** (4), 292–306.

Griliches, Z., 1992, The Search for R&D Spillovers, *Scandinavian Journal of Economics*, **94**, 29–47.

Hall, B.H., A.N. Link, and J. T. Scott, 2003, Universities as Research Partners, *Review of Economics and Statistics*.

Jaffe, A.B., 1986, 'Technological Opportunity and Spillovers of R&D: Evidence from Firms' Patents, Profits and Market Value,' *American Economic Review* **76**, 984–1001.

Jaffe, A.B., 1989, 'Real Effects of Academic Research,' *American Economic Review* **79**(5), 957–970.

Jaffe, A.B., M. Trajtenberg, and R. Henderson, 1993, Geographic Localization of Knowledge Spillovers as evidenced by Patent Citations, *Quarterly Journal of Economics* **63**, 577–598.

Kleinknecht, A., T.P. Poot, and J. O. N. Reijnen, 1991, Formal and Informal R&D and Firm Size, in Acs, Z. and D.B. Audretsch (eds): *Innovation and Technological Change. An International Comparison*, Ann Arbor: University of Michigan Press, 84–108.

Kohn, M. and J.T. Scott, 1982, 'Scale Economies in Research and Development: The Schumpeterian Hypothesis,' *Journal of Industrial Economics*, **30**, 239–249.

Krugman, P., 1991, *Geography and Trade*, Cambridge: MIT Press.

Link, A.N. and B. Bozeman, 1991, 'Innovative Behavior in Small-Sized Firms,' *Small Business Economics* **3**(3), 179–184.

Link, A.N. and J. Rees, 1990, 'Firm Size, University Based Research, and the Returns to R&D,' *Small Business Economics*, **2**(1), 25–32.

Link, A.N., 1995, 'The Use of Literature-Based Innovation Output Indicators for Research Evaluation,' *Small Business Economics* **7**(6), 451–455.

Lucas, R. E., 2001, Externalities and Cities, *Review of Economic Dynamics*, **4**, 245–475.

Lucas, R. E. and E. Rossi-Hansberg, 2002, On the Internal Structure of Cities, *Econometrica*, **70**, 1445–1476.

Mansfield, E., 1968, *Industrial Research and Technological Change*, New York, NY: W.W. Norton, for the Cowles Foundation for Research Economics at Yale University, pp. 83–108.

Mansfield, E., 1981, 'Composition of R&D Expenditures: Relationship to Size of Firm, Concentration, and Innovative Output,' *Review of Economics and Statistics*, **63**, November, 610–615.

Mansfield, E., 1983, 'Industrial Organization and Technological Change: Recent Empirical Findings,' in John V. Craven (ed.), *Industrial Organization, Antitrust, and Public Policy*, The Hague: Kluwer-Nijhoff, pp. 129–143.

Mansfield, E., 1984, 'Comment on Using Linked Patent and R&D Data to Measure Interindustry Technology Flows,' in Z. Griliches (ed.), *R&D, Patents, and Productivity*, Chicago, IL: University of Chicago Press, pp. 462–464.

Mansfield, E.,1995, 'Academic Research Underlying Industrial Innovations: Sources, Characteristics, and Financing,' *The Review of Economics and Statistics* **77**, 55–65.

Mansfield, E., 1998, 'Academic Research and Industrial Innovation: An Update of Empirical Findings,' *Research Policy* **26** (7–8), 773–776.

Mansfield, E., A. Romeo, M. Schwartz, D. Teece, S. Wagner and P. Brach, 1982, *Technology Transfer, Productivity, and Economic Policy*, New York: W. W. Norton.

Marshall, A., 1920, *Principles of Economics*, 8th ed. London: MacMillan.

Mueller, D.C., 1967, 'The Firm Decision Process: An Econometric Investigation,' *Journal of Political Economy*, **81**(1), 58–87.

Orlando, M.J., 2000, *On the Importance of Geographic and Technological Proximity for R&D Spillovers: An Empirical Investigation*, Kansas: Federal Reserve Bank.

Romer, P.M., 1986, Increasing Returns and Long run Growth, *Journal of Political Economy*, **94**, 1002–1037.

Santarelli, E., and A. Sterlachinni, 1990, Innovation, Formal vs. Informal R&D, and Firm Size: Some Evidence from Italian Manufacturing Firms, *Small Business Economics*, **2**, 223–228.

Scherer, F.M., 1965a, 'Firm Size, Market Structure, Opportunity, and the Output of Patented Inventions,' *American Economic Review* **55**, 1097–1125.

Scherer, F.M., 1965b, 'Size of Firm, Oligopoly and Research: A Comment,' *Canadian Journal of Economics and Political Science* **31**, 256–266.

Scherer, F.M., 1967, 'Market Structure and the Employment of Scientists and Engineers,' *American Economic Review* **57**, 524–530.

Scherer, F., M., 1982, 'Inter-Industry Technology Flows in the United States,' *Research Policy,* **11**, 227–245.

Scherer, F. M., 1983a, 'Concentration, R&D, and Productivity Change,' *Southern Economic Journal* **50**, 221–225.

Scherer, F.M., 1983b, 'The Propensity to Patent,' *International Journal of Industrial Organization*, **1** 107–128.

Scherer, F.M., 1984, *Innovation and Growth: Schumpeterian Perspectives*, Cambridge, MA: MIT Press.

Scherer, F., M., 1988, 'Testimony before the Subcommittee on Monopolies and Commercial Law,' Committee on the Judiciary, U.S. House of Representatives, February 24.

Scherer, F.M., 1991, 'Changing Perspectives on the Firm Size Problem,' in Z.J. Acs and D.B. Audretsch, (eds.), *Innovation and Technological Change: An International Comparison*, Ann Arbor: University of Michigan Press 24–38.

Schumpeter, J.A., 1942, *Capitalism, Socialism and Democracy*, New York, NY: Harper and Row.

Scott, J.T., 1984, 'Firm Versus Industry Variability' in R&D Intensity, in Z. Griliches (ed.), *R&D, Patents and Productivity*, Chicago, IL: University of Chicago Press, pp. 233–248.

Modeling the Impact of Technical Change on Emissions Abatement Investments in Developing Countries

Michael Gallaher[1]
K. Casey Delhotal[2]

ABSTRACT. The cost of greenhouse gas (GHG) mitigation over time depends on both the rate of technical change in leading-edge technologies and the diffusion of knowledge and capabilities throughout international markets. This paper presents a framework developed by the U.S. Environmental Protection Agency (EPA) and RTI International (RTI) for incorporating technical change in non-CO2 GHG mitigation projections over time. An engineering (bottom-up) approach is used to model technical change as a set of price and productivity factors that change over time as a function of technology advances and the location of developing countries relative to the technology efficiency frontier. S-shaped diffusion curves are generated, which demonstrate the maturity of the market for a given technology in a given region. The framework is demonstrated for coal mine methane mitigation technologies in the United States and China, but it is applicable for the full range of technology adoption issues.

Key words: technology transfer, diffusion, climate change

JEL Classification: O33

1. Introduction

Edwin Mansfield was an early pioneer in the description of the diffusion of industrial technology. His work on the diffusion of robotics and flexible manufacturing systems highlighted the importance of the firm's perceived adoption costs, rate of return, and risk associated with technology investments (Mansfield, 1989, 1993). Mansfield's early work set the stage for more sophisticated econometric analysis (Geroski, 2000). However, all these efforts build on the principle that technical information diffuses throughout a population, reducing costs, and generates S-shaped adoption paths over time. Information lowers the cost (and risk) of adoption by reducing the leaning curve and increasing the effectiveness of new technologies. This paper follows Mansfield's work, applying these principles to the adoption of emissions abatement technologies in developed and developing countries. The paper develops a bottom-up engineering approach for modeling technology change that provides insights into the factors underpinning the S-shaped diffusion curves observed in the empirical and qualitative literature.

The diffusion of information and technical change are key drivers in the adoption of abatement technologies. This is particularly important in developing countries where the diffusion of new technologies and supporting infrastructures significantly affect the installation and maintenance costs of emerging technologies. The availability of cost-effective abatement options over time depends on both the rate of technical change in newer mitigation technologies and the rate of diffusion of established mitigation practices and technologies. New technologies follow a life cycle where early installation and operating costs are high but then decrease for later installations as methods are refined. Technical improvements lead to reductions in capital and labor

---

[1] RTI International
3040 Cornwallis Road
Research Triangle Park, NC 27709
E-mail: mpg@rti.org
[2] U.S. Environmental Protection Agency
1200 Pennsylvania Avenue NW, 6202J
Washington, DC 20460

costs and increase the reduction efficiency of mitigation options. In addition, knowledge spillovers and the expiration of patents lead to increased competition that lowers market prices.

Analyses of historical data have shown that inter- and intra-firm diffusion of new technologies typically follows a gradual S-shaped process. Griliches' (1957) early work on the diffusion of hybrid corn shows that the rate at which a new technology is being used slowly increases at first, then increases more rapidly, and then continues to increase but at a decreasing rate, forming an S-shaped curve. Griliches characterized the observed pattern as a logistic curve. Mansfield (1968) also found that a logistic S-shaped curve fit the diffusion of diesel locomotives in the U.S. railroad industry. In addition, Mansfield found that although the shapes of most diffusion curves may be similar, the length of time associated with the diffusion process can vary significantly across different industries and technologies.

The S-shaped diffusion can theoretically be motivated by decreasing cost and/or information models. One popular explanation of S-shaped curves is the epidemic model of information diffusion (Geroski, 2000). Similarly Rogers (1995) motivates the S-shaped diffusion curve in terms of innovators, early adopters, takeoff adoptions, and late adopters. He describes diffusion as a social process where early adopters reduce the uncertainty for later adopters of the innovation. In this way, the communication of knowledge and experience from peers is equally important as the dissemination of knowledge through consensus guidelines and academic publications.

In a related fashion, technology adoption plays an important role in the timing of potential emissions reductions. Expensive installations by early adopters serve to demonstrate the technology, lowering the perceived risk for following adopters. In addition, early adopters develop solutions for integrating new technologies into legacy systems, hence lowering costs to later adopters. In this way, it is the heterogeneous cost and benefit characteristics of individual sources that determine the rate of adoption, with entities in the tails of the distributions significantly affecting the timing of adoption by "mainstream" or "typical" entities.

This paper presents a framework developed by the U.S. Environmental Protection Agency (EPA) and RTI International (RTI) for incorporating technical change into the marginal cost of methane gas mitigation projections over time. An engineering-economic (bottom-up) approach is used to model technical change as a set of price and productivity factors that change over time as a function of specific technology life cycles and the location of countries relative to a technology efficiency frontier. The framework is demonstrated for coal mining emission reduction technologies in China, but it is applicable for the full range of technology adoption issues.

2. Introducing technical change into marginal abatement cost analysis

Marginal abatement curves (MACs) are an important input into the modeling of global climate change and policy alternatives to reduce greenhouse gas (GHG) emissions. Similar to marginal cost curves, MACs express the quantity of emissions a country might be willing to abate at a given carbon price.

MACs commonly describe the adoption potential of a single or suite of emission reduction technologies. As shown in Figure 1, MACs present emissions reductions (on the horizontal axis) as a function of the price of carbon (on the vertical axis). As the market value of abatement (expressed as tons of carbon equivalent [TCE][1]) increases, more abatement options become economically viable. Analysts and policy makers use these curves to assess the impact of potential carbon taxes or emissions trading programs.

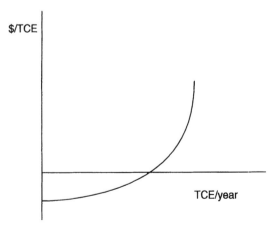

Figure 1. Marginal abatement curves (MACs).

Because climate change is a global issue, MACs are needed for both developed and developing countries. For example, coal production in China is projected to approximately double over the next 30 years, making it by far the leading source of methane in the coal mining sector. EPA has developed MACs reflecting the cost of mitigating methane emissions for several major economic sectors and countries (EPA, 1999, 2001, 2003). The International Marginal Abatement Curve (I-MAC) model (EPA, 2003) provides a methodology that can be applied to similar analyses using country-specific data, yielding reliable mitigation projections that can be integrated into a wide range of climate control models.

The construction of the MACs is based on a standard net present value formula equating costs of mitigation to the dollar value of the benefits. This is often referred to as an engineering cost or bottom-up modeling approach.[2] Capital and operating costs are estimated, along with the technology's ability to lower emissions, and are then used in this type of investment model to project potential technology adoption.

Previous analyses have been based on then-current costs and reduction efficiencies. This paper introduces technical change in the MACs by incorporating changes in technical efficiency, (which change input prices and factor productivity) and in technology diffusion (which change the share of domestic vs. foreign labor, capital, and material inputs). At any point in time, a heterogeneous population of coal mines has different costs and benefits associated with adopting abatement technologies. As a result, it is financially attractive for some mines to adopt and others not to adopt. As costs decrease because of technology advances and learning by doing, more mines will adopt, tracing out the S-shaped diffusion curve. In developing countries, substitution away from foreign inputs greatly decreases costs due to the underlying differential in wages.

As shown in Figure 2a, the result of technical change and technology diffusion is that the MACs shift outward over time, increasing emission reductions for any given carbon price. This implies that as costs of abatement decrease over time, adoption of mitigation technologies is likely to increase, making potential mitigation policies or programs more effective. Holding price constant over time, the diffusion curve of the technology being modeled can then be determined as shown in Figure 2b.

3. MACs as a function of technical change

Incorporating technical change into MACs is important for accurately modeling climate change scenarios and the impact of policy alternatives. However, prior to describing our approach to integrating technical change, we begin with a brief review of how MACs are developed.

MACs are generated by calculating the "break-even" price where different abatement technologies (for different entities) become economically viable. Restated, the calculation determines what carbon price (P) is needed for revenues from the project to equal the cost of the project (i.e. $NPV(P) = 0$). After the abatement potential and break-even price are computed, the MAC curve is constructed by ordering, from least expensive (lowest break-even price) to most expensive (high-

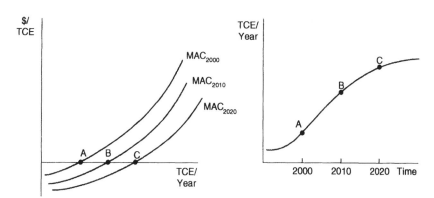

Figure 2. Modeling technology change helps identify the diffusion path of new technologies.

est break-even price), all of the technology options across all entities. The MAC approaches the total (technically feasible) abatement potential asymptotically as the carbon price becomes extremely large (i.e. as the options become very expensive).

The discounted cash flow analysis uses the fixed cost, recurring cost, and total revenue (or value of emission reduction) of each technology option to calculate the break-even price. The investment decision used to solve for the break-even price is expressed as

$$\text{NPV}(P) = 0$$
$$= -\text{CC} - \Sigma(\text{O\&M}/(1+R)^t)$$
$$+ \Sigma(\text{ER}^*P/(1+R)^t)$$

where P is the price in dollars per ton of carbon equivalent (\$/TCE);

ER the emissions reduction (TCE) achieved by the technology;

R the discount rate;

T is the the option's lifetime;

CC the one-time fixed-cost of capital, and

O&M the recurring operation and maintenance costs of the technology.

Technical change and technology diffusion affect the price of inputs, the productivity of inputs, and the overall reduction efficiency of abatement options. The components of the discounted cash flow analysis are defined in terms of price (p), input productivity (z), and reduction efficiency (r):

$$\text{CC} = \text{fn}(p, z)$$
$$\text{O\&M} = \text{fn}(p, z, r)$$
$$\text{ER} = \text{fn}(r)$$

O&M costs are a function of reduction efficiency because they are defined as operating and maintenance costs net of energy benefits from using captured methane as a fuel source. An overview of the abatement technologies modeled and the engineering cost analysis is provided in the following section.

4. Estimating MACs for underground coal mining

We apply the framework described above to methane abatement options for underground coal mines for the United States and China. China, which accounts for approximately 45% of total world coal mine methane emissions, also has the greatest abatement potential for any positive carbon equivalent price.

The methodology to construct MACs builds on EPA's engineering-economic cost analysis for the United States (EPA, 2001, 2003). The approach calculates a technology option's one-time investment costs and annual O&M costs and operating benefits. Benefits include both emission credits and energy offsets from using the captured methane as a fuel.

Three coal mine abatement options are included in the analysis: (1) degasification (degas), where wells are drilled to capture the methane before mining operations begin; (2) enhanced degas, where advanced drilling technologies are used and low grade gas is purified; and (3) ventilation abatement methane (VAM), where the low concentrations of methane contained in the mine ventilation air are oxidized to generate heat for process use. Appendix A contains additional information on these three coal mine abatement options. A detailed engineering description can be found in Delhotal et al. (2003).

For U.S. coal mines, engineering costs for each abatement option were calculated based on mine characteristics, such as annual mine production, gassiness of the coal deposits, and methane concentration in ventilation flows. Table I provides a summary of the one-time investment costs, annual operating and maintenance costs, and benefits from using the captured methane as an energy source.

5. Integrating technical change into MACs

Technical change has the potential to shift MACs for methane emissions down and out over time as abatement potential increases and net costs decrease. The result is that the marginal cost of methane abatement will decrease, leading to greater potential emissions reductions at any given carbon price. The impact of technical change is broadly categorized as either shifting the asymptote of the curve or altering the shape/position of the curve.

Technical change's impact on technical potential (asymptote)

Figure 3 summarizes the key parameters that determine the share of methane emissions that

TABLE I
Summary of average abatement costs and benefits for US coal mines

	Average costs/benefits ($millions)		
	Degas	Enhanced degas[a]	VAM
One-time costs			
Compressor capital	$1.00	$0.39	N/A
Gathering line capital	$0.90	$0.20	N/A
Processing capital	$0.04	$2.56	N/A
Ventilation capital	N/A	N/A	$18.64
Miscellaneous capital	$0.38	$0.14	N/A
Annual costs			
Drilling capital	$0.50	$0.36	N/A
Drilling materials	$0.94	$0.31	N/A
Compressors energy (kWh)	$0.33	$0.13	N/A
Gathering lines labor	$0.25	$0.96	N/A
Processing materials	$0.13	$0.18	N/A
Ventilation operating costs	N/A	N/A	$0.91
Miscellaneous labor	$0.28	$0.12	N/A
Annual after-tax benefits			
Methane sold or purchases offset	$0.97	$0.34	$2.78
Depreciation tax benefits	$0.02	$0.24	$0.14

N/A – Not applicable.
[a]Incremental costs and benefits in addition to degas (Option 1).
Source: RTI International (2003); Coal Methane Model, Research Triangle Park, NC: RTI International.

can be abated as a function of the mine and technology characteristics. This is referred to as the technical potential. The technical potential defines the vertical asymptote of the MAC in Figure 1. The technical potential can change over time as

- baseline emissions changes;
- mine characteristics change;
  - share of underground vs. surface mines and
  - share of methane that can be liberated and recovered via pre-mine drilling (degas)
- limitations of VAM technology decreases (currently require methane concentration >0.15%); and
- reduction efficiency of degas and VAM technologies increase.

All of the factors will potentially change over time as a result of enhancements to existing technologies or introduction of new processes and procedures. For example, in the United States, advances in surface mining are projected to decrease underground mining activities, reducing the technical potential for methane abatement.[3] Also, VAM technology is projected to improve over the next 20 years, decreasing the technical applicability concentration level below 0.15% methane. Table II provides the assumptions affecting technical potential over time that are used in the analysis for US mines.

Technical change's impact on economic potential

The economic potential (or projected adoption level) is a subset of the technical potential and is captured in the shape of the MAC. Economic viability of abatement options is a function of the reduction efficiency discussed above and price and productivity factors that influence the cost-benefit analysis. Figure 4 provides an overview of the approaches used to integrate technical change into the shape of the MACs. The general approach is to disaggregate abatement costs and benefits into component activities (e.g., drilling, gas moving, gas processing) in terms of their input factors (e.g., capital, labor, materials, and energy) and then use price and productivity trends to account for technical change over time.

Trends in factor inputs may vary by region or country. For example, in developing countries where skilled labor is in short supply, average labor productivity may increase at a faster rate

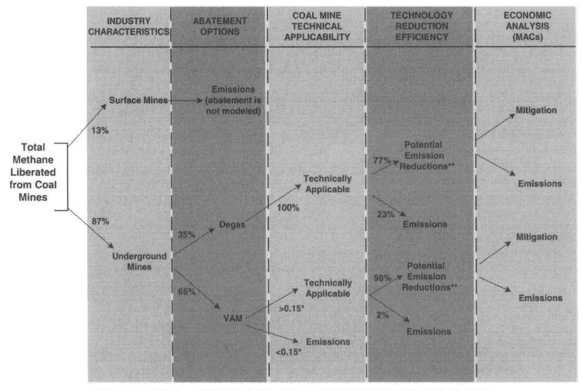

Figure 3. Key parameters in coal mine model. **The asymptote refers to the MAC curve approaching a limit of total potential reductions. The curve goes inelastic at a given point because of the engineering limitations of current technologies.

compared to developed countries (learning by doing). In contrast, trends in the energy consumption of abatement technologies may be the same across countries throughout the world because most of the equipment is supplied by a common group of developed countries (i.e. United States, European Union [EU], or Japan).

To capture this richness of differing technology trends across countries, input costs for abatement options are separated into factors of production: capital, labor, material, and energy. Changes in these input factors resulting from technical change can be expressed in terms of price and efficiency trends. Price trends reflect

TABLE II
Trends affecting technical potential over time for US coal mines

	2000	2030
Baseline emissions in billions of cubic feet (liberated from coal mining activities, surface and underground)	131.1	130.5
Share of underground mines	87%	75%
Share of gas liberated by degasification (vs. VAM)	36%	39%
Technical applicability for VAM	0.15%	0.075%
Reduction efficiency degas	77%	87%
Reduction efficiency VAM	97%	98%

Note: Trend assumptions are based on expert judgment and are not intended to represent official analysis by EPA.

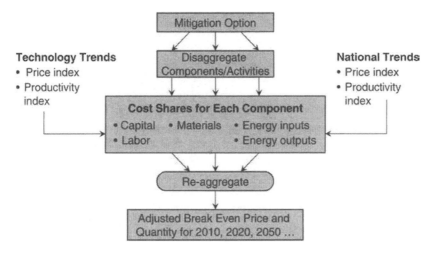

Figure 4. Approach for integrating technical change into MACs.

regional changes in supply and demand and production costs. Efficiency (productivity) trends reflect regions' adoption of new production technologies, with information dissemination that affects skill levels of the local labor force.

Table III presents price and efficiency trend projections for the United States. The price and quantity trends are then used to adjust one-time costs and annual costs to reflect technology change over time. A similar approach is used to incorporate technology change into annual benefits, where benefits are separated into avoided energy inputs (purchases of gas or electricity) and energy sales (gas injected into a pipeline) and recalculated after applying changes in price and changes in quantity due to increased reduction efficiency.

6. Developing Chinese coal mine MACs and trends

In addition to the United States, mine-level data were also obtained for China. However, detailed engineering cost estimates were not available for the Chinese mines. As a result, regression analysis was used to map U.S. costs onto Chinese mines as a function of coal production and methane liberated from individual Chinese mines. Separate regressions were run for each cost component/factor listed in Table A.1 (e.g. annual drilling costs, one-time compressor costs), and separate sets of regressions were run for each of the three abatement options. The coefficients were then applied to the known value of coal production and methane liberated for the Chinese mines to generate cost components for each abatement technology. The regression results are provided in Appendix B.

TABLE III
Annual trends in the United States

	Price change per year (%)	Rate of efficiency change per year (%)
Capital	−0.02	−0.01
Material	−0.02	−0.01
Labor	0.04	−0.02
Energy (electricity)	−0.01	−0.01
Energy (natural gas)	−0.02	N/A

N/A – Not applicable.
Source: U.S. Department of Energy, Energy Information Agency (EIA) (2003); *Annual Energy Outlook 2003 with Projections to 2025.* Washington, DC: EIA.

Cost adjustments to reflect domestic inputs

Costs estimates were then adjusted to reflect price differences in domestic inputs. It is likely that input costs for labor, capital, and materials may differ significantly. For example based on studies by the World Bank, wage rates in China are approximately 5% of U.S. wage rates for comparable occupations. Cost components were then adjusted by international price indices. Each country has a price index for labor capital, materials, and energy expressed relative to U.S. prices.

The first row in Table IV lists input price factors for China relative to U.S. prices. The price of electricity and natural gas in China is 62 and 63% of U.S. prices, and the price of materials in China is 4% of U.S. prices. The third row indicates the relative share of domestic versus foreign inputs for each factor. For example, in 2000, 100% of capital for the three abatement options is imported (mostly from Japan, the United States, and EU). For materials, high technology replacement parts, such as drill bits and compressor parts, are imported. However, experts said that approximately 50% of annual material costs are supplied by domestic producers (Schultz, 2003). The price indices for China, along with the share of domestic inputs, are used to calculate the weighted price factors for energy, labor, capital, and materials. As discussed in the following section, the share of domestic inputs is assumed to increase over time, reflecting technology and information transfer from developed countries to China.

Key parameters and trends for Chinese mines

For underground coal mining in China, several of the parameters shown in Figure 3 are different from the U.S. mines. For example, there are virtually no surface mines in China. As a result, 100% of coal mining activities are assumed to be labor-intensive underground mining through 2030. In addition, the share of methane liberated from underground mines that can be potentially captured through degas pre-drilling is assumed to be less in Chinese mines compared to U.S. mines. This is because geologic and reservoir conditions in these countries are generally described as having high gas contents, but they have low permeability, are prone to outburst, and have tight strata in the interburden between coal seams. Therefore, it is more difficult to produce and liberate gas under these conditions. For these reasons, degasification options were only applied to 33% of methane emissions baseline (as opposed to 36% in the United States), with the market potential increasing it to 38% by 2030 (as opposed to 39% in the United States) (Schultz, 2003).

Trends used in the analysis of abatement options for Chinese coal mines are presented in Table V.

7. Results

Applying the trends listed in Tables II and V, shifts in the MACs for the United States and China were developed from 2000 to 2030. Figures 5a and 6a show the MACs for 2000, 2010, 2020, and 2030. The magnitude of the shifts reflects both changes in abatement technologies and trends in the share of underground vs. surface mining. For example, after 2020, the shift in the U.S. MACs slows because underground mine production is projected to decrease slightly. However, technology improvements continue, driving down costs, which in turn increase the adoption of abatement technologies for any given price. In contrast, the MACs for China shift out and downward steadily, reflecting the decreasing technology costs and the growth in underground mine production.

Figures 5b and 6b show the diffusion of abatement technologies over time. The diffusion curves show the abated quantity (MMTCE) over time where $/TCE = 0 (i.e. where abatement options are economically viable with no incentives). The

TABLE IV
2000 price factors for selected countries

	Price factors				
	Gas	Electricity	Labor	Capital	Materials (annual nonenergy)
China	0.62	0.63	0.03	0.03	0.04
U.S.	1.00	1.00	1.00	1.00	1.00
Share domestic	100%	100%	25%	0%	50%
Weighted	0.62	0.63	0.27	0.97	0.52

Source: For gas, electric, labor, and materials, price factors were obtained from EPA's IMAC Model (EPA, 1999, 2001). For capital, import shares (WTO, 2002) were used to weight international capital price factors (KPMG, 2002).

TABLE V
Trends affecting technical potential over time for Chinese coal mines

	2000	2030
Baseline emissions in billion cubic feet (liberated from coal mining activities, surface and underground)	424.7	817
Share of underground mines	100%	100%
Share of gas liberated by degasification (vs. VAM)	33%	38%
Technical applicability for VAM	0.15%	0.075%
Reduction efficiency degas	77%	87%
Reduction efficiency VAM	97%	98%
Domestic share of labor	75%	100%
Domestic share of capital	0%	80%
Domestic share of materials	50%	88%

U.S. diffusion curve flattens out over time reflecting that many of the coal mining abatement technologies in the United States made significant penetration in the 1990s and that they are in the tail end of their adoption life cycle (past the inflection point of the S-shaped diffusion curve). In contrast, these technologies are in their early stages of adoption in China, and the S shape of the diffusion curve is more visible with the inflection point occurring around 2015.

Sensitivity analysis

The diffusion curves presented in Figures 5b and 6b are the result of simultaneously applying several technology feasibility, efficiency, and import trends. Each contributes to lowering the cost and/or increasing the benefits associated with abatement technologies and hence shifts the MACs. Sensitivity analysis was conducted to investigate which trends have the most significant impact on the MACs over time. Two scenarios are modeled for the development of Chinese diffusion curves: the first focuses on the rate of change in the technical applicability and reduction efficiency of abatement technologies, and the second focuses on the share of domestic vs. foreign labor, capital, and materials used in the mitigation options. Table VI presents the lower and upper bounds used in the sensitivity analysis for the two scenarios.

The sensitivity analysis for Scenario 1 (technical applicability and efficiency) is presented in Figure 7. The lower and upper bounds are shown as a range for the diffusion curve. Similarly, Figure 8 presents the lower and upper bounds for the sensitivity analysis for Scenario 2 (the share of domestic inputs). The two sensitivity scenarios indicate that the diffusion curves are more sensitive to the projected trends in the share of domestic inputs and less sensitive to projected changes in technical applicability and reduction efficiency. This is due to the abundant availability of low-wage labor in China and the relative maturity of abatement technologies for coal production.

8. Conclusions and next steps

The inclusion of technical change in MACs over time is important because it provides researchers and policy makers more accurate behavioral responses to potential future carbon prices. The methodology outlined above presents a bottom-up, engineering approach for the development of technology diffusion curves and provides detailed insights into the origins of S-shaped diffusion curves, whereas historically, analysis of technology diffusion has employed econometric or qualitative methods.

The approach for integrating technical change into the projected adoption of abatement technologies is illustrated for the coal mining sector and MACs are generated for the United States and China in 2000 and 2030. Projected changes over time in technical applicability and reduction efficiency, and in the share of domestic versus foreign inputs, lower the cost and increase the benefits of abatement technologies. This in turn shifts MACs downward, potentially increasing adoption at any give carbon price.

Sensitivity analysis shows that resulting diffusion curves are most sensitive to the rate of growth in the share of domestic inputs used in the

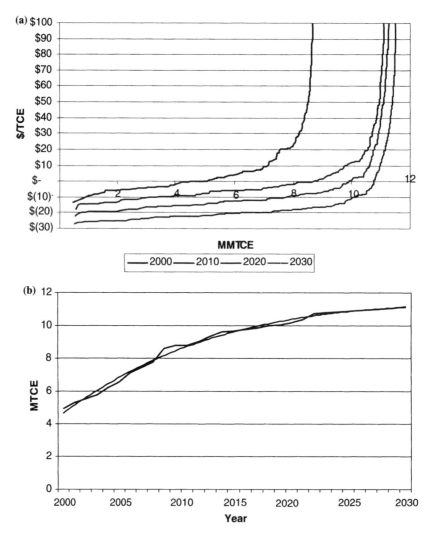

Figure 5. (a) Shift in U.S.'s MAC Over 30 years, (b) U.S. diffusion curve ($/TCE = 0).

mitigation options. The analysis shows that the United States is more mature user of coal mine abatement technologies and is therefore farther along the diffusion path. In contrast, in developing countries such as China, that are in the early stages of technology diffusion, increased domestic production of mitigation options and use of domestic labor will decrease costs and provide more cost-effective opportunities for reduction.

This conclusion may provide insights into how to motivate emission reductions outside of developed countries where many of the "no-regrets" options have already been implemented. Technical assistance and information transfer programs may yield greater emission reductions compared to R&D expenditures in developed countries or direct financial aid for developing countries. Technical assistance would allow developing countries to accelerate the adoption of domestically produced mitigation technologies at lower costs and that are maintained by lower-cost domestic labor. Lower project and O&M costs lead to more profitable projects, allowing for more cost-effective actions overall. Stimulating adoption of mitigation projects in developing countries would capture previously untapped reduction potential and significantly lower the cost of climate policy.

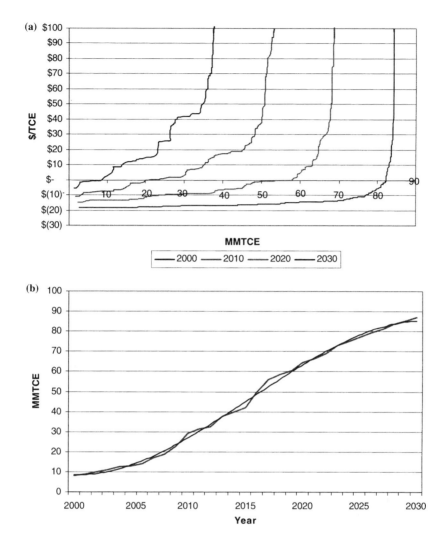

Figure 6. (a) Shift in China's MAC over 30 years, (b) China's diffusion curve ($/TCE = 0).

TABLE VI
Trends affecting technical potential over time for Chinese coal mines

	2000	2030 Lower bound	2030 Original projection	2030 Upper bound
Scenario 1				
Technical applicability for VAM	0.15%	0.10%	0.075%	0.05%
Reduction efficiency degas	77%	82%	87%	92%
Reduction efficiency VAM	97%	97.5%	98%	98.5%
Scenario 2				
Domestic share of labor	75%	85%	100%	100%
Domestic share of capital	0%	40%	80%	100%
Domestic share of materials	50%	69%	888%	100%

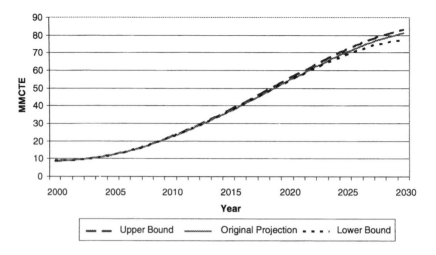

Figure 7. Sensitivity analysis for China: Scenario 1.

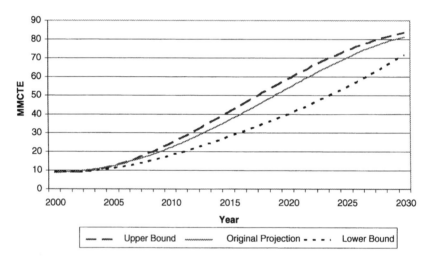

Figure 8. Sensitivity analysis for China: Scenario 2.

Appendix A

Coal mining abatement options

This appendix describes the three specific coal mining abatement options that are modeled associated with methane emissions from underground mines:

- **Degasification and pipeline injection:** High quality methane is recovered from coal seams by drilling vertical wells up to 5 years in advance of a mining operation or horizontal boreholes up to 1 year before mining. Most mine operators exercise "just-in-time management" of gate road development; subsequently, horizontal cross-panel boreholes are installed and drain gas for 6 months or less. Long horizontal boreholes are used by only a few operators in the United States. In some cases high quality methane also can be obtained from gob wells. Gob gas methane concentrations can range from 50% to over 90% (EPA, 1997). The gas recovered is injected into a natural gas pipeline requiring virtually no purification. This option assumes that gob gas sales decline over time because of declining levels of concentration. EPA reports that of the methane recovered from drainage, 57% can be directly used for pipeline injection. This is referred to as a 57% recovery efficiency for this technology (EPA, 1999).

- **Enhanced degasification, gas enrichment, and pipeline injection:** Methane is recovered in the same fashion as the first option using vertical wells, horizontal boreholes, and gob wells. In addition, the mine invests in enrichment technologies such as nitrogen removal units (NRUs) and dehydrators, used primarily to enhance medium-quality gob well gas by removing impurities. This option also assumes tighter well spacing to increase recovery. The enrichment process and tighter spacing improve recovery efficiency by 20% over the first option discussed above (EPA, 1999).
- **Flow reversal oxidizers:** These technologies have the potential to be applied to the methane emitted from a coal mine's ventilation air. It is not economically feasible to sell this gas into a pipeline because of extremely low concentration levels (typically below 1.0%). However, by ducting ventilation air with methane concentrations in excess of 0.15% into a flow reversal oxidizer, approximately 97% of the methane from the ventilation air could be mitigated, generating useful heat as a by-product.

These abatement options are broken into their basic components and activities, as indicated in Table A.1. Trends in the price and efficiencies of each component are applied to integrate technology changes over time. As shown in Table A.1, degas and enhanced degas coal mine options employ similar activities. Both include drilling, compressors, gathering lines, and other fixed costs. Enhanced degas includes processing to improve the quality of the gas.

The VAM abatement option has different components, specifically the oxidizer unit(s) and ducting necessary to connect the oxidizer(s) to the ventilation system evas.

TABLE A.1
Components of coal mining abatement options

Cost component	Markets	Description	Degas	Enhanced degas	VAM
Drilling	Annual capital	Drilling is continual through the life of the mine; thus, capital costs are classified as "annual" costs. Costs are proportional to annual coal production.	√	√	
	Annual materials	Material costs for drilling are estimated based on the volume of methane liberated.[a]	√	√	
	Annual labor	Annual labor costs related to drilling.	√	√	
Compressors	One-time capital	Number of compressors is proportional to the amount of methane liberated per unit time.[b]	√	√	
	Gas	Natural gas used by compressors is proportional to the amount of methane liberated per unit time.	√	√	
Gathering Lines	One-time capital	Costs are proportional to coal production.	√	√	
	Annual labor	Annual costs are primarily labor related to moving the lines each year.[c]	√	√	
Other Fixed Costs	One-time capital	Costs are proportional to coal production. Capital costs include safety equipment, licenses, and designs.[d]	√	√	
Processing	One-time capital	Costs are proportional to both coal production and methane liberated and include dehydrators and enrichment units.[e]		√	
	Annual materials	Annual costs are primarily the material used for maintenance.		√	
VAM	One-time capital	Costs are proportional to both coal production and the flow of VAM. Capital costs are primarily oxidizer units, fans, and ducts.			√
	Annual labor	Annual costs are primarily the labor associated with running the oxidizer.			√

[a]Material costs are related to the development rate of mines (i.e. access to drill boreholes) or the actual amount of drilling. However, because this information was not available, the volume of methane liberated was used as a proxy.
[b]Methane production levels of a typical mine site will ramp up in a step-wise fashion until a point is reached that new wells replenish production of depleted wells and production becomes flat. Compression is added as appropriate during the increase in production.
[c]In some instances it may cost more in labor to move in-mine gas pipelines than to install a new line and leave old lines in the workings.
[d]Other fixed costs may also include monitoring, reclamation, and gas ownership (royalties).
[e]Processing one-time capital costs are related to the gas recovery technique that is used. For example, more processing will be required for gob gas recovery than inseam.
Source: RTI International (2003); Coal Methane Model. Research Triangle Park, NC: RTI International.

Appendix B

Cost estimates for Chinese mines

Detailed engineering cost information was not available for Chinese underground coal mines. Thus, costs were estimated as a function of mine production and liberated methane, which was obtained from the EPA report *Reducing Methane Emissions from Coal Mines in China: The Potential for Coalbed Methane Development* (EPA, 1996).

Regression analysis was used to estimate cost relationships based on the known costs for the given 56 U.S. mines as a function of coal production and/or methane liberated. Individual regressions were run for each cost component/factor listed in Table A.1 (e.g., annual drilling costs, one-time compressor costs), and separate sets of regressions were run for each of the three abatement options. The coefficients were then applied to the known value of coal production and methane liberated for the Chinese mines to generate cost components for each abatement technology. The regression results are provided in Table B.1.

TABLE B.1
Regression results

Type of cost (by option)	R^2	Constant	Coal production coefficients ($ per MM tons/yr)	Methane liberated coefficients ($ per MM cf/yr)
Annual drilling capital				
Degas	0.5497	150,464 (1.93)	165,468 (7.25)	
Enhanced degas	1.0		115,000 (–)	
Annual drilling materials				
Degas	0.9845			42 (59.07)
Enhanced degas	1.0			13 (–)
Compressor capital				
Degas	0.9918			423 (81.77)
Enhanced degas	1.0			164 (–)
Compressor energy				
Degas	0.9872	87 (0.10)		14 (64.49)
Enhanced degas	1.0			5.5 (–)
Gathering lines capital				
Degas	0.9999	397,020 (939.70)	159,785 (1,433.02)	
Enhanced degas	0.9986	5,738 (3.35)	58,809 (129.95)	
Gathering lines labor				
Degas	0.9999	510 (2.42)	79,892 (1,433.02)	
Enhanced degas	0.9968	2,869 (3.35)	29,404 (129.95)	
Processing capital				
Degas	(–)	40,000 (–)		
Enhanced degas	(–)	1,888,500 (–)		
Processing materials				
Degas	0.9927	51 (64.08)	2,096 (2.54)	
Enhanced degas	1.0	132,000 (–)		
Other fixed capital				
Degas	1.0	765 (2.42)	119,839 (1,433.02)	
Enhanced degas	0.9968	4,304 (3.35)	44,107 (129.95)	
Other fixed labor				
Degas	0.9999	25,510 (120.76)	79,892 (1,433.02)	
Enhanced degas	0.9968	27,869 (32.50)	29,405 (129.95)	
VAM (Option 3)			Coal Production	Methane Concentration
Capital	0.8445		3,315,380 (6.56)	10,438 (6.71)
Labor	0.8809		170,950 (8.04)	488 (7.45)

Notes

1. cubic foot of methane is contains 0.0001 tons of carbon equivalent (TCE). Thus, 1 million metric tons of carbon equivalent (MMTCE) is equivalent to 9.1 billion cubic feet (bfc) of methane.
2. A wide range of models have been used to assess the economic consequences of climate change strategies. These models can be broadly categorized as either using top-down or bottom-up approaches. Top-down models, such as computable general equilibrium (CGE) models, typically tie emissions directly to economic activity such as the production of goods or the consumption of fossil fuels. In contrast, bottom-up models typically incorporate detailed engineering cost analysis to characterize specific technologies when investigating GHG controls.
3. Few mitigation options are available for surface mining; hence, most of the methane is liberated into the atmosphere (surface mining also releases less methane per ton of coal mined).

References

Delhotal, K.C., M.P. Gallaher, and M. Martin, June 24, 2003, 'Technical Change in Energy-Related Methane Abatement,' presented at the International Energy Workshop (IEW) Conference in Vienna, Italy.

Geroski, P.A., 2000, 'Models of Technology Diffusion,' *Research Policy* **29**, 603–625.

Griliches, Z., 1957, 'Hybrid Corn: An Exploration in the Economics of Technological Change,' *Econometrica* **48**, 501–522.

KPMG Competitive Alternatives, 2002, Comparing Business Costs in North America, Europe, and Japan. Available at <www.competitivealternatives.com/main.htm>. Obtained on August 4, 2003.

Mansfield, E., 1968, *Industrial Research and Technological Innovation*, New York: Norton.

Mansfield, E., 1989, 'The Diffusion of Industrial Robots in Japan and the United States,' *Research Policy* **18**, 183–192.

Mansfield, E., 1993, 'The Diffusion of Flexible Manufacturing Systems in Japan, Europe and the United States,' *Management Science* **39** (2), 149–159.

Rogers, E.M., 1995, 'Lessons for Guidelines for the Diffusion of Innovations,' *Journal of Quality Improvement* **21** (7), 324–228.

RTI International, 2003, *Coal Methane Model*, Research Triangle Park, NC: RTI International.

Schultz, L., June 2003, Personal communication between Mike Gallaher and Lee Schultz.

U.S. Department of Energy, Energy Information Agency (EIA), 2003, *Annual Energy Outlook 2003 with Projections to 2025*, Washington, DC: EIA.

U.S. Environmental Protection Agency (EPA), 1996, *Reducing Methane Emissions from Coal Mines in China: The Potential for Coalbed Methane Development*, Washington, DC: EPA.

U.S. Environmental Protection Agency (EPA), 1997, *Technical and Economic Assessment of Potential to Upgrade Gob Gas to Pipeline Quality*, 430-R-97-012, Washington, DC: EPA.

U.S. Environmental Protection Agency (EPA), 1999, *U.S. Methane Emissions 1990–2020: Inventories, Projections, and Opportunities for Reductions*, EPA 430-R-99-013, Washington, DC: EPA.

U.S. Environmental Protection Agency (EPA), 2001, *Addendum Update to U.S. Methane Emissions 1990–2020: Inventories, Projections, and Opportunities for Reductions*, Washington, DC: EPA.

U.S. Environmental Protection Agency (EPA), 2003, *U.S. Coal Methane Engineering Cost Analysis*, Washington, DC: EPA.

World Trade Organization (WTO), 2002, *International Trade Statistics 2001*, France. Available at <www.wto.org/english/res_e/statis_e/stat-toc.e.htm>. Obtained on August 3, 2003.

Index of Names

Abernathy W., 81, 83
Abramovitz M., 169, 268
Acemoglu D., 11, 106
Achilladelis B., 51, 57
Acs Z., 129, 285, 286
Adams J.D., 99, 103–106, 285, 286
Aghion P., 11, 49, 57
Alexander R.C., 169, 171
Alic J.A., 169
Allen R.C., 47, 48, 57
Allison J.R., 218, 230
Andersen E.S., 268
Anderson S.P., 49, 57
Angelis D., 83
Antonelli C., 267, 268
Armour H., 39, 42
Arnold E., 279
Arora A., 101, 106, 223, 224, 226, 228, 230, 231
Arrow K.J., 49, 57, 63, 66, 69, 70, 83, 156, 157, 169, 170, 267, 268, 285, 289
Astebro T., 253, 256
Atkinson S.H., 213, 216
Audretsch D.B., 142, 160, 170, 271–274, 285–288
Auerswald, P., 81, 83, 155, 158–162, 169, 170
Ausubel J.H., 267
Autant-Bernard C., 285
Azoulay P., 102, 106

Bain J.S., 275, 279
Balachandra R., 51, 57
Baldwin W.L., 122, 124, 126, 284
Barclay I., 51, 52, 58
Barfield C., 84
Barnow B.S., 146, 151
Bartenbach K., 244
Barton J.H., 208, 217, 222, 230
Barzel Y., 17, 25
Battisti G., 253, 257
Bauer L.L., 102, 107, 184, 192, 193
Baumol W., 56, 57
Beardsley G., 84, 97, 100, 105, 107, 143, 151
Benkler Y., 46, 55, 57
Berger P., 169, 170
Bessen J., 49, 157

Birdzell L.E., 154, 171
Bizan O.,106
Black G., 285, 289
Blanchard O.J., 83
Bloch F., 174, 184
Boer F.P., 83
Bok D., 216
Boldrin M., 55, 57
Bond S., 249, 250, 256, 257
Bound J., 283, 289
Bozeman B., 274, 289
Brach P., 42, 84
Brandenburg R., 99, 100, 103, ,105, 107
Branscomb L.M., 81, 83, 155, 160, 169, 170, 215
Bratt E.C., 263, 268
Breitzman T., 230
Breschi S., 244
Bresnahan T.F., 55, 57
Brod A., 175, 184, 192
Brodley J.F., 174, 184
Brooks H., 169
Brynjolfsson E., 40, 42
Buckley P., 42
Burns A.F., 264, 268
Bush V., 95, 97, 155

Caballero R., 65, 83
Cain G.G., 151
Cainarca G., 253, 257
Cameron G., 83
Cameron H., 268
Canepa A., 248, 250, 251, 257
Cannon P., 83
Carpenter R.E., 249, 250, 257
Carter A.B., 169
Casson M., 42
Caves R., 271, 274
Ceccagnoli M., 226
Chamberlin E.H., 48, 57
Chan S., 38, 42, 84
Chandler A.D., 39, 42, 159, 170, 281, 289
Cherington P.W., 157, 161, 169, 170
Chesbrough H., 41, 43, 169, 170

Chiang E.P., 106
Christensen C.M., 159, 170
Christie A.F., 244
Cleveland W.S., 256, 257
Coase R.H., 41, 42, 62, 83, 158, 170
Cockburn I.M., 4, 101, 105–107
Cohen W.M., 62, 83, 99, 101, 104–107, 151, 195, 196, 202, 208, 222, 225–231, 235, 244
Cole A.H., 39, 42
Colombo M.G., 257
Colyvas J., 240, 244
Combs K.L., 173, 174, 178, 181–187, 192
Cooper B., 28
Cooper J., 4, 6
Crépon B., 142, 151
Crow M., 244
Cummins C., 289
Cyert D., 28

D'Aloisio S., 244
D'Aspermont C., 174, 184, 185
Darby M., 71, 83
Dasgupta P., 82, 83, 240, 244
David P., 27, 81–83, 240
Davies S., 251, 257
De Fraja G., 174, 185
de la Grandville O., 11, 12
de Palma A., 57
Deeds D., 84
Delhotal K.C., 305
Devereux M., 249, 257
Diamond A.M., 5, 6, 259, 268
Dick A., 185
Dixit A.K., 57, 100, 107
Dosi G., 32, 41, 42, 84, 264, 268
Dreyfuss R.C., 244
Duguet E., 142, 151
Dunne T., 252, 257

Eaton B.C., 48, 49, 57
Eisenberg R.S., 217, 221–225, 237, 241, 244
Elias E., 83, 84
Elrod T., 51, 57
Elston J., 257
Enos J.L., 47, 57
Epstein G.L., 169
Evans J., 37, 268
Evenson R., 299, 230

Fabricant S., 169, 264, 268
Fazzari S., 249, 250, 257
Feldman M.P., 142, 285, 289
Feller J., 58

Fellner W.J., 2, ,16, 25, 169
Finan W., 81, 84
First H., 244
Fischer S., 83
Fisher F.M., 288, 289
Fisher J., 268
Fitzgerald B., 58
Flamm K., 81, 84
Florida R., 170
Foray D., 85
Foster J., 267, 268
Franke N., 46, 48, 58
Frankel M., 267, 268
Freeman C., 59, 259
Friar J.H., 51, 57

Gaita K.L., 244
Galbraith J.K., 281, 289
Gallaher M.P., 305
Gallini N.T., 46, 58
Gaston J.F., 264, 268
Geiger R.L., 236, 244
Gelijns A., 244
George B., 42
Georghiou L., 264, 268
Geroski P.A., 260, 267, 268, 292, 305
Gibbons M., 268
Giudici G., 250, 257
Glenday R., 268
Goldberger A.S., 151
Golec J., 25
Gompers P.A., 161, 170, 215
Goodacre A., 248, 257
Gouriéroux C., 132, 142
Grabowski H.G., 4, 282, 289
Graham A., 81, 84
Graham S., 230
Grandstrand O., 41, 42
Grant R.M., 31, 42
Greene W.H., 114, 126, 147, 151
Greenland S., 254
Greenstein S., 55, 57
Griliches Z., 3, 61, 62, 70, 80, 83, 84, 87, 97, 103, 107, 129, 139, 142, 145, 146, 151, 156–158, 170, 208, 247, 259, 289, 292, 305
Grindley P.C., 207, 208
Grossman G.M., 49, 58, 174, 185

Hagedoorn J., 187, 192
Hall B.H., 39, 42, 80, 83, 84, 129, 142, 146, 151, 169, 170, 195, 197, 198, 201–208, 217, 218, 222, 225, 229, 230, 243, 244, 247–250, 253, 257, 274, 289
Hamburger M., 84

Hamilton K., 230
Hand J., 38, 42
Hannan T.H., 252
Harhoff D., 5, 26, 48, 58, 226, 230, 256, 257
Hart O.D., 49, 58
Hartmann G.C., 169, 170
Hayek F.A., 41, 42
Heller M.A., 217, 221–225, 230, 241, 244
Helpman E., 49, 58
Henderson R.M., 4, 81, 84, 101, 105–107, 229, 230, 240, 244, 285
Henkel J., 48, 53, 58
Herstatt C., 46, 58
Hicks D., 225, 229, 230
Hicks J.R., 16, 25, 264, 268
Hinloopen J., 174, 185
Hinzmann B., 83
Hirshleifer J., 124, 126
Hissam S., 58
Hoffman W.G., 264, 268
Horsley A., 59
Hotelling H., 49, 58
Howitt P., 49, 57
Howlett M.J., 244
Hubbard R.G., 247, 249, 257
Husic F., 58
Hymer S., 42

Ireland N., 267, 268

Jacquemin A., 174, 184
Jaffe A.B., 42, 58, 65, 82–84, 103, 107, 118, 126, 129, 142, 207, 208, 215–218, 220, 223, 230, 244, 274, 285, 288, 289
Jankowski J., 190, 192
Jensen J.L., 106
Jeppesen L.B., 53, 58
Jervis P., 57, 59
Jewes J., 155, 170
Jokisch M., 53, 54, 58
Jones C., 75, 83, 84
Jorde T.M., 174, 185
Jorgenson D., 82, 84
Justman M., 81, 84, 85

Kaiser U., 174, 185
Kalbfleisch J.D., 256, 257
Kamien M.I., 146, 151, 174, 185
Kaplan S., 250, 252, 257
Karshenas M., 252, 253, 256, 257
Kash D.E., 82, 84, 158, 170
Katz M.L., 243, 244
Kauffman S., 170
Keilbach M., 274

Keller J.H., 169, 170
Kelman A.P., 51, 58
Kendrick J., 169
Kenney M., 170
Kesinger J., 42
Kilger C., 244
Kim J., 195, 208
Kim W., 81, 84
Kingsland S.E., 268
Kingston W., 222, 230
Kislev Y., 229, 230
Kitch E.W., 25
Kleinknecht A., 282, 289
Klepper S., 267, 268, 278, 279
Klevorick A.K., 42, 65, 71, 75, 81, 84, 104, 107, 208, 230, 244
Knight K.E., 47, 58
Kodama F., 170
Koenig G., 218, 230
Kohn M., 125, 126, 288, 289
Kortum S., 195, 208, 229, 230
Kreps D., 42
Krugman P., 285
Kukies J., 26
Kuznets S., 27, 157, 169, 263, 264, 268
Kwasnicki H., 268
Kwasnicki W., 268

Lagace B., 83, 84
Lakhani K.R., 48, 58
Lamoreaux N., 107
Lancaster K., 49, 58
Landau R., 57, 107, 218
Lanjouw J.O., 220, 225, 230
Lazonick W., 161, 170
Lee J.Y., 41, 42
Lehmann E.E., 274
Lemley M.A., 218, 230
Lerner J., 48, 58, 195, 206, 208, 215, 216, 218, 229, 230
Leslie S.W., 169, 170
Lessig, L., 55, 58
Lester R., 159, 170
Lev B., 42
Levin J., 223, 230
Levin R.C., 36, 41, 42, 101, 107, 202, 208, 223, 226, 227, 230, 234, 244
Levin S., 169, 170
Levine D., 55, 57
Levinthal D.A., 62, 83, 151
Levy J.D., 279
Leyden D.P., 192
Lichtenberg F., 146, 147, 151
Liebeskind J., 240, 244

Lim K., 47, 58
Link A.N., 81, 82, 84, 95, 97, 102, 107, 146, 151, 184, 185, 187, 188, 192, 193, 274, 285, 288, 289
Linn J., 106
Lippman S., 34, 42
Lipsey R.G., 49, 57
Lissoni F., 244, 267, 268
Lobo J., 170
Los B., 147, 151
Lotka A.J., 263, 268
Lucas R.E., 288, 289
Lûthje C., 46, 56, 58

Machlup F., 42
Maddala G.S., 127
Maddison A., 169, 170
Mahajan V., 268
Mairesse J., 83, 84, 134, 142, 151, 257
Mansfield E., 1–7, 20, 21, 25, ,27, 31–33, 37, 40–42, 51, 55, 58, 61–63, 65, 80–84, 87, 97, 99, 100, 103–107, 129, 130, 139, 142–146, 151, 153–159, 167–173, 185, 209, 216, 226, 230, 233, 234, 244, 247, 251, 257, 259, 260, 267, 271, 274, 275, 279, 281, 284, 289, 291, 292, 305
Marcu M., 103, 106
Mariotti S., 257
Marschke G., 195, 208
Marshak T.A., 157, 160, 171
Marshall A., 285, 289
Martin J., 42
Martin M., 305
Martin S., 126, 127, 175, 185
Maskin E., 49, 57
Mauborgne R., 81, 84
Mayer C.P., 248, 257
Mazzoleni R., 218, 230, 244
McDowell J.M., 252, 257
McGroddy J., 159, 161, 169, 171
McMillan S., 84
Medda G., 145, 147, 151
Medoff M., 41, 42
Mensch G., 81, 85
Merges R., 221, 223, 230, 241, 244
Merrill S., 230, 231
Metcalfe J.S., 267–269
Meyer P., 169, 267, 269
Mickey J., 254, 257
Miotti L., 70, 85
Modigliani F., 28
Mohnen P., 70, 85, 134, 142
Monfort A., 142
Montobbio F., 244
Morck R., 40, 42
Morrison P., 46, 47, 58
Mowery D., 84, 102, 107, 230, 236, 237, 240, 244

Mueller D.C., 289
Mulkay B., 257
Muller E., 185, 268, 282
Myers M.B., 170

Nadiri I., 81, 83, 85
Narin F., 84
Nelson R.R., 2, 7, 16, 22, 25, 27, 41, 42, 66, 70, 81, 84, 85, 106, 107, 156, 159, 169, 170, 171, 184, 185, 208, 217, 218, 221, 223, 229, 230, 231, 241, 244, 245, 248, 257, 259, 267–269
Nordhaus W.D., 25, 49, 58
Nuvolari A., 48, 58

O'Sullivan M., 161, 170
Ofek E., 169, 170
Ogawa S., 52, 58
Oi W.Y., 49, 58
Olivastro D., 230
Ordover J.A., 174, 185, 243, 244
Oriani R., 129, 142
Orlando M.J., 285, 289
Orsenigo L., 84, 230

Pakes A., 226
Paleari S., 250
Panzar J., 57
Parapatt S.J., 208
Pavitt K., 130, 143
Peck M.J., 3, 20, 25, 156, 170
Perloff J.M., 49, 58
Petersen B.C., 249, 250
Peterson S.R., 126
Petit P., 268
Phelps E., 156
Piekarz R., 38, 42
Piga C.A., 146, 151
Pigou A.C., 62, 85
Pindyck R.S., 100, 107
Pisano G.P., 84, 102, 107, 230
Polyani M., 30, 31, 41, 42
Poolton J., 51, 52, 58
Poot T.P., 289
Popp D., 25
Portney P.R., 126
Poyago-Theotoky J., 174, 185
Prentice R.L., 256, 257
Prescott R., 263, 269
Pry R., 268
Pryor F.L., 279

Quillen C.D., 222, 226, 231

Raff D., 107
Raporport J., 58, 84, 97, 107, 143, 151, 185, 268
Ray T., 268
Raymond E.S., 48, 58
Redmond W.H., 51, 58
Rees J., 187, 193, 274, 288, 289
Reijnen J.O.N., 289
Reimers N., 244
Reiter S., 169, 171
Rhodes R., 171
Riggs W., 47, 59
Rivkin J., 158, 171
Roan S., 126, 127
Roberts J., 58
Robertson A.B., 57, 59
Rochet J., 37, 43
Rogers E.M., 292, 305
Röller L.H., 48, 59
Romeo A., 42, 58, 84, 97, 107, 143, 151, 185, 268
Romer P.M., 15, 26, 49, 59, 71, 85, 169, 171, 285, 289
Rosenberg N., 27, 47, 59, 85, 107, 154, 169, 171, 244, 267, 269
Rosenbloom R., 169
Ross D., 26
Rossi-Hansberg E., 288, 289
Rothwell R., 51, 59, 268
Royston P., 257
Ruffin R., 62, 85
Rumelt R., 34, 42
Ruttan V.W., 26
Rycroft R., 82, 84, 158, 170

Sachwald F., 70, 85
Saint-Paul G., 57, 59
Salant S.W., 185
Saloner G., 57, 59
Salop S.C., 49, 58
Salter W.E.G., 267, 269
Sampat B.N., 236, 237, 244
Samuel W., 42
Samuelson P.A., 268
Santarelli E., 288, 289
Sattinger M., 49, 59
Saviotti P.P., 268, 269
Sawers D., 170
Schankerman M., 41, 43, 83, 85, 146, 151, 220, 225, 226, 230, 231
Scherer F.M., 4, 5, 7, 17, 20, 22, 23, 25, 26, 38, 43, 106, 107, 139, 146, 151, 170, 226, 231, 259, 281–284, 289, 290
Schianterelli F., 249
Schmalensee R., 57, 275, 279
Schmidt K.M., 57, 59
Schmitt N., 48, 58
Schmookler J., 3, 16, 26, 49, 59, 65, 85

Schnee J., 84
Schnitzer M., 57, 59
Schultz L., 298, 305
Schumpeter J.A., 1, 15, 16, 24–27, 154–157, 160, 169, 171, 281, 290
Schwartz M., 42, 84, 107, 170
Scotchmer S., 57, 58, 221, 231
Scott J.T., 82, 84, 95, 97, 109, 111, 112, 114, 117, 118, 120–127, 151, 193, 274, 284, 288–290
Senge P., 81, 84
Shaffer S., 178, 184, 185
Shah S., 46–48, 58, 59
Shaked A., 275, 279
Shannon C., 43
Shapiro C., 174, 175, 185, 222, 225, 231
Shell K., 156, 169, 170, 171
Sherman G.R., 169, 171
Shin H., 184, 185
Shivakumar R., 175, 184
Siegel D.S., 103, 107, 146, 147, 151
Silberston Z.A., 226, 231
Silpo D.B., 174, 185
Simon H., 28
Simons K.L., 278, 279
Smith B., 84
Smith D.K., 169, 171
Solow R.M., 1, 27, 156, 171
Spence M., 49, 50, 59
Starkey K., 106
Stavins R.N., 126
Steinmueller W.E., 57, 59
Stennek J., 175, 185
Stephan P.E., 274, 285
Sterlachinni A., 288, 289
Stern S., 58, 230
Stigler G.J., 9, 264, 269
Stiglitz J.E., 49, 57, 248, 257
Stillerman R., 170
Stiroh K., 82, 84, 85
Stix G., 106, 107
Stoneman P., 247–253, 256, 257, 268, 269
Storey D.J., 257
Suárez F., 278, 279
Sutton J., 105–107, 271, 274, 275, 279
Szulanski G., 31, 43

Tahar G., 268
Tamarkin M., 25
Tassey G., 63, 64, 71, 81–85, 193
Taylor C.T., 226, 231
Taylor T., 57
Teece D.J., 29, 31, 33, 39, 40–43, 84, 101, 107, 169, 171, 174, 207, 208

Temin P., 288, 289
Teubal M., 81, 84, 85
Thies S., 53
Thirtle C.G., 26
Thisse J.F., 57
Thurik A.R., 160, 170
Tirole J., 37, 43, 48, 54, 58, 59
Toivanen O., 249, 251, 257
Tombak M.H., 48, 59
Tonks I., 248
Toole A., 84
Townsend J., 59
Trajtenberg M., 42, 207, 208, 244, 285
Triplett J., 253
Trognon A., 142
Trow M., 236, 244
Tybout R.A., 3, 7, 142

Urban G.L., 46, 59
Utterback J., 81, 83, 85, 260, 267, 269, 278, 279

van Reenen J., 80, 256, 257
Varian H.R., 55, 59
Verspagen B., 151
Vianelli S., 263, 269
Villani E., 58
Vivarelli M., 146
von Hippel E., 46, 47, 52, 58, 59, 101, 107, 222, 231
Vonortas N.S., 192, 193

Wagenvoort R., 250, 257
Wagner S., 42, 51, 58, 84, 97, 107, 143, 151, 170, 185
Wallerstein M.B., 42
Walsh J.P., 106, 107, 208, 229, 231, 244
Warning S., 274
Warshofsky F., 225, 231

Weaver W., 43
Webster O.H., 222, 226
Wein H.H., 158, 170
Weiss A., 248
Weitzman M.L., 157, 171
Westhead P., 107, 257
Wild P., 268
Willard G.E., 279
Williams J., 75, 83, 84
Williamson O.E., 39, 43
Willig R.D., 57, 174, 185
Windsor C.P., 263, 269
Winter S.G., 41, 42, 81, 84, 85, 107, 159, 171, 208, 230, 244, 268
Witt U., 268, 269
Wolf B., 48, 58
Wooldridge J., 143
Wooster J.H., 279
Wright G. 57
Wright M., 107

Yang S., 40, 42
Yeung B., 40, 42
Yi S.S., 184, 185
Yoffie D.B., 57

Zang I., 146, 151, 185
Ziedonis A.A., 244
Ziedonis R.H., 195, 197, 201, 202, 207, 208, 217, 218, 220, 222, 225, 229, 231, 243, 244
Zimmerman D.L., 244
Zingales L., 250, 252
Zucker L., 71, 83
Zuscovitch E., 85